330.954
Sn5c

65969

DATE DUE			
GAYLORD M-2			PRINTED IN U.S.A.

Ceylon:
An Export Economy
in Transition

Publications of
The Economic Growth Center

LLOYD G. REYNOLDS, *Director*

Ceylon:
An Export Economy
In Transition

DONALD R. SNODGRASS
Advisor to Economic Planning Unit
Prime Minister's Department
Government of Malaysia

A Publication of
The Economic Growth Center
Yale University

1966

RICHARD D. IRWIN, INC.

Homewood, Illinois

First Printing, August, 1966

PRINTED IN THE UNITED STATES OF AMERICA
Library of Congress Catalog No. 66–14542

Series Foreword

This volume is one in a series of studies supported by the Economic Growth Center, an activity of the Yale Department of Economics since 1961. The Center's Research program is focused on the search for regularities in the process of growth and structural change by means of intercountry and intertemporal analyses. The emphasis is on measurable aspects of economic growth and on the development and testing of hypotheses about the growth process. To provide more reliable statistical tests of theoretical hypotheses, the Center is concerned with improving the techniques of economic measurement and with the refinement of national data systems. The Center provides a home for the International Association for Research in Income and Wealth, which moved its headquarters from Cambridge University, England in 1962. The Center library endeavors to achieve a complete intake of significant economic and statistical publications from about 80 of the larger countries of the world.

Book-length studies supported by the Center are printed and distributed by Richard D. Irwin, Inc. Reprints of journal articles are circulated as Center papers.

LLOYD G. REYNOLDS, *Director*
GUSTAV RANIS, *Associate Director*
HUGH T. PATRICK, *Assistant Director*
SHANE J. HUNT, *Assistant Director*
MARIAM K. CHAMBERLAIN, *Executive Secretary*

Preface

Before asking the reader to plunge into a volume as large as this one, an author should make some attempt to explain what it is he thinks his book is trying to do and for whom it is written. The title of this volume, like most titles, is to some extent misleading. By referring to Ceylon, an export economy in transition, I intend to announce my goal of examining the economic development over a considerable stretch of time of one particular economy which I consider to be a fairly typical example of the type of economic structure which has already been identified and referred to as the export economy by Wallich, Levin, and others.[1] The main area of interest of this book is to analyze the structure of the export economy and study its growth, especially with regard to the influence of structure upon growth. This has involved studying the development of the economy from the dawn of its modern economic history, which is placed sometime in the 1840's, up to the present day. Despite this lengthy period of interest, however, I did not intend to write an economic history of Ceylon. The approach used here has deliberately been selective in its choice of subject matter and limited in its methodology. The following points are called to the reader's attention.

All parts of the 120-year period just referred to are not studied with equal intensity. The long period from the 1840's up to World War II is frankly regarded as being of interest primarily as a "classical" background for the evolution of the economy in more recent times. This is not to imply that the early period is inherently uninteresting or to deny that the economy underwent important economic changes during this first century of its modern economic development. Some of the more relevant of these for economic growth and structure are in fact brought out in the text. What is contended is that all of these changes were quite consistent with the maintenance of the particular type of economic system referred to here as the classical export economy—"classical" because the main features of its enclave system of primary production were

---

[1]Henry Christopher Wallich, *Monetary Problems of an Export Economy* (Cambridge: Harvard University Press, 1950) and Jonathan V. Levin, *The Export Economies* (Cambridge: Harvard University Press, 1960).

typical of those found in a large number of Asian, African, and Latin American economies during the Nineteenth and early Twentieth Centuries. As the text moves on to more recent times, the 1940's are examined in increased detail as the period in which the forces that produced what Levin has called "the revolt against the export economy" began to gather force. The main period of interest, however, is the one which begins with independence in 1948. As a result of the "revolt"—which can also be described as an attempt to reorient the economy towards comprehensive economic development—the economy entered into a period of fundamental transition, during which it moved ever farther away from the classical pattern. The nature of the attempt to make this transition a successful one in the sense of accelerating national economic development, the advances made and the problems encountered, form the primary area of concern in this volume. The transition in Ceylon has not to date been a very successful one and during the early 1960's it took on a somewhat different and grimmer tone. The account ends with some speculation about what future growth and structural transition is to be expected.

In trying to analyze the evolution of Ceylon's economy, certain types of explanatory forces have been singled out for emphasis, while others have been treated less thoroughly or ignored. The book generally limits itself to economics, bringing in political, social, psychological, and other influences only when they are most obviously relevant to the economic analysis. Insofar as noneconomic forces are regarded as being important, this volume cannot claim to present a full explanation of Ceylonese economic development. Even within the general category of economic factors, there is some unevenness of treatment. The main emphasis has been placed on quantitative, macroeconomic materials, supplemented by more intensive study of key sectors and the main actions of the government. No attempt has been made to survey all types of economic activity. Short-run factors (e.g. problems of trade instability), monetary as opposed to "real" phenomena, and detailed consideration of policy questions have deliberately been eschewed. Instead, the efforts of the author have been concentrated on trying to analyze the main economic factors influencing the secular growth of Ceylon's national output and the alteration of her economic structure.

I hope that the foregoing volume will be of at least some value to three types of readers: those interested respectively in Ceylonese economic development, in the growth of export economies, and in the development process in general. All three groups will presumably find something of significance for them in Chapter 1 of the book, which tries to bring out in explicit terms the main lessons of Ceylon's economic experience for development economics. Their relative interests in the remainder of the text and in the Statistical Appendix, however, will probably vary. Ceylonese and others interested in Ceylon *per se* will, I hope, find the entire work interesting and relevant, but others may not. The Statistical Appendix will be useful primarily to those who wish to have detailed quantitative information for use in further analysis of Ceylon's economic development, individually or as part of a comparative study. However, it is my hope that after going through Chapter 1 even readers who have no previous knowledge of Ceylon will see in it a fascinating subject for a case study of the development of an export economy and will want to read the entire volume.

The debt which I owe to the many individuals and institutions who provided advice and assistance in the writing of this book is very great. It is with genuine pleasure that I single out the most important of these for special mention here.

Without question my largest debt is to the Economic Center for affording me the rewarding experience of participating in its Country Analysis Program. Particular thanks are due to Professors Lloyd G. Reynolds and Gustav Ranis for the unfailing helpfulness and confidence they have shown me. The Economic Growth Center is entirely responsible for the financing of this study, including the cost of a 13-month stay in Ceylon in 1962-63, as well as research and clerical expenses.

Another institution which rendered especially valuable assistance was the Central Bank of Ceylon which, with its highly trained staff and fine library facilities, gave me an excellent informal base of operations during my period of field research. Other individuals and government departments in Ceylon whom I approached for assistance were invariably cooperative and helpful. The officers of the Department of Census and Statistics should be singled out for special mention in this regard. Finally, the Ford Foundation, my present employer, is to be thanked for providing typing services during the late stages of the work.

A long series of research assistants and typists have helped in the mechanical aspects of assembling this volume. In the former category, Messrs. John McGowan, A.E.C. Fernando, James Neal and Andrew Pianim have assisted at various stages of the research. Many different people have typed parts of succeeding drafts of the manuscript, but particular thanks are due for the large amount of work done by Mr. G.W. de Alwis, Mrs. Rosemary Ingham, Mrs. Margaret Oscanyan, and Mrs. Kim Symes.

Finally, I must acknowledge the large intellectual debt that I owe to the friends and former colleagues who submitted to lengthy discussions of problems posed by various aspects of the study and read through all or part of the draft manuscript. Professors Gustav Ranis, Lloyd Reynolds, Richard Ruggles, and Gerald Helleiner of Yale, Professor Henry Oliver of Indiana University, Dr. Ponna Wignaraja of the World Bank, Dr. Ian vanden Driesen of the University of Ceylon, and Mr. N.S. Karunatileke of the Central Bank of Ceylon read through all of an earlier draft and made a great number of useful comments. Other valuable discussions were provided by Professors Donald Mead and Hugh Patrick of Yale. Mr. Etienne van de Walle of the Office of Population Research at Princeton University was kind enough to read over the demographic sections and make a number of observations which have, I hope, improved them. To all of these persons I owe a profound debt of gratitude, as well as apologies if the ideas they expressed failed to find their way into the text or did so only in garbled form. In the final analysis, of course, the responsibility for all statements made in the book is fully my own.

D.R.S.

Kuala Lumpur, Malaysia
August, 1966

Table of Contents

List of Tables

PAGE

STATISTICAL APPENDIX

Chapter 1

Economic Development
and the Case of Ceylon

The estate revolution that gripped Ceylon, a hitherto sleepy island colony which had been acquired by Great Britain from Holland some 50 years earlier, in the 1840's was typical of the profound economic transformations wrought throughout the world by the rapid expansion of international trade during the nineteenth century. As it did in a host of other countries, the greatly increased flow of international commerce created in Ceylon for the first time on a substantial scale the chief characteristics of a modern economy: specialized, capital-using, wage labor-hiring production for a cash market, in this case a foreign market. In Ceylon the attentions of modern economic enterprise centered first on coffee, then on tea and, still later, rubber, all grown primarily within the confines of a plantation system. The particular nature of the product specialization, however, is not the critical characteristic of Ceylon's economy during this period. Rather, what is fundamental is the basic nature of the plantation system, which underwent relatively little modification as it shifted its attentions from one crop to another. Viewed more broadly, plantation agriculture can be classed with the whole range of extractive industries which in various countries formed the basis of what can be called the classical export economy. As already noted in the Preface to this volume, colonial Ceylon formed an excellent example of this type of economic structure. The present chapter attempts to draw out the common characteristics of the export economy from the Ceylon case study presented in succeeding chapters and to highlight the main implications of the study for the analysis of development.

For purposes of this examination of structural change and growth in the Ceylon economy, the economic history of the island since the 1840's can usefully be divided into two or perhaps three periods of development (see Table 1-1). Like all attempts to divide history into unique stages, this one is liable to criticism on the grounds that there is substantial continuity between successive eras and that the

1

TABLE 1-1

Schematic Representation of Modern Ceylon's Economic Development

Features	Period 1 Classical, or colonial economy, c. 1840–c. 1946	Period 2a Transitional, development-oriented, or independent economy, c. 1946–c. 1961	Period 2b Transitional, development-oriented, or independent economy, c. 1946–c. 1961
A. Factor supplies			
1. Labor	a. Modern sector: available in unlimited supply at legal wage from India b. Traditional sector: growing at 1% a year	Growing steadily at 2.2%	Growing at over 2% and accelerating a bit
2. Land	a. Modern sector: at first, good land available very cheaply in unlimited quantities; later (c. 1910) land worth cultivating at current export prices exhausted b. Traditional sector: growing slowly: as fast as peasant population up to the 1920's, then less fast	Growing very slowly and at great expense via land development	Same as 2a
3. Capital	a. Modern sector: easily available, at first from abroad, then from undistributed profits b. Traditional sector: unmonetized accumulation; slow	Limited supply, mainly through taxation of export agriculture and rest of modern sector; some foreign aid; also sale of foreign assets	Same as 2a, except that foreign assets became virtually exhausted and domestic saving rate may fall
B. International flows			
1. Current	Mainly between modern sector and abroad; traditional sector largely unmonetized; international trade very free	More flow between domestic sectors and between traditional sector and abroad; some redirection of flows by government; international trade relatively free, but increasingly restricted toward end of period	Flows between domestic economy and abroad tightly controlled; further increased flows between domestic sectors

2. Capital............	Between modern sector and abroad; investment in both sectors financed mainly by reinvestment of surplus	Modern sector taxed and proceeds used for public investment in peasant agriculture, industry, and overhead capital	Same as 2a
C. Growth rates			
1. Sectoral............	a. Modern sector: fast while new estate industries are opening up, then slower b. Traditional sector: very slow	Export sector relatively slow; industries favored by government policy (rice, industry) fast	Industries producing for home market have greater demand stimulus, but all sectors face shortages of capital and intermediate goods; net result uncertain
2. Overall............	Fast while new estate industries are opening up and export prices are good, then slow	Mediocre, since export industries are undynamic and import substitution and export promotion efforts are weak	Probably slower because of capital and capital-goods shortages, despite increased pressure for import substitution

Factors Determining Dividing Lines between Periods

Between 1 and 2a	Between 2a and 2b
1. Independence (emphasis on development, end of migration, new fiscal policies, etc.) 2. Population explosion	1. Exhaustion of external assets caused by political and demographic bias toward external imbalance and insufficiency of domestic saving and capital inflow 2. Tight import restriction, reducing living standards, restructuring imports, and rising demand for locally produced goods

break between them is not so sharp as is implied by the specification of distinct periods. However, like any useful identification of historical stages, the distinctions made here are based on the fact that fundamental, discontinuous changes did take place at certain times in the country's development, with the new period in each case being basically different in some important ways from the old, however great the remaining similarity between them.

This book takes little notice of the premodern period of Ceylonese economic development. It begins with the establishment, from the 1840's on, of the classical export economy. Like the later periods of development which followed it, the economic structure of this era is conveniently specified with reference to two types of criteria: the nature of the supply conditions of the factors of production and the pattern of economic flows among the sectors of the economy and between the economy and the rest of the world.

As in so many other countries, the effect of international trade was to create a dual economy, that is, two broad sectors which differed radically from each other in patterns of resource use and technology and which had relatively few economic interrelations between them. The modern sector, which centered around the estates but also included a variety of supporting commercial, financial, transportation, communications, and other service activities undertaken by both the private sector and the government, depended mainly on foreign entrepreneurship, immigrant labor, and either imported or reinvested capital. It utilized just one important indigenous resource—extensive land suitable for the cultivation of tropical tree crops. This land and the cheap, plentiful immigrant labor were organized on modern commercial lines in a capitalized and technologically advanced but highly labor- and land-intensive system. The crops chosen had to satisfy two requirements: they had to be those for which there was a large and growing demand in the industrializing countries of the West and they had to be capable of being produced efficiently using large quantities of the easily obtained factors, land and labor. Once these two conditions were satisfied, the resulting returns to the relatively scarce factors, capital and entrepreneurship, were handsome indeed. How the modern sector of Ceylon's economy, in its particular historical and geographical context, obtained the factor supplies it required is described in Chapter 2. To summarize briefly, labor was available in virtually unlimited supply from impoverished South India, good land could at first be obtained at nominal cost and in practically limitless quantities from the colonial government (later, the supply of land worth cultivating at prevailing world prices for Ceylon's crops was exhausted), and capital as well was easily acquired, first from abroad, then increasingly through reinvestment of the large modern-sector profits.

The impressive development of the modern sector which ensued had little immediate impact on Ceylon's traditional sector, the economic life of the country which had existed prior to the coming of estate agriculture. The technology employed in traditional economic activity, which was overwhelmingly agricultural in nature, was ages-old and tradition-bound. The supplies of factors of production available to traditional-sector producers grew only very slowly. The labor force, held in a virtual balance of high birth rates and high death rates, increased at only about one percent a year. The supply of land was extended only very slowly and painfully. Capital accumulation took place mainly in its nonmonetized form and was slow in pace. As in so many other countries, the contrast between the two parts of the economy was striking and tended to persist stubbornly through time. The classical export economy was thus what has been called a dual economy.

Why did the rise of the estates in Ceylon create a dual economy and why did this condition persist through so long a period of the nation's economic development? At one level of explanation, the answer is that there was scarcely any economic interrelationship between the two segments of the economy and hence the "spread effects" of modern-sector growth to the traditional sector were negligible. The products of the modern sector were of course sold abroad. The factors of production were similarly obtained from foreign sources, except for estate land, most of which had been completely unused or only lightly used by the traditional sector before the formation of the estates. Almost all the intermediate goods used by modern-sector producers and almost all the articles they consumed were imported. The forces of the market thus hardly came to play upon the traditional sector at all. There was little favorable "spread effect" of modern-sector development on the traditional sector, but neither was there much unfavorable "backwash effect." The two sectors were virtually in different countries.[1]

On a more fundamental plane, of course, one must ask *why* the economic dealings between the two sectors were minimal. The literature of economic development offers two basic explanations of

----

[1]The use of the terms spread and backwash to represent the external economies and diseconomies respectively of the development of one sector of an economy on the rest of the economy or one economy on the rest of the world was originated by Gunnar Myrdal. See *Economic Theory and Under-Developed Regions* (London: Gerald Duckworth & Co., Ltd., 1957).

dualism, the sociological and the technological. The leading exponent of social dualism, of course, is Boeke, whose essential thesis is that "Asians are different," i.e., that their behavior is inherently incapable of being analyzed in terms of Western economic theory.[2] The implication of immutable cultural differences present in Boeke's thinking is rejected by most modern economists, who have criticized his work[3] and provided a fundamental alternative to his main hypothesis. The alternative hypothesis, which has been referred to as technological dualism, is however less clearly applicable to the case of estate versus traditional agriculture dualism than it is to a split between industry and agriculture in general.[4] It states that factor proportions in the modern sector are either fixed by technical conditions at a highly capital-intensive position or are viewed as such by producers in the modern sector; traditional-sector factor proportions are variable; since labor is relatively plentiful, labor-intensive methods are used. Various writers[5] have generalized from this starting position and sketched out a process of economic development based upon capital accumulation in the modern sector, which progressively expands and gradually draws into its employment the labor surplus from the traditional sector, ending with the elimination of technological dualism itself. The way Ceylon and other economies in which the modern sector centers on plantation agriculture differ from this general picture is that even though labor is relatively more productive in the modern sector, the latter, too, is relatively labor-intensive, using from the start large numbers of unskilled laborers. The idea of a modern sector which does not require a large labor force is thus not applicable here. The plantations *did* need a sizable labor force and we must ask ourselves why the indigenous traditional sector did not do more to satisfy the need. There appear to be two possible answers, between which it is difficult to choose (indeed, there is no reason to regard them as mutually incompatible): cultural factors and alternative economic opportunities. Ceylon in the mid-nine-

[2]J. H. Boeke, *Economics and Economic Policy of Dual Societies* (New York: Institute of Pacific Relations, 1953).

[3]E.g., Benjamin Higgins, "The Dualistic Theory of Underdeveloped Areas," *Economic Development and Cultural Change*, January, 1956.

[4]The notion of technological dualism has been developed by Benjamin Higgins, *Economic Development* (New York: W. W. Norton & Co., Inc., 1959), pp. 325–333. An earlier treatment was R. S. Eckaus, "The Factor Proportions Problem in Underdeveloped Areas," *American Economic Review*, September, 1955.

[5]W. Arthur Lewis, "Economic Development with Unlimited Supplies of Labour," *The Manchester School*, May, 1954; John C. H. Fei and Gustav Ranis, *Development of the Labor Surplus Economy* (Homewood, Illinois: Richard D. Irwin, Inc., 1964).

teenth century was not a densely populated country. Moreover, it was favored by nature with a benevolent climate and advantageous conditions for the cultivation of the traditional peasant crops. Compared to the relatively easy life offered by nature to traditional-sector producers, the wages paid by the early estates were probably not attractive. It was undoubtedly also true that there were elements in traditional Sinhalese culture, especially in the up-country, where it retained a purer form than it did in the low country, which had experienced long association with commercially minded Europeans, that created a dislike for wage labor. These attitudes were surely malleable, however; the essential reason why they did not change more rapidly is probably that, with a large supply of cheap Indian labor easily available, the estates never offered a wage which was high enough to attract large numbers of indigenous Ceylonese into the modern sector. This simple hypothesis about the relative returns to economic activity in the traditional and modern sectors appears to be a third possible explanation of dualism, since it rests on neither immutable cultural traditions nor on fixed capital-intensive technology in the modern sector. It can be applied, however, only to cases where ready access to immigrant labor held wages below levels which might have provided a bigger incentive for labor to move from the traditional to the modern sector.

The growth potential of the classical export economy, as long as there is a foreign market for its modern-sector products and as long as its land and labor supplies hold up, is very great. This growth takes place primarily through the extension of plantation agriculture to ever-greater land areas, the immigration of a continuously growing labor force, and the progressive reinvestment of sectoral profits. Since it takes place in response to world demand, economic growth is limited almost entirely to modern-sector production, which thus increases rapidly as a percentage of domestic output. To the extent that the proceeds of this increasing production are not remitted abroad, income levels within the modern sector rise correspondingly. The traditional sector, whose economic life has not been fundamentally transformed, shares little in the increase in national income (although the government may to a limited extent begin to serve as an instrument for broadening the distribution of the benefits from export production). Thus, it scarcely makes sense to talk about the growth of an export economy as such. The growth is virtually limited to the modern sector; it is really artificial to add the two sectors together and refer to the growth of the national economy, although somewhere along the line a long, slow process of transformation does begin in the traditional sector.

The first check which the expansion of plantation agriculture receives is likely to be the gradual depletion of the supply of cheap land upon which it depends. The value of the land depends upon the price fetched by the end product in the world market, of course. During the twentieth century the growth of world demand for primary exports (with the notable exception of petroleum) has tended to retard as time goes by. The demand for food products is income-inelastic and the demand for industrial raw materials, which was initially highly elastic, has become much less so as synthetic substitutes for the various natural products have been developed in the industrial countries. In consequence, the prices of primary products in international trade, while they have not necessarily moved adversely relative to prices of industrial products as the Singer-Prebisch thesis suggests,[6] at least have generally ceased to rise. This means that the supply of land which can profitably be planted with each crop is eventually exhausted and the pattern of growth which has been known in the past must come to a halt. When export prices decline sharply, as they did in the 1930's, the shock is of course severe. In any case, after the supply of good land is virtually used up further rises in output come to depend on the intensification of production through increased use of other factors relative to land and through improvements in technology. Plantation agriculture is by no means unamenable to technical change, as the experience of the estate industries of Ceylon and other export economies shows, but the process of raising output by this means is still likely to be less dramatic than the production gains which were recorded in earlier times by the opening of vast tracts of land to estate enterprise. Thus, for both supply-side and demand-side reasons, the growth of export receipts has been much less rapid in the twentieth century than it was in the nineteenth.

At approximately the same time as these changes in world market conditions and in the availability of factors of production at home took place, most export economies underwent some important non-economic changes which altered the whole direction of economic development and eventually created strong pressures for structural change. The main changes were political. The worldwide independence movement of the mid-twentieth century radically increased the demands made on the export economies by their citizens. As the governments of these countries passed into the hands of leaders

---

[6]Among the many references are Hans Singer, "The Distribution of Gains between Investing and Borrowing Countries," *American Economic Review Papers and Proceedings,* May, 1950 and Raoul Prebisch, "The Role of Commercial Policy in Underdeveloped Countries," *American Economic Review Papers and Proceedings,* May, 1959.

with some sort of popular mandate, economic policy quickly developed into what Levin has termed the revolt against the export economy.[7] The failure of the classical export economy to provide sufficiently higher and more evenly distributed levels of income, its short-term instability, and even (irrationally) its mere association with colonialism came increasingly under attack. The pressures for faster economic growth and structural diversification grew. In Ceylon as in many other export economies, demographic pressures were added to the political ones. Dramatic reductions in death rates without corresponding declines in birth rates brought rapidly accelerated population growth. This added urgency to the drive for faster income growth, which was invariably viewed as being impossible within the economic framework of the past. These political and demographic pressures so altered the environment for economic change that it is useful to identify a second major period of export-economy development, which begins with (though it was not primarily created by) World War II. About that time a new type of economic structure began to emerge; it might be called the development-oriented export economy, or, since it is still very much in a state of flux, the transitional export economy.

The ways in which the transitional export economy differs from the classical form can conveniently be defined with reference to the two criteria used earlier, the supply conditions of the factors of production and the pattern of intersectoral flows. Labor supply lost the flexibility it had possessed in earlier times, since nationalism led to the essential elimination of international migration; under the influence of rapid overall population growth, its rate of growth probably rose. The supply of land could, as in the recent past, be increased only with great difficulty and expense. Capital thus became a strategic factor in the growth process, as did technical change. The free private international capital flow of earlier days had largely died out and was only fractionally replaced by foreign economic aid. The export-sector surpluses which previously had furnished a principal source of investment finance remained, however; capturing a large portion of these surpluses through taxation and using them to finance investment in other parts of the economy —peasant agriculture, industry, and overhead capital—came to be a fundamental principle of development strategy. Technical modernization in both plantation and peasant agriculture began to be stressed. Invariably, the attempts to force the pace of economic

---

[7]Jonathan V. Levin, *The Export Economies* (Cambridge, Massachusetts: Harvard University Press, 1960).

development and change its nature created pressures for the integration of the economy, i.e., a breaking down of its dualism.

Just what type of development strategy should be pursued in an export economy at this juncture and even whether a massive governmental effort need be launched at all are matters which have received extensive discussion in world economic literature and, of course, in the countries themselves. In part, the question is one of an apparent conflict between the neoclassical theory of international trade and more recent thought on the subject of economic growth. The neoclassical conclusion was that free international trade was invariably of benefit to all participating nations and, moveover, that it was an engine of economic growth. This nineteenth-century optimism about the chances of a nation's enjoying simultaneously the maximum benefits of international trade and economic growth is jarringly inconsistent with the pessimism about the returns to developing countries from international trade common in our own day and the emphasis in current development prescriptions on developing production for the home market.[8] This change in attitudes toward international trade is readily understood in the light of the two phases of development through which Ceylon and other export economies have passed. It is hardly surprising that conclusions based on the experience of the classical and the transitional periods respectively should be strikingly different. During the era of the classical export economy the advantages of international trade for both primary producing countries and the industrializing countries were evident; international trade theory based on static comparative advantage seemed to provide a suitable exposition of these gains. International trade was indeed an engine which produced the type of economic growth experienced by the export economies during their "classical" phase. As already noted, however, it was limited export-sector growth, not general growth of the entire economy, which trade created. Around the middle of the present century, two things changed. As noted previously, one change was that on both the supply and the demand sides the income-increasing potential of primary production for export began to decline. More important, however, was the fact that the rate of economic growth

---

[8]Chenery has stated succinctly the conditions required for a theoretical reconciliation of trade and growth theory: ". . . . it is necessary to discard [from neoclassical trade theory] the assumption of equilibrium in factor markets, to allow for changes in the quantity and quality of factors of production over time, and to take account of internal and external economies of scale." Hollis B. Chenery, "Comparative Advantage and Development Policy," *American Economic Review*, March, 1961, p. 46.

expected of the economy rose sharply. The revolt against the classical export economy created a parallel revolt against neoclassical trade theory in its relation to economic growth. Diligent searching discovered shortcomings in the theory (see footnote[8], above), which could be used as justification for intervention in international trade. Intellectual weaknesses of the neoclassical theory aside, increasing external imbalance resulting from the accelerated growth of aggregate demand (itself caused by imperfectly executed efforts to raise the growth rate of real output) forced many transitional economies into a position of increasing protectionism.[9] The pressing question of the hour came to be that of development strategy: what economic policy would provide the greatest increase in the growth rate? In particular, since capital was the scarcest factor of production, what allocation of investment was optimal? A bewildering variety of investment criteria were put forth in economic literature. Granted that the seeming conflict with international trade theory could be resolved by following the nation's dynamic comparative advantage (i.e., one based on true alternative costs to society of the various factors of production and on future factor endowments, taking account of potential external and internal economies of scale), how was that to be discovered?

In Ceylon, policy makers wrestled with this problem, but to no avail. At various times, attempts were made to justify the allegedly inherent superiority of industry over agriculture (or vice versa), of export production over production for home use (and the reverse), and so on. No completely convincing answer to the dilemma was ever found, although it is clear from the discouraging failures encountered in Ceylon's case that the policies actually followed were hardly optimal. Indeed, there is probably no simple, general solution to the problem. The location of an export economy's dynamic comparative advantage doubtless depends heavily on the nation's particular present and likely future resource endowments. Country size also enters in. For large countries the possibility of exploiting dynamic external economies through a policy of balanced growth may hold some appeal but for small countries such as Ceylon and most other export economies (small in terms of population and, in the immediate future at least, income) considerable specialization is necessarily a part of any sound long-term strategy. Like most of the other small countries which are seeking a viable alternative to the classical export economy, Ceylon cannot hope to expand all

---

[9]Whether for adequate reasons or not, these countries generally rejected the neoclassical remedy for external imbalance, exchange rate devaluation.

kinds of production simultaneously without having to pay an enormous price in terms of efficiency. For this reason, countries of this type will inevitably continue to depend heavily on international trade, although the nature of the commodities traded will necessarily undergo fundamental changes. Kuznets states that the principal problems of small nations seeking to develop their economies are small area and population, limited natural resources, and greater difficulties in maintaining national security. He cites as a partially compensating advantage a political and social homogeneity which may permit small countries to recast their domestic institutions into a shape which will promote economic growth and international trade more readily and painlessly than might a larger country.[10] Unfortunately, Ceylon's example shows that even small countries can be heterogeneous and that the social concensus required for an effective growth effort may still be hard to obtain. Indeed, the past operations of the classical export economy, which introduced foreign labor and entrepreneurship and established for them a dominant position in the economy and society, tended to create social heterogeneity and a serious potential cause of political friction in the export economy.

Aside from the question of which sectors investment should have been channeled into, it is clear that Ceylon failed to take full advantage of the opportunities open to it as a development-oriented export economy. Fei and Ranis have concisely indicated how international trade can be used as an engine of general, economy-wide growth in this economic structure. They cite four significant advantages which the export economy derives from its contact with the international market. (1) Most importantly, the export sector represents a highly efficient production function by which the economy may transform the food and industrial consumer goods imports used mainly by workers in the export sector into imported capital goods and raw materials; the transformation is made much more efficiently through the export sector than by any other route. (2) The economy may choose from a wide range of technological alternatives assembled by a process of trial and error over a considerable period of time in the industrial countries; it should thus be able to select capital goods for import which are suited to its resource endowment and development strategy. (3) It can obtain from foreign sources providing grants and loans on easy terms capital which can be used to pursue whatever development strategy it de-

---

[10]S. Kuznets, "Economic Growth of Small Nations," in International Economic Association, *Economic Consequences of the Size of Nations,* ed. E. A. G. Robinson (New York: St. Martins Press, 1960).

cides to embark upon; this capital will not possess the severe limitations in direction and impact possessed by the private capital inflows of the classical period, nor will it be so costly. (4) Through a generally overvalued exchange rate, it can implicitly tax exporters and subsidize capital-goods importers, above and beyond any taxes and subsidies which are levied explicitly.[11]

All of these advantages represent potentials which are available to be exploited by the development-oriented export economy. But they are certainly not guarantees of success, as the abortive attempts of Ceylon to take advantage of them demonstrate. While Ceylon's general development strategy was essentially based upon an attempt to use these potentials, it fell short of success in several ways. (1) The transformation of receipts from the old export crops from providers of consumer goods to providers of capital goods and materials was for a long time undertaken far too half-heartedly; when a serious effort was made of necessity in the early sixties, the wrong policy instruments (direct controls rather than indirect measures) were probably used. (2) The application of borrowed technology to agriculture and industry in Ceylon, while responsible for much of the output growth of the period, fell far short of potentials. (3) Foreign loan and grant sources were not exploited to as full an extent as they might have been. (4) The overvalued exchange rate, when taken in the context of the failure to restructure imports, simply worked as a subsidy on imported consumer goods.

Another significant point of Ceylon's postwar experience is the fundamental relationship it indicates among three factors: the social consensus referred to previously, short-term instability, and long-term economic growth. Because no adequate public commitment to make the sacrifices which would have been required if an acceptable long-term growth rate were to be achieved (essentially, this would have meant a much higher domestic saving ratio) was ever extracted by a weak government, the success of the development policy was seriously jeopardized by external instability. If an export economy is to grow rapidly and still remain reasonably open to the import commodities which are essential to the satisfaction of both its consumption and its investment goods needs, then it must match whatever proportion of its domestic investment is not financed by capital inflows with domestic saving. Failure to do so results in excess aggregate demand. Excess demand, if allowed to persist, will eventually force a sealing off of the economy from past sources of imports. This will reduce living standards in the short

---

[11]Fei and Ranis, *op. cit.*, pp. 298–99.

run and, more important, create supply-side obstacles to new investment (shortages of investment and intermediate goods not produced at home), as well as further tendencies towards the autarky which a small country can ill afford. It will also accelerate a desirable restructuring of the economy through forced import substitution, but with the high setup costs involved in creating an industrial sector virtually from scratch the economy will be slow to generate internal surpluses anywhere other than in the old export sector. Unless enormous sacrifices are extracted from the public (and to achieve these would require discipline of a very high order) the investment rate may well fall and the pace of economic growth may decelerate. The inability of the country to finance the import bill to which it had previously become accustomed, in short, not only causes popular suffering but it deprives the government of some of the development alternatives which it had enjoyed before, since all policy proposals must now pass rigid balance of payments tests. The moral is that in developing export economies it is best to be cautious about the growth of aggregate demand, protecting the country from the kind of situation just described. Sacrifices are best made early, voluntarily, and piecemeal, rather than being forced upon the country wholesale later on. The unpredictability of export receipts often makes it hard to assess precisely the secular trend in the external balance, but it is probably better to be overly conservative than to suffer the consequences described above. Here again, the need for the creation of a national consensus favorable to growth is more than evident.

In the case of Ceylon, the transitional stage of economic development was marked by a failure to hit upon an adequate growth strategy and by a seeming inability to maintain external stability in the face of public demands for immediate rises in consumption levels. The kind of blanket imposition of import prohibitions just mentioned was thus required. It took place in the early 1960's and ushered in what is referred to in Table 1.1 as phase 2b of the development of the economy—2b because while most of the structural characteristics of period 2a (the development-oriented export economy with essentially free access to imports) remained, one key factor had changed when import trade came under tight governmental control. During period 2a a fundamental problem of inducing private investment outside of export agriculture was that market forces (static, private comparative advantage) worked against it and the government was slow to provide measures which would produce the necessary redirection of market incentives. With the supply of imports abruptly and severely constrained, this problem disappeared. In its place were the even greater problems mentioned in the preceding paragraph. Surely the ambiguities and other difficulties of period 2a are preferable to the mutually reinforcing antigrowth forces of period 2b. Fortunately, it is in regard to this progression from stage 2a to stage 2b that one may cease to think of Ceylon as typical of all export economies. There is nothing inevitable about the transition; its prevention depends entirely on the astuteness of public policies.[12] The world contains examples of export economies in both stages, those which can still afford to remain essentially open to all kinds of imports and those which have had to restrict sharply the access of their nationals to imported goods. Surely the lesson of Ceylon is of great relevance to those countries which are still in stage 2a. If they can maintain their external balance and convert their import bills from largely consumer goods to largely producer goods they need never enter stage 2b. For countries already in stage 2b perhaps the greatest consolation which can be offered is that slow, painful growth is still possible and that regional cooperation in trade policy and investment allocation may yet permit them to gain many of the benefits of specialization and international trade as well.

---

[12]Indeed, if import flows are controlled and restructured through the gradual but timely application of import duties and selective direct controls, most of the advantages of period 2b can be attained while minimizing its frustrations.

Chapter 2

Historical Background: The
Rise of the Estates

The "export economy," an economic system in which productive activity is heavily oriented toward supplying a few primary commodities to the world market and consumption is largely made up of imported goods, is often identified with colonialism. For most of the period studied here Ceylon was both an export economy and a colony. But the beginnings of the export economy in Ceylon did not coincide with the country's colonization. The island had been a European fief for three and a quarter centuries before it emerged with dramatic suddenness in the 1840's as a veritable model of the export economy. Portugal and Holland had each enjoyed a century and a half of rule of the island, but their effective sovereignty had always been limited to a narrow coastal belt. Their economic interests had been similarly circumscribed, consisting mainly of trade in native-grown cinnamon, pearls, ivory, and the other exotic commodities for which Ceylon had been renowned since ancient times. The Portuguese had failed in efforts to subjugate the Kandyan kingdom of the hinterlands and the Dutch formulated a policy of leaving the feudal political, social, and economic structure untouched to as great an extent as was consistent with their control of the prized cinnamon trade. The seizure of Holland's coastal forts by the British in 1796 had no immediate effect on this situation. The British valued the island for strategic reasons—its proximity to India and the fine natural harbor at Trincomalee—and apparently gave little thought at first to its potential economic worth.

COFFEE

The economic side of British interests in the early years centered on the cinnamon trade[1] and not even the extension of European rule to the whole island for the first time in 1815 had any profound

---

[1] See Colvin R. de Silva, *Ceylon under the British Occupation, 1795–1833* (Colombo: The Colombo Apothecaries Co., Ltd., 1962), Vol. 2.

effect on its economic structure. Although Ceylon had throughout recorded time been a participant in international trade it was only with the revolutionary introduction of the coffee plantation in the 1840's that it became a classic example of the export economy. An export economy can be defined as one with not merely a high ratio of imports and exports to national income, but one in which all the important macroeconomic quantities—government revenues and expenditures, private investment, imports, and national income itself—possess a strong functional dependence upon the level of export receipts. This Ceylon very clearly became during the decade of the 1840's and remained, certainly throughout the rest of the colonial era, and in some respects to the present day.

The effect of the coffee revolution on the economy was electric. In the words of its leading historian,

> Bringing with it new modes of economic behaviour and a host of concepts foreign to the prevailing economic system, it ate quickly into the foundations of the existing structure. Capitalism had arrived, and it is with its advent that the Island's modern economic history takes its start. A virile commercial agriculture soon displaced in importance the old pursuits of the people and within the short space of a few years coffee had made itself responsible for almost a third of the Government's income. The stake was large enough to render it the State's most favoured child. In the years that followed the planters' problems came to be regarded as synonymous with those of the country, and in the quest to solve them,—an undertaking to which the Government lent its energetic support—much that was new was introduced with startling rapidity. Thus did Ceylon dance to the coffee-growers' tune for the greater part of the 19th century. In the process a new economic structure began slowly to evolve. The factors of production,—land, labour and capital, took on a new meaning; roads, railways and ports appeared where there had been none before, political affairs were invested with a novel significance, and class in the modern sense of the term began its slow growth. Along with these developments a money economy emerged, bringing with it a consciousness of prices, profit, wages, rent and credit . . .[2]

The sudden rise of the coffee industry in the 1840's is apparently attributable to the confluence at that time of a number of favorable factors. Britain had developed a taste for coffee during the eighteenth century as consumption of wine dropped, but previous supplies had come first from the East Indies and later increasingly from the West Indian colonies. In Ceylon, on the other hand, the

---

[2]I. H. van den Driesen, *The Economic History of Ceylon in the Nineteenth Century*, Vol. 1, *Plantations, Land and Capital* (unpublished English manuscript of Sinhalese book; 1961). As will become evident in the following pages the section of this monograph which deals with the coffee industry depends heavily on van den Driesen's work.

plant had long been grown by the peasants, but never as a cash crop. Sporadically, it had been Dutch policy to offer incentives to native producers and the British at first tried this, too, but in 1823 the first coffee plantation was set up and in the following year Sir Edward Barnes, a man who had unbounded confidence in the future of coffee in Ceylon, became governor. Incentives were given to estate production in the form of abolition of an export duty, exemption of coffee land from the land tax, repeal of import duties on agricultural and manufacturing equipment, and exemption from feudal labor dues of those employed in coffee growing.[3] Despite these powerful incentives production failed to respond very much until a good foreign market opened up. By the 1830's all conditions were right: the early experimental plantations had begun to evolve a greatly improved technology, the discriminatory import duty in favor of West Indian coffee which Great Britain had previously maintained was equalized, and the plantation system in the West Indies was disrupted by the freeing of the slaves who had provided its labor force.

Ceylon's coffee output responded strongly to the more favorable environment. From 1834 to 1842 export volume rose fivefold,[4] yet the latter year was only the threshold of the era when coffee was king. From that year up to 1849 a further rise to three times the 1842 level was recorded (see Table 2–1). Ceylon ousted West Indian coffee from the British market: in 1827 Ceylon had supplied only 1,800,000 pounds of coffee to Britain (versus 29,400,000 from the West Indies), but by 1847 it was supplying 19,500,000 (the West Indian contribution had fallen to 5,300,000 pounds).[5]

In 1846 something happened which was unprecedented in the economic history of Ceylon up to that time: the island felt the effects of a world depression. Coffee prices fell from 41s. per hundredweight in 1845 to 28s. in 1848. Considerable new planting had been done earlier, when prices were still high, so total output of coffee continued to rise rapidly, but sales of government land to planters fell off precipitously. Van den Driesen estimates that perhaps 10 percent of the estates being farmed in 1847 had been abandoned by 1849[6] and official data show a decline in planted acreage of nearly 25 percent.[7] Many planters were ruined and estates changed hands

---

[3]*Ibid.*, pp. 47–48.
[4]See Table 2–1.
[5]van den Driesen, *op. cit.*, p. 55.
[6]*Ibid.*, p. 79.
[7]These acreage data were probably compiled on a "care and maintenance" basis. That is, acreage which had not been uprooted but had merely fallen into disuse was removed from the total. This explains why the recovery of acreage in the ensuing prosperity was so rapid.

at prices representing a fraction of what had been their value just two years before. Yet, as time proved, the frightening depression of 1847–49 was just the first of several such incidents in the history of Ceylon's export economy. Even for the coffee industry, which itself proved to be only a transient feature of the longer-lived economic structure, two extremely prosperous decades lay ahead.

The 1850's and 1860's were the years when King Coffee reigned supreme. Over that twenty-year span the area planted with the crop rose swiftly and the quantity exported more than tripled. Prices moved steadily upward during the fifties and then remained stable at favorable levels during the sixties. With the coming of the seventies, however, this golden era drew to a close. The fall of coffee, which began during that decade, was even more dramatic than its rise; within the span of just fifteen years the industry went from peak prosperity to utter ruin. The cause of coffee's ultimate downfall made its first appearance in 1869: *Hemileia vastatrix*, the coffee-leaf disease. This fungus, which ultimately destroyed the Ceylon industry, also struck the coffee industries of India and Java, but spared Brazil, thus going far to determine the future pattern of supply to the world market. The appearance of the disease coincided, as it happened, with a rapid rise in world prices, in which the unit value of Ceylon's coffee exports more than doubled between 1872 and 1876. Attempts were made to combat the fungus: for instance, Liberian plants were substituted for the Arabian variety in some cases, but they proved to be even more susceptible to the disease. Soaring prices, however, assured that for the time being coffee growing remained profitable. The area planted, which had been rising at a relatively modest pace, began to increase more rapidly. New parts of the island were introduced to coffee cultivation. Meanwhile, the fungus had caused year-to-year instability (a pattern of alternating good and bad years emerged) and a steady downward trend in per acre yield. In this race between rising prices and acreage on the one hand and falling yields on the other, the revenue-increasing forces remained ahead throughout the seventies. Export volume hit its peak in 1870, but 1879, with its average price of 119s. per hundredweight and its total export proceeds of nearly £5,000,000, was in these respects one of the very best years in the industry's history.

Meanwhile, however, per acre yields were slipping fast as the fungus spread. During the 1870's, while prices soared, increasingly high-cost production areas, upon which nothing had ever been grown in the past, had been planted with coffee. Yields on these new lands were low but at the prices of the seventies even this low-yield cultivation was remunerative. At the same time, the spread of the leaf disease had been reducing yields on the older coffee lands. After 1879 the world price fell as Brazilian coffee began to come onto the world market in increasing volume. This drop in price was not particularly sharp and prices were still far above the levels of the prosperous sixties, but the leaf disease had spread too far. Per acre yields were now so low that thousands of acres suddenly became unprofitable. The fall in price, when combined with the continuing effects of the fungus, spelled disaster for the Ceylon industry. Acreage declined rapidly in the early 1880's, going from nearly 300,000 acres to just over 100,000 by 1886. Yields, too,

TABLE 2-1

THE CEYLON COFFEE INDUSTRY, 1834–86*

(Annual Figures and Annual Averages)

Year	Export Volume (000 Cwts.)	Export Unit Value† (s./Cwt.)	Area Planted‡ (000 Acres)	Yield§ (Cwts./Acre)
1834......	26	30	..	..
1835–39....	46	47	..	..
1840–44....	97	49	23	4.2
1845–49....	260	33	51	5.1
1850–54....	344	40	59	5.9
1855–59....	537	48	138	3.9
1860–64....	615	51	199	3.1
1865–69....	939	52	243	3.9
1870–74....	881	66	276	3.2
1875–79....	795	108	310	2.6
1880–84....	433	89	259	1.7
1885......	316	78	139	2.3
1886......	179	89	110	1.6

*Here, as elsewhere in this monograph where quantitative data are used and questions of statistical accuracy arise, the reader is urged to refer to the Appendix, where he will find more detailed statistics and an evaluation of their quality. Statistical detail has been held down in the text so as to lessen boredom. Also, every effort has been made to avoid misleading or overly concrete uses of data in the text, but many of the statistical materials used cannot be properly evaluated by the reader unless he refers to the Appendix essays on statistical quality, the relevant Appendix tables, and the footnotes attached to these tables. Ideally, this warning should be repeated at dozens of points throughout the text, but space considerations forbid it, so the reader must regard this single note as a blanket warning.

†Export value in shillings divided by export volume in hundredweights; this is not to be interpreted literally as a measure of price, since a small part of the rise in the later years represents the displacement of lower-priced peasant coffee by estate coffee (see Table 2–3). Also, there seems to have been a conventional aspect to these price data: e.g., in 1873 a sudden upward adjustment was made in the conventional price used in making customs estimates, to allow for the rise in the actual price which had been taking place over the previous several years

‡See footnote # to Table A–37, Appendix.

§Exports in hundredweights divided by area planted; the measure is distorted by the inclusion of immature acreage in varying degrees at different times.

Source: Department of Statistics and Office Systems, *Ceylon Blue Books.*

continued their downward trend. By 1886 the Ceylon coffee industry was, for all practical purposes, dead.

Although remote in time from the main interests of this study, the history of the coffee industry is worth examining in some detail because it set the pattern for the later development of the plantations (the fact that it was tea, rubber, or coconut that was planted in later years did not fundamentally alter the structure of the system) and the plantations in turn monopolized the center of the stage throughout the colonial period. All the characteristics which remained basic to the plantation system in Ceylon, at least up to independence in 1948, made their first appearance in the nineteenth-century coffee industry: British ownership and management of most estates, including almost all the largest ones; provision of finance by British banks and "agency houses"; large-scale, factory-style operation of the estates using massive forces of Indian labor specially imported for the purpose; control of the import-export trade by the British; virtually complete reliance on imported supplies of capital equipment, estate supplies, and even food for the labor force; virtually complete reliance on foreign—especially British—markets for the product. These key characteristics had important consequences for the working of the economy and its capacity for economic growth.

The Ceylon peasant had grown coffee in a casual manner, only slightly different from the gathering of wild berries in the jungle which had preceded coffee's organized cultivation. The peasant simply planted a few bushes in his garden and then allowed them to mature, not bothering either to weed or to fertilize them. Often he picked the berries before they had reached full ripeness so as to win his continuous competition with the birds, who might otherwise devour the ripe berries. Once picked the berries had to be dried, so as to aid the stripping of the outer pulp from the kernel ("coffee bean") inside. Sometimes, to make the stripping of the pulp from the kernel easier, the peasant soaked the berries in water. This also increased the weight of the coffee and added to the peasant's revenues, since he sold the coffee by weight to itinerant tradesmen, who carried it to Colombo, but it did make for lower quality. The lack of care, the premature picking, and the wetting that the coffee often received all went together to reduce the quality of the end product. Clearly there was much room for improvement in this casual technology of coffee growing.

The estate system of coffee cultivation was evolved gradually by the early British planters in Ceylon. They had little experience elsewhere to rely upon in devising their methods of production, because they and their Dutch contemporaries in Java were the world's pioneers in large-scale commercial coffee cultivation. The estate revolution consisted of growing the crop on a large scale (the average European estate was perhaps 100 acres in extent; see page 23, below) and raising both average yields and quality levels by the application of scientific agriculture. As time went by, the precise methods of spacing the trees, shading, interplanting with other crops, pruning, weeding, and manuring that were best suited to Ceylon's estate country were determined. The coffee bushes were "topped" to make them spread out and achieve a larger growth of berries. They were given constant attention throughout the year. The continuous maintenance that was required and the handpicking of the berries, which occurred at several times during the year but especially at the main three-month harvest season, created huge requirements for labor. The drying and pulping of the picked berries was done in a factory attached to the estate (or, in the case of the smaller estate, in the factory of a nearby large estate). The beans were then carefully graded and sent off to Colombo to be shipped abroad. Bringing together the capital required to build up one of these estates, the land needed for the planting of the trees, and the sizable labor force (about two workers to the acre) necessary to maintain, harvest, and process the crop called for prodigies of entrepreneurial effort. But adequate supplies of each factor of production were found somehow.

Land for plantation development was purchased from the Crown. With the conquest of the Kandyan kingdom in 1815 all the land in the central part of the island which was not at that time occupied—and this meant vast stretches of forest land—was taken over by the Crown. As it happened, this was the land which later proved suitable for coffee cultivation and it was the sale of Kandyan land by the Crown to planters that furnished the starting point for the estate cultivation of coffee. This land, for which there was little alternative use (but see pages 28–29), was at first sold to British investors at a nominal price of five shillings per acre; the government even defrayed the cost of surveying the plot that the investor selected. Beginning in 1833, when only 146 acres of Crown land were sold, the demand for this land rose very rapidly and in 1840 an all-time record was set when 78,686 acres were sold.[8] In just four years, 1840–43, some 230,000 acres of land were sold by the government, mostly to developers of coffee estates.[9] Not all sales were made to Europeans and not all were for use in the coffee industry,

---

[8]*Ibid.*, p. 59.
[9]*Ibid.*, p. 59.

but records show that between 1844 and 1860, while sales continued at a pace somewhat less hectic than that of the early forties, government land sales of all types totaled some 150,000 acres and of these over 105,000 acres represented land in the coffee-producing areas sold to Europeans; of the remaining sales, to natives, most were also in the coffee country.[10] The average sale to a European between 1833 and 1860 was 97 acres; this can be taken as a first approximation of the size of the average coffee plantation.[11]

During the land rush of the early 1840's speculation ran wild as investors bought up government land at the five-shilling price and resold it not long after at three or four times as much. The government lacked adequate personnel to do a good job of surveying land before selling it and the result was a wave of land litigation. In June 1844 the speculative bubble was pricked by an edict declaring that in the future no land would be sold before being surveyed and that the price would be raised to 20s. These measures immediately struck down speculation. Coffee acreage continued to grow despite a much lower rate of government land sales by means of cultivation of previously purchased but unplanted acres. The growth of the industry was thus not stifled but the era of virtually free land was over. This policy change, coupled with the effects of the 1847–49 depression, which weeded out the less efficient producers, meant that the days when almost anyone could make money in coffee were also ended.

From 1850 to 1857 the area under coffee tripled, rising at a much faster rate than can be explained by reference to government land sales. After about 1860 a new era of massive land sales began. The Surveyor-General's Department had finally been organized in an efficient enough way to cope with requests to buy land as fast as they came in and the prosperity of the 1850's and 1860's created a brisk demand. During the sixties about 35,000 acres a year were sold, but it was not such good land as had been sold in earlier decades and prices were higher now. After *Hemileia vastatrix* struck in the seventies, the volume of land sales remained sizable but the makeup of the buyers changed. Less of the new land went into coffee (though total coffee acreage did continue to grow) and more was bought by peasants.[12]

During its formative years, then, the coffee industry enjoyed easy

[10]*Ibid.*, pp. 122–23.

[11]*Ibid.*, p. 125.

[12]By the 1880's the government had accelerated the work of repairing old irrigation works and building new ones. Most of the land sold during that decade was located near such works and was used by its peasant purchasers for traditional agriculture—mostly rice cultivation. See van den Driesen, *op. cit.*, p. 154.

access to cheap land. Later, the cost of land rose but extension of the area cultivated continued. Only in the early eighties did the spread of the fungus and the reversal of the rising price trend put a stop to the process of extending coffee cultivation to new land. When these two events occurred the Ceylon coffee industry melted away in the course of a very few years.

Labor was one of the first problems encountered by the pioneer planters. The indigenous inhabitants of the plantation area, the Kandyan Sinhalese, had been under European domination for only about 20 years when the coffee industry began and their acquaintance with the money economy was slight. In 1833 the government attempted to create a supply of wage labor for the estates by abolishing the feudal Kandyan system of service tenure *(raja-kariya)*. The expectation that this action would force large numbers of Kandyans into the labor market proved to be mistaken. The Kandyans continued to prefer their traditional village existence to the regimented life and work of the estates. Whether their refusal to work on the estates was purely a cultural matter or whether the wage income offered by estate labor was not better than the fairly good subsistence income which, thanks largely to nature, the traditional system provided, one cannot say. Data on the point are inconclusive. In any case, given the preferences of the Kandyans, the wage income offered was not sufficient to bring about their conversion into estate laborers. Yet coffee, perhaps more than any other estate crop, requires a large, disciplined labor force. An alternative source of labor had to be found if the industry was to grow.

Large-scale Indian immigration to Ceylon, which began in earnest around 1839, provided the answer. Two factors distinguished the South India of this time from neighboring Ceylon. One was the much more severe poverty of the mainland, arising out of the pressure of population (by establishing peace among a previously warring people the British accentuated this problem) on natural resources generally inferior to those of Ceylon. The other was the greater experience of South Indians with industrial routine (their extensive weaving industry had been ruined by British free trade).[13] By 1839 word had spread among the Tamils of South India that relatively well-paid employment was available in Ceylon and the exodus began. The journey to the coffee country was a rigorous one, involving a sea voyage to Colombo, or more often, Talaiman-

---

[13] This is not to imply that any large number of immigrant plantation workers in Ceylon had personally been industrial workers, let alone weavers, in the past, but merely that South Indian society had had much more experience with wage labor than had Kandyan society.

nar, the port closest to the mainland, and then a walk of more than 150 miles to the planting region. The earliest immigrants came of their own initiative, in gangs of 25 to 100 headed by a "kangany", who negotiated for the gang and subsequently acted as their foreman. They came with the idea of staying only long enough to amass some modest savings but many never saw India again.

The trickle of 1839 soon became a flood. Arrivals swelled from about 3,000 in 1839 to 77,000 in 1844.[14] Throughout the 1840's and 1850's the inflow averaged over 50,000 persons a year, with the return flow to India standing at about half that amount (see Table 2–2). The new labor was cheap (its wages amounted to only 18s. per month[15]), but it had all the usual disadvantages of transient labor. At first (see Table 2–2), the men rarely brought their wives and children and the resulting separation from normal family life provided a motive for a quick return to India; later, as a Tamil community began to form in the estate country, more families came. Despite a remarkable expansion of immigration in the 1840's, there continued to be a shortage of labor in Ceylon up to the end of the decade. Then, with the island's first depression setting in, immigration fell off precipitously and many of the workers who had taken up residence in Ceylon returned to their homeland. In 1848 arrivals totaled only 32,000.[16] Besides the depression, another factor in the reduced immigration was the extreme difficulty of the trip the immigrants had to make and the exploitation to which they were prey. In the early fifties the Ceylon government, in an attempt to increase the supply of labor to the estates, began to take some responsibility for immigrant labor. Medical services and amenities at ports and major planting centers were set up and this, along with the revival of prosperity, again swelled the tide of immigrants. Arrivals rose to 58,000 by 1858 and in the last years of the coffee era the figure was about 100,000 a year. By the 1880's the accumulation of Indian estate laborers and their families permanently settled in Ceylon amounted to about 200,000.[17]

Because of the economic and cultural differences between the

---

[14]I. H. van den Driesen, "The Need for Immigrant Labour," (unpublished manuscript, 1963), p. 12.

[15]*Ibid.,* p. 13.

[16]I. H. van den Driesen, *The Economic History of Ceylon in the Nineteenth Century,* Vol. 1, p. 18.

[17]*Ibid.,* p. 19. This contemporary estimate refers to the number who stayed from year to year, not the number in Ceylon at harvest time. The 1871 census gave 537,800 as the total Tamil population of Ceylon, of which Ferguson (A. M. and J. Ferguson, *The Ceylon Directory for 1874* [Colombo, 1874], p. 414) estimated that only 115,000 were estate laborers and their families (the rest were "Ceylon Tamils", a group of considerably longer residence in Ceylon, centered in the Northern and Eastern Provinces).

TABLE 2–2

MIGRATION OF INDIAN ESTATE LABORERS, 1839–72*

(Annual Averages, Rounded to Nearest Hundred)

| Period | ———Arrivals——— | | | ———Departures†——— | | | ———Net Inflow——— | | |
	Men	Women and Children	Total	Men	Women and Children	Total	Men	Women and Children	Total
1839–42....	4,800	400	5,300	6,400	500	6,900	−1,500	−100	−1,600
1843–49....	46,600	1,500	48,100	23,500	800	24,300	23,100	800	23,800
1850–59....	48,600	7,500	56,100	36,300	2,700	39,000	12,200	4,900	17,100
1860–72....	52,400	17,300	69,700	54,700	12,400	67,100	−2,300	4,800	2,600

*Source: A. M. and J. Ferguson, *The Ceylon Directory for 1874* (Colombo, 1874). p. 244. Small discrepancies in totals are due to rounding.
†The official figures have been inflated by 25 percent here, as a rough allowance for unregistered departures, which were put at 25 percent of registered ones by a contemporary source.

estates and the villages, the Tamil immigrants lived almost completely apart from the Sinhalese natives of the island. They lived in barracks-like "lines" provided by the estates, had their own bazaars adjacent to the estate land, and followed Hinduism in a predominantly Buddhist country. To as great an extent as the British, they represented a foreign enclave in Ceylon.

Capital was self-generating, once the coffee industry had been established on a prosperous footing. The first investors were those most familiar with Ceylon's potential, the civil and military officials stationed there. As interest in coffee rose to fever pitch under the stimulus of cheap land, however, a wave of small investors poured in from outside. In 1844 the minimum cost of setting up a plantation was perhaps £3,000[18] and many of the small operators obtained part of this sum in the form of advances on future crops. British-owned banks in Ceylon and "agency houses" (which supervised the operation of the estate and shared in its returns until the owner had paid off his debt) came to invest large sums in coffee mortgages. Because the banks and agency houses were in British hands and were extremely reluctant to extend credit to Ceylonese (and lent only at high rates of interest when they did) estate ownership was at this time almost entirely European. Native coffee production, which also enjoyed a considerable boom, was strictly on a small-holding basis.

Almost all of Ceylon's coffee output went into the British market. Between 1868 and 1872, for example, 3,654,200 hundredweights,

[18]I. H. van den Driesen, *The Economic History of Ceylon in the Nineteenth Century*, p. 27.

94.7 percent of the total quantity exported, went to the United Kingdom. Most of the total was intended for consumption there, though a small proportion was re-exported.[19]

Estate development falls into two periods, with the 1847–49 depression serving as the dividing line between them. In the early days credit was freely extended and with its aid an immense number of Englishmen in all walks of life poured into the industry. The depression bankrupted many of the smaller operators, sobered the banks and agency houses, and ushered in an era of calm rationality. During the postdepression period and right up to the disaster of the late seventies, a well-managed coffee estate must have been at least a tolerably profitable enterprise. A well-informed contemporary writer put profits at 25 percent of sales. However, the same authority states that by the time the coffee era was over not more than one-tenth of the estates had succeeded in making a fair return on their capital.[20] Just how profitable the industry as a whole was is hard to say. In any case, it makes little sense to talk in terms of overall averages, since deviations between the most efficient estates and the least efficient were probably very great.

One characteristic feature of the later estate industries, corporate ownership and management of estates, did not become dominant during the coffee era. Even in the 1870's, after corporations had swallowed up many former partnerships and individual proprietorships, over two-thirds of the estates in operation were still owned by individuals. About a third of these individual owners lived on their property and managed it, while the rest left the management in the hands of an agency house.[21]

When the coffee era ended there was remarkably little evidence of its former prosperity left. As Ferguson, a contemporary observer, laments,

The accumulated profits made during the time of prosperity, which elsewhere, e.g., England, form a reserve fund of local wealth, to enable the sufferer from present adversity to benefit by past earnings, were so far as the planters were concerned, wanting in Ceylon. There was no reserve fund of past profits to fall back upon, no class of wealthy Europeans enriched by former times of prosperity . . . circulating the liquidated profits of former industry, when the period of adversity and depression arrived . . . Ceylon, in fact, in the best days, used to be a sort

---

[19]A. M. and J. Ferguson, *The Ceylon Directory for 1874* (Colombo, 1874), p. 243.

[20]Ferguson, quoted in van den Driesen, *The Economic History of Ceylon in the Nineteenth Century*, Vol. 1, p. 197. This is a rough estimate, since, unfortunately, there are no detailed statistics on rates of return on capital.

[21]*Ibid.*, p. 189.

of incubator, to which capitalists sent their eggs to be hatched, and whence a good many of them received from time to time an abundant brood, leaving sometimes but the shells for our local portion.[22]

No doubt the benefits of the coffee era to the European commercial class (which Ferguson represented)—and still more to the Ceylonese—were transient. But time was to demonstrate that a valuable national capital had been built up. The entrepreneurial experience, physical capital, developed land, and trained labor which had resulted from the coffee experience proved in time to be transferable, in large measure, to the cultivation of other estate crops.

During its days of supremacy, the plantation coffee industry completely dominated Ceylon's economy. It was at this time that the outlines of the plantation-centered economic structure came to be defined. Other segments of the economy were profoundly affected by the rise of the estates.

The traditional sector was influenced in two important ways. The estates sometimes took over lands to which the villagers felt they had traditional rights (even though the government designated them as "Crown lands"). At the same time, the peasants were offered a prospect of making a cash income through smallholder coffee production.

The seriousness of the estate incursions on the peasants' lands remains a major point of debate in Ceylonese economic history to this day. It is, on the one hand, certain that the lands taken by the planter were not those on which the Kandyan peasant depended most—his precious paddy (rice) lands, which were located in the wet up-country valleys and were not suited to coffee cultivation. On the other hand, the traditional agricultural system worked on a combination of these muddy lowlands with the highland, which performed important secondary functions—acting as grazing land and also as an area in which the peasant planted fruits and vegetables and, in a system of shifting cultivation, supplementary food grains. The loss of vast areas of highland, even though most of it was not actually in cultivation, did no doubt reduce peasant welfare. In a few cases entire villages were moved to make room for estates, but on the whole such severe and immediate hardship seems to have been rare. The greatest losses suffered by the peasants were indirect ones, whose effects were not fully felt until the twentieth century. Then, when the acceleration of rural population growth caused people to press much more heavily on the remaining land,

---

[22]Quoted in *ibid.*, p. 197.

there was less of a reserve of lightly cultivated land to fall back upon and the Kandyan peasantry came rapidly to a condition of severe land scarcity.

The good market for coffee offered by the spread of marketing facilities, on the other hand, presented the villager with an attractive profit-making opportunity. Even before estate development gained momentum, in the second through the fourth decades of the century, smallholder coffee production expanded by nearly tenfold,[23] encouraged by peace and good administration and reflecting an increasingly commercial outlook on the part of the villager. Later, estate output eclipsed that of the smallholders, whose product was generally inferior in quality and commanded a much lower price on the London market (see Table 2–3). Still, throughout the prosperous 1850's and 1860's the smallholders managed to account for about a quarter of the total output (although because they earned a lower price for their product they received only a bit more than 20 percent of the export proceeds).[24] At its peak the total area planted with smallholder coffee reached just over 50,000 acres.[25] This was not more than about five percent of the total cultivated area involved in peasant agriculture throughout Ceylon, but in the up-country (Kandyan) areas, to which the climatic requirements of coffee cultivation limited the crop, the percentage was considerably higher. Peasant plots were usually quite small, so perhaps 100,000 or more Kandyan agriculturalists were involved in coffee cultivation at its height. In the seventies, however, peasant production was the least well equipped to withstand *Hemileia vastatrix*. It dropped off sooner and more rapidly than estate output and its share in the total market fell to less than ten percent. Thus, while coffee introduced the Ceylon peasant to the notion of producing for a cash market its ultimate debacle may have made him more reluctant to assume the risks involved in market production in the future.

Other than these two impacts, the effects of the coffee estates on the traditional village economy were remarkably few. There was little trading in either end products or factors of production between the estates and the villages. Estate coffee, of course, was

---

[23]*Ibid.*, p. 44.
[24]*Ibid.*, p. 101. Some of the proceeds of peasant coffee were used to build up the capital stock of the industry: in the 1850's some progressive peasant producers began to imitate the methods of production used on the European estates. Additional proportions of the newfound income went to buy land, build better houses, and send rural sons to the new government schools; the beginnings of a new local aristocracy, based on economic success, can be traced back to the coffee era.
[25]See Table 2–10.

almost exclusively for export. The modern equipment, fertilizer, etc. needed to run an estate were all imported. Even the food to feed the estate labor force, which might conceivably have been bought from the peasant, was imported; Table 2–4 shows the rise in imports of the few simple items consumed by the coolies which resulted from the expansion of the coffee estates. In a fundamental sense the economic system of the village was left untransformed by the coffee experience. Some bitterness had been aroused over land rights, a certain number of peasants had made some money growing coffee and a few others working on estates, more had been indirectly affected through the opening of their native districts to modern transportation and communications, but basically the impact of coffee on the peasant economy was slight.

TABLE 2–3

ESTATE AND SMALLHOLDER COFFEE EXPORTS, 1849–86*

(Annual Figures and Annual Averages)

Year	Estate Volume (000 Cwts.)	Estate Unit Value (s.)	Smallholder Volume (000 Cwts.)	Smallholder Unit Value (s.)	Smallholder Volume share (%)
1849......	210	33	127	18	38
1850–54....	237	44	118	33	33
1855–59....	360	50	162	39	31
1860–64....	450	54	132	40	23
1865–69....	747	54	192	40	20
1870–74....	749	82	135	55	15
1875–79....	720	105	75	77	9
1880–84....	405	91	27	58	6
1885......	295	80	21	50	7
1886......	169	90	10	70	6

*Source: For years up to 1870: Ferguson, *op. cit.*, p. 242; for 1870 on: van den Driesen, *The Economic History of Ceylon in the Nineteenth Century*, p. 107 (his source was the Department of Statistics and Office Systems, *Ceylon Blue Books*). The Ferguson figures relate to the twelve months ending on October 10 of each year. This fact, and differences between Ferguson and the *Blue Books*, explain the discrepancies which exist between this table and Table 2–1.

Aside from the setting up of the estates themselves, the coffee boom also marked the beginnings (or at least the significant expansion) of the commercial wing of Ceylon's economy. The British banks which opened branches in the island and the British commercial firms which were set up to service the estates have already been mentioned. The emergence of modern commerce can be closely identified with the growth of Colombo, which had gone from an insignificant town in pre-European days to a city of 120,000 by the end of the coffee era. Although the British commercial firms were heavily concentrated in the capital they were functionally mere appendages of the estates.

To a considerable degree the government, too, came to be an appendage of the estates. In 1833 a Legislative Council was set up to govern the colony and by the forties the planters were an important force on the council, working for measures close to their own interests, particularly improved transportation to quicken and cheapen the process of moving estate supplies up to the planting areas and coffee down. At times transportation difficulties became intolerable as the inadequate roads disintegrated under the fury of the monsoons and a great urgency was imparted to the planters' drive to gain more and more political power. Roads were built as fast as government revenues permitted (although still more slowly than the planters demanded), even to the extent of allocating 15 percent of government expenditures to road building. Not until the completion of the Colombo-Kandy railroad in 1867, however, was the central part of the island really opened up. The railroad reportedly cut transportation costs for the coffee estates by as much as 60 to 75 percent.[26]

TABLE 2-4

SELECTED IMPORTS, 1837–72*

(Annual Averages)

Period	Cotton Goods (£000)	Rice (Cwts.)	Rice (£000)	Fish (£000)
1837–39........	162.5	798.2	166.9	6.6
1840–49........	184.6	1,689.3	295.6	14.8
1850–59........	313.8	2,727.8	323.1	42.1
1860–69........	707.6	4,197.4	1,185.9	67.2
1870–72........	883.7	4,793.9	1,558.0	81.5

*There is no way of knowing what part of these imports were consumed by estate laborers. Other segments of the population also received higher incomes as a consequence of estate prosperity and their consumption of these things may also have risen. The goods are, however, those which would be consumed in overwhelming proportions by the lower income groups. They are in any case indicative of the growing link between the estate and commercial sectors, on the one hand, and the world economy on the other.

Source: Ferguson, *op. cit.*, p. 243.

In one sense, the planters might justifiably argue that the government should devote a large proportion of its budget to expenditures on their behalf, for it was they who were providing the bulk of its revenue. Prior to the coming of coffee the Colonial Office had

[26]I. H. van den Driesen, *The Economic History of Ceylon in the Nineteenth Century*, p. 23.

dreamed of placing the colony on a self-supporting basis, but the pearl fisheries and cinnamon crops they counted on to balance the budget often fell short of that goal. In 1843–45, however, the combination of export duties on coffee and land sales proceeds produced a surplus of £133,000.[27] Despite the depression which hit immediately thereafter the government tried to maintain its previous level of expenditures on public works and other activities. Revenues fell sharply and large deficits resulted. The government reacted by trying to tax the peasants, who had hardly been touched by taxation up to this point. A number of irritating minor taxes, including a partial reinstatement of the feudal *rajakariya*, were levied. A rural insurrection was the consequence. By trimming expenditures and waiting for the recovery, the government finally weathered the depression. Surpluses accrued throughout the fifties and sixties and were used to finance extra-budgetary public works expenditures. By the 1870's government revenues were running at about £1,500,000 a year, over three times what they had been in the forties.[28] These unprecedented government receipts were used to continue the work of improving the island's transportation system. In the two years 1871 and 1872, for instance, some £600,000 (26 percent of total government expenditure) was spent on public works, mostly road and railroad construction and maintenance.[29] With the collapse of coffee in the 1880's, total government revenues fell off by more than a third, but by that time the foundations of what were to be excellent road and railroad networks had been laid.

TEA

When coffee fell with such a resounding crash in the 1880's the planters were left with land lying idle, a trained labor force available (some of the Tamil laborers had by now settled in Ceylon and others could be recalled from South India), and an organizational system embodying the accumulated knowledge of half a century at their disposal. Quite naturally, they began casting about for an alternative crop to which these assets might be applied. Actually, some years before coffee collapsed its eventual demise had been foreseen by a few farsighted planters and officials and the search for a substitute had begun. Cinchona (quinine) was the first alternative crop tried. From its beginnings in 1870 the cinchona industry expanded to an 1885 peak, at which 39,000 acres were cultivated and 12,000,000 pounds exported, at a value of over Rs. 4,000,000

---

[27]*Ibid.*, p. 85.

[28]*Ibid.*, p. 112.

[29]Ferguson, *op. cit.*, p. 270. This excludes the regular expenditures of the government railroad, some of which went for maintenance.

(£387,000).[30] Although some estimates of the world market for the crop had been glowing, the London market was soon glutted with exports from Ceylon. The price of quinine per ounce fell from 12s. to 1s. 5d. during the decade of the eighties and the crop was abandoned as a plantation endeavor.[31]

Another crop tried as a substitute for coffee was cocoa. It had some past history in the island as a smallholder crop, but suitable land proved to be too limited in supply for cocoa to be widely adopted on an estate basis. It did, however, serve as an important crop in some of the middle-country areas which were later to become the domain of rubber and it has continued to the present day as an item of subsidiary cultivation for both estate and peasant producers.

At first, then, tea was just one of several alternatives to coffee being considered by Ceylon's planters. Early experiments with the crop in the 1840's were not encouraging, but twenty years later varieties imported from Assam (where an expansion of estate production was already under way) were successfully cultivated on several estates in Ceylon. For the time being, however, coffee served as a complete distraction from serious efforts to grow tea commercially. The growth of the tea industry proceeded in close step with the decline of coffee (see Table 2–5).

Once the failure of coffee was a clear and indisputable fact and the imperfection of such crops as cinchona and cocoa as replacements for it had been shown, interest came to center on tea. Early hindrances to the development of the industry were the generally bankrupt financial standing of the planters, their lack of technical information on tea, and the shortage of tea planting materials in Ceylon. All of these were in time overcome and in 1886 the passing of an era was marked when for the first time acreage in tea exceeded acreage in coffee. Thereafter, the tea industry expanded rapidly. The area planted rose by some 20,000 acres a year for the remainder of the century and output underwent a tenfold increase. Then, in the late 1890's, a decline in world prices set in as the expansion of demand, of which the United Kingdom furnished by far the largest component, was finally overtaken by the growth of world supply. Production costs had been running around 6d. a pound in the eighties (about Rs. 0.35)[32] and as long as a pound of

---

[30]S. Rajaratnam, "The Growth of Plantation Agriculture in Ceylon, 1886–1931," *Ceylon Journal of Historical and Social Studies*, January-June, 1961, p. 3.
[31]*Ibid.*
[32]*Ibid.*, p. 8. The Ceylon rupee (singular: Re.; plural: Rs.) had been worth about 2s. up to the early 1870's but it then depreciated to about 1s. 4½d. Its present official value is about 1s. 6d. or approximately U.S. $0.21.

tea continued to fetch Rs. 0.70 (1s.), as it did in the 1880's, or even Rs. 0.50, as it did in the 1890's, the estates remained highly profitable. By the turn of the century Ceylon was producing about a quarter of the world's tea,[33] a proportion which has remained remarkably stable ever since, but many estates were in trouble. Even after prices began to rise again during the first decade of the twentieth century, profits for many operators were slim and many planters changed over to rubber when it appeared on the scene.

In 1907 world demand began to rise after a period of stagnation as the threat of competition from Chinese green tea was finally quashed and British per capita consumption resumed its upward trend.[34] At the same time, Ceylon planters adopted the policy of plucking more finely than before, sacrificing the very rapid growth of output which they had tried for in an earlier, stronger world market and concentrating on producing a tea of higher quality. World War I brought developments which were almost identical to those experienced later during World War II: strong demand, rising shipping costs and shortages of shipping space, short supplies of artificial fertilizers (before the war these had come mostly from Germany), and eventually replacement of the free market by a system of bulk purchases at contracted prices by the British government. Over the protests of the planters, the price for the bulk purchases was set at the average level for the three prewar years; 90 percent of Ceylon's output was purchased at this price at the height of the war.[35] With costs rising, the planters were totally unable to capitalize on the war.

After the war the industry was left with large stocks on hand in Ceylon. An output-restriction scheme was essayed by the planters' associations in both India and Ceylon and it, along with the recovery of demand, was responsible for the strong upward trend in prices which ensued in 1920–22. In the course of the decade, however, overproduction again developed (thanks in part to the emergence of the Netherlands East Indies upon the scene as a major producer) and prices slipped off. By this time Ceylon tea was enjoying a 10 to 30 percent premium over the prices of teas from other sources. The industry was thus able to remain profitable

---

[33] See V. D. Wickizer, *Coffee, Tea and Cocoa: An Economic and Political Analysis* (Stanford, California: Stanford University Press, 1951), p. 157, for estimates of world exports at various times.

[34] Between 1907 and 1914 it rose by nearly one pound. S. Rajaratnam, "The Ceylon Tea Industry, 1886–1931," *Ceylon Journal of Historical and Social Studies,* July-December, 1961, p. 189.

[35] *Ibid.,* p. 191.

TABLE 2–5

THE CEYLON TEA INDUSTRY, 1880–1939
(Annual Averages)

Year	Estimated Output* (000,000 Lbs.)	Area Planted† (000 Acres)	Export Unit Value‡ (Rs./Lb.)	Yield Per Acre§ (Lbs.)
1880–84......	1	23	0.79	52
1885–89......	17	185	0.60	91
1890–94......	71	281	0.49	252
1895–99......	119	388	0.41	306
1900–04......	151	425	0.36	355
1905–09......	175	468	0.41	373
1910–14......	193	493	0.46	391
1915–19......	205	498	0.52	413
1920–24......	187	418	0.81	447
1925–29......	236	449	0.90	525
1930–34......	243	558	0.59	435
1935–39......	231	497	0.75	465

*Exports (see Table A–52, Appendix) plus estimated local consumption, the latter taken as zero through 1899, with a smooth growth from zero to three pounds per capita in 1953 (the latter figure is from Central Bank of Ceylon, *Survey of Ceylon's Consumer Finances*, 1954).
†See footnote † to Table A–37, Appendix.
‡Export value divided by export volume.
§Estimated output divided by area planted. In the 1920's, it seems likely that an understatement of acreage led to an overstatement of yields.

throughout the twenties (though its costs were also somewhat higher than those of producers in other countries).

Ceylon's favored position in the world market stood it in good stead when the depression of the 1930's struck. Ceylon tea fell less in price than any other tea in the world market[36] and export proceeds from tea were more nearly maintained than those earned by the island's other export crops (see Table A–52, Appendix). In 1933 the International Tea Regulation Scheme,[37] a model of its kind, went into effect and prices were restored to their predepression levels.

[36]*Ibid.*, p. 195.
[37]In the International Tea Regulation Scheme, the major producing countries (India, Ceylon, and the Netherlands East Indies) sought a solution to the problem of worldwide overproduction. An aggregate output figure was agreed upon each year and apportioned among the participating countries (the actual signatories of the International Tea Agreement, which created the scheme, were the various national producers' associations, but in each country the government passed legislation to enforce the decisions of the associations). The scheme, which was one of the most soundly planned and successfully executed of all the international commodity control measures which proliferated during the thirties, lasted until the beginning of the war. For further details, see Wickizer, *op. cit.*

In terms of the organization of production, tea was—and still is —the classic example of the plantation crop. It followed quite closely the pattern of the estate system first set up in Ceylon to grow coffee, making only minor refinements in it. In many cases, the same land, capital, and labor were applied to tea as had been used in coffee. Most of the old coffee estates were in time converted to tea (although not always under the old ownership and management) and they formed the nucleus for the new industry. Even where new resources were drawn into the industry (and as early as 1894 the total acreage under tea surpassed the peak coffee acreage) a similar organizational system prevailed.

The Ceylon tea industry has always been one of large estates, European-run and European-owned in the main. One of the more substantial estates, with its hundreds of meticulously planted, carefully drained, and flawlessly maintained acres is a thing of beauty as well as an extremely valuable capital asset. To keep it beautiful and valuable, the constant attentions of a trained and dedicated supervisory staff and the exertions of a small army of workers are required. (Tea is not so labor intensive as coffee was, however: where coffee required two workers per acre, tea has generally used a bit less than one.) A tea bush takes three or four years to come into bearing and, with all the facilities which must be provided, setting up a going estate may take six to ten years. Once planted, the bushes remain productive for a very long time (even today, with most bushes 50 years old or more, there has been little replanting), but only with constant attention. The basic reason why continuous care is needed is that the tea "bush" is not naturally a bush at all, but a tree which must be continually pruned so as to induce it to grow out (and thus expose the greatest possible leaf area to the sun) and not up, as is its natural inclination. This, along with the need to fertilize, weed, drain, and so on, necessitates a large maintenance force. Plucking the bush remains an unmechanized process, also requiring hordes of laborers, because of the high degree of selectivity required. The only leaf that should be plucked is the "flush," the young and tender leaves on the new shoots; the older, coarser leaves would be too strong and bitter to make a desirable beverage. This means that the pluckers, who are traditionally women, must go over the bushes with great frequency (it can be as often as every three days) to assure that the flush is plucked and not allowed to age.

All of these technical characteristics go together to explain the short-term price inelasticity of tea output. To maintain the value of an estate as a capital asset over the long run, a fairly steady rate of output is an absolute necessity. Roughly the same amount of flush must be plucked each year, regardless of the price tea is bringing in the market. Underplucking would mean a failure to keep the bush properly thinned; overplucking would strip it and endanger its future productive potential. Only extremely sharp price changes would alter short-run profit opportunities by a large enough amount to justify such deviations from the policies designed to maintain the value of the bush in the long run. Of course, if a sharp price change is expected to last over a number of years action either to plant new areas with tea or to allow some of the present acreage to go out of production might be indicated. But such sudden, sharp alterations in market conditions have been rare in the industry's history. In their absence, the long-term rationality of keeping production on an even keel generally outweighs any temptation to raise or lower output much in the short run.

The economies of scale in tea production are considerable. Wickizer puts the optimum estate size at 500 acres.[38] Besides the economies realized in the field, there are also very considerable economies available to the large estate in the processing of the green leaf. While there has been little mechanization of the field work over the years, the factory work—drying, grading, rolling, and packing the tea—has long been a mechanized operation. This essentially industrial work is traditionally done on the estate and only a large estate can afford a factory. Small estates and peasant producers must sell their green leaf to estates possessing factories and, because of their weak market position, suffer considerably thereby.

Despite the residual supplies of land, labor and capital remaining after the coffee era ended, the expansion of the tea industry soon created a need for more. After the old coffee lands had been planted with tea, new lands began to be opened up. This, fortunately, was easy to do because tea can be grown at a much wider range of altitudes than coffee (varying, in Ceylon, from near sea level to over 5,000 feet). A new boom in the sale of Crown lands developed. To meet rising demands for labor, more Tamil labor was imported. Official statistics, which are undoubtedly overstated, show the net inflow of Indian estate laborers rising to 334,000 in the 1890's, after a relatively small inflow of 122,000 in the eighties, then continuing at a pace of 316,000 in the first decade of the present century and 430,000 in the second.[39] The 1921 census reported an Indian Tamil population of 602,700, perhaps three times as many

---

[38] Wickizer, *op. cit.,* p. 180.
[39] See Table A–15, Appendix. The overstatement of net inflow results from an understatement of departures. See footnote † to Table 2–2, page 26.

Indian Tamils (who were almost all estate laborers) as there were in Ceylon at the height of the coffee days. Capital continued to come from British banks and agency houses, as well as from internally generated funds, which were often substantial. One increasingly important development was a rise in the degree of corporate control over tea acreage. Companies replaced individual proprietorships and, in time, merged into larger corporations having control over several estates. By the time the first official data were gathered in the 1950's, over 60 percent of the total industry acreage and about 75 percent of the estate acreage was held by corporations.[40]

Smallholders in tea held a position similar to that occupied by their predecessors in coffee. They developed in the wake of the more profitable estate industry, operating on small plots with less efficient methods and making relatively little use of hired labor. The fact that they had to rely on nearby estates to buy and process their green leaf put them in a disadvantageous market position and they thus had to settle for relatively low prices. Nevertheless, by 1935 there were nearly 70,000 tea smallholdings, accounting for some 11.8 percent of the total area cultivated.[41] Many of these holdings were only intermittently cultivated, however, and it is safe to say that they accounted for less than ten percent of total output. They can thus be dismissed as a minor force in the industry. Nor was smallholder tea cultivation more than a minor factor in opening the traditional sector to the influences of the market. At most about five percent of total peasant land was ever devoted to tea (see Table 2–10, page 49) and in only a few areas did smallholder tea production ever become an important economic activity.

RUBBER

As with tea, rubber's beginnings as a plantation crop in Ceylon derived from the fact that the main crop of the time ran into difficulties. The weak prices for tea which prevailed in the early years of this century, up to 1907 (see Table 2–5), made some planters search for a more profitable crop. Rubber, which was just beginning to be demanded in large quantities by the industrial countries, was fetching attractive prices. From just 1,750 acres in 1900 the Ceylon acreage went to some 150,000 by 1907.

The Ceylon rubber boom, though dramatic, was not so overwhelming as the contemporaneous upsurge of the Malayan rubber

----

[40]See Table A–38, Appendix.
[41]See Table A–39, Appendix.

industry. Two factors—the relative scarcity of good uncultivated rubber land (most suitable land was already under tea) and the revival of tea prices after 1907—limited the expansion of Ceylon's industry. Nevertheless, growth was rapid. By 1913 rubber earned about three-fourths as much foreign exchange as tea. In 1917, with the industry enjoying war-inflated prices,[42] it actually surpassed tea for the first time in export value. Because of rubber's five- to seven-year gestation period, it was not until about 1917 that the full fruits of the first extensive plantings began to be realized. This new production would have corrected the general excess demand in the world market if the war had not intervened. Despite the difficulties of importing supplies and finding shipping space for the bulky export product, the volume of exports continued to grow during World War I. At the war's end, however, demand fell off and prices plummeted to less than half their 1919 level by 1921.

In 1922 the Stevenson Restriction Scheme came into effect and in the following year prices rallied.[43] Despite the scheme, Ceylon's acreage continued to rise (see Table 2–6). The limitation of the Stevenson Scheme to the British colonies (an attempt to enlist the Netherlands East Indies was unsuccessful) doomed it to ultimate failure, although for a time the growth of the automobile industry in the United Kingdom and especially the United States brought prosperity to the industry. Acreage, output, and exports all rose steadily throughout the decade of the twenties and by 1929 Ceylon claimed about a tenth of the world's acreage, ranking a poor third behind Malaya and the Netherlands East Indies. Prices, however, hit a peak in 1925 and then began to decline. This particular fall in prices was indicative of the failure of the Stevenson Scheme to prevent world oversupply, but soon the world depression set in and demand dropped catastrophically. The bottom fell out of the world market.

The sensitivity of the Ceylon rubber industry to the depression of the thirties was extreme. Prices sank. Ceylon's rubber proved to be in an especially poor competitive position. Much of the country's

---

[42]As an industrial raw material, whose production had to be encouraged, rubber was allowed to benefit more from the war-inflated world demand conditions than was tea. See page 34.

[43]The Stevenson Restriction Scheme was an early attempt at international commodity control. It allocated production quotas and controlled planting within the British empire, notably in Ceylon and Malaya, but was never extended to a large enough percentage of world production to be completely successful. It was allowed to lapse in 1928. See P. T. Bauer, *The Rubber Industry* (Cambridge, Massachusetts: Harvard University Press, 1948), for further details.

acreage was already getting old (40 percent of it had been planted before 1911). Some of it had been planted at altitudes which were too high and on ground which was too hilly. In many cases cultivation techniques that were inappropriate to the industry had been transferred intact from tea cultivation (e.g., clean weeding, which resulted in extensive erosion in the hilly rubber country).[44] Furthermore, legal minimum wages remained under the influence of the relatively prosperous tea industry and declined very little. There are references in official documents to considerable reductions of output in the early thirties; according to the director of agriculture some 40 percent of the tappable area was left untapped in 1932 and about half of the Indian laborers who had been employed in 1929 had by then been laid off.[45] The quantity exported declined, though perhaps by less than might be expected. Prices fell toward the vanishing point. In 1932, with prices at one-quarter of their 1929 level, output was down 39 percent. By 1934 a new international output restriction scheme (this time including the Dutch and all other important producers) went into effect and prices began to recover. Soon after, a partial recovery of demand, based partly on German rearmament and partly on the subsequent limited revival of civilian demand and upsurge of military needs elsewhere, set in and the market improved further. By 1939 the rubber industry was back on the road to good health and in the following year it felt the beginnings of a new boom.

With the shift to rubber, the estate sector in Ceylon moved away from the classic model which had been initiated in coffee cultivation and later transferred virtually intact to tea. Like tea and coffee, rubber is a tree crop, but unlike them it requires very little maintenance to continue to thrive, nor is constant harvesting required. A rubber tree is easily planted, takes approximately 5 to 7 years to come into full bearing, and may be tapped at varying rates thereafter for the 25–30 years of its productive life. Even if conscientiously maintained, it uses less than half as much labor per acre as tea. Moreover, if left untapped for a year or two its future productivity will actually be enhanced:

Some bark removal is . . . inevitable [in tapping a rubber tree] and this naturally varies not only with the skill of the tapper but also with the frequency of tapping and with the tapping system adopted. If a tree is left untapped bark reserve will be greater, with the possibility of higher yields later; where bark removal exceeds bark renewal it will

---

[44]*Ibid.*, p. 51.
[45]*Ibid.*, p. 54.

eventually be necessary to suspend or slow down tapping, or else to tap on imperfectly renewed bark . . .[46]

This relationship between present and future output is diametrically opposed to the relationship in tea cultivation, where present plucking enhances future output. Rubber output is thus more easily varied than that of tea, the range of possibilities running all the way from letting the tree stand idle to "slaughter tapping" it, that is, tapping so fast that proper bark renewal is impossible and the tree is permanently damaged. The level of current output depends in large part on the level of prices. More precisely, it depends on the relationship of present prices to expected future prices; output foregone this year raises potential future output and if the level of expected prices relative to present ones justifies it, present output will be sacrificed so as to raise future yields.

TABLE 2–6

THE CEYLON RUBBER INDUSTRY, 1900–19

(Annual Averages)

Year	Estimated Output* (000,000 Lbs.)	Area Planted† (000 Acres)	Export Unit Value‡ (Rs./Lb.)	Yield Per Acre§ (Lbs.)
1900–04......	. . .	7	. . . .	. . .
1905–09......	. . .	98	. . . .	. . .
1910–14......	. . .	199	. . . .	. . .
1915–19......	65	244	1.60	265
1920–24......	84	390	0.76	214
1925–29......	133	494	0.99	269
1930–34......	148	. . .	0.20	. . .
1935–39......	128	611	0.42	209

*Through 1936, equals exports; thereafter, actual output data from the *Administration Report* (henceforth abbreviated: *A.R.*) of the *Rubber Controller* have been used.
†See footnote ‡ to Table A–37, Appendix.
‡Export price divided by export volume.
§Estimated output divided by area planted; to a greater degree even than with other crops, these figures vary with changes in the ratio of bearing acres to the total planted; they are thus not a sensitive measure of changes in intensity of cultivation or of technological progress.

Rubber technology is inherently much simpler than that of tea. The "manufacturing" process which must be gone through after the latex is tapped consists simply of adding an acid to hasten coagulation and rolling and drying the coagulated latex into one of two popular forms, sheet or crepe. No mechanical power need be used. The water can be pressed from the latex using hands and feet and

---

[46]*Ibid.*, p. 1.

the final drying can be left for the sun to achieve. More commonly, however, simple power machinery and a smokehouse are employed.

It should be clear from this brief description that rubber is naturally much more of a smallholders' industry than tea. The economies of scale in the industry are evidently much smaller. Moreover, the location of good rubber land—at the middle altitudes, closer to the bulk of the peasant population than tea—made the crop appealing to smallholding peasants. So, from the early days of the industry in Ceylon, smallholders have played a significant role. In 1936, the first year of official data collection on the subject, smallholders were found to hold 21 percent of the island's rubber acreage. However, this percentage holds only under the arbitrary definition that an estate is any holding ten acres or more in extent. About 40 percent of Ceylon's rubber land in the 1930's was in holdings of less than 100 acres.[47] Rubber smallholders in Ceylon typically use the cultivation of the crop as a supplementary sideline, shifting their attentions from rubber to their other agricultural or nonagricultural interests when rubber prices decline and back to rubber when they rise. When they decide to tap they hire casual labor from the village and when they are not tapping their trees stand almost completely unattended.

Aside from the greater importance of the smallholder segment of the industry, rubber also brought other changes in the familiar pattern of resource use in the estate sector. The less regular need for labor meant that local workers employed on a casual basis were heavily relied upon, even by the estates. Of the 540,000 Indian estate workers in Ceylon in 1929, perhaps no more than 100,000 were employed on rubber estates. Capital flowed into rubber cultivation from a wide variety of sources, ranging from large British corporations with holdings in various parts of Ceylon and often Malaya and India as well to peasants with just a few acres planted.

COCONUT

With coconut, the third of modern Ceylon's three great export crops, one moves still further away from the classic plantation system. Cultivation of the coconut palm in Ceylon goes back, apparently, to ancient times and the palm was the "Tree of Life" to the Ceylonese peasant (*Kalpa Vriksha* in Sanskrit) long before it became a plantation crop. One of many similar quotations suggests its vital role in the village economy:

The leaves are used for roofing, mats, baskets, torches, fuel, manure, whilst the stem of the leaf is utilised for fences, pingoes and fishing rods.

---

[47]See Table A–39, Appendix.

Pickles and preserves are made of the cabbage or cluster of unexpanded leaves. The sap forms toddy, from which arrack is distilled. By evaporation, jaggery (a form of sugar) is obtained. Acetic fermentation produces coconut vinegar. The unformed nuts are utilised in medicine. The milk of the young nut makes a refreshing drink. The meat itself is used to make curry and generally in cooking. The oil from the nut is useful in medicine, for anointing the hair, to make soap, candles and to provide light. Cattle are fed on the poonac or copra cake. From the shell of the nut, drinking cups, charcoal, toothpowder, spoons, medicine, beads, receptacles and knife-handles are manufactured. The coir is used for mattresses, cushions, ropes, cables, cordage, canvas, fishing nets, brushes, fuel and floor-mats. The trunk, sometimes called porcupine-wood, is used for rafters, lathes, sailing boats, troughs, furniture, buttons and firewood. The roots of the tree are used for medicinal purposes.[48]

The coconut industry is dominated by smallholders, to an even greater extent than rubber, with which it shares many technical characteristics. Even more than the rubber tree, the coconut palm can live without systematic human attention. Weeding, fertilizing, and pest control all enhance yields, of course, but they are not at all necessary. The tree will go on producing dozens of nuts per year without them. It is very long lived, although after 50 or 60 years senility sets in and the yield drops. The tree is easily grown in small plots and even in gardens attached to houses. In the wet zone low country, where soil and climatic conditions are favorable, one finds them everywhere.

Aside from its almost endless village uses, which generally absorb about half of Ceylon's total harvest, the coconut palm produces five products of commercial value which are traded internationally: copra (the shredded meat of the nut, intended for later pressing into coconut oil), oil, poonac (the residual cake left after the oil is pressed out of the copra), desiccated (dried and finely shredded) coconut, and coir (coconut fibre, derived from the husks). The copra is used as a raw material to obtain oil, the oil is employed in food products (as an input into the manufacture of margarine and as a cooking oil) and in soap, the poonac serves as a cattle feed, the desiccated coconut goes mainly into the confectionery industry, and the coir fibre competes with other natural and man-made fibres in a variety of uses: mats, brooms, rope, and so on.

Information on the coconut industry, because of the dominance of the smallholders and also because coconuts never came under an international regulatory agreement as did tea and rubber, has always been sparse. Table 2–7, however, summarizes what is known or can be estimated about its development up to World War II. Because

---

[48]*Report of the Coconut Commission,* Sessional Paper (henceforth abbreviated: S.P.) XII of 1949, pp. 11–12.

of its long-standing role as a peasant crop, coconut has always accounted for a much larger total area planted than any of the more purely plantation-type crops (see Table 2–10, page 49). From 1870 through the 1930's coconut output and acreage grew at a fairly steady rate. During this growth process, mainly in the first decades of the twentieth century, the plantation began to take a place in the industry. Unlike the tea or rubber estate, the coconut plantation was almost always locally owned. As time went by it came to represent an important transitional step taken by the village landowner on the way to becoming a member of the urban elite. In later days, many of Ceylon's leading politicians were to be coconut landowners. Only for the post-World War II period are data available, but in 1951 only 20 to 25 percent of the island's coconut acreage appeared to be on estates.[49] Of the estates, 84.9 percent were in the hands of Ceylonese individuals, while only 7.7 percent were evidently in foreign hands (owned by non-Ceylonese companies or individuals).[50] The foreign role in the industry is somewhat understated by these figures, however, in view of the fact that the processing of coconuts, unlike that of tea and rubber, is not usually done on the estate, but at a separately located and owned mill. The mill may be a very simple affair or it may be a modern factory. A small number of modern British-owned mills process a high proportion of the coconuts grown in Ceylon.

Under the beneficent influence of attractive and steadily rising export prices, coconut acreage and production expanded steadily up to World War I. After the war, the growth of acreage appears to have slowed down (though it may be that the overestimation of acreage in the earlier period is what creates this impression), while output continued to rise. In the world market for coconut products, and desiccated coconut in particular, Ceylon was a leading supplier in the 1920's. Its position was undercut, however, by the increased entry of the Philippines into the world market in the twenties; the American market for desiccated coconut, for instance, was lost to the Philippines, which enjoyed a preferential tariff. Then the effects of the depression were felt. Despite the popularity of the coconut as an article of domestic consumption (which might be expected to work for greater price elasticity of supply in the export market), exports in terms of nut equivalents were higher in the depressed thirties than they had been in the prosperous twenties. Prices fell by more than half.

---

[49] Department of Census and Statistics, *Census of Agriculture 1952*, Vol. 3, 1956; see Table A–39, Appendix, and footnote § attached to it.

[50] See Table A–38, Appendix, and its footnote #.

TABLE 2-7

THE CEYLON COCONUT INDUSTRY, 1870-1939

(Annual Averages)

Period	Estimated Output* (000,000 Nuts)	Area Planted† (000 Acres)	Yield per Acre‡ (Nuts/Acre)	Coconut Oil — Export Volume§ (000 Cwts.)	Coconut Oil — Unit Value§ (Rs.)	Copra — Export Volume§ (000 Cwts.)	Copra — Unit Value§ (Rs.)	Desiccated Coconut — Export Volume§ (000 Cwts.)	Desiccated Coconut — Unit Value§ (Rs.)
1870-79	374	...	...	174	12.37	36	7.45	...	......
1880-89	433	582	830	311	12.45	127	8.28		
1890-99	611	818	747	443	13.93	169	10.17	76‖	20.52‖
1900-09	861	920	936	554	13.20	545	11.43	187	17.91
1910-19	1,091	972	1,122	493	28.58	1,122	15.67	326	28.41
1920-29	1,507	1,076	1,401	610	27.17	1,789	16.70	775	25.56
1930-39	1,674	1,076	1,556	1,111	11.89	1,399	7.25	653	10.34

*Through 1936, estimated by taking nut equivalents of coconut-product exports (suggested in Department of Census and Statistics, *Census of Agriculture 1952*, Vol. 3, 1956, p. 10) and adding an assumed 115 nuts per capita annually (from Central Bank of Ceylon, *Survey of Ceylon's Consumer Finances*, 1954, p. 29); from 1937 on there are official figures, similarly estimated (see Table A-32, Appendix).
†See footnote § to Table A-37, Appendix.
‡Estimated output divided by area planted.
§Source: Table A-52, Appendix.
‖1892-99

PEASANT AGRICULTURE

Just what happened to peasant agriculture during a century of estate development between 1840 and 1939 is hard to say. Reliable data on output are totally lacking and the only available quantitative indications of levels of activity come from information on resource use in the sector. It would be a mistake to think of this sector, which provided a livelihood for the major part of the population during the period, as static. In fact, its population grew and the quantity of resources available to it underwent some changes. On the other hand, it is clear from an examination of income levels and other quantitative indicators of well-being and technology levels in 1939 that the estate revolution bestowed relatively few immediate benefits on the peasant sector.

The opportunities to earn higher incomes offered to the peasants by the estate revolution were limited in number and character. Once the pattern of immigrant labor and imported supplies was established (that is, ignoring the very difficult question of whether the Sinhalese were given an economic incentive to work on the estates or provide food for them) the number of transactions taking place between the estate and village economies was small. Estate inputs were almost all imported. In time, Sinhalese peasants came to supply a fair proportion of the labor services used by the estates (by the 1930's, some 100,000 Ceylonese were working on the estates, making up about 20 percent of the labor force), but this remained a minor tie between the two worlds of the estate and the village. Smallholding was a second link, which in time involved a relatively small number of peasants in producing coconuts and rubber (and an even smaller number tea) for the market. The great majority of peasants, however, had no contact at all with the estates.

In most instances (especially in the case of up-country tea) the estates were not physically contiguous with the peasant areas, but even where they were (as was frequently the case with low-country tea, rubber, and coconuts) there were remarkably few economic relations between the sectors. The villager grew paddy (rice) to feed himself and his family, often enjoyed the easily gained produce of a few coconut trees, and relied on a small plot of garden or "highland" to furnish fruits and vegetables to supplement his diet. His ideal was self-sufficiency and the ideal came close to being realized in practice. His technology was primitive—even draft animals were considered a luxury, available only to the relatively well-to-do peasant—and his per capita income was correspondingly low, much lower than that of the plantation sector (though the estate income was distributed so unevenly that the estate laborer was probably very little better off than his village counterpart). Fortunately for the Ceylon peasant, nature was generally kind—especially in the rich wet zone which comprises the southwest corner of the island. In the wet zone two rice crops were easily grown each year; in the remaining dry zone (which is dry only in comparison to the richly watered wet zone) two crops were possible but, in the absence of good irrigation, rather unlikely.

During the first hundred years of estate development, technology in the peasant sector, which had been essentially unchanged for centuries, underwent no apparent transformation. Up to the 1920's, peasant population grew at only about one percent a year (see Table 2–8). A high incidence of infant deaths and periodic outbreaks of malaria were the main forces keeping the rate of natural increase down in the face of a high birth rate. In addition, there were gradual population losses to the cities and the estates. The supply of land to the peasants also expanded slowly but steadily, partly through the gradual restoration of the extensive ancient irrigation works which exist in many parts of the island, so only after 1920 did the ratio of population to cultivated land in the peasant sector begin to rise. Despite frequent claims in Ceylon to the contrary, the estates seem to have cut very little into the supply of arable land available to the peasant. In other ways, however, the effects of the estates on resource availability in the peasant sector may have been more harmful. It is probably true that the growth of the estates did reduce the reservoir of land available for future expansion of traditional cultivation and thus did bring about suffering among the peasants later, in the twentieth century, when their population began to rise rapidly. And what actual diversion of land there was from the peasants to the estates did not involve paddy land, but rather the supplementary pasture and "chena" land (land used for the occasional slash-and-burn cultivation of secondary grains) of the Kandyan peasants. The disappearance of good pasture land may be the reason why the ratio of draft animals to rural population, after rising in the late nineteenth century, fell almost continuously during the twentieth (see Table 2–9).

Despite the lack of quantitative information on the history of the traditional sector, the broad outlines of the estates' influence on it are clear: the effects of estate development on the village were relatively minor in quantity and indirect in nature. The economic opportunities offered to the villager were relatively few. The negative impact of diverting land from the peasants was of consequence only with the passing of time, and even then the indignities suffered

TABLE 2–8

ESTIMATED CULTIVATED LAND AND POPULATION IN THE PEASANT AGRICULTURAL
SECTOR, CENSUS YEARS, 1871–1959

Year	Cultivated Peasant Land* (000 Acres)	Annual Growth Rate since Previous Year	Peasant Population† (000s)	Annual Growth Rate since Previous Year (%)	Peasant Population per Acre
1871.............	954	...	1,831	...	1.9
1881.............	1,092	1.4%	1,996	0.9	1.8
1891.............	1,243	1.3	2,219	1.1	1.8
1901.............	1,370	1.0	2,541	1.1	1.9
1911.............	1,544	1.2	2,818	1.0	1.8
1921.............	1,676	0.8	3,051	0.8	1.8
1931.............	1,809	0.8	3,921	2.5	2.2
1946.............	2,076	0.9	4,941	1.6	2.4
1953.............	2,206	0.9	6,044	2.9	2.7
1959‡............	2,351	1.1	7,297	3.2	3.1

*Source: Table A–36, Appendix. "Peasant land" consists of paddy acreage, plus "other" crops, plus certain proportions of coffee, tea, rubber, and coconut cultivation: 20 percent of coffee, 10 percent of tea, 20 percent of rubber, and 60 percent of coconut. Each of these embodies an estimate of the proportion of total acreage under the crop which consisted of holdings under 10 acres. From 1946 on, actual percentages are used for tea and rubber (see Table A–39, Appendix) and part of the rise in peasant land after 1931 consists of land bought from estates by smallholders.

†Rural population from Table A–18, Appendix, minus estate population; the latter is taken as equal to Indian estate population from 1931 on (see Department of Census and Statistics, *Statistical Abstract of Ceylon, 1961*, p. 185); before that the assumption is that the land-labor ratio in the estate sector during the 1920's applies in all periods. This formulation leaves Sinhalese estate workers in the peasant sector, which is probably desirable, since they tend to be peasants at heart and only casual estate workers.

‡1959 was not a census year, so the origins of the data used are somewhat different from those of the other years (see Tables A–18 and A–36, Appendix).

TABLE 2–9

DRAFT ANIMALS AND POPULATION IN THE PEASANT AGRICULTURAL SECTOR, CENSUS
YEARS, 1871–1959*

Year	Draft Animals (000s)			Draft Animals Per Hundred of Peasant Population		
	Buffaloes	Cattle†	Total	Buffaloes	Cattle†	Total
1871.........	...	997	.....	..	54	..
1881.........	281	1,056	1,337	14	53	67
1891.........	393	1,065	1,458	18	48	66
1901.........	521	1,477	1,998	21	58	79
1911.........	462	1,465	1,927	16	52	68
1921.........	419	1,386	1,805	14	45	59
1931.........	528	1,052	1,580	13	27	40
1946.........	522	1,080	1,602	11	22	32
1953.........	656	1,229	1,885	11	20	31
1959.........	781	1,486	2,267	11	20	31

*Peasant population is the same total as was used in Table 2–8; data on draft animals are from Table A–40, Appendix. Small discrepancies are attributable to rounding error.

†Cattle in Ceylon are used mostly as draft animals; there are few dairy cattle.

by the peasants might as logically be ascribed to the acceleration of their rate of population growth as to the effect of the estates in limiting the amount of land available for the expansion of peasant agriculture; that, after all, was ultimately limited by nature in any case.

THE ESTATES AND ECONOMIC GROWTH

The first century of Ceylon's modern economic development—from the coming of the coffee estate in the 1840's to World War II —was utterly dominated by the emergence and subsequent growth of estate agriculture. Roughly, the century can be divided into a number of periods, each distinguished on the basis of what was happening in the estate sector at the time: the rise of coffee and establishment of the estate system, about 1845–70; coffee's decline, 1870–88; the rise of tea and rubber up to World War I, 1888–1913; war and peace prosperity, 1913–29; and the depression of the thirties. Anticipating a bit the subject matter of later portions of this book, one might add that the 1939–46 period was dominated by the special circumstances surrounding World War II and the

TABLE 2–10

AREAS CULTIVATED BY ESTATES AND PEASANTS, CENSUS YEARS, 1871–1959*

(Thousand Acres)

	1871	1881	1891	1901	1911	1921	1931	1946	1953	1959
Estate Land:										
Coffee	214	228	45	5	—	—	—	—	—	—
Tea	—	12	235	366	412	376	456	490	505	502
Rubber	—	—	—	2	148	312	451	507	482	477
Coconuts	200	210	304	339	412	410	430	428	428	428
Total	413	450	584	711	971	1,099	1,337	1,426	1,415	1,408
Export Smallholdings:										
Coffee	53	57	11	1	—	—	—	—	—	—
Tea	—	1	26	41	46	42	51	63	70	78
Rubber	—	—	—	—	37	78	113	152	176	191
Coconuts	300	315	456	508	618	615	645	643	643	643
Total	353	373	493	550	701	735	808	858	888	911
Nonexport Crops:										
Paddy	544	549	563	670	645	727	811	913	964	1,124
Others	58	169	186	150	199	215	190	305	353	315
Total	601	718	750	820	843	941	1,001	1,218	1,317	1,440
Total peasant area	954	1,092	1,243	1,370	1,544	1,676	1,809	2,076	2,206	2,351
Total cultivated area	1,367	1,542	1,826	2,081	2,516	2,775	3,146	3,501	3,620	3,758
Annual rate of increase	....	1.2%	1.7%	1.3%	1.9%	1.0%	1.3%	0.7%	0.5%	0.6%

Source: Table A–36, Appendix. The split of export crop acreage between estates and peasant smallholdings prior to 1946 is based on an assumed constancy of their relative shares in total acreage. See footnote to Table 2–8, page 48. Small discrepancies are attributable to rounding error.

post-1946 era by the political fact of independence. Within the unchanging framework of an economy which is heavily dependent on its estate sector, each of these periods has its own particular growth experience (see Table 2–11). Total exports (and presumably national output, though there are no data) rose and fell with coffee in the early decades. During the 1888–1913 period it was tea which propelled the economy forward; the rise of the tea industry is mainly responsible for the fact that overall export volume moved upward at a 6.2 percent annual rate during these years. In the 1913–29 period the estate sector experienced its most rapid growth—7.7 percent a year; in this period, rubber, growing faster than tea ever did, provided the main impetus. Thus, up to 1929 coffee, tea, and rubber had each served in turn as a leading sector, an engine of growth for the economy. After 1929 no sector boomed. The depression brought output declines for all three of the leading crops, attributable to the weakened state of world markets. When World War II began, demand rose sharply and the growth of overall export volume resumed; supply-side limitations on production (shortages

TABLE 2–11

ANNUAL RATES OF INCREASE IN OUTPUT AND EXPORT VOLUME, 1845–1960

Period	Coffee Export Volume*	Tea Output†	Rubber Output‡	Coconut Output§	Combined Export Volume Index‖
1845–70	6.4%	–	–	...	...
1870–88	−12.7	∞	–	2.4%	...
1888–1913	− ∞	8.7%	∞	3.0	6.2%
1913–29	–	1.8	13.2%	2.8	7.7
1929–39	–	−0.9	−4.4	−0.2	−1.5
1939–46	–	2.6	6.6	−3.0	4.0
1946–60	–	3.2	0.3	2.6	1.8

*Source: Department of Statistics and Office Systems, *Ceylon Blue Books.*

†Prior to 1900, output is assumed equal to exports; from 1900 through 1932 a factor for local consumption (per capita consumption from Ceylon Bank of Ceylon, *Survey of Ceylon's Consumer Finances,* 1954, times estimated population) is added in; from 1933 on, actual production figures from the *A.R. of the Tea Controller* are used.

‡Prior to 1937 output is taken as equal to exports; from 1937 on, actual production data from the *A.R. of the Rubber Controller* are used.

§Total output is taken as the nut equivalents of exports of the three leading coconut products, plus estimated local consumption (per capita consumption from the 1953 consumer finance survey times estimated population).

‖Because of frequent changes in the composition of Ceylon's exports, computing a long-term index of export volume poses a formidable index-number problem. Using either constant weights from any single year or period or current-year weights causes gross distortion, the former toward understatement and the latter toward exaggeration. A third alternative was thus elected here: the 115-year period was divided into seven subperiods; within each subperiod, first-year weights were used; the subperiod indexes were then linked together to provide a combined export volume index for the entire 115 years. The resulting index rises from an 1888 base of 100 to 450 by 1913 and 1,475 by 1929, falls to 1,268 by 1939, then rises again to 1,669 in 1946 and 2,143 in 1960. Based on Table A–52, Appendix.

of capital equipment, fertilizers, and export shipping space), along with British bulk-purchase policies (see Chapter 4, pages 74–75, 78), held the growth of output and exports in check and at the war's end aggregate exports were only slightly in excess of the 1929 level. Since 1946 the volume of production has resumed its upward movement, but at a much slower rate than previously. Much more will be said of this later.

Each of the estate industries appears to have followed a life cycle in its development which, up to a point, differs remarkably little from crop to crop. There exists a foreign market for a crop which can be grown profitably in Ceylon. Dramatically, a local industry springs up. In its first dynamic stage of development, the industry's acreage grows by leaps and bounds and so, with a suitable lag to allow for the gestation period, does its output. Soon output per acre, measured using gross acreage planted as the denominator, is growing rapidly as more and more acres reach optimal bearing age.[51] Meanwhile, world demand, which may have been increasing rapidly in the earliest years of the industry, has settled down to a relatively slow rate of growth and other countries have made extensive plantings of the crop; world prices stabilize and perhaps drop a bit. Within Ceylon, returns to the marginal acre planted have been falling as the cultivation of the crop is extended to less and less suitable land. Soon a point is reached beyond which additional investments in the Ceylon industry, most of which must compete with alternative uses of capital in the world capital market, no longer yield a return that is greater than returns from alternate investments. When acreage reaches this point its expansion halts abruptly. Barring any large and permanent increase in the world price there will be little more expansion of acres planted in the future. After a lag of a few years, output also stagnates. Employment, which had been rising briskly in the early years, stops growing. An interregnum in the industry's growth is ushered in. Coffee, tea, and rubber all demonstrate the pattern up to this point. Beyond this interregnum, however, there is the possibility of a second phase of development. Here, there is room for considerable variation among cases. If output is to grow during this second stage it must rise mainly through technical change; in particular, since land is the scarcest factor of production, there must be increases in output per acre. A variety of circumstances—involving the rate at which scien-

---

[51]There is also likely to be some improvement in the technology of the industry during this period and this accelerates the rise of output per acre. However, the main contribution to increasing land productivity during this period is probably made by the maturing of the trees.

tific research makes new techniques available, the market and other incentives (including government subsidies) given to planters to induce them to adopt improved methods, and the adequacy of the planters' response[52]—determine whether these increases are achieved.[53]

Table 2–12 shows these trends in tea, rubber, and coconut. Tea and rubber had similar growth experiences up to the 1920's and similar stagnation thereafter. Coconut's initial period of rapid growth, if it had one (and it may not have), is lost in the mists of prestatistical antiquity. The years since 1946 show a variety in the latest phase of development. The tea and coconut industries have been able to accelerate their rates of output growth through faster rises in productivity, while rubber, hampered by generally less favorable markets and (in the short run) replanting,[54] has not.

It is clear that the estate sector of Ceylon's economy has repeatedly demonstrated its capacity to grow, both by bringing new resources under its command and by improving the efficiency of its resource utilization. What are the implications of this capacity for the aggregate growth of the economy? As one would expect, similar long-run data on the growth of the peasant and urban parts of the economy are lacking, so it is impossible to say just how fast Gross Domestic Product (GDP) has grown historically. However, a rough but conservative estimate of overall growth is possible. If the whole modern sector is assumed to have accounted for half of Ceylon's real GDP on the average from 1888 to 1939 (a very rough assumption), if its annual growth rate is taken to be 5.1 percent (this is the growth rate of the combined export volume index in Table 2–11), and if constant output per head is assumed in the rest of the economy, then the overall growth rate works out to

---

[52]The operation of each of these factors with respect to tea, rubber and coconut in the post-World War II economy is examined below, Chapter 6, pages 133–52.

[53]There is no inherent reason why output *must* stagnate after total acreage stops rising. The upsurge in productivity could follow close on the heels of the exhaustion of suitable land supplies. It could even precede it, though this is less likely because while cheap land is still available planters have little incentive to work for higher yields per acre. One should not be arbitrary about this question of timing. It can be argued, for example, that with tea and rubber it was only the coincidental appearance of the depression soon after the expansion of acreage ceased which produced the period of output stagnation which is observable in the statistics.

[54]Paradoxically, rubber was the crop in which by far the most replanting with greatly improved strains was done in the postwar period. Few returns from this replanting had become evident by 1960, though; see Chapter 6, pages 143–49.

TABLE 2-12

SUBPERIOD TRENDS IN TEA, RUBBER, AND COCONUT, 1888–1960*

(Average Annual Growth Rates: %)

Subperiod	Output	Acreage	Employment	Output per Acre	Output per Employee
Tea:					
1888–1913	8.7	3.0	...	7.3	...
1913–29	1.8	} 0.5	} 1.2†	} 0.2	} 0.0
1929–39	−0.9				
1939–46	2.6	−0.1		3.1	
1946–60	3.1	0.4	0.5	2.5	2.6
Rubber:					
1888–1913	....	...	...	...	...
1913–29	13.2	5.3	} 4.9†	7.5	...
1929–39	−3.1	1.4		−4.5	...
1939–46	6.7	0.5		6.1	...
1946–60	0.2	0.4	−0.1	−0.1	0.3
Coconut:					
1888–1913	3.0	1.6	...	1.3	...
1913–29	2.8	0.8	...	2.0	...
1929–39	−0.2	} 0.7	...	} −1.3	...
1939–46	−3.0		...		...
1946–60	2.7	0.0	1.7	2.7	0.9

*Sources: Tables 2–5, 2–6, 2–7, 6–8, 6–12, 6–13; A–12, A–26, and A–37.
†1911–46.

3.2 percent a year.[55] Since population growth averaged about 1.4 percent annually from 1888 through 1939 (see Table A–14, Appendix), this implies an annual rate of growth for real Gross Domestic Product per capita of about 1.8 percent. While not a spectacular growth rate, this is a discernible one and is definitely significantly different from zero. There is thus evidence that over the last century the trend of Ceylon's domestic product has been distinctly upward and at a rate somewhat faster than population growth.

This growth record is rendered more impressive by the diversity

---

[55]That is, real output is thought to have risen at a 5.1 percent rate in the modern sector and 1.4 percent in the traditional sector; 3.2 percent is the mean of these two rates. This is a conservative estimate. There is no profound reason to believe that per capita output in the traditional sector was actually constant. There is little quantitative information to go on, but a reasonable guess might be that the slow-working influences of capital accumulation and technical change more than offset the increasing pressure on the land (which started only in the 1920's) and created a slow upward trend in per capita output in the traditional sector between 1888 and 1939. How rapid such an increase might have been, however, cannot possibly be estimated.

of products which went into its compilation. Coffee, then tea, and (briefly during World War I) rubber all served in their turn as the leading earner of foreign exchange (see Table 2–13). Several times, a reverse in the world market for one good stimulated the development of another profitable commodity. The one consistent principle in the history of the estate sector has been a continual sifting through the array of possible export crops by actual and potential entrepreneurs, who have repeatedly discarded the infeasible and picked the most profitable for their attention. Of course, in world depressions the prices of all primary products drop and adaptability is to no avail. Ceylon was hit several times during the plantation era by depressions and the impact was often considerable. But in each case the estates rode out the depression and recovered with income and output levels higher than ever. Fluctuations were the price of the higher income levels afforded by the plantation system. Individual estate companies often went bankrupt but the system itself continued as virile as ever.

TABLE 2–13

SHARE OF LEADING CROPS IN TOTAL EXPORT RECEIPTS,
SELECTED YEARS, 1891–1959*

(Percent of Total)

Year	Tea	Rubber	Coco-nut Oil	Copra	Desic-cated Coconut	Other Products†	Total Export Receipts (Rs. 000,000)
1891.....	52.3	—	9.1	1.6	...	....	58
1900.....	58.4	....	7.3	4.3	2.4	27.6‡	92
1913.....	37.7	26.3	7.2	9.0	3.4	16.4	233
1929.....	48.6	20.5	4.3	6.2	2.8	17.6	423
1939.....	57.3	20.6	4.1	2.2	2.2	13.6	328
1949.....	61.1	11.5	11.4	2.0	2.4	11.6	1,064
1954.....	65.1	16.0	5.8	2.6	3.8	6.7	1,724
1959.....	58.9	16.8	6.6	2.9	4.2	10.6	1,773

*Source: Tables A–52 and A–56, Appendix.
†Includes minor coconut-product exports (poonac, coir, whole coconuts), other minor domestic exports, and re-exports.
‡Includes rubber.

One side of the historical record of the estate sector, then, is the not inconsiderable amount of economic growth it provided for Ceylon. There is another side, however: the failure of estate development to touch off any remarkable growth or transformation of the rest of the economy. Despite a century of estate development, the average income in 1939 of Ceylon's 5,916,000 people was only about Rs. 140 (or, converting at the then-current exchange rate,

U.S. $46 in 1939 prices);[56] it had been higher—about Rs. 190 (some U.S. $60) in the late twenties—but had suffered in the depression. Other quantitative indicators for 1939 point to a very poor country. The birth rate was very high, 35.9 per thousand, and the death rate was also substantial (22.0); of every 1,000 live births, 166 infants died in their first year. The population was about 85 percent rural. In the fields of public health and education considerable progress had been made and standards in Ceylon exceeded those in most other Asian countries. Still, much remained to be done: fewer than 40 percent of the nation's school-age children were actually in school and infectious and parasitic diseases, which medicine and public health could in time eradicate, accounted for 20 percent of all deaths in the island. Most of Ceylon's rural population relied heavily on the traditional cultivation of paddy (rice), yet per acre yields in the crop were among the lowest in the world. The main reasons for the continuing poverty of the traditional agricultural sector were the primitive technology and the small quantities of cooperative resources the peasants had to work with. The average paddy holding was just over one acre and, with supplemental holdings of other kinds, the typical peasant family had no more than perhaps three acres to work. Mechanical power use was sparse; electricity consumption amounted to some 25 kilowatt hours per capita a year in 1939 and even this was almost entirely limited to the cities and the estates. Even draft animals were in short supply; there was only one buffalo for every eight rural persons and one cow or bull for every four. Low incomes were the inevitable consequence of such low levels of resource use.

The coexistence of so poor an economy in general and a peasant sector in particular with a prosperous estate sector raises a serious question. It is clear that the estates did not create the poverty. But even so, why did they not eliminate it? The failure of the estates to transform Ceylon's economy must be considered in detail. The explanation for it lies in the basic structure and dynamics of the pre-World War II economic system.

---

[56]Warnasena Rasaputram. "The Influence of Foreign Trade on the Level and Growth of National Income of Ceylon, 1926–57" (unpublished Ph.D. dissertation, University of Wisconsin, 1959), p. 133. Data supporting the other statements made in this paragraph appear in the Appendix.

Chapter 3

The Structure and Dynamics
of the Classical Economy

THE DUALISTIC EXPORT ECONOMY

Both the strengths and the weaknesses of Ceylon's colonial economy grew out of its basic structure and dynamics. In structure, the economy was a veritable model of what might be called a dualistic export economy. There are two identifying features of this kind of economy: (1) close dependence of national income on foreign trade and (2) a split of the economy into two sectors, one modern in organizational structure and technology, producing for the world market, and the other traditional in both these regards, producing for the immediate village market. Dualism can be and has been defined in many different terms: capitalistic versus subsistence, monetized versus nonmonetized, export versus domestic, and a positive versus a zero marginal product of labor. In Ceylon prior to the 1940's the various criteria would in practice have given closely coincident definitions of the two sectors, which, however defined, were clearly visible. In the present study the general terms "modern" and "traditional" will be used to identify the two sectors. The modern sector can be said to have consisted of the estates, the financial and commercial establishments of Colombo and a few smaller cities, and the central government.[1] The traditional sector was made up of the villages and depended preeminently upon agriculture, with a sprinkling of native crafts and traditional service occupations. The classic purity of the Ceylonese case is illustrated by the clarity of this two sector division and the near absence of any in-between or third case. Not until after World War II did a

---

[1] For completeness, one should also include (1) the embryonic industrial sector (notably the construction and the tea and rubber machinery building industries) which grew up around the plantation sector and perhaps (2) local government, which has always been a minor institution in Ceylon, having narrowly circumscribed functions and spending no more than about five percent as much money each year as the central government. Neither was of any great importance in the classical economic system, however.

56

significant "third sector," comprising industrial and urban activities not directly related to plantation agriculture, develop.

The dualism of the economy was very nearly perfect. The estate and peasant economies touched at relatively few points. There was little blurring of the sectoral lines. The coconut industry was a mixed form, containing both tiny subsistence gardens and huge capitalistic estates, but in the other export industries, tea and rubber, smallholders were relatively unimportant and produced less than 15 percent of the crop. The rest of the economy did not count for much. There was a small plumbago (graphite) mining industry; an unimportant remnant of the old spice trade, the principal commercial activity of Portuguese and Dutch times; and only the barest rudiments of a manufacturing sector (almost no modern industry —unless the processing operations attached to the tea-, coconut-, and rubber-growing industries are counted—and cottage industries which compared most unfavorably with those of neighboring India). For even the simplest manufactured goods the reliance on imports was virtually complete.

By way of qualification, however, it might be mentioned that the two generalizations of the preceding paragraph—that there were few economic interrelations between the modern and the traditional sectors and that the dividing line between the two sectors was distinct—tend to hold less firmly for, say, the 1920's and 1930's than for earlier decades. The development of the coconut industry by Sinhalese entrepreneurs, for example, was mainly a twentieth-century phenomenon. The opening of areas close to the estates or to the larger towns to modern transportation also had an integrating effect. By World War II the entire wet zone low-country region surrounding Colombo had become thoroughly commercialized. Subsistence production had all but disappeared and many of the area's residents moved freely among traditional, estate, and urban activities. By contrast, many other parts of the island were left virtually untouched by the century of economic development which ended in 1939.

The relative importance of the modern and traditional sectors during the classical period can be defined with reference to the proportions of the labor force employed in each of them and by their relative contributions to national output.

Ceylon's labor force, once the plantation system was firmly established in the late nineteenth century, split on about a 40–60 basis between the modern and traditional sectors. This proportion remained remarkably stable up to World War II. As Table 3–1 indicates, some 30 percent of the available labor force was utilized on the estates, another 30 to 35 percent in traditional agriculture, and the remaining 35 to 40 percent in nonagricultural pursuits. Of the 40 percent employed outside agriculture, some fell into the modern sector and some into the traditional. No precise division can be made, but perhaps three-fourths should be considered to have been attached to the traditional sector, mostly in service occupations. Thus 40 percent and 60 percent serve as rough estimates of the relative importance of the two sectors in terms of labor employed. If total population, as distinct from labor force, were used as a basis for division, the modern sector would be somewhat smaller than 40 percent, owing to the tendency for estate workers to be transients with no family present in Ceylon.

TABLE 3–1

SECTORAL ALLOCATION OF LABOR FORCE, CENSUS YEARS, 1881–1953*

Year	Estates	Traditional Agriculture	Other Sectors	Total: All Sectors	Estates	Traditional Agriculture	Other Sectors
		(In 000s)				(Percent of Total)	
1881...	623		408	1,031	60.4		39.6
1901...	441	624	589	1,653	26.7	37.7	35.6
1911...	562	540	652	1,753	32.0	30.8	37.2
1921...	620	734	864	2,218	27.9	33.1	39.0
1946...	783	556	1,272	2,612	30.0	21.3	48.7
1953...	856	680	1,445	2,982	28.7	22.8	48.5

*Source: Table A–26, Appendix. Small discrepancies are attributable to rounding.

The relative contributions of the modern and traditional sectors to national income during the classical period are somewhat more difficult to determine. No doubt the contribution of the modern sector had undergone a substantial rise up to the late 1920's, the first period for which even crude national accounts estimates are available. Looking at these rough estimates of national income[2] and at foreign trade statistics, one sees that exports, which were mostly the product of the modern sector, were running about 35 to 40 percent of national income. Adding in the contribution of government and the few other goods and services produced by the modern sector for local use, one reaches the conclusion that something like half of the total national income was produced by the 40 percent of the labor force employed in the modern sector.

[2]See Warnasena Rasaputram, *"Influence of Foreign Trade on the Level and Growth of National Income of Ceylon, 1926–57"* (unpublished Ph.D. dissertation, University of Wisconsin, 1959).

INTERSECTORAL FLOWS

The economy of Ceylon up to World War II, then, can be regarded as consisting of a modern and a traditional sector, both open to trade with each other and with the outside world. However, the overwhelming bulk of trade flows ran from the modern sector to the outside and back again. Few goods and services flowed between the traditional sector and the modern sector or between the traditional sector and the outside. The government, an institution with a potential for changing the pattern of intersectoral flows, was small at the time and did little to alter this basic pattern. The pattern can be illustrated in a rough and incomplete way with respect to one fairly typical prewar year—1929.[3]

There are no data available which would provide a quantitative estimate of trade between the modern and the traditional sectors in 1929, but the flow was certainly very small. As already noted, the estates depended on the village neither for productive inputs nor for end products. The same was true, perhaps to a lesser degree, of the small but growing urban wing of the modern sector. It, like the estates, leaned heavily on foreign sources to satisfy its needs. Of course, the village did succeed in selling some export produce, some food, a very few other types of goods, and a variety of services to the modern sector. Such cash incomes, which doubtless increased through time, were used to add members to the growing urban and estate elites and to enrich some of the more fortunate or more industrious residents of the villages. But relative to the tremendous size of the trade flow linking the modern sector to the rest of the world the value of this flow must have been miniscule.

Although some 60 percent or more of Ceylon's population in 1929 depended on the traditional sector for its livelihood, nearly all of the country's foreign trade was conducted by the modern sector. As Table 3–2 shows, more than three-fourths of the nation's exports in 1929 had their origins in the modern sector. Furthermore, virtually all exports at least passed through the hands of the modern-sector export-import firms. Coconut products constituted the main export crop of the traditional sector, bringing in some Rs. 35,600,000 (about 44 percent of the sector's total export receipts). Tea and rubber each accounted for about half as much revenue to the traditional sector as coconut products and a few minor products made

---

[3]The *magnitudes* of the flows outlined in this section differ considerably from those which might be measured for other years of the classical period. The *pattern* of flows, however, would be much the same for any year from the 1840's through the 1930's.

up the rest. However, the great bulk of export receipts—some 78.6 percent of the total in 1929—accrued to the modern sector, including the enormous sum of Rs. 188,400,000 from tea.

TABLE 3–2

BREAKDOWN OF RECEIPTS FROM DOMESTIC EXPORTS BETWEEN
MODERN AND TRADITIONAL SECTORS, 1929*

(Rs. Millions)

Item	Modern Sector	Traditional Sector	Total
Food, drink, and tobacco:	202.1	32.7	234.8
Tea†	188.4	16.8	205.2
Desiccated coconut‡	4.9	7.0	11.9
Others§	8.9	8.9	17.7
Raw materials:	96.2	45.0	141.2
Rubber‖	73.4	13.2	86.6
Coconut oil‡	7.4	10.6	18.0
Copra‡	10.8	15.5	26.3
Minor unmanufactured coconut products	1.9	2.5	4.4
Plumbago (graphite)	2.7	—	2.7
Others#	—	3.2	3.2
Manufactured goods#	—	3.7	3.7
Domestic exports	298.3	81.4	379.6
Percent of total	78.6	21.4	100.0

*As the following notes make clear, this is only a rough breakdown. Small discrepancies are attributable to rounding.

†Ten acres is the dividing line between smallholdings and estates; the acreage ratio was taken to be that of 1935 (88.2 percent estate) and yields on smallholdings were assumed to be two-thirds of estate yields per acre.

‡All coconut output is divided on the basis of the 1946 acreage ratio (31.9 percent estate) and the assumption that smallholder yields are two-thirds of estate yields.

§Assumed 50–50; includes minor estate crops, spices, etc.

‖Acreage ratio taken as in 1936 (78.7 percent estate); smallholder yields assumed to be two-thirds of estate yields.

#Arbitrarily allocated entirely to traditional sector; actually contain small proportions of modern-sector output.

Sources: Tables A–39, A–52, and A–53, Appendix; Department of Commerce, *Thirty Years Trade Statistics of Ceylon (1925-1954)*, Vol. 1.

Table 3–3 breaks down 1929 imports among several categories: consumption goods, Western-style and traditional, intermediate goods, and investment goods. The Western-style consumption goods amounted to 16.8 percent of total retained imports at this time. Since the European population was no more than 7,000 or 8,000, less than 1 percent of the total, the figure is indicative of both the much higher income levels enjoyed by the few Europeans in Ceylon and the spread (which was later to become much wider) of Western

TABLE 3–3

BREAKDOWN OF RETAINED IMPORTS AMONG CONSUMPTION GOODS, WESTERN-STYLE
AND TRADITIONAL, INTERMEDIATE GOODS, AND INVESTMENT GOODS, 1929*
(Rs. Millions)

Item	Consumption Goods Western-style	Consumption Goods Traditional	Intermediate Goods	Investment Goods	Total
Food, drink, and tobacco:	27.5	147.1	3.8	—	178.4
Rice	—	99.5	—	—	99.5
Sugar	—	15.8	—	—	15.8
Fish	0.9	10.2	—	—	11.1
Curry stuffs	—	5.8	—	—	5.8
Other food	18.4	15.2	3.8	—	37.4
Drink	4.6	—	—	—	4.6
Tobacco	3.6	0.6	—	—	4.2
Raw materials:	—	—	30.2	—	30.2
Fertilizers	—	—	15.2	—	15.2
Other	—	—	15.0	—	15.0
Manufactured goods:	33.6	38.4	33.4	49.9	155.4
Cotton goods	—	25.7	—	—	25.7
Motor vehicles	5.5	—	—	9.5	15.0
Iron and steel and their products	—	—	—	14.7	14.7
Gasoline	4.8	—	8.3	—	13.1
Machinery	—	—	—	7.8	7.8
Kerosene	—	7.6	—	—	7.6
Other	23.3	5.1	25.1	17.9	71.4
Total	61.1	185.5	67.4	49.9	364.0
Percent of total	16.8	51.0	18.5	13.7	100.0

*As in Table 3–2, there is some roughness inherent in the arbitrary assignment of items to one category or another; however, the existence of a finely detailed summary of imports in the source considerably reduces errors arising from this difficulty. Retained imports are taken as 1929 imports minus 1929 re-exports, with no adjustment for changes in stocks. Small discrepancies are attributable to rounding.
Source: Department of Commerce, *Thirty Years Trade Statistics of Ceylon (1925–1954)*, Vol. 1.

modes of living to the Ceylonese population. The Ceylonese consumers of Western-type goods may at this time have numbered 10,-
000 or 20,000. They were largely limited to Colombo and consisted
of persons with high-level positions in the estates, commerce, and the
government, as well as a small but growing independent Ceylonese
middle and upper class, made up of landowners and professionals
in law, medicine, and similar fields. Traditional consumption
goods, which accounted for just over half the import bill in 1929,
consisted mostly of staple foods (especially rice), with basic manufactured goods like cotton textiles, kerosene, and matches rounding
out the total. No division of these goods between modern and traditional sector consumers (e.g., between villagers and estate workers) can be made, since the consumption patterns of the two groups

were similar in many respects. One can speculate that most of these goods went to the estates and to urban consumers, though the villager, too, had by this time become dependent on foreign sources of such things as cloth, matches, and kerosene and used much of his meager cash income to buy them. The intermediate and investment goods which made up the remaining 37 percent of the import bill went almost exclusively to the modern sector—the estates, commerce, and the government. Almost all the raw materials, tools, and construction materials employed by the traditional sector were of native origin.

Like the outside world, the government of Ceylon in 1929 dealt mainly with the modern sector. The government was much smaller then than it was to become later (its consumption and investment expenditures together amounted to about 14 percent of Gross National Product, compared with the 19.4 percent disposed of by the 1960 government)[4] and its later function as an instrument of intersectoral redistribution had hardly been used yet. The revenues of the government in 1929 came mainly from customs duties (49.0 percent of total revenues), nontax receipts (32.1 percent), and excise taxes (16.1) and only to a small extent from direct taxation.[5] By far the greater proportion of revenue was raised in the modern sector; the traditional sector was barely touched by the revenue system. Import duties, the largest single revenue source, were levied at an average rate of 9.5 percent of the total c.i.f. value of imports. About a third of this duty was raised from imports of traditional food items (much of which was destined for consumption by estate laborers), but the rest fell on consumption, intermediate, and investment good imports of the modern sector and on items which were subsequently re-exported.[6] About 80 percent of the total sum raised from export duties, of which tea provided by far the largest share, fell on estate exports.[7] The average rate of export taxation was just 3.1 percent of the value of domestic exports.[8] There was no income tax, either on companies or individuals. The nontax revenues of the government were mostly payments for services performed for the modern sector—land sales proceeds, surveying fees, tolls, electricity charges, port and warehouse duties, etc.

---

[4]Rasaputram's data (*op. cit.*) put GNP in 1929 at about Rs. 775,000,000 (p. 121); for 1960, see the Appendix.

[5]See Table A–65, Appendix.

[6]Department of Commerce, *Thirty Years Trade Statistics of Ceylon (1925–1954)*, Vol. 2; this is for 1930.

[7]*Ibid.*

[8]During the following year, with the onslaught of the depression, export taxation was temporarily abandoned.

Similarly, the expenditures of the government were in large measure the costs of providing services to the modern sector. Table 3–4, which provides a rough functional breakdown of expenditures in the 1928/29 budget, shows this. Aside from the fairly heavy burden of administrative cost and the light defense burden which it bore, the government confined its activities to providing services which were of direct or indirect benefit to the estates. This is not

TABLE 3–4

FUNCTIONAL BREAKDOWN OF CENTRAL GOVERNMENT
EXPENDITURES, 1928/29*

(Rs. Millions)

Administration		27.0
Defense		2.3
Economic services		35.0
Social services		21.9
Education	10.3	
Health	11.5	
Transfer payments		18.7
Interest on public debt		11.2
Pensions		7.5
Extraordinary expenditures†		21.0
Total		144.6

*This breakdown, which is based on *The Report of the Colonial Auditor for 1928/29*, is necessarily rough; it is only approximately comparable with the data for later years presented in Table A–66, Appendix.

†Nonrecurrent expenditures of the Irrigation, Public Works, Railway, and Electrical Departments; this figure serves as a rough measure of government investment.

to imply, however, that government activity left other segments of the population untouched. Many of the services that were provided —electricity, roads, railroads, and others—yielded substantial benefits to other parts of the economy and society as well as to the estates.[9] Two areas in which the colonial government had a particularly profound impact on the traditional economy were education and health services. In the early nineteenth century education had been left mainly to private institutions, but as time went by the government took on an increasing responsibility in this area and

---

[9]It can be argued that the main reason these services were provided not only to the estates but to parts of the peasant economy as well is that they approached the character of public goods and, once provided to the estates, necessarily had to be consumed by the traditional sector, too. It is no doubt true, however, that government motivations in these areas were mixed and that the public goods argument provides only part of the explanation.

rapidly rising educational standards resulted.[10] Public health services, too, improved rapidly in quantity and quality during the twentieth century. Development in both fields was stimulated when Ceylon gained internal self-government in 1931. Both educational and health services were usually best in Colombo, next best on the estates, and poorest in the villages, but nevertheless there was considerable benefit to the whole country.

THE GROWTH POTENTIAL OF THE CLASSICAL SYSTEM

The dynamics of Ceylon's classical export economy were extremely simple. Export earnings provided the exogenous stimulus, and national income—as well as almost every other economic magnitude—adjusted accordingly. In the traditional sector the sensitivity to changes in foreign earnings was of course much less than in the modern sector, but for the economy as a whole both secular growth and short-term fluctuations originated principally in the world market. The only other influence on the welfare of the peasant was the immemorial natural cycle of weather and disease.

Given the existence of a sizable foreign demand for products which could be grown efficiently on Ceylon's estates, the other requirement of a growing modern sector was a plentiful supply of the factors of production. This Ceylon's estates found in their early days either by drawing from outside the country, as they did for British capital and entrepreneurship and for Indian labor, or by putting to use hitherto unexploited resources located within Ceylon (e.g., Crown land). All of these resources could be brought into play within the modern sector without producing more than a minimal disturbing impact on Ceylon's traditional sector.

(1) *Labor supply* to the estates, as has been seen, was almost perfectly elastic at prevailing wage rates. The failure of the Sinhalese peasant to join the estate labor force in any great numbers, whatever its reason, is one of the main explanations of the economy's dualism. With estate wages set by statute, labor ebbed and flowed between the plantation areas and South India according to seasonal, cyclical, and secular variations in the estates' needs for workers.

---

[10]See Tables A–19 and A–20, Appendix. Here, too, government action can be explained in terms of a desire to promote an efficiently operating modern sector. The need of the estates, the commercial firms, and the colonial government itself for English-educated clerks is often given credit for the early development of education in Ceylon, though, again, other motivations doubtless entered in. Similarly, it could be contended that action in the field of public health was at least partly motivated by a desire to avoid the disruption of estate work by epidemics among the labor force.

There was a similar flow, though a much smaller one, between the estate and Ceylon's own villages. Although there were some frictions involved in getting labor from India and even some labor shortages in the early days (see Chapter 2, pages 24-26), labor was generally plentiful and it must be said that the plantation system could not have been established in Ceylon in the absence of Indian immigrant labor.

(2) *Land* was the only factor of production which could not be brought in from outside. In the early coffee period good land was available to European planters in unlimited supply and at nominal cost and some planters reaped enormous profits as a consequence. But this golden age soon passed. By the last two decades of the nineteenth century the scarcity of land well suited for tea cultivation had become the main factor in limiting the further expansion of production. Similar problems were encountered with coconuts, for which adequately watered land was the scarce factor, and later with rubber. After the 1920's, total estate acreage stagnated (see Table 2-10, page 49). Since Ceylon provided only a relatively small fraction of total world supply in its leading export crops, increases in its production of them would generally have little effect on world prices. Given the output of other producing countries, Ceylon itself could hardly "spoil" the market for any of them. Factors of production other than land were still in ready supply, so it was the exhaustion of the quantity of land capable of being planted profitably at prevailing prices (coupled in some cases with a decline in world price arising out of *worldwide* overexpansion) which provided the initial check to further output growth in the case of each plantation crop. Rates of return on the marginal acre planted with a crop declined as total acreage was progressively extended and in time, given the world price, acreage reached a point where further extension became unprofitable. Coffee attained this point in the 1860's and only the soaring prices of the seventies induced the area planted to rise above 240,000 acres.[11] For tea the limit was reached in the first decade of the twentieth century.[12] In retrospect, one can see that rubber acreage reached the limits of profitable expansion during the late 1920's; in fact, a considerable amount of overly optimistic planting did go on into the early 1930's, but as prices fell steeply and costs remained relatively inflexible it proved to be unprofitable. Coconut, which never experienced the rapid inflow of European capital and enterprise that tea and rubber enjoyed,

---

[11]See Table 2-1, page 20.
[12]See Table 2-5, page 35.

took longer to come to the point where all the acres which could be planted profitably were already in cultivation: it could be said to have arrived there around World War I. The apparent stability of coconut acreage since then has been remarkable.[13] Thus, in each of these industries there came a time when, barring spectacular increases in the world price, extension of the acreage planted became infeasible. From this time on, output necessarily had to stagnate—unless yields per acre could be raised. Until means could be found to raise yields land was to be the limiting factor of production.

(3) *Capital* was generally less of a problem than land. In eras of prosperity it was generated in considerable amounts by the internal profitability of the estates. Once the estates were planted and the need for further capital expenditures was slight, they returned handsome dividends to their shareholders. Rippy found that 20 British plantation companies operating in Ceylon paid a median dividend of 19.0 percent over the first half of the twentieth century, not counting stock dividends, which were substantial during the early years of the century. During their best 5-year subperiod within this 50-year span, these corporations paid a median dividend of 50.0 percent! By the late 1940's their average dividend had not fallen, but was running at 19.1 percent. An additional group of 42 companies had only slightly less impressive payout ratios. They had a median dividend of 14.8 percent between 1911 and 1950 and 36 of them were still paying at a rate of 13.3 percent in the late forties (the other 6 had disappeared, through mergers or otherwise).[14] These 62 companies, while no doubt not a completely representative group, constitute a substantial fraction of the universe of British plantation companies operating in Ceylon (Rippy puts the total of companies registered in the United Kingdom to grow tea or rubber in Ceylon between 1880 and 1950 at 200).[15] Over the estate sector as a whole such rates were perhaps exceptional but they give some indication of the power of the estates, at least the more efficient ones, to supply their own needs for capital. To the extent that external finance was needed, agency houses and British banks were willing to make short-term advances on the security of future crops. The estates seldom suffered for lack of capital.

If world price levels were favorable, the estate sector, facing a

---

[13]This apparent stability is partly attributable to lack of information; see footnote § to Table A–37, Appendix.

[14]J. Fred Rippy, "Trinidad and Ceylon: Two Profitable British Colonies," Lyle W. Shannon (ed.), *Underdeveloped Areas* (New York: Harper & Brothers, 1957), pp. 247–52.

[15]*Ibid.*, p. 248.

demand curve of very high elasticity with respect to price and possessing easy access to the necessary factors of production, had a tremendous capacity for economic growth. By contrast, the traditional sector was left generally untouched by the growth-inducing forces active in the modern sector or, indeed, by any other influences which might cause a rapid rise in per capita income. The peasant economy created its own demand or, rather, its subsistence production was relatively unresponsive to market stimuli. The exception, of course, was peasant smallholders of export crops, who were generally highly responsive to market stimuli. In fact, they were often overresponsive, planting too much of whatever crop appeared attractive at any given moment on land that was not really suitable. For this reason and because of their technical and market disadvantages relative to the estates, smallholders made much lower returns per acre than estates did from the same crops.

In general, smallholder production of export crops had only a marginal impact upon the giant mass of the traditional economy. The main reason for the failure of smallholder export agriculture to have a more profound influence is probably that only a fraction of the total land area controlled by the peasant sector was technically suited to producing tea, rubber, or coconuts for a cash market. Even with coconut, which was widely produced in most wet zone peasant areas, yields were seldom high enough to leave any substantial surplus over and above the consumption needs of the producer's family. Unwillingness to abandon old systems of cultivation and a lack of technical knowledge may be additional explanations. In any event, most peasants remained tied to the traditional modes of cultivation, in which paddy farming assumed an almost mystic position at the center of rural life and the raising of coconuts and a wide variety of secondary crops for use within the village economy played a secondary role. Within this traditional sector little happened to disturb the old equilibrium. Labor force grew slowly as peasant population increased (see Table 2–8, page 48), but with the gradual loss of people to the cities and the estates, as well as the slow growth of complementary resources available to the peasant producer, it probably did not swell so rapidly as to apply downward pressure to rural incomes.[16] The supply of peasant land (Table

---

[16]There is little direct evidence on output trends for peasant crops or on price movements for the marketed proportion of traditional sector output. One has only the estimates of population density to serve as indirect evidence on the trend of peasant real income. Yet, given the absence of worsening pressure on the land up to the 1920's, real per capita income in the traditional sector was probably at least constant, if not slowly rising.

2–8) was never reduced absolutely by the rise of the estates, but continued to grow slowly from year to year. Reclamation of formerly irrigated areas in the dry zone accelerated its growth somewhat. In terms of capital equipment, of course, the peasant producer was desperately wanting and there is no evidence as to just how fast he may have been able to augment his meager capital stock. Under the circumstances, the traditional sector could hardly be expected to be a focal point for economic growth and it is unlikely (see Chapter 2, pages 52–53) that it experienced any marked rise in output per head during the colonial era.

Demand originating within the economy of Ceylon thus had very little to do with the growth of the classical export economy. The peasants lived in their semisubsistence world, buying little that had not been produced in their own immediate neighborhood. The estates (and the urban sector which supported them) relied heavily on imports, both for inputs into their production processes and for consumption. Two further considerations also helped to restrict the growth of internal demand:

(1) *Government finance* played only a small role in the economy. As has already been seen, the colonial government took little interest in influencing economic trends via fiscal policy or the composition of its expenditures. Instead, it generally reacted passively to demands that it attend to the most basic needs of the colony, especially those of the planters. According to conventional doctrine, colonial governments were expected to live within their revenues; these of course, depended on the tax base, which meant mainly the modern sector (see pages 62–63). Had the government been willing to impose heavier taxes on the export sector, it could have done so. Because of the elasticity of world demand for Ceylon's exports and the low elasticity of supply, the incidence of additional taxation would have been on the export producers and, as has been seen, the after-tax profits existing in the sector were considerable and could have supported a heavier tax load. The government, however, had no such ambitions. It conceived of its role as maintaining law and order, providing transportation and other utility services to the estates, and improving health and educational levels. The colonial administrators, who were typically capable men, depended for the revenues needed to finance these services on the tax and nontax receipts generated by the modern sector. In prosperous times they often accomplished their limited assigned tasks quite successfully.

(2) *Monetary developments*, whether conscious policy or spontaneous event, were effectively prevented from having any important impact on the economy by the "currency board system" of note

issue and the British commercial banking tradition. The currency board scheme, which was in effect from 1884 to 1949, provided for a 100 percent backing of the government's note issue by British and Indian notes and government securities. These assets were purchased mostly out of export receipts, so their supply in Ceylon was closely related to the country's foreign trade fortunes. This system made currency supply yet another magnitude which was closely dependent upon export returns. The banking system was almost exclusively in British hands (prior to 1938 the only rivals to the British in the banking field were a few small Indian banks and one short-lived attempt to found a Ceylonese bank) and lent almost exclusively to the planters and the export-import trade. Naturally, the hallowed practice of making only self-liquidating short-term business loans was followed. The supply of credit was thus almost as closely linked to exports as was the currency supply, except that in the case of credit it was anticipated export receipts which gave rise to the creation of money (not, as with currency, actual realized receipts), so that had it not been for the extreme conservatism of the banks the overextension of credit and perhaps occasional panics would have been possible.[17]

In sum, the structure and dynamics of Ceylon's classical export economy were such that the modern sector was capable of extensive growth and short-term fluctuations as severe as those of any advanced economy. The fluctuations were largely determined by world prices for Ceylon's exports, something which the country could not affect. Growth, too, was possible only with the all-important existence of favorable prices for tea, rubber, and coconut products in the world market. For the foundation of each plantation industry prices had to be high enough (and the expectation had to be that they would remain favorable long enough) to justify clearing and planting considerable land areas. Later, when the return on newly planted areas fell to near zero, output tended to stagnate and little further planting was done unless prices took a sharp upward turn. Once the continued extension of the area planted became unprofitable, further increases in output depended mainly on the ability of producers to increase per acre yields profitably. Although the standard of how high the price had to be for the estates

---

[17]There was just one famous bank collapse in Ceylon's colonial monetary history. In 1884 the Oriental Bank, which had been left with large holdings of coffee mortgages at the time of the collapse of the coffee industry, failed. This was the largest bank in the colony at the time and its failure gave rise to a government note issue and the currency board system. On this whole subject, see H. A. de S. Gunasekera, *From Dependent Currency to Central Banking in Ceylon* (London: G. Bell and Sons, Ltd., 1962).

to maintain or increase their level of output declined once the trees were planted, still the future development of the industry depended strictly on the uncontrollable variable, world price trends. The economy itself generated only a negligible amount of demand for tea and rubber, although the existence of the coconut industry was partly based on home demand.

As for the peasant sector, it received little direct stimulus from the growth of the modern sector. Its traditional patterns of resource allocation, technology, and commercial structure were relatively little altered by the rise of the estates. In the context of what has happened since 1939, however, it is possible to see that the colonial system had some important indirect implications for the future of the peasant economy. The two most important of these derived from activities of the colonial government which have been continued and extended by the government of independent Ceylon, with dramatic consequences. They are the development of public health services, which was instrumental in slashing the death rate after World War II and forever upsetting the population balance which had existed in the colonial economy, and the spread of education, which eventually produced as profound changes in the qualitative aspects of the labor force as the population explosion did in the quantitative.

Finally, the colonial economy might also be viewed in terms of the surpluses of production over consumption that were generated and how these surpluses were used. As noted earlier, the estates produced enormous surpluses. What became of them? It has been seen already that some of the money was reinvested in the estates themselves and that other large sums were remitted as dividends to shareholders outside Ceylon. Lesser amounts also went to locally resident British and Ceylonese individuals,[18] who spent them in large part to build up and maintain a consumption level far above that of the Ceylonese masses. The growth of the estate sector and its continued prosperity, then, increased dividend levels for foreign shareholders and increased consumption levels within a growing enclave in Ceylon itself, but it did not materially raise levels of expenditure on Ceylon-produced goods and services, nor did it provide a surplus to be invested in other parts of Ceylon's economy. This is the fatal flaw of economic growth within the classical export economy model: the "spread effects" of modern sector growth to the traditional sector are very slight. Thus, when world price movements or an exhaustion of supplies of good land coupled with tech-

---

[18]The profits from estate coconut cultivation, while smaller in the aggregate than those of tea and rubber, probably gave the largest locally retained surplus.

nical stagnation bring an end to the estate sector's growth there is no other dynamic sector to fall back on and economic growth itself ceases.

Within the classical framework and in the absence of fortuitous rises in export prices, the only way that Ceylon's economy could grow after the 1920's was by increasing per acre yields in estate crops. Even after the "abnormal" depression and war periods had passed, however, the nature of the world continued to be such that this appeared to offer only a meager chance of substantial economic growth. The alternative was to break out of the classical model, change the structure of the intersectoral flows, increase internal demand, capture the surplus generated by the estate sector and use it for investment in other parts of the economy, and try to transform both the traditional and the modern sector, the former by techno-logical modernization and the latter by diversification and indus-trialization. It is the emergence of these alternative growth oppor-tunities and attempts to pursue them that are of most interest in the more recent period of Ceylonese development.

Chapter 4

New Forces in the Export Economy

Although Ceylon's economy in 1939 was vastly different from what it had been a century before it still conformed closely to the export economy pattern, to which it had clung so long. The depression had been a trying experience for the country, cutting export earnings at one point to only 38 percent of their 1926 pre-depression peak level. The expansion of the plantation sector and the roads, schools, hospitals, and other public facilities that went with it had abruptly ceased. To add to the trials of the thirties, a severe malaria epidemic had ravaged the country in 1935 and 1936. Yet the fruits of past economic growth within the export economy mold were visible in several aspects of Ceylonese life. Income per capita was high relative to what it had been in the past and compared quite favorably with the South Asian regional average. In 1938, according to the Department of Census and Statistics (CSD), GNP in current prices was Rs. 652,000,000; this amounted to Rs. 112 per capita or, using the import price index as a crude deflator (if anything, it deflates too much), Rs. 509 per capita in 1953 prices.[1] Literacy had advanced to a rate of about 60 percent.[2] And the educational and health systems were strong and growing.

In 1939 over 800,000 students were enrolled in the nation's schools, representing about 40 percent of the total population of school age.[3] More than 21,000 teachers were employed in this educational venture.[4] The students were about evenly divided between

---

[1] For the GDP figure (actually, the total is "national income" as defined by the CSD, which also includes income earned abroad by Ceylonese nationals), see Table A-1, Appendix; for the import price index, see Table A-50, Appendix.

[2] See Table A-23, Appendix.

[3] See Table A-19, Appendix. Since 1939 is not a census year, there are no data on population of school age; however, the total number of pupils in 1939 is a higher percentage of *total* population than is total number of pupils in 1946; since the 1946 population was, if anything, younger than the 1939 population and since 41.1 percent of the school-age population was enrolled in the latter year, it can be deduced that *at least* 41.1 percent of the population of school age—and probably more—was enrolled in 1939.

[4] Ministry of Finance, *Economic and Social Development of Ceylon (a Survey), 1926–1954* (Colombo, 1955), p. 90.

government schools and private government-assisted schools, with a very small additional number attending unaided private institutions. The nation's school system was thus nearly halfway down the road to universal education at this point. As has been seen, the government had played a major role in this development, in establishing government schools (mostly in the villages) and aiding private schools on the estates and in the towns.

Health services, by Asian standards, were similarly advanced. Not counting private nursing homes, there were 120 hospitals in Ceylon in 1939, containing over 10,000 beds, roughly one for every 500 persons in the population.[5] More than 400 doctors worked in them, along with some 3,000 employees of other kinds.[6] Like Western education, Western medicine had a potent cultural effect as it spread through the countryside. It helped to lay the foundations for the period of change upon which the economy was about to embark.

A note should also be added here on developments in the political sphere. By the Donoughmore Constitution of 1931 the island had been granted adult suffrage and a considerable measure of internal self-government. During the thirties a nucleus of future political leaders began to form. A State Council, consisting of 50 elected members and 8 appointees of the Crown, was set up to legislate on internal affairs and 7 of its members also took on the duty of administering the 7 ministries dealing with domestic matters: Home Affairs; Agriculture and Lands; Local Administration; Health; Labour, Industry, and Commerce; Education; and Communications and Works. D. S. Senanayake, later to become the first prime minister of independent Ceylon, took the portfolio of Agriculture and Lands.[7] One result of this constitutional change was that interest in diversification of the economy and possible industrialization came to the fore with the new leaders. The *Report of the Ceylon Banking Commission,*[8] which appeared in 1934, reflected this new interest. It expressed support for the ideas that industry should be encouraged, that it had been impeded hitherto by the profitability (up to the depression) of the estates, and that the formation of an indigenous bank would aid its development. An Indian advisor produced a list of 12 industries which he felt were suited to Ceylon's resource endowment and market conditions and was criti-

---

[5] *Ibid.* p. 99.
[6] *Ibid.*
[7] For a detailed account of Ceylon government in the Donoughmore period, see Sir Charles Jeffries, *Ceylon—The Path to Independence* (London: Pall Mall Press, Ltd., 1962), pp. 66–75.
[8] *Report of the Ceylon Banking Commission,* S.P. XXII of 1934.

cized for being too unambitious.[9] Then, in 1936 the Executive
Committee on Labour, Industry, and Commerce came under the
chairmanship of G. C. S. Corea, a vigorous proponent of industrial
progress via government pilot plants, research aid, and other
assistance. The State Council in the late thirties was sympathetic to
tariff protection for industry and two industries which had been
founded, matches and soap, received assistance of this kind. The
Bank of Ceylon, a joint public-private undertaking, was founded
in 1938 over British opposition. Work on the hydroelectric scheme
at Laxapana, which had been started in the 1920's by the British
but abandoned when the depression hit, was resumed in 1937.
Several pilot plants were put up and the planned industrialization
program was just beginning to gather momentum when the outbreak of World War II intervened. Thus, little that was tangible
was done in the 1930's, but considerable intellectual ferment had
been stirred up. Another economic consequence of internal self-
government was the development under D. S. Senanayake of plans
for extensive resettlement of peasants in the dry zone but here, too,
there was little time for action.

The forces of change which had begun to build up in the thirties
came to full maturity in the forties. Three developments of that
decade can be said to have brought the classical era of the export
economy to an end and ushered in a period of transition to an uncertain future: the war, independence, and revolutionary changes
in the island's pattern of population growth.

WORLD WAR II

Of the three great forces of change operating on Ceylon's economy in the 1940's, the war was in some ways the least important
in its long-run effects. In common with the depression of the
thirties, it was largely a repetition of past experience. Like World
War I before it, the Second World War called a halt to the usual
pattern of development of the export economy, but in itself it provided no reason why the old economic order should not be reestab-
lished soon after the cessation of hostilities. Indirectly, however,
by virtue of the fact that it hastened the end of British rule in South
Asia, the war was to become an important watershed in Ceylon's
economic development.

As had nearly all other influences on the economy up to that
time, the war first made itself felt in the foreign markets. Immedi-

---

[9] On this point and for a full treatment of thinking about industrialization,
see Henry M. Oliver, "The Industrialization of Ceylon: Opinions—Policies,
1916–1951," *Ceylon Economist*, November, 1956, pp. 175–225.

ately after hostilities began in 1939 Britain put into effect a scheme to assure unbroken supplies of its normal food and raw materials imports from the colonies. Contracts were to be entered into for the purchase of most of the colonial produce at "fair" prices for bulk delivery to the United Kingdom. By 1942 almost all of Ceylon's exports had come under such a contract: tea, rubber, copra, coconut oil, and plumbago, amounting to 97 percent of total exports by value.[10] Prices were first set at prewar levels[11] and later adjusted to compensate producers for increases in production costs; they were renegotiated annually. It is quite clear that the net effect of the bulk purchase contracts was to hold Ceylon's export prices substantially below the level they would have reached on a free world market. Export prices rose by about 80 percent during the course of the war (see Table 4–1), while import prices more than tripled. Further, since production costs were reduced by certain measures, notably the food subsidies, designed to damp the rise in the cost of living, Ceylon taxpayers were actually subsidizing British tea drinkers in even greater measure than might be thought.

Meanwhile, prices of all kinds of imports—food, other consumer goods, raw materials, and capital goods—shot up. Many of these goods, in fact, became completely unavailable. For items that could still be obtained short supplies and enormously increased freight and insurance rates combined to push prices far above past levels. The shortage of imports had both external and internal consequences. Externally, it meant that Ceylon's barter terms of trade deteriorated sharply, to the point where a unit of exports brought less than half as much in terms of imports as it had in 1939. But, despite the unfavorable turn in the terms of trade, Ceylon ran large trade surpluses throughout the war.[12] The fact that export value consistently exceeded the value of imports despite the deteriorating terms of trade is attributable to a rise in export volume (see page 78), coupled with a sharp decline (by more than a third) in the aggregate volume of imports, which came about mainly because people often just could not find imported goods to buy at any price. Ceylonese piled up external assets, especially sterling balances, in unprecedented quantities. Between 1939 and 1945 foreign assets worth approximately Rs. 1,000,000,000 were amassed. Internally, the effects of the trade situation were to create the most

---

[10]J. B. Kelegama, "The Ceylon Economy in the War and Post-War Years," *Ceylon Economist*, May, 1957, pp. 318–370.

[11]For instance, in the case of tea each estate had to sell at the average price its produce had realized in the period 1936–38.

[12]See Table A–56, Appendix.

TABLE 4-1

PRICES, OUTPUT, AND EXTERNAL ASSETS, 1939–50

Year	Export Prices*	Import Prices*	Terms of Trade†	Export Volume‡	Real Export Receipts§	Cost of Living‖	National Income# Current Prices (Rs. 000,000)	National Income# 1939 Prices	External Assets¶ (Rs. 000,000)
				(1939 = 100)					
1939....	100	100	100	100	100	100	652△	652△	275
1940....	110	118	93	101	100	103	.....	...	324
1941....	121	141	86	99	91	113	.....	...	435
1942....	138	209	66	111	78	150	.....	...	521
1943....	145	291	50	113	60	182	.....	...	672
1944....	169	345	49	108	60	184	.....	...	960
1945....	179	323	55	97	64	203	1,990	616	1,260
1946....	193	332	58	108	70	211	2,268	683	1,210
1947....	248	373	66	103	73	232	2,608	699	947
1948....	248	400	62	117	75	239	2,879	720	998
1949....	266	382	70	117	85	237	3,056	800	964
1950....	359	391	92	128	110	250	3,868	989	1,133

*Source: Tables A–50 and A–51, Appendix; these are the Department of Census and Statistics indexes.

†Export price index divided by import price index.

‡Source: CSD indexes in Tables A–48 and A–49, Appendix.

§Index of export value, merchandise exports only, from Tables A–56 and A–57, Appendix, divided by import price index, i.e., the "purchasing power of exports."

‖From Table A–71, Appendix; the index grossly understates increases in consumer prices over this period, even for low-income groups, because of its heavy weighting of rationed and price-controlled items and its omission of the black market.

#Unpublished CSD data; the constant-price figures have been deflated by the import price indexes and so are probably conservative. Dividing these figures by population suggests that not until 1950 was the 1938 level of real per capita income regained.

¶Source: Table A–60, Appendix.

△1938.

attractive domestic market for Ceylon-produced goods in history and, at the same time, to place considerable obstacles in the way of entrepreneurs seeking to satisfy that demand. In addition to normal sources of money income, the war added to the income stream additional sums originating in the large export surpluses which were run in every year of the war,[13] the modest budget deficits incurred by the government,[14] and a considerable volume of military expenditure arising out of the fact that after 1944 Ceylon became the headquarters for the Allied operations in the Southeast Asian sector.[15] On the other hand, machinery, building sup-

---

[13]Merchandise surpluses totaled more than Rs. 800,000,000 over the course of the war. See Table A–56, Appendix.

[14]Actually, the government ran war deficits only at the height of the war, in 1941/42 and 1942/43. See Ministry of Finance, *Economic and Social Development of Ceylon (op. cit.)*, p. 110.

[15]Kelegama *(op. cit.)* estimates that by 1944 military expenditure in Ceylon exceeded Rs. 400,000,000 annually, more than a quarter of national income at the time.

plies, and raw materials from foreign sources became virtually un-obtainable. Despite the difficulties, there were war-induced in-creases in the production of manufactured goods. Meanwhile, the output of most export products and (apparently) food stagnated.

Both the government and private businessmen responded to the drastically reduced supply of imported manufactures. On the gov-ernment side, action was taken to get plants producing a wide variety of products into operation as rapidly as possible. In some cases, plants which had originally been intended to function as pilot projects were thrown into the production of far larger quan-tities than they had been intended to make; in other cases heroic efforts were made to take over vacant buildings, to adapt second-hand machinery designed for some other purpose, to hire and train a labor force, and to begin production as soon as possible. On this basis government plants were soon opened to manufacture hats, coir products, and leather goods. These pioneers were followed in 1942 and 1943 by a plywood mill, an acetic acid plant, a quinine factory, and a steel-rolling mill based on the utilization of scrap, as well as glass, ceramics, and paper operations. Costs and prices were high and the quality of the end product was low, but in the sellers' market of the early forties no one objected. Through 1945, at least, most of the government factories made profits.[16] For the time being, they served their purpose. After the war ended and im-ported manufactures began to flow into the island again the gov-ernment factories quickly demonstrated their unsuitability as a base for peacetime industrial development. It soon became clear (though not so soon and not so clear as to keep the government from losing millions of rupees in trying to keep the plants open) that unless a very high level of tariff protection was provided, the great majority were uneconomic, even after substantial overhauls.[17] The govern-ment plants did have the effect of providing the government with valuable first experience in the industrial field, but they were prob-ably, in the net, an unfortunate phenomenon, since they served to divert its attention from other methods of encouraging industrial development for a period of several years.

Private manufactures, too, responded to the challenge of the

---

[16]*A.R. of the Acting Director of Industries for the Years 1940 to 1947 (Part I: October, 1940, to September, 1947)* (Colombo, 1948), pp. 11-16.

[17]There is, of course, the possibility that even though these plants made accounting losses after 1945 they were in social terms a net gain. One could argue that the resources they employed had few alternative uses and that the social benefits of the industrial experience involved were great. But whatever the potential social benefits of industrialization in general, the wartime gov-ernment plants certainly represented an inefficient way of exploiting them.

sellers' market. Local handicrafts in particular enjoyed a golden era, as consumers who had never before used them turned to Ceylon-made brooms, rugs, textiles, and other goods which could be produced with the materials at hand. As with the government plants, however, the market abruptly crashed at the end of the war and the only lasting effect of the boom was the disillusionment with which it left those who suffered from its sudden end. Modern private industry, mainly because of its inability to find substitutes for imported materials and equipment which were no longer available, seems to have responded less impressively than government factory output and handicrafts. Nevertheless, Kelegama mentions that sawmills and factories producing molded rubber goods, batteries, eau de cologne, packing chests, toilet goods, bricks and tiles, plywood, hosiery, lacquered goods, glass, ink, matches, soap, cigarettes, sealing wax, twine, paper, chocolate, and many others appeared during the war and that a few of these plants survived the transition to peacetime.

Estate producers, facing compulsory deliveries of all or nearly all their output at prices which were adjusted to the rapidly rising level of production costs only with a lag, had little incentive to increase production. Tea exports rose only from an average of 221,-000,000 pounds in the late thirties to 254,000,000 in the war years; tea prices had risen by only 36.5 percent. Rubber, which was essential to the British war effort and in desperately short supply after the fall of Malaya and the Netherlands East Indies to the Japanese, got more favorable price treatment (wartime prices averaged 171.0 percent of the late-thirties prices) and was slaughter tapped. Output jumped from 128,000,000 pounds to 218,000,000. Coconut exports were channeled into the form of copra; the volume of copra exported rose from 1,198,000 hundredweights to 2,208,000, largely at the cost of other coconut products, whose prices rose sharply as a result of this limitation in supply. In terms of nut equivalents, total exports of coconut products actually fell, from 1,024,000,000 nuts a year in the late 1930's to 880,000,000 during the war; the percentage of output consumed domestically rose from 37.4 to 44.2. For export crops in general, then, output and export responses were clearly related to the price incentives offered to their producers.[18]

Producers of rice and other food crops for local consumption generally failed to respond to the increased demand for their products, mainly because they were given little incentive to do so.

---

[18]In all these calculations, "late thirties" means 1935–39 and "war years" means 1940–45, both periods inclusive. Source: Table A–52, Appendix.

The food shortage worsened as the war went on. The government took direct action. In 1940 importers of many basic foods were required to purchase some fixed proportion of any commodities they imported in the local market. Three years later estates of 35 acres or more in extent were required to devote some proportion of their land to domestic food production. Then, in 1942, a standing offer was made to purchase any quantity of paddy at Rs. 2.50 a bushel. There were few purchases made at this price and by 1944 a levy of two to three bushels per acre was imposed. Then all production over a fixed allowance for own consumption became liable to compulsory purchase.[19] There are no adequate data on the response of food production to all of these blandishments but what evidence there is suggests that it was not impressive. At no time was a really attractive price incentive offered to producers (some of whom left the village to take advantage of the many remunerative opportunities for wage labor) and even if one had been offered the primitive nature of production and marketing for peasant crops at the time doubtless would have rendered the supply extremely inelastic. Rice imports, meanwhile, fell to about a quarter of their 1939 level. Consumption was cut back and other grains (notably Australian wheat) were substituted.

With imports falling, at low ebb (1942), to 60 percent of their 1939 level[20] and local production utterly unable to satisfy the soaring volume of demand, inflation ensued. The 103 percent increase recorded by the official cost-of-living index between 1939 and 1945 greatly understates the actual rise in consumer prices, even of goods consumed by the common man. The import price index more than tripled (see Table 4–1) and had not rationing been introduced consumer prices would have gone up by about this much, too. Rice rationing, combined with fixed retail prices for the basic ration, was introduced early in 1942. In time the majority of consumer goods was covered by rationing. As the prices of food imports rose, the government embarked upon a policy of maintaining the retail price of rationed foodstuffs and absorbing the difference as a subsidy. Up to September, 1947, some Rs. 97,000,000 was spent on food subsidies. As subsequent experience was to prove, this policy was one of the few events of the World War II period with major long-run implications.

With the war's end, conditions changed rapidly. The prewar level of imports was restored by 1947. By the following year imports in

---

[19]For a comprehensive discussion of policy toward food producers during the war, see Kelegama, *op. cit.*
[20]See Table A–48, Appendix.

all major categories were markedly higher than prewar.[21] Price controls and rationing were generally eased soon after the war ended and, amid rapidly rising domestic prices, the flow of imports resumed. In this one instance of postwar disequilibrium prices paid for imports were largely determined in Ceylon, since locally available supplies were inadequate to meet the demand and the prices of those goods which did arrive were bid up. Exports increased, too, but not so rapidly as imports. The late 1940's saw much reduced surpluses (and even, in 1947, a deficit) on merchandise account. During 1947 a quarter of Ceylon's wartime-amassed external assets went to meet the backlog of consumption demand,[22] but thereafter the decline was arrested. Rises in export volume and prices helped to replenish the stock of assets. An agreement was reached with the United Kingdom to bolster the British balance of payments by limiting the rate at which Ceylon could expend its holdings of sterling assets and this helped slow down the rise in Ceylon's import bill. Between them, these two factors served to stabilize the level of foreign assets. Late in 1949 the Ceylon rupee was devalued, in step with the pound sterling, and export receipts (especially those from rubber, which was the main product Ceylon sold to the dollar area) were greatly stimulated. The Korean War, which followed close on the heels of devaluation, then turned the balance of payments around again and brought about a new period of asset accumulation.

One of the most notable points about World War II's economic effects is their general impermanence. With the resumption of normal import flows the great majority of the war-induced manufacturing plants, both government and private, collapsed. The initial impulse of the policy makers was to return to the prewar structure of taxes, expenditures, and controls. Ceylon did not achieve full independence until early in 1948 and even after Ceylonese gained complete control of the reins of government the desire to bring into being an economy of a markedly different type from that of the thirties took some time to form and become fully articulated. Consequently, the late forties was a period of stagnation in agricultural output[23] and collapse in industrial output.[24] The legacies of the war era were surprisingly few: food subsidies, a set of direct controls which

---

[21]*Ibid.*

[22]The volume of consumer goods imports in 1948 was 28 percent higher than the prewar (1938) level, while intermediate goods were only 3 percent higher than prewar and investment goods 11 percent. Consumer durables were being imported at an especially high rate. See Table A–48, Appendix.

[23]See Table A–32, Appendix.

[24]There are no data to support this statement, only impressions gathered from contemporary accounts.

was seldom used in the next few years but never completely abandoned, substantial foreign balances, a few plants to form the nucleus of a government industrialization drive, and an estate sector which had just emerged from a time of high production and considerable capital consumption.[25]

INDEPENDENCE

After 17 years of internal self-rule, Ceylon gained full independence on February 4, 1948. The effects of this political transformation on economic structure and growth were to show themselves only through time, but they were ultimately to be revolutionary in their impact on the export economy. As time was to show, independence changed several of the key elements of the classical system, contributing in large degree to the increasing difficulty of maintaining the colonial pattern of international trade flows during the 1950's. Much of what the government of independent Ceylon has done will be recounted in later portions of this monograph, but a summary here in terms of the key characteristics of the export economy, which were discussed in the preceding chapter, will help to underline the ultimate impact of the independence achieved in the late forties.

Labor supply was the main factor of production affected by independence. The free ebb and flow of Indian estate labor to and from Ceylon began to be limited as soon as an independent government was set up in Colombo. One law or regulation after another added to the constriction of the Indian labor supply. The flow of Indians out of Ceylon during the war had been strongly reversed in the late 1940's, but after 1950, under the influence of the new policy, the net flow was steadily outward again. In 1954 immigration virtually ceased. The estates were now cut off from the unlimited pool of labor on which they had relied for so long. The Ceylon nationalists had hoped to gain from this cessation of immigration an upsurge of estate employment for Ceylonese. Their hopes of repatriating the 770,000 Indians then living on the estates were frustrated, however, by the refusal of the Indian government to recognize their Indian nationality.[26] Since Ceylon has granted

---

[25]In none of the estate industries had proper maintenance procedures been followed during the war, since overriding emphasis had been laid on raising current output. In all cases replanting had been neglected. The situation was worst, however, in rubber, where years of slaughter tapping had hastened the aging of the industry's trees and sharply reduced their productive potential.

[26]Only much later, in 1964, was an agreement concluded with the Indian government defining the position of these "stateless" individuals. At that time India finally agreed to the repatriation of the majority, while some 300,000 were to receive Ceylon citizenship.

citizenship to only a small fraction of these people, they remain stateless to this day. As a nationalistic device to expand job opportunities for Ceylonese, however, the policy has been a failure. The natural increase of the present Indian estate population has continued to provide accretions to the labor pool on the estates over a period in which total estate employment has grown only slowly, so relatively few openings for Ceylonese have been created.

The impact of independence on the other factors of production, land and capital, was more limited. The efforts of the colonial government to expand the total land area available for cultivation through colonization and increased irrigation were continued and at times redoubled but the net effect was slight relative to the continuing population-induced rise in the demand for land among the peasantry. The supply of private foreign capital was largely shut off, but with the frequently unspectacular state of world markets for primary products during the years since independence it is unlikely that it would have poured into Ceylon in any great quantity even if the country had remained a British colony.

In the field of economic policy, independence made all the difference. The new government bore no commitment to the colonial concepts of limited government and the use of automatic policy rules such as balanced budgets and 100 percent currency reserves (Chapter 3, pages 68–69). Although the United National Party governments which ruled Ceylon up to 1956 were conservative relative to the governments which later succeeded them, the unbalanced budget as a tool of development policy gradually gained quasi-respectability and in almost any area of activity one might choose to examine both the scope and the magnitude of the government's responsibilities became greater. In the monetary area, the creation of the Central Bank of Ceylon in 1950 marked the introduction of the possibility that monetary policy might become an active influence on the path of economic development. The emergence of other new financial institutions contributed to this trend. The independent influence of the Central Bank has proved to be relatively small in practice, but the potential remains.[27]

---

[27]The Central Bank has been prevented from having a larger independent role in economic development by (1) the relative unimportance of internal, controllable monetary factors as compared with largely uncontrollable balance-of-payments influences in an export economy and (2) the fact that it has been dominated by the central government proper and used chiefly as a means of financing budget deficits. Because of their lack of independent significance for the operation of the economy, the policies of the Central Bank will receive little attention here. The standard reference is H. A. de S. Gunasekera, *From Dependent Currency to Central Banking in Ceylon* (London: G. Bell and Sons, Ltd., 1962).

Most important of all, independence greatly increased the sensitivity of all kinds of policy formation to popular desires. It is for this reason that a whole new economic role for the government evolved. Whereas the colonial government had played a relatively small role in the economic life of the country and had concentrated its activities on the provision of services to the estate sector, the government of independent Ceylon aspired to a much larger role and sought to bring about a basic restructuring of the economy. Gradually, at times incoherently, the outlines of a new economic policy emerged. The level of taxation on the estates was to be raised very sharply and the surpluses earned by them were to be captured by the government for ultimate reinvestment in other parts of the economy. Levels of current expenditure on transfer payments and social services were also to be increased substantially. In addition, the government would enter increasingly into the direct planning of economic activity and especially the design of projects intended to build up a modern industrial sector. The direction in which the government was propelling the economy was not always clear, but one thing was certain: the government, which in colonial days had been a minor and generally passive economic institution, had now become the most important force for good or ill in the nation's economic development.

POPULATION GROWTH

The environment in which the government and other actors on the economic scene had to perform, however, was profoundly altered by the dramatic population boom which started in 1946. A sudden acceleration of the rate of natural increase, followed by a considerable period of very rapid population growth, is a common occurrence in today's underdeveloped world, but nowhere, perhaps, has the phenomenon been so spectacularly illustrated as in Ceylon. The population boom in Ceylon has made a major contribution to the destruction of the classical export economy, though one which is difficult to assess with precision. Before any attempt is made to evaluate the economic effects of the population boom, a brief review of the demographic facts is in order.

Basically, Ceylon's story is one of a spectacular fall in the death rate, the product mainly of a strikingly successful public health campaign. The story is similar to what has happened elsewhere in recent years, but the magnitudes involved and the radical nature of the changes wrought make the case of Ceylon one of the most sensational examples of the global trend.

The bare outline of what happened is best represented through the medium of the official vital statistics, which in this instance can be accepted as generally accurate (see Tables 4–2 and A–14, Appendix).[28] The immediate, striking change is easily stated. Between 1945 and 1947 the birth rate rose slightly (from 35.9 per thousand of population in the official data to 38.5), the death rate was cut by a third (from 21.5 to 14.0), and the rate of natural increase, as a result, leaped upward from 1.4 percent to 2.5. After 1947 the death rate continued to follow a generally declining trend and the rate of natural increase rose a bit more. Throughout the 1950's it ran at about 2.7 percent.

TABLE 4–2

RATES OF BIRTHS, DEATHS, NATURAL INCREASE, INFANT AND MATERNAL DEATHS, 1900–59*

(Annual Averages)

Period	Births per Thousand of Population	Deaths per Thousand of Population	Natural Increase (Percent)	Infant Deaths per Thousand Live Births	Maternal Deaths per Thousand Live Births
1900–09....	38.1	28.9	0.9	180	....
1910–19....	37.8	30.1	0.8	195	....
1920–29....	39.6	26.9	1.3	183	....
1930–39....	36.7	23.5	1.3	174	....
1940–44....	36.5	19.7	1.7	133	14.2†
1945–49....	38.1	16.1	2.2	112	11.5
1950–54....	38.6	11.6	2.7	77	5.3
1955–59....	36.6	9.9	2.7	66	3.8

*Source: *Reports of the Registrar-General on Vital Statistics.* For annual figures, as well as comments on the reliability of these data, see Table A–14, Appendix.
†1941–44.

The fall in the death rate was evident within all the various segments of the population classified by locality, sex, "race" (in Ceylon this term is used in reference to the island's diverse ethnic groups), or age. Its biggest single cause was a large and highly successful campaign to control malaria. In addition, other factors work-

---

[28]The question of how much reliance to put in these data is to some extent open to debate. As noted in the Appendix (pages 301–2, 305–7), Ceylon's past experience with the collection of population data had been long enough that relatively high standards had been established by the middle of the twentieth century. A conservative rule of thumb would be to assume a ten percent margin of error and look with suspicion at any apparent changes in death rates, birth rates, etc. of less than that amount. Thus, in the context of the present paragraph, the legitimacy of the apparent rise in the birth rate from 35.9 to 38.5 per thousand might well be questioned but the fall in the death rate from 21.5 to 14.0 cannot possibly be.

ing for lower death rates, which had been in operation for several decades, continued to cut deaths further in the post-1946 period: rising living standards, improved public health facilities, "the development of a public health conscience" (to quote the director of Medical and Sanitary Services at the time), free milk and midday meals for school children, etc. But such things work very gradually through time. For the sudden reversal of trend that took place in the late forties, the conquest of malaria is largely to be credited.

In 1935 a terrible epidemic of malaria struck Ceylon. Before it died down, sometime during the following year, over 50,000 persons had lost their lives. For 1935, the vital statistics show more deaths registered than births. The infant death rate shot up from 173 per thousand live births in 1934 to 263 in 1935. During the peak year of 1935 alone, 5,454,781 cases of malaria were said to have been treated at government hospitals and dispensaries[29]—this at a time when the estimated total population was 5,608,000. While there is some double counting in the dispensary statistics, it is true to say that the great majority of Ceylonese suffered a case of malaria in 1935. Malaria deaths during the year totaled 47,315 according to the government's count, nearly 1 percent of the population.[30]

The malaria epidemic of 1935–36 was one of the most telling and certainly the best documented of its type, but it was by no means the only one in the history of Ceylon. Others had come at frequent intervals and struck equally high proportions of the population, though the numbers infected and killed were not so great. But the effects of epidemic malaria on the country were probably not so important as those of endemic malaria.

Endemic malaria had played a key role in Ceylon's history. In many parts of the country, especially in the dry zone of its north and east, it was an ever-present menace to human existence. Many historians accord malaria a key role in the downfall of the ancient Sinhalese civilization, which was centered in the dry zone, and it is certainly true that over the preceding century it had been a major hindrance to efforts to resettle population in the dry zone and make greater use of its agricultural potential. The malarial season in the dry zone coincided with the period of greatest agricultural activity, making life there doubly hazardous. The effects of the disease in sapping the energies of the labor force can best be suggested by the fact that from 1926 to 1946 malaria cases treated at government

---

[29]*A.R. of the Director of Medical and Sanitary Services for the Year 1935,* p. 28.

[30]This and the other figures in this paragraph are from various issues of the *Report of the Registrar-General on Vital Statistics.*

hospitals and dispensaries averaged 40.3 percent of the population per year.[31] It is not surprising that malaria was thought of in much the same matter-of-fact way as residents of the Temperate Zone regard the common cold.

For years prior to 1946 the government of Ceylon had been greatly concerned about malaria. In many respects Ceylon had a superb public health record: smallpox, yellow fever, cholera, plague, and other infectious diseases which were still scourges elsewhere in the tropics had been brought under control in Ceylon and were unlikely ever to be a major problem again.[32] Malaria thus came to command increasing attention. Year after year it was the leading cause of death and after the 1935-36 epidemic ravaged the island, a malaria control unit was set up in the Department of Medical and Sanitary Services. This unit oiled rivers and streams and took other steps to prevent the breeding of mosquitoes. The increased attention was not enough, however, to overcome the disease. Epidemics in 1939-40 and 1945-46 each succeeded in killing about 20,000 persons in a two-year period. Something more was needed.

The "something more" was added in the late forties as the result of a sudden technological breakthrough. In November, 1945, a program of killing adult mosquitoes by spraying houses in malarial areas with a DDT solution was inaugurated in the Anuradhapura district (in the heart of the dry zone and one of the worst regions for malaria). As the success of the new chemical became increasingly apparent the program was broadened and by 1946 some 200,-000 houses were being sprayed once every 6 weeks. The following two years saw spraying spread to the entire island. The number of houses included in the spraying rounds rose to 1,800,000 in 1947 and 3,400,000 in 1948.[33] The success of the campaign, as revealed in Table 4-3, was stunning.

Almost as spectacular as the completeness of the victory over malaria was the low cost at which it was achieved. The total cost of the campaign in the crucial 1946-48 years was in the neighborhood of Rs. 6,000,000.[34] And for this expenditure literally millions of lives were saved.

As Table 4-3 suggests, preventive measures are not to be given all the credit for the abatement of malaria deaths. In 1957-58 the

---

[31] Based on figures given in the *A.R. of the Director of Medical and Sanitary Services* for 1935 (p. 28) and 1948 (p. 86).

[32] See Table A-24, Appendix.

[33] *A.R. of the Director of Medical and Sanitary Services* for 1947 (p. 31) and 1948 (p. 83).

[34] Ibid.

TABLE 4–3

MALARIA MORTALITY AND MORBIDITY, 1930–60

Period	Deaths	Cases	Rates per Million of Population Deaths	Cases
1930–39 (annual average).	8,210	2,427,766	1,475	436,154
1940	9,169	3,413,618	1,535	571,604
1941	7,132	3,220,360	1,154	521,604
1942	5,143	3,225,477	832	522,006
1943	6,765	2,141,329	1,074	340,109
1944	5,609	1,672,478	871	259,621
1945	8,521	2,539,949	1,281	381,947
1946	12,578	2,768,385	1,835	403,908
1947	4,557	1,350,521	648	191,917
1948	3,349	775,276	462	107,023
1949	2,403	681,624	302	91,432
1950	1,903	610,784	248	79,550
1951	1,599	448,100	203	56,894
1952	1,049	269,024	130	33,320
1953	722	106,350	87	12,829
1954	447	37,464	52	4,397
1955	268	19,929	31	2,285
1956	144	43,158	16	4,823
1957	177	35,086	19	3,828
1958	105	61,711	11	6,573
1959	82	1,736	9	180
1960	61	460	6	46

Source: *Reports of the Registrar-General on Vital Statistics.*

first post-DDT epidemic broke out. Cases treated in government hospitals and at dispensaries rose sharply from their previous low of about 20,000 in 1955. But deaths, with the exception of a small temporary rise in 1957, continued to fall. For this fact, improvements in curative medicine (e.g., the development of improved substitutes for quinine) must be credited. The 1957–58 revival of the disease led to a U.S. grant of $388,840 to expand the malaria control unit with a view to the utter eradication of the disease within five years.[35] This goal is rapidly being achieved and soon malaria will be as much of a rarity in Ceylon as cholera or plague.

If the death and birth rates of 1930–46 can be taken as a standard of comparison, there were nearly 1,500,000 more people alive in Ceylon at the end of 1960 than there would have been had not the demographic pattern changed. Yet, on a similar calculation only about 143,000 of these people were alive because they had been saved from a death by malaria. That is, only about a tenth of those

[35]A.R. *of the Director of Health Services* for 1960.

whose lives were saved would have died from malaria itself. However, many more people—in fact, roughly six times as many—were
added to the population by the indirect effects of malaria control
on the birth rate and on deaths from other causes. Newman estimates that nearly 1,000,000 of the 1,500,000 people just mentioned
owed their lives directly or indirectly to the antimalaria campaign.[36]
The indirect effects of malaria prevention have been felt more
gradually through time than the direct effects. They include sharp
declines in the rates of mortality among infants and childbearing
mothers, as well as much reduced rates of death from infectious
diseases other than malaria itself.[37] Along with other slow-moving
influences on the death rate, these indirect effects account for the
further decline of the death rate to its 1960 level of only 8.6 per
thousand.[38] Also, by 1960 the infant death rate had sunk to little
more than one-third its traditional level and the maternal death rate
to only a fifth the rate per thousand live births of past decades.

Besides malaria eradication, what has caused these continuing
declines in death rates? To some extent, the saving of lives among
mothers and infants is attributable to the spread of midwifery, pre-
natal and baby clinics, and maternal hospitalization. This trend is
associated with a broader one, which has had a deep-seated influence for better health: the tremendous extension of education which
has taken place in postwar Ceylon. Infectious diseases in general
(particularly, aside from malaria, typhoid) have also declined
sharply in importance (from 21.1 percent of all deaths in 1946 to
7.7 percent in 1959),[39] but this trend is closely interrelated with
malaria eradication and the decline in infant and maternal deaths,
so it should not be thought of as strictly an independent phenome-

---

[36]Newman compared birth and death rates in malarial regions of Ceylon
with rates in areas which had always been free of the disease, both before and
after 1946. Using regression analysis, he estimated the sum of malaria eradication's direct and indirect effects on population growth, through both the death
rate and the birth rate. His estimates give 60 percent of the credit for the
acceleration of population growth to malaria control and 40 percent to other
causes. Peter Newman, *Malaria Eradication and Population Growth* (Ann
Arbor, Michigan: University of Michigan; to be published).

[37]A number of chains of indirect causation lead from malaria eradication to
faster population growth. For instance, mothers are in better health and therefore death rates of both mothers and infants in childbirth are lower; the typical
mother thus has more children during her lifetime and a higher percentage of
them survive. Only by a research technique such as Newman's (see footnote
36) can one hope to evaluate all such indirect effects of malaria's eradication.

[38]On paper, this is lower than the American death rate, but the comparison
is not quite a fair one. Ceylon has a much younger population than the United
States and this distorts a comparison of deaths per thousand of population.
Also, the degree of underreporting is undoubtedly greater in Ceylon.

[39]See Table A–24, Appendix.

non. The extent of recent improvement in death rates from infectious diseases other than malaria, however, is rendered especially striking by the fact that many of these diseases were already comparatively rare in Ceylon. No other major causes of death show particularly noteworthy declines. Some, like cancer (because of the increased longevity of the population and perhaps because of improved diagnosis as well) and violent deaths of various kinds have actually become more prevalent. Aside from the outstanding and interrelated examples of malaria and other infectious diseases and of afflictions of infancy and childbirth, the fall in the death rate has ranged widely across the spectrum of causes.

Several factors enter into this continuing and wide-ranging aspect of death rate decline. Certainly, the slow-working but important forces of education and rising living standards are of some relevance. Moreover, the fact that the composition of the population has shifted markedly toward a lower average age should not be overlooked; this phenomenon, itself a result of the accelerated rate of population growth, has a mild depressing effect on deaths measured per thousand of population. It cannot be denied, however, that the availability of public health services has been greater in the postwar period than in the prewar and has improved slowly since the late 1940's, despite the rapid increase in population. Table 4–4 shows that there has been improvement in the quantitative provision of health services relative to total population and it is also true that there has been a notable spread of these facilities geographically, bringing Western medicine to the villager for the first time in many areas.

Has Ceylon's birth rate, meanwhile, shown any notable trends? With the rate of natural increase now at 2.7 percent, some observers are anxiously scanning the horizon for a sign of decline in the birth rate. And indeed, if one takes the era of the 1950's as an observation period, a slight fall in the official birth rate is discernible. This decline (from 40.2, an exceptionally high figure in the light of past experience, in 1950 to 36.6 in 1960) is too small, however, to fall definitely outside the range of likely statistical error (see footnote 28, page 84) and probably no great significance should be attached to it. In any case, the decade of the fifties shows no overall birth rate decline as compared with previous decades. And what many students of population consider to be the basic sociological preconditions for a significant fall in the birth rate—the thoroughgoing urbanization and industrialization of the society (is education, which has swept Ceylon in recent years, an additional or alternative precondition?)—do not seem to have been satisfied yet in Ceylon, or at best have been only partially satisfied. On present evidence, then, it seems unlikely that there will be any significant fall in the birth rate in the immediate future and that if it comes at all it will lag well behind the decline in the death rate, perhaps by some decades. An additional reason for believing that Ceylon can expect a continuation of roughly its present high rate of natural increase is that the government has not as yet even taken a stand on the question of making a conscious effort to reduce the rate of population growth through birth control. Despite the fact that no strong religious taboos would be impinged upon, the government, for reasons that are obscure, has taken no action in this area. It does, however, permit private organizations like the Planned Parenthood League to operate in Ceylon.

TABLE 4–4

POPULATION RELATIVE TO BEDS, DOCTORS, AND MINOR HOSPITAL
EMPLOYEES IN GOVERNMENT HOSPITALS, SELECTED
YEARS, 1929–60*

Year	Persons per Hospital Bed	Persons per Doctor	Persons per Minor Employee
1929......	572	15,347	2,231
1938......	567	15,918	1,999
1945......	425	12,938	1,822
1946....	408	12,261	.....
1947......	385	......	.....
1948......	381	10,334	.....
1949......	376	11,594	.....
1950......	385	11,392	1,328
1951......	388	10,529	1,161
1952......	388	10,486	1,103
1953......	388	10,724	1,146
1954......	368	10,467	1,057
1955	359	9,163	1,011
1956......	351	9,074	1,023
1957......	347	9,678	987
1958......	341	8,345	883
1959......	345	8,212	781
1960......	340	8,105	796

*These figures exclude private nursing homes and doctors in private practice, but these are relatively unimportant, catering only to the wealthy. Source: Ministry of Finance, *Economic and Social Development of Ceylon (a survey) 1926–1954*, (1955), p. 6; Department of Census and Statistics, *Statistical Abstract 1962*, p. 75.

Accompanying the very much more rapid growth of aggregate population since 1946 have been some important changes in the population's composition. Migration trends, while not involving

1assive numbers of people, have combined with natural increase
o produce some alterations in the makeup of the population. The
arly war years—1939–42—saw net emigration from Ceylon of
71,000, as Indians in particular returned home in time of trouble.
.he danger past, the late forties saw a reversal of this flight. From
944 through 1949 the official data show a net inflow of 305,000
ersons. However, the desire to "Ceylonize" employment soon
rought about stricter legislation, which radically changed migra-
ion trends. From 1950 on the net flow was consistently outward.
After 1954 the legal immigration of Indian estate laborers was
lrastically cut and after 1957 it all but ceased. The result, over the
.946–60 period, was a net outflow of 24,000 Indian plantation work-
rs (these are official figures; the illicit flow cannot, of course, be
neasured, but it is rumored to have been considerable and prepon-
lerantly in the direction of Ceylon). Ceylonese legislation has also
een instrumental in the expulsion of 127,000 other Indians, in-
luding estate workers' families, over the period. In addition, there
vas net emigration of 3,000 Europeans (i.e., Caucasians) and 6,000
Ceylon citizens during the fifties.[40] From the economic point of
view, these departures from Ceylon are important because they
nvolved some of the groups which had made the largest contribu-
:ions to Ceylon's economy in the past. Indians and Europeans, in
particular, had played major roles in the development of the colonial economic system and their emigration (which was a reflection of their diminished political power) cost the modern sector
valuable skills and experience which it would take some time to
replace.

Another point about the composition of the population concerns
urbanization and the way it is coming about. Urbanization in Ceylon has run counter to a strong natural tendency for the percentage
of the population located in rural areas to rise. Both birth rates and
death rates are higher in the rural districts than in the cities, but
the resulting rate of natural increase is substantially higher outside
the urban areas. In 1960, for example, Colombo residents had a
birth rate of 31.2 per thousand, a death rate of 8.1 per thousand,
and thus a rate of natural increase of 2.3 percent. Dwellers in
towns and cities other than Colombo had rates of 31.9, 8.4, and 2.4
respectively. The all-island rates for the year were 36.6, 8.6, and
2.8, so it can be deduced that the birth rate for the rural population
was 37.6 per thousand, the death rate was 8.6, and the rate of

---

[40]All figures are from the *Reports of the Registrar-General on Vital Statistics.*

natural increase was 2.9 percent.[41] If the rural-urban differentials for 1960 can be accepted as typical, then it is clear that in the absence of migration to the cities there is a strong tendency for the proportion of the populace dwelling in rural areas to rise. In fact, however, urbanization (defined as the percentage of the population living in towns of 20,000 or more) increased from 9.9 percent to 12.9 between 1946 and 1960.[42] Redefinition of administrative boundaries (especially the incorporation of former villages surrounding Colombo into large suburban towns) had something to do with this rise in urbanization. Mainly, however, it was internal migration which more than overcame the natural tendency for rural population to grow more rapidly than urban. There was a steady migration from rural areas into a number of medium-sized towns in various parts of the island, several of which crossed the rural-urban dividing line of 20,000 persons between 1946 and 1960. Colombo itself grew relatively slowly (and fell as a percentage of total population), but its suburbs, as well as several secondary towns, boomed. Economically, rural-urban migration is important because it reflects primarily the "push" of labor out of the most crowded traditional agricultural areas which arose from worsening land scarcity. Also, of course, the fact that employment in the towns was expanding somewhat more rapidly than rural employment exerted some "pull" of potentially higher incomes. It is probable, however, that the migrants' hopes were in large measure frustrated and that the main effect of the migration was to convert rural, traditional-sector underemployment into open urban unemployment.

One more point about the anatomy of population growth in Ceylon might be made, namely the fact that the age-sex structure of 1960 is probably quite different from that of 1946. The upswing in the rate of natural increase, abetted by the particularly sharp fall in the infant death rate, has raised the proportion of the population in the lower age brackets. And the steep drop in the maternal death rate, together with the emigration of a disproportionate number of males who had been working in Ceylon on a temporary basis, has raised the ratio of females to males.[43] The main economic importance of these tendencies is that they increase the "dependency ratio" of nonworking to working population.

---

[41]Source: *Report of the Registrar-General on Vital Statistics* for 1959 and 1960. These official figures are not to be interpreted with complete literalness, but they surely indicate a correct direction of difference.

[42]Source: 1946 census and *ibid*.

[43]Somewhat rough calculations—based on the author's estimation of the age-sex structure in 1960, which derived from the 1953 census, birth registrations, age-sex-specific death registrations, and net migration—suggest that the percentage of the population that is under 15 years old rose from 39.2 to 41.1 between 1946 and 1960 and the percentage that is female from 46.6 to 47.8

Rapid population growth such as Ceylon has experienced since he late 1940's puts a strain on the economy. It has the dual effect of raising the consumption needs of the nation and, at least potentially, increasing the productive capacity which can be used to satisfy those needs. By definition, a high rate of population increase means that for the level of real per capita income—or any given rate of increase in it—to be maintained, aggregate output must grow more rapidly than would be necessary if population were not increasing so fast. If the higher rate of output growth is not achieved, then one of two things must occur: either resources must be transferred from the production of investment goods to the production of consumption goods so as to keep per capita consumption levels constant[44] or else consumption levels must fall. But what chance does rapid population growth itself offer of inducing the faster output growth which it requires?

When population growth accelerates, the rate of increase of the labor force also rises. This means that there is some addition to the potential output of the economy. But will *actual* output rise and, if so, will it rise by enough to offset the consumption effect of population growth? Two considerations suggest that any offset to the consumption effect will be only partial.[45] For one thing, the additions to the labor force must find employment in at least as high a proportion as the old, existing labor force. In a country with a considerable unemployment-underemployment problem, this may not be possible. And secondly, the employment found by the new labor must be at least as productive as that enjoyed by the existing workers.[46] In the absence of technical change this is not likely. Since the complementary factors of production are almost certain in an

---

Ceylon's population has always exhibited an unusually high masculinity ratio). Although one would expect there to be changes in both these directions, the percentage variations found are so small as to be of questionable statistical significance.

[44]This is only a short-run solution, however. In the longer run, lowering the ratio of investment to national output is likely to reduce the rate of output growth and thus work *against* the solution of the problem.

[45]There is an additional problem, which is mainly a short-run transitional difficulty. For a short time after population growth has accelerated, the growth rate of the labor force may be considerably lower or higher than that of total population, depending on precisely how the faster population growth has come about. That is, the proportions in which workers and nonworkers are added to the population may be quite different from their relative shares in the previous total population. Such differences tend to disappear in time, however. See page 96.

[46]Logically, various combinations of employment and productivity increase could be used to produce the necessary output gain. Thus, even if only a small percentage of the additional labor found employment the needed output could result if the new employment were productive enough. Without technical change, however, it is hard to see how this could come about.

underdeveloped country to be growing less rapidly than labor supply (one, land, is fixed in supply and the other, capital, is probably growing less rapidly than labor and is unlikely to be spurred on to more rapid growth by accelerated population increase[47]) the law of diminishing returns ensures that the new labor will be less productive than the old and that past consumption levels will be difficult to maintain. In the net, then, population increase in an underdeveloped country is almost certain to raise consumption needs more rapidly than it increases national output. To offset this negative effect on the economy there must be rises in the productivity of labor. Such rises can come about either through an acceleration of the rate of capital accumulation, to the point where it is sufficiently higher than the rate of labor force growth to substitute for land and keep output per man from falling, or else via technical change.

Thus runs the conventional doctrine on the economic effects of population growth. With a few minor modifications to fit the special circumstances of the Ceylon case, it provides a good general framework for viewing this new element introduced into Ceylon's export economy in the late 1940's. Its general conclusion, that rapid population growth had a net effect of depressing real output per head, holds in the present case. The fact that the level of real income per capita actually rose rather than fell over these years, as later parts of this monograph will show, is attributable to the achievement of substantial productivity increases in several parts of the economy.

As has been seen, Ceylon's classical export economy was a delicately balanced mechanism. The world prices for the country's export crops and the amount of suitable land available for each crop defined the limits within which the system worked. Labor and capital flowed to the modern sector in the quantities demanded. The government budget was balanced. The traditional sector was left largely to itself, trading little with either the modern sector or the world. Imports tended to equal exports. The acceleration of population increase affected this pattern in two fundamental ways:

(1) It accelerated and regularized the rate of growth of labor supply. Along with the cessation of immigration, the faster growth

---

[47]Indeed, one would expect that a more rapidly growing population would require that a larger percentage of national income be devoted to satisfying consumption needs and to providing overhead capital (housing, educational facilities, etc.) for the ever-increasing population, thus leaving a smaller proportion for directly productive investment. Capital stock, especially the stock of directly productive capital, would thus rise more slowly.

of the labor force from natural causes meant that a more rapid and unavoidable growth of total labor supply had been substituted for the low long-run growth rate and the short-run tendency toward automatic adjustment of supply to demand that had been characteristic of colonial days. Although aggregate labor supply probably grew no faster than it had over certain periods of large-scale immigration in the past, now the demand for labor to work on the estates and in related industries was increasing much less rapidly than it had on past occasions of rapid labor force growth. Gradually, labor supply in the national labor market moved out of line with the level of demand for labor at statutory levels of wages; unemployment and underemployment rose.[48] The faster and steadier growth of labor supply created a pressing need for economic growth and diversification, particularly the creation of more jobs outside the estates.

(2) The other effect of accelerated population growth, however, was that the consumption needs of the country rose more rapidly. To some extent, this increase was translated into effective consumption demand. The marginal propensity to consume (and especially the propensity to consume imported goods) was high. As aggregate income rose and as income redistribution schemes further swelled the receipts of low-income groups (see Chapter 5, pages 118–20), consumer demand increased rapidly. Because of the accelerated population increase, consumption probably rose somewhat more rapidly than it would have had the same growth of national income been combined with slower population growth. On the other hand, the acceleration of population growth probably did relatively little to raise the rate of growth of national income. Thus, while faster population growth increased the need for economic growth and diversification it may also have had the effect of raising the ratio of consumption to income, depressing the saving ratio (and thus, if it is true that faster population growth did not markedly accelerate the growth of national income, aggregate savings), and inhibiting the investment needed to create a larger and more diversified economy. Just how important this depressing effect on saving might have been in quantitative terms, however, is hard to say. The population boom also made some contribution to the emergence of persistent current account deficits in the balance of

---

[48]As in colonial days, the estates and other parts of the modern sector have continued to be covered by minimum wage legislation. Excess labor supply thus tends to result in open unemployment rather than underemployment; in the traditional sector, of course, the consequence of excess labor supply is more likely to be underemployment. See Chapter 5, pages 100–103.

payments from 1952 on, though it was not the main factor working for external imbalance during this period.

One final note, relating to the special demographic characteristics of the 1946–60 period to be studied in the following chapters, might be added here. Aside from the fact that the rate of population growth has been very much more rapid since 1946 than before, it is also relevant to notice that it increased very rapidly. This quick acceleration has meant that the age structure which prevailed in the late 1940's and in the 1950's was somewhat different from the one which will exist after an extended period of population growth at the new, higher rate. The upswing in the rate of natural increase probably raised the proportion of young people in the population, whereas continued rapid population growth will eventually swell the higher age brackets and shift the age distribution back to something more like its old shape. In the meantime, however, the rapidity of the acceleration has contributed to a rise in the dependency ratio and has thus increased the potential negative effect of rapid population growth on real per capita income. However, this additional negative potential might not have been realized, since even if more of the new additions to the population had been workers they might very likely not have found productive employment. The high levels of unemployment and underemployment among the labor force already in existence suggest that this could well have been the case.

The three new factors of the 1940's which have been highlighted in this chapter—World War II, independence, and the population boom—all set the stage for a new period of Ceylon's economic development, which because of a basically altered economic structure and a new set of economic policies was to be fundamentally different from its earlier development experience. This period is examined in detail in Chapters 5 through 7.

Chapter 5

The Transitional Economy:
Structure and Dynamics

During the fifteen years following the conclusion of World War II Ceylon's economy continued to expand. As was appropriate to the changed environment which the forces discussed in the preceding chapter had brought about, however, its growth during this period followed a rather different pattern from the growth which Ceylon had experienced previously and had different economic effects. A detailed examination of sectoral and aggregate growth during the 1946-60 period forms the substance of Chapter 6. The present chapter will try to demonstrate fully the implications of the postwar environment, which, it will be contended here, created an economic system that was fundamentally different from the one which preceded it. Roughly coinciding with the political transformation from colonialism with limited self-rule to full independence was an economic change from what might be called a colonial or classical export economy to a development-oriented export economy. The most characteristic structural features of the pre-World War II economy—the high proportion of exports and imports in GNP and (though to a diminishing degree) the dualism of the economy—continued into the new period. Other important features, however, especially the relative growth rates of the factors of production, basic public policy, and the pattern of resource flows within the economy, changed markedly. It is these changes which justify identifying the economy of these years as a basically different economic system from that of prewar Ceylon. However, the economic system of the 1946-60 years in time began to reveal a tendency to be unviable; during the late fifties it became increasingly difficult to maintain its characteristic pattern of external trade and finally in 1960-61 the economy was forced to undergo a further marked transformation. The 1946-60 economy, then, must be considered a transitional system, one which created a trend toward yet another type of economy, which in turn was to represent an even sharper departure from the classical model.

The move from a classical colonial-type export economy to the independent, development-oriented variety during the late 1940's was a less radical economic change than the rise of the export economy itself a century before had been. Most of the structural characteristics of the earlier form (described in Chapter 3) continued to exist after World War II and most of the rules governing the economy's potential for economic growth were unchanged, too. The attention of the present chapter, however, will be concentrated on those elements which *did* change. They are important enough to merit some emphasis. The key changes are easily stated in summary form. First of all, the new economic system had to operate under different growth rules for factor supplies from those which had prevailed in prewar days. Labor supply, because of faster natural growth of population and greatly reduced migration, grew more steadily and, in the long run, faster than before. The supply of land available for agricultural expansion came to be severely limited and subject to exploitation only at extremely high cost.[1] Increasing the capital stock also became very difficult, since capital inflows from abroad were very small and the domestic saving ratio was low. Secondly, within this framework of unfavorable relative factor growth rates, increasingly serious efforts were made to force the pace of economic development. A series of development plans was drawn up and attempts were made to raise the volume of investment in the economy and direct it into patterns which would create rapid increases in national output. Thirdly, and largely as a result of this change in basic public policy, a somewhat different set of intersectional flows came into being after independence. In particular, the dualism of the economy gradually tended to break down as the former traditional sector became more involved in selling food to the modern sector and in this way gained greatly increased cash receipts, which it used largely to buy more goods from abroad. Also, to a limited degree, an industrial "third sector," producing goods for the home market, began to emerge. And finally, the government of Ceylon tried to mobilize savings to support its development effort; since the only really significant source of savings was the modern sector and in particular the estates, the chief government strategy for resource mobilization became one of taxing plantation agriculture very heavily and using the surpluses thus captured for investment elsewhere in the economy. This in itself produced further tendencies for the economic structure to change.

---

[1] This had also been the case during the later portion of the classical period, from about the 1920's on.

Each of these basic changes—the new rules governing factor supplies, the development commitment of the government, and the altered pattern of intersectoral resource flows—will be examined in turn.

FACTOR SUPPLIES: LABOR

The overriding influence on labor supply after 1946 was the new phenomenon of extremely rapid population increase. With the link to the Indian labor market virtually severed and migration between Ceylon and other countries slight, the country's labor supply came for the first time to be closely dependent upon the natural growth of the domestic population. Whereas in the past labor supply had grown in close step with demand, now a steep upward trend independent of demand became evident. The particular pattern by which Ceylon's rate of natural increase accelerated, however, tended to moderate population's immediate impact on labor supply. The rise in the proportions of women and children in the population contributed to this effect, as did a trend not discussed up to now— a swift rise in the number of students. As a result, labor force rose less rapidly up to 1960 than it might have if the same aggregate population rise had been realized in some other manner.

Ceylon's labor force, as estimated for various years by the author, is given in Table 5–1.[2] The nature of the impact made by population growth clearly emerges from these calculations. While population grew at 2.7 percent annually, the labor force increased at only 2.2 percent and thus fell slightly as a percentage of the population, from 37.7 to 35.4.[3] It is clear that the effect of the demographic upswing on the labor force was in large part delayed by the very nature of population increase. Putting it in numerical terms, while the population swelled by more than 3,000,000, fewer than 1,000,000 persons were added to the labor force. This growth pattern temporarily raised the dependency ratio and had the effect of postponing until the 1960's much of the unemployment and underemployment problem which would be expected to result from growth in labor supply unmatched by increases in labor demand. If roughly the

---

[2] The methodology used to calculate labor force, employment, and unemployment is described in the Appendix, pages 287–300.

[3] The same question of statistical accuracy which was encountered in connection with the demographic data of the preceding chapter again arises apropos of these labor force and employment figures. Again, caution would dictate the use of a ten percent rule for statistical significance (see Chapter 4, page 84). By this rule, the fall of the labor force as a percentage of population, although supported by external logic, cannot be regarded as being of assured statistical significance.

present birth and death rates continue through the sixties, as they are likely to do, the proportion of young people in the population will gradually begin to decline again as some of the post-1946 swell moves into the upper age brackets. A fall in birth rates, if it comes, will accelerate this tendency for the population to age. In any case, the rise of school attendance among young people must eventually taper off—although it is not likely to do so for some time yet—and this will induce the labor force to stop falling relative to population. For these reasons, the rate of growth of the labor force can be expected to accelerate during the 1960's, possibly even to the point where the labor force begins to rise again as a percentage of population. When that happens, unemployment and underemployment will soar—unless something is done to accelerate the growth of employment opportunities.

TABLE 5–1

POPULATION AND LABOR FORCE, 1946–60*

(Thousands)

Year	Population	Labor Force	Labor Force as a Percentage of Population
1946	6,854	2,583	37.7
1947	7,037	2,630	37.4
1948	7,244	2,690	37.1
1949	7,455	2,758	37.0
1950	7,678	2,831	36.9
1951	7,876	2,886	36.6
1952	8,074	2,957	36.6
1953	8,290	3,012	36.3
1954	8,520	3,077	36.1
1955	8,723	3,162	35.8
1956	8,929	3,235	36.2
1957	9,165	3,268	35.7
1958	9,388	3,354	35.7
1959	9,625	3,415	35.5
1960	9,896	3,502	35.4

*Source: See the Appendix, pages 289–94.

Up to 1960, however, Ceylon's economy appears on the basis of fragmentary evidence to have been successful in opening up job opportunities nearly as fast as the supply of labor grew. The author's estimates suggest that population growth added 919,000 persons to the labor force from 1946 to 1960.[4] As nearly as can be discovered, some 803,000 of these persons were able to find jobs,

---

[4]See Table 5–1.

TABLE 5-2

Estimated Employment by Industry, 1946-60*

(Midyear Averages in Thousands)

Industry	1946	1947	1948	1949	1950	1951	1952	1953	1954	1955	1956	1957	1958	1959	1960
Agriculture, fishing, etc.	1,425	1,453	1,470	1,460	1,525	1,530	1,563	1,574	1,587	1,618	1,647	1,676	1,692	1,709	1,729
Agriculture	1,385	1,413	1,430	1,419	1,484	1,488	1,521	1,531	1,543	1,573	1,602	1,630	1,645	1,662	1,681
Estates	632	644	646	619	668	656	672	664	657	667	677	684	678	674	683
Tea and minor crops	499	509	517	501	535	516	530	526	531	539	547	555	555	551	560
Rubber	117	119	111	99	112	119	121	118	104	104	106	104	101	99	100
Coconut	16	16	17	19	21	20	21	20	22	24	24	25	22	24	23
Other	753	769	784	800	816	832	849	867	886	906	925	946	967	988	998
Fishing, hunting, forestry	40	40	40	41	41	42	42	43	44	45	45	46	47	47	48
Mining and quarrying	8	9	9	10	11	12	12	13	12	11	11	10	9	8	7
Construction	46	47	48	46	50	49	51	51	52	55	58	60	62	64	67
Manufacturing	195	185	175	210	193	199	254	273	277	308	337	352	345	361	378
Electric, gas, water	4	4	4	4	4	4	4	4	4	4	5	5	5	5	5
Trade, commerce, finance	173	186	189	196	298	225	221	222	221	235	233	237	233	252	253
Transport and communications	87	89	89	90	92	94	94	94	93	108	105	111	103	129	133
Services n.e.c.	293	298	303	309	313	319	324	329	337	344	351	358	365	373	382
Government n.e.c.	68	77	83	90	97	103	110	116	106	108	106	102	122	142	148
Total	2,299	2,348	2,370	2,415	2,493	2,535	2,633	2,676	2,689	2,791	2,852	2,911	2,936	3,043	3,102

*See Source notes, pages 294-98 in Appendix. Minor discrepancies are attributable to rounding.

TABLE 5-3

THE STRUCTURE OF EMPLOYMENT, 1946 AND 1960, AND ADDITIONS TO
EMPLOYMENT, 1946-60*

Sector	1946 Employment		Additions to Employment, 1946-60			1960 Employment	
	(000)	% of Total	(000)	% of Total	% Increase	(000)	% of Total
Primary.........	1,425	62.0	304	37.9	21.3	1,729	55.7
Estate.........	632	27.5	51	6.4	8.1	683	22.0
Other.........	793	34.5	253	31.5	31.9	1,046	33.7
Industry.........	253	11.0	204	25.4	80.6	457	14.7
Services.........	621	27.0	295	36.7	47.5	916	29.5
Total..........	2,299	100.0	803	100.0	34.9	3,102	100.0

*Source: Table 5-2. Minor discrepancies are attributable to rounding.

leaving the unemployment rate only a little higher in 1960 than it
had been at the beginning of the period.[5] For this record to be
achieved, it was necessary that considerable restructuring of the
employment pattern take place. The estate sector provided only
51,000 new jobs, so the brunt of labor absorption had to be taken
up by other industries. Manufacturing, with 183,000 new jobs
created, transportation and communications (46,000), and construction (21,000) took up some of the slack and the rest of the newly
employed went into areas where their productive contributions to
society were perhaps less great: traditional agriculture (245,000);
trade, commerce, and finance (80,000); services not elsewhere
classified (89,000); and government n.e.c. (80,000). The changing
employment pattern led to a decline in the relative importance of
primary employment, while industrial employment underwent a
rapid relative and absolute rise and service employment a more
gradual one (see Table 5-3). At least to some extent, then, the
pattern of relative employment change between 1946 and 1960 can
be regarded as a transition toward a more "modern" economic
structure. With a substantial traditional sector remaining in 1960,
however—peasant agriculture alone still accounted for a third of
total employment—the transition plainly had a long way to go before the whole economy could be said to have been modernized.

The labor force and employment estimates presented here
suggest that job openings were expanded rapidly enough from 1946
to 1960 to keep the unemployment rate from rising substantially.[6]

---

[5]For this and the other employment change figures, see Table 5-2. The
conjecture that percentage unemployment increased very little rests on rather
shaky evidence; see pages 102–4, in the Appendix, pages 298–300.

[6]See pages 298–300, Appendix.

Iowever, the estimates are rough enough that they may mask a ertain amount of increase. There were no regularly collected statistics or comparable surveys conducted at various times over the period which might either verify or upset the tentative conclusion hat percentage unemployment did not rise significantly.[7] In any ase, in an economy with as large a traditional sector as Ceylon till has, unemployment does not serve as a very comprehensive measure of the underutilization of labor resources. Especially in rural areas (excluding the estates), an increasingly unfavorable ratio of population to complementary resources is more likely to manifest itself in some form of underemployment than in outright unemployment. A sample survey undertaken by a team from the International Labour Organisation in 1959[8] found very high levels of underemployment, though it did not, of course, indicate whether these levels had increased substantially over the preceding 10 or 15 years. In addition to the 10.5 percent of the labor force which it found to be completely unemployed in 1959, the survey revealed that 45.4 percent of the rural labor force was underemployed, in the sense of working fewer than 40 hours a week on a year-round basis; the comparable percentage for the urban labor force was 29.0. However, if the desires of the persons involved to work more hours a week were taken into account, the severity of underemployment appeared to be much less: 18.8 percent of the rural labor force and 11.2 percent of the urban were working fewer than 40 hours per week *and* declared themselves available for additional hours of work.[9] Clearly, in measuring underemployment the exact percentages one obtains are always heavily dependent upon the way underemployment is defined. Precise percentages aside, however, it is obvious that Ceylon's economy, especially its traditional rural sector, contains sizable pools of untapped labor resources.

FACTOR SUPPLIES: CAPITAL

Independent Ceylon inherited as a legacy from the colonial era a considerable stock of private and public capital. Notable in the

---

[7]However, there *is* good independent evidence which substantially corroborates the estimate of unemployment for the year 1959 by itself. The author's estimate (page 299) was that 10.9 percent of the labor force was unemployed in that year, while an ILO survey (see following footnote 8) reached an entirely independent estimate of 10.5 percent. See pages 298–300. in the Appendix.

[8]International Labour Organisation, "Report to the Government of Ceylon on the Employment, Unemployment and Underemployment Sample Survey of Ceylon, 1959" (unpublished, 1960), a summary of which is published as "A Survey of Employment, Unemployment, and Underemployment in Ceylon," *International Labour Review* (March, 1963), p. 247–257.

[9]*Ibid.*, p. 255.

latter category were the school, hospital, road, railroad, harbor, and communication systems which had been built up to a high standard over the years. Among the various types of private capital, the estates themselves formed by far the most significant item, though in their case the value of the legacy was qualified by the fact that much of their ownership still resided in the hands of the British. In the late forties, the foreign-owned share of the tea industry was over 50 percent and that of rubber 40 (foreign-owned coconut acreage amounted to less than 10 percent of the total; see Table A–38, Appendix). British firms also controlled substantial fractions of the modern industrial and service sectors. A further difficulty was that after a long period of undermaintenance, fostered by the depression and the war, the value of both private and public assets had undergone some deterioration.

Efforts to expand the capital stock have, of course, taken a central position in Ceylon's attempts at economic development since the late forties. The basic aims of the Ceylon government between 1946 and 1960 were at least to maintain public social and economic capital at per capita levels no worse than in the past, to maintain and modernize the estate sector, and to diversify the economy, especially by building up industry. Essentially, then, the leading growth sector of colonial days—the estates and the commercial activities that were intimately associated with them—was to be little more than maintained in this new investment strategy, while the bulk of the available investment fund was to be used in promoting the growth of other sectors.

During the rapid growth periods of plantation agriculture (see Chapter 3, page 66) capital had been obtained relatively easily, either from private foreign investors or from the reinvestment of surpluses generated by the profitable operation of plantation agriculture itself. After 1946, however, the problem of obtaining capital either internally or externally became acute. Internally, the government's strategy of capital accumulation had to face difficulties in extracting surpluses from the profitable sectors of the economy (still notably the estates), in avoiding the temptation to use too high a proportion of revenue collections for current purposes or for relatively unproductive overhead capital uses, and finally in deciding how best to allocate what remained to directly productive investment projects.[10] Relatively little directly productive government investment had emerged from this process through 1960 and what investment there had been had not proven productive enough

---

[10]For a discussion of these problems, see below, Chapter 7, pages 187–207.

o generate substantial surpluses and thus hasten the process of
apital accumulation. Investment from sources other than the
;overnment lagged far behind what might have been hoped for.
'rivate domestic entrepreneurs generally showed reluctance to make
ubstantial investments, basically because profit opportunities in
he old lines of activity (e.g., estate agriculture) seemed generally
tot to warrant them[11] and possible new lines (especially pro-
luction for the local market) were deemed too uncertain a pro-
'ider of profits.[12] It need hardly be said that independence meant
considerable change in the availability of foreign private capital.
The potential foreign investor faced all the difficulties of the local
private investor just mentioned and in addition possessed a greater
'ear of political uncertainty and a concern that he might receive
liscriminatory treatment at the hands of the government. New
'oreign private investment during the fifties did not, in fact, amount
to enough to offset the outflows of capital which took place in the
early years of the decade as a result of purchases of British assets in
Ceylon by Ceylonese individuals. Aid from foreign governments *did*
prove to be a fairly important source of investment funds from the
mid-fifties on. In general, however, capital scarcity remained severe
and provided one of the main checks to economic growth during
the 1950's.

Quantitatively, less is known about investment than about almost
any other aspect of Ceylon's postwar development, but it appears
that expenditures on gross fixed investment totaled some Rs. 6,800,-
000,000 over the years 1950–60 inclusive.[13] Of this total, just half,
Rs. 3,400,000,000, was spent by government. A further Rs. 1,500,000,-
000 went for private residential construction. Fixed capital formation
by private enterprises lagged throughout most of the period; it
totaled Rs. 1,900,000,000 for the 11 years together, but over Rs.
600,000,000 of that sum came in the upsurge of private investment
which started in 1959. On the average, gross fixed investment ran
at about 12 percent of GNP.[14] Beyond this, little can be said. Noth-

---

[11]Because of the high cost of planting estate crops relative to the returns
that might be expected from it, little was done. Output growth through more
intensive use of the land area already in cultivation, especially when combined with better materials and techniques, *was* often a profitable proposition and most of the output expansion which occurred came about in this
way. See the sections on tea, rubber, and coconut in Chapter 6.

[12]See Chapter 6, pages 171–173 for a fuller discussion of public policy and
private investment in the postwar period.

[13]See Table A–7, Appendix. Since there are no good investment data or balance of payments accounts for the late 1940's, all of the statements made in this
paragraph will relate to the years 1950 through 1960.

[14]11.6 percent of GNP in current prices and 12.2 percent of real GNP, according to Tables A–2 and A–3, Appendix.

ing precise is known about the industrial distribution of investment expenditures. The extent to which these gross expenditures represent net additions to the capital stock can be calculated only roughly. If 5 percent of GNP is accepted as a reasonable estimate of depreciation,[15] then net fixed investment in current prices over the 1950–60 period works out to just 6.6 percent of GNP.

The role played by international capital flows can hardly be described as favorable. The net flow of private long-term direct investment throughout the period as a whole was out of the country, in the sum of Rs. 182,000,000, 1950–60 inclusive. Most of this represented purchases of foreign holdings in Ceylon—estates and mercantile houses in the main—by Ceylon nationals.[16] The movement of private long-term portfolio investment was also adverse (Rs. 128,000,000), reflecting purchases of securities from foreigners by Ceylonese. Offsetting in part the outflow of private long-term capital was a net inflow of government long-term capital. It amounted to only Rs. 208,000,000 during the 1950–60 period, however, and thus did not fully counterbalance the outflow of private long-term capital. Including both kinds of flows, then, Ceylon was a net exporter of long-term capital during this vital phase of its economic development.[17]

FACTOR SUPPLIES: LAND

Since 1871 the total land area under cultivation in Ceylon had been rising at a rate of somewhat more than one percent a year.[18] With the gradual exhaustion of the supply of good cultivable land and the rising costs of clearing, irrigating (where necessary), and planting, however, it had become progressively more difficult to maintain the past growth rate. In the postwar period, with the rural population rising much more rapidly than in the past and the existing cultivated area thus coming under severe population pressure, efforts were made to accelerate the growth rate of this cultivated extent.

---

[15]See pages 256–257 in Appendix.

[16]This net outflow takes into account only the proportion of such purchases which took place during the 1950's. There was also a considerable number of similar asset acquisitions during the 1940's.

[17]But when movements of *short-term* capital are included Ceylon was a net capital importer in 1950–60. Looking at the current account of the balance of payments and equating a current account deficit with a capital inflow, one obtains a net inflow of Rs. 443,000,000 for 1950–60. Nearly the entire amount of this capital inflow (Rs. 422,000,000; see Table A–60, Appendix) can be accounted for by sales of external assets held by Ceylonese banks and the Ceylon government to foreigners. For complete balance of payments data, see Table A–57, Appendix.

[18]See Table 2–10, page 49.

The main way in which new acreage had been brought under cultivation in the past was by the sale or "alienation" of public or "Crown" land to agriculturalists. In the early days of the coffee and tea industries the alienation of Crown land had provided the estate owner with immense quanities of land, but in the postwar period almost all such sales were made to the peasantry.[19] In fact, to supplement the rapidly diminishing quantity of Crown land suitable for any cultivation at all, a program was put into operation under which the government bought up estate land for subsequent resale to the peasantry; this program, however, did not amount to much in practice during the 1950's (see Table 5–4). The other prong in

TABLE 5–4

LAND ALIENATION, 1950–60*

(Acres)

Year	Alienated to Peasants		Alienated to Middle-class Ceylonese	Coloniza-tion Schemes	Total: All Alienation
	Total	Of which Acquired from Estates			
1950........	39,485	.....	1,942	16,253	57,680
1951........	36,614	.....	5,369	7,306	49,289
1952........	32,573	.....	1,959	9,304	43,836
1953........	18,137	.....	922	13,107	32,166
1954........	24,359	2,216†	12,210	12,753	49,322
1955........	22,262	2,156	9,663	12,586	44,511
1956........	31,884	499	14,048	13,910	59,842
1957........	34,248	1,362	8,393	16,017	58,658
1958........	26,183	2,290	5,460	22,505	54,148
1959........	25,701	1,646	19,575	7,326	52,602
1960........	15,270	1,534	6,414	6,234	29,918
Cumulative total, 1950–60...	306,716	11,703‡	85,955	139,301	531,972

*Totals are net of cancellation of allotments (for reasons of nondevelopment of the land, non-residence, failure to make annual payments, etc.). Source: *A.R.s of the Land Commissioner.*
†Prior to 1954 a total of 12,686 acres had been acquired and alienated.
‡1954–60.

the government's traditional land policy, like the sale of Crown land a holdover from colonial days, was the colonization of the dry zone through the building of new communities near newly built or renovated major irrigation schemes. This program, too, continued through the 1950's, but the pace was slow and the cost high.

---

[19]There has also been a program of alienation to "middle-class Ceylonese," but the amount of land alienated under this scheme has been small and the actual development of the land alienated has lagged; see Table 5–4.

Through all the government programs together, about 50,000 acres a year were transferred to nonestate agriculture, but not all of this by any means went directly into cultivation.

Only minor new plantings of export crops were made during the period and since land-hungry smallholders bought out some of the previously existing estates the total estate acreage actually registered a slight decline. In all, only 257,000 acres were added to the total area cultivated between 1946 and 1959, although including purchases from the estates the peasant sector managed to increase its holdings by 275,000 acres.[20] The annual rate of increase in total cultivated area fell to 0.5 percent, less than half its historical rate, and in the peasant sector the population density rose from 2.4 to 3.1 persons per cultivated acre.[21]

In sum, then, the supplies of land and (probably) capital available to Ceylon's economy rose less rapidly from 1946 through 1960 than they had over the preceding century and population increased much more rapidly. Taken in a static technological context, this new and unfavorable constellation of factor growth rates could only lead to declining levels of real income per capita. Fortunately, however, technology was not static. Chapter 6, which tells the story of postwar economic growth, analyzes the key role played by productivity increases in the output expansion which took place during these years. First, however, some attention should be given to the other changes which had taken place in the structure and dynamics of the export economy.

DEVELOPMENT PLANNING[22]

Like virtually all of the countries which have attained independence since the end of World War II, Ceylon embarked upon an attempt at centrally directed economic development. As is to be expected, the history of development planning in Ceylon reveals the common problems which have been encountered in most of these countries. One of these difficulties, a striking one in Ceylon's case, is the failure of much of what was written into the various plans to be translated into effective policy decisions and hence implemented. A history of development planning is thus not the same

---

[20]See Table 2–10, page 49.

[21]See Table 2–8, page 48.

[22]This section is intended to provide only an introduction to government plans for economic development. Questions of development policy recur throughout this and the following chapters. In particular, the effects of the main public policies influencing the growth of the various sectors of the economy are dealt with in Chapter 6, while the problem of financing government economic activities, as well as the basic question of what development strategy might have been more successful than the one actually attempted, are discussed in Chapter 7.

thing as a history of development policy. Even if regarded only as expressions of outlook, however, mere intellectual exercises, Ceylon's plans are worth examining in some detail. At the very least they help describe the problems of the economy and show how the government proposed to go about solving them. A brief historical review of economic planning in the postwar period will thus serve to define the general nature of Ceylon's development strategy.

Economic planning of a sort began even before independence. In the *Post-War Development Proposals* of 1946, ministry plans to smooth the conversion to peacetime production and ". . . to raise the standards of living by designed action, to maintain full employment, and to provide [the people] with the opportunities to lead a fuller life"[23] were published. Added together, the ministry proposals took on the appearance of a national plan, but they did not really represent a coordinated program for economic development. They envisioned the spending of Rs. 1,739,000,000 on capital projects by the government and laid out the general order of priorities which reigned throughout the United National Party (U.N.P.) regime.[24] Communications and works (Rs. 560,000,000), agriculture and lands (Rs. 420,000,000), and education (Rs. 372,-

[23]*Post-war Development Proposals* (1946), p. v.

[24]For the information of readers not familiar with the subject, the bare outline of independent Ceylon's political history is presented at this point. From the granting of full independence in 1948 through the general election of April, 1956 Ceylon was ruled by the United National Party. The U.N.P. had been formed by D. S. Senanayake, who served as prime minister until his death in a riding accident in 1952. He was succeeded by his son, Dudley Senanayake, who resigned "for reasons of health" just over a year later in the wake of serious unrest caused by the government's efforts to correct the severe budgetary and external payments imbalance which had resulted from the steep fall of export prices in 1952. Sir John Kotelawala then became prime minister. In 1956 the U.N.P. suffered an overwhelming surprise defeat in the general election at the hands of S. W. R. D. Bandaranaike's Mahajana Eksath Peramuna coalition, of which the new prime minister's Sri Lanka Freedom Party formed the cornerstone. The main cause of the M.E.P.'s victory is generally thought to have been a Sinhalese-Buddhist linguistic-cultural-religious reaction against the rather Westernized outlook of the U.N.P., coupled with frustrated expectations on the part of the rapidly growing group of the educated unemployed and underemployed (see I. D. S. Weerawardana, *Ceylon General Election, 1956* [Colombo: M. D. Gunasena & Co., Ltd., 1960]; W. Howard Wriggins, *Ceylon: Dilemmas of a New Nation* [Princeton, New Jersey: Princeton University Press, 1960] ch. 9). Bandaranaike governed, with some minor changes in the structure of his coalition, until his assassination by a Buddhist monk in September, 1959. Thereafter, a period of extreme political instability ensued, which was finally ended by the assumption of the prime minister's position by Mrs. Sirimavo Bandaranaike, the late prime minister's widow, after the second (July) general election of 1960. Mrs. Bandaranaike remained prime minister up to March, 1965, at which time independent Ceylon's sixth general election was held, resulting in the election of a U.N.P.-centered coalition government and the resumption of the premiership by Dudley Senanayake.

000,000) were to receive the bulk of the funds.[25] Diversification of agriculture, the promotion of dry zone colonization by peasant agriculture, and the building of infrastructure were given prime emphasis. Plantation agriculture was generally ignored and industry received only a nominal allocation. Emphasis on industrialization was in fact deliberately scorned: the ministers proclaimed that they could think of few prospectively efficient industries; the level of protection would be reduced in the future so as to prevent the formation of inefficient industry.

Although the *Post-War Development Proposals* did not really constitute a national development plan, they did represent the kind of thinking which guided policy through the early U.N.P. years. Central government investment expenditure grew from year to year, rising from about Rs. 150,000,000 in 1947/48 to over Rs. 300,000,000 in 1951/52 and 1952/53. However, investments in electricity, land development, and other projects were cut back in the adjustment to the post-Korean commodity slump; central government capital expenditure fell to just over Rs. 250,000,000 in 1953/54. The cut was restored in the following year and the total continued to run at about Rs. 300,000,000 through the rest of the U.N.P. era.

Several flurries of activity in the field of planning during the remaining U.N.P. years had relatively little effect on actual investment allocations.[26] With the formation of the Colombo Plan in 1950 the Ceylon government was called upon to submit a six-year development plan for the period beginning in mid-1951. Its submission was an extremely modest proposal to invest Rs. 1,359,000,000 in the economy, Rs. 503,000,000 of it in agriculture, Rs. 375,000,000 in social services, Rs. 297,000,000 in transportation and communications, and much smaller sums in power and industry. The plan was purely a pro forma exercise and probably had no influence on policy.[27] Then in late 1951 came the visit of a World Bank team, which produced an exhaustive analysis of Ceylon's development prospects and also a proposed development plan for the years 1953-59.[28] Another modest program, the World Bank's proposal

---

[25]*Post-War Development Proposals*, p. 51.

[26]The 1947/48 and 1948/49 budget speeches were published by the Department of Information as *A Six-Year Plan for Ceylon* (1950), which they were only in the general sense that they stated long-run government intentions in several fields.

[27]See Commonwealth Consultative Committee on South and South-East Asia, *Report on the Colombo Plan for Co-operative Economic Development in South and South-East Asia* (London, 1950), pp. 28–32.

[28]International Bank for Reconstruction and Development, *The Economic Development of Ceylon* (Baltimore, Maryland: Johns Hopkins Press, 1953).

ooked for government investment of Rs. 1,600,000,000 over the six-year period. Its emphasis was predominantly on agriculture (and on rrigation and land development within agriculture), transportation, and power; health and education also received substantial allotments but industry was virtually neglected.[29] The report thus reflected the familiar U.N.P. priorities but became a political football when it was attacked by politicians to the left of the government for being insufficiently ambitious in both its growth and its structural transformation goals. In any case, the plan had little influence on actual investment allocations, less because of the raging debate over national priorities than because soon after its publication commodity prices fell and growth began to take a back seat to stabilization policies.

Only in 1954 was a serious plan produced by the Ceylon government itself. *The Six-Year Programme of Investment 1954/55 to 1959/60* was only a plan for government investment and not a full national plan but it did represent an attempt to coordinate the investment decisions of the various ministries and fit them into a general framework. The plan indicated a desire on the part of the government to accelerate its investment rate; total planned government investment over the six years amounted to Rs. 2,529,000,000. The system of priorities had changed little from earlier periods: public utilities and agriculture between them were to receive about 70 percent of the aggregate sum invested; social services were downgraded somewhat but industry remained a minor concern. Like its predecessors, the *Six-Year Programme* was destined to have little effect on policy. The U.N.P. government which drew it up remained in office only long enough to write the budget in two of the six years covered by the *Programme* and when the Mahajana Eksath Peramuna (M.E.P.; People's United Front) came to power in 1956 it brought with it quite a different idea of how public investment should be allocated; the *Six-Year Programme* thus became a dead letter.

Although questions of development policy played only a small and indirect role in the 1956 election, the new government did come into office possessing a conviction that economic development was being mismanaged and that improvements were called for. Of two things in particular was it convinced: that the government should

---

[29]That is, it received only a small allocation of public investment. The IBRD proposal, like *The Six-Year Programme of Investment 1954/55 to 1959/60*, of the National Planning Council, which followed it, was based on the stated premise that industry was primarily a field for private rather than public investment.

play a more vigorous role in development and that the promotion of industry should be given a much higher priority than it had received hitherto. The M.E.P. government set about drawing up a new national plan which would express these convictions. An unprecedented degree of interest in planning was engendered by the *Ten-Year Plan* which finally emerged in 1959. The new plan was for the first time a plan for the whole national economy, embodying programs for the government to follow not just in regard to public investment but also in other aspects of government policy including ways of influencing the decisions of the private economy. The plan was designed, according to its chief architect, as an exercise to show that despite the relatively unimpressive growth record of the immediate past it was possible to draw up a plan containing reasonable magnitudes which could overcome basic Ceylon's economic problems and set income and employment upon a satisfactory growth path.[30] As such, it appeared at the time to be an ambitious plan, but not one that was beyond the capacity of the economy to finance and implement. For public and private sectors together total investment over the 10 years 1959–68 was to come to Rs. 13,600,-000,000; this meant annual investment of Rs. 1,360,000,000, as compared with the then current figure of about Rs. 800,000,000.[31] Relative allocations were greatly altered from past plans: agriculture was downgraded and industry moved far up the priority scale (agriculture was to get Rs. 3,100,000,000 in total investment, industry Rs. 2,700,000,000); investment in social services, transportation and communications, and other areas trailed behind in positions of secondary importance. Technically an elegant document, the *Ten-Year Plan* then went on to calculate in great detail the policy ramifications in various sectors of its proposals. But as things were to happen, it too failed to become a working document.

A combination of changes in the economic environment and political instability doomed the carefully worked out *Ten-Year Plan*. Within just a few months of its publication the prime minister, Bandaranaike, was assassinated and the worst period of political turmoil since independence was ushered in, featuring three governments, two general elections, and innumerable minor political crises in the course of less than a year. Simultaneously, the economic position of the country approached crisis proportions. The paralysis of

---

[30]Gamini Corea, former secretary of the Planning Secretariat, in an interview, June 27, 1963.

[31]The climb was to be gradual, from about Rs. 700,000,000 in 1959 to approximately Rs. 900,000,000 in 1960, and so on, up to more than Rs. 2,000,000,000 in 1968.

decision making which followed naturally from this political ferment helped to worsen the economic situation. As in the past, political interests came to dominate economic interests and, when attention could be spared for economics, short-term improvisation took precedence over long-term calculation. Thus planning, although it had made great strides in terms of the quality of documents produced, failed once again to establish itself as a major influence on investment policy.

Although no single clear and consistent set of investment priorities emerged from Ceylon's experience with development planning, continuously increasing concern over economic development in general is evident in the increasing size and sophistication of the plans which were drawn up. Clearly the magnitude of public investment was to increase rapidly, even if it proved impossible to raise it as fast as the plans demanded. Since the government did not propose to renege on its substantial commitments to provide current services to the public, this posed a massive financing problem. Those sectors of the economy which possessed or could generate substantial surpluses would have to bear increasingly heavy tax burdens. In simplest terms, this mean that the estates and the high-income elite created by them would be taxed so as to develop the remainder of the economy, notably industry and peasant agriculture. This was a potentially revolutionary proposition, since now for the first time the large surpluses generated in the plantation sector could be reinvested in other parts of the economy, breaking down its dualism and leading to economic diversification.[32]

INTERSECTORAL FLOWS

While the causes of output growth since World War II are the concern of the following chapter, it is relevant to note here simply that the total volume of transactions—of almost all types—engaged in by the Ceylon economy was much higher after the war than it had been at any time in the past. The real output of all the major export crops was markedly higher than it had been in prewar days (see Table A–32, Appendix) and production in other sectors had risen noticeably, too. In terms of rupees, of course, the sharp rises which had taken place in virtually all prices since the 1930's had magnified the rise in the total volume of transactions. All the goods flows of the colonial economy—between the modern sector and abroad, between the modern and traditional sectors, between the

---

[32]See Chapter 7, pages 187–207, for a discussion of some of the problems of public finance which this development effort encountered.

TABLE 5-5

DISTRIBUTION OF RECEIPTS FROM TEA AND RUBBER EXPORTS, 1946–60

Year	Export Receipts*	Total Costs†	Export Duties‡	Company Taxes§	After-Tax Profits‖	Total Costs	Before-Tax Profits	Taxes	After-Tax Profits
			(Rs. 000,000)				Percentage of Export Receipts		

A. Tea

Year									
1946	379	300	9	25	45	79	21	9	12
1947	567	335	92	56	83	59	41	26	15
1948	590	373	113	55	49	63	37	28	8
1949	650	400	113	55	82	62	38	26	13
1950	752	406	131	91	124	54	46	30	16
1951	800	493	164	68	75	62	38	29	9
1952	723	504	115	57	47	70	30	24	7
1953	825	497	139	119	71	60	40	31	9
1954	1123	599	214	194	116	53	47	36	10
1955	1194	618	300	173	104	52	48	40	9
1956	1044	608	221	142	72	58	42	35	7
1957	1016	594	238	126	58	58	42	36	6
1958	1131	622	281	156	72	55	45	39	6
1959	1045	665	198	125	58	64	36	31	6
1960	1096	674	139	203	79	61	39	31	7

B. Rubber

Year									
1946	227	...	6	...	...	..	..	..	..
1947	136	...	—	...	...	..	..	..	..
1948	142	...	—	...	...	..	..	..	..
1949	123	...	—	...	...	..	..	..	..
1950	401	...	18	...	...	..	..	..	..
1951	572	...	75	...	...	..	..	..	..
1952	363	201	44	65	53	55	45	30	15
1953	329	212	33	53	32	64	36	26	10
1954	276	210	31	22	13	76	24	19	5
1955	350	237	37	48	29	68	32	24	8
1956	293	196	53	29	15	67	33	28	5
1957	300	199	60	28	13	66	34	29	4
1958	258	181	49	20	9	70	30	27	3
1959	298	182	45	48	22	61	39	31	7
1960	378	207	53	86	33	55	45	37	9

*Source: Department of Commerce, *Thirty Years Trade Statistics of Ceylon (1925–1954)*; Department of Census and Statistics, *Statistical Abstracts.*

†Cost per pound (see Tables 6–8 and 6–12) times pounds exported (sources: *A.R.s of the Tea Controller; ibid.*).

‡Sources: *ibid.*

§The prevailing rate of company taxation (see note # to Table 6–7) times before-tax profits.

‖Before-tax profits, minus export duties and company taxes.

traditional sector and abroad, and within the two sectors themselves —had increased in size. In addition, however, they had undergone some changes in relative magnitude. The data which one would need to outline in detail the flow of goods and services between the two domestic sectors and between each of them and the rest of the world are not available, but the broad pattern of these flows and the ways in which they differed from the flows typical of the colonial economy can be specified.

The flow between the modern sector and abroad continued along much the same lines as before; the estates and modern-sector processing and commercial concerns continued to export much the same array of products as they had in the 1930's. The proceeds of these exports continued to go to pay the wages and salaries of the labor and supervisory staffs employed on the estates,[33] to buy imports of estate supplies and equipment from abroad, and to provide profits for the corporate and individual owners of the estates. Other fractions of the proceeds went to the export-import firms, managing agencies, and banks associated with estate agriculture and were similarly distributed. The group of persons who received a sufficient income from their direct or indirect association with the modern sector to afford themselves a more-or-less Western standard of living increased in number and widened to include unprecedented numbers of Ceylonese.[34] Increasingly, however, another claimant to the returns from export agriculture made its influence felt. Through export taxation and the taxation of corporate and individual incomes the Ceylon government gained a rising share of total export receipts.

Tables 5-5 and 5-6 assemble some information on export proceeds from the three leading export crops during the years 1946-60 and on how these proceeds were distributed. Returns from the export of tea, which was the leading earner of foreign receipts, rose fairly steadily throughout the period, while proceeds from rubber and coconut followed little or no upward trend. As nearly as one can tell, all three crops remained highly profitable throughout the postwar era.[35] and had the government not intervened the same very

---

[33]A larger proportion of the labor employed on the estates was now made up of Sinhalese peasants working on a full- or part-time basis than had been the case in colonial days, so the flow of income from the modern to the traditional sector via this route was increased.

[34]The absolute number of Europeans in Ceylon declined after independence and Ceylonese took their places on the estates and in the mercantile firms to an increasing degree. The continuing process of education raised the number of professionally trained Ceylonese doctors, lawyers, and accountants and they, too, took their places in the westernized enclave. A Ceylonese journalist has referred to these westernized Ceylonese, who absorbed many Western values along with their economic associations, as the Brown Sahibs. See Tarzie Vittachi, *Brown Sahib* (London: Andre Deutsch, Ltd., 1962).

[35]The figures on profits as a percentage of export receipts are rough estimates only (see footnotes to Tables 5-5 and 5-6). In any case, a better measure of profitability would be percentage return on capital, rather than sales. But

(Continued on next page)

TABLE 5-6

DISTRIBUTION OF RECEIPTS FROM COCONUT PRODUCTS EXPORTS, 1946-60*

Year	Export Receipts†	Export Duties‡	Ex-Estate Costs§ —(Rs. 000,000)—	"Margin"‖	Percentage of Export Receipts Export Duties	Ex-Estate Costs	"Margin"
1946.........	56	—	29	27	—	52	48
1947.........	93	8	29	57	9	31	61
1948.........	152	30	44	77	20	29	51
1949.........	168	34	58	77	20	35	46
1950.........	248	36	59	153	15	24	62
1951.........	320	47	97	176	15	30	55
1952.........	232	28	104	100	12	45	43
1953.........	244	32	95	117	13	39	48
1954.........	212	35	75	102	17	35	48
1955.........	225	33	102	90	15	45	40
1956.........	213	28	92	93	13	43	44
1957.........	156	18	61	78	12	39	50
1958.........	164	16	58	89	10	35	54
1959.........	244	26	76	142	11	31	58
1960.........	152	24	54	74	16	36	49

*Includes only the three leading coconut-products exports (coconut oil, copra, and dessicated coconut), which together account for some 90 percent of total coconut-products exports by value.
†Source: Department of Commerce, *Thirty Years Trade Statistics of Ceylon (1925-1954)*; Department of Census and Statistics, *Statistical Abstracts*.
‡Source: *Ibid.*
§Since processing is done away from the estates these figures are not to be compared with the similar ones for tea and rubber; aggregate cost is cost per thousand nuts times export volume, with coconut products exports expressed in terms of standard nut equivalents.
‖Includes transportation cost from estate to factory, processing, transportation form factory to ship, company taxes, and profits. This measure should move roughly with industry profits (aggregate or as a percentage of sales), except that the rising level of company taxation through the period would make actual profits tend downward more rapidly than "margin".

high dividend rates as had been paid in prewar times (see Chapter 3, page 66) could probably have been paid out to domestic and foreign shareholders during this period as well. Export duties, which had had a limited currency for short periods in the past, became a permanent feature of the tax structure after independence. Rates of export taxation were varied from time to time as world prices and per unit costs within Ceylon changed, the government's goal being to leave the export producer with a constant profit margin per unit exported. Increases in export value thus swelled the duty revenues of the government. The intention was that a rise in export value which was attributable to increases in

since there are no data on capital invested in the export industries no estimate of this rate can be made. However, the basic implication of the tables, that before-tax profit levels, especially in tea, were substantial throughout the period, is probably basically correct.

prices should create no gain for the producer,[36] but a rise in value caused by output increases should benefit him, since he now sold more units at a constant profit margin per unit. Profits after export duties had been paid, however, were subject to income taxation at rates which rose continually throughout the period. The combined result of the export duties and the income taxation was that the aggregate after-tax profits of the tea industry did not rise secularly, despite the steady upward trend in production (Table 5–5), while profits from rubber and coconut, which experienced less satisfactory output trends, generally declined. The government thus succeeded in capturing an ever-increasing proportion of the total proceeds of export agriculture through taxation. The government's share in proceeds from the export of tea went up from about 19 percent in the late 1940's to some 34 percent by the latter part of the 1950's, while the share remaining to the estate owners declined from about 12 percent to roughly 6. For rubber, the relative shares can be estimated only starting in 1952, when the government took 30 percent and the estate owners 15; by 1960 these proportions had shifted to 37 percent for the government and 9 percent for the owners. Data on coconut production are too weak to provide even rough numerical estimates, but it is probable that a similar trend in relative shares existed there, too.[37]

What was true of export agriculture applied to other parts of the modern sector as well. The steady rise in rates of taxation on corporate incomes and on personal incomes in the upper ranges led to the government's taking a larger and larger share of modern-sector income. As Table 5–7 shows, the taxation of corporate profits,

---

[36]The system did not work strictly according to its goals, however. Lags in duty rate changes sometimes left producers with a very high per unit profit margin after a rapid price rise or an inordinately low one after a sudden drop. At one point an attempt was made to overcome this problem by using a "sliding scale," with specific duty rates which varied automatically with changes in market prices. The system soon had to be abandoned, however, because it proved to be susceptible to price rigging by large dealers in export produce, who manipulated the timing of their shipments so as to lessen their duty payments.

[37]If these tax shares in export receipts are taken as measures of the incidence of taxation on producers it must be on the assumption that world demand for the products exported was infinitely elastic, since this is the only case in which the entire weight of export taxation would fall upon the producers, as is assumed when one classifies export duties as direct taxes on producers. For purposes such as the present one, this is probably not too bad as a broad assumption, though world demand for Ceylon tea is clearly less elastic than demand for its other exports and for none, of course, is elasticity literally infinite.

which was already very heavy in 1950, moved upward still further as the decade of the fifties progressed. Despite a marked rise in corporate profits before taxes, after-tax profits did not show an upward trend and taxes of various kinds, principally the corporate income tax, absorbed the entire increment in corporate profits.

TABLE 5–7

DISTRIBUTION OF CORPORATE PROFITS, 1950–60

Year	Before-Tax Profits*	Taxes†	After-Tax Profits	Divi-dends‡	Retained Earnings	Taxes	Percentage of Before-tax Profits Divi-dends	Retained Earnings
			(Rs. 000,000)					
1950.......	484	358	126	58	68	74	12	14
1951.......	609	460	150	93	57	76	15	9
1952.......	583	447	136	77	59	77	13	10
1953.......	599	453	145	61	84	76	10	14
1954.......	669	525	144	176	−32	78	26	−5
1955.......	700	613	88	79	9	88	11	1
1956.......	799	649	149	110	39	81	14	5
1957.......	795	655	140	31	109	82	4	14
1958.......	799	646	154	88	66	81	11	8
1959.......	761	607	153	...	...	80	————20————	
1960.......	756	620	136	...	...	82	————18————	

*Source: Tables A–2 and A–5, Appendix. This sum represents corporate profits after the payment of excise taxes and import duties, the receipt of subsidies, and the deduction of capital consumption allowances, but before the payment of direct taxes; export duties are classified as direct taxes. The total thus consists of the following items from the Appendix tables: 2K2 + 2L + 2M1 − 5A3d(1) − 5G1.

†Includes all taxes paid by corporations other than excise taxes and import duties, which are considered to be indirect taxes.

‡These estimates were made by Rasaputram in connection with his saving study (W. Rasaputram, "Savings of the Ceylon Economy, 1950–59," *Central Bank of Ceylon Bulletin*, January, 1961, p. 10–31), but never published. They were received by the author by personal communication from Rasaputram.

Aside from the fact that ever larger proportions of the surplus accruing from modern-sector economic activity were being appropriated by the government for its own uses, other important changes in its distribution and use were taking place. As a result of the spread of education among the Ceylonese and their purchases of assets from the British, the size of the westernized high-income elite was growing, even as Westerners themselves began to leave the island. The coincidence of the Korean commodity boom with the large-scale transfer of ownership to Ceylonese greatly enhanced the economic position of this elite. The wealth amassed by this expanding group was largely used by them to build up, as far as possible, a Western standard of living. The accoutrements of this standard of living—radios, automobiles, canned foods, watches, and so on—virtually all had to be imported. Table 5–8 shows how import outlays on some representative luxury consumer goods increased. As the table suggests, these outlays rose strongly during and immediately after the Korean commodity boom. Although there was some retrenchment in 1953–54 it does seem that the boom caused a permanent upward shift in the standard of living expectations of the elite. Of course, if export proceeds had continued indefinitely at their 1950–51 levels these imports would have emerged not as extravagant luxury consumption but as the natural accompaniment of the higher income level produced by a successful export economy. It is only in retrospect, now that the far less buoyant long-term trend of export prices has revealed itself, that it has become evident that the island's consumption level had utterly outreached its resources. In this light, as Joan Robinson has said, it is seen that "Ceylon has tasted the fruit before she has planted the tree."[38] During the bad-to-mediocre export years of the mid- and late-fifties it was only the previously accumulated stores of foreign assets which permitted the country to live beyond its means. The standard pattern during these years came to be for large import surpluses to be run and financed by the sale of foreign securities held by Ceylon's banks and government (see Chapter 7).

While the economy was thus becoming so consumption-oriented, what was happening to the structure of production? In the absence of effective government intervention there was very little pressure for any marked change in the old production pattern. The incentives to make new investments in the traditional fields of endeavor had largely disappeared and in the context of the wide-open economy of the fifties there was relatively little hope for successful investment in import-substituting lines. Thanks mainly to the government's subsidy scheme for peasant food producers (see Chapter 6) there was a considerable expansion of traditional agriculture. In fact, much of the economic surplus generated in the modern sector which was taken by the government in higher taxes found its way into the traditional sector, either as government current or capital expenditures designed to improve the welfare of the peasant or as food subsidies. A considerable (though unfortunately immeasurable) redistribution of income was thus effected. This income redistribution, coupled with rising food sales to the modern sector, had the effect of producing a minor consumption boom among the peasantry to parallel the free spending of the high-income elite. The consumption demands of the peasants were of course for a

---

[38] Joan Robinson, "Economic Possibilities of Ceylon," in *Papers by Visiting Economists*, Planning Secretariat (1959), p. 41.

more modest class of goods—much of their additional income went for improved food and clothing—but because of the purity of its export-economy structure Ceylon was heavily dependent on imports even for these humble necessities and the peasants, too, made their contribution to the worsening external balance of the economy.

TABLE 5–8

EXPENDITURES ON IMPORTS OF SELECTED LUXURY CONSUMER GOODS, 1948–60*
(Annual Averages in Rs. Millions)

Item	1948–50	1951–52	1953–54	1956–58	1959–60
Jam, marmalade, etc........	0.5	1.2	0.9	1.4	1.4
Apples and grapes..........	0.9	3.2	3.7	3.2	4.9
Coffee.....................	2.6	3.4	2.7	2.5	2.9
Beer......................	1.5	3.7	2.9	2.3	3.5
Whisky...................	0.7	1.0	1.2	1.2	1.2
Tobacco...................	3.6	3.0	3.0	5.1	6.4
Patent medicines...........	4.2	7.4	9.6	14.2	17.9
Sewing machines (domestic)..	1.2	4.5	4.8	8.7	11.3
Refrigerators (domestic).....	....	....	....	1.4	2.5
Automobiles...............	15.5	35.6	23.1	33.6	51.5
Automobile tires...........	1.8	3.2	3.6	4.5	7.2
Dry cell batteries..........	2.6	6.6	4.2	4.5	3.9
Radios....................	....	....	....	5.8	10.7
Watches...................	....	....	....	7.8	22.2

*Sources: Department of Commerce, *Thirty Years Trade Statistics of Ceylon (1925–1954)*; Department of Census and Statistics, *Statistical Abstracts*. Because of the changes made in the system of commodity trade classification during this period early figures for some items are difficult to obtain.

In terms of current goods and services flows, then, the 1950's saw some redirection of modern-sector demand from abroad to the domestic traditional sector. The redirection, however, was limited in amount and did not serve to outweigh the effect on the balance of payments of increasing demands by both the modern and the traditional sector for imported consumer goods. To only a limited degree was the integration of Ceylon's economy (i.e., the strengthening of flows between its two broad sectors) achieved.

With the prodigious growth in national consumption which was taking place it was clear that substantial output growth was becoming an increasingly pressing necessity. As Chapter 6 makes clear, Ceylon's economy did in fact achieve substantial output gains during the decade of the fifties. After the Korean War, however, the trend in export prices became unfavorable and, taking into account the factors which held production gains in export agriculture to relatively modest proportions, the hope of achieving increases in export proceeds sufficient to match the rise in the import bill began to fade. The government, which encouraged export agriculture through replanting subsidies at the same time as it levied an increasingly heavy tax burden on the sector, had a strategy for solving this basic economic problem of the 1950's. It aimed to reform the classical export economy, restructuring it through induced import substitution and to a lesser extent through export promotion so that a higher growth rate could be achieved with no significant restriction of import flows. This strategy, which is discussed in some detail in Chapter 7, must be judged a failure in view of the breakdown of import flows after 1960, but it nevertheless contained many of the elements of a sound development strategy. Its failure is primarily attributable not to its inappropriateness but to the slowness of the government to perceive and enunciate its policy clearly and to the pressure of other political and economic forces which kept the strategy from being fully implemented.

It has already been noted (pages 113–118) that the economic surplus generated by the economy, and particularly by its modern-sector export agriculture, during the postwar era was sizable and that an increasing share of it was being appropriated by the government through taxation. It is hardly necessary to point out that this capture of the surplus from export production had an immense potential for altering the structure of the economy, since now the surplus, which had in the past either been used for reinvestment in plantation agriculture or had been paid to foreign shareholders, became available for investment in parts of the economy other than export agriculture itself. The attempt to do just that formed a major part of the government's development strategy, but its fruits in terms of output diversification and import substitution had been modest indeed through 1960.

It has been seen that the power of modern-sector producers to save was greatly reduced by the fact that the government appropriated the major share of their profits through taxation. Nevertheless, as Table 5–9 shows, corporate saving remained the most important single source of investment finance throughout the decade. The intention of the government development strategy, of course, was that the government itself should do the saving for the modern sector, run a current account surplus, and use this surplus to finance public investment. Political pressures, however, often intervened and caused a diversion of large sums originally intended for investment expenditure to the maintenance of current government services in the face of rising population and heavy public demand for these services. As a consequence, there was only one year during the decade of the fifties—1955 (see Table 5–9)—in which government saving was a more important component of investment finance than income retained by producers. The third internal source of in-

TABLE 5-9

Sources of Investment Finance, 1950-60

(Rs. Millions)

	1950	1951	1952	1953	1954	1955	1956	1957	1958	1959	1960
Corporate saving	251.7	278.4	256.6	267.8	293.7	215.5	269.0	276.6	296.1	373.0	373.0
Capital consumption allowances	139.0	143.0	138.0	148.0	167.0	169.0	183.0	210.0	235.0	305.0	305.0
Retained earnings	112.7	135.4	118.6	119.8	126.7	46.5	86.0	66.6	61.1	68.0	68.0
Personal saving	266.0	266.0	−20.0	79.0	226.0	302.0	255.0	126.0	256.0	284.0	284.0
Government saving	144.6	132.5	36.2	129.8	288.7	283.7	253.8	139.4	28.8	−72.7	15.6
Subtotal: Internal financing	662.3	676.9	272.8	476.6	808.4	801.2	777.8	542.0	580.9	584.3	672.6
Deficit of nation on current account	−150.0	−89.1	441.1	169.8	−284.4	−289.5	122.5	352.7	152.9	205.8	221.1
Statistical discrepancy	−130.8	−53.2	−101.2	−9.8	−78.4	98.5	−268.2	−184.9	23.0	21.7	−109.0
Total: Gross domestic capital formation	381.5	534.6	612.7	636.6	445.6	610.2	632.1	709.8	756.8	811.8	784.7
(Percent of Total Less Statistical Discrepancy)											
Internal financing	129.3	115.2	38.2	73.7	154.3	156.6	86.4	60.6	79.2	74.0	75.3
Corporate saving	49.1	47.4	35.9	41.4	56.0	42.1	29.9	30.9	40.4	47.2	41.7
Personal saving	51.9	45.3	−2.8	12.2	43.1	59.0	28.3	14.1	34.9	35.9	31.8
Government saving	28.2	22.5	5.1	20.1	55.1	55.4	28.2	15.6	3.9	−9.2	1.7
External financing	−29.3	−15.2	61.8	26.3	−54.3	−56.6	−13.6	39.4	20.8	26.0	24.8

Source: Table A–7, Appendix.

vestment financing, personal saving, was also an important component of total saving, except in years of serious export slump such as 1952–53 and 1957. At such times the convergence of falling personal incomes and rigid customary living standards served to raise consumption as a proportion of personal income and squeeze personal saving to very low levels (in its worst year, 1952, personal saving even turned negative). As the decade wore on, however, all internal sources of finance taken together increasingly failed to cover the total volume of investment and it became necessary to resort to foreign sources of finance. In the absence of any substantial capital inflows, this meant primarily that the foreign assets Ceylon had accumulated during World War II and the Korean War boom had to be sold off to finance the current account deficit in the balance of payments. This does not necessarily mean, of course, that the investment program which the country carried out was incapable of being financed domestically. It does mean, however, that if this investment program—or a larger one—were to have been internally financed then the growth of private and public consumption expenditures would have had to be held more firmly in check than it was.[39]

SUMMARY

The economic structure characteristic of the colonial export economy was in many ways carried intact into the period of independence. Beginning in the late 1940's, however, the economy had to operate within a less favorable combination of factor growth rates than had existed in earlier times—labor growing faster, land and perhaps capital more slowly. Meanwhile, the Ceylon government launched increasingly ambitious efforts to speed the nation's economic development. These efforts created one important structural change, namely that a large share of the surplus of the highly productive export agricultural sector was appropriated by the government with an eye to its reinvestment in peasant agriculture and in industry. All these circumstances together combined to produce a transitional form of the export economy, consciously oriented toward economic development but possessing a number of thorny problems which would make development difficult and eventually come to menace the continued existence of the transitional system itself. The following chapter will examine the successes and failures of the development-oriented economy in terms of output growth, after which Chapter 7 will focus more closely on the characteristic problems of Ceylon's transitional export economy.

---

[39]For further discussion of the problems of excess aggregate demand and investment finance, see Chapter 7.

Chapter 6

Growth in the Transitional Economy

Given the less favorable combination of factor growth rates which emerged during the "transitional" 1946–60 period, as compared with those of the "classical" era, how much production growth could Ceylon's economy be expected to achieve in the first decade and a half following World War II? As the output data reviewed in the present chapter reveal, the economy did manage to expand at a fairly brisk rate despite some ups and downs. The sectoral pattern of growth was rather featureless. The stimulus for the kind of export-sector development which had provided the motive power for most of the island's past economic growth had become greatly weakened, on both the demand and the supply sides. On the other hand, the efforts of the government to promote the growth of other sectors and thereby diversify the structure of production met with only qualified success. No focal point for really rapid economic development emerged. As a result, the overall rate of output growth, though certainly not insignificant, was not high enough to support the rapid increase in consumption expenditures which took place —it is obvious now that consumption should not have been allowed to increase so rapidly as it did, of course—and thus did not suffice to solve the nation's mounting economic problems.

NATIONAL OUTPUT

Just how rapid was Ceylon's economic growth during the "transitional" period? In looking at GNP growth over these years, the researcher has the choice of three main series of data: the official estimates made by Ceylon's Department of Census and Statistics; the United Nations figures, which are reported by the Census and Statistics Department on the basis of a general (but not complete) conformance with UN definitions; and the estimates of the present author, which can best be described as the UN data revised to fit the Economic Growth Center's integrated accounts format as closely as possible.[1] These three series produce somewhat

---

[1]The Appendix gives a detailed description and critique of all three series.

different totals for GNP but the estimates are usually no more than five percent apart (see Table 6–1). Moreover, there is only a negligible discrepancy among the overall growth rates implied by the three sets of data.[2] All three suggest that GNP at current market prices rose at an average rate of 4.5 percent a year, 1950–60. Only one series, the official one, goes back before 1950. It indicates a 7.2 percent annual growth rate for the entire 1946–60 period, buoyed up by a massive 11.3 percent annual rate between 1946 and 1950. However, these figures of the late forties antedate some of the better sources of data underlying the national accounts estimates, so it is at least possible that they somewhat exaggerate the growth of those years.

The general price level increased only very gradually during the 1950's. What inadequate deflator series there are suggest inflation at a rate of only 0.5 percent a year,[3] leaving 4.0 percent as the annual increase in real Gross National Income.[4] In the late forties price increases were more rapid. On the basis of a rough calculation, it seems likely that the GNP deflator rose by 31 percent between 1946 and 1950. However, improvement in the terms of trade during those years tended to offset the effect of increases in the prices of food and other internally produced goods and services and the deflator of GNI rose by only 4 percent.[5] Thus, it appears that between 1946 and 1960 price increases could not have amounted to more than one percent a year. If the Census and Statistics De-

---

[2]This is true only for the period as a whole. Year by year there *are* significant differences among the three series in implied growth rates.

[3]See pages 252–253, Appendix.

[4]Three different concepts representing the overall level of economic activity are employed in this section: Gross National Product, Gross National Income, and Gross National Expenditure. When measured in current prices, of course, these are simply the same aggregate viewed from three points of view: the flow of net output during the year, the income generated by that flow, and the expenditure made on the output. All three concepts give identical totals. When a deflation is made to constant prices however, the distinction between the prices paid for national output and the prices which must be paid for the goods and services the nation consumes becomes important; export prices enter into the calculation of the former deflator and import prices into the latter. Changes in the terms of trade alter the purchasing power of given national physical output and hence real national income. Thus when an aggregate expression of real output is called for in the narrative, real GNP is used, but when the income-producing implications of national production are being considered real GNI is the appropriate measure.

[5]W. Rasaputram ("Gross National Product of Ceylon at Constant [1948] Prices," *Central Bank of Ceylon Bulletin,* January, 1956, pp. 8–16) provides a deflator for the 1947–50 period which rises by 21 percent and the fact that the Colombo cost-of-living index rose in 1947 by 10 percent and the import price index by 12 percent suggests that the 1946–47 rise was about 10 percent.

partment figures for the late forties can be accepted, then the real growth rate, 1946–60, was 6.5 percent.

Real Gross National Income per capita (in 1953 prices) by the Center measure rose from Rs. 587 to Rs. 677 between 1950 and 1960. Its upward climb was not a steady one, however. During export booms in 1951 and again in 1955 peaks were reached which were followed by short-term declines. Still, in 1960, not a particularly good year for Ceylon's main export commodities, real per capita income was at its highest level of the decade. Taking all the ups and downs of the fifties into account, real GNI per head had grown at an average annual rate of 1.4 percent since 1950 (that had been a better-than-average year for Ceylon's exports, so the choice of a 1950–60 time period is in this sense a conservative one). It is worth noting, however, that since the early and mid-fifties featured export booms and the late 1950's did not, real per capita income in 1956–60 averaged only 2 percent higher than real income per head in 1950–55. By 1960 real income per capita had reached a level of U.S. $142 (1953 prices) at the official rate of exchange (the unsatisfactory nature of comparisons of this sort is well known, but no attempt will be made here to provide a more sophisticated estimate of Ceylon's real per capita income in dollar terms).

Looking at national output in terms of industrial structure, one

TABLE 6–1

Gross National Product at Current Market Prices,
1946–60*

(Rs. Millions)

Year	Official Concept	UN Concept	Center Concept
1946	2,268	....	....
1947	2,608	....	....
1948	2,879	....	....
1949	3,056	....	....
1950	3,868	4,046.7	4,170.5
1951	4,619	4,752.9	4,888.9
1952	4,507	4,492.9	4,606.2
1953	4,491	4,679.2	4,900.7
1954	4,748	4,950.7	5,050.9
1955	5,234	5,546.7	5,701.8
1956	5,096	5,087.8	5,146.9
1957	5,200	5,331.0	5,422.9
1958	5,493	5,622.0	5,783.1
1959	5,753	5,996.2	6,162.1
1960	6,033	6,301.2	6,476.3

*Source: Appendix.

TABLE 6–2

GROSS NATIONAL INCOME, TOTAL AND PER CAPITA,
AT CONSTANT (1953) PRICES, 1950–60

Year	Real GNI (Rs. 000,000)	Real GNI per Capita (Rs.)
1950	4,510.2	587
1951	4,918.4	624
1952	4,627.8	573
1953	4,900.7	591
1954	5,267.5	618
1955	5,802.7	665
1956	5,217.1	584
1957	5,382.1	587
1958	5,847.1	623
1959	6,279.7	652
1960	6,698.6	677

Source: Tables A–3 and A–14, Appendix.

sees a certain amount of apparent structural change during the 1950's. Some of this is real and some only apparent. What most quickly strikes the eye in Table 6–3 is the gradual but definite decline in the relative importance of agriculture and related activities, from 49.8 percent of Gross Domestic Product in 1950 to 44.7 in 1960. A fall in the relative importance of export crops is entirely responsible for this decline, since "other" agriculture exhibits a sharply rising trend. The three major export crops taken together fell from 36.7 percent of GDP in 1950 to 22.5 at the end of the period. This fall is explained partly by declines in export prices, absolutely and relative to the prices of the goods and services produced by other sectors, and partly by declines in the output of coconut and rubber,[6] but mainly by the fact that overall real output in export agriculture tended to grow more slowly than output in the more rapidly expanding parts of the economy: manufacturing; administration and defense; electricity, gas, and water; and banking, insurance, and real estate. Of the remaining sectors, two—transport and communications and wholesale and retail trade (in part because of their close ties to estate agriculture)—decline relatively. Mining and quarrying is now nearly moribund. Construction continues to boom. Ownership of dwellings remains a constant fraction of income. And miscellaneous services has risen a bit in relative importance. These changes appear to constitute a slow but

---

[6] 1950 was a year of exceptionally high rubber output, called forth by the sharp price increases which followed the outbreak of the Korean War.

distinct movement away from agriculture and production for foreign markets and toward domestically oriented urban pursuits. However, care is required in the interpretation of these current-price data.

TABLE 6–3

INDUSTRIAL ORIGIN OF GROSS DOMESTIC PRODUCT AT CURRENT FACTOR COST,
1950 AND 1960*

	1950		1960		Percentage Increase,
Industry	Rs. 000,000	%	Rs. 000,000	%	1950–60
Agriculture, fishing, and forestry	1,963.7	49.8	2,716.7	44.7	38.3
Tea and minor estate crops	660.6	16.8	817.3	13.5	23.7
Rubber	387.3	9.8	210.2	3.5	−45.7
Coconut	398.0	10.1	331.1	5.5	−16.8
Other	517.8	13.1	1,358.1	22.4	162.3
Mining and quarrying	6.2	0.2	5.8	0.1	− 6.5
Manufacturing	154.6	3.9	314.2	5.2	103.2
Construction	278.8	7.1	571.7	9.4	105.1
Electricity, gas, and water	17.6	0.4	47.6	0.8	170.5
Transport and communications	294.1	7.5	347.3	5.7	18.1
Wholesale and retail trade	325.0	8.2	473.0	7.8	43.5
Banking, insurance, and real estate	14.0	0.4	52.5	0.9	275.0
Ownership of dwellings	281.7	7.1	406.5	6.7	44.3
Public administration and defense	199.6	5.1	482.8	8.0	141.9
Services n.e.c.	406.9	10.3	654.6	10.8	60.9
GDP at factor cost	3,942.2	100.0	6,072.7	100.0	54.0

*Source: Table A–8, Appendix. Domestic rather than national product is used here because factor payments to abroad, the data which would be needed to obtain national product by industry of origin, are not available in an industrial breakdown.

A less ambiguous view of the changes which took place in the structure of the economy would be provided by a complete restatement in constant prices of the data in Table 6–3. The information on prices and output which would be needed to make a thorough deflation of the table are lacking, but some notion of the broad sectoral trends in real output can be gained by expressing agricultural output and total Gross Domestic Product (GDP) in constant-price terms and letting real GDP originating in the secondary and tertiary spheres (where both price deflators and indexes of real output are weak) be determined as a residual. This is done in Table 6–4. Looking at that table, one sees that the relative declines in the primary and export-crop shares are to some extent genuine ones, applying to physical production as well as output value. Part of the decline in the share of export agriculture, however, is clearly a result of price trends unfavorable to it. On the other hand, peasant agriculture has been somewhat less dynamic than Table 6–3 implies, since relative prices have shifted in its favor.[7] In real terms, the output of the peasant agriculture sector and the whole nonagriculture sector have been rising at about the same rate. Export agriculture has grown more slowly and has fallen behind, even in real terms. The reasons for these limited structural changes will be considered later in this chapter.

TABLE 6–4

ESTIMATE OF GROSS DOMESTIC PRODUCT BY INDUSTRIAL ORIGIN AT FACTOR COST
OF 1953, 1950–60

(Rs. Millions)

| | —Agriculture, Forestry, Fishing— | | | | | All | | As a % of GDP: | |
| | Tea and Minor Export Crops* | Rub-ber† | Coco-nut‡ | Other§ | Total | Other Indus-tries‖ | GDP# | Export Crops | All Agri-culture |
Year									
1950......	595	336	334	839	2,104	1,679	3,783	33.4	55.6
1951......	633	310	379	889	2,211	1,998	4,209	31.4	52.5
1952......	615	285	417	1,022	2,339	2,015	4,354	30.2	53.7
1953......	666	292	396	921	2,275	2,320	4,595	29.5	49.5
1954......	712	278	384	1,142	2,516	2,123	4,639	29.6	54.2
1955......	738	278	442	1,263	2,721	2,355	5,076	28.7	53.6
1956......	729	282	426	1,066	2,503	2,087	4,590	31.3	54.5
1957......	773	289	350	1,179	2,591	2,423	5,014	28.4	51.7
1958......	802	296	327	1,298	2,723	2,559	5,282	27.0	51.6
1959......	802	271	373	1,291	2,737	2,809	5,546	26.1	49.4
1960......	850	287	349	1,476	2,962	2,957	5,919	25.1	50.0
Percentage change, 1950–60:									
	42.9	−14.6	4.5	75.6	40.8	76.1	56.5		

*Figure for 1953 from Table A–8 times the output index (1953 = 100) for tea implied in Table A–32, Appendix.
†*Ibid.*
‡*Ibid.*
§A residual: figure for agriculture, forestry, and fishing for 1953 from Table A–8 times the author's index of agricultural output (see Table A–31, Appendix), minus the sum of the three preceding items.
‖A residual: real GDP minus the sum of the four preceding items.
#GDP at current factor cost from Table A–8 divided by the implicit price deflator of GNP (see Table A–72, Appendix).

The fruits of the output growth represented by the foregoing national accounts data were used primarily to obtain sizable increases in private and public consumption during the fifties. Despite a 29 percent increase in population between 1950 and 1960 private consumption per head (in prices of 1953) rose from Rs. 440

---

[7]Producer prices for food crops generally rose from 1950 up to 1952, then remained fairly stable over the remainder of the decade. The general trend of export prices, after the peaks of the early fifties, was downward.

to Rs. 525, or by nearly 20 percent.[8] Public consumption went up even faster, rising to almost two-and-a-half times its 1950 level by 1960. If sustainable, these would have been impressive long-run rates of improvement in living standards. Unfortunately, time was to demonstrate that these consumption increases had been prematurely realized. As will become clear in the following chapter, the long-run development of Ceylon's economy would have been better served if consumption gains during the fifties had been held to more modest proportions and a larger share of the increment in national output had been reinvested.

OUTPUT PER WORKER

The reader might well ask at this point how it was possible for output to rise faster than population in a period when the labor force was rising relatively slowly, when land resources had been pushed to the point of diminishing returns, when foreign markets for export products were not especially favorable, and when capital stock was not being augmented at a particularly impressive rate. The answer to the question is—and logically would have to be—that the economy experienced sufficient growth in output per unit of labor employed to keep total production rising at least a short distance ahead of population growth. How great were these productivity increases, in which sectors of the economy did they occur, and what were the causal mechanisms which brought them about?

Since estimates of income originating and employment by industry for the years 1950–60 have already been made (Tables A–8, Appendix and 5–2, respectively) it is now statistically possible to divide the first by the second and derive estimates of value added per man employed. The relative levels of productivity in the various parts of the economy and, to the extent that the data permit, the comparative rates of productivity growth by industry, should thus be revealed.

Table 6–5 gives the resulting view of productivity levels by industry. Although this table absorbs all the errors inherent in its two component tables, it does tell much about the structure of the economy in the fifties. In it, the highly capitalized, "modern" industries are easily identified by their high levels of value added per worker. Outstanding among these, as might be expected, is the electricity, water, and gas industry, where a high degree of capitalization is a virtual necessity. (The even higher level implied for construction is overstated; its employment denominator is too low, since it includes only those who do construction work as a pri-

---

[8]The figures in this paragraph are derived from Table A–3, Appendix.

TABLE 6-5

VALUE ADDED PER WORKER

(Average, 1950–60)*

Industry	Value Added per Worker (Rs.)
Agriculture, fishing, forestry	1,444
Tea and minor estate crops	1,364
Rubber	1,458
Coconut	3,999
Other	1,202
Mining and quarrying	536†
Manufacturing	786†
Construction	8,152‡
Electricity, gas, and water	7,350
Transport and communications	2,648
Wholesale and retail trade ⎰ Banking, insurance, and real estate ⎱	1,894
Ownership of dwellings	§
Public administration and defense	3,090
Services n.e.c.	1,518
All nonprimary industries	1,992
All industries	1,798

*Source: Value added by industry from Table A–8, Appendix; employment data are from Table 5–2, except that figures for the industries within the primary sector had to be revised. The breakdown between estate and other agriculture had to be altered to reflect *total* employment in the production of each of the major export crops, i.e., on smallholdings as well as estates. These new estimates along with notes on sources and methods, are given in the Appendix, pages 296–298.

†Even though there is reason to believe that mining and manufacturing are not so productive relative to other industries in Ceylon as in most countries (see text), these figures are implausibly low. It is quite possible that employment in these industries has been overstated, perhaps because of the prevalence of part-time employment in mining and handicrafts, and that the estimate of value added per worker has thus been depressed.

‡Overstated; see text.

§Not applicable; income originating in this "industry" is also excluded from the figures for all nonprimary industries and for all industries.

mary economic activity and excludes the thousands who are engaged in it on a part-time basis.) Export agriculture (especially rubber and coconuts, where the land-labor ratio is much higher than in tea) also appears in the table as a relatively productive industry. On the other hand, the mining and quarrying and manufacturing industries (the latter includes handicrafts) were still rather primitive affairs technologically in the fifties and had low value added per man; in the case of manufacturing, heavy reliance on imported raw materials is an additional possible explanation of the low productivity found.[9] As in most countries, value added per worker is higher in industrial and service activities taken as a

[9] Even so, the figures in the table are probably understatements; see footnote † to Table 6–5.

whole than in agriculture. But in Ceylon the ratio of productivity in agriculture to productivity in such industries is relatively high. Estate agriculture is obviously a "modern" industry and even "other" agriculture and primary activities yield about 60 percent as much value added per worker as the average for all nonagricultural activities together.

As Table 6–6 indicates, real output per worker rose by about one-fourth between 1950 and 1960. But this overall figure conceals marked variations in the rate of productivity growth over various segments of the period and among different sectors of the economy. Only tea—and, to a lesser extent, nonexport agriculture—experienced a really strong and steady growth of output per worker throughout the decade. Rubber and coconut enjoyed peaks during export booms in the early and middle parts of the decade, then stagnated. Since the real output of the individual nonagricultural industries cannot be measured (see pages 128–129) that whole large and amorphous sector must be treated as one. Its productivity growth pattern approximates that of agriculture taken as a whole, being more rapid than that of rubber or coconut cultivation but slower than that of tea or peasant agriculture, which emerge as the two most dynamic industries identifiable in these data. For the economy in the aggregate, a somewhat higher rate of increase is obtained than for either of the major sectors, by virtue of the fact that there has been some shift in the allocation of the work force: the proportion employed in primary activities, which have generally lower productivity levels, fell from 61.2 percent in 1950 to 55.7 in 1960.[10]

Thus it can be seen that rates of output and productivity growth have differed widely among industries. No simple pattern of stagnant and dynamic sectors is visible in these data, however. The markedly greater dynamism of the export sector which often held in the past is no longer evident. At the same time, no obvious tendency for new industrial activities to grow more rapidly than old agricultural pursuits has emerged. On the contrary, two of the most dynamic industries, tea cultivation and peasant agriculture, go far back into Ceylon's history. A closer look at the most important

---

[10]The mere fact that the *average* productivity of labor is higher in one sector (e.g., industry) than in another (e.g., agriculture) does not prove that the *marginal* productivity of labor is also higher, as it must be if a simple reallocation of labor from one sector to the other is to raise the average productivity level in the economy as a whole. In this case, however, productivity in all industries taken together rose more than productivity in either agricultural or nonprimary activities taken separately, so one can infer that not only the average but the marginal worker must also have been more productive in the nonagricultural sector.

ndustries seems to be required if one is to find out just what the causes of the new pattern of output and productivity growth which he economy has experienced have been.

TABLE 6-6

VALUE ADDED PER WORKER IN CONSTANT (1953) PRICES, 1950-60*

(Rupees)

Year	Agriculture, Fishing, and Forestry	Tea and Minor Estate Crops	Rubber	Coconut	Other Agriculture	Other Industries†	Total†
1950	1,380	1,094	1,750	3,884	1,193	1,443	1,517
1951	1,445	1,155	1,498	4,075	1,304	1,694	1,660
1952	1,496	1,183	1,411	4,299	1,374	1,596	1,654
1953	1,445	1,273	1,460	4,352	1,212	1,818	1,717
1954	1,585	1,306	1,487	4,129	1,499	1,637	1,719
1955	1,682	1,362	1,433	4,857	1,597	1,719	1,819
1956	1,520	1,333	1,382	4,630	1,326	1,433	1,609
1957	1,546	1,388	1,424	3,763	1,433	1,649	1,722
1958	1,609	1,435	1,518	3,940	1,518	1,744	1,799
1959	1,602	1,417	1,457	4,287	1,484	1,810	1,823
1960	1,713	1,476	1,495	4,106	1,685	1,857	1,713
Percentage increase, 1950-60:	24.1	34.9	−14.6	5.7	41.2	28.7	25.8

*Sources: Tables 5-2, 6-4, and A-8, and A-12, Appendix.
†Excludes income originating in ownership of dwellings.

EXPORT AGRICULTURE: TEA

As had been the case in the past, the growth of all of Ceylon's traditional export industries depended heavily on what happened to world demand. Foreign demand for each of these crops was viewed by the planters in terms of prices in the Colombo market.[11] Along with production costs and taxes, the level of the Colombo price for the commodity they produced determined the estates' profits. Profitability, in turn, determined their willingness to expand production. Although output was not easily varied in the short run regardless of price levels, steady long-run growth in output required that the general level of prices be satisfactory relative to costs and taxes; it was also desirable that it did not fluctuate too violently from year to year. To be sure, short-term price upswings did produce handsome profits, but if the price was expected to fall back to some (subjectively) normal level in the future, they afforded no incentive to expand output, aside from any limited increases

[11]Actually, much Ceylon produce is sold in other markets—e.g, London for tea and Singapore for rubber—but prices in these markets move very closely in line with Colombo prices.

which could be achieved immediately, in the few months over which prices might reasonably be expected to remain at boom levels.

It is often said that estate producers are at the mercy of world prices, a force which is completely beyond their control. This is true, but it is only part of the story: it is also correct to say that both the individual producer and the country which produces only a small share of the world's total supply of a commodity are offered great opportunities to benefit from their almost perfectly competitive position.[12] If they can work on the cost side of the profit equation and lower their production costs they can benefit from the fact that this will have little effect on price and most of the gains they make will be theirs to keep, rents accruing to the relatively more efficient producers. This benefit accrues only to the individual producer or nation which succeeds in lowering costs *relative to other producers;* if *all* producers cut costs together and demand does not change, prices will fall and everyone will lose (assuming the usual price inelastic world demand curve for primary products). But both individual estates and Ceylonese producers as a group can gain from relative cost reduction, regardless of the world price level. Their welfare and the amount which they can profitably produce thus depend not only on world prices, a force outside their control, but also on their ability to cut per unit costs and make an expansion of output profitable, something which is very much within their control.

Of the three main export crops, it was tea that experienced price movements which came closest to satisfying the criteria of a good environment for industry growth which have been outlined. With the freeing of the tea trade from its restrictive wartime shackles in the late forties, prices climbed to a level, in 1950, nearly twice the controlled wartime price.[13] As an article of final consumption and not an industrial raw material, tea did not share to any appreciable degree in the heady Korean boom enjoyed by rubber and coconut products. After a Rs. 2.11 per pound average price in 1950, three

---

[12]The role of atomistic seller on a highly competitive world market more neatly fits Ceylon's rubber and coconut producers than it does its tea industry. During the late 1940's and the 1950's Ceylon's approximate shares in total world exports (excluding re-exports) were 33 percent for tea, 5 percent for rubber, only 2 percent for copra, and 24 percent for coconut oil (Source: Food and Agricultural Organization of the United Nations, *Trade Year Books,* Rome, various years). Moreover, much of Ceylon's tea (the highgrown variety, accounting for about 40 percent of its total output) is significantly differentiated in quality from tea supplied by other major producers, like India, and thus to some extent has its own market.

[13]See Table A–73, Appendix.

TABLE 6–7

EXPORT TEA: PER UNIT VALUE, COST, TAXES, AND PROFIT*

(Rupees per Pound)

Year	F.O.B. Unit Value†	Minus: Costs‡	Before-Tax Profits§	Export Duty‖	Company Taxes#	After-Tax Profits
1946......	1.298	1.029	0.269	0.030	0.086	0.153
1947......	2.007	1.188	0.819	0.327	0.197	0.295
1948......	1.994	1.261	0.733	0.381	0.187	0.165
1949......	2.121	1.306	0.815	0.369	0.179	0.267
1950......	2.567	1.385	1.182	0.449	0.311	0.422
1951......	2.555	1.575	0.980	0.525	0.216	0.239
1952......	2.316	1.615	0.701	0.367	0.184	0.150
1953......	2.437	1.467	0.970	0.410	0.350	0.210
1954......	3.126	1.668	1.458	0.594	0.540	0.324
1955......	3.309	1.711	1.598	0.832	0.479	0.287
1956......	2.918	1.700	1.218	0.617	0.398	0.203
1957......	2.879	1.683	1.196	0.675	0.357	0.164
1958......	2.997	1.648	1.349	0.745	0.414	0.190
1959......	2.646	1.684	0.962	0.500	0.316	0.146
1960......	2.736	1.684¶	1.052	0.347	0.508	0.197

*This table attempts to estimate the value of a pound of exported tea and what happens to the proceeds. Returns to the tea industry from the local sale of tea are not considered.

†Export proceeds (source: Department of Commerce, *Thirty Years Trade Statistics of Ceylon (1925–1954)*; Department of Census and Statistics *Statistical Abstracts*) divided by export volume (source: *A.R.s of the Tea Controller*).

‡Ex-factory costs per pound of tea, as estimated by the Department of Census and Statistics from sample survey data (source: Department of Census and Statistics *Statistical Abstracts*), plus a 10 percent additional allowance to cover transportation and handling costs from factory to ship and taxes levied for health programs, tea research, etc.

§Unit value minus costs.

‖Source: Department of Commerce, *Thirty Years Trade Statistics of Ceylon (1925–1954)*; Department of Census and Statistics *Statistical Abstracts*; equals export duty collections divided by quantity exported.

#Profits remaining after costs and export duties have been subtracted from total export proceeds, *times* the prevailing rate of company taxation (including income tax on companies, profits tax, and—for early years—excess profits duty). This assumes all producers to be companies, of course; individuals pay taxes at various rates and no attempt has been made to adjust for this.

¶Provisional.

mediocre years ensued. With production costs inflated after Korea and taxes rising (see Table 6–7), profit margins sagged. However, output, adjusting with a lag to the 1950 price rise, continued to increase. As it turned out, this rising volume of output was a tremendous asset to the planters and the country, since in 1953 a strong upsurge of prices occurred and export proceeds swelled. The estates benefited through rising profits and the government through unprecedented tax collections. The good prices lasted, with only a little weakening, through mid-1956 and during this period tea virtually supported the economy. Thereafter prices fell from the prevailing average of Rs. 2.11 a pound to about Rs. 1.85, where they remained with remarkable steadiness for the rest of the decade.

TABLE 6–8

PRODUCTION, ACREAGE, EMPLOYMENT, AND PRODUCTIVITY IN TEA, 1946–60

Year	Production* (000 Lbs.)	Acreage†	Lbs. per Acre	Employment‡ (000s)	Lbs. per Employee
1946	282,911	551,370	531	536	528
1947	298,526	553,463	539	537	556
1948	298,791	554,578	539	538	555
1949	298,559	555,330	538	539	554
1950	306,215	558,304	548	544	563
1951	326,279	564,160	578	548	595
1952	316,842	569,648	556	520	609
1953	343,033	573,129	599	523	656
1954	366,738	574,877	638	545	673
1955	380,013	570,807	666	542	701
1956	375,578	567,785	661	547	687
1957	397,775	570,016	698	557	714
1958	413,155	571,640	723	559	739
1959	413,130	576,179	717	566	730
1960	434,709	580,736	749	576	755

*Source: *A.R.s of the Tea Controller*.
†*Ibid.*
‡See Table A–12, Appendix.

Production, meanwhile, continued to rise at an annual rate of about four percent and export receipts increased accordingly.

Aside from these price trends the other determinants of the industry's financial well-being between 1946 and 1960 were movements in per unit cost levels and government tax policies. On the former score, a considerable degree of success was enjoyed in industry cost control. Quite rapid increases in cost per pound were recorded during the worldwide inflation of the late 1940's and early 1950's, amounting to more than 50 percent through the Korean period. Thereafter, however, it proved to be possible to increase the productivity of the resources employed in the industry fast enough to prevent any significant rise in unit costs. The average hourly earnings of labor employed in the industry, which form the main element of cost in so labor-intensive an industry, rose from Rs. 0.18 in 1948 to Rs. 0.26 in 1951 by virtue of the prosperity of the late forties and early fifties. Since then they have been held firmly in place through the government's dominance of the wages boards system of wage determination and by 1960 they had risen only to Rs. 0.30.[14] Meanwhile, output per worker was rising (see Table

[14]See Table A–29, Appendix. Wage determination in Ceylon's largest industries, which is handled through tripartite "wages boards," is often more easily explained with reference to political than to market criteria. During the 1948–51 period the living costs of tea estate workers rose by some 10 to 15

6-8) and average weekly hours were falling somewhat. What emerged was an approximately constant per unit margin on a rising volume of production. This would have generated enormous profits had it not been for the government policy of appropriating through taxation large proportions of any increases in receipts, whether generated by price increases, volume increases, or cost reductions. Export duties were frequently adjusted to allow for price changes and the rate of company taxtion went steadily and steeply upward, just doubling between 1946 and 1960. The government thus raised its share of before-tax profits to more than 80 percent.[15] Profit rates on sales were forced downward and aggregate profits did not rise despite the ever-increasing volume of exports.

Despite the limited opportunities for profit which government tax policies left them, tea producers managed to write an impressive record of industry growth. Thanks largely to the gradual adoption of a series of technical improvements (see pages 138–140), output grew steadily—in the aggregate, per acre cultivated, and per worker employed. Table 6-8 summarizes these achievements. It shows output rising at an average annual rate of about three percent and rising very steadily, almost regardless of price trends, the weather, or other factors which have a major influence on the output of most crops. The absence of sharp year-to-year fluctuations is largely attributable to the technical qualities of tea cultivation which encourage long-run profit maximization and make any response to short-term stimuli difficult (see Chapter 2, pages 36–37). The fact that output grew at all is striking, however, especially in view of the fact that from 1946 to 1960 acreage increased by only 5.3 percent and employment by a mere 7.5 percent. Almost all the increase in output can thus be attributed to productivity increases, which are reflected in Table 6-8 by virtually equiproportional rises in output per acre and output per man. What explains these rises?

---

percent and it was thought equitable to compensate them for this increase; in addition, the generous profit levels enjoyed by the estate companies were considered adequate to merit a rise in real wages for the work force and money wages were raised by 45 percent overall. By contrast, after 1951 no such case could be made on equity grounds. Moreover, most tea estate workers, being Indian Tamils, were disenfranchised during the early 1950's and their unions thus lost political power. Government policy generally opposed wage increases and hourly earnings went up by only about 15 percent from 1951 to 1960. Since there were some slight increases in living costs over this period, real wages rose by even less.

[15]See Table 5–5. The proportions in the table all depend on an assumption of infinitely elastic demand for Ceylon tea. Actually, of course, demand is less than perfectly elastic, so some of the tax is paid by the consumer and does not really come out of producer profits. To the extent that this is true, the percentage rate of taxation on producers is reduced.

Ceylon's tea industry has remained basically an estate industry. If anything, the only major organizational change which took place, the widespread purchases of former British estates by Ceylonese— the share of sterling companies and non-Ceylonese individuals in total acreage declined from well over half to about 40 percent[16]— appears to have led to some drops in yields.[17] Part of the reason for these declines in efficiency was that a certain amount of subdivision of estates took place subsequent to their sale. There are tremendous variations among tea holdings in yield per acre, with the larger, better managed estates often achieving yields twice as large as those on the smallholdings and smaller "estates" of under 100 acres.[18] Accordingly, it became necessary for the government to step in and arrest the trend toward subdivision. It is also likely that at least temporary reductions in the level of managerial skill had something to do with the yield declines which took place. Despite these changes in ownership and management, however, striking increases in efficiency were registered over the period 1946–60 as a whole. What accounts for the generally rising yields is the willingness of producers, within the limits of profitability, to accept technical innovations and the fact that such innovations became available at a fairly impressive rate over the period in question.

Perhaps the most important yield-raising factor is the greatly increased use of fertilizer, especially as compared with the shortage years during and immediately after the war. Ceylon as a whole immensely increased its fertilizer consumption between 1946 and 1960 (see Table 6–9) and while it is not possible to say just what proportion of the additional fertilizer went into tea, it is certain that the industry was in the vanguard of the new trend.[19] Table 6–9 shows that fertilizer consumption increased most during periods of export boom (in 1951 and again in 1954–55), when it offered one of the few ways to get quick increases in estate output. But there is also a strong upward secular movement, indicating that even

---

[16]See Table A–38, Appendix.

[17]An unpublished survey made by the Central Bank of Ceylon suggested that this was generally the case.

[18]The 1952 Census of Agriculture showed a yield of 642 pounds of made tea per acre for the modern estates (defined as those which were 20 acres or more in extent, had 10 or more resident laborers, and had its census schedule filled out in English), which implied an average of only 335 pounds per acre for the rest of the industry. See Department of Census and Statistics, *Census of Agriculture 1952. Part I, Tea Plantations.*

[19]Data supplied the Tea Controller's Department suggest that perhaps half the total—and probably more than half of the increment of recent years—goes into tea.

after each boom receded estate superintendents found it profitable to continue to use fertilizer in larger quantities than prior to the boom.

TABLE 6–9

IMPORTS OF THE MAIN ARTIFICIAL FERTILIZERS, 1946–60*
(Thousand Cwts.)

Year	Sulfate of Ammonia	Super-phosphates	Muriate of Potash
1946	591	24	135
1947	881	68	150
1948	946	2	111
1949	1,087	10	259
1950	996	14	371
1951	1,726	10	482
1952	1,027	18	242
1953	1,459	34	440
1954	1,792	47	588
1955	.....	...	...
1956	1,951	69	918
1957	2,428	161	767
1958	1,953	26	702
1959	2,841	65	852
1960	2,577	19	781

*These are actually the most important fertilizer materials. None of them are produced in Ceylon, although the mixing of them into prepared fertilizer is done there. Source: Department of Commerce, *Thirty Years Trade Statistics of Ceylon (1925–1954)*, Part I; Department of Census and Statistics, *Statistical Abstracts*.

Aside from increased fertilizer use, the other important productivity-raising factor was the technical work done by the government's Tea Research Institute in developing new strains of tea, improving production methods, and taking preventative action against diseases and pests. Perhaps the most serious natural threat faced by the industry during this period was the outbreak of blister blight, a fungus which was first noticed in Ceylon in 1946. Experiments carried out by the Tea Research Institute suggested a copper solution as the best disease-preventing device and a vigorous campaign by planters and the government succeeded in bringing the menace under control by 1952. Despite the impressive level of estate technology which had been reached in the past, a number of modifications in planting technique suggested by the Institute also played an important role in the productivity increases of the 1950's.

It can be surmised that adoption of the various improved techniques had by 1960 not spread much beyond the circle of the largest and most up-to-date plantations. And in the case of the new strains of tea, which were potentially the most important contribution of the Tea Research Institute, even these most advanced segments of the industry proved to be hard to persuade. By 1956 the Institute had perfected strains which, when grown with generous quantities of fertilizer, could yield 2,000 pounds or more of made tea per acre —this at a time when the industry's average yield was only 661 pounds.[20] In most cases, the estates were still tending their original tea bushes. Replanting was called for, since tremendous gains were evidently realizable (although not all plots could achieve 2,000 pounds per acre; this yield was possible only under nearly ideal conditions). But the prospective cost was staggering. In materials and labor alone it amounted to something between Rs. 2,000 and Rs. 6,000 an acre.[21] And the cost in terms of the output which would have to be foregone during the replanting process was even greater. Two years of a soil-reconditioning grass crop normally had to intervene between the uprooting of the old tea and the planting of the new. Then, once the new tea was planted it would be a further three to five years before anything approaching full bearing was reached. Based on 1956 prices and per acre yields, this might mean a revenue loss of from Rs. 6,000 to Rs. 10,000 per acre. On the other hand, the fall in productivity connected with the aging of the tea bush had proved to be very gradual and in fact, as has been seen, was being offset easily by increased fertilization and improved techniques. This lessened the incentive to replant still further and it is not surprising that the planters were reluctant to enter into so costly a process for gains which it would take so long to realize.

Very little replanting was done until the advent of the government's replanting and rehabilitation subsidy schemes. Only with the passage by Parliament of these new subsidy provisions in late 1958 did the refurbishing of the industry begin at all. The government offered estates a replanting subsidy of Rs. 2,500 an acre, to be paid in six instalments at various stages of the uprooting, reconditioning, and replanting operations. Clearly, this by no means covered all the costs of replanting, but it did make a start (by 1958 prices were down but yields were up since 1956, leaving the value of output foregone in replanting perhaps a bit lower, say Rs. 5,000 to Rs. 9,000). The goal of the scheme was to replant a total of 30,000 acres with high-yielding clones during the first six years of its operation, but by the end of 1960 only 3,074 acres had been uprooted for replanting and a mere 1,129 had actually been

[20]See *A.R. of the Tea Controller* for 1956, p. 8.
[21]*Ibid.*

replanted with the new varieties.[22] The tea controller, reporting on this disappointing performance, blamed the shortage of the new plants available for replanting and the general lack of experience of planters and officials with replanting (this was the first major tea replanting to be attempted anywhere in the world). In fact, however, the relatively modest amount of the subsidy, the fact that prices rose slightly between 1958 and 1960, the continuing climb of per acre productivity, and the extreme reluctance of the European estates to trade present output for future output in what they considered a hazardous political environment were probably more important factors.

Much more seriously in need of rehabilitation than the estates were the smallholdings. Smallholders numbered about 87,000 in 1954 and controlled some 12 percent of industry acreage, which they worked by methods vastly less efficient than those employed by the estates.[23] In addition to the inadequacy of their technical information, the smallholders also had serious problems relating to market structure. They lacked adequate sources of credit to finance the purchase of fertilizer and to retrieve themselves from their perennial indebtedness to the estate factory owners who processed their tea. Government policy was to attack both the technical and the market problems through a scheme of cooperatives, which were to disseminate materials and information and operate processing factories. But by 1957 only 25 Tea Producers' Co-operative Societies had been founded. With the advent of the Tea Replanting Subsidy Scheme, intended to enhance estate output, a new start was made with the smallholdings as well. More than replanting the smallholders needed a general improvement in production practices, as well as an increase in the stand of tea bushes per acre. For them, the Tea Rehabilitation Subsidy Scheme was launched, offering subsidies of Rs. 300, 100, and 250 per acre respectively for increasing the stand, improving conservation methods, and buying fertilizer. The goal was to rehabilitate some 30,000 acres in 6 years. By the end of 1960 (that is, after 2 years of the scheme) some 9,000 acres had been supplied with additional plants and about 13,000 had received the subsidy for soil conservation.[24] Moreover, permits had been issued for thousands of additional acres and work under the scheme was accelerating rapidly. The drive to bring standards of operation on smallholdings closer to estate levels thus appeared to be going well.

---

[22]*A.R. of the Tea Controller* for 1960, p. 43.
[23]*A.R. of the Tea Controller* for 1957, p. 9.
[24]*A.R. of the Tea Controller* for 1960, p. 45.

It should be clear from what has been said here that the Replanting and Rehabilitation Subsidy Schemes will in time effect substantial increases in the productive capacity of Ceylon's tea industry. Yet it is equally obvious that through 1960 their net effect on output must have been nil, even negative. They could thus have made no contribution to the sizable increases in output and productivity recorded between 1946 and 1960. It is really impossible, however, to account in a completely satisfactory way for all the sources of productivity change in tea (or, for that matter, in any industry). Some of the observed increase in output per employee and per acre is attributable to the application of new techniques and the rest simply to more intensive use of resources in conjunction with previously known technology. The percentage share assignable to each is very hard to spell out. In the case of tea, increased fertilizer use and the adoption of new production techniques developed by the Tea Research Institute obviously made important contributions to rising productivity but how much of the credit they deserve one cannot say precisely. In this connection it is worth noting that foreign estate owners had a threat of nationalization hanging over them in the late 1950's and even though the government later denied repeatedly that it contemplated any takeover in the immediate future it has been rumored that some estate companies responded by intensifying production so as to use up capital and evade the restrictions on capital repatriation through increasing profit remittances. Clearly this phenomenon, if important, calls into question the legitimacy of some of the productivity rises in tea, but just how widespread the practice has been one cannot say.

In relation to the substantial increases in output per worker which took place, employment trends in the industry are worth a bit of attention. Total employment in the industry, which is the island's leading employer, rose by only 40,000 or so at a time when 150,000,000 pounds of made tea were added to annual production. Part of the rise in output per employee is attributable to the fact that the structure of employment in the industry underwent a considerable shift. The proportion of work alloted to children fell sharply but the share done by women went up, leaving men with a reduced percentage of the industry's employment, though there were about 25,000 more male workers employed in 1960 than in 1950. The number of managerial, technical, clerical, and other non-laboring jobs in the industry underwent a substantial increase, but these remained only a small percentage of the total. As a provider of national income and foreign exchange tea thus did a far better job than as a provider of new employment. Technical improvement in the industry appears to have been neutral as regards the use of labor and land as productive inputs—i.e., the labor-land ratio was substantially the same in 1960 as it had been in 1950.

TABLE 6–10

THE STRUCTURE OF TEA EMPLOYMENT, 1950–60*

(Thousands)

Year	Managerial, Technical, Clerical, etc.	Men	Workers Women	Children†	Total Employment
1950	8	231	234	59	532
1951	8	226	229	54	516
1952	8	232	240	49	530
1953	8	234	243	40	526
1954	8	240	246	37	531
1955	11	241	254	34	539
1956	11	244	259	32	547
1957	13	246	264	32	555
1958	13	248	266	28	555
1959	13	250	269	20	551
1960	13	256	275	16	560

*Refers to employment reported under the Wages Board Ordinance. These totals include some employment on cocoa, cardamom, and pepper estates, as well as rubber workers on estates which produce both tea and rubber; they are not comparable to the totals in Table 5–2. Minor discrepancies are attributable to rounding.

†Defined as males below the age of 16 and females below 15.

Source: *A.R.s of the Commissioner of Labour.*

EXPORT AGRICULTURE: RUBBER

If all three of the major estate industries had done as well as tea in the late forties and fifties the economic history of the period would have had to be written quite differently. But for rubber and coconut the situation was not so favorable. The wartime development of a synthetic rubber industry in the United States had demonstrated that the future of the world's natural rubber industry, especially in the debilitated form in which it emerged from the slaughter tapping (in some parts of the world) or neglect (in others) of the war years, was dim. And in the more immediate future, the disappearance of the military component of world demand and the release of previously accumulated American stockpiles depressed prices. The year 1949 marked the nadir of the postwar slump; in that year the average Colombo price of RSS No. 1 sheet fell to Rs. 0.57 a pound, after a wartime peak of Rs. 0.98.[25]

---

[25]See Table A–73, Appendix.

Output, too, was off—about ten percent below the wartime level. With the sudden outbreak of war in Korea, the picture changed drastically. Colombo market prices soared to Rs. 1.55 per pound in 1950 and Rs. 2.15 in 1951. Production responded quickly, hitting a high of 254,000,000 pounds in 1950, a figure which exceeded both the previous record and, incidentally, anything which has been achieved since. Output per acre and per man also rose sharply as trees which had been left idle since World War II were brought back into production. But for Ceylon the Korean episode was disappointingly short-lived. By 1952 the price was back down to Rs. 1.38 per pound and the trend since that year has been distinctly downward.

With demand from the Western industrial countries dropping off after Korea, Ceylon was rescued from the worst effects of the slump by the sudden appearance on the scene of a new large buyer. Communist China was in need of considerable quantities of natural rubber from an assured supply and in December, 1952 a bilateral trade agreement—the first of many for Ceylon—was signed. The agreement stipulated that Ceylon would sell China 50,000 metric tons of sheet rubber each year for the next 5 years. This quantity came to almost the entire sheet rubber production of the island and over half of its current production of all types of rubber. In return, Ceylon was to import 27,000 tons of rice a year from China. The prices set for Ceylon's rubber—32d. a pound for grades 1, 2, and 3, 29d. for grades 4 and 5—were good and became especially attractive when offered as a one-year guarantee in a falling market. The price which Ceylon agreed to pay for Chinese rice, £54 a metric ton, was also favorable. In December, 1952, the rubber commissioner, acting as the purchasing agent of the government, began to buy sheet from producers at Rs. 1.35 a pound for shipment under the agreement.

During 1953 and 1954 prices continued their downward trend. In Ceylon, prices paid by the rubber commissioner to producers of sheet rubber remained constant while crepe prices, reflecting the world trend, fell. Crepe production fell relative to sheet. But in the second year of the agreement with China, Ceylon was forced to agree to a reduced price scale—28d. for grades 1, 2, and 3 and 25d. for grades 4 and 5. Still, China was paying a premium over the world market price. In late 1954, with prices still depressed, a further cut of 1d. per pound was negotiated. Then, in mid-1954, world prices suddenly recovered. A Ceylon delegation left at once for Peking. The Chinese agreed to continue buying Ceylon rubber at above-market prices and a formula was worked out: China was to pay a premium of 5d., 4d., or 3d. above the price in the Singapore market, depending on the level of that price (that is, the higher the free market price, the smaller the premium paid by China). In the following year the formula was retained but the premiums were cut (they now ranged between 1d. and 4½d.). When a new five-year agreement was signed in 1957 the premium paid by China, which had been ebbing away slowly for five years, disappeared entirely. The new pact, which came into effect in January, 1958, called for a minimum annual exchange of Rs. 95,-000,000 worth of goods in each direction, including at least 30,000 metric tons of rubber bought by China and 200,000 metric tons of rice imported by Ceylon. Although the Ceylon delegation naturally pleaded for the continuation of some price premium, the Chinese steadfastly declined to grant one, using the argument that they could not afford to set a precedent which could be used as a talking point by other countries (notably Indonesia) with which they might enter into similar agreements.[26] In lieu of a premium, China established an aid program, which would give Ceylon Rs. 15,000,000 a year for the 5-year life of the agreement. On the basis of 30,000 metric tons a year, this aid was equivalent to a price premium of Rs. 0.23 (4d.) per pound.

The second agreement with China remained in effect through the end of the decade. Its adherence to world prices and the greatly reduced volume of rubber exported reduced the advantages of the agreement to Ceylon, but it still remained a saving grace for Ceylon producers. China continued to be the leading purchaser of Ceylon rubber.

Meanwhile, in the free market, the familiar ups and downs had continued. Prices surged upward in 1955 and 1956, then plunged precipitously. With an average Colombo price for grade 1 sheet of Rs. 0.93, 1958 was the worst year since 1949. Some recovery took place in the following year, but there was scant cause for optimism at the decade's end. A spectre haunted the world market for natural rubber—synthetic production, which increased every year and was rapidly approaching the world total for natural rubber production. Ceylon's exports to the United States—once its leading customer but by now the world's greatest synthetic producer—fell. More and more, sales had to be directed toward those countries which had rubber-using industries but little synthetic production so far; this meant largely the Communist bloc. By 1960 the world price for natural rubber was well on its way toward Rs. 1.00 per pound, a

---

[26]See *A.R. of the Rubber Controller* for 1957, p. 11; these Administration Reports are the main source for this description of the workings of the China rice-rubber agreements.

crisis level for most producers. It was becoming increasingly apparent that unless costs could be cut substantially the industry was doomed.

TABLE 6–11

EXPORT RUBBER: PER UNIT VALUE, COST, TAXES, AND PROFIT*

(Rupees per Pound)

Year	F.O.B. Unit Value†	Costs‡	Before-Tax Profits§	Export Duty‖	Company Taxes#	After-Tax Profits
1946	0.995	....	....	0.025	....	....
1947	0.748	....	....	0.001	....	....
1948	0.688	....	....	—	....	....
1949	0.629	....	....	—	....	....
1950	1.530	....	....	0.069	....	....
1951	2.534	....	....	0.332	....	....
1952	1.760	0.974	0.786	0.214	0.316	0.256
1953	1.544	0.993	0.551	0.154	0.248	0.149
1954	1.360	1.035	0.325	0.153	0.107	0.065
1955	1.578	1.068	0.510	0.166	0.214	0.130
1956	1.581	1.058	0.523	0.285	0.158	0.080
1957	1.453	0.963	0.490	0.291	0.136	0.063
1958	1.253	0.877	0.376	0.237	0.096	0.043
1959	1.455	0.886	0.569	0.221	0.234	0.114
1960	1.620	0.886 ¶	0.734	0.224	0.367	0.143

*The table tries to estimate what happens to the proceeds from a pound of exported rubber. Latex exports and local sales of rubber, both minor items, are excluded.
†Export proceeds divided by export volume; source: Department of Commerce, *Thirty Years Trade Statistics of Ceylon (1925–1954)*; Department of Census and Statistics, *Statistical Abstracts*.
‡Footnote ‡ to Table 6–7 applies here, too.
§Unit value minus costs.
‖Source: Department of Commerce, *Thirty Years Trade Statistics of Ceylon (1925–1954)*; Department of Census and Statistics, *Statistical Abstracts*.
#See footnote # to Table 6–7.
¶Provisional.

The survival of the industry in the 1950's was largely attributable to successful cost control. What data there are (see Table 6–11) show a declining trend in cost per pound late in the decade. The decline was associated with a stabilized industry wage level[27] and some slight rises in productivity. The latter represented early returns on a dramatic reformation of the industry undertaken in the late fifties, of which more presently. Up to 1960, however, the industry profit rates before taxes ran a bit lower than those in the tea industry. These before-tax earnings were taxed, through export duties and company taxation, at much the same rate as tea profits,

---

[27]Average hourly earnings in rubber rose more than tea wages through 1953, from Rs. 0.18 an hour to Rs. 0.34, but thereafter they ceased to go up. The 1960 figure was Rs. 0.33. See Table A–29, Appendix.

so after-tax earnings were lower, too, running consistently less than ten percent of sales after 1952. As with tea, variations in efficiency among producing units were wide (this was even more true in rubber, where smallholders formed an important part of the industry) and many small operations must have been running at a loss, just managing to cover their variable costs. Had it not been for the promised benefits of replanting, the industry would have been in a very serious plight by 1960. Table 6–11 gives an estimate of the financial results for the fifties (see also Table 5–5, page 114).

Table 6–12 summarizes the physical performance of the industry through 1960. Output, employment, and total land input showed no secular trend at all over this 15-year span. Only in the decline of acres in bearing and the rise in yield per bearing acre does one sense the beginnings of the industry's rejuvenation. The 1960 yield of 418 pounds per bearing acre had been matched or exceeded in the past, but only when very attractive world prices induced intensive tapping; this latest high-yield figure, by contrast, reflected the beginning of production from newly planted high-yielding clones and foretold much better yields in the future.

TABLE 6–12

RUBBER: OUTPUT, ACREAGE, EMPLOYMENT, AND YIELD, 1946–60

Year	Production* (000 Lbs.)	Acreage† Total	Acreage† Bearing	Lbs. per Acre Total	Lbs. per Acre Bearing	Employ- ment‡ (000s)	Lbs. per Employee
1946	210,560	635,251	610,578	331	345	194	1,085
1947	199,360	634,142	418,432	314	476	190	1,049
1948	212,800	633,215	624,765	336	341	190	1,120
1949	200,480	629,450	568,484	319	353	189	1,061
1950	254,240	655,225	617,225	388	412	192	1,324
1951	235,200	655,501	617,001	359	381	207	1,136
1952	216,160	656,879	615,583	329	351	202	1,070
1953	220,886	657,427	608,802	336	363	200	1,104
1954	210,414	659,209	604,175	319	348	187	1,125
1955	210,179	660,985	581,866	318	361	194	1,083
1956	209,191	659,247	568,970	317	368	204	1,025
1957	219,887	660,725	550,443	333	399	203	1,083
1958	224,439	664,836	541,219	338	415	195	1,151
1959	205,397	668,178	519,706	307	395	186	1,104
1960	217,898	668,948	521,832	326	418	192	1,135

*Source: *A.R.s. of the Rubber Controller.*

†Bearing acreage excludes areas which have been newly planted or replanted within the previous six years and areas which are left untapped. The figures for 1950 and later years are official estimates of the rubber controller, while those for the earlier period are made by the author on the basis of statistics on new planted, replanted, and untapped extents (the latter data are a bit weak, so the estimates before 1950 are less reliable than those after). Source: *A.R.s. of the Rubber Controller.*

‡See Table A–12, Appendix.

As far back as 1947 a committee appointed to investigate the situation had reported that some 175,000 acres of Ceylon's rubber trees were uneconomic by reason of their being past their most productive age.[28] In view of this, a replanting program was urged. But with prices depressed and long-term prospects hazy estate owners were not prepared to act on this recommendation. Nor did the government seem ready to offer sufficient inducement. Then, when prices rose sharply in 1950–51, producers continued to be uninterested in replanting, instead concentrating on very heavy tapping of their trees to maintain present output. As a consequence, more and more trees approached a state of exhaustion. In his 1951 report the rubber commissioner estimated that the uneconomic acreage had risen to about 200,000 acres.[29] Now, with prices falling, producers professed themselves interested in replanting but unable to afford it. In 1953 the government stepped in with the Rubber Replanting Subsidy Scheme.

Under the new scheme a subsidy was offered amounting to Rs. 700 per acre for large estates (100 acres or more), Rs. 900 for small estates (10-100 acres) and Rs. 1,000 for smallholders (less than 10 acres) to replant with high-yielding varieties developed by the Rubber Research Institute. The subsidy was to be paid in instalments, so as to ensure proper execution of all the operations connected with replanting: clearing the land, new planting, and care of the young trees for the six years or so before they begin bearing. Each stage was to be inspected by the Rubber Controller's Department. The initial program was to run for five years and replant 65,000 acres. However, the response of producers was much more enthusiastic than had been anticipated and by the end of the fifth year (1957) over 90,000 acres had already been replanted under the subsidy scheme.[30]

A second five-year scheme was inaugurated. Its more ambitious goal was to replant a further 110,000 acres and thus virtually eliminate the island's uneconomic acreage. By the end of 1960, with two years still to go on the second five-year scheme, a total of 151,043 acres had been replanted.[31] In terms of extent replanted the scheme had been a huge success. This was seven years after the start of the first subsidy scheme and the first trees planted under it were just coming into bearing. As has been seen, however, the

[28]E. W. Whitelaw and S. F. H. Perera, *Report on the Rubber Industry of Ceylon* (S.P. XVIII of 1947).

[29]*A.R. of the Rubber Controller* for 1951, p. 11.

[30]*A.R. of the Rubber Controller* for 1959, p. 39.

[31]*A.R. of the Rubber Controller* for 1961, p. 46.

greatly improved yields which were made technically possible by replanting had barely begun to show themselves. Still, a sound foundation had been laid for the industry's future and the advent of attractive prices could be expected to call forth record crops.

The first five-year scheme was paid for by the producers themselves, through an addition to the export duty on rubber.[32] Toward the end of the first five-year period, in late 1957, the precipitous fall in prices and the ensuing complaints of producers led to the suspension of this special levy. In any case, the Rs. 15,000,000 of economic aid to be received from China during the 1958–62 period had been granted for the specific purpose of financing the second rubber replanting scheme. It was estimated that the cost of the second five years of replanting would be Rs. 20,000,000 a year and that the government would make up the Rs. 5,000,000 not covered by Chinese aid out of general revenues; the estimate turned out to be substantially correct.

Thus after some years of trying Ceylon achieved striking success during the late 1950's in inducing planters to replant their overage rubber with the new high-yielding strains. Actually, it was the severe productivity-reducing effects of senility which forced the planters to this step, leaving them only the choices of replanting or getting out of the industry. In view of the doubtful prospects of natural rubber, one might indeed ask whether the latter alternative might not have been preferable. Certainly it was in the national interests of China, still far away from self-sufficiency through synthetic rubber production and desirous of realigning Ceylon's foreign trade toward the Communist bloc, to subsidize this commitment. But was it in Ceylon's best interest? The complete returns are not yet in, but many technical experts are now saying that replanted natural rubber should be able to compete successfully with synthetic production and if this is so Ceylon was definitely right in moving to assure its share of world output.

EXPORT AGRICULTURE: COCONUT

The postwar story for coconut products draws elements from the experience of both tea and rubber. Like tea prices, the prices of coconut products on the world market rose substantially in the late forties. Like rubber prices, they reached completely unpre-

---

[32]The fact that the producers themselves paid for the subsidy program suggests that the whole affair might have been left to estate initiative. However, by taxing all producers and returning the tax in the form of a subsidy only to those estates which replanted the government created a more powerful incentive to replant than would have existed otherwise.

cedented heights during 1950 and 1951 and then suffered a steep plunge in 1952. Thereafter, world prices for coconut products shared with rubber prices a tendency to vary sharply from year to year, while not showing the downward trend taken by rubber prices. In general, then, the pattern of price changes for coconut products was less favorable than that of tea, though it was considerably less dismal than that of rubber.

TABLE 6–13

Coconuts: Output, Employment, and Productivity, 1946–60*

Year	Estimated Output† (000,000 Nuts)	Estimated Employment‡ (000s)	Output per Man (000 Nuts)
1946	1,361	67	20.3
1947	1,339	71	19.2
1948	1,765	76	23.2
1949	1,763	81	21.8
1950	1,877	86	21.8
1951	2,129	93	22.9
1952	2,344	97	24.2
1953	2,223	91	24.4
1954	2,159	93	23.2
1955	2,485	91	27.3
1956	2,391	92	26.0
1957	1,965	93	21.1
1958	1,836	83	22.1
1959	2,099	87	24.1
1960	1,964	85	23.1

*Data for coconuts are of a generally lower quality than those for tea or rubber. The last estimate of total acreage was made in 1946. An educated guess is that the area planted has changed little since that time, so output per acre must have followed a path much like that of estimated output.

†Reconstructed from exports and estimated domestic use. Source: Department of Census and Statistics.

‡See Table A–12, Appendix.

However, Ceylon coconut producers showed an inability to benefit from their not unfavorable environment. Profits during the occasional price upsurges were limited by the fact of short-term supply inelasticity, which meant that the maximum production effort was mistimed, coming only after prices fell to or below previous levels.[33] Similarly, the industry showed inflexibility in its response to longer-run problems. During the late 1950's the coconut industry came increasingly under a shadow: the approaching senility of many of its trees. Attemps to forestall the problem were only par-

---

[33] See Table 5–6, Chapter 5, for what fragmentary financial data there are on the industry.

tially successful (see below). Export volume, which had climbed steadily during the late forties and early fifties, stopped rising and then, by the latter part of the decade, began to dip below levels of previous years. Part of the reason for the decline in exports was the rapid growth of the local market (Ceylonese, whose numbers were of course increasing rapidly, consume some 110 coconuts per head annually), but total output, too, dropped off, far more than demand conditions justified (see Table 6–13). This fact reflected the mounting problems of the industry.

Why did output drop? Coconut production is much more of a smallholders' affair than tea or even rubber and this fact provides part of the answer. The agricultural census of 1952 revealed that only about 25 percent of coconut acreage was located on estates and only 17.1 percent on estates of 100 acres or more.[34] Similarly, it indicated that only 20,000 acres out of a total slightly greater than 1,000,000 were under corporate rather than individual ownership.[35] This is preeminently an industry composed of villagers' smallholdings and the even tinier town and village gardens which surround most low-country houses. Yet the census of agriculture suggested that while large estates did enjoy a measurable advantage in yield per acre over small estates it was a relatively unimportant one; moreover, the small estates themselves apparently had yields which were no higher than those of the smallholdings.[36]

The structure of the industry must bear some responsibility, however, for getting coconut production into the plight in which it found itself in the 1950's. Coconut producers had paid scant attention to fertilizing and other methods of raising yields and in particular had never made a practice of regularly replacing worn-out trees with new ones. By the 1950's more than half the island's trees had passed the age of 50 and were well beyond their period of maximum productivity.[37] In 1956 the government launched an at-

---

[34]See Table A–39, Appendix.

[35]See Table A–38, Appendix.

[36]The census indicated an average per acre yield of 2,117 nuts for estates of 100 or more acres, contrasted with only 1,850 on the smaller estates. But, on the basis of 1951 estimated output and 1946 acreage, the yield for the whole industry, including smallholdings, was 1,990; estimated smallholders' yields as a residual work out to an average of 2,028 nuts to the acre, actually more than the average yield on small estates. Of course, if any marked expansion of acreage occurred between 1946 and 1951 the smallholders' yields may be somewhat overestimated. Still, it is certain that coconut cultivation does not exhibit the wide productivity gap between estates and smallholdings that is evident in tea and rubber. See Department of Census and Statistics, *Census of Agriculture 1952*, Vol. 3. *Coconut Plantations*, p. 14.

[37]*Ibid.*, p. 11.

tempt to arrest the deterioration of the industry through the subsidized distribution of fertilizer and seedlings. Although the problems of the two industries were similar, it is clear that the incentives given to coconut producers to rehabilitate their lands were much smaller than those received by the rubber planters. The subsidies offset only a minute fraction of the costs of replanting, especially when the implicit cost of foregoing output for several years while the newly planted seedlings are maturing is taken into account. Just how much progress had been made by 1960 in terms of acres replanted is not certain, but in the late fifties enough seedlings were being distributed at subsidized prices to replant about 22,000 acres a year.[38] Thus not more than ten percent of the island's coconut acreage had been replanted by the end of the decade. The future of the industry, with poor practices continuing relatively unchecked and the march of senility perhaps checked but certainly not reversed, was not bright.

DOMESTIC PEASANT AGRICULTURE[39]

It is an intriguing deviation from simple stages-of-economic growth notions that one of Ceylon's most dynamic sectors in the 1950's—in terms of output and productivity and certainly in employment growth—should have been the "primitive" peasant agricultural sector. Yet consider the facts. The gross output of its primary crop, rice or paddy,[40] rose by two-and-a-half times from 1946 to 1960 (though the gross output of its other products rose more slowly).[41] The value of its contribution to GDP rose by 75 percent during the 1950's.[42] Value added per worker (in constant prices) went up by roughly 40 percent over the same period.[43] It employed, at this much higher level of productivity, about 245,000 more persons than

---

[38]About 1,300,000 seedlings were distributed in both 1959 and 1960. See Department of Census and Statistics, *Ceylon Year Book*, 1960, p. 66 and 1961, pp. 66-67.

[39]This sector is defined here so as to exclude all tea, rubber, and coconut production. Tea and rubber are consumed domestically only in minute quantities and produced mainly on estates, but coconut is a genuine borderline case. Since splitting output, income, etc. between estates and smallholdings, exports and domestic consumption, and so on can be difficult and arbitrary it is often convenient to assign an entire industry to one or the other group. Even though it has been treated here as an export industry and is not covered in the present section, coconut production has many of the characteristics of domestic peasant agriculture.

[40]The usual practice in Ceylon is to refer to the plant and the unhusked grain as paddy and only the husked grain as rice.

[41]See Table A–31, Appendix.

[42]See Table 6–4.

[43]See Table 6–6.

it had in 1946; it thus accounted for about 30 percent of the total increase in employment over the period.[44] All the data point to a dynamic sector, discovered in a most unlikely place. With the ancient cultural roots of paddy farming and the failure of the colonial economic system to bring the forces of the market to bear upon it, one would expect it to be a backward, stagnant sector. And at the end of World War II that is exactly what it was. This fact makes its rapid transformation in the postwar period all the more striking.

Several factors played a part in turning this ancient but long neglected part of the economy into a growth point, but basically the astonishing growth of peasant agriculture is a tribute to the sheer strength of market incentives. Fundamentally, paddy output grew so fast because producers were rewarded for their production by guaranteed purchase at prices which were not only unprecedented in past experience but represented a subsidy of approximately 50 percent over world market prices. Before a detailed account of how the subsidy scheme achieved its effect is presented, some background information on the Ceylon peasant's traditional crop should be sketched.

The question of paddy output is a complicated one, involving as it does hundreds of thousands of small peasant cultivators and a tangled web of social and economic problems: technology, knowledge, ancient custom, economic incentive, cooperative action, tenure relationships, law, and government administration. Starting with people, the great majority of the nearly 1,000,000 persons employed in peasant agriculture during the fifties spent at least part of their time cultivating paddy; the total number dependent in some way on paddy production—as dependents of paddy cultivators or as transporters, millers, etc. of paddy or as *their* dependents—must have numbered 4,000,000 or 5,0000,000.

In mode of production, paddy is strictly and undeniably a peas-

---

[44]See Table 5–2, Chapter 5. How productive was this additional labor? This is an interesting question but one which cannot be answered precisely for lack of evidence. At the same time as output per man was going up at a reasonably brisk pace the underemployment of labor in rural areas was also rising. Much of the apparent increase in employment may thus have made little contribution to the sector's output. If this is the case, then the actual rise in productivity—in terms of output per man-hour or output per effective man-equivalent—was far greater than is apparent in the aggregate data. The contribution of productivity increase to higher agricultural output was thus somewhat greater than the data suggest and the contribution of employment increase less. Also, of course, the rising underemployment in peasant agriculture meant that the overall record of the economy in providing jobs for the growing labor force was less good than it might appear at first glance.

ant crop. Despite a few unsuccessful experiments in the past, there is no large-scale production of the crop in Ceylon today. Plots are, almost without exception, very small. According to a survey carried out by a visiting FAO expert, based on the *Maha* crop[45] of 1953–54, about 36 percent of the parcels which form the actual working units were less than ½ acre in area; 45 percent fell into the one-half to one-and-a-half-acre range, 10 percent more centered around 2 acres, and fewer than 1 percent were greater than 10 acres in extent.[46] A corroborative view of the size distribution of plots was given by the 1946 census. Working with holdings rather than parcels (i.e., with the total extent worked by one man, tenant or owner, whether in a single geographically contiguous parcel or not), it obtained findings similar to those of the later study.[47] More than 60 percent of the holdings (which, however, represented only 22.8 percent of total paddy land) were of an acre or less. A third of the holdings and almost half the land were in the 1- to 5-acre class and the 1.1 percent of the holdings that the census found to be over 10 acres in extent accounted for 16.3 percent of the land. There are no comparable estimates for different years so it is impossible to substantiate one's suspicion that the average size of plot is slowly declining. The average holding was 1.2 acres in 1946 and the average parcel was 1.0 acre in 1953–54. This may be indicative of falling plot size, but basically what it shows is that the working units are smaller than the holdings as a result of the latter's fragmentation into noncontiguous plots.

Of the 771,908 paddy holdings enumerated in the census of 1946, 60.8 percent (representing 55.1 percent of the land) were owner cultivated.[48] Various tenancy arrangements regulated the cultivation of the remainder, but by far the commonest was the *ande* system, a sharecropping arrangement, often based on a nominal equal sharing of the crop by landlord and tenant ("nominal" because the tenant was commonly in debt to the landlord and thus ended up giving him more than half the output all told). In 1946 *ande* tenancy applied to about one-quarter of the holdings and land in paddy. Roughly half the remaining holdings, 6.8 percent of the total, were held on *thatumaru* basis—a system by which co-owners of a plot rotate its cultivation among themselves, the cultivator in any particular season receiving all the output. Other arrangements —lease for cash, cultivation by a hired worker, etc.—were less

---

[45]See page 155.
[46]See Table A–39, Appendix.
[47]*Ibid.*
[48]See Table A–38, Appendix.

common. The economic significance of the tenancy contract lies in the extent to which it inhibits production, either in the current season or—by discouraging land improvements—in future seasons. All in all, the inhibitions placed on the cultivator in Ceylon at this time were perhaps not so great as those often found in peasant cultivation elsewhere. The main favorable factor was the high percentage of owner-cultivated land. But where *ande* tenancy existed its effects were severely deleterious to efforts to obtain output above the minimum needed to sustain the cultivator's family; the need to share increments of production so generously with the landlord inhibited effort and also discouraged capital formation by the tenant, who often had no security of tenure. Nor was *thatumaru* much better; it gave no disincentive to greater production efforts in one's own year of cultivation, but the difficulty of deciding who should expend time and money to improve the plot must have been a sharply limiting factor on capital formation. The kind of tenancy which most encourages productive effort and land improvement—a fixed rent in money or kind, accompanied by a fairly long lease—was very rare.

Traditionally, paddy cultivation occupies a central position in village culture. It is *the* basic economic activity, around which a large part of the social and religious life of the villagers revolves. Thus, it is natural that the techniques of rice production should themselves have become highly traditionalized over the centuries. Paddy is grown throughout Ceylon. The pattern of cultivation varies somewhat, especially between the wet and dry zones, but something like the following can be taken as the traditional procedure. Two crops are grown each year: the *Maha* ("great") season, dependent on the northeast monsoon, which is sown sometime between July and November and harvested five or six months later, and the *Yala* ("lesser") season, which relies on the southwest monsoon, is usually sown between February and June, and is harvested in about four months (quicker, and therefore lower-yielding varieties are generally sown in *Yala*). In much of the dry zone there is little *Yala* cultivation, because of the absence of the southwest monsoon. Paddy cultivation takes place on "asweddumized" paddy land, that is, land which has been ridged in preparation for flooding. First, however, the earth is broken up; this is usually done with a crude wooden plow pulled by one or two bulls or buffaloes, but where the land is marshy or the cultivator very poor a man wielding the traditional mamoty (a large, heavy hoe) does the job. Water, either from irrigation works or rain, is then allowed to flow into the paddy field and stand for several days; at this time buffaloes may be driven through the field to break up the clods and muddy the water, the ideal being a uniform, soupy texture. Seed paddy, which has been saved from the previous crop, is allowed to germinate for about three days and then sown broadcast. After the young shoots rise to a height of six inches or so, water is permitted to flood the field, though care is taken to avoid drowning the plants. Within a month the paddy has reached a stage after which no more care need be given to it until the crop is ready to harvest. For three to five months there is hardly any work to be done, but when the time for harvest is reached all the labor available is needed to get the crop in quickly. The cultivator's whole family is enlisted and additional laborers may be hired on a cash or cooperative basis. The next step, threshing, typically takes place on a mat-covered hard dirt floor made in the middle of the field and is done by driving bullocks around and around a central post, letting their hooves separate the grain from the stalk (sometimes, when small amounts of paddy are involved, the threshing is done by human feet). Winnowing, the separation of the husk from the kernel, is accomplished simply by tossing the grain in the air, allowing the husk to blow away and the kernel to fall again to the floor. Now all that remains to be done is to measure the harvest and (where the plot has been tenant cultivated) divide it between the cultivator and the owner, who is sure to be present, either himself or in the person of a representative.[49]

One other possibly production-inhibiting circumstance surrounding traditional paddy cultivation deserves mention. The village economy has always been riddled with debt. The average cultivator is continually—and in some cases continuously—indebted to the village shopkeeper and often to his landlord as well. These lenders provide him with both consumption and production loans—at a traditionally usurious rate of interest—in the season preceding harvest, take a substantial part of the harvest in the form of a loan repayment when the time comes, and frequently renew their profitable lending business soon thereafter. When the inevitable happens and the presence of too little water—or too much (both are common occurrences in Ceylon)—ruins the crop, peasant indebtedness rises by leaps and bounds. Thus, the cultivator is frequently unable to build up a surplus to use for land development and, indeed, may

---

[49]Of the many accounts of traditional paddy culture that are available, the main source used here is a description of a small wet zone village by Bryce Ryan, and others, *Sinhalese Village* (Coral Gables, Florida: University of Miami Press, 1958), pp. 15–22.

TABLE 6–14

PADDY OUTPUT, ACREAGE, AND YIELD, 1946–60

Year	Output* (000,000 Bushels)	Area Sown† (000 Acres)	Yield‡ (Bushels per Acre Sown)
1946.............	17.2	....	....
1947.............	16.7	....	....
1948.............	18.7	....	....
1949.............	23.1	....	....
1950.............	22.0	1,066.0	20.6
1951.............	22.0	1,073.5	20.5
1952.............	28.9	1,161.9	24.9
1953.............	21.9	1,046.9	20.9
1954.............	31.1	1,253.8	24.8
1955.............	35.7	1,346.9	26.5
1956.............	27.5	1,203.6	22.8
1957.............	31.3	1,207.6	25.9
1958.............	36.6	1,382.2	26.5
1959.............	36.4	1,330.2	27.3
1960.............	43.0	1,468.4	29.4

*Equals the sum of the *Maha* and *Yala* crops harvested in a given calendar year; see Table A–32, Appendix.

†Equals acres sown in the *Yala* season plus acres sown in the *Maha* season. Source: Department of Census and Statistics, *Statistical Abstracts*.

‡Column 1 divided by column 2; yield is more commonly expressed in terms of bushels per acre *harvested;* not all of the acres on which paddy is sown are harvested (because of drought, flooding, etc.), so these yield figures are somewhat lower than those figured on the conventional basis. For the latter, see Table A–33, Appendix.

not even be able to obtain the tools and materials needed for the full exploitation of his land in the short run.[50]

It can be seen that traditional paddy cultivation in Ceylon follows very closely the standard pattern of peasant cultivation everywhere. All the common characteristics are there: small holdings, fragmentation of even these small holdings into still smaller working units, a technology which has come down virtually unchanged from the dawn of known time and is hallowed by traditional

---

[50]Do usurious village moneylenders inhibit productivity growth? Despite the many features of the system which are disadvantageous to the cultivator it is true that the traditional moneylender performs a valuable economic function: supplying working capital to the perenially illiquid cultivator. This service in itself may well *increase* the ability of the farmer to exploit his land productively. If, however, traditional moneylending is compared with the alterative government, cooperative, or private credit systems which might be devised to replace it, it is clear that it is productivity-inhibiting, since the credit it provides is more expensive and subject to quicker repayment than the funds which would be available through a reformed credit system. It is thus not the presence of the traditional moneylender *per se* but the absence of superior sources of credit which inhibits productivity growth.

usage,[51] tenancy arrangements which give the cultivator scant incentive to make lasting improvements on the land and little enough to strive for increased output in any given season, and an enmeshing web of indebtedness which keeps the cultivator from accumulating any sort of surplus and holds him perpetually in the power of his creditors, the village shopkeeper and the landlord.

Yet it is in this context that the remarkable output and productivity gains outlined in Table 6–14 were scored. How were these achievements made? For one thing, paddy cultivation in Ceylon was backward relative to paddy cultivation elsewhere in the world and this opened up the possibility of quick gains through the adoption of foreign techniques. The smallness of the country and the relatively high standard of literacy were other favorable factors. But all of these were merely permissive; the positive, dynamic force behind the output growth was a successful, multifronted government campaign, reinforced by potent price incentives.

One front in the campaign was technical. No scientific experimentation was needed to show that the adoption of various improved practices could raise yields enormously. Practices which were standard elsewhere—especially in Japan, where yields per acre were running about four times as high as those in Ceylon at this time—were scarcely employed at all in Ceylon. These included transplanting rather than broadcast sowing, the use of pure-line seed, row planting, harrowing, the use of insecticides, and even such basic operations as fertilizing and weeding. The Department of Agriculture and the Department of Food Production (later reorganized as the Department of Agrarian Services) embarked upon an intensive campaign of demonstration and propaganda. Attempts were made to persuade peasants to adopt several specific improved techniques and, beginning in 1954, a more ambitious campaign was launched to bring about a full-scale conversion to the Japanese method of cultivation,

. . . the special features of which are the selection of good seed, transplanting in wide-spaced rows so as to facilitate weeding and intercultivation, the use of heavy dressings of artificial fertilizer in two applications and the practice of mechanical weeding.[52]

The adoption of the Japanese method by a few of the more progressive cultivators where conditions were favorable (a sizable labor force is needed for the extremely labor-intensive trans-

---

[51]And even religion; religious rites accompany several of the steps in traditional paddy cultivation just described.

[52]A.R. of the Director of Agriculture for 1954, p. 7.

planting process and in some areas this cannot be obtained) produced striking results. By 1956 the Director of Agriculture was reporting yields ranging from 60 to 150 bushels per acre on land cultivated by the Japanese method, with an average of about 70 (this at a time when the all-island average was 30 bushels).[53] In 1957 it was estimated that 20,700 acres were being cultivated using the entire system.[54] But this was only a drop in the bucket, representing a mere 2.5 percent of the acreage sown in the 1957–58 *Maha* season. Even in regard to the piecemeal improvements, gains during the fifties were very limited (see Table 6–15). This bodes well for the future, since it shows how much potential for future gains remains to be realized, but it indicates that only a small proportion of the output and productivity gains observed up to 1960 can be explained by improved techniques.

TABLE 6–15

USE OF IMPROVED PRACTICES, MAHA 1959–60 AND YALA 1960*

| | *Maha* 1959/60 | | *Yala* 1960 | |
	Extent (Acres)	% of Total	Extent (Acres)	% of Total
Transplanting in rows............	8,968	1.0	2,633	0.5
Transplanting, not in rows.......	54,899	6.0	7,447	1.4
Sowing in rows.................	19,100	2.1	9,360	1.7
Harrowing.....................	6,552	0.7	4,874	0.9
Pure-line seed.................	59,800	6.5	23,898	4.4
Total Acres Sown..............	920,747	100.0	547,659	100.0

*Source: Department of Census and Statistics, *Statistical Abstract*, 1961, pp. 200–201.

A certain further contribution to increased paddy output has been made by the extension of irrigation facilities which has paralleled the development of new peasant land already discussed (Chapter 5, pages 106–108). Water availability is a crucial factor in paddy cultivation and since ancient times Ceylon has depended heavily on irrigation to increase the chances that the right quantity of water will be available when needed. Reliance on irrigation is especially heavy in the dry zone, where rainfall, though not light, is narrowly concentrated in four months (October through January) and is unpredictable, leaving the area liable to both drought and flooding. The ancient solution is to build reservoirs ("tanks" in Ceylon parlance) to trap the water, along with canal systems to carry it

[53]*Ibid.*, 1956, p. 7.
[54]*Ibid.*, 1957, p. 10.

to the fields. Through the efforts of the Department of Irrigation the proportion of the paddy crop that was artificially watered was raised substantially during the fifties. Table 6–16 tells the tale in brief. Even with irrigation, of course, the dependence of the crop on the vagaries of the monsoon is not eliminated; it *is* lessened, however, and an important step toward higher and steadier levels of output is thus taken.

TABLE 6–16

DISTRIBUTION OF PADDY ACREAGE BY WATERING SYSTEM, 1950 AND 1960*

| Crop | Major Irrigation Schemes | | Minor Irrigation Schemes | | Rainfed | |
	Acres Sown (000s)	% of Total	Acres Sown (000s)	% of Total	Acres Sown (000s)	% of Total
Maha, 1949/50....	131.3	19.5	140.5	20.9	400.3	59.6
Maha, 1959/60....	258.2	28.1	239.0	26.0	423.2	46.0
Yala 1950.........	114.8	29.1	64.8	16.4	214.5	54.5
Yala 1960........	196.4	35.8	140.7	25.7	210.8	38.5

*Source: Department of Census and Statistics, *Statistical Abstract*, 1952 and 1961.

A few other technical factors deserve mention. To go with the advice given by extension workers, the government has been producing simple agricultural implements of improved design—plows, harrows, rotary weeders, and row seeders. The fertilizer subsidy is another case of the government's trying to bracket new techniques and new materials. Since 1951 a one-third subsidy has been given to cultivators who buy fertilizer through cooperative societies for use on paddy land. The subsidy has led to a rapid increase in fertilizer use during the 1950's: by the end of the decade over 20,000 tons of paddy fertilizer were being bought through the co-ops each year (this does not count additional amounts being purchased through private dealers).

Although it is not possible to assign a precise quantitative significance to each factor working for greater paddy output, it should be clear that improved techniques by themselves cannot count for more than a fraction of the observed increase in output. The great bulk of Ceylon's paddy land was being farmed in 1960 by much the same methods as had been employed in 1946, yet some 40 percent more land was being sown each year and each acre was yielding nearly half again as much grain as before. By far the most important reason for these gains in acreage and yield was the existence of the Guaranteed Price Scheme (GPS). The effect of the GPS was to induce paddy farmers to plant more land and to cultivate it more intensively; in the end, it succeeded in doing nothing less than converting the island's leading subsistence crop into a major cash crop.

The GPS, which provides for government purchases of paddy and certain other products of peasant agriculture, was inaugurated in 1948. Its primary aim was to ease the flow of peasant food crops to the domestic market by lessening the economic power of the middleman and offering the peasant producer a fair and stable price for his output; implicit in the notion of a "fair" price, however, was a degree of subsidization. The 1948 dating is somewhat deceptive, since in practice the incentive offered for increased output has increased gradually through time as the effectiveness of the scheme's administration has risen. The mechanics of the GPS are as follows. The government authorizes a producers' cooperative society to act as its agent in a given village. The society buys the produce from the cultivator at the government-set price (this price is reviewed annually by the minister of agriculture, but for paddy it has remained constant at Rs. 12 a bushel since 1952) and subsequently resells it to the government at the guaranteed price, plus a commission and reimbursement of transport costs. The government then ships the grain either to a government-owned mill or, more likely, to a government-licensed private mill for milling. In the final step, the milled rice is distributed to consumers under the rice-rationing scheme.

The proportion of the paddy crop which was purchased under the GPS rose during the fifties from a mere one percent to over half the total. In physical terms, there was a hundredfold increase, from 221,000 bushels collected in 1950 to nearly 22,000,000 in 1960 (see Table 6–17). Both the rapid rise in the amount collected and the continuing tendency for large quantities of paddy to be marketed outside the GPS are significant. The rise is not, in the main, explained by increased subsidization. The guaranteed price has remained at Rs. 12 ever since 1952; previously, it had been Rs. 7 (to February 28, 1950), Rs. 8 (to March 31, 1951), and Rs. 9 in succession. So only in 1950, 1951, and 1952 can increased purchases be attributed to a higher absolute government purchase price. To some extent, however, the increase in GPS purchases since 1953 can be explained by the rise of the guaranteed price *relative to the free market price,* since the latter has fallen slightly. When the Department of Census and Statistics collected its first data on free market paddy prices in 1953 it found the producer price on the open market to be above the newly established GPS price of Rs. 12 in 8 of Ceylon's 9 provinces (in the ninth, Western Province, it was

Rs. 11.94). By 1960 the situation had altered sharply: by that time
only three provinces were found with a free market price of Rs. 12
or greater. In most areas, therefore, the free market price fell from
1953 to 1960, making sales to government a more attractive outlet
to the cultivator than they had been. All this does not answer one
fundamental question, though: why, in the 6 provinces where the
free market price was below Rs. 12, did not everyone sell to the
GPS? Why was any paddy available on the free market? The
key to this riddle lies in the administrative effectiveness of the
scheme.

TABLE 6–17

GPS PURCHASES AND TOTAL PADDY OUTPUT, 1950–60*

Year	GPS Purchases (000 Bushels)	Total Output (000 Bushels)	GPS Purchases as a % of Total Output
1950.........	221	22,000	1.0
1951.........	592	22,000	2.7
1952.........	1,535	28,900	5.3
1953.........	311	21,900	1.4
1954.........	3,372	31,100	10.8
1955.........	12,918	35,700	36.2
1956.........	9,454	27,500	34.4
1957.........	13,111	31,280	41.9
1958.........	16,261	36,600	44.4
1959.........	16,642	36,400	45.7
1960.........	21,836	43,000	50.8

*Source: Department of Census and Statistics, *Statistical Abstracts.*

One important part of the GPS, for instance, is the functioning
of the cooperative societies which act as the government's purchasing agents. These societies have to be formed by the cultivators
themselves and then be officially recognized by the government;
both processes are fraught with delays. The number of such societies
in existence grew from about 200 at the beginning of 1950 to more
than 5,000 by the end of 1960; aggregate membership mounted to
roughly 700,000, which should have included the great majority of
paddy farmers in the country, but some of these societies were in
fact defunct and not more than half the cultivators were actually
members of an active society.[55] Naturally, the existence of an active

---

[55]The figures are from the *A.R. of the Director of Food Production* for
1954, p. 10, and the *A.R. of the Commissioner of Agrarian Services* for 1959,
p. 56. The last estimate was made by the director of agriculture in his 1960
A.R., p. 159.

cooperative society in his village is a necessary prerequisite for a cultivator's selling his crop under the GPS.

Another important question, though one which cannot be answered precisely, is the extent to which the system has functioned as planned. The scheme lends itself to fraud and an astonishing variety of abuses have been uncovered. Many abuses grow out of the indebtedness of the cultivator and his constant need for liquid assets. Some shopkeeper or other enterprising middleman with transportation facilities at his command will show up at harvest-time with a spot cash offer: Rs. 8 a bushel, say, for the crop, to be paid immediately in cash. The farmer can get Rs. 12 under the GPS, but even assuming that there is a cooperative society in his village and that it can buy his crop—many societies have been unable to buy their members' crops because they lacked the storage facilities needed to keep the produce until representatives of the government come to purchase it—he will have the problem of getting the paddy to the co-op himself (and poor peasants do not even have bullock carts). In addition, it may be sometime before he actually receives payment from the society, which is likely to be so illiquid that it will have to wait for the government to pay *it* for the paddy before it can pay the farmer. Transportation difficulties and his crying need for money combine to induce the peasant to sell now for ready cash. The middleman, if he is willing to push enterprise over the line of legality, can then make some arrangement to take the crop to the cooperative society himself and sell it for Rs. 12 a bushel, though this privilege is supposed to be open only to cultivators.

This ploy is only one of several kinds of abuse possible under the GPS. There are others, related to the wide gap between the artificially high GPS paddy price and the artificially low consumer price of rice, to the fact that paddy is milled by hundreds of registered private millers and transported in both its unmilled and its milled state over long distances where checking is not feasible, and to the presence of large quantities of paddy and rice in the hands of middlemen.

Aside from the increases in the level of price support already noted, the main cause of the increase in GPS paddy purchases is the success of the government in widening the coverage of the system, providing additional facilities, and mitigating abuses. During the late fifties attempts were made to move ahead on three measures which interlock with price subsidies to make them more effective output inducements: credit provision, land reform, and crop insurance.

The cooperative societies, among their other functions, channel government credit to the cultivator. Loans are made for various purposes, the most important among them being for seed paddy, fertilizer, and other cultivation expenses. In recent years loans of about Rs. 15,000,000 have been extended annually. But the program has had a spotty history. The default rate on these loans has always been very high and the total amount defaulted grows every year. And in any case the system of cooperative rural credit has made no more than a superficial impression on the overall structure of rural credit. The Survey of Rural Indebtedness of 1957 found that the co-ops furnished only 3.9 percent of all rural credit, while "undesirable sources of credit" accounted for 48 percent.[56]

The desire to do something about the production-inhibiting effects of some forms of land tenure—especially *ande* tenancy—was first expressed in the Paddy Lands Act of 1953. The act provided for security of tenure and maximum levels of rent for paddy-farming tenants, as well as the enforced leasing of paddy lands not at present in cultivation. The act was proclaimed effective in two of the island's (then) 20 revenue districts, but it proved to be unenforceable and had little impact. In 1958 another attempt was made. A new Paddy Lands Act was passed, embodying much the same features as the earlier act, but written so as to be more easily enforced and administered. It gave lifelong security of tenure, as well as the power to assign tenancy rights to an heir; there was only one escape clause: within five years of the passage of the act, the landlord could evict his tenant, provided that he would cultivate the land himself. Other features of the new act were the fixing of maximum rents and the creation of village cultivation committees, which were elected by all the paddy cultivators in the village and had the responsibility of administering many sections of the act.

In 1958 the security of tenure provisions were applied throughout Ceylon and the rest of the act, which came into effect only through ministerial decree, to the Colombo and Hambantota districts. A few months later, although the commissioner of agrarian services complained that he lacked the staff to administer the act efficiently,[57] it was extended to four more districts. The first reaction to the act was an islandwide spate of evictions; the great majority of these were illegal under the act, but it proved to be hard to take effective legal action against them. For one thing, while the security of tenure provisions of the act applied to the whole island, the provisions

---

[56]Department of Census and Statistics, *Survey of Rural Indebtedness* (1957).
[57]*A.R. of the Commissioner of Agrarian Services* for 1958, p. 55.

embodying sanctions for eviction were applicable only to the de-creed districts; in the rest of the island the tenant had no legal recourse. Even in the decreed districts the number of such cases clogging the courts was so great that it was not unusual for a case to take two years to complete. The initial impact of the act was thus harmful to the tenant cultivator.

The Paddy Lands Act of 1958 was amended twice (in 1958 and again in 1959) in an attempt to block illegal evictions and make the cultivation committees a more effective instrument of the act's intentions (they were being weakened in many areas by the re-fusal of the landlords to cooperate). By 1960, despite considerable legislative and administrative effort, little overall progress had been made.

Crop insurance is the most recent device tried in the continuing attempt to raise rice production. The scheme, a simple one involving the collection of premiums from all cultivators and the payment of benefits of those whose crops suffer misfortune from natural causes, was initiated on a pilot basis in 1959. By 1960, then, it had no measurable effect on output, though it does appear to have promise for the future. The hope is that the peasant can be induced by the insurance to modify his traditional conservatism (which, for in-stance, leads him not to plow his land until the village tank is full, thereby wasting time and—through evaporation—water) and take more justified risks.

Only in rough terms can one say what the major causes of rising paddy output and productivity have been. The GPS has clearly been an important influence and extension services, the fertilizer subsidy, colonization, and improvements in irrigation have all cer-tainly had *some* effect. On the other hand, the value of some other elements in the government program—land reform, cooperative credit and crop insurance—was still more of an open question in 1960. It seems obvious, however, that the cornerstone of the whole program and by far the most important inducement to increase output and intensify land use has been the GPS. Its existence and, even more important, its progressive effectuation during the fifties have worked a virtual revolution in the peasant economy. For the first time paddy has been established as a cash crop and the peasant has been taught to think of it as such. This change in attitude caused much more paddy to be grown and a far higher proportion of the crop to be marketed rather than consumed on the farm.[58]

[58]Just what percentage of paddy output was marketed in any given year is difficult to estimate. Part of the rise in GPS purchases represents an increase in total paddy marketings and part only a transfer of the distributive function

(Continued on next page)

An incidental result was that the GPS created an environment in which producers became more economically minded and in such an environment many of the other efforts of the government are likely to meet with more success. A large area of potential future gains has thus been created. The GPS has, in fact, been so successful that the government has begun to wonder how it will be able to go on paying the subsidy bill if producers continue to expand output and sell increasing proportions of it to the government. Of course, the magnitude of the subsidy might be questioned, particularly at this point. Quite likely, the job could be done in the future with a more modest subsidy, though Ceylon's political history suggests that it would be a brave minister of agriculture who would actually take the step of reducing it.

Gains in output and productivity in most of the minor peasant crops grown in Ceylon have been much less impressive than those recorded in paddy production. The basic reasons for this are that the inducements offered to expand output have been less attractive than the rice subsidy and that the vigorous response to the rice subsidy has diverted land and effort away from some of the minor crops. Table 6–18 summarizes the trend of output in 13 of the leading minor crops, showing the effect of acreage changes and variations in per acre yields on production. If the crops listed in the table can be taken as representative of all minor food crops (and, in general, they can) and if the rather unreliable statistics on minor food crops can be trusted (this is less certain) it can be said that output rose by about 70 percent between 1950 and 1960 and that this rise was entirely attributable to increased output per acre, the area devoted to minor food crops actually falling slightly over the decade. According to the table, yields rose even more rapidly in the minor crops than in paddy, but the stagnation of acreage held the aggregate volume of output to a percentage increase only three-fourths as great as that of paddy.

Many of these minor crops have traditionally been grown by the villager, as an adjunct to his main occupation as a paddy cultivator, to satisfy his family's limited demand for foodstuffs to supplement

---

from private traders to the government. There are no data on the private rice trade, so it is hard to assess the relative importance of these two effects. The private trade remained an important medium for the marketing of rice at the decade's end, so considerably more than 50 percent of the total output must have been marketed in 1960. The commercialization of rice production went so far, in fact, that some paddy producers began to sell all their output and buy milled rice through the rationing scheme for their family's consumption; in this way they took advantage of both aspects of the subsidy, once as producers and again as consumers.

their staple diet of rice. These are known as "highland" crops, meaning that they are grown on land which is too high and dry for paddy cultivation. Others of the crops in Table 6–18, especially the secondary grains—kurakkan, maize, and mineri—are grown mainly on a chena basis, in shifting plots hacked from the jungle, planted for a year or two, then left to lie fallow for a decade or more. In neither case would one expect to find scientific farming methods practiced, but in several instances the data do show the same kind of striking rise in yield exhibited by paddy. The technical advisory and subsidization efforts of the government have

TABLE 6–18

MINOR FOOD CROPS: CHANGES IN OUTPUT, ACREAGE, AND YIELD, 1950–60

Crop	% Change in Output*	% Change in Acreage†	% Change in Yield‡	Area Sown in 1960 (000 Acres)
Kurakkan	− 12.7	− 13.7	− 1.2	88.8
Maize	1.6	− 8.5	11.0	36.8
Mineri	95.4	75.9	11.1	6.5
Green gram	647.5	9.2	584.5	11.6
Cowpea	979.0	216.0	241.5	8.1
Manioc	41.1	− 39.2	132.1	112.3
Sweet potatoes	51.2	− 44.3	171.5	31.2
Potatoes	28.6	101.0	− 34.0	1.0
Chilies	19.6	36.1	− 12.1	31.3
Onions	53.5	97.1	− 22.1	14.3
Ginger	15.9	21.4	− 4.5	5.7
Tumeric	102.3	29.4	56.3	3.4
Pepper	99.6	51.2	32.0	19.7
Weighted average§	70.5	− 2.9	79.6	——

*Source: Department of Census and Statistics, *Statistical Abstracts*. Refers to the total output during the two growing seasons.
†Source: *Ibid*. Refers to the total area sown in the two growing seasons.
‡Output index divided by acreage index.
§Weighted by total acreage planted in 1960.

been applied to minor crops as well, though usually with less vigor. Most—though not all—of the crops in Table 6–18 have been covered by guaranteed prices throughout the fifties, but the level of support offered has generally been lower and the collection network has been less well developed than for paddy. Many of the co-ops have preferred dealing exclusively in paddy, which comes to them in larger volume and yields higher commissions, and have discouraged farmers from selling them minor crops covered by the GPS. Only for maize and onions have GPS collections ever exceeded ten percent of estimated annual production.[59]

The nonagricultural part of the primary sector is not very important in Ceylon's economy. Its main component is fishing, a traditional economic activity similar in many ways to peasant agriculture. The official statistics indicate a rise in total catch of 15.1 percent from 1950 to 1960.[60] The data for all years are definitely understated and cannot be taken literally, but the fact that Ceylon's fish imports have risen only very gradually suggests that the general picture they give of very slowly rising output is likely to be correct. During the late fifties in particular attempts have been made to reform the industry and make its operation more commercial, mainly by improving marketing facilities and providing better equipment, such as light outboard motors. The basic problems of the industry remained to be solved in 1960, but the measures taken up to that time were largely responsible for the rapid rises in annual catch which seem to have occurred late in the decade.

INDUSTRY

Industrial activity was only an insignificant part of Ceylon's economy before World War II. By 1960 the industrial sector remained small but some noteworthy developments had taken place. From 1946 to 1960 total employment in industry expanded from about 250,000 to some 450,000 or from 11 to 15 percent of aggregate employment.[61] The industrial contribution to Gross Domestic Product grew similarly: in 1950 it amounted to 11.7 percent of the total; by 1960 it had risen to 15.5.[62] According to the best available output index, industrial output stood at 135.0 in 1960, with 1952–56 equal to 100.[63] This considerable overall increase masked some divergent trends within the sector. It has already been noted (pages 126–129) that mining declined, manufacturing and construction grew noticeably, and utility output climbed steeply. Another useful way of looking at the sector is in terms of (1) small-scale and (2) large-scale industry; the latter category can be split further into (*a*) private and (*b*) government operations. A brief glance at how each of these fared in the period since 1946 is called for.[64]

---

[59]See Department of Census and Statistics, *Statistical Abstracts.*

[60]See Table A–34, Appendix.

[61]See Table 5–2, Chapter 5. "Industry" here includes mining and quarrying; construction; manufacturing; and electricity, gas, and water.

[62]See Table 6–3.

[63]See Table A–41, Appendix; the index leaves something to be desired but it probably gives an accurate general picture.

[64]The discussion throughout this section is hampered by the lack of reliable

As in most countries, small-scale industry is one of the sectors of the economy about which least is known. Official Ceylon government definitions cut the sector into three parts: (1) cottage industry (firms run wholly or largely by family labor as a full-time or part-time occupation); (2) small-scale industry, narrowly defined (firms using hired laborers: fewer than 20 or, if no motive power is used, fewer than 50); and (3) handicraft industry (cottage or small-scale industries making products which require the use of artistic skill and craftsmanship in their manufacture).[65] Categories (1) and (3) include handloom weaving, carpentry, pottery, coir products, gold- and silverwork, bamboo products, and similar trades, all of which have some basis in Ceylon's ancient traditions. Category (2) covers the smaller units found in almost all the island's manufacturing industries, as well as in construction. Of output and employment trends in categories (1) and (3) little is known; of category (2) it is virtually correct to say that nothing is known, since no organized inquiry into this area of economic activity has ever been made.

As has been noted, all forms of industry boomed during World War II. The market was willing to absorb any available local output and the only important limitations on production were the shortages of capital equipment and raw materials. Small industry, because it worked with little capital and relied heavily on local materials, was able to benefit from this situation even more than large industry. When the war ended and the normal flow of imports was gradually restored, the shock to small-scale producers was correspondingly severe. It appears that the resulting disillusionment of the participants in cottage and handicraft industries has been a powerful deterrent to the development of those industries ever since. Government policy did attempt to rehabilitate various of the cottage and handicraft industries after the shock of postwar readjustment. For a long time, however, the development of rural industry was thought of primarily as a form of unemployment relief and no systematic attempt was made to establish some of the more promising rural crafts on a sound competitive basis. Only toward the end of the decade did this attitude begin to change.

Although the coir products industry was the largest of this group in terms of output and employment, it was handloom textiles which

and comprehensive data on most aspects of industrial development before 1960. The foregoing paragraph summarizes the few such bits of information that are available.

[65]A.R. of the Director of Rural Development and Cottage Industries for 1955, pp. 48–49.

received the most government attention. Elements of the government program were the establishment of demonstration centers, assistance of producers through cooperative societies (these two measures were extended to most of the cottage and handicraft industries), and protection from foreign competition through the Industrial Products Act. Under the latter provision, which was instituted in 1949 to cover towels, banyans (a widely worn man's garment similar to an undershirt), and sarongs (the other half of the standard working-class man's attire), ratios were set requiring merchants importing such goods to buy fixed proportions of locally produced articles at the same time. Protection was later increased by tightening up the ratios and extending the coverage of the act to other textile products. By the end of the decade, with cottage output bolstered by the production of one modern private spinning and weaving mill, self-sufficiency in these textile goods had been attained. Further attempts to build up the cottage-weaving industry were now taking the form of increasing efficiency by establishing power weaving centers in selected villages and making other organizational and technical improvements so as to permit a reduction in the degree of subsidization given by government policies.

This was the most successful cottage-industry program. The other industries, despite sporadic attempts to develop them, appeared to be in dire straits at the decade's end. Many were feeling heavy competitive pressures from newly developing modern industry; e.g., handmade bricks from locally produced machine-made bricks, pottery from the growing domestic output of aluminum and plastic ware. All in all, the progress of small-scale industry appears to have been uneven and slow in the fifties, with the exception of handloom textiles. The future of the sector was beclouded. It was clear that the potential of cottage and handicraft industry as a means of soaking up underemployed rural labor, teaching rudimentary industrial skills, and, with proper organization, producing efficiently a wide variety of useful articles, was considerable, but little of this potential had been realized by 1960.

When private large-scale industry was surveyed in the 1952 *Census of Industry* it was found to consist of some 700 establishments, employing 53,000 persons and producing value added of Rs. 224,700,000 with a productive capital employed of Rs. 355,-800,000. Value added per man employed averaged Rs. 4,203.[66] In

---

[66]Department of Census and Statistics, *Census of Industry 1952*, pp. 10–11. The scope of the census included establishments which met three criteria: (1) they had not less than five paid employees; (2) they employed a capital of not less than Rs. 3,000; and (3) they used mechanical power in at least part

terms of both employment and value of output, the most important industries were engineering (which included producers of tea and rubber machinery, truck bodies, etc.), coconut and oil milling, printing and bookbinding, and coir fibre and coir goods. Smaller contributions to employment and output were made by firms in other areas: plumbago mining, salt, rice milling, confectionery, brewing and distilling, soft drinks, tobacco, textiles, lumber, rubber goods, fertilizer mixing, soap, matches, ceramics, cement, and electricity. The sector was small and almost all the industries included clearly fell into one of three categories; (1) those processing locally produced raw materials for export and, to a lesser degree, for local consumption; (2) those producing for local use goods which were too bulky to import cheaply; and (3) a small number of industries which existed because of protection in earlier times (notably matches). About a quarter of these enterprises were corporations, but they were the larger ones and produced 64 percent of the output.[67] Some of these corporations were locally owned, but more often foreign-owned organizations (British or sometimes Indian) were dominant. Most of the sector was in private hands, but there were areas (the utilities, as well as cement and ceramics) in which government plants had been established.

There are no data on large-scale industry for 1960 or any other year near the end of the period being studied here which would give us a clear picture of just how much expansion had taken place in the sector up to that time and what form it had taken. It is evident, however, that while the sector's growth had been considerable relative to the small base from which it had started in the immediate postwar years, large-scale industry had still not taken its place as an important part of the economy. Not until import duty rates on some consumer goods began to rise sharply in 1958 did significant production of consumer goods for the local market begin to develop. Up to that point the story of private industrial investment had been primarily one of unsuccessful government policy attempts to induce local and foreign capital to enter the industrial field. Meanwhile, a parallel (and often competing) effort was being made to set up a public industrial

---

of their operations (p. 2). Mining, manufacturing, construction, and gas and electric utilities were covered. Many small-scale establishments were obviously excluded and even within the chosen field of purview coverage was far from complete. Of the list of establishments to which questionnaires were sent, about 85 percent responded (p. 4); those which failed to answer were predominantly the smaller operations, but, on the other hand, the list probably suffered from some omissions.

[67] *Ibid.*, p. 14.

sector. This effort met with a discouraging series of setbacks. A brief look at government policy with respect to private capital and at public industrial enterprise will serve to show why Ceylon's attempts to industrialize during the 1950's did not meet with greater success.

Although there is only fragmentary evidence relating to the subject, it seems probable that with import duties at their relatively low levels of the early and middle fifties there were few activities into which large-scale industry could have been pushed profitably. Even existing firms made, in general, low returns on their invested capital, especially late in the decade as the rate of company taxation rose to over 60 percent of before-tax profits.[68] Potential returns period relative to what could be earned on capital invested in trade, plantation agriculture, or real estate. Only at the very end of the decade, at the same time as the after-tax profits of the old established firms fell, did they begin to rise to attractive levels (new firms could obtain concessions on direct taxation and on import duties on capital equipment and raw materials, so their profit prospects were superior to those of the older firms). But while private returns on industrial investment were low there is good reason to believe that the marginal social product of investment in industry was much higher. If the economy was ever to achieve significant industrialization a beginning had to be made in accumulating industrial experience and directing the attention of entrepreneurs away from their traditional fields of operation in agriculture, trade, and real estate. Active government encouragement was thus not only necessary if any appreciable volume of private industrial investment was to take place, it was also highly desirable. The disappointing performance of private industry during this period must thus be attributed mainly to the inadequacies of public policy.

At first the government relied primarily on short-term tax concessions to spur investment. These were first offered in 1949 and later extended and liberalized. No perceptible success came of this policy, perhaps because even the complete exemption from direct taxation for three years which was offered in 1951 held no appeal on marginal investments in industry were probably low during this for a firm which was unlikely to earn large profits during its early

---

[68]M. Ramachandran, "Finances of Manufacturing Companies in the Post-War Period," *Central Bank of Ceylon Bulletin,* December, 1963, pp. 10–15, found that six of the leading manufacturing corporations made after-tax returns on their invested capital which fell from 5.6 percent in 1948–50 to 5.5 percent in 1951–53, to 5.1 in 1954–56, and finally to only 3.3 percent in 1957–61.

years of operation in any case and would then be liable to taxation at any rate chosen by the government thereafter. Foreign firms were especially wary of the risks involved in industrial investment in Ceylon. Periodic attempts were made to reassure them, including a general statement of policy regarding foreign investment which was made in 1955.[69] The latter pronouncement was in fact too general, since while it welcomed foreign investment and granted various kinds of tax relief it failed to spell out precise criteria for acceptable investment (each case was left subject to individual negotiation), gave no guarantee that announced policies would not be changed in the future, and spoke vaguely of the desirability of hiring large proportions of Ceylon nationals.[70] In any case, the government changed hands within a year and once again the established policy was in doubt.

Meanwhile, attempts to build up a publicly owned industrial sector were under way. At first the emphasis was on maintaining what had been built up during the war. These plants (see Chapter 4, page 77), which had earned large profits during the war, began to make huge losses soon after the war's end. It eventually became necessary to subject them to sweeping reorganization.[71] In 1955 the government's cement, ceramics, leather products, oils and fats, and plywood plants were converted into public corporations. During the U.N.P. regime, which lasted until 1956, relatively little was done to build up this nascent public industrial sector. Three factors appear to have hindered progress in this area: (1) the initial preoccupation with the reorganization of the older plants, (2) the philosophical preferences of the U.N.P. government for agriculture and for private enterprise, and (3) the financial stringency which prevailed from 1952 up to 1955, as virtually all types of government expenditure were adjusted to the much lower revenues available after the Korean War.

After the accession of the M.E.P. government in 1956 a new attitude toward government economic activity became dominant. It found expression in a sharp rise in government industrial invest-

[69]M. D. H. Jayawardane, Minister of Finance, *Government Policy in Respect of Private Foreign Investment in Ceylon* (1955).

[70]See Reinhard Kövary, *Investment Policy and Investment Legislation in Under-developed Countries* (New York: Taplinger Publishing Co., 1960), for a critique of this approach to attracting foreign capital.

[71]The *Report of the Commission on Government Commercial Undertakings* (S.P. XIX of 1953) found fault with the government plants on technical grounds and criticized their organization as arms of government departments. It recommended closing some plants, selling others to private industry, and converting the rest into public corporations.

ment. Through 1960, projects to produce caustic soda and chlorine (1956), ilmenite (1957), sugar (1957), salt (1957), cotton yarn (1958), brick and tile (1959), and hardboard (1959) were launched. Together, they represented an investment of about Rs. 120,000,000.[72] Like their predecessors, the new industrial plants usually ran into delays in construction and further difficulties in breaking in new equipment and untrained labor and getting production up to planned capacity. At the end of 1960 the situation was as follows.[73] On an invested capital of nearly Rs. 200,000,000, output worth about Rs. 50,000,000 at prices inflated by heavy protection was being produced. Employment had been furnished for just over 3,000 men. Only four corporations (Ceylon Ceramics, Ceylon Plywoods, D. I. Leather Products, and Ceylon Cement) had ever been able to show a one-year profit and only one, the cement corporation, had shown an ability to earn substantial profits with any consistency. Of course, several plants were still either under construction or in the break-in stage at this point, but it is still basically correct to say that the state industrial corporations had performed disappointingly in terms of output, employment, and import competitiveness and had been an expensive experiment in government economic initiative.

Besides the difficulties of project execution which are invariably encountered in a country's initial efforts at industrialization, many of the problems of Ceylon's state factories are traceable to shortcomings of program and project conception. The industrialization program as a whole was foredoomed to make only a minor immediate contribution to national welfare in terms of employment provided and output produced. With an average capital per worker requirement of Rs. 67,000 (see preceding paragraph) and given the limited availability of investment funds, the creation of large-scale industrial projects could not begin to solve Ceylon's pressing short-term job-creation needs. And at a capital-output ratio of approximately four to one (see above) possible immediate returns in the form of output were quite limited. Nor was import competitiveness likely to come for some time; even the list of factories for which there was good reason to anticipate *ultimate* competitiveness (e.g., cement and ilmenite because of reliance on local raw materials, brick and tile because of the cost advantages of producing close to the ultimate market) was soon exhausted. The program can be defended mainly as a means of gaining experience with modern in-

---

[72]See Table A–70, Appendix.

[73]See Table A–70, Appendix, for the data upon which these estimates are based.

dustrial production in a country which had had hardly any such experience in the past. But the newfound experience was gained at a high cost.

In addition to the inherent limitations of the industrialization program, individual projects were dogged by faulty planning. The world market for ilmenite was badly overestimated. Growing sugar on a large-scale basis proved to be much harder than had been anticipated. The wrong kind of papermaking machinery was ordered at first. These trials, too, can be rationalized as ways of gaining valuable experience, but again they were costly.

Part way between government and private enterprise lay an experiment in the jointly financed corporation. This organizational form was tried with a small number of medium-sized companies—producing, for example, asbestos cement, light bulbs, glassware, and flashlight batteries—but under the M.E.P. government the emphasis put on it declined and it was not extended to a large number of industries.

Although the upsurge in industrial investment which started about 1958 and accelerated after 1960 was largely *not* a product of conscious government policies to promote industry, it may have received a boost from the publication for the first time in 1957 of an attempt to define exactly the government's views on the proper role of government and private initiative in the industrial sector of Ceylon's economy.[74] Three lists were published. One list, of seven industries, defined the area reserved to government production. It was composed of *some* of the industries in which government had or was planning plants: (1) iron and steel; (2) cement; (3) chemicals; (4) fertilizers; (5) salt and its by-products; (6) mineral sands; and (7) sugar, power alcohol, and rayon. The second enumerated 23 areas open to government corporations, mixed corporations, or private corporations; the possibility of more than one of these forms operating in any one industry was specifically mentioned. This list was made up of generally lighter industries, such as textiles, tires and tubes, bicycles, ceramics, glassware, paper, etc. The third list, containing 82 industries, most of them producing light consumer goods, defined areas reserved to private enterprise (though prolonged negotiations with the government over tax and tariff concessions were necessary for profitable operation in almost all cases). This policy statement, although it did not represent a very dynamic approach to industrial development, may have served as a precondition for the later expansion,

---

[74]*A.R. of the Director of Industries* for 1957, pp. 32–34.

especially in the areas covered by the third list, where most of the post-1958 activity centered.

One industrial area in which government initiative did succeed in bringing about a tremendous expansion was electric power. The development of Ceylon's ample hydroelectric potential had begun under the British in the late 1920's, but the depression and then a world war had interrupted the work. As soon as possible after the war ended construction was resumed and in 1950 the first hydro-generation facility ("Stage I" at Laxapana) was opened, with a capacity of 25 megawatts. Although there had been fears that Stage I would provide more power than would be needed for many years to come, capacity generation was actually reached by December, 1952. Financial stringency followed by delay in obtaining a World Bank loan and then prolonged construction delays put off the opening of Stage IIA, with another 25 megawatts, until late 1958. By 1960 a Stage IIB expansion of hydro and thermal capacity was under way and a Stage III hydro project was under investigation. Demand showed a distinct tendency to grow as rapidly as supply conditions allowed and between 1946 and 1960 nearly a six-fold increase in government power generation, from 53,000,000 kilowatt hours to 302,000,000 took place.[75] Private power generation, which had dwarfed government generation prior to the hydro era, grew more slowly and declined to secondary importance.[76] Unfortunately, although the main purpose of the power program had been to promote industry most of the newly generated electricity went for relatively unproductive uses in homes and government offices.

SERVICES

Having said something about output and employment trends in agriculture and industry, one is left with that large and heterogeneous mass, the service sector, to analyze. Between 1946 and 1960 the service sector absorbed nearly 300,000 additional workers; its employment grew more rapidly than that of agriculture—though more slowly than industrial employment—and it thus raised its share in total employment from 27 to about 30 percent.[77] What is the economic significance of this increase in service-sector employment? No government ever deliberately sets out to raise aggregate employment in services, though there are several high-productivity portions of the sector which it might try to enlarge. Services can be

---

[75]See Department of Census and Statistics, *Statistical Abstract 1962*, p. 229.
[76]See Table A–43, Appendix.
[77]See Table 5–3, Chapter 5.

among the most modern parts of the economy and they can be among the most backward. To complicate matters still further, problems of measuring output and productivity are much more acute for services than they are for goods-producing sectors.

Looking at income originating in the service sector, one sees that during the 1950's it rose slowly as a percentage of Gross Domestic Product at current factor cost: from 28.5 percent of the total in 1950 to 29.5 in 1960.[78] Estimated output per employee also increased, climbing from Rs. 1,746 in 1950 to Rs. 2,195 in 1960; this is an increase of about 26 percent.[79] What is not known is how much of this rise represents growth in real output and how much price increases. There is some evidence to suggest that prices of services rose somewhat more rapidly during the fifties than did prices of goods.[80] Since real output per man employed in the economy as a whole rose by 25 percent over the decade of the fifties[81] it is evident that in real terms productivity in the service sector rose distinctly less than productivity in other areas. Does this mean, then, that the service sector has been used as a haven for the disguised unemployed, perhaps soaking up labor which has moved out of agriculture?

Something can be learned by looking at the four main parts of the service sector separately, as is done in Table 6–19. The sector can be split into (1) trade, commerce, and finance; (2) transportation and communications; (3) other government services (i.e., those not already included in a functional category); and (4) other private services. This breakdown is useful in some ways, but it still leaves lumped together in each subcategory groups with widely divergent productivity levels and economic implications: bank employees with shopkeepers, export shipping workers with bullock-cart drivers, doctors with domestic servants, and government engineers with the peons who swarm around every government office.

---

[78]See Table 6–3. Income originating in the service sector is taken to be the sum of transportation and communications; wholesale and retail trade; banking, insurance, and real estate; public administration and defense; and services n.e.c. Income originating in ownership of dwellings is excluded from the total so as to make the income figures comparable with the employment totals.

[79]Obtained by dividing income originating (Table A–8, Appendix) by estimated employment (Table 5–2).

[80]The "miscellaneous" component of the consumer price index, which includes services other than housing and goods other than food, clothing, and fuel, rose by 29 percent in the fifties; some of this rise is attributable to luxury goods but service prices also rose. See Table A–71, Appendix.

[81]Real GDP (Table A–3, Appendix) divided by total employment (Table 5–3).

TABLE 6–19

EMPLOYMENT AND OUTPUT PER MAN IN THE SERVICE SECTOR: 1950 AND 1960*

Industry	Net Output per Man (Current-Price Rupees)		Employment (000s)		% Change in Employment, 1950–60
	1950	1960	1950	1960	
Trade, commerce, and finance.......	1,630	2,077	208	253	21.6
Transportation and communications...	3,197	2,611	92	133	44.6
Government n.e.c....	2,058	3,262	97	148	52.8
Services n.e.c........	1,300	1,714	313	382	22.0
Total: Services......	1,746	2,195	710	916	29.0

*Source: Tables A–8, Appendix, and 5–2, Chapter 5.

Since there are no census data for the terminal year to give an idea of what has happened to the employment totals for each of these small categories, one cannot say which types of groups are growing. One does get the strong impression that the number of professionals in the country—doctors, lawyers, accountants, and, to a lesser degree, engineers and scientists—is increasing rapidly, but in only a few cases are there data to prove this. In terms of broad aggregates, the figures in Table 6–19 indicate that it is the two groups with the highest productivity levels, transportation and communications and government not elsewhere classified, which have experienced the most rapid increases in employment. The services n.e.c. group, which is likely to contain the highest proportion of disguised unemployment, grew slowly and, in addition, experienced a fairly rapid rise in the value of its per capita output. The addition of approximately 50,000 persons to government payrolls in the 1950's is especially difficult to interpret. Apparent productivity did rise substantially in this sector, but all this means is that the salaries of government employees went up (since it is virtually impossible to measure the output of government employees, conventional national accounting simply assumes it to be equal to the labor input, as measured by wages and salaries paid). There has been no indication, however, that the Ceylon government has used government employment as a form of unemployment relief.[82] Instead, the main reason for the rapid expansion of government employment is simply that the scope of government activities has grown rapidly

---

[82]There *have* been cases in which the Public Works Department, unde: political pressure, has shifted from using heavy construction equipment t(more labor-intensive methods. Many economists would feel that such a mov(was in line with economic rationality for a labor-surplus country like Ceylon.

as the population has risen and the government has become more active in more fields of social and economic endeavor.[83]

Within the bounds of the very incomplete information pertaining to the service sector, then, one is inclined to say that it has not been used to any marked extent as an artificial way of absorbing additions to the labor supply for whom there would otherwise be no work. The proportion of very low-productivity workers in the service sector remains high relative to what it would be in a more developed country, of course, but there is no evidence that it has risen very much during the 1950's. A fair part of the increase in service-sector employment can be accounted for by rises in the numbers of relatively high-productivity service occupations—professionals and, if one agrees with the foregoing argument, government servants. Of course, this situation could change sharply in the future: as the labor force grows more rapidly and the development of industry and the estates fails to absorb more than a fraction of the new workers, the service sector could become more and more of a reservoir of underemployment.

SUMMARY

Real national output rose by 57 percent in the 1950's, despite the fact that the labor force increased by only 24 percent, the supply of arable land by only 8 percent, and the capital stock too by only a small percentage. Allowing for a moderate decline in the terms of trade, real national income increased by 49 percent. With a population increase of 29 percent, the economy was thus able to record a noticeable rise in real income per head. The saving grace of the situation was the fact that some key sectors of the economy, especially rice and tea production, were able to achieve substantial increases in output per man employed and per acre of land used. Government policy was partly responsible for these productivity increases, particularly in the case of rice cultivation, but in other instances its role was negative or unimportant. The economy did not depart markedly from its past economic structure but it did benefit from the emergence within that structure of some new focal points of economic growth. The resource-extensive growth of plantation agriculture and the modern sector which supported it was replaced by technical innovation and increasingly intensive use of resources in tea cultivation and peasant agriculture and by a fairly rapid rise of the still small industrial sector. For the time

[83]For instance, the gradual take-over by the government of almost all of the country's school system added thousands of teachers and other school employees to the government payroll.

being, this pattern of growth proved to be an acceptable successor to the old pattern and an adequate answer to the Malthusian challenge as well. By the latter part of the fifties, however, it was becoming increasingly evident that this pattern of growth was not likely to provide a definitive solution to the longer-run economic problems of the country and that if not carefully managed it might in the end bring about its own destruction. This side of independent Ceylon's economic experience is examined in Chapter 7.

Chapter 7

Problems of the Transitional Economy

The transitional economic system which prevailed in Ceylon during the late 1940's and the 1950's was, as has been seen, no absolute failure when it came to providing a fairly reasonable rate of national income growth. True, the rise in real income per capita which it produced was not especially impressive and it tended to slow down during the late 1950's, but even to have maintained a constant per capita income level within the context of such unfavorable relative growth rates of the factors of production would have been no inconsiderable achievement. Indeed, in the present later and unhappier day one hears talk of economic development designed to "broaden" Ceylon's economy, that is, to find productive employment for its rapidly growing labor force that will suffice just to maintain the present per capita income standard. A duplication of the growth record of the 1950's would thus be considered an ambitious goal today.

There was an important sense, however, in which the performance of the transitional economic system proved to be totally inadequate. This inadequacy was only vaguely perceived by some observers during the fifties, but it came into sharp focus soon after the dawning of the new decade, the 1960's. The basic proof of the inadequacy of what has been referred to here as the transitional economy is to be found in the fact that while a determined attempt was made to maintain the island's historical tradition of relative openness to all kinds of imports the government found it necessary in 1960–61 to abandon precipitately the free flow of imports into the country and to institute a stringent set of direct controls over foreign trade and payments. Of course, signs of the progressive unviability of the transitional system were observable during the 1950's for those who chose to see them. They took the form of persistent and increasingly large deficits in the balance of payments, deficits which not only appeared in the current account but, because of the grossly insufficient level of capital inflow, also showed themselves in increasing magnitudes in the basic balance. The deficits were financed primarily by the sale of the nation's accumulated foreign assets; the level of those assets, which dropped almost continuously throughout the fifties and approached the vanishing point as the decade drew to a close, set a limit on the length of time over which this trend could continue. Official attention was drawn to the dwindling of the foreign assets from time to time and various preventative measures were taken, but they were never sufficiently vigorous to stem the tide.

While the external deficits and the declining foreign assets were the overt signs of the failings of Ceylon's transitional economy, however, they were not in themselves the basic problem. The fundamental underlying problem was that no method was ever devised to allocate a sufficient quantity of resources to investment. There were basic difficulties, never wholly resolved, of laying out a viable investment program through national development planning and of implementing and financing it through public and private efforts. Part of the reason for the failure on the financing side was, of course, the scantiness of capital flows from abroad. But weak as these flows were they did not present so great an obstacle to the achievement of a successful growth pattern as did the failure to call forth anything like enough domestic saving. This failure to provide internal finance for an adequate volume of investment was undoubtedly the most important shortcoming of Ceylon's transitional economy. It is, of course, simply the over-consumption problem discussed in Chapter 5 looked at from a different point of view. In both the private and public sectors, too large a proportion of total resources was devoted to current expenditure and too small a share allotted to meeting the needs of the future. To make matters worse, the limited investment which did materialize was too inefficiently allocated to provide a really rapid growth of income and, along with it, the saving potential of the nation. Had there been a larger volume of investment, less rapid growth of private and public consumption, and a more efficient allocation of investment expenditure to productive uses it might have proven possible to ride out the balance of payments deficits and, through a combination of export promotion and import substitution, establish a new external balance which would have been consistent with rapid output and income growth. Unfortunately, this successful growth pattern never emerged. The problems were not solved and by the beginning of the sixties they had brought about the downfall of the transitional economy as it had existed during the first decade and a half of independent Ceylon's economic experience.

This chapter examines the fatal flaws in the transitional economic system. It looks first at the fundamental saving-investment problem itself, including the difficulties of public finance which formed an important part of it, then at its visible manifestation, the balance of payments crisis of the late fifties.

CONSUMPTION AND SAVING IN THE PRIVATE SECTOR

It has already been noted that one characteristic of Ceylon's economy in the 1950's was an exceedingly buoyant consumption level. Both private and public current expenditure tended to increase rapidly—in retrospect, far too rapidly—throughout most of the decade. The overconsumptionist tendencies of the government will be dealt with in the following section, as one of the factors which prevented the government from channeling to investment a sufficiently large quantity of resources. However, the private sector, too, shared this inability to save in large enough quantities.

The disposable income received by the private sector could be used for any one of three purposes. It could go for consumption expenditures. Alternatively, it could be devoted to foreign remittances, as was a significant percentage of the income received by the Indian estate laborers. Or it could be saved. From the point of view of the economy of Ceylon, transfers abroad were equivalent to consumption of imported goods, since the money flows involved were not only not available for investment within Ceylon but did in fact create additions to the foreign claims on the country. In 1950 (see Table 7–1) 82.6 percent of Ceylon's GNP became disposable income for the island's households. Of this sum, which amounted to nearly Rs. 3,500,000,000, 90.3 percent was spent on consumption, an additional 2.3 percent went for transfers abroad, and only 7.5 percent was saved. The household sector thus contributed a sum of Rs. 266,000,000 in saving for the finance of investment. While this saving rate was not an especially impressive one its continuation over the entire decade would at least have resulted in the contribution of nearly Rs. 3,600,000,000 in investment finance by the household sector. However, the actual outcome was far less favorable.

The stark fact is that over the decade of the 1950's as a whole the private sector spent on consumption and on transfers abroad virtually the entire increment to disposable income which economic growth during the period made available to it (see Table 7–2). Personal saving, which at one point appeared to be growing satisfactorily, became utterly stagnant. Consumption in the aggregate rose over the decade by some Rs. 1,800,000,000 and increased its percentage share of disposable income from about 90 percent to 94. Personal saving had started the decade at 7.5 percent of disposable income but it never touched so high a percentage again; over the entire 11-year period it averaged just 4.9 percent. Such high and rising consumption rates could not help but pose a serious threat to the economy's capacity for continued growth.

TABLE 7–1

THE GROWTH OF DISPOSABLE INCOME AND ITS DISPOSAL, 1950–60*

(Rs. Millions)

Year	GNP	Disposable Income	Consumption	Household Saving	Transfers to Abroad
		Aggregates			
1950........	4,170.4	3,443.4	3,218.8	266.0	80.5
1951........	4,888.9	4,091.2	3,788.6	266.0	89.8
1952........	4,606.2	3,886.0	3,890.4	−20.0	116.8
1953........	4,900.7	4,043.5	3,908.5	79.0	65.8
1954........	5,050.9	4,012.9	3,793.9	226.0	71.4
1955........	5,701.8	4,695.4	4,210.4	302.0	84.5
1956........	5,146.9	4,090.2	4,013.7	255.0	89.7
1957........	5,422.9	4,404.0	4,387.7	126.0	75.1
1958........	5,783.1	4,776.9	4,410.5	256.0	85.4
1959........	6,162.1	5,082.2	4,713.0	284.0	63.5
1960........	6,476.3	5,273.6	5,011.1	284.0	38.7
		Increments			
1950–51.....	718.5	647.8	569.8	0	9.3
1951–52.....	−282.7	−205.2	101.8	−286.0	27.0
1952–55.....	1,095.6	809.4	320.0	322.0	−32.3
1955–56.....	−554.9	−605.2	−196.7	−47.0	5.2
1956–60.....	1,329.4	1,183.4	997.4	29.0	−51.0
1950–60.....	2,305.9	1,830.2	1,792.3	18.0	−41.8

*Source: Table A–4, Appendix.

What were the causes of this disproportionate buoyancy of consumption? Some of the factors involved have already been discussed. The annual data showing levels of consumption and saving from 1950 to 1960 which appear in Table 7–1 suggest that a basic reason for the rapid rise of consumption expenditures during the period was the effect of the two export booms which the country experienced on customary living standards. The booms of 1950–51 and 1955 appear to have had a kind of irreversible "ratchet" effect on aggregate consumption expenditures. The strong upsurge of GNP in 1950–51 was followed by an equally strong rise of consumption. Consumption rose only with a lag, however, so that in 1950 and 1951 the ratio of consumption to disposable income was

TABLE 7–2

AVERAGE AND MARGINAL RATES OF CONSUMPTION AND SAVING,
1950–60* (Percent)

Year	Consumption/ Disposable Income	Consumption plus Transfers Abroad/ Disposable Income	Saving/ Disposable Income
	Average Rates		
1950	.903	.925	.075
1951	.914	.936	.064
1952	.976	1.005	−.005
1953	.964	.981	.019
1954	.927	.945	.055
1955	.916	.934	.066
1956	.921	.941	.059
1957	.956	.973	.027
1958	.928	.946	.054
1959	.931	.944	.056
1960	.939	.947	.053
Average, 1950–60	.934	.952	.049
	Marginal Rates		
1950–51	.984	1.000	0
1951–52	−.648†	−.819†	1.819†
1952–55	.525	.472	.528
1955–56	.825‡	.803‡	.197‡
1956–60	1.023	.970	.030
1950–60	1.013	.990	.010

*These rates have been worked out on the basis of a slightly different defi-
nition of disposable income than is used elsewhere, e.g., in Table 7–1. Here disposable income is taken as the sum of consumption, transfers abroad, and saving;
the statistical discrepancy which is present when this sum, which should conceptually equal disposable income, is compared with the aggregate as calculated in
Table A–4, Appendix, has thus been eliminated.

†Consumption and transfers abroad both rose while disposable income was
falling.

‡Consumption and saving both fell while disposable income was falling.

Source: Table 7–1.

robably lower than in previous years (figures for the late forties
ʰhich would be comparable to the data in Table 7–1 are not avail-
ble, but this was surely the case). In 1952, when the export boom
ame to its sudden end, with a consequent drop in GNP and dis-
osable income, consumption was still rising; the consumption ratio
ₐcreased sharply. Through 1953 and 1954, relatively unimpressive
ₓport years, consumption remained fairly stable at its higher post-
oom level; consumption ratios remained higher than they had
een in 1950–51 (and perhaps higher than they had been in the
ₐte 1940's, though there are no data to substantiate this). Ac-
ually, by 1954 the ratchet was beginning to loosen, as both ag-
regate consumption and the ratio of consumption to disposable

income fell slightly. Household saving, which had completel
disappeared during the post-Korean episode, began to regain ;
more normal level. Then came the second export boom of th
fifties, the 1955 tea boom. Again GNP and disposable incom
leapt upward and consumption, this time with a shorter lag, fo
lowed. The second boom was milder and shorter lived than th
first but again consumption fell very little from its new, higher
boom-inspired level.

After 1955 there were no more export booms but GNP and dis
posable income grew at a steady and fairly rapid rate. As had bee
the case earlier in the decade, consumption absorbed the entir
increase in disposable income. By this time it was becoming clea
that the nation's consumption standards had become pegged at a
unrealistically high level. The rapid increase of Ceylon's popula
tion continued to push aggregate consumption expenditures u
each year and certain other factors also made their contribution
the egalitarian redistribution of income brought about by the foo
subsidies and other welfare policies of the government, as well as
at the very end of the decade, speculative purchases of impor
goods by those who saw signs of approaching import control an
sought to beat the restrictions. Transfers abroad were restricted b
the progressive tightening of exchange control from 1958 on bu
the money which was thus prevented from flowing abroad appear
to have gone almost entirely into consumption rather than saving
In the end, household saving in 1960 was only slightly higher i
absolute terms than it had been in 1950 and its rate, at 4.
percent, was much lower. Over the decade as a whole household
saved only Rs. 2,324,000,000.

What of the saving of private corporations? It has already bee
noted (see Table 5-7) that corporate retained earnings amounte
to only a very small sum during the 1950's, perhaps Rs. 500,000,000
600,000,000.[1] Although before-tax corporate profits grew substan
tially during the decade taxes took the entire increment and th
volume of corporate saving, while it varied from year to year, ex
hibited no rising trend.

In sum, then, the tendencies at work in the private sector durin
the 1950's were for the nation's ambitious and boom-fed consump
tion standards to push hard on a gradually rising level of dispos
able income and for the increasing magnitudes of corporate profi
to be drained off via taxation. Between them, these phenomen
severely limited the saving capacity of the private sector. Accor

---

[1] The exact total for 1950–60 cannot be ascertained because there is no est
mate of dividend payments in 1959 and 1960 (see Table 5-7).

ingly, the main burden of responsibility for the generation of investment finance fell upon the government. The government made no attempt to avoid this responsibility. Indeed, this pattern of saving and investment was in keeping with the basic development strategy of the time. Had the resources which came under government control been saved and efficiently invested in sufficient proportion, then the failings of the private sector would have been much less harmful. However, this did not take place.

THE GOVERNMENT ROLE: REVENUE

The government's attempt to provide the necessary volume of saving and investment on its own was frustrated on two main counts. One was the difficulty of raising a sufficient volume of revenue; the unsuitability of the inherited colonial revenue system for the new policy goals, the difficulty of adapting it to these new aims, and the frequent conflicts with other goals of tax policy created one whole series of problems. The other basic frustration was that the revenue that was raised had to overcome competition from the alternative uses to which it could be put—transfer payments and current expenditures on goods and services—before it became available for investment; often the short-term pressures for these current uses outweighed the desire to invest, with harmful effects for the nation's development.

The main means of financing the government's contribution to economic development was the central government revenue system. Other methods of diverting resources to the government's purposes assumed some importance at times—drawing down foreign assets, assuming loan liabilities at home and abroad, and even, by the late fifties, virtual resort to the printing presses—but the prime source of finance continued to be the revenue system of tax and nontax receipts.

Like so much else in Ceylon, the government revenue system was a legacy from colonial days. Its main characteristic was a strong reliance upon indirect taxes levied on foreign trade flows. In 1947/48, the first financial year of independent Ceylon, it brought in just over Rs. 500,000,000.[2] Of this total, about 60 percent was provided by customs duties, which had long contributed 50 to 75

---

[2]Various delimitations of the government sector can be made. In this section reference is to the central government, including such quasi-commercial activities as health services, posts and telecommunications, and port facilities, but excluding the government-run railroad and electrical networks. Local government, which never during the period accounted for more than five percent of total government expenditure and had nearly half of even this modest level of expenditure financed by central government grants (see Tables A–66 and A–68, Appendix), is excluded.

percent of government revenues, depending on the vicissitudes of foreign trade. Import duties, which had been the largest single source of revenue ever since the nineteenth century, accounted for revenue of Rs. 177,000,000 in 1947/48; they were collected at an average rate of about 18 percent of the c.i.f. value of imports. Export duties brought in an additional Rs. 137,000,000, 14 percent of total export value f.o.b. Besides these major revenue sources, several minor ones (e.g., port dues) also depended on foreign trade.

Direct taxes were in existence but underdeveloped. A bare total of Rs. 100,000,000 was raised in 1947/48 from the various direct taxes: a personal and corporate income tax, a profits tax, an estate tax, and pension contributions. The base for these taxes was extremely narrow (e.g., the individual income tax applied to fewer than two percent of the country's income recipients;[3] the bases of the other direct taxes were similarly narrow).

The rest of the government's tax revenues were supplied by a stamp tax and various excise duties. The former covered a wide variety of legal transactions and the latter centered on gasoline, tobacco, and liquor. All told, tax receipts made up 85 percent of central government revenues; the remainder came from charges for services and property income of various kinds.

This revenue structure was a reflection of the classical economic structure. The heavy dependence of national income on foreign trade was the main reason for the parallel concentration of the tax burden on the trading sector. It was not, however, the only reason. Ease of administration and collection, the desire of the colonial ruling class to avoid the more severely progressive forms of direct taxation, the fact that the colonial regime had no need for more extensive revenues, and an extremely low ability to pay on the part of the masses also helped to shape the revenue structure. Independence introduced a desire for more rapid growth, some restructuring of the economy, more equal income distribution, and additional social services. The revenue system was called upon to serve a multiplicity of social ends—to redistribute income, foster the growth of particular sectors, discourage certain kinds of consumption, and so on. Probably its most important task, however, was to raise the additional funds needed to finance the development program.

Table 7–3 shows the increases in government revenues which

---

[3]The exemption limit at this time was Rs. 4,800 annual income. Even by 1953, after marked increases in income levels, less than two percent of the economically active population was earning this much (see Central Bank of Ceylon, *Survey of Ceylon's Consumer Finances,* 1954, Table 10).

were effected between independence and the end of the fifties. These increases, which amounted to 157.2 percent in all, were by no means inconsiderable. Yet, inevitably, they left something to be desired. If the government was to be the main saver in the economy and the volume of investment was to be raised, then it was necessary that the share of national income collected from tax and non-tax sources be increased. However, despite scores of increases in tax rates throughout the period and a full-dress attempt to revise the system of direct taxation toward its end, doing this proved to be very difficult.

TABLE 7–3

CENTRAL GOVERNMENT REVENUES, 1947/48–1960/61*

(Rs. Millions)

Year	Export Duties	Import Duties	Direct Taxes	Commodity Taxes	Nontax Revenues	Total Revenues	% of Gross National Income
1947/48	137.0	177.0	100.5	64.0	62.1	540.6	17.0
1948/49	149.1	180.2	117.7	62.8	66.2	576.0	16.9
1949/50	167.6	188.3	128.0	65.0	74.4	623.3	15.0
1950/51	282.7	245.0	144.3	84.6	75.7	832.3	17.1
1951/52	227.3	259.9	218.1	78.3	86.2	869.8	17.3
1952/53	193.2	250.6	243.5	92.8	87.8	867.8	17.4
1953/54	259.1	244.1	231.3	100.6	99.6	934.8	17.8
1954/55	370.7	258.2	219.7	95.4	119.8	1,063.8	18.5
1955/56	322.1	286.3	313.6	112.1	122.8	1,156.9	20.2
1956/57	323.9	303.6	282.6	131.9	112.6	1,154.6	20.1
1957/58	325.0	292.0	278.7	147.9	137.1	1,180.7	19.3
1958/59	328.9	367.0	218.2	160.9	142.5	1,217.5	18.9
1959/60	327.2	406.5	215.2	190.9	143.6	1,283.4	19.1
1960/61	303.6	435.3	313.9	190.6	147.1	1,390.5	....

*Source: Table A–65, Appendix; Department of Census and Statistics, *Statistical Abstracts.* Minor discrepancies are attributable to rounding.

The main reason revenue collections tended to be inelastic with respect to income growth was that they relied so heavily on the taxation of foreign trade at a time when the trade sector was generally lacking in dynamism. Despite a general upward trend in duty rates it proved hard to raise the proportion of the tax base collected (see Table 7–4). Part of the problem was conflict with other policy objectives. For example, it is axiomatic that excluding imports to protect local industry or to reduce a balance of payments deficit limits the usefulness of the import duty as a revenue device; prior to 1960, however, attempts to use import duties for these other purposes were limited in their ambitions and in any case often failed to achieve them, so revenue did not suffer much in practice.

A more important limitation on the expansibility of duty receipts was the elasticity of demand for imports in Ceylon; there comes a point at which further duty rate increases will reduce quantity demanded by enough to cut into duty receipts and by 1960 this point was being reached for many goods. Export duties ran into even clearer limits as revenue sources. Although the government was willing to tax exports at a very high rate (see Chapter 5) it still had to be careful not to bankrupt the estates, which because of the elasticity of world demand for Ceylon's products and the inelasticity of supply had to bear the main burden of the tax. Customs duties as a whole were capable of only a little expansion relative to national income, as Table 7–4 shows.

TABLE 7–4

EXPORT AND IMPORT DUTIES AS A PERCENTAGE OF THEIR TAX BASE
AND OF GNP, 1947/48–1959/60*

Year	Export Duty as a Percentage of Exports f.o.b.	Import Duty as a Percentage of Imports c.i.f.	Customs Revenue as a Percentage of GNP
1947/48......	13.8	16.0	11.2
1948/49......	15.4	17.6	10.9
1949/50......	13.6	17.5	9.7
1950/51......	14.9	16.8	11.9
1951/52......	14.6	15.9	10.7
1952/53......	13.9	15.6	9.9
1953/54......	15.7	16.2	10.7
1954/55......	20.1	18.0	12.3
1955/56......	18.1	18.6	11.9
1956/57......	19.6	16.4	12.1
1957/58......	23.3	18.6	11.4
1958/59......	18.4	18.2	12.2
1959/60......	12.2	19.5	12.3

*All data are in terms of financial years; GNP is the Census and Statistics Department concept. Source: *Ceylon Customs Returns;* Department of Census and Statistics, *Statistical Abstracts.*

Over most of the period from independence to 1960 direct taxes showed greater elasticity, relative to both their tax base and national income, than customs duties. Primarily as a result of a long series of rate increases but also because of income spurts in 1951/52 and 1954/55 the relative impact of these taxes rose steadily (see Table 7–5). Still, the highest percentage of national income ever mobilized via direct taxation was only 6.1 percent, in 1955/56. Direct taxes on individuals (income and estate taxes) averaged about one or two percent of personal income. The basic reason for these slight

TABLE 7–5

DIRECT TAXES ON INDIVIDUALS AS A PERCENTAGE OF
PERSONAL INCOME AND TOTAL DIRECT TAXES
AS A PERCENTAGE OF NATIONAL INCOME,
1947/48–1959/60*

Year	Direct Taxes on Individuals as a Percentage of Personal Income	Total Direct Taxes as a Percentage of National Income†
1947/48	...	3.6
1948/49	...	3.9
1949/50	...	3.5
1950/51	1.4	3.3
1951/52	2.1	4.8
1952/53	2.3	5.4
1953/54	2.2	4.9
1954/55	1.9	5.3
1955/56	2.3	6.1
1956/57	2.1	5.5
1957/58	2.1	5.1
1958/59	1.7	3.8
1959/60	1.5	3.6

*Source: Table A–65, Appendix; Department of Census and Statistics, *Statistical Abstracts.*
†National income is measured by the Census and Statistics Department concept.

yields was of course the narrow range of application of these taxes. During the 1953/54 assessment year, to take just one example, only 46,014 individual income tax assessments were made, covering income of Rs. 598,700,000, or 14.5 percent of all personal income earned during the period.[4] This narrowness of the tax base persisted throughout the period and greatly limited the possibilities of direct taxes as devices for expanding total government revenues. Starting in 1958/59 direct tax collections and especially income tax receipts underwent an absolute decline. The cause of this decline was an overloading of the administrative machinery (already heavily burdened by the cumbersome procedure used in applying the income tax) which resulted from the precipitate application of succeeding and sometimes contradictory rounds of direct tax reform. These difficulties had largely been overcome by 1960/61.

Commodity taxes and nontax revenues, almost by their very nature, are limited and inelastic sources of government revenues. Excise taxes were raised very rapidly during the late 1950's but

[4] *A.R. of the Commissioner of Inland Revenue* for 1954, p. 15; some further assessments covering the year in question were made later, so the coverage was actually a bit broader than the above figures suggest.

they remained a relatively unimportant part of the revenue system. The only reform which could have elevated commodity taxes to a major role would have been the levy of a general sales tax; this was talked about from the mid-fifties on and actually instituted in 1962, but badly mismanaged and withdrawn a few days after its introduction. Most of the nontax revenues—fines, charges, sales— were incidental by-products of government policies of various types —land policy, the existence and profitability of state corporations, the amount of business done by the ports—and were not generally subject to much manipulation for revenue purposes.

Taking all revenue sources together, how successful was the attempt of the government to appropriate an ever-increasing share of national income? Through the mid-fifties a considerable degree of success was achieved (see Table 7–3). In 1955/56, revenues, riding the crest of the tea boom, topped 20 percent of Gross National Income for the first time. But it was only after that year that serious efforts were made to reform the tax system and achieve massive increases in revenues[5] and these attempts were not notably successful. By 1960, in fact, the proportion of national income collected had actually slipped slightly. The main reason for this slippage was that export markets were weak and export duty collections were thus actually lower than they had been in the mid-fifties.[6] The economic growth of the latter half of the decade centered on production for the local market and much of the new output was produced by newly founded firms which enjoyed various exemptions from direct taxation. Then there was the administrative disruption connected with the new tax system. And finally, many suspect that higher rates of direct taxation meant increased tax evasion, though this cannot be proven. In sum, the revenue system, although its achievements were considerable, had not completely overcome its basic weakness of being heavily dependent on foreign trade and thus not well suited to an economy in which the relative importance of trade was gradually declining. Still, for any government of an underdeveloped country to collect much more

---

[5] A visit and a set of recommendations by Nicholas Kaldor (*Suggestions for a Comprehensive Reform of Direct Taxation*, S.P. IV of 1960) formed the starting point for these reforms, but not all of Kaldor's recommendations were followed and he cannot in any case be held fully accountable for the confusion surrounding the various turnings of government tax policy.

[6] The export duties were officially specific duties but they were in one sense a form of progressive taxation, since rates were raised when prices went up and lowered when they fell, in both cases more than proportionally. When export income rose as a result of expanding output, however, export duty rates did not necessarily go up.

than 20 percent of Gross National Income in tax revenue is highly unusual. All in all, the revenue side of Ceylon government finance can be considered to have been much better managed during this period than was the expenditure side.

THE GOVERNMENT ROLE: EXPENDITURES

Reference has already been made to the ever-rising demand for government expenditures of all kinds. These expenditures can be divided into four basic categories: (1) expenditure on current goods and services (which may or may not be closely related to economic development); (2) expenditure on capital goods; (3) transfer payments and subsidies; and (4) net loans of the government to private and local government bodies. Table 7–6 shows the broad trends in each of these as far as the central government is concerned for the years from independence through 1960.

TABLE 7–6

TYPES OF CENTRAL GOVERNMENT EXPENDITURE, 1947/48–1960/61*

Year	Current Rs. 000,000	% of Total	Capital Rs. 000,000	% of Total	Transfer Rs. 000,000	% of Total	Net Loans Rs. 000,000	% of Total	Total Expenditure
1947/48	260.6	44.0	152.5	25.7	172.7	29.1	7.1	1.2	592.9
1948/49	293.6	42.5	209.2	30.3	158.6	22.9	29.7	4.3	691.1
1949/50	321.7	40.4	241.6	30.4	141.5	17.8	90.9	11.4	795.7
1950/51	383.6	43.1	228.7	25.7	246.4	27.7	31.9	3.6	890.6
1951/52	420.7	36.3	320.7	27.7	382.7	33.1	33.4	2.9	1,157.5
1952/53	457.3	41.0	316.5	28.4	278.6	25.0	62.4	5.6	1,114.8
1953/54	470.1	50.6	253.8	27.3	147.9	15.9	57.8	6.2	929.8
1954/55	526.2	54.1	295.1	30.3	191.0	19.6	−39.0	−4.0	973.3
1955/56	547.1	44.8	307.8	25.2	288.4	23.6	79.1	6.5	1,222.4
1956/57	595.3	42.5	298.8	21.3	341.4	24.4	164.5	11.7	1,400.1
1957/58	684.6	47.1	350.4	24.1	406.5	28.0	12.9	0.9	1,454.2
1958/59	790.1	47.6	363.0	21.9	451.5	27.2	55.6	3.3	1,660.3
1959/60	847.5	48.6	357.2	20.5	480.4	27.6	56.9	3.3	1,742.0
1960/61	871.7	46.3	399.0	21.2	549.3	29.2	61.4	3.3	1,881.4

*Source: Table A–66, Appendix. Minor discrepancies are attributable to rounding.

While all kinds of expenditure rose substantially over this 12-year period the various rates of increase were by no means equal. Central government capital expenditure went up by 162 percent but transfer payments rose 218 percent and current expenditure increased by 234 percent. The type of expenditure which presumably contributed most to the economic growth of Ceylon thus fell as a percentage of the total. Government investment started out at about a quarter of total central government spending and on two different occasions was pushed by strenuous efforts up to 30 percent, but by the decade's end it had dropped back again to little more than 20 percent of the total. Current expenditures and transfer payments also had their ups and downs, but by the end of the period they were proportionally a little greater than they had been at the beginning. Current expenditures and transfers were not without their contributions to economic growth but in general Ceylon's government finance during this period is a story of the more essential kinds of expenditure from the point of view of growth being crowded out by the less essential. The cause of this phenomenon was political. At all times during the period the effective political pressures for consumption and transfer spending greatly outweighed the drive to create new capital assets. It was the government's misfortune to be committed in a fairly rigid way to roughly constant per capita expenditures on a variety of consumption services—notably public education and health services—and to the provision of subsidized food and other forms of transfer payments, also on a per capita basis. The rapid increase in the size of the population for which these services had to be provided, coupled in some cases with rises in the per unit cost of providing the services, pushed the total bill to the government up at a brisk pace. Caught between these rising service bills and the relative inelasticity of government revenues, capital expenditures suffered.

These commitments to provide current services had had their origins in the decade of the forties. For example, food subsidization for the consumer started as a natural outgrowth of wartime rationing, but both the subsidization and the rationing were permitted to linger on long after their initial justification had disappeared. During the war the program had been a relatively expensive one, since consumer prices were held constant while the cost of imported rice rose, but in the late forties increased world food supplies brought the cost down and reduced the burden on the government. Then during the Korean War period the government undertook to provide cheap food as one means of blocking increases in living costs. By 1952 these efforts had resulted in rice being sold to the consumer at less than one-third its imported cost. In 1951/52 a third of government expenditures went into transfers and subsidies, with food subsidies bulking large within the total. The government tried to back out of its onerous commitment. In July, 1953, it announced that all net subsidization of food would cease. Violent demonstrations and Ceylon's first forced change of government followed. The political commitment to food subsidies was sealed, once and for all. The U.N.P. government, anxious to make up for past misdeeds, raised the per capita rice ration to 2 measures a week for all persons in November, 1954[7] (it had previously been 2 measures for manual workers and 1¼ measures for all others) and cut the price from 55 cents to 50 cents in May of the following year. Under the M.E.P. government which followed in 1956 the price was eventually reduced to 25 cents. These moves to liberalize the food subsidy simply reinforced the effects of population rise on the total subsidy bill.

TABLE 7–7

TYPES OF SUBSIDY AND TRANSFER PAYMENTS, 1950–60*

(Rs. Millions)

Year	Subsidies				Transfer Payments					Total: Subsidies Plus Transfers
	To Food Producers	To Public Corporations	To Private Firms	Total	Interest on Public Debt	Social Security Benefits	Food "Subsidy"	Other	Total	
1950...	0.8	6.8	6.3	13.9	20.2	31.4	59.0	47.6	158.2	172.1
1951...	0.3	8.5	6.0	14.8	21.9	35.5	160.4	54.8	272.6	287.4
1952...	0.1	10.9	6.1	17.1	24.8	40.4	217.5	65.4	348.1	365.2
1953...	1.7	18.1	7.2	27.0	31.1	43.4	96.7	61.8	233.0	260.0
1954...	8.9	14.6	2.2	25.7	35.3	50.7	9.5	56.3	151.8	177.5
1955...	55.5	36.4	5.0	96.9	33.6	52.1	−8.6	57.5	134.6	231.5
1956...	43.4	55.1	8.3	106.8	34.2	63.4	42.6	71.2	211.4	318.2
1957...	68.8	55.4	17.7	141.9	35.7	70.2	38.3	86.9	231.1	373.0
1958...	85.1	61.4	31.0	177.5	37.9	80.5	35.5	99.1	253.0	430.5
1959...	89.3	62.4	22.9	174.6	46.3	91.8	68.8	95.7	302.6	477.2
1960...	124.9	57.9	9.9	192.7	57.0	94.8	81.9	100.0	333.7	526.4

*Source: Table A–5, Appendix. This table differs from Table 7–6, in that it includes all levels of government, goes by calendar rather than budget years, and nets out transfers from central government to local governments; its total is thus not comparable to the figure for transfer expenditure in Table 7–6.

After the events of 1953, however, transfers to consumers via the food subsidy began to slip somewhat in importance relative to other types of subsidies and consumer transfers. As Table 7–7 shows, subsidies to food producers (already discussed in Chapter 6) and to government corporations and transfers to individuals in the form of social security benefits, welfare payments of various kinds, and interest on the public debt came to assume much greater importance. The general line of explanation for most of these is similar to that of the food subsidies: the government took on fairly ambitious commitments in each of these areas, then stuck with them as their total cost climbed. In only one case, that of subsidies to public corporations, was it the adoption of new policies (in

---

[7] A "measure" equals about two pounds.

this case the founding of new public corporations, most of which proved to be unprofitable, at least at first) rather than the continued execution of old policies which was the key to the soaring transfer expenditures. As regards producer subsidies, the impact of the commitment on economic growth was by no means entirely negative, however, as the story of the GPS paddy scheme suggests.

The mechanism working to increase current government expenditure on goods and services was very similar to the one operating on transfer payments. The colonial government had assumed fairly ambitious obligations in the areas of education, health care, transportation, and communications. The independent government accepted these obligations in all cases and in several areas enlarged upon them. For instance, the already impressive commitment in education was enlarged to a guarantee of free education from kindergarten through university. Of course, facilities could not readily be provided to allow literally everyone who wanted this free education to have it, especially at the highest levels, but a valiant attempt was made. Despite a 50 percent rise in the school-age population between 1946 and 1960[8] the percentage of these young people who were enrolled in school was raised from just over 40 percent to more than 60 percent.[9] Hundreds of new schools were opened and thousands of teachers hired. The literacy rate and other indicators of educational achievement rose. The story for health services is similar. Despite heavy pressures on facilities enough new hospital beds were provided and enough nurses and doctors trained to raise the level of medical services relative to total population. In other areas, such as road maintenance and telephone service, past standards were sometimes permitted to deteriorate but in general the commitment to maintain past services and do this on a per capita basis where appropriate was recognized and met.

It would not be correct to regard the provision of current services by the government as entirely competitive with economic growth. Most current services can be construed to contribute *something* to growth, though some types are clearly more closely related to it than others. Table 7–8 breaks current expenditure into two categories: *general* expenditures, which represent the "overhead cost" of government and bear only a tenuous relation to economic growth, and *developmental* expenditures, which by supporting investment outlays on either human or physical resources make a direct con-

---

[8]See Table A–16, Appendix.
[9]See Table A–19, Appendix.

TABLE 7–8

CURRENT GOVERNMENT EXPENDITURE ON GOODS AND SERVICES, 1950–60*

(Rs. Millions)

Year	Admin-istra-tive	De-fense	Total	% of all Cur-rent	Edu-cation	Health	Other Social	Eco-nomic	Total	% of All Cur-rent	Total Cur-rent
		General					Developmental				
1950.....	88.6	7.6	96.2	28.1	97.8	65.2	7.2	75.8	246.0	71.9	342.2
1951.....	106.9	11.1	118.0	29.5	108.9	72.6	9.8	90.2	281.5	70.5	399.5
1952.....	103.5	18.4	121.9	27.7	122.8	84.7	12.8	98.4	318.7	72.3	440.6
1953.....	115.3	29.2	144.5	30.7	126.8	88.9	12.5	97.3	325.5	69.3	470.0
1954.....	120.4	30.2	150.6	31.1	125.5	91.7	22.0	94.0	333.2	68.9	483.8
1955.....	138.6	27.5	166.1	31.3	134.7	95.3	22.3	112.4	364.7	68.7	530.8
1956.....	148.7	31.2	179.9	31.7	149.9	104.0	22.9	111.4	388.2	68.3	568.1
1957.....	167.8	41.2	209.0	32.7	171.9	112.4	18.7	126.4	429.4	67.3	638.4
1958.....	179.3	66.2	245.5	32.9	198.5	126.4	33.1	142.1	500.1	67.1	745.6
1959.....	188.9	71.9	260.8	31.4	232.3	144.6	51.6	142.2	570.7	68.6	831.5
1960.....	198.7	71.3	270.0	30.9	201.0	146.4	95.1	161.3	603.8	69.1	873.8

*Source: Table A–5, Appendix.

tribution to the development effort. As the table suggests, trends in the respective proportions of current expenditure devoted to those two types of activities left something to be desired. Through 1958 general expenditures rose faster than developmental expenditures. In part this rapid rise in the overhead costs of government was attributable to increasing military expenditures: Ceylon had been fortunate in needing to devote only a very small percentage of its resources to military uses at first, but internal unrest—principally in 1953, 1957, and 1958—eventually led to a tenfold increase in military spending over the decade. Administrative expenditures also moved steadily upward, however, as government employment rolls lengthened and wage and salary increases were granted to various groups of government employees. Only in 1959 and 1960 was the lid placed on general expenditures; at that time their rate of increase was finally slowed down by enough to permit the percentage of current expenditure going into developmental uses to be raised (though it nevertheless remained below its 1950 level in 1960). The rise in expenditures on education and health has already been commented upon. Government commitments in most other areas of social services and for all economic services were less firm, so these areas tended to be squeezed in a manner similar to capital expenditures. Only in the last two years of the decade were substantial increases in spending on these important services —community development, irrigation maintenance, road repair, and many others—achieved.

Left to compete on rather unequal terms with expenditures on current goods and services, government investment in Ceylon has had a checkered history. Through 1960 it increased neither so much nor so regularly as current spending. Besides having to compete disadvantageously with current expenditures, capital expenditure faced two additional liabilities. For one thing, planning investment projects is more difficult than continuing or even extending current spending programs; often investment projects must be integrated into a full-blown national plan and this entails still more time-consuming delays. Secondly, even after investment plans are drawn up investment expenditure is harder to execute than current spending; capital expenditures have thus tended to take up a smaller proportion of actual government spending than of budget allocations originally voted by Parliament.

TABLE 7–9

GENERAL GOVERNMENT REVENUE AND EXPENDITURE, 1950–60*

(Rs. Millions)

| Year | Total Revenue | Current Expenditures | | Current Surplus | Fixed Investment | Overall Surplus |
		Goods and Services	Transfer Payments and Subsidies			
1950........	658.9	342.2	172.1	144.6	222.4	− 77.8
1951........	819.4	399.5	287.4	132.5	241.3	−108.8
1952........	842.0	440.6	365.2	36.2	308.3	−272.1
1953........	856.5	470.0	260.0	126.5	292.9	−166.4
1954........	926.4	483.8	177.5	265.1	264.2	0.9
1955........	1,029.4	530.8	231.5	267.1	315.3	− 48.2
1956........	1,112.3	568.1	318.2	226.0	335.1	−109.1
1957........	1,124.1	638.4	373.0	112.7	328.2	−215.5
1958........	1,150.0	745.6	430.5	− 26.1	345.4	−371.5
1959........	1,191.7	831.5	477.2	−117.0	355.2	−472.2
1960........	1,363.3	873.8	526.4	− 36.9	378.7	−415.6

*Source: Tables A–5 and A–7, Appendix. The current surplus shown in this table represents a slightly different concept from the current surplus of Table A–7, in that grants from foreign governments are considered a component of total government receipts there, whereas here they are regarded as a means of financing the deficit.

Table 7–9 brings together totals covering all the main categories of public finance for the general government sector in the period 1950–60. All the trends just discussed are visible in this table, in addition to which the overall balance of revenues and expenditures is given. As the table shows, the surplus of revenue over current expenditures, which had been an invariable characteristic of Ceylon government finance since colonial days, declined rapidly during the late fifties and finally disappeared, as current expenditures on both goods and services and transfer payments and subsidies climbed rapidly and the growth of government revenue lagged behind. The addition to the total expenditure bill of public investment, which rose quite modestly during the course of the decade, caused ever larger overall deficits to be run. The government thus became an increasingly expansionary influence on the economy, in fact, as will be seen shortly, a dangerously overexpansionary influence. One further trend in public finance, which exacerbated the expansionary effect of the government during this period, is not shown in the table. It pertains to the means by which the growing budgetary deficit was financed. Up to the last four years of the period relatively little use was made by the government of the more blatantly inflationary forms of deficit finance. Sizable proportions of the debt incurred in the earlier years were financed by foreign grants and loans and by domestic nonbank borrowing. From 1956 on, however, increasing resort was had to means of finance which amounted to little more than use of the printing press—borrowing from the Central Bank, "administrative borrowing" from government trust funds, and drawings from government cash balances and reserves.[10] The government's net impact on aggregate demand was of course accentuated by this development.

One does not have to be a proponent of strict fiscal orthodoxy to be appalled by the course taken by Ceylon government finance during the late 1950's. However valid the arguments for deficit finance as a means of bolstering aggregate demand and restoring national output to capacity levels in other economic contexts, they are clearly inapplicable to the case of a developing export economy, where the pressing need is to increase domestic saving and investment while guarding against fatal damage to the balance of payments. This end can hardly be promoted by government dissaving (i.e., a surplus of current expenditure over total revenue), which adds to demand pressures while doing little to accelerate economic growth. A more promising policy for the Ceylon government to have pursued at this stage would have been to run current surpluses and use these surpluses, as well as any funds which became available through foreign grants and loans, for investment purposes. Instead, public finance contributed to the squeezing of investment by

---

[10]See Table A–67, Appendix, for a precise breakdown of the central government deficit by means of finance. Comparable data for the general government sector, to which the discussion in the text pertains, are not available.

current expenditures while making major additions to the pressures on the balance of payments.

THE QUESTION OF INVESTMENT PRIORITIES

Aside from the massive problem of investment finance, the nation was also faced with the basic issue of how best to allocate among alternative uses whatever volume of investment could in fact be financed. This question arose in regard to both the direct allocation of public investment and the measures to be taken to influence indirectly the flow of private investment. In short, it was an important part of the larger, fundamental problem of determining the appropriate strategy for the island's economic development, to which each successive national plan addressed itself (see pages 108–113). This problem had several dimensions. There were the universal issues of public investment in overhead capital versus directly productive facilities, of export promotion versus import substitution, of agriculture versus industry, and of private versus public enterprise, as well as the more peculiarly Ceylonese question of estate versus traditional agriculture. In the Ceylon context, most of these issues boiled down to the fundamental sectoral question: To what degree should the development of traditional agriculture, estate agriculture, and industry respectively be stressed? This question was asked by every government of Ceylon during the period being studied, both of itself and of notable outside consultants,[11] but the breakdown which eventually ensued in the development effort shows that no completely satisfactory response was ever received. Even now, reviewing the successes and failures of the period and making use of the incalculable advantage of hindsight, it is hard to

---

[11]The visit of a star-studded panel of visiting economists in 1958 and 1959 did nothing to resolve the dilemma of sectoral priorities. In his "Reflections on the Economic Problems of Ceylon" (Planning Secretariat, *Papers by Visiting Economists*, pp. 7–21) John R. Hicks came out for emphasis on traditional agriculture as the only sector which offered a real hope of increasing employment fast enough to absorb the rapidly growing labor force and one area in which considerable productivity gains could be made with little capital cost. Nicholas Kaldor ("Observations on the Problem of Economic Development in Ceylon," pp. 23–33), by contrast, noted that Ceylon owed what prosperity it had realized so far to its plantation agriculture and urged further concentration on that relatively productive sector: "Contrary to the widespread belief according to which a 'colonial' economy is necessarily at a disadvantage as compared with countries which do not depend on the exports of primary products for their livelihood, it seems to me that it is the further development of the plantation economy which provides the means for a rapid increase in Ceylon's national wealth." (p. 25). And in the third paper in the volume ("Economic Possibilities of Ceylon," pp. 35–71) Joan Robinson rounded out the list of possible sectoral emphases by stressing industry as the ultimate solution to Ceylon's economic problems. It is no wonder that the discussion within Ceylon was inconclusive.

define the optimal strategy for the country's economic development. Still, one should try.

Two clearly defined subperiods in the development of official thinking on the subject can be distinguished within the 1948-60 era dealt with here. The dividing line between them is political. If only because D. S. Senanayake, the founder of the United National Party and Ceylon's first prime minister, was passionately interested in the development of peasant agriculture, the U.N.P. in its early years of power stressed the building up of traditional agriculture, especially its extension to a broader land area through land development and irrigation schemes. Overhead facilities, especially education, health, power, and transportation, also ranked high on the U.N.P.'s priority list. Industrial development was generally left to the private sector. The estates began to be used as a means of financing the entire development program and were thus taxed increasingly heavily; their regeneration through replanting was effectively assured, but this was essentially a defensive operation. It was not expected that export markets would expand very rapidly and no noteworthy attempts were made to accelerate the growth of export receipts, in either traditional or new product lines. On the other hand, the failure to achieve rapid industrial development meant that the substitution of local production for imports (with the notable exception of rice) proceeded very slowly. In short, while the U.N.P. government was probably not guilty of so many errors of commission as the coalition governments which succeeded it, it is liable to criticism for having allowed the economy to drift too long without putting into operation a workable long-term development strategy.

The U.N.P.'s approach to development was partly a product of party ideology and partly a natural, if shortsighted, reaction to the fact that the early 1950's were good years for Ceylon's economic well being. As the decade wore on and the prospect darkened the U.N.P. government experienced a heightened concern for the economy's future and began to act with increasing boldness (as in the *Six-Year Programme of Investment*). When the M.E.P. government replaced the U.N.P. in 1956 both ideology and circumstances dictated a bolder course still. Under the M.E.P. regime priority in the allocation of public investment shifted from overhead capital and agriculture to directly productive assets and industry. In the field of plantation agriculture and particularly in the industrial area this change brought the government into direct conflict with private capital; despite attempts to carve out a niche for each and thus create a basis for coexistence foreign private capital in particular received a serious fright. The deteriorating external position of the economy suggested the need to lend a larger measure of protection to local industry, however, so despite the increasingly hostile attitude of the government during the late fifties policies were implemented which led to a sharp increase in the rate of private investment. In sum, while the U.N.P. policies were benevolent but too mild those of the M.E.P. were more aggressive but often ominous in their implications for the private economy.[12] Partly because of its evident short-comings and partly because it had a far narrower margin for error and delay than the U.N.P. had enjoyed, the M.E.P. policy was even less successful than that of its predecessor had been in combining economic growth with balance of payments stability. Both parties thus made their contributions to the economic debacle of the early 1960's.

Before describing that debacle, however, one might pause to ask the obvious question posed by Ceylon's problem of investment priorities. What development strategy might in retrospect have saved the transitional economic system and made it possible to avoid the harsh austerity of the sixties? Aside from the evident need to devote a larger proportion of its output to investment, what changes in basic policy should have been adopted? Ceylon's economy had traditionally been dependent upon the exportation of primary products, but now it was rapidly developing a sizable labor surplus, which could not possibly be absorbed by the export sector. With prospects for any substantial expansion of the income earned by traditional exports similarly dim, the need to restructure the economy had clearly become imperative. And with capital becoming increasingly scarce in relative terms the need to invest

---

[12]From the point of view of private capital there was the further problem of knowing just what government policy was. To some extent, this ambiguity is inevitable under a coalition government. When Bandaranaike first took office, for example, he made the leader of one of the parties which was a junior partner in his coalition, Trotskyite Phillip Gunawardene, minister of agriculture. Before long Gunawardene was announcing plans for a full-scale nationalization of foreign-owned estates. The minister was in time forced out of the cabinet by the enmity of some of its less radical members but regardless of his departure and despite a flat ten-year indemnity from nationalization which was subsequently proclaimed by the prime minister much harm was done to the morale of the foreign estate companies in particular and to that of private capital in general. Here and in other sections of this volume the account given of personalities and policies does no more than hint at the obstacles to Ceylon's economic development created by events in the ever-lively political sphere. For much of the period covered here, further detail is given by Henry M. Oliver, *Economic Opinion and Policy in Ceylon* (Durham, North Carolina: Duke University Press, 1957), and by W. Howard Wriggins, *Ceylon: Dilemmas of a New Nation* (Princeton, New Jersey: Princeton University Press, 1956).

where the marginal unit of capital would yield the maximum return was also obvious. But where was that? What investment allocation could have reconciled the separate but interrelated goals of restructuring the economy, raising national output, and providing employment for the expanding labor force, while at the same time managing to avoid gross external imbalance?

The analysis of Chapter 6 has already suggested two areas— estate technology, including replanting, and the intensification of rice cultivation—in which returns to investment appear to have been very high. In these areas investment by both the public and the private sectors yielded handsome returns. The decade of the fifties saw the basis created for an increasingly efficient agricultural sector. However, much more could have been done. To cite just one example, despite considerable discussion and even some concrete proposals, no national rice research institute of the type which had proved so effective an agent for enhancing productivity in the tea and rubber industries was ever founded. Nor was anything like a comparable volume of research effort put into any of the crops which might have formed the basis for agricultural diversification as the old crops received. In short, the promotion of the long-run efficiency of Ceylon's agriculture, although an area of relative success during the 1950's, could have been made to yield much larger benefits.

Building up the efficiency of export agriculture, however, was inevitably a long-term project. In fact, whatever amount of export promotion of any type was actually feasible during the fifties (and it was probably not great) was likely to be of limited immediate benefit to the country. To permit the life of the relatively open economy of the 1950's to be extended into the sixties at all it would have been necessary to work far sooner and far more effectively for import substitution. This necessity for import substitution implies that the two areas of highest priority, which should have been stressed above all others, were consumer goods manufacturing and food production. Food production, as already noted, was an area of relative though not unqualified success. In the industrial area, however, it has been seen that public policy failed badly. For significant import substitution of manufactured products to have occurred it would have been necessary to give those industries which had a reasonable chance of ever achieving an efficient standard of operation substantial protection from foreign competition and effective direct encouragement early in the decade. Given Ceylon's relatively small population and modest per capita income level, the efficiency criterion implies that it was small and medium-scale (and therefore presumably private) plants producing primarily consumer goods which should have received first attention. Had a clear, consistent policy toward private industrial investment been enunciated in, say, the early fifties and then maintained substantially intact throughout the decade, and had it been combined with a reasonable degree of protection from external competition through a rationalized tariff structure, then Ceylon would have been well on the way to industrialization by 1960. The cheap and easy access to imports which the Ceylonese consumer enjoyed throughout most of the decade would have had to be fairly sharply curtailed, but the degree of austerity needed would have been far milder than that which mas made necessary later by the failure to evolve and implement a satisfactory policy. Moreover, a foundation for future growth and a conceivable eventual end to austerity would have been laid. Some external deficit and a controlled rundown of the country's foreign assets would doubtless have occurred, but these resources would have been used to finance the importation of intermediate and investment goods rather than articles of luxury and semiluxury consumption. The latter could have been prohibitively taxed in cases where import substitution was plausible; where it was not, heavy but not prohibitive duties could have been used to stem the flow of expenditures on consumer goods imports, while at the same time providing a much-needed supplement to government revenue.

Import duties were not the only policy tool which could have been used to prevent gross external imbalance during the development effort. In principle, at least, direct trade controls and rupee devaluation were alternative instruments which could have been employed. However, the objections to the use of either are great. The argument against direct controls is administrative. Direct controls are precision instruments *if* the basic policy to be enforced is clearly spelled out down to the finest detail and *if* the administrative machinery is able to enforce the policy. In Ceylon, as in most underdeveloped countries, the government administration was already under strain because of the many new responsibilities it had acquired in the past few years. The argument for allowing the forces of the market to help implement policy, as they do under a system of indirect controls such as tariffs, should have been compelling (although in fact when the government finally did enact severe trade sanctions in 1960 it chose direct controls over trade and payments as its main instruments). As a third alternative, rupee devaluation could have been used as a means of restoring external equilibrium. This would have served to reduce the import bill and would, like higher tariffs or direct controls, have created incentives for investment in import-substituting industries. However, devaluation on the scale which would have been needed if external equilibrium were to be regained at relatively low tariff levels would have involved a sudden, discontinuous reduction of customary living standards. Furthermore, it would have raised the prices of *all* imported goods, intermediate and capital goods as well as consumer goods. All in all, selective tariff manipulation would appear to have been the most desirable policy tool to have adopted for major emphasis.

But even without going into all the possible arguments for and against alternative methods of restoring equilibrium one can see that it is quite possible to imagine a development strategy which would have provided at least as high a growth rate as the economy enjoyed during the 1950's while at the same time offering at least partial answers to the saving, employment, and structural change problems and leaving the economy in far better condition to face the 1960's. Answers to the various questions of investment priorities —agriculture versus industry, overhead capital versus direct production, private enterprise versus public—would have flowed naturally from this strategy. Agriculture, both plantation and peasant agriculture, would have received heavy emphasis because of the attractive rate of return offered by investment in intensive agriculture and because of its considerable potential for employment creation. Industry of a certain type would have been another area stressed, with small-scale private organization preferred on efficiency grounds. Some of the more lavish outlays on overhead capital, for example expenditures on traditional academic education and on power production for household consumption, would have been trimmed. It is true that these improvements in investment allocation would not have been adequate to guarantee sustained development unless a considerably larger volume of investment had been made. However, if the government had encouraged rather than frustrated private investment and if it had managed the resources at its own disposal more effectively it could have brought about a considerable rise in national saving and investment. Most important of all, rapid and effectively managed economic growth would have generated a considerable increase in saving and investment potential in its own right.

The contrast between this idealized picture of the economic development Ceylon might have had during the first years of its independence and what actually happened is sobering. Despite the limited successes described in Chapter 6, the problems of the transitional economy which have been discussed in the present

TABLE 7-10

THE GROWTH OF AGGREGATE SUPPLY AND DEMAND, 1950–60*

(Rs. Millions)

	1950	1951	1952	1953	1954	1955	1956	1957	1958	1959	1960
Gross Domestic Product	4,225	4,953	4,652	4,939	5,098	5,763	5,202	5,474	5,824	6,199	6,521
Minus: Exports	1,617	1,968	1,565	1,698	1,914	2,071	1,846	1,796	1,912	2,079	2,079
Equals: Internal supply	2,608	2,985	3,087	3,240	3,183	3,693	3,356	3,678	3,912	4,120	4,442
Private consumption	3,219	3,789	3,890	3,909	3,794	4,210	4,014	4,388	4,411	4,713	5,011
Gross investment	391	535	613	637	446	610	632	710	757	812	785
Public consumption	342	400	441	470	484	531	568	638	746	832	874
Total: Aggregate demand	3,952	4,723	4,944	5,015	4,723	5,351	5,214	5,736	5,913	6,356	6,670
Aggregate demand *minus* internal supply†	1,344	1,737	1,857	1,775	1,540	1,659	1,858	2,058	2,001	2,237	2,228
Excess aggregate demand‡	–273	–230	292	77	–374	–412	12	262	89	158	149

*Source: Table A–2, Appendix. Occasional small discrepancies are attributable to rounding error.
†This aggregate is identical to imports of goods and nonfactor services.
‡I.e., imports of all goods and services (including factor services) minus all exports. This total is derived from the national accounts and thus differs slightly from the equivalent figure in the balance of payments. A negative total denotes a surplus.

chapter gradually came to dominate the economic scene. The fundamental failures in regard to the finance and allocation of investment led directly to the balance of payments crisis of the late fifties.

EXTERNAL IMBALANCE

In the context of the export economy, one can define excess aggregate demand as the amount by which the total volume of expenditures by the economy on local output and imports exceeds the economy's supply capacity, i.e., its ability to satisfy this demand, either through domestic output for local use or through imports purchased out of export receipts. As a result of all the difficulties discussed in earlier sections of this chapter, the development of Ceylon's economy during the 1950's had a tendency to produce excess aggregate demand. It first appeared in 1952–53 as a result of the coincidence of the commodity slump with large expenditures out of the incomes that had been earned in the preceding boom. Not until 1956, however, did excess demand become a persistent feature of the economy (see Table 7–10). Then, based on the swelling consumption expenditures of the household sector and fed by the deficit finance of the government, it became the major problem with which public policy had to cope. The failure to provide adequate domestic saving and the shortcomings of the allocation pattern of the investment which did take place limited the growth of the economy's supply capacity, as did the unfavorable price trends which occurred in the export markets during the latter part of the decade. The government, faced with the necessity to hold this excess demand within safe limits or else accept the unpleasant consequences, proved unequal to the challenge.

The basic structure of the export economy assured that this growing excess of demand over the supply capacity of the economy tended to be expressed almost entirely in increased imports of the many kinds of consumer and producer goods for which the economy was still largely dependent on foreign suppliers. Rising domestic prices, coupled with some induced increases in local production of the demanded goods, which would have been a major result of excess aggregate demand in other economic environments, did not occur on any significant scale. Price levels in Ceylon, as in all export economies, continued to be dominated by trends in world markets rather than by factors internal to the domestic economy.[13]

---

[13]Only in the short run can local demand have much effect on the level of goods prices in an export economy. If, say, an unexpected surge takes place in local demand for some particular good, prices do rise, but this is purely a

(Continued on next page)

Thus no incentive for increased production was created by the excess demand situation. Instead, there were only serious foreign payments difficulties.

The tendency for excess aggregate demand to arise during a period when attempts are being made to force the growth and diversification of an export economy is anything but surprising. Indeed, serious efforts to expand national output generally imply domestic investment in excess of domestic saving and hence excess aggregate demand. Financing this excess demand and the external deficit which it is likely to create is an essential part of the development problem and one which requires careful management. In Ceylon during the 1950's it did not receive it.

Within any export economy there are clearly defined limits to the amount of excess demand which can safely be tolerated. Excess demand expresses itself as a deficit in the goods and services account of the balance of payments. It is a deficit in this account that is the likely, even unavoidable consequence of attempted development. What is intolerable, however, is a prolonged deficit in what might be called the basic balance of payments. The basic balance includes not only goods and services flows but also current transfers (the sum of these two, of course, is the current account balance) and autonomous capital flows.[14] Developing export economies

---

short-run, disequilibrium phenomenon. In a matter of weeks or months increased imports will flow into the country to answer the rise in demand and prices will fall back to their previous level. In equilibrium, prices of imported goods are invariably equal to prices in the supplying countries, plus margins for shipping costs, import duties, and dealers' costs and profits. Since goods which are both produced and consumed locally are relatively unimportant and are usually in close competition with imports, their prices, too, are decisively influenced by world prices. Services, which often cannot be imported, are in a different position. It is possible in an export economy with restricted access to immigrant labor for wages to be driven up by either a general shortage of labor at going wages or by a shortage of some particular types of labor. If this occurs, the reaction in the goods market is again primarily one of increased imports, not, in the long run, higher prices or increased local production. Ceylon during the period being studied generally had ample supplies of labor, even for most of the specialized skills employed in the economy, so the latter situation did not arise (although it had upon occasion in the past).

[14]The concept of "autonomous capital flow" represents an attempt to distinguish between two types of items in the capital account of the balance of payments: (1) those which represent international capital flows occurring independent of the balance of current account items; and (2) those which represent means of financing current account deficits (or investing the proceeds of current account surpluses). The former category is taken here to consist of changes in long-term liabilities to foreigners, whether private or official. All short-run capital movements are considered to be means of finance, as are changes in the long-term foreign assets of the country (e.g., long-maturity sterling securities).

are likely to have large current account deficits, for more than one reason. There is the buoyant goods and services demand already mentioned. In addition, since foreign entrepreneurship played a central role in the past development of the economy and is still likely to be a significant factor, the goods and services deficit is likely to be swelled by a substantial outflow of profits and interest paid abroad. Moreover, the historical legacy of immigrant labor is almost certain to result in an additional large outflow of current transfers in the form of immigrant remittances. All things considered, the current account deficit is likely to be large. Whether the probable deficits on goods and services and on current transfer payments create a basic external deficit depends, of course, on the direction and size of autonomous capital flows. While some current account deficit is virtually inevitable it is to be hoped that a deficit in the basic balance of payments *can* be avoided, or, if it occurs, that it can be righted within a relatively short time. The ability of a country to tolerate a basic balance of payments deficit depends upon the quantity of foreign assets it possesses which can be sold off to finance the deficit and on the facilities for short-term financing through the acceptance of its liabilities by foreigners it can uncover, but it is in any case basically limited. Foreign asset accumulations, however large, are finite in quantity and the willingness of foreign businesses and governments (although not necessarily international institutions) to provide short-term credits disappears quickly if an extended series of deficits is run. The developing country is thus faced with the necessity to avoid basic deficits altogether, or, if it runs them at all, to see that they are safely eliminated, either by accelerated real output growth or by improved control over monetary outflows, well before the availability of financing runs out.

It was thus almost inevitable that Ceylon was called upon to face the problem of external imbalance as its efforts to develop were intensified. That it failed to solve the problem and was eventually forced to accept the bitter consequences of that failure was not inevitable.

It is always difficult in a situation in which a country runs successive external deficits to isolate the particular item or items which "caused" the deficits. All parts of the balance of payments make their contributions. Even accounts which show credit balances may be to blame if their magnitudes are not so large as they could or should be. A brief item-by-item survey, however, will help to suggest the nature of the various contributions made to the worsening condition of Ceylon's external accounts.

Table 7–11 presents the net position of the key categories of Ceylon's balance of payments in the late forties and the fifties. It shows that up to the last four years of the period the island generally ran a surplus on merchandise account, the only exception to this tendency being the postboom adjustment years of 1952 and 1953. Against this merchandise surplus was usually credited a deficit on invisible items of varying but considerable size, as well as a steady net outflow of private remittances and immigrant transfers, which went mainly to India. This pattern, it can be presumed, was similar to the one which had prevailed for some decades; it can be judged to be a characteristic feature of the export economy. The fact that merchandise imports were kept at a level substantially lower than that of merchandise exports permitted large foreign remittances to be made out of profits and wages without creating any serious current account deficit. Ever since the end of the

TABLE 7–11

SELECTED ELEMENTS OF THE BALANCE OF PAYMENTS, 1948–60*

(Rs. Millions)

Year	Merchandise Surplus	Current Account			Autonomous Capital Inflow†	Basic Balance‡	Increase in Foreign Assets§	Other Balancing Items‖
		Surplus on Invisibles	Net transfers from Abroad	Overall				
1948.........	94	. . .	. . .	24	. . .	. . .	51	. . .
1949.........	37	− 6	− 59	− 28	. . .	. . .	− 34	. . .
1950.........	239	− 33	− 69	137	− 26	111	169	− 58
1951.........	238	− 72	− 77	89	− 65	24	84	− 60
1952.........	− 297	− 45	− 104	− 446	− 17	− 463	− 343	− 120
1953.........	− 138	25	− 45	− 158	− 22	− 180	− 233	53
1954.........	340	9	− 43	306	50	356	304	52
1955.........	415	− 31	− 61	323	− 42	281	285	− 4
1956.........	196	− 59	− 55	82	− 43	39	47	− 8
1957.........	− 95	− 61	− 39	− 195	− 18	− 213	− 214	1
1958.........	− 89	− 41	− 23	− 153	8	− 145	− 129	− 16
1959.........	− 183	− 13	− 12	− 208	8	− 200	− 199	− 1
1960.........	− 203	− 39	22	− 220	22	− 198	− 193	− 5
Cumulative totals:								
1948–60.......	554	. . .	. . .	− 447	. . .	. . .	− 405	. . .
1950–60.......	423	− 360	− 506	− 443	− 145	− 588	− 422	− 165

*Unless otherwise noted, the source for all items is the balance of payments (see Table A–57, Appendix).

†Defined as net inflow of long-term capital on private or public account, minus net changes in long-term foreign assets held by the government and Ceylonese banks. Source: Central Bank of Ceylon, *Annual Reports of the Monetary Board to the Minister of Finance.*

‡Defined as current account surplus (deficit), minus any autonomous capital outflow (inflow).

§Source: Table A–60, Appendix.

‖A residual; consists of declines in short-term liabilities to foreigners, plus errors and ommissions.

period of sizable estate plantings, it is likely that a pattern much like this, with the current account approximately balanced, had been the rule.

The balance of payments of the late 1940's and early 1950's did have one feature which was new, however. That was the steady net outflow of long-term capital which was taking place. This outflow resulted primarily from sales of assets which had previously been foreign-owned to Ceylon nationals. Many tea and rubber estates and a wide variety of commercial establishments—newspapers, hotels, department stores, etc.—changed hands during these years. Capital outflows of this type, which were heaviest during the years 1950–52, were large enough to outweigh all the autonomous capital inflows that the island received. As a result, the cumulative basic balance did not show any great surplus over the period ending in 1956, as did the merchandise account and even the overall current account balance. The nation was thus less well equipped than it might have been to withstand the really serious balance of payments pressures which developed after 1956.

With the waning of the mid-decade tea prosperity the merchandise account swung into a state of persistent deficit. This was the period of large-scale demand creation. Almost the entire impact of the excess demand which resulted was felt in the external balance. As the payments position worsened, increasingly stringent measures were taken by the government to arrest the deterioration. These measures primarily took the form of direct trade and exchange controls and struck first at private remittances and capital repatriation, then increasingly at goods and services trade. The flow of current transfers out of the country was severely limited and the outward flow of private long-term investment, which had slowed down in the mid-fifties but had been revived by the election of the M.E.P. government in 1956, was virtually halted. The merchandise account, however, continued to deteriorate right up through the end of the decade. The cumulative basic deficit for the decade of the fifties, fed by cumulative deficits on invisibles, transfers, and autonomous capital, finally mounted to the sum of Rs. 588,000,000.

There were two basic ways in which Ceylon could finance this enormous deficit. It could draw down its accumulated foreign assets or it could take on more short-term liabilities to foreigners. The extent to which the latter alternative was really open to it, of course, depended upon the willingness of foreigners to supply goods and services on receipt of such IOU's. In fact, only in 1952 did increasing foreign liabilities serve as an important means of financing the deficit. Over the rest of the period and particularly during the uniformly deficit years of the late 1950's the full brunt of financing fell upon the external assets. The level of the country's foreign assets and the rate at which they were being dissipated thus served as the best indicators of how much excess demand was being financed through external deficits and how long this process could be continued.

There is a sense in which the total value of foreign assets furnishes the best indication of the continued viability of an export economy. Regardless of what rate of economic growth is being achieved an export economy cannot continue to function in its familiar way with a deficit in its basic balance of payments. If a basic deficit is permitted to persist for too long a time total foreign assets will eventually be exhausted and there will be no means remaining to finance further deficits. A sharp reduction of the import bill to a level which can be financed solely by the remaining items which go into the basic balance of payments will then become an absolute necessity.

During the late 1950's Ceylon's economy entered a period in which there was indeed a strong and persistent tendency toward basic external imbalance. The growth of aggregate demand within the economy greatly increased import demand at the same time as the export booms which had periodically replenished the stock of foreign assets in the past ceased to recur. To restore external equilibrium in this new, less favorable environment it would have been necessary to restrict the flow of imports into the country to a level that could be financed without rapid rundowns of external assets through the application of much higher rates of import duty. A similar effect could have been achieved through the use of direct controls or rupee devaluation or some combination of these policy tools. Whichever policy instruments were chosen, two steps would have been required: (1) to recognize the new situation for what it was—a basic disequilibrium, not just a brief unfavorable episode in an essentially viable economic structure—and (2) to institute measures strong enough to regain basic balance. Neither of these steps was taken until, by the end of 1960, the country's foreign assets had become so badly depleted (see Table 7–12) that the action required was drastic and painful in the extreme.

As noted earlier, a timely application of direct or indirect controls over imports would also have formed part of a workable strategy for economic development. While a rationally designed protective duty structure would be rather different from a structure intended primarily to achieve external balance (the former would presumably give greatest protection to simple mass consumption goods which could be produced easily and profitably in Ceylon, while the latter would emphasize the limitation of luxury and semi-luxury imports) there would nevertheless be considerable overlap. This protective side effect did in fact accompany the harsh controls imposed in and after 1960 but, because the government had waited too long to make a determined effort to act, stabilization became to some extent a goal which conflicted with development, rather than harmonizing with it, as it would have if imposed in a milder form at an earlier date. The controls instituted in the early sixties had an initial effect of stimulating the growth of production for the local market but because the external assets had been permitted to decline to precarious levels imports of intermediate and investment goods as well as consumption goods had to be tightly curtailed in time and much of the growth-promoting effect was lost (see Chapter 8).

TABLE 7–12

Foreign Assets, 1946–60*

Year	Foreign Assets, End of Year (Rs. 000,000)	Change in Assets During Year (Rs. 000,000)	Cumulated	Assets in Terms of Months of Imports†
1946	1,210.3	− 49.6	− 49.6	20.9
1947	947.3	−263.0	−312.6	11.8
1948	997.9	50.6	−262.0	13.4
1949	963.7	− 34.2	−296.2	11.3
1950	1,132.9	169.2	−127.0	11.6
1951	1,216.8	83.9	− 43.1	9.5
1952	873.8	−343.0	−386.1	6.1
1953	640.4	−233.4	−619.5	4.7
1954	944.3	303.9	−315.6	8.2
1955	1,228.8	284.5	− 31.1	9.2
1956	1,275.7	46.9	15.8	9.7
1957	1,061.9	−213.8	−198.0	7.2
1958	933.2	−128.7	−326.7	6.5
1959	734.0	−199.2	−525.9	4.5
1960	541.3	−192.7	−718.6	3.2

*Source: Tables A–56, A–57, and A–60, Appendix.
†Includes merchandise imports only; taking account of invisible imports as well would lower all of these figures slightly.

The impact of the fall in the external assets which took place throughout the fifties is forcefully demonstrated when one considers the fact that the burgeoning population and the slowly rising per capita income level were applying constant pressure to the import bill and continuously increasing the need of the country for external reserves. In terms of the value of imports in the preceding year, Ceylon had on hand at the end of 1946 foreign assets equivalent to nearly 21 months' purchases (see Table 7–12). At the top of the Korean boom, on the other hand, the figure reached not quite 12 months. In 1954 it peaked again, but at less than ten. And by the end of 1960 it had fallen to just over three months and could not go much lower.

CONCLUSION: WHERE CEYLON FAILED

Having examined some of the successes of the attempt to accelerate the expansion of Ceylon's economy after independence, as well as some of the problems that this effort created, and before going on to a discussion of the period since 1960, it is appropriate to ask where Ceylon failed. That the development effort was a failure, at least by some important criteria, cannot be denied. The violent and hasty imposition of severe import and exchange controls from December, 1960 on, the hardships imposed on the island's inhabitants since that time, and the deceleration of growth which has resulted all point to a fundamental failure of some kind. Where the development effort of the 1950's fell short was not, as has been seen, in failing to provide a reasonably satisfactory rate of real output growth but in failing to deal adequately with the expenditure flows which took place as a natural consequence of this growth. The high consumption and import propensities in the private sector, the sluggishness of public revenues, the shortcomings of public investment allocation, the failure to stimulate an adequate volume of private investment—none of these inadequacies were necessarily fatal to the continued smooth functioning of the economy. They all helped to reduce the rate of output growth that was attainable and they all contributed to the mounting balance of payments pressures but external equilibrium could have been achieved at the resulting lower growth rate had adequate public policies been enacted. The emergence of excess aggregate demand is normal in the development context but it makes a great deal of difference in what proportions current and capital expenditures respectively are being financed via external deficits. A higher growth rate could have been produced by converting more current expenditure to investment. But regardless of the investment ratio, it was absolutely essential that close attention be paid to the problem of external imbalance. The disaster which overtook Ceylon in 1960 could have been averted only if the deficits in the basic balance of payments had been corrected well before the depletion of the foreign assets took place. Some planned rundown of these assets from their high postwar levels would have been defensible, of course, but once a prudent minimum level had been reached it would have become absolutely necessary to hold the growth of imports within limits consistent with basic balance in the external accounts, if not year by year at least over a series of three or four years. Since this was not done by choice during the late fifties it was forced on the government by necessity during the early sixties. Unfortunately, the fact that it was done some years later than it should have been done and by necessity rather than choice was to prove to be a crucial distinction.

Chapter 8

The 1960's and Beyond

By the end of 1960 it had become completely impossible to maintain the free flow of imports into Ceylon. Years of excess demand had led to the virtual disappearance of the country's foreign assets. It had ceased to be possible to cover the balance of payments deficit by drawing down foreign assets. Loans from abroad did not come close to bridging the gap. Now there was no alternative left but to cut imports to a level which would be consistent with basic balance in the external accounts. This drastic course of action had to be taken without delay. The government, which had been fighting for balance of payments stability ever since the mid-fifties with the use of an array of direct and indirect controls on foreign trade and payments, now felt compelled to take major steps toward comprehensive direct government control of all foreign transactions.

Starting with the 1957/58 budget, the emphasis in import duty policy had gradually been turning away from revenue raising and toward protection of infant industries and attempted correction of the economy's external imbalance. Throughout the late 1950's increases in duty rates were employed in conjunction with increasingly stringent exchange control in an attempt to bring the volume of foreign payments under control. The 1957/58 budget cut import duties on capital equipment and raw materials, at the same time raising some consumer luxuries to a 100 percent duty rate. In the following year, luxury automobiles were hit with a virtually prohibitive tariff. Again in 1959, there were duty reductions for materials, some increases to protect the final products of nascent local industries, and further duty increases for cars, gasoline, and watches. Despite these attempts to improve the external balance of the economy, the balance of payments position continued to deteriorate rapidly through 1959. The 1960 budget increased import duties once more. As in past years, cars, gasoline, liquor, and tobacco were prime targets for increased taxation. This was the ninth consecutive year of increases in duty rates and the steadily rising tariff level was at last beginning to have some visible impact on the aggre-

216

gate value of imports. Total merchandise imports, which had been rising almost continuously for six years, finally leveled off. The hoped-for recovery of exports failed to materialize, however; once again, a large deficit was run and the decline in external assets continued unabated.

Ceylon's policy on import duties in the late 1950's was not successful in achieving what came to be its main goal, righting the increasingly precarious balance of payments. This is not to say that it would have been impossible to bring about balance of payments stability through primary, or perhaps even sole, reliance on import taxation, rather than resorting to the comprehensive system of direct controls imposed in the early 1960's. It is an axiom of economic policy that anything which can be achieved through direct controls can also be done through the application of taxes and subsidies of sufficient magnitudes. The failure of Ceylon's duty rate policy was thus that the rate increases enacted were too little and too late to correct an imbalance as large as the one which actually developed. Had another export boom emerged unexpectedly to restore the balance, as policy makers at the time must have wished, the crisis would have been solved—at least for the time being. A measure of the failure of the import duty policy to achieve its balance of payments goal is the relative success it enjoyed in revenue collection. Duties which keep out imports cannot collect revenue and the fact that receipts from import duties soared to over Rs. 400,000,000 a year shows that the goods were still flowing in abundance despite the high duties (some of these flows were speculative, based on the belief held by many traders that the situation was serious and that ample stocks should be obtained before more severe sanctions were imposed). Probably the basic failing of Ceylon's policy makers at this time was that they continued to think of balance of payments defense as a cyclical problem which could be counted upon not to persist for more than three or four years at a time. They failed to understand the strong economic, political, and demographic forces within the economy working for persistent deficits and thus underrated the need to bring imports under control and encourage more actively the restructuring of the economy. Taking advantage of hindsight, one can now surmise that even if there had been another export boom it would only have served to postpone the day of judgment, not to cancel its appearance.

In January and August, 1961, the government finally took vigorous action. The measures taken included still more increases in import duties: a five percent surcharge was added to the general duty and additional five percent increases were levied on a wide range of goods. More important, however, textiles, many food items, and a large number of manufactured goods were placed under quantitative import restriction for the first time. Several luxury items, notably automobiles and watches, were banned outright by the simple expedient of declaring that no more licenses would be issued for their importation. From now on, import duties were to be abandoned as the chief tool of commercial policy and import and exchange controls would come to play the dominant role. The framework for a system of state-managed foreign trade and payments was established. Now all that remained to be done to create a completely government-controlled trading system was to extend these measures to a wider and wider variety of transactions and eventually to every type of dealing which enters into the balance of payments.

Although the time span required for an adequate historical perspective is lacking, it is quite possible that future economic historians will date the beginning of yet another phase in the development of Ceylon's export economy from January 2, 1961. Like the economy of the immediate postwar years, the system now prevailing in Ceylon displays a considerable degree of continuity with the one which preceded it. Indeed, aside from the revolutionary changes in the availability of imports, the essential economic trends of the postwar decade and a half—population pressure, the stagnation of export receipts, the expansion of traditional agriculture, and the government's development effort—continued to be as evident during the sixties as they had been in the fifties. If the Ceylon government had been able to achieve external stability during the late fifties through a gradual, timely application of indirect and direct trade and payments controls, then the later period would have merged imperceptibly into the earlier. The failure to reconcile external balance with the reasonably rapid economic growth of the 1950's, however, meant that in one vital sense a different economic environment was created in 1961. From that time on into the foreseeable future, the nation's economy would move ever farther away from the classical export economy model. The free international trade flows characteristic of the classical economy would be subject to increasingly tight control. The availability of imports would decrease sharply. Emphasis on local production and import substitution would necessarily rise. To the extent that domestic production could not make up for the drastically reduced supply of imports, living standards were likely to decline. Excess aggregate demand, whose impact had formerly been felt almost exclusively in the balance of payments, would now be turned inward. Both industrialization and price inflation would thus become real possibilities for the first time. On the other hand, import substituting industry, with a more than adequate market now available for its output, would begin to face increasingly strong supply-side constraints in the form of difficulties in obtaining necessary imported materials and equipment. But regardless of the degree of success achieved, it was to be a far different world from that of the classical export economy.

SINCE 1960

On the basis of its performance during its first four years of existence, the strengths and weaknesses of the controlled economy can be tentatively assessed. Hopefully, a fairly close examination of the experience of this short period will give some basis for guessing about what future transitions and how much economic growth are in store for Ceylon's economy in the years to come.

Unlike the import duty rate changes and milder forms of direct control which had been used in the late 1950's, the stern measures taken in 1961 were strikingly effective in their initial task of controlling overall import volume. The physical quantity of imports, which by 1959 had risen to 145 percent of the 1953 level, was slashed by 20 percent as a result of these measures. To put this feat of economic control in perspective, one should bear in mind the inexorable pressures pushing imports up. In only one previous year since World War II (1953) had import volume failed to rise. Not only were the direct controls unprecedentedly effective in holding down the overall volume of imports but they also succeeded in discriminating, according to a predetermined scale of priorities, among broad categories of imported goods, concentrating their restrictive efforts on those deemed less essential to the national welfare. Food imports fell relatively little. Within the food category, a sharp distinction was made between staple foodstuffs on the one hand and luxury and semiluxury food and drink items on the other. Staples, which by this time were imported and sold largely by the government or by cooperative organizations, were little effected by the controls and continued to be imported in approximately their past volume. Canned goods, spirits, and other foods of the less essential type were put under severely limited quotas or banned outright. Among other consumer goods, textiles had previously been subject to more controls than other consumer goods and were thus hit relatively lightly at this point (though textile supplies were tightly curtailed later, in 1963). It was consumer goods other than food and textiles which were most easily identified as nonessential imports and thus felt the full brunt of import restriction. As Table 8-1 indicates, these goods as a class suffered a 70 percent drop in import volume from 1960 to 1962. Many luxury consumer goods which had once been imported in considerable quantities were now cut to zero.

TABLE 8-1

IMPORT VOLUME AND STRUCTURE, 1958–63*

	1958	1959	1960	1961	1962	1963
			(Rs. Millions)			
Imports (current prices)†.	...	2,176	2,209	1,972	2,070	2,014
	Indexes (1958 = 100)					
Consumer goods.........	100	112	111	83	78	65
Food and drink.......	100	111	104	96	90	85
Textiles., ...	100	89	86	75	74	42
Others.............	100	129	148	49	45	25
Intermediate goods......	100	121	121	118	131	124
Investment goods.......	100	131	117	102	116	93
All imports............	100	116	113	91	92	79

*Source: Central Bank, *Annual Report of the Monetary Board to the Minister of Finance* for 1963.
†These figures, which include both visible and invisible items, are derived from a new Central Bank series which originates in 1959 and are not directly comparable with any earlier data.

The drastic policy changes of 1961 brought about little immediate improvement in the balance of payments.[1] Export volume rose by 4 percent in 1961 and a further 7 percent in 1962, then suffered a 3 percent decline in the following year. But export prices declined in both 1961 and 1962, leveling off in 1963. As a result, export receipts did not rise. When invisible items are added in, export value followed a downward path, going from Rs. 1,796,000,-000 in 1960 to Rs. 1,725,000,000 in 1963. Through 1962, however, falling import prices kept the purchasing power of exports (income terms of trade) on the rise. With 1960 = 100, the income terms of trade worsened to 96 in 1961 but improved again to 106 in 1962, thus nearly keeping abreast of population growth. But in 1963 prices of imported food and other consumer goods rose sharply and the income terms of trade index sank to 93.

As a result of all these volume and price changes the current deficit in the balance of payments was reduced in size but not eliminated. It was brought down from Rs. 220,000,000 in 1960 to

[1]The source of all data in this paragraph and the following one is the Central Bank of Ceylon, *Annual Report of the Monetary Board to the Minister of Finance* for 1963.

Rs. 94,000,000 in 1961, but crept back up to Rs. 144,000,000 in 1962 and 146,000,000 in 1963. After a slump in 1961, there was a significant rise in autonomous capital inflows: from Rs. 11,000,000 in 1961 to Rs. 38,000,000 in 1962 and Rs. 79,000,000 in 1963. These increased flows helped reduce the amount of further external financing needed. Still, there remained a basic deficit to be covered somehow: Rs. 83,000,000 in 1961, Rs. 106,000,000 the next year, and Rs. 67,000,000 in 1963. Foreign assets could not fall much further (they did drop from Rs. 541,300,000 at the end of 1960 to Rs. 462,-300,000 at year-end 1963), so a rise in external liabilities, particularly two drawings from the International Monetary Fund, had to be used as the main means of financing the continuing deficit. In sum, while the rapid deterioration of the external accounts which had characterized the late fifties was arrested there was no reversal of the earlier trend. Although production for export continued to rise quite satisfactorily, declining prices in the world market kept export value from going up. And, despite the severity of the new controls and the fillip they gave to import-substituting local industry, imports were not reduced by a large enough amount to eliminate the deficit entirely.

Meanwhile, the fiscal operations of the central government kept the economy brimming over with excess demand. The central government deficit for 1960/61—Rs. 490,800,000—was the largest ever, breaking the 1959/60 record by some Rs. 40,000,000.[2] Again in 1961/62 a deficit of about Rs. 500,000,000 was run, while in the following year the size of the deficit was reduced by some Rs. 50,000,000.[3] The effect of these continuing large deficits on aggregate demand was moderated, however, by two key monetary phenomena. For one thing only a small proportion of the debt was monetized. The money supply rose at a relatively modest rate through 1962 (as defined in Table A–61, Appendix, it rose by 6.7 percent in 1961 and 1.1 percent in 1962), then accelerated (11.4 percent). Secondly, the public showed a striking willingness to hold onto currency, presumably on the assumption (which was without doubt irrationally optimistic) that while there were few goods available which were worth buying at current prices supplies would improve in the future and prices would fall. The bank debits tax, the prohibition in 1961 on the opening of new accounts

---

[2]See Table A–67, Appendix.

[3]The data needed to make a precise comparison of the 1961/62 and 1962/63 government deficits with deficits of earlier years were not available to the author at the time of this writing; the former deficit was, however, very close in size to the one run in 1960/61 and the latter was a bit smaller.

in foreign-owned banks by Ceylon nationals, and, worst of all, the fear that the government might freeze or even confiscate bank accounts created a move away from demand deposits and into currency. Total demand deposits fell from 1960 through 1962 (Rs. 588,900,000 at the end of 1960, 571,600,000 in 1961, and 565,600,-000 in 1962), then rose again in 1963 (Rs. 595,500,000). Currency in circulation, meanwhile, climbed steadily, from Rs. 595,300,000 at year-end 1960 to 692,200,000 in 1961, 712,600,000 in 1962, and 828,400,000 in 1963. The extent to which the public was using this currency as a store of value rather than to satisfy its current transactions needs is indicated by the rapid rise in the number of Rs. 100 bills outstanding. This denomination, the largest issued, is too big to be used in any but a very few transactions in Ceylon but is admirably suited for hoarding purposes. The value of Rs. 100 notes issued shot up from Rs. 148,400,000 at the end of 1960 to Rs. 211,900,000 by the end of 1961, then continued to climb briskly and was up to Rs. 275,300,000 by December, 1963. Of course, it was naive of people to believe that while the government could tamper with demand deposits it could not touch currency and to doubt that prices would continue to rise. The more sophisticated recognized the fallacy in this thinking and instead bought real property of various kinds.[4]

For all of these reasons not so much price inflation as one might expect was created by the abrupt imposition of strong import controls. Of course, there was some upward pressure on prices. Just how much is hard to define. The official consumer price index, which is heavily weighted by subsidized and price-fixed items, had been rising at an annual rate of only 0.7 percent throughout the fifties; after 1960 its rate of climb accelerated a bit: to 1.3 percent in 1961, 1.4 in 1962, and 2.4 in 1963.[5] Even allowing for the considerable understatement which is obviously inherent in this index the rate of increase of consumer prices in general was relatively moderate. Of course, many prices which were not included in the consumer price index, particularly those of consumer goods used mostly by the middle and upper income groups and

---

[4]The public *as a whole* had no choice, of course, but to hold the money supply issued by the government and the banks (though it could alter the proportions held in currency and bank deposits respectively). Those with inflationary expectations presumably bought tangible assets, even at prices which were grossly inflated by past standards, and the others held cash. Cash, especially large bills, was also attractive to those who held wealth acquired through illegal operations of various kinds.

[5]Central Bank of Ceylon, *Annual Report of the Monetary Board to the Minister of Finance* for 1963; Table 4–1.

those suitable for use as a store of value, rose more rapidly. An illustrative case of this type was used-car prices, which doubled in the course of about two years. Prices of intermediate and investment goods, the importation of which had been less severely curtailed, presumably rose less than those of consumer goods in general. How much inflation one says there has been since 1960 is thus clearly dependent upon the particular types of goods one wishes to price. And, even though price increases have perhaps not been so great as one might expect given the severity of the shortages which developed, an important step had been taken: the tie with world prices had been severed and there was now the possibility of an inflation of considerable magnitude.

Price movements aside, the import controls surely brought about a stagnation, if not a decline, in real income levels. Different economic groups were affected in proportion to their previous consumption of imported goods. Thus the middle-class man suffered a very clear decline in real income, since even though he generally retained his former employment and received much the same money income as before many of the goods he had previously consumed were no longer available at any price and many others which were still available were subject to periodic shortages and greatly inflated prices. The ordinary man entered into a period of more modest austerity. While the prices of the necessities of life were held close to their past levels, many of the semiluxuries occasionally consumed by the average family had become unavailable or had risen steeply in price. During 1964 cloth was made subject to rationing. Moreover, the ordinary workingman was more likely to have been affected by the rising level of unemployment and underemployment which seems to have ensued during the early sixties. While some new jobs were created in import-substituting industries, other sectors (wholesale and retail trade, especially the large import firms and department stores of Colombo) experienced sharp declines in employment. Meanwhile, the long-term pressure of population on capital and land resources continued unabated. Depending on how one reads the statistics, there was either a stagnation or a decline in the average level of real per capita consumption between 1959 and 1963; certainly there was an unmistakable decline after 1960.[6]

---

[6]Using Central Bank aggregate consumption figures (Central Bank of Ceylon, *Annual Report of the Monetary Board to the Minister of Finance* for 1963, p. 27), the CPI as a deflator, and population estimates from the Registrar-General's Department and from the 1963 Census, apparent consumption per capita in 1959 prices rose from Rs. 486 in 1959 to Rs. 513 in 1960. Thereafter, however, figures of Rs. 480 for 1961, Rs. 477 for 1962, and Rs. 482 for 1963 were recorded. These data are doubtless biased upward to some extent,

(Continued on next page)

While the declining level of per capita real consumption was the obvious negative side of the post-1960 changes in the economy, there was also a positive side: the diversification (though not necessarily the growth; see below) of national output was definitely accelerated. The abrupt choking off of imports of a wide range of goods upon which the middle class and, to a lesser extent, the ordinary man, had learned to rely created for the first time an extremely attractive market for domestic manufacturers of the simpler consumer goods. There was a great flurry of new activity in these areas. Delays in obtaining tax concessions and import licenses for machinery and supplies and in clearing other bureaucratic details often hampered but did not prevent the rise of a host of small private manufacturers. As already noted, the new import controls were capable of distinguishing quite sharply among the various broad classes of imported goods. Until the balance of payments situation worsened still further in 1963–64, intermediate and investment goods continued to flow into the country in even larger quantities than before the controls were imposed. At a lower level of aggregation, however, the new controls were often arbitrary. Although they had proven to be an effective means of reducing the volume of imports and altering its structure, they did not solve the problem of allocating efficiently the available volume of producer-goods imports among promising entrepreneurs. Many local producers, especially new manufacturers of goods not previously made in Ceylon, encountered difficulties in obtaining permission to import the goods they required to set up or expand their operations. And after two years of direct controls on consumer goods imports had not brought about sufficient improvements in the balance of payments, the controls began to cut increasingly into imports of intermediate and investment goods. This is evident in the import figures for 1963 (Table 8–1) and became the occasion for loud complaint by many of the new manufacturers as the controls were tightened further in 1964.

Despite their many faults, however, the controls did achieve one thing for which official policy had long striven with only slight success: a channeling of the proven abilities of the local entrepreneurial class out of the old familiar lines—estate agriculture, real estate, and trade—and into manufacturing. Previously, entrepreneurs had been reluctant to enter manufacturing, but now they showed no

---

since the downward-biased CPI is an inadequate deflator and the 1963 preliminary census count seems a bit low relative to the estimates made for earlier years by the Registrar-General's Department. It is probable, then, that real per capita consumption actually fell—perhaps considerably—from 1959 to 1963.

tendency to be discouraged by the capital shortages, lack of skills and technical knowledge, inexperience, or other problems to which their former inactivity had long been ascribed. The products of these small manufacturers—jams, pickles, chocolates, shirts, pots and pans, and an almost endless list of similar consumer products—were often crude but they usually improved as time went by and some even succeeded in gaining the favor of a critical, import-coddled public.

It is too soon to say just what effects the closing of the economy to so many imports will have on the overall rate of economic growth. In the early sixties the economy experienced growth rates

TABLE 8–2

GROSS NATIONAL PRODUCT AND MAIN COMPONENTS, 1959–63

	1959	1960	1961	1962	1963
In Current Market Prices (Rs. 000,000)*					
Private consumption............	4,678	4,991	4,849	5,010	5,309
Government consumption........	881	911	926	979	1,011
Gross domestic fixed capital formation...................	1,069	966	978	1,031	982
Change in stocks...............	−11	−47	67	2	12
Exports of goods and services.....	2,016	2,011	1,907	1,966	1,914
Imports of goods and services.....	2,176	2,209	1,972	2,070	2,014
Gross Domestic Product.........	6,457	6,622	6,755	6,919	7,213
Net factor income from abroad....	−37	−44	−40	−47	−52
Gross National Product..........	6,420	6,578	6,715	6,872	7,161
At Factor Cost of 1959					
Gross National Product (Rs. 000,000)†....................	5,854	6,078	6,260	6,493	6,611
GNP per capita (Rs.)‡..........	608	614	616	622	617
Gross National Income (Rs. 000,000)§....................	5,854	6,064	6,087	6,391	6,349
GNI per capita (Rs.)...........	608	613	599	612	593

Annual Growth Rates (Percent)

	1959– 1960	1960– 1961	1961– 1962	1962– 1963	Average 1959– 1963
GNP in current market prices...	2.5	2.1	2.3	4.2	2.8
GNP at 1959 factor cost.......	3.8	3.0	3.7	1.8	3.1
Real GNP per capita..........	1.0	0.3	1.0	−0.8	0.4
GNI at 1959 factor cost........	3.6	0.4	5.0	−0.7	2.1
Real GNI per capita...........	0.8	−2.3	2.2	−3.1	−0.6

*Source: Central Bank of Ceylon, *Annual Report of the Monetary Board to the Minister of Finance* for 1963, pp. 25–26.

†*Ibid.*, p. 33.

‡These and the other per capita figures are based on midyear population estimates which grow from 9,625,000 in 1959 to 10,712,000 in 1963. See *ibid.*, p. 22.

§Allows for changes in the terms of trade by deflating export value in current prices by the import price index rather than by export prices; see Table A–3, Appendix, and the last note attached to it.

which were noticeably lower than those of the fifties, but problems of transition and an unfavorable turn in export prices were at least partly to blame for this slackening of the rate of expansion. As Table 8–2 shows, real output rose from 1959 through 1963 at a pace which was somewhat more rapid than the rate of population increase. But the growth rate was lower than the rate during the fifties—3.1 percent, as compared with about 4.0 for the preceding decade. And even though the volume of imports had been brought under control the vagaries of world price movements continued to exercise a dominant power over Ceylon's national welfare. Because of generally falling export prices and the rise of import prices in 1963, the growth rate of Real National Income was forced down below population's growth rate. During the first four years of the sixties real GNI grew at a satisfactory rate only in 1960 and 1962 and averaged only 2.1 percent annually overall.

TABLE 8–3

INDEXES OF INDUSTRIAL PRODUCTION, 1958–62*

(1952–56 = 100)

	1958	1959	1960	1961	1962
Mining and quarrying..	53.3	73.0	101.0	87.1	86.8
Manufacturing........	113.8	124.5	133.0	139.0	151.3
Electricity...........	140.7	157.5	174.4	185.0	202.3
Industrial production ..	114.2	125.1	135.0	141.1	152.3

*Source: Table A–41, Appendix; Development Division, Department of Industries. There is a distinct possibility that increases in manufacturing output after 1960 arising from small-scale private activity are understated in this table (see footnote 11).

Despite generally falling world prices production of the leading export commodities was higher in most cases. Tea production swelled impressively, going from 413,000,000 pounds in 1959 all the way to 485,000,000 in 1963. Rubber output, responding to a price increase, rose to 218,000,000 pounds in 1960 (by reducing their inventories, dealers managed to export 235,000,000 pounds), slipped in 1961, then rose again amid declining prices through 1963. Output in 1963 was 231,000,000 pounds but the average unit value f.o.b. was only Rs. 1.23 per pound. Coconut output was generally higher, too, partly in a belated response to 1959 export price increases which had since been reversed.[7] Total production for export

---

[7]For all these data, see Central Bank of Ceylon, *Annual Report of the Monetary Board to the Minister of Finance* for 1963, pp. 35–44.

was 13.0 percent higher in 1963 than it had been in 1959 but falling prices converted this gain into a 1.8 percent fall in value terms.[8]

In physical terms, production for domestic use appears to have grown at much the same rate as output for export; official data give the 1959–63 increase as 13.1 percent.[9] Paddy output and yield continued their strong upward trends, even though interrupted by bad years in 1961 and 1963; gross output rose by 34.8 percent from 1959 to 1963.[10] Industrial production was also growing at a good pace, but it was still too small a proportion of national output to influence the overall growth rate very much.[11]

THE FUTURE

Any attempt to discover the fundamental meaning of Ceylon's economic experience in the brief period since the government began to build up its system of comprehensive import controls must necessarily develop into a consideration of what the future holds in store for Ceylon. It has been contended here that the growth experience of 1946–60 was essentially different from that of the preceding hundred years as a result of basic changes which took place in the economic environment, especially during the 1940's. Many of the opportunities open to the economy in the years to come will be the same as it had (but did not always exploit successfully) in the recent past. Most of the familiar problems will remain, too; some may worsen steadily. To some extent, however, the environment for economic growth in the 1960's is rather different from that of the 1950's.

There is reason to believe that tight import control has become a permanent feature of Ceylon's economy. Both exchange control

---

[8]*Ibid*, pp. 23, 33.

[9]*Ibid*.

[10]*Ibid*, p. 35

[11]Did the growth of industrial production accelerate markedly after 1960? The evidence on this question is contradictory. The data in Table 8–3 indicate that output continued to rise at roughly the same rate as in the late fifties (which was higher than that of earlier years) but did not accelerate. Casual observation suggests that these figures must understate the rises of the early sixties. Furthermore, annual surveys made by the Central Bank conclude that the value of industrial output rose by 5.8 percent in 1961, 17.0 percent in 1962, and 11.3 percent in 1963 (Central Bank of Ceylon, *Annual Report of the Monetary Board to the Minister of Finance* for 1963, p. 117). These are current-value figures, so they no doubt reflect a certain amount of price inflation. Moreover, there is reason to suspect that the coverage of the survey has improved considerably over the years, creating a further upward bias. The Central Bank data thus appear to be even harder to interpret than those of the Development Division. All that can be concluded with safety is that industrial production rose rapidly between 1960 and 1963, as fast as in the preceding period or perhaps somewhat faster.

and import control have gradually been tightened since their initial stiffening in 1961. During 1962, for instance, the percentage of total imports which were subject to individual licensing was raised from 17 percent to 48 percent of the 1961 import bill; by the end of 1963 coverage had been extended to 60 percent.[12] Although these controls may conceivably be partially relaxed in the years to come, it does seem likely that Ceylon will never again in the foreseeable future be open to the free flows of imports which it enjoyed during more than a century of modern economic development. True, if another export boom similar to that of the early fifties were to develop there would doubtless be some easing of the controls once more, but such an occurrence could only be a temporary reversal of the trend. The long-term forces working against the restoration of external balance at reasonably low import duty rates are too great. They would soon serve to reestablish the tendencies noted throughout the 1950's. Ceylon's rising population, coupled with the slowness of the increase in export production and the unfavorable trend of export prices, make it extremely unlikely that plantation agriculture will ever again generate enough export receipts to finance all the import needs of the island's population. In any case, to think in terms of another export boom is to indulge in fantasy. Predicted world price trends for all of Ceylon's major traditional exports are downward. The more likely course of events is that it will be necessary to exercise tight control over the flow of imports into Ceylon indefinitely.

This probable continuation of strict import control is what is likely to distinguish the 1960's (and very probably a considerable period beyond the present decade) from the 1950's. The import restrictions will have effects on consumption and on production within Ceylon. On the consumption side, it is safe to predict that the controls will continue to deprive Ceylon's citizens, especially the middle and upper income groups, of the wide range of foreign goods which they had become accustomed to consume as the main benefit of international trade and the global division of labor. Depending on the outcome of events within Ceylon and in world markets, consumer austerity may tighten or loosen slightly in the future but the consumption standards of the fifties will not be

---

[12]This is in terms of 1961 imports; as a percentage of 1962 or 1963 imports the figures would be lower, since by this time the structure of imports was changing in response to the controls themselves. See Central Bank of Ceylon, *Annual Reports of the Monetary Board of the Minister of Finance* for 1962 (p. 56) and 1963 (p. 52).

restored until a new period of rapid output growth has been inaugurated. On the production side, the main effect of import control will continue to be the encouragement of output diversification through the creation of a sellers' market for consumer goods, industrial and agricultural. At the same time, extremely severe or inefficiently administered import control can make the satisfaction of this new demand for local output difficult by creating shortages of producer goods. Whether in the net the growth rate of local production for domestic use will be enhanced or reduced is hard to say. Demand pulls one way, supply the other.

In general, the growth of Ceylon's economy in the future will depend on two broad types of factors: the scope of unexploited technical possibilities for output expansion remaining in the economy and the extent to which private economic action and public policy succeed in realizing these potentials. As in the past, the potentials are very great; the limiting factor is sure to be the human ingenuity required to exploit them. A brief review of the situation with regard to Ceylonese agriculture, industry, and economic growth in general should serve to highlight the critical factors upon which successful future development within the present economic structure will depend.

Unless starved of necessary materials and equipment, industry in Ceylon is almost certain to grow more rapidly in the sixties than it did in the fifties. In other broad sectors of the economy, the potentials for output growth remain much what they have been in the recent past. As already noted, the situation in the export sector varies sharply among the three leading industries. Despite the failure of government attempts to initiate wholesale replanting, gradual improvements in tea technology have continued to raise output at a satisfactory pace (better than four percent a year, 1959–1963). Still, yield gaps between the best-managed plots and the worst remain very large and the room for productivity growth is far from exhausted. Tea prices, however, are if anything weaker than they were in the 1950's. The main growth in world consumption is in the Middle East, where the demand is largely for low-quality tea. If Ceylon sells increasing proportions of its output in this market, as seems likely to occur as an increasing share of Ceylon exports come under bilateral trading arrangements, it will do so only at the cost of a decline in unit value. The demand for high-quality teas, Ceylon's traditional specialty, centers in the high-income Commonweath countries and will grow very slowly, if at all (beverage preferences in some of these countries, e.g., Australia, are turning from tea to coffee.) In summation tea will remain in the future what it has been in the recent past: a steady and reliable but not very dynamically growing source of export receipts.

Ceylon rubber in recent years has become something of an enigma. Despite enthusiastic and widespread replanting, output has grown relatively slowly. Since a long-term price decline is expected, industry efficiency is at a premium; only highly efficient producers will be able to expand or at least maintain export receipts by increasing output fast enough to compensate for price declines. But by the end of 1964, despite the fact that political instability in Southeast Asia had held prices at higher levels than had been anticipated earlier, Ceylon's output had stagnated and loud complaints were being heard from the industry about the depressed state of the world market. Why the replanting program had not lowered costs to the point where large output increases became profitable, even at the low prices of the sixties, was not at all clear.

The position of the coconut industry is the least promising of all. The industry continues to contain a high proportion of senile trees, with replanting proceeding at too slow a pace to bring about any great change in the situation. Domestic consumption continues to rise, cutting into the exportable surplus. World prices for copra and coconut oil, responding to the worldwide surplus of oils and oilseeds, are following a declining trend. All in all, it seems inevitable that coconut products will provide a progressively smaller share of Ceylon's export earnings in the future.

The overall prospect for Ceylon exports, then, is not bright. No minor export products appear to be in a position for substantial growth, so the total export prospect remains overwhelmingly dependent on the position of the three main crops. A summation of their prospects shows that only if tea continues to perform satisfactorily and if rubber output picks up (it may, since the unimpressive performance of 1963 has been ascribed to an excess of rainfall)[13] can total export proceeds be expected to rise significantly in the years to come. A repetition of the experience of the 1950's, when total export receipts rose at an annual rate of just over two percent, is probably about the best that can be hoped for. Under the least favorable circumstances imaginable, Ceylon's export proceeds could follow the example of Indonesia's and decline absolutely over time. Which outcome, or what intermediate case, emerges depends on what happens to the basic political environment and on the ability of policy makers to exploit the consider-

---

[13] *Far Eastern Economic Review 1965 Yearbook* (Hong Kong, 1964), pp. 116–117.

able potentials for output increases which still remain in Ceylon's export industries.

Potential production gains in agricultural production for domestic consumption are even more impressive. If the analysis of Chapter 6 is correct and the considerable rises in paddy production which took place during the 1950's were mainly a response to the price incentive offered by the GPS, made with increased fertilizer application but with little further modification of technique, and not primarily a result of the government's campaign to improve methods of production by a number of devices, then the potential for increased rice production is very great indeed. No one can doubt that the possible effects on output of the Japanese method, land reform, crop insurance, and other aspects of the government program are considerable. From World War II to the present, average paddy yields have risen from approximately 25 bushels per acre to over 35. This is an impressive gain, but when a comparison is made with the average yield in Japan, roughly 100 bushels an acre, it is evident that the room for further intensification of paddy cultivation is even greater than the historical increase. While a great number of technical considerations would go to determine whether an average yield of 100 bushels an acre is a technical possibility in Ceylon or not, the data on improved cultivation practices (Table 6–15, Chapter 6) make it clear that the spread of methods used on the best-farmed plots to all paddy land would have revolutionary consequences. The possibility of increasing the degree of self-sufficiency and diminishing the need for rice imports is thus great. From the late forties to the early sixties the growth of domestic paddy production was fast enough to offset the rapid rise of rice consumption and decrease slightly the relative dependence on imports, from about 55 percent to 45. But even the latter percentage must be regarded as extremely high when one considers the staple position of rice in the Ceylonese diet, the inevitably rapid growth of consumption needs as population rises, the slow increase in the availability of foreign receipts out of which to buy imported rice, and the enormous opportunity cost of using these receipts to buy food rather than producer goods. The reduction of this percentage would have to be an important part of any campaign to restructure Ceylon's import bill and bring about a further relative shift from consumer to producer goods. With luxury consumer goods imports now cut to the bone, rice has become an increasingly important part of total imports (about 15 percent in the early 1960's).

For peasant crops other than paddy, the chances of sizable increases in output are similarly good on technical grounds, ultimately, perhaps, even better, since attention has been focused mainly on paddy so far. What any progress in increasing peasant agricultural output depends on is a continuation of active government encouragement (especially increased success in providing extension services and in creating an appropriate legal framework), plus the availability of pure-line seed, fertilizers, and other material requisites of improved cultivation practices.

Throughout Ceylon agriculture, in fact, technical production possibilities are still far in excess of actual current output. In the future as in the recent past, output gains must come almost entirely from improved per acre yields. But in none of the major crops— tea, rubber, coconut, or rice—does an ultimate doubling of current per acre yields seem out of the question. Moreover, such yield levels could probably be reached simply by the application of currently known techniques to all of Ceylon's present acreage. The additional benefits which could be derived from further technological advance are impossible to imagine. As in the past, however, actual production will inevitably continue to lag far behind maximum physical possibilities. Not all possible production increases are economic in the sense of repaying their cost. But many economic increases are not in fact realized because of producer inertia and ignorance. Obviously, it is the speed with which public policy succeeds in overcoming these latter obstacles that will primarily determine how fast agricultural output will grow.

Looked at from an aggregate rather than a sectoral viewpoint, the main problem of Ceylonese economic growth appears to be the same as it was during the fifties: the difficulty of developing a large enough volume of saving and investment to produce really rapid output growth. Indeed, this problem is likely to be more severe in the future than it was in the recent past. The pressure of population growth, causing increments in national income to be used for consumption rather than investment purposes, shows no sign of abating, since the rate of population growth itself shows none. The main source of domestic saving in the past, surpluses growing out of export prosperity, will continue to be available in the future, but now, with consumption standards depressed below the customary levels of the past, consumers will feel more inclined than ever to spend increases in their incomes on consumer goods and if export receipts rise significantly the government will be under severe pressure to ease import restrictions and let consumption of imported goods rise. The position in regard to capital inflows is not likely to be radically different—although private inflows may well be smaller and intergovernment flows larger than in the past—so investment finance will remain largely dependent upon domestic saving. To increase domestic saving significantly, a really severe domestic austerity will now be required, as compared with the modest braking of the growth of private and public consumption expenditures which would have accomplished this aim in the periods of export prosperity during the 1950's. With memories of higher past consumption levels still fresh and resentment of even the present degree of austerity strong, public consent to still larger sacrifices, unless impossible to avoid or very convincingly justified, is unlikely to be forthcoming. The prospect for substantially increased domestic saving and investment is thus not bright.

The problem of finding employment for the labor force which is likely to emerge in the coming years will probably be even more difficult to solve than the problem of raising per capita income, to which, of course, it is closely related. The natural consequences of past demographic trends, abetted perhaps by a slowing down of the spread of education as bottlenecks in the provision of educational facilities grow worse, will gradually raise the rate of growth of the labor force from the 2.2 percent annual rate of the fifties toward the population growth rate of about 2.6 percent. By 1970, unless there is an unexpectedly sharp decline in the birth rate, Ceylon will have a population of close to 13,000,000 persons and a labor force of perhaps 4,500,000. Even very rapid growth of industrial output will absorb very little additional labor. The government plants built so far have been highly capital-intensive (see Table A–70, Appendix) and the ones under construction or being contemplated at the present writing—steel, tires and tubes, grain milling, and fertilizers—are even more so. The type of small-scale private industry which has proliferated since 1960 is less capital-intensive but it will provide employment for only a tiny fraction of the available labor. Perhaps with increases in the prices of imported factors of production relative to domestic factors private firms will be induced to use more labor-intensive methods than they otherwise would. Even using high projections of industrial output, however, it is clear that the main burden of providing jobs for new workers will continue to fall, as it did in the fifties, on the agricultural and service sectors, where relatively unproductive uses of labor resources will continue to provide an alternative to complete inactivity. Even here, however, Ceylon's rapidly rising educational level will pose a serious problem. Increasing education means that many new entrants to the labor force rule out employment in virtually all of agriculture and much of the service sector as unbefitting to their social and intellectual level. Outside of industry, the only jobs open to their consideration are thus professional and clerical service occupations. It is hard to say which aspect of the unemployment problem is more forbidding: the aggregate problem of finding jobs for some 100,000 new workers annually or the difficulty of obtaining suitable employment for the much smaller but growing number issuing forth from the Ceylonese educational system each year.[14]

Is concentration on production for the local market a blind alley for Ceylon? Is not its relative factor endowment still better suited for specialized export production and does not a reorientation of production toward the home market offer only the prospect of a particularly inefficient form of autarky? There are two major limitations to the industrialization of Ceylon: lack of almost all of the raw material inputs needed for modern industry except hydro-electric power[15] and the smallness of the present national market for most finished goods. The former consideration dictates that industry must be based either on processing local agricultural raw materials or on imported materials. There is some possibility (already being explored) of extending the processing of Ceylon's traditional export crops further: e.g., by manufacturing "instant" tea from green leaf or by producing automobile tires. Aside from these possibilities, which are obviously quite limited, and unless large-scale production of some agricultural raw material which has not been a major product of Ceylon in the past—such as cotton or sugar, both of which have been tried with scant success—can be developed, the main reliance will have to be put on imported raw materials. This is a serious limitation, but not necessarily a fatal one, as the Japanese and Hong Kong success stories show.

The barrier posed by the smallness of the national market may

---

[14]One's enthusiasm for rapid educational expansion in a country like Ceylon must be qualified by an awareness of the costs of misdirected or premature education. It is common for a growing educational system in such a country to continue to concentrate its attention on the traditional academic-type education which had previously been provided in small quantities for the elite, rather than changing over to the more technically oriented mass education that is needed by a modernizing economy. This creates a supply of graduates that is badly out of line with available employment opportunities. In Ceylon, education expanded so fast relative to the growth and diversification of the economy that by the late fifties there came to be an excess supply of almost all types of trained labor. Aside from tying up resources in educational plant which might have been used more productively elsewhere, this kind of imbalanced and overly ambitious educational expansion creates a serious political problem by continually adding to the numbers of frustrated, underemployed or unemployed, but articulate persons in the society.

[15]Ceylon has little mineral wealth; there are some iron deposits but as of 1966 these seemed to be of no commercial value.

be a more difficult one to overcome. In part, the growth of income and population will solve this problem over time by enlarging the national market. But at no conceivable level of per capita income will Ceylon be able to support an efficient automobile-producing operation, for example. This is an extreme case, but it is true that the list of goods for which a substitution of local production for imports can be made quickly and easily will very soon be exhausted. The smallness of Ceylon's population and the still low per capita income level place a fairly definite limit on the number of commodities which can be produced in Ceylon purely for the local market now or in the immediate future without an enormous sacrifice of efficiency. Almost immediately, then, economic policy will be faced with three alternatives: to be satisfied with the degree of industrialization already achieved, to press on regardless with increasingly inefficient plants requiring ever-increasing degrees of subsidization, or to seek foreign markets for industrial exports, presumably in countries which are trying to bring about a similar change in the structure of their own economies and are similarly penalizing or excluding foreign competition. The first two alternatives are unacceptable. The chances for a reasonably efficient industrial sector depend on Ceylon's being able to escape from the autarkic pattern they imply and enter into international trade in manufactures. Such trade will probably not be possible along conventional, multilateral lines. It may be conducted through bilateral barter agreements of the kind which the Ceylon government concluded with various Communist-bloc and underdeveloped countries during the late fifties and early sixties.[16] A far better solution would be through some sort of multilateral regional trade and cooperative development system, which would seek to stimulate trade and rationalize the pattern of investment over a broad segment of underdeveloped Asia. Unfortunately, no real prospect that this kind of arrangement would emerge was visible during the mid-sixties. All in all, the obstacles to full-scale industrial development in Ceylon are formidable, though certainly not altogether insurmountable.

In the final analysis, it behooves the author of a strictly economic work such as this to refrain from making any unqualified predictions about future economic growth in Ceylon. Certainly the immediate economic prospects for significant improvement in the material welfare of the island's people are far less good than those existing at the granting of independence 17 years ago. It is the failure of economic policy makers to recognize and adjust to the

---

[16]During 1964 Ceylon began exporting auto batteries to Burma, which represented a very modest beginning in the exportation of manufactures.

profound changes in economic environment which took place over a period of time but were especially conspicuous during the 1940's that is largely to blame for the dissipation of the earlier opportunities and the deterioration of Ceylon's prospects. By failing to create a rapidly expanding yet externally balanced transitional economy they brought on the forced structural changes of the early sixties and the recent declines in consumption standards. Still, virtually all of the technical possibilities for output growth which were available to Ceylon in 1948 remain open to it today. The type of development strategy which could have dealt successfully with the challenges of the fifties can still be implemented, although the resources with which to effect it are sadly depleted now. This means that the sacrifices which the population will have to bear if rapid growth is to be achieved are at present considerably greater than those which would have produced the same result 10 or 15 years ago. Yet because predicting future economic growth in Ceylon is less a matter of defining economic potentials than of assessing human ability to realize those potentials it becomes impossible for the economist to say just what the future holds. To comprehend fully why Ceylon's technical potentials were not more completely realized in the recent past and predict whether they are likely to be in the future, one would have to possess a full understanding of all the factors guiding the evolution of Ceylonese society—psychological, sociological, and political as well as economic. And that clearly goes far beyond the chosen range of this volume. From the historical perspective of 120 years of modern Ceylonese economic development, only one thing is certain: the search for an economic system that will provide a politically acceptable and economically viable replacement for the classical export economy will continue.

Statistical Appendix

A. INTRODUCTION

This Appendix is designed to serve two purposes. One is to give, in greater detail and with more careful annotation as to sources and reliability, some of the most important statistics cited in the text of this monograph. The second is to provide a source of economic data which can be mined by future students of Ceylon's economy and by those interested in economic development in a broader focus. With this latter intent in mind, the range and quantity of data included in the Appendix go far beyond the statistical input requirements of the text. The usefulness of this Appendix as a source of information for others is enhanced by the fact that as far as possible its format has been rendered comparable with the similar appendixes to be found in all the country analysis monographs produced by the Economic Growth Center at Yale University. In time, this will mean that if an investigator wishes to compare any one of dozens of economic series in, say, Ceylon, Ghana, and Greece (the Center plans to complete 25 to 30 of these studies in all) he can do so with the assurance that considerable effort has been expended in trying to make the series genuinely comparable.[1] It is the Center's hope that this will turn out to be a major contribution to the advancement of the empirical study of economic development in general.

There are three substantive parts to this Appendix. The first two deal with special topics relative to the post-World War II period for which detailed consideration of statistical materials seems especially important: national economic accounts and trends in labor supply and use. The third consists of a wide range of basic historical series of economic data. Each of the three parts contains critical comments and descriptions of sources and methods as well as the tables themselves.

B. NATIONAL ACCOUNTS
1. Introduction

The development of national accounting in Ceylon began in 1947, when B. B. Das Gupta published a set of national income

---

[1]For an exposition of the terms of reference within which the data-gathering and data-evaluating aspects of the Country Analysis Program are being carried out, see Economic Growth Center at Yale University, *A System of National Economic Accounts and Historical Data* (New Haven, Connecticut, 1964).

estimates as an appendix to the *Report of the Commission on Social Services.*[2] His pioneering work covered the years 1937, 1938, 1942, 1943, and 1944. It is no longer necessary for a student of the subject to concern himself directly with the Das Gupta estimates. In 1952 a standardized system of accounts computation emerged which, though influenced by Das Gupta's work, differed from it in many ways. The new system, which was formulated by the then Director of Census and Statistics, K. Williams, was immediately enthroned as the official national accounting system, which it has remained to the present day.[3] Recently, the Census and Statistics Department (which will be informally cited here as CSD) prepared revised estimates going back through 1947 on Williams' method, with an additional total for 1938.[4] Moreover, private estimates which follow closely Williams' methodology extend back to 1926.[5] For continuity over a considerable period of time Williams' system is unrivaled.

When judged by other standards, though, the official accounts leave much to be desired. This will become clear in the exposition and critique which follows. The system of definitions and measurement techniques used was well designed to suit the economic structure and data problems existing in Ceylon at the time but economic change is rendering it obsolete and, in any case, it fails in many ways to meet modern international standards, as defined, for instance, by the Statistical Office of the United Nations.[6] Thus, Williams' system, which was preserved intact for more than a decade, is now giving way to revisions. Later parts of this essay will discuss the revisions made so far (and more are sure to come), which have derived from two sources: (1) the Central Bank of Ceylon (CBC) has, in its *Annual Reports* of 1958 and succeeding years, improved estimation procedures in several areas and also provided first estimates of magnitudes which do not feature in Williams' system and (2) the Census and Statistics Department, in responding to the annual "National Accounts Questionnaire" sent out by the UN Statistical Office, has computed modified versions of the official (Williams) estimates which are more in line with ac-

---

[2]*Report of the Commission on Social Services,* S.P. VII of 1947.

[3]K. Williams, *The National Income of Ceylon* (Colombo, 1952).

[4]See Table A–1.

[5]Warnasena Rasaputram, The Influence of Foreign Trade on the Level and Growth of National Income of Ceylon, 1926–57 (unpublished Ph.D dissertation, University of Wisconsin, 1959).

[6]United Nations, Statistical Office, *A System of National Accounts and Supporting Tables* (Studies in Methods, Series F, No. 2, Rev. 1, New York, 1960); United Nations, Statistical Office, *Methods of National Income Estimation* (Series F, No. 8, New York, 1955).

cepted international practice. Finally, the accounts formulated by the present writer to fit into the Economic Growth Center's integrated system (see Tables A–2 through A–8) are based on the UN figures but deviate from them in several instances, in adding items which should be a part of the UN accounts but have not been included for Ceylon to date and by providing finer breakdowns in some areas than have been presented so far.

Thus four different accounts systems are used at some time in this monograph: Williams' system (because of its continuity), the CBC revisions (for the first light they throw on areas not previously illuminated), the UN accounts (for their closer conformance to world standards), and the revised UN figures of the Center integrated accounts (for, hopefully, a new high in comprehensiveness and international standardization). To use each of these systems intelligently and to be able to distinguish actual changes in economic aggregates from purely statistical phenomena which arise from the quirks of each particular accounting system, it is necessary to have some understanding of the makeup and weaknesses of each. Promoting that understanding is the goal of this essay.

2. *Williams' (CSD) System*

Since Williams' system is Ceylon's official system of national accounting and since it is the parent schema from which all later accounting frameworks have been derived, it is worth outlining and criticizing in some detail.[7]

Two definitionally identical aggregates are generated by Williams' scheme. Its author titled them Gross National Product (GNP) and Gross National Expenditure (GNE), but they do not correspond to the generally accepted definitions of these terms. The conversion to the commoner definitions is, however, simple. Both GNP and GNE are valued at factor cost, but the addition of indirect taxes net of subsidies puts them on a market price valuation basis. Both include income earned abroad gross, not net, of income paid out to foreigners and thus correspond neither to Gross National Product nor to Gross Domestic Product (GDP) in the accepted definitions, but produce a total which in the case of Ceylon is higher than either of these. There are also some less important deviations from standard practices.

Gross National Product is the sum of ten separately computed items.

---

[7]However, readers who are not interested in the item-by-item description and critique may skip the next few pages and turn to page 249.

1. Domestic Exports. Total value of domestic exports as given in the *Customs Returns* minus 50 percent of the value of fertilizer imports and 100 percent of total imports of tea chests and acetic and formic acid, all of which are assumed to have been used as inputs in the production of domestic exports. This quantity is the net value (or a bit more than the net value, since the list of imported raw materials which has been netted out is not complete) of Ceylon's domestic exports, consisting mainly of agricultural output but also including a smattering of mined or manufactured items, as well as some value added by the industrial processing of agricultural exports. For all items, distribution costs incurred before

TABLE A–1

CEYLON'S OFFICIAL (WILLIAMS) NATIONAL ACCOUNTS, 1938–60*
(Current Prices, Rs. Millions)

	1938	1945	1946	1947	1948	1949	1950	195
A. "Gross National Product"								
1. Domestic exports	255	572	699	815	911	982	1,469	1,7
a. Tea	172	288	381	567	590	650	752	8
b. Rubber	47	218	227	137	143	125	405	5
c. Coconut	26	69	69	103	167	190	281	3
d. Other	19	15	40	29	37	41	56	
Minus: imported materials used	− 9	− 18	− 18	− 21	− 26	− 24	− 25	−
2. Local produce for Ceylon consumption	138	553	588	707†	763	764	890	1,0
a. Rice	29	112	124	136	163	180	190	2
b. Coconuts and coconut oil	14	35	47	84	87	79	115	
c. Tea	5	14	15	14	26	26	35	
d. Other food crops	28	188	173	195	180	173	198	
e. Tobacco	1	4	4	3	4	5	6	
f. Livestock products	14	45	46	70	102	100	106	
g. Fish	8	27	29	24	26	27	32	
h. Industrial products	29	81	98	108	115	118	141	
i. Betel and areca nut	4	23	25	30	27	25	30	
j. Firewood	2	8	10	12	10	9	11	
k. Other	4	16	17	21	23	22	26	
3. Trade, nonexport	53	180	192	252	263	277	344	
4. Transport, nonexport	29	112	120	136	136	143	166	
5. Professions	16	40	49	52	50	51	54	
6. Personal and domestic services	42	166	182	205	230	239	246	
7. Rent	25	41	43	44	48	52	58	
8. Capital development	30	119	136	109	162	233	273	
9. Government	50	194	239	255	283	295	336	
10. Income from abroad	14	13	20	33	33	20	32	
"Gross National Product"	652	1,990	2,268	2,608	2,879	3,056	3,868	4,

the goods reach customs are included. The total, though it is easy to obtain because of the relatively high quality of the customs statistics on which it relies, is a great hodgepodge conceptually. As an expression of the net output of domestic export goods it is rough, with a bias toward overstatement arising from the incompleteness of raw materials subtraction. The implied assumption that 50 percent of all imported fertilizer finds its way into export production is an arbitrary one. Moreover, no allowance has been made for changes in stocks, so while errors may be expected to average out over a number of years, for any given year there may be a considerable under- or overstatement of production under this head.

TABLE A–1 (Continued)

Ceylon's Official (Williams) National Accounts, 1938–60*

(Current Prices, Rs. Millions)

	1952	1953	1954	1955	1956	1957	1958	1959	1960
A. "Gross National Product"									
Domestic exports...........	1,381	1,457	1,676	1,836	1,613	1,538	1,613	1,644	1,727
a. Tea...................	723	825	1,123	1,194	1,044	1,021	1,131	1,045	1,096
b. Rubber...............	373	338	285	347	293	300	258	298	378
c. Coconut..............	259	274	243	259	237	196	199	285	238
d. Other................	53	49	63	72	78	71	63	64	62
Minus: imported materials used...................	− 27	− 29	− 38	− 36	− 39	− 50	− 38	− 48	− 47
Local produce for Ceylon consumption................	1,271	1,260	1,299†	1,426	1,292	1,375	1,463	1,552	1,701
a. Rice.................	344	291	330	391	276	310	365	379	470
b. Coconuts and coconut oil.	131	157	157	126	139	145	165	169	151
c. Tea..................	32	36	42	40	44	47	49	51	53
d. Other food crops........	317	316	292	333	317	326	311	327	354
e. Tobacco..............	7	9	7	9	9	10	15	15	14
f. Livestock products.......	136	141	154	174	140	142	117	137	135
g. Fish.................	33	29	30	41	46	52	54	60	69
h. Industrial products......	178	192	196	215	222	240	278	321	354
i. Betel and areca nut......	45	41	42	43	49	50	52	34	37
j. Firewood.............	11	11	12	12	12	13	14	14	14
k. Other................	37	37	39	42	38	40	43	45	50
Trade, nonexport...........	407	332	287	296	334	354	402	425	440
Transport, nonexport.......	191	192	187	212	237	258	267	294	311
Professions...............	57	57	64	67	68	72	80	81	82
Personal and domestic ervices.....................	279	288	300	312	324	337	348	356	361
Rent....................	76	82	84	97	108	125	124	130	134
Capital development........	409	377	367	443	497	479	512	556	545
Government..............	394	411	451	496	566	602	634	667	695
Income from abroad.......	42	35	33	49	57	60	50	48	49
oss National Product".......	4,507	4,491	4,748	5,234	5,096	5,200	5,493	5,753	6,045

(Continued on next page)

TABLE A–1 (Continued)

Ceylon's Official (Williams) National Accounts, 1938–60*

(Current Prices, Rs. Millions)

	1938	1945	1946	1947	1948	1949	1950	195⟩
B. "Gross National Expenditure"								
11. Imported consumption goods at market value	253	650	752	1,116	939	1,032	1,259	1,52
12. Consumption of local produce at market value	188	824	842	993	1,054	1,097	1,314	1,55
a. Rice	34	148	177	160	226	266	281	29
b. Coconuts and coconut oil	23	53	67	102	107	118	159	18
c. Tea	6	21	21	28	32	33	38	3
d. Other food crops	39	269	247	281	255	243	320	40
e. Tobacco	1	6	6	4	6	6	9	1
f. Livestock products	22	64	66	108	126	127	142	15
g. Fish	11	40	41	39	44	42	46	7
h. Industrial products	43	174	164	208	215	228	264	31
i. Betel and areca nut	5	33	35	44	39	35	43	4
j. Firewood	3	11	15	17	14	13	15	⟩
k. Other	5	24	23	27	30	31	37	4
Minus: government local purchases	− 4	− 19	− 20	− 25	− 40	− 45	− 40	− 4
13. Personal and domestic services	56	197	219	243	268	276	281	3⟩
14. Rent	23	39	41	40	43	47	52	6
15. Travel	11	46	51	40	42	44	45	5
16. Government current expenditure	71	200	246	276	298	335	387	4⟩
17. Remittances and travel abroad	25	46	38	27	70	94	122	1⟩
18. Dividends and interest payable to nonresidents	56	112	110	99	80	43	72	⟩
19. Gross domestic capital formation	50	182	210	170	229	330	396	5⟩
a. Government	13	70	79	71	124	184	213	2
b. Private	37	112	131	99	105	146	183	3
20. Net change in foreign assets	− 22	−110	− 50	−263	42	− 55	143	1⟩
21. *Minus:* import and excise duties net of subsidies	− 61	−190	−177	−153	−141	−175	−202	−1⟩
22. Statistical discrepancy	2	− 6	− 14	20	− 45	− 12	− 1	—
"Gross National Expenditure"	652	1,990	2,268	2,608	2,879	3,056	3,868	4,6⟩

2. *Locally Produced Articles Consumed in Ceylon.* This item consists of eleven subitems. Among them they cover nearly all such output in the economy, though often very roughly.

a. *Rice.* Gross paddy output is estimated by multiplying a figure for total acreage harvested by an average yield figure obtained (in recent years) by a sample survey; net output of paddy is gross output minus an assumed two bushels an acre for seed. Net output is valued at the producers' prices prevailing in the various growing

TABLE A–1 (CONTINUED)

CEYLON'S OFFICIAL (WILLIAMS) NATIONAL ACCOUNTS, 1938–60*

(Current Prices, Rs. Millions)

	1952	1953	1954	1955	1956	1957	1958	1959	1960
B. "Gross National Expenditure"									
1. Imported consumption foods at market value	1,426	1,417	1,270	1,425	1,443	1,643	1,556	1,774	1,831
2. Consumption of local product at market value	1,727	1,720†	1,732	1,849	1,711	1,799	1,854	1,952	2,172†
a. Rice	391	368	393	412	303	322	330	280	352
b. Coconuts and coconut oil	153	197	202	185	190	198	215	226	194
c. Tea	38	42	49	49	55	59	61	59	64
d. Other food crops	447	456	403	451	414	425	418	470	521
e. Tobacco	13	11	9	11	11	13	20	20	20
f. Livestock products	182	179	200	219	189	199	168	180	175
g. Fish	50	36	44	65	60	68	70	79	89
h. Industrial products	373	344	339	357	384	407	466	560	667
i. Betel and areca nut	65	59	60	61	70	72	74	49	53
j. Firewood	16	16	17	17	18	18	19	19	20
k. Other	49	48	49	52	48	50	54	54	59
Minus: government local purchases	− 50	− 31	− 33	− 30	− 31	− 32	− 41	− 44	− 52
. Personal and domestic services	325	336	351	367	384	400	415	424	433
. Rent	68	74	76	88	98	113	111	117	121
. Travel	57	83	89	114	119	138	129	150	158
. Government current expenditure	472	535	405	564	685	719	830	853	879
. Remittances and travel abroad	170	108	105	119	126	113	122	102	72
Dividends and interest payable to nonresidents	66	61	68	94	98	92	77	69	76
Gross domestic capital formation	609	559	500†	624	693	697	724	865	861
a. Government	307	314	298	353	396	377	412	426	426
b. Private	302	245	200	271	297	320	312	439	435
Net change in foreign assets	−346	−230	288	260	25	−236	− 60	−195	−208
Minus: import and excise uties net of subsidies	− 65	−185	−299	−282	−277	−285	−263	−328	−349
Statistical discrepancy	−	13	25	12	− 9	7	− 43	− 30	− 1
oss National Expenditure"	4,509	4,491	4,748†	5,234	5,096	5,200	5,493†	5,753	6,045

*Source: Department of Cenus and Statistics, unpublished data and *Statistical Abstract of Ceylon 1961*. ᵉ of the pre-1956 figures, which are unpublished, are revisions made by the Department of estimates ᵗished in earlier editions of the *Statistical Abstract*.
†Does not equal the sum of its components; error present in original.

regions and, where applicable, at the ruling price under the government's Guaranteed Price Scheme (GPS). Distribution costs, as with all subitems under this item are figured separately and included in items 3 and 4.

b. *Coconuts and Coconut Oil.* Total consumption is estimated by assuming that in each district it has remained at the per capita level which was revealed by the family budget survey of 1949[8] and adjusting for population growth. It is then valued at district producers' prices. As with other subitems under this item whose production for local use is estimated on the basis of 1949 consumption, the estimate here is likely to be seriously out of date.

c. *Tea.* 1949 per capita consumption is multiplied by total population and a producers' price supplied by the tea controller.[9]

d. *Other Food Crops.* Two types of crops are included here: (1) grains, pulses, and root crops; and (2) vegetables and fruits. Output and price data similar to those for rice—but less dependable —are used to compute the value of output at factor cost.

e. *Tobacco.* Includes the value of locally produced tobacco consumed in the form of cigars and chewing tobacco only. From estimated production is subtracted exports and the quantity used in local cigarette production (the latter is included under h, below). Small-scale production of cigars and chewing tobacco is thus included here rather than under cottage industry; since the tobacco is valued at growers' prices, any value added by the industrial production and distribution of these products is ignored.

f. *Livestock Products.* The item includes animals slaughtered for food, increase in livestock population, and production of milk and eggs. District producer prices are used for valuation, but the output data are very weak and the estimate is thus a rough one.

g. *Fish.* Official Department of Fisheries data on catches and prices are used. These totals are thought to be considerably understated.

h. *Industrial Products.* Factory and cottage production are handled separately. Data on the former, giving gross value of output, value of imported raw materials used, and domestic exports of factory output are obtained from the Department of Industries and used to estimate net retained factory output. Since until quite recently there were very few factories involved, many of them government-owned, the task has not been too difficult. On cottage industry there is no direct information at all and an indirect—and most unsatisfactory—method is used. The income earned by persons engaged in cottage industry according to the 1946 census is simply adjusted for the change in total population and the consumer price index (CPI) since 1946. This figure is in crying need of revision: a recalculation on the basis of the 1953 census would be a small

---

[8]*The New Consumer Price Index,* S.P. VI of 1953.
[9]*A.R. of the Tea Controller,* various years.

improvement; a survey of cottage industries would be a much greater one.

i. and j. *Betel and Areca Nut; Firewood.* These estimates are also based on 1949 per capita consumption, population increase, and changes in consumer prices.

k. *Other.* Finally, since there is no inherent test for comprehensiveness in this item, an addition of three percent of the total of subitems above is made to cover production not already accounted for. It is likely that the range of items produced in Ceylon for local consumption has widened over the last decade and will continue to do so, so understatement of an ever-increasing magnitude can be expected to result from this arbitrary allowance for uncovered production.

3. and 4. Trade and Transport in Goods Other than Export. These two items, which for reasons that will become obvious can be treated collectively, are probably the weakest ones in concept and method in Williams' system. They are intended to include trade and transport in domestically produced goods for local consumption and in imports (distribution costs of domestic exports are included in item 1, while those of reexports, a small item, escape inclusion altogether). Domestically produced and consumed goods are valued at retail prices. From this total retail value are subtracted the producers' value of the same goods (i.e., item 2), government purchases, and excise taxes net of subsidies. The resulting sum is then multiplied by .5, on the assumption that half of these goods are marketed and the other half used by their producers for own consumption.[10] Of this quantity, which represents total distribution costs incurred on locally produced goods for domestic consumption, 70 percent is assumed to accrue to trade and 30 percent to transport (this crucial assumption is said by Williams[11] to have its origin in a sample survey but the details of the survey do not seem ever to have been published). Total distribution cost of imports of consumption goods is estimated, by class of good, on the basis of average spread between the retail and c.i.f. prices of a sample of goods in each class. For other imports, distribution costs are arbitrarily assumed to be 35 percent of c.i.f. value. In both cases total distribution cost is allocated between trade and transport on a 70-30 ratio. After distributive costs of imports and locally produced and consumed items are summed up, a deduc-

[10]The source of the assumption is the 1951 rural economic survey. See *Final Report of the Economic Survey of Rural Ceylon, 1950–1951,* S.P. XI of 1954.

[11]See Williams, *op. cit.,* p. 15.

tion is made for the rent of commercial buildings (which is assumed to be 25 percent of total urban rents).

Much can be said in criticism of this item. It is obvious that far too much weight has been placed for far too long on the assumed proportions of 50 percent of total domestic nonexport output being marketed and the 70-30 split between trade and transport. Moreover, a really important conceptual error has been pointed out in the CBC revisions:[12] in item 12 below, "market value of consumption of local produce," all local production for domestic use is valued at retail prices. But here distribution costs are assumed to have been incurred only on the marketed half. Hence, the GNP and GNE concepts, which are supposed to be definitionally identical, are not in fact the same. Either market valuation of consumption expenditure should be revised downward or an imputed distribution cost should be added to the production side (the Central Bank—see below, pages 251–252—chooses the latter course).

To goods transport, whose calculation has been described, is added passenger revenue on the railways and buses. To get net output in this sphere, the cost of imported motor fuels, lubricating oils, tires and tubes, and spare parts is subtracted out. Coverage of passenger transport is incomplete, both as to types of transport covered and imported inputs deducted.

5. Professions. Government employees are excluded, being counted under item 9. For private professionals, two different approaches are used. For those who are subject to income tax, earnings are estimated from tax records (an arbitrary 18 percent addition is made to allow for underreporting). For other professions, of which a list has been compiled from the 1946 population census, 1946 earnings have been used as a base and multiplied by indexes of total population and wage rates, on the assumption that it is these things which determine professional income. As in other cases when this kind of calculation is used, direct information would be greatly preferable. Also, there is some suspicion that the list of professions used is outdated.

6. Personal and Domestic Services. This covers domestic services, hotel and restaurant services, and other private personal services. The procedure used is identical to the one just described in connection with professions not subject to income tax and suffers from the identical shortcomings.

7. Rent. What Williams intended this item to include is not

---

[12]See Central Bank of Ceylon, *Annual Report of the Monetary Board to the Minister of Finance* for 1961, pp. 50–51.

clear, but in practice it consists of total urban rents (total rents of dwellings is the commoner category). Total assessed rental value of urban buildings is obtained from the larger classes of local government: municipal councils, urban councils, and town councils. The estimates are very much on the low side because rural rents are totally ignored and also because the legally assessed values of urban rental property are likely to be lower and rise more slowly than the actual market values.

8. *Capital Development.* This category is split into two sub-items: government and private.

a. *Government.* This is the sum of expenditure under several headings of the central government budget: capital expenditure from the revenue budget; loan fund expenditure (i.e., specially budgeted capital works expenditures); deferred maintenance reserve account; reserve, extension, and renewal funds; Colombo Plan and other foreign-aid projects; Rubber Rehabilitation Scheme; and others. In other words, government capital expenditure is identified in accounting terms—by what accounting head the expenditure falls under—rather than by a direct examination of the actual goods purchased or created. To obtain net government capital goods output, government capital goods imports are deducted. Two major criticisms can be made of this procedure. One is that a more precise identification of capital expenditure would be desirable. The other is that by accepted international standards the definition of capital formation used is too broad, especially with regard to the inclusion of repair and maintenance expenditures. For a further comment, see page 248.

b. *Private.* Included here are (1) the value of building construction net of imported materials used; (2) erection cost of imported machinery; (3) cost of clearing and opening new land for tea, rubber, and coconut plantations; and (4) value of locally manufactured tea and rubber machinery less the value of imported parts and accessories used in their manufacture. The biggest item—and, unfortunately, the weakest—is the first. There is no direct information on the volume of building construction that is at all reliable, so an indirect method devised by Williams has been used. An informal inquiry made by him in the Public Works Department and among private contractors revealed that approximately 30 percent of their building costs consisted of imported materials. Accordingly, gross value of construction is taken to be 10/3 of the value of imported construction materials and net value to be that total minus the cost of the imported building materials. As to adequacy of measurement, this technique is obviously deficient; it takes no account of the changes in the ratio of imported materials to value of building construction that have undoubtedly taken place over the years. As to concept, it is not clear what is included: was it seriously intended by Williams to include rural construction, which clearly involves a much lower import component than the kinds of construction undertaken by the organizations he questioned? The point has never been made explicitly, but it probably does not. A further conceptual error is that import duties on building material imports have not been subtracted out, as they should be in a factor cost estimate. Incidentally, the measurement of construction in this way means that local production of building materials is included here under "capital development" rather than under industrial output.

The other components of private capital formation are less weak. Acreage of new estates opened up is obtained from various departments and valued at a subjective estimate of the average cost of opening up a new acre. Simple lack of data and inertia seem to account for the failure to include new acreage under paddy and other crops in these estimates. Replanting should also have been included (rubber replanting, insofar as it is subsidized by the government, has been included—incorrectly—under government capital formation, but tea and coconut replanting have been ignored). The erection costs of imported machinery are assumed to be 30 percent of the c.i.f. value. Information on the local manufacture of tea and rubber machinery is obtained directly from their few makers. A final criticism which must be made of these estimates of capital formation is that there seems to be some double counting as between the public and the private sectors: when the government lets out a contract to private contractors, the value of the construction appears in both accounts.

9. Government. The remaining net output of government is measured by wages and salaries paid to government employees.

10. Income from Abroad. This consists of the total of three balance of payments items: "foreign travel," "investment income," and "private donations and migrant transfers." As already noted, these items are taken gross and not net of the corresponding payments to foreigners. In any case, the item appropriate to a national income estimate would include only the second of these, i.e., *factor* income from abroad.

Gross National Expenditure is the sum of twelve items.

11. Imported Consumption Goods at Market Value. This item includes both private and government imports of consumer goods. Government imports of rice, flour, and sugar are divided between subsidized and free market distribution and priced accordingly.

Private imports are valued at c.i.f. value plus import duties plus distribution costs as estimated in items 3 and 4.

12. Consumption of Local Produce at Market Value. This item corresponds exactly with item 2, except that valuation in this case is at retail prices collected by the CSD.

13. Personal and Domestic Services. The totals under items 6 and 7 are reproduced here and expenditure on newspapers and cinemas (motion pictures) is added. The added items are estimated directly and their totals should be accurate, but the failure to include certain other types of services results in some understatement.

14. Rent. Rent in item 7 is multiplied by 12/10, the multiplication being intended to convert it from net rental income to gross rental payments of tenants. A further deduction of 25 percent is made to allow for business rents. These adjustments are apparently arbitrary and could well be reexamined with an eye to possible revision.

15. Travel. Direct estimates (see item 4) of consumer expenditure on internal travel by trains and buses make up this item.

16. Central and Local Government Current Expenditure on Goods and Services. This is arrived at as a residual: from total government expenditure are subtracted transfer and capital items. The criticism made under item 8a about weaknesses of identifying capital expenditure through conventional government accounts applies here as well.

17. Remittances and Travel Abroad. Source: the balance of payments.

18. Dividends and Interest Payable to Nonresidents. This item is also from the balance of payments.

19. Gross Domestic Capital Formation. This includes all the components of item 8, plus the value of imported capital goods.

20. Net Change in Foreign Assets. From the balance of payments.

21. Minus: Import and Excise Duties Net of Subsidies. This subtraction, whose source is the government accounts, converts GNE from a market price to a factor cost basis and makes it comparable with the GNP estimates already made.

22. Statistical Discrepancy.

This completes a detailed exposition and critique of Williams' system, which has regulated official usage in Ceylon up to the present day. The system has many weaknesses. Conceptually, the aggregate that it produces is not of major interest, but this is a minor point since either GNP or GDP conventionally defined is easily obtained by a simple conversion. Methodologically, the system's weaknesses are those of the basic data and those arising from the reliance placed on rough estimation techniques which depend on certain assumed parameters. These parameters in several cases derive from purely subjective estimates and even where they were originally based on objective studies they are often outmoded now. Better parameter estimates are available in most cases—e.g., from the 1953 Central Bank Consumer Finance Survey, the 1958 Urban Budget Survey, and the 1959 Survey of Employment, Unemployment and Underemployment[13]—and should be used. A shift to these newer estimates would effect considerable improvements in the accuracy of measurement with no change in the basic data inputs, though problems of comparability with earlier estimates would arise. Also, the 1953 census and, when available, the 1963 census could be used. A somewhat different problem is that Williams' system is almost impossible to work with in a disaggregated form: income by sector of origin, capital formation by type, and other breakdowns of interest cannot easily be extracted from it. Finally, there are no checks for comprehensiveness. Among the more obvious omissions are rural housing use and construction and inventory investment (though changes in livestock inventories are erroneously included under consumption).

It is interesting to note, however, that these shortcomings with regard to precision of definition and measurement and to comprehensiveness make *relatively* little difference in the measurement of economic growth.[14] The ease with which production for export and a few other important output components (e.g., rice production, government services) can be measured makes it easy to compute *fairly* good growth rates of national output. The absolute *size* of GNP according to the various accounting systems is less similar. The CSD concept of GNP is a consistently much smaller economic aggregate than GNP as measured by the United Nations or Center systems. When computing growth rates, then, it makes relatively little difference—at least, over a fair stretch of time—which system one uses; in talking about absolute levels, though—say in comparing per capita income figures—one must be careful to adjust for definitional and measurement differences.

Williams' system was admirable for the time and place of its

---

[13]Central Bank of Ceylon, *Survey of Ceylon's Consumer Finances,* 1954; *Report of the Committee to Revise the Cost-of-Living Index.* S.P. II of 1959; International Labour Organisation, "Report to the Government of Ceylon on the Employment, Unemployment and Underemployment Sample Survey of Ceylon, 1959" (unpublished draft report) (1960).

[14]See Chapter 6, pages 124–125.

inception. It maximized reliance on the one really good set of statistics existing in an immediately postcolonial open economy—those of foreign trade—and required only a minimum of other data. It was an excellent pioneering effort but it has unfortunately been allowed to reign supreme for far too long after other systems became feasible. Now its weaknesses are widely recognized and a wholesale revision will undoubtedly take place just as soon as the inertia built up over the years can be overcome. In the meantime, the limited improvements made by the CBC and by the CSD in conjunction with the UN questionnaire have provided alternative estimates to the official ones.

3. The Central Bank Revisions

When the Central Bank began to publish national accounts estimates (in its 1958 *Report*) it did so for a purely practical reason: it is required by law to publish an economic review of the preceding year every March and because of lags in data collecting and processing the official CSD estimates were—and are—not available until after midyear. At first the bank merely worked up preliminary estimates based strictly on Williams' definitions but using projections and other rough estimates in place of the basic data that were not yet available. For political reasons it was felt that competitive estimates were to be avoided, so the bank's figures were played down at first. The passage of time has, however, rendered Williams' system increasingly obsolete—especially in the sense that the more sophisticated economic analyses being done by the bank and others required estimates of many aggregates which did not appear in Williams' system and were not easy to derive from it—and so, for the first time in its 1961 *Report,* the CBC began to revise the CSD methodology. The 1961 estimates (which also covered 1959 and 1960) were accompanied by a methodological note outlining the major departures from previous practices. Further changes were announced in the 1962 bank *Report.* There is no need to summarize these changes in detail, since those who require detailed knowledge of them can consult the relevant *Annual Reports,* but the main drift of the bank's innovations can be indicated.

(1). The category "domestic exports" was transposed to "production for export" by adding in changes in locally held stocks of export commodities; the netting out of imported raw materials was made more comprehensive and the handling of reexport trade and the distribution costs of export goods was also improved.

(2). "Trade" and "transport" were revised by making a somewhat improved allowance for nonmarketed production of locally produced and consumed goods and by imputing distribution costs on this type of production (this change was needed to make the output and expenditure sides of Williams' accounts balance—see page 246). Coverage was also expanded slightly.

(3). The estimates for "rent," "services," and Gross Domestic Capital Formation were all broadened. Initial—but overly conservative—calculations were made of rural rents. Financial services were measured for the first time. And a wider range of imported machinery, along with the growing domestic production of cement, were allowed for under investment.

(4). *Net Factor Income from Abroad* was correctly redefined to be net of payments to the rest of the world and to include only factor payments, not foreign travel, private donations, or migrant transfers.

(5). On the expenditure side, various minor improvements were made. Coverage of nonfactor service imports and of goods and services purchased in Ceylon by nonresidents was improved.

(6). Finally, various reclassifications were undertaken to highlight aggregates which did not feature in Williams' system.

Thus, some of the weaknesses of the CSD system which were mentioned in the preceding section have already been corrected by the CBC. The CBC accounts improve upon the official estimates for the years since 1959 for which they have been compiled. Not being the official statistical agency, the bank has not redone CSD estimates for earlier years. Even between the 1961 and 1962 bank *Reports* the accounting systems used differ to some extent. The CBC accounts thus represent an improved interim system, useful for analyses of recent years but limited in their application to longer periods of time by their incomparability with other systems. They are part of a continuing improvement of Ceylon's national accounts. It is said that more corrections will be made in future editions of the Central Bank *Report*. In any case, the situation is in flux and a major revision, possibly a joint product of the Central Bank and Census and Statistics, is to be expected in time. Just how soon this needed change will come is an imponderable.

Besides introducing refinements in the measurement of GNP in current prices, the Central Bank also contributed the first constant-price estimates in 1956. The methodology first used to deflate GNP to constant prices is described in W. Rasaputram, "Gross National Product of Ceylon at Constant (1948) Prices," *Central Bank of Ceylon Bulletin* (January, 1956), pp. 8–16. A few minor changes have been made in the method of deflation since that time (e.g.,

1956 and later 1959 prices were used) but the basic procedure remains unchanged. Mainly because of the paucity and weakness of price indexes for Ceylon (see pages 304–305), the deflation of current value estimates by an appropriate price series is often difficult. Import indexes for Ceylon are heavily dependent on the base period chosen for their construction and their widespread use in the deflation process adds an arbitrary element. The frequent use of the consumer price index (especially in the case of rent) contributes an upward bias to apparent real income growth. And the treatment of government consumption (real product is measured by gross wages and salaries paid) adds a further upward bias. In some cases physical output series can be used instead of deflated value series but such cases are limited and, in any case, the physical series are generally far from perfect. It must be concluded that the estimates of real product are not only rougher than the current price estimates but have a distinct tendency to overestimate real income growth. It is interesting to note that in its 1962 *Annual Report* the CBC acknowledges this bias and promises a complete revamping of its real GNP series.

4. The Census and Statistics Department and the UN Questionnaire

While the Central Bank has taken the lead in improving the official system of national accounting, the main impetus for change at the Census and Statistics Department has come from the annual necessity to reply to the "National Accounts Questionnaire" sent out by the Statistical Office of the United Nations. The UN asks national statistical services to conform "as closely as possible" to the UN System of National Accounts (SNA) and to indicate major deviations by footnotes. Barring internal inconsistency in the return that is sent in, it is published as received in the annual *Yearbook of National Accounts Statistics*. In the *Yearbook* the "major deviations" noted by the national statistical service are indicated by footnote, but aside from that the user is given no indication of how the data were compiled and just how close they come to the UN standards. In the case of Ceylon one would want to know how the CSD figures are adjusted to bring them into line with the SNA totals—if this, indeed, is how the questionnaire is answered—and what new estimates have been made. The final, crucial, question is: how closely do the reported figures correspond with the SNA definitions?

Ceylon replies to six of the nine tables asked for in the questionnaire: (1) expenditure on GNP; (2) industrial origin of GDP;

(3) distribution of the national income; (4) composition of gross domestic capital formation; (5) composition of private consumption expenditure; and (6) external transactions. The three which it has not as yet furnished are (1) the finance of gross domestic capital formation; (2) receipts and expenditures of households and private nonprofit institutions; and (3) general government revenue and expenditure. Most of the data needed to fill in these last three can be obtained from various studies and calculations made by the Central Bank. The following paragraphs outline the procedure followed by the CSD in filling in the UN questionnaire.[15]

1. Expenditure on Gross National Product. Indirect estimates of most of the items included in the current-price portion of this table can be made by manipulating the totals of the expenditure side of Williams' accounts. Private consumption, imports, and exports are obtained in this way. In accord with UN procedure, more of government expenditure is classified as consumption and less as investment than under CSD practices. The only item which is totally missing in Williams' system is change in stocks. Various calculations have been used from time to time by the CSD in providing the UN with an estimate of this item, resulting in noncomparable figures in various issues of the *Yearbook*. The methods used to convert expenditure on GNP to constant prices have already been commented upon.

2. Industrial Origin of Gross Domestic Product. Williams' system of GNP calculation is partly an industrial system, so obtaining income originating in most of the two-digit industries identified in the International Standard Industrial Classification (ISIC) is not difficult. There are cases, though, in which special adjustments are needed. "Domestic exports" in the CSD system is an amalgam of various industries and is treated thus: mineral and manufacturing industries are broken out and reassigned to the appropriate categories; the resulting total is reduced by seven percent to allow for distribution costs (which are arbitrarily apportioned between "trade" and "transport") and credited to the ISIC category "agriculture, forestry, hunting, and fishing." Thus the industrial processing of tea and rubber (but not coconut) remains in agriculture. Other industries are identified in a generally satis-

---

[15]The account will be an imperfect one. There is no written manual of procedure on this matter and each occupant of the relevant office in the department has had to devise his own methods. These methods have changed—presumably improved—through time. Both the 1962 and the 1963 *Yearbooks* contained revised estimates, apparently designed mainly to incorporate the CBC revisions already noted. The account given here was received orally in 1963 from the then-current national accounts officer.

factory way, except for construction and ownership of dwellings, which err mainly in ignoring the rural sector.

3. *Distribution of the National Income* is a very difficult table to compile from Ceylonese sources. Its first item, compensation of employees, consists of the central and local government wage bills, an estimate of corporate wages, and the service component of GNP under the CSD system. The estimate apparently errs in two important ways. By including all income originating in the service "industry" it must take in a great deal of entrepreneurial income. Working in the opposite direction is the apparent failure to include wages paid in kind, a major part of the compensation of corporate employees on the estates. Of the various forms of property income, rent should include all net rental income of persons, not just on dwellings but on the places of operation of businesses and governments as well; the UN figures seem to include all such rental income up through 1956, but in 1957 something slipped and from that year on rent in this table corresponds with total rent payments as an item of personal expenditure. The other elements of income from property—interest, dividends, and corporate transfer payments—are available only as a single total for the three of them; their source is income tax returns, corporate reports, and other kinds of information on business. Corporate retained earnings are estimated from corporate records, as are corporate direct taxes. Finally, income from unincorporated enterprises is computed strictly as a residual, being the difference between national income estimated by making the necessary subtractions from GNP and the sum of the other items of the present table, which have been calculated separately.

4. *Composition of Gross Domestic Capital Formation.* This table has two parts: gross domestic capital formation by type of capital good and by type of purchaser. Since the various types of capital goods are handled separately in the CSD system, the first part of the table poses no problem, except that construction of dwellings and other new buildings cannot be distinguished from each other. The division by type of purchaser is made on a rougher basis than the UN would like, being simply a public-private one, with private enterprises and public corporations being lumped together on the one side and government enterprises and general government on the other.

5. *Composition of Private Consumption Expenditure.* Two methods are used to calculate consumer expenditure on the various categories of this table. Where possible, a national balance sheet method is used, taking production minus exports plus imports and

valuing the resulting quantity at current market prices. In the relatively minor cases where total output is not known, indirect estimates are made on the basis of family budget surveys, assuming per capita consumption to be fixed either in absolute terms or as a percentage of total consumption expenditure. The latter method is of course the less desirable, since it assumes away changes in consumption patterns.

6. External Transactions. This table merely repeats information from the balance of payments accounts.

How close, then, do Ceylon's responses to the "National Accounts Questionnaire" come to the specifications of the SNA? The question is made hard to answer by the fact that there exists no definite format in the Census and Statistics Department for answering the questionnaire. There have been procedural changes through the years (mostly in the direction of a closer compliance with SNA stipulations), not all of which have been mentioned in the narration just completed. In general, though, several shortcomings of the Ceylon responses stand out. All either remain uncorrected at present or else have been corrected only in the last one or two responses and are thus a feature of the data for most of the years in question.

Estimates of personal consumption expenditure run the risk of not being comprehensive; the three percent allowance for "other goods" may be adequate for a low-income society with a narrow range of goods and services consumed, but its tendency to ignore items such as the cost of operating personal automobiles, several kinds of recreation, and the cost of financial services will tell in time, as incomes rise. Government consumption expenditure, in the same table, is presented unadjusted on the financial year (October 1–September 30) for the central government and on a calendar basis for local governments; otherwise SNA standards seem to be attained. Gross domestic fixed investment suffers the sins of its original means of estimation (see pages 247–248); the need for more direct measurement of fixed investment is a crying one. Also, own account rural construction using indigenous raw materials deserves attention. Increase in stocks has been dealt with in a generally inadequate manner and has been noncomparable from year to year; by 1962, a fair degree of coverage had been achieved, thanks largely to the simplicity of the island's economy and the fact that there are very few important types of stocks. Valuation has been made at current market prices.

Finally, mention should be made of depreciation. This is a notoriously difficult item to compute and it has yet to be handled adequately in Ceylon. At first the estimate required for the UN questionnaire (the aggregate does not appear in Williams' system) was estimated directly from an examination of corporate income statements, tax returns, etc. This yielded a figure which was obviously far too low and the attempt to measure depreciation directly was eventually abandoned. The present practice is simply to assume that it amounts to 5 percent of GNP and that Net National Product is therefore 95 percent of GNP.

5. The Center Accounts

In compiling the Center national accounts tables used in this monograph,[16] consideration was given to the strengths and weaknesses of the systems just described. Because the Economic Growth Center had decided to use SNA definitions and a system of accounts which bear a close kinship to the SNA, the UN figures for Ceylon were taken as a starting point for the present calculations. The reason that the UN data could be only a starting point is simply that the Ceylon data published in the UN *Yearbook* fail in the several ways already mentioned to measure up to the SNA standards. Of the various shortcomings they possess, some of the more obvious ones have been remedied here. In several cases the shortcoming was an omission and it has been corrected by the addition of a rough estimate of the magnitude in question: this remedy reflects the belief that even a very rough estimate is a better approximation of the true quantity than zero, which is the magnitude implied if the item is simply ignored.

For each year, 1950 through 1960, eight tables have been prepared. They present in integrated fashion a statistical description of (A-2) Gross National Income and Expenditure at Current Market Prices; (A-3) Gross National Expenditure at Constant (1953) Prices; (A-4) Personal Income, Outlay, and Saving; (A-5) General Government Revenue and Current Expenditure; (A-6) External Transactions; (A-7) Gross Domestic Capital Formation and Saving; and (A-8) Industrial Origin of Gross Domestic Product at Factor Cost. They are closely akin to the UN tables on Ceylon in subject matter as well as approach, but there are some important deviations. These will be pointed out in a general way now. Detailed source notes on the Center tables follow the tables themselves.

A-2. *Gross National Income and Expenditure at Current Mar-*

---

[16]The tables themselves appear on pages 269–279; they are followed by detailed, item-by-item, notes on sources and methods.

ket Prices. This subject is handled in a manner similar to that of the two UN tables it replaces,[17] except for these differences. On the expenditure side of the account, there is some additional detail shown and, more important, two major additions and two key alterations have been made. The additions are rural house rents (both paid and imputed) as an element of private consumption expenditure and rural subsistence construction as a component of gross domestic fixed capital formation. The alterations come in the estimation of increase in stocks and government expenditure, both capital and current.

Rural house rents were computed as follows: Total rural population for each year was estimated on the basis of data from the 1946 and 1953 population censuses and estimates of the Registrar-General's Department. Average household size was then computed, the sources of information being the 1946 census and the 1953 consumer survey (the slight growth trend appearing between these two dates was interpolated and extrapolated for other years). Dividing rural population by average size of household gave a figure for total number of rural houses. The average monthly rent which the 1953 census showed to apply to rented rural houses was assumed to apply to all rural houses and the multiplication of the estimated number of houses in existence in 1953 yielded the rural house rent bill for that year. For other years the 1953 average rent figure was deflated by the CPI with a one-year lag and multiplied by the corresponding total number of houses.

The estimates of rural subsistence construction interlock with these rent calculations. The change in number of rural houses was computed by comparing annual totals which had been reached in the manner just described. An estimate of the average cost of constructing a rural house—presumably for 1959—appears in the *Ten-Year Plan* (p. 473); it was applied directly to 1959 and, after deflation by the CPI, to other years. The average cost of construction for each year was then multiplied by the estimated number of new houses to obtain the item "rural subsistence construction." It should be mentioned that these estimates are probably on the low side, since the Planning Secretariat, which made up the *Ten-Year Plan,* was most interested in the quantity of resources which would have to be mobilized through the market to fulfill the housing plan and may not have taken full account of the input of own account labor in costing the housing needs of the country.

---

[17]Tables 1 (first part) and 3 in the United Nations, Statistical Office, *Yearbook of National Accounts Statistics.*

The figures on increase in stocks which appear in the UN tables are not used here for two reasons: they are quite inadequate in their method of computation in the early years of the period, whereas for later years, when their adequacy is very much greater, they are noncomparable, both to the earlier figures and to each other. An entirely new and reasonably consistent series was thus constructed. To the potential user of these figures, though, the warning should be issued that they bear little or no resemblance in their results to any earlier stock estimates for Ceylon and there is no satisfactory way of checking their accuracy. If any reliance is to be put on them, it must be based on the circumstantial evidence of the method of their calculation, which is outlined here. The figures include stocks of tea, rubber, and livestock, and trade stocks of imports and locally produced goods for domestic consumption; from 1953 on they also include government-held food stocks (rice, flour, raw sugar, and white sugar); this last is the one break with year-to-year consistency in the series. Inventories in the economy are covered with a fairly high degree of comprehensiveness: manufacturing inventories are very small because the manufacturing sector itself is so small and stocks of coconuts and minor export goods are the only other ones omitted (coconut inventories are inherently incapable of being measured because the only available production estimates are based on the nut equivalents of the various coconut product exports plus estimated local consumption). Tea inventory change is taken as production minus exports minus estimated local consumption, all figures being based on the *A.R. of the Tea Controller;* valuation is at the average Colombo market price. Rubber inventory change is estimated in the same way, except that the figures on local consumption, which are based on surveys of local users of rubber by the rubber controller, are more accurate; they are valued at the average Colombo market prices for RSS 1 sheet. In both of these cases the method of computation is faultless in principle but likely to be somewhat unreliable in practice because it involves subtracting one large number (exports) from another (production) and the resulting small difference (inventory change) is thus likely to be much more inaccurate than either of the numbers themselves. Inventory change among the various forms of livestock is measured using population figures reported to the divisional revenue officers (a three-year moving average was used to smooth out idiosyncratic year-to-year fluctuations in these notoriously erratic but probably unbiased numbers) and prices consisting of the unweighted all-island average as collected by the CSD for 1960 and a deflation by the CPI for earlier years. Trade inventories of imports and domestically produced goods for local consumption have not been included in any previous inventory estimate; no information on them exists, so for want of a better source the approximate ratio for the United States of one percent of sales per year (an average of the years preceding and following the year-end in question) was used to provide some sort of figure (the item turned out to be quite small, so it really has little effect on the overall totals). Finally, stock data for government-held food are from the *A.R. of the Food Commissioner;* changes are valued at Colombo wholesale prices.

Government current and capital expenditure was derived from the newly drawn up accounts for general government revenue and expenditure which are described below (pages 263–265) and differ somewhat from the UN figures.

Distribution of Gross National Income (at market prices) corresponds quite closely to UN Table 3 (see page 255), which, however, is worked out on a factor cost basis. Only a few new or revised figures appear in the table. Payments by producers to individuals have been split into (1) wages and salaries; (2) employer contributions for social security; and (3) income in kind. The first of these is taken straight from the UN table. The second is zero in value up to the beginning of the Employees' Provident Fund Scheme in 1959, after which the proportion of fund revenues contributed by employers had to be calculated indirectly. Total contributions made by both employees and employers are given in the *A.R. of the Commissioner of Labour.* The act which created the fund provided for minimum contributions of six percent of wages by participating employers and four percent by employees. Higher contributions are permissible but it was thought reasonable to assume that total contributions broke down between employers and employees on a 60-40 ratio and the amount contributed was divided accordingly. The third item, income in kind, was added here. The estates make substantial compensation in the form of free goods and services. Only the most important of these, free rice, is included here. An estimate for 1948[18] put the value of free food issued by estates at Rs. 4,700,000. This estimate was extended to other years by multiplying it by indexes of rice prices and estate population. Since in the UN table the last two items were apparently left uncounted and thus must have wound up in the residual item, income of unincorporated enterprises, they are subtracted out of that item here.

_____

[18]"Labour Conditions in Ceylon", *International Labour Review* (December, 1949), p. 581.

To rental income of persons has been added the item already computed to cover rural house rents (the tacit assumption being that all rural rent paid or imputed becomes net rental income). The percentage of total rental income that is imputed to owners of owner-occupied housing has been estimated using information from the 1946 and 1953 censuses.

Entrepreneurial income ("Income of Unincorporated Enterprises" in the UN table) has had rural subsistence construction added to it, on the assumption that this construction is not done by corporations. Both in the UN total and here it serves as a residual item, since there is no direct information on the subject. Accordingly, the statistical discrepancy which developed when GNP measured by the product approach was compared with GNP by the income approach was subtracted from this item.

An unorthodox procedure in the handling of taxes should be noted here. Export duties, one of the major sources of revenue for the central government in Ceylon, are considered by the UN to be indirect taxes (see *Yearbook of National Accounts Statistics* 1960, p. xvi), but the CSD regards them as direct taxes on corporations and, for once, their procedure was given preference here over that of the UN. The key consideration in principle is the incidence of the tax: does it fall on the producer or purchaser of the good? The general answer to the question is that it depends on the elasticities of supply and demand. In the particular case of Ceylon's export crops, the answer is clear-cut: the elasticity of supply is very low (most production plans must be made a considerable time in advance and a shift to other lines of production is very difficult) and the elasticity of demand is very high (Ceylon is, in fact, a nearly perfect competitor in the world markets for rubber and coconut products—though less so in tea—and a small change in its prices while the prices of other suppliers of these products remained constant would mean a great change in the demand for Ceylon's products). The tax therefore falls almost entirely on the producers and amounts to a direct tax on the plantation companies.

Subsidies are strictly defined here as producer subsidies. Often in Ceylon the entire "rice subsidy," which is really in large part a transfer payment to consumers rather than a subsidy to producers, is erroneously counted here.

Finally, since the aggregate dealt with here is *Gross* National Income, some estimate of capital consumption allowances must be added in. As already mentioned, earlier estimates used in national accounts must be adjudged failures, being obviously too low in value. The figures used here probably err on the low side, too, but they are at least the product of a careful direct study of corporate accounts[19] and may thus be considered the best available. They may or may not be an improvement on the simple assumption that depreciation is five percent of GNP (see page 257).

A–3. *Gross National Expenditure at Constant (1953) Prices* is, of course, the result of a deflation of the first part of Table A–2. The accuracy of the table is severely limited by the inadequacy of the price indexes available for use as deflators; the weaknesses of these have been cited elsewhere. Private consumption expenditure is deflated by the all-items CPI; food by the food component of the CPI; housing by the overall CPI lagged one year and the fuel and light component of the CPI, currently weighted (the rent component of the CPI was eschewed for reasons which are mentioned elsewhere); and other consumer expenditure by the clothing and miscellaneous components of the CPI, currently weighted. General government consumption expenditure for 1953 and later years was deflated by the index implied in UN Table 1; the UN furnishes no deflation for earlier years, so the index used by Rasaputram in estimating constant price GNP (see *Central Bank of Ceylon Bulletin,* January, 1956) was used (but the fit between the two indexes at their 1953 juncture was not good). An identical procedure was followed in the deflation of gross domestic fixed capital formation. Increase in stocks was deflated by an index which grew out of the stock change estimates already described: price indexes were calculated for each of the goods whose stock changes were traced; the overall index was obtained by current weighting (a double weighting by the value of the stock and the value of the change in the stock was used). Exports and imports were deflated, respectively, by the export and import price indexes compiled by the CBC. The sum of all these items was taken to be Gross Domestic Product at 1953 prices. Net factor income from abroad was deflated by the overall implied deflator of GDP and subtracted from the GDP total to get expenditure on gross national product in real terms. Real Gross National Income, though, is a somewhat different concept: it was taken to be the same as expenditure on GNP, except that "net foreign investment" (i.e., exports of goods and services minus imports) was measured as a single quantity and always deflated by the import price index (whether net foreign investment was positive or negative). This last concept measures changes in the ability of Ceylon nationals

---

[19]W. Rasaputram, "Savings of the Ceylon Economy, 1950–59." *Central Bank of Ceylon Bulletin* (January, 1961), pp. 10–31.

to acquire goods and services and allows for the "terms of trade effect" on their real income.

A-4. *Personal Income, Outlay, and Saving* poses no special problems and it is hard to see why the corresponding UN table from the "National Accounts Questionnaire" has not yet been filled in by the CSD. The probable reason is a lack of trust in the personal savings figure which emerges as a residual after consumption expenditure has been subtracted out of personal income and taxes and transfers have been allowed for. In the present instance the unreliable residual is not used, but the findings of Rasaputram in his savings study[20] are utilized instead, along with a statistical discrepancy.

A-5. *General Government Revenue and Current Expenditure,* by contrast, was the most difficult of the new tables to compile. The fundamental problem was to derive a consolidated budget on a "general government" basis (i.e., with all levels of government included but with public corporations and other autonomous producing units taken out). This problem has been solved here in a fairly rough manner. The starting point was the economic and functional reclassification of the central government accounts done by the Central Bank and published in its recent *Reports.* These accounts were further adjusted by netting out the Railway and Electrical Departments, the most obvious producing units included within the confines of the accounts (separately chartered public corporations had already been excluded). The resulting figures for budget years (which end on September 30) have been adjusted to calendar years by the simple expedient of taking three-fourths of the budget year which ends on September 30 of the calendar year in question and adding in one-fourth of the total for the next budget year. This elementary adjustment should give a satisfactory estimate of receipts and expenditure within given calendar years for all but the very most discontinuous forms of revenue and expenditure. Local government was then added in, but the degree of refinement possible in its handling was much less than with the central government. For the larger classifications (municipal councils, urban councils) a considerable but nonstandard breakdown of revenues and expenditures can be made; for the smaller units (town councils, village committees) no breakdown at all is available. In general, it has been necessary to leave the producing activities of local government in the "general government" accounts.

---

[20]*Ibid.*

The main tasks to be accomplished were to split government revenue among four sources (direct taxes on households, direct taxes on corporations, indirect taxes, and income from property and entrepreneurship), to break down expenditure by function, and to distinguish between current and capital expenditure.

The Central Bank data, once the Railway and Electrical Departments were removed, provided the information for the revenue breakdown. The only remaining task was to split the revenue from certain direct taxes between corporations and households. The most important of these was the income tax, for which the proportion of tax assessments falling on households and corporations respectively are published (in the *A.R. of the Commissioner of Income Tax, Estate Duty and Stamps,* later called the *A.R. of the Commissioner of Inland Revenue*) but the corresponding proportions of tax collections are not. An estimate of the division of actual collections was made by taking the assessment proportions, using a three-year moving average to smooth out eccentric deviations, and introducing a two-year lag to allow changes in the assessment ratio to be reflected in the collection ratio. Receipts from the bank debits tax were divided between firms and households on the same ratio as existed in their total deposits (data on this were from the *Central Bank of Ceylon Bulletin,* various issues). For local governments a few arbitrary assumptions had to be made about sources of revenues (basically, that the revenues of town councils and village committees came from the four possible sources in the same proportions as did the revenues of urban councils).

For the functional classification of expenditure, the work of the Central Bank was relied on where the central government was concerned. Local governments once again had to be dealt with via arbitrary assumptions, but their expenditures are very small relative to those of the central government.

In distinguishing between current and capital expenditure the procedure of neither the Central Bank nor the UN was followed. The resulting estimate of government capital expenditure lies somewhere between the two, being smaller than that of the Central Bank and larger than that of the UN (the difference is obviously one of definition of the line between current and capital, so when the estimate of capital formation rises the estimate of current expenditure shrinks correspondingly). The bank's work was used as a starting point. From its total for capital expenditure, investment by the Railway and Electrical Departments was subtracted, military investment was transferred to current expenditure, and "expenditure on capital repair and maintenance" was similarly reclassified. The resulting estimate, as noted, is somewhat larger than the one in the UN accounts. Part of the reason for the difference is that the central government data were not adjusted to a calendar year basis when reported to the UN by the CSD; adjusted data (such as those used here) would be expected to be somewhat higher than unadjusted ones, since they include a portion of the (usually higher) expenditure in the following budget year.

A–6. *External Transactions* corresponds exactly with UN Table 6, except that the items on current transfers to and from the rest of the world in that table have never been filled in. This is puzzling, since the figures are easily available in the balance of payments accounts published by the Central Bank.

A–7. *Gross Domestic Capital Formation and Saving* is comprised exclusively of material which has already appeared in earlier tables. The fit of the items in the table gives some indication of the accuracy of the measurement in all the preceding tables. The results in this case are not too good, since many of the items in this table —change in stocks, income retained by producing units, and household saving—are those for which the measurements available are weakest. All in all, this is the most inadequate table of the series and the area in which future reorganizers of Ceylon's national accounts might well concentrate their efforts (though in large part the improvement of these estimates implies the improvement of the whole accounting system).

A–8. *Industrial Origin of Gross National Product* derives mainly from UN Table 2 (see pages 254–255). The two tables are, in fact, identical, except for three points of deviation. The items "construction" and "ownership of dwellings" have had added to them rural subsistence construction and rural house rents respectively. Any other deviations between GNP at factor cost in the UN and the present accounts are mainly explained by differing treatment of taxes and subsidies; since these are mainly matters between the government and agricultural producers, the statistical discrepancy between the two estimates has been added to income originating in agriculture. The only unjustifiable element in this procedure is that there is also some difference in income originating in government (i.e., government's total wage bill) and no attempt has been made to allow for this.

6. Using the Center Accounts

Besides the creation of improved accounts, another purpose of a methodological study such as this is to determine how much confidence may be placed in a given set of accounts when using them. Two fundamental questions must be asked. Are the aggregates correctly defined? Are they accurately measured?

Questions of definition have already been dealt with above. In brief, it has been found that the "Gross National Product" of the CSD system deviates in several ways from GNP as usually defined. The UN accounts adhere more closely to standard definitions, but the Center accounts make still more progress in this direction by adding two quantities (rural subsistence construction and rural house rents) which bring the production frontier to precisely the point at which the UN itself recommends that it be drawn: to include all market production, plus the own account production of food and housing. Similarly, each of the components of GNP has now been aligned quite closely with standard definitions, a considerable advance over Williams' scheme (this was accomplished mainly by the CSD in responding to the "National Accounts Questionnaire"). The user of the accounts presented here may thus rest assured that their elements have been defined to coincide with present international practice (in general, with UN recommendations).[21]

But how accurately has measurement been able to approximate the ideals represented by the definitions? With problems of definition now generally solved, the question of the reliability of the estimates reduces to one of the quality of the basic data and the appropriateness of the measuring techniques employed in turning them into national accounts estimates. Ceylon's basic data, as later sections of this Appendix make clear, are relatively good—exceptionally fine for a country of such a low per capita income level. In most areas, it has been possible to devise fairly reliable estimates of the important aggregates of national accounting. On the other hand, corroborating estimates that could give the user of the accounts greater confidence in them have generally not been worked out (for instance, in Table A-3 income of unincorporated enterprises must be taken as a residual). In its broadest sense, the question of statistical reliability is unanswerable in any precise way and each reader must form his own subjective judgment from the methodological description given in this Appendix. In a narrower sense, though—and an important one—the question of measurement resolves itself to one of bias. In particular, many elements of the CSD system (on which, after all, the other systems are based) have been calculated using population data and some estimate of the per capita value of the flow involved. Is any right to draw conclusions

---

[21]See *A System of National Economic Accounts and Historical Data, op. cit.*

about levels and trends in per capita—or, indeed, gross—income for-
feited thereby?

The items in the CSD total "GNP" which are based in part on
population are 2b (coconuts and coconut oil, locally consumed);
2c (tea locally consumed), part of 2h (industrial products; only
cottage industry is estimated from population); 2i & 2j (betel,
areca nuts, and firewood locally consumed); 2k (miscellaneous
goods locally consumed), part of 3 and 4 (trade and transport of
locally produced and consumed goods; only trade and transport
of those goods which are listed above has been estimated—indirectly—with population as a base); 5 (professional services); and
6 (personal and domestic services). The key question is: are these
likely in fact to grow more rapidly or more slowly than the other
elements of GNP? CSD "GNP" has been growing at about 4.5
percent a year since 1950, at a faster rate than population, so tying
these items to population growth produces a downward bias unless
they have actually grown at a much lower rate than other items.[22]
Subjectively, there seems no particular reason for expecting this to
be so. Levels of consumption of coconuts, tea, etc., per head would
be expected to rise, not fall, and the proportion of professionals in
the populace—and their incomes in the total—should rise.

POPULATION-BASED ESTIMATES AS A PERCENT
OF CSD "GNP"

1946	21.6	1951	18.5	1956	18.8
1947	22.7	1952	19.1	1957	19.4
1948	22.0	1953	19.6	1958	19.8
1949	20.9	1954	18.9	1959	19.5
1950	19.1	1955	17.2	1960	19.0

Note: For items 2h (industrial products) and 3 and 4 (trade and transport
of locally produced goods for domestic consumption), the proportions of the
total item falling into the population-based category was taken to be that of
1951, 45 and 32 percent respectively. At least in the case of industrial products, where factory production has actually risen faster than cottage industry, this leads to some overstatement in later years.

Putting the matter another way, what has happened to the population-based items as a percentage of GNP? As the table below
shows, they have fallen slightly. This is another way of saying that
other items have grown faster and that the use of population-based

---

[22]Actually the comparison should be between *real* income growth and
population, but the CSD publishes no constant price estimates. Since price
increases have been at a rate below one percent per annum, the essential
points remain valid; GNP has increased faster than population and items
which are not estimated from population faster than those that are.

estimates may well impart a downward bias to income growth. Thus, the basic conclusion to be garnered from a study of GNP growth—that income per head has been slowly rising—is shown by a detailed study of national accounts methodology at least not to be overly optimistic. The use of population in estimating Ceylon's GNP does not lead to upward bias. It seems more likely that any bias is slightly downward. Other minor instances of biased estimates have been noted in the discussions of specific items above, but they are of relatively little import. The general user can accept the estimates without concern that they produce a warped picture of actual trends in the economy.

7. Concluding Note

This section has reviewed the development of national accounting in Ceylon, showing the way in which the estimates of the present author were able to build upon earlier work. It is not meant to imply that these latest estimates represent any pinnacle of achievement in the field. On the contrary, the evolution is continuing and they will doubtless soon be superseded in many ways. If, however, they represent improvements in some regards over what has gone before and if they serve in their turn as the basis for further advances, then they will have served their purpose.

8. The Center Accounts

TABLE A-2

Gross National Income and Expenditure at Current Market Prices

(Rs. Millions)

	1950	1951	1952	1953	1954	1955	1956	1957	1958	1959	1960
Expenditure on Gross National Product											
A. Private consumption expenditure	3,218.8	3,788.6	3,890.4	3,908.5	3,793.9	4,210.4	4,013.7	4,387.7	4,410.5	4,713.0	5,011.1
1. Food	1,521.7	1,812.1	1,983.8	1,986.6	1,922.6	2,140.9	2,018.3	2,278.3	2,233.9	2,348.2	2,441.4
2. Clothing	263.3	313.4	321.7	324.5	312.8	349.3	331.1	311.4	293.8	369.8	431.0
3. Rent	278.8	288.5	302.6	310.5	315.0	329.5	349.8	373.7	376.1	381.5	393.1
4. Durables	1,155.0	1,374.6	1,282.3	1,286.9	1,243.5	1,390.7	1,314.5	1,424.3	1,506.7	1,613.5	1,745.6
5. Other											
B. Government current expenditures	342.2	399.5	440.6	470.0	483.8	530.8	568.1	638.4	745.6	831.5	873.8
1. General expenditures	96.2	118.0	121.9	144.5	150.6	166.1	179.9	209.0	245.5	260.8	270.0
2. Developmental expenditures	246.0	281.5	318.7	325.5	333.2	364.7	388.2	429.4	500.1	570.7	603.8
C. Gross fixed capital formation	410.1	525.1	616.8	546.9	478.2	588.0	608.0	673.6	683.5	821.0	840.8
1. Government fixed capital formation	222.4	241.3	308.3	292.9	264.2	315.3	335.1	328.2	345.4	355.2	378.7
2. Residential construction	75.4	117.1	131.7	104.6	118.7	156.2	157.7	164.4	160.7	164.9	156.4
Of which subsistence:	20.3	22.5	21.0	23.9	22.5	22.4	26.0	25.4	25.9	27.3	26.9
3. Enterprise fixed capital formation	112.3	166.7	176.8	149.4	95.3	116.5	115.2	181.0	177.4	300.9	305.7
D. Change in stocks	− 19.6	9.5	− 4.1	89.7	− 32.6	22.2	24.1	36.2	73.3	− 9.2	− 56.1
E. Exports of goods and services	1,617.0	1,967.7	1,564.7	1,698.2	1,914.3	2,070.5	1,845.9	1,795.5	1,912.1	2,079.2	2,078.5
F. *Less:* Imports of goods and services	1,344.0	1,737.3	1,856.7	1,774.8	1,540.1	1,658.8	1,857.5	2,057.5	2,001.3	2,236.7	2,227.6
G. Gross Domestic Product	4,224.5	4,953.1	4,651.7	4,938.5	5,097.5	5,763.1	5,202.3	5,473.9	5,823.7	6,198.8	6,520.5
H. Net factor income from abroad	− 54.0	− 64.2	− 45.5	− 37.8	− 46.6	− 61.3	− 55.4	− 51.0	− 40.6	− 36.7	− 44.2
I. Gross National Product	4,170.5	4,888.9	4,606.2	4,900.7	5,050.9	5,701.8	5,146.9	5,422.9	5,783.1	6,162.1	6,476.3
Distribution of Gross National Income											
J. Payments by producers to individuals	3,347.5	3,889.5	3,634.0	3,925.9	3,980.6	4,678.8	4,006.4	4,284.2	4,648.7	4,910.9	5,185.9
1. Compensation of employees	1,820.9	2,052.7	1,965.9	2,045.3	2,173.0	2,458.1	2,321.4	2,409.1	2,509.0	2,583.4	2,698.5
2. Entrepreneurial and property income	1,526.6	1,836.8	1,668.1	1,880.6	1,807.6	2,220.7	1,685.0	1,875.1	2,139.7	2,327.5	2,487.4
3. Business transfer payments											

(Continued on next page)

TABLE A-2 (Continued)

Gross National Income and Expenditure at Current Market Prices
(Rs. Millions)

	1950	1951	1952	1953	1954	1955	1956	1957	1958	1959	1960
K. Income retained by producers	251.7	278.4	256.6	267.8	293.7	215.5	269.0	276.6	296.1	373.0	373.0*
1. Capital consumption allowances	139.0	143.0	138.0	148.0	167.0	169.0	183.0	210.0	235.0	305.0	305.0*
2. Retained earnings of corporations	112.7	135.4	118.6	119.8	126.7	46.5	86.0	66.6	61.1	68.0	68.0*
L. Payments by producers to government	605.4	757.7	757.5	765.1	837.6	938.0	1,012.5	1,039.7	1,053.7	1,099.1	1,167.1
M. *Less:* Adjustments	34.1	36.7	41.9	58.1	61.0	130.5	141.0	177.6	215.4	220.9	249.7
1. Subsidies	13.9	14.8	17.1	27.0	25.7	96.9	106.8	141.9	177.5	174.6	192.7
2. Interest on public debt	20.2	21.9	24.8	31.1	35.3	33.6	34.2	35.7	37.9	46.3	57.0
3. Statistical discrepancy											
N. Gross National Income	4,170.5	4,888.9	4,606.2	4,900.7	5,050.9	5,701.8	5,146.9	5,422.9	5,783.1	6,162.1	6,476.3

*Preliminary.

TABLE A–3

Gross National Expenditure at Constant (1953) Prices

(Rs. Millions)

	1950	1951	1952	1953	1954	1955	1956	1957	1958	1959	1960
A. Private consumption expenditures	3,381.1	3,823.0	3,953.7	3,908.5	3,851.7	4,164.6	3,942.7	4,409.7	4,450.6	4,794.5	5,198.2
1. Food	1,593.4	1,885.6	2,103.7	1,986.6	1,920.7	2,158.2	2,070.1	2,301.3	2,238.4	2,376.7	2,567.2
2. Clothing	258.0	250.7	266.3	324.5	325.8	359.4	335.1	305.6	278.0	332.6	375.1
3. Rent	250.9	299.0	300.8	310.5	307.9	325.9	348.1	373.0	365.9	363.7	374.0
4. Durables	1,278.8	1,387.7	1,282.9	1,286.9	1,297.3	1,321.1	1,189.4	1,429.8	1,568.3	1,721.5	1,881.9
5. Other	370.3	435.7	484.7	470.0	549.1	589.1	641.2	659.5	779.9	865.2	923.7
B. Government current expenditures	484.2	481.3	531.7	546.9	545.3	646.9	669.6	592.4	662.3	843.8	859.7
C. Gross fixed capital formation	1,540.0	1,549.4	1,596.6	1,698.2	1,724.6	1,784.9	1,709.2	1,726.4	1,874.6	1,961.5	1,960.8
D. Change in stocks	− 19.2	8.9	− 4.3	89.7	− 35.5	26.4	28.8	45.4	94.7	− 11.6	− 72.4
E. Exports of goods and services	1,701.2	1,720.1	1,856.7	1,774.8	1,656.0	1,863.8	2,087.0	2,165.8	2,274.2	2,513.1	2,557.8
F. Less: Imports of goods and services											
G. Real Gross Domestic Product	4,055.2	4,578.2	4,705.7	4,938.5	4,979.2	5,348.1	4,904.5	5,267.6	5,587.9	5,940.3	6,312.2
H. Net factor income from abroad	− 51.8	− 58.6	− 46.0	− 37.8	− 45.5	− 56.9	− 52.2	− 49.1	− 39.0	− 35.2	− 43.1
I. { Real Gross National Product	4,003.4	4,519.6	4,659.7	4,900.7	4,933.7	5,291.2	4,852.3	5,218.5	5,548.9	5,905.1	6,269.1
{ Real Gross National Income	4,510.2	4,918.4	4,627.8	4,900.7	5,267.5	5,802.7	5,217.1	5,382.1	5,847.1	6,279.7	6,698.6

TABLE A-4

Personal Income, Outlay, and Saving

(Rs. Millions)

	1950	1951	1952	1953	1954	1955	1956	1957	1958	1959	1960
Receipts											
A. Payments by producers to individuals	3,347.5	3,889.5	3,634.0	3,925.9	3,980.6	4,678.8	4,006.4	4,284.2	4,648.7	4,910.9	5,185.9
1. Compensation of employees	1,820.9	2,052.7	1,965.9	2,045.3	2,173.0	2,458.1	2,321.4	2,409.1	2,509.0	2,583.4	2,698.5
a. Wages and salaries	1,816.0	2,047.6	1,960.1	2,037.6	2,166.3	2,451.6	2,314.6	2,402.3	2,502.2	2,569.7	2,625.8
b. Social security contributions										6.5	65.2
c. Income in kind	4.9	5.1	5.8	7.7	6.7	6.5	6.8	6.8	6.8	7.2	7.5
2. Entrepreneurial and property income	1,526.6	1,836.8	1,668.1	1,880.6	1,807.6	2,220.7	1,685.0	1,875.1	2,139.7	2,327.5	2,487.4
a. Unincorporated farm income } b. Unincorporated nonfarm income	1,150.0	1,413.2	1,250.8	1,453.2	1,374.3	1,733.1	1,167.2	1,378.9	1,522.8	1,853.4	1,992.5
c. Rental income	281.7	295.5	307.2	316.6	319.0	338.5	359.8	385.7	389.1	394.5	406.5
Of which owner occupied:	172.5	174.3	177.8	178.6	177.5	181.6	188.8	196.9	196.4	195.3	198.3
d. Interest and dividends	102.8	136.1	118.3	119.3	123.0	158.0	167.2	120.0	107.5	89.6	98.7
e. *Less:* Interest on consumer debt	7.9	8.0	8.2	8.5	8.7	8.9	9.2	9.5	9.8	10.0	10.3
3. Business transfer payments	138.0	250.7	323.3	201.9	116.5	101.0	177.2	195.4	215.1	256.3	276.7
B. Transfer payments from government	11.4	12.7	13.2	7.1	4.6	7.0	6.4	8.8	7.4	7.6	7.2
C. Transfer payments from abroad											
D. Personal Income	3,496.9	4,152.9	3,970.5	4,134.9	4,101.7	4,786.8	4,190.0	4,488.4	4,871.2	5,174.8	5,469.8
Outlays and Saving											
E. Private consumption expenditures	3,218.8	3,788.6	3,890.4	3,908.5	3,793.9	4,210.4	4,013.7	4,387.7	4,410.5	4,713.0	5,011.1
1. Food	1,521.7	1,812.1	1,983.8	1,986.6	1,922.6	2,140.9	2,018.3	2,278.3	2,233.9	2,348.2	2,441.4
Of which subsistence:	394.5	458.8	521.8	529.4	520.3	550.0	367.8	488.3	496.5	497.4	553.8
2. Clothing	263.3	313.4	321.7	324.5	312.8	349.3	331.1	311.4	293.8	369.8	431.0
3. Rent	278.8	288.5	302.6	310.5	315.0	329.5	349.8	373.7	376.1	381.5	393.1
Of which owner occupied:	172.5	174.3	177.8	178.6	177.5	181.6	188.8	196.9	196.4	195.3	198.3

	1,155.0	1,374.6	1,282.3	1,286.9	1,243.5	1,390.7	1,314.5	1,424.3	1,506.7	1,613.5	1,745.6
4. Durables											
5. Other											
F. Payments to government	53.5	61.7	84.5	91.4	88.8	91.4	99.8	84.4	96.3	92.6	196.2
1. Social security contributions	4.9	5.7	7.1	6.0	6.4	6.9	7.6	8.0	8.8	20.7	120.0
2. Personal taxes	48.6	56.0	77.4	85.4	82.4	84.5	92.2	76.4	87.5	71.9	76.2
3. Other	80.5	89.8	116.8	65.8	71.4	84.5	89.7	75.1	85.4	63.5	38.7
G. Transfer payments to abroad	266.0	266.0	− 20.0	79.0	226.0	302.0	255.0	126.0	256.0	284.0	284.0*
H. Personal saving	−121.9	− 53.2	−101.2	9.8	− 78.4	98.5	−208.2	−184.8	23.0	21.7	− 60.2
I. Statistical discrepancy											
J. Personal outlay and saving	3,496.9	4,152.9	3,970.5	4,134.9	4,101.7	4,786.8	4,190.0	4,488.4	4,871.2	5,174.8	5,469.8

*Provisional

TABLE A-5

General Government Revenue and Current Expenditure

(Rs. Millions)

	1950	1951	1952	1953	1954	1955	1956	1957	1958	1959	1960
Receipts											
A. Payments by producers	605.4	757.7	757.5	765.1	837.6	938.0	1,012.5	1,039.7	1,053.7	1,099.1	1,167.1
1. Corporate profits taxes	78.6	101.0	140.0	149.0	139.6	151.8	206.1	196.2	163.1	131.9	147.5
2. Property taxes	13.4	13.6	14.1	16.1	16.5	14.4	18.4	19.1	21.3	22.3	23.2
3. Commodity and transaction taxes	443.9	567.0	529.1	521.4	599.2	684.0	685.8	708.9	733.8	820.2	870.5
a. Excise	45.1	49.4	52.7	62.7	64.5	60.2	72.6	84.0	97.0	114.9	135.5
b. Sales											
c. Turnover											
d. Customs	398.8	517.6	476.4	458.7	534.7	623.8	613.2	624.9	636.8	705.3	735.0
(1) Import duties	202.4	248.8	257.6	249.0	247.7	265.3	290.6	300.7	310.9	376.8	411.2
(2) Export duties	196.4	268.8	218.8	209.7	287.0	358.5	322.6	324.2	325.9	328.5	323.8
e. Other											
4. Other business taxes and fees	35.3	43.4	38.7	42.9	44.5	47.7	57.6	66.4	72.5	63.2	74.6
5. Property income paid to government	27.1	30.8	33.7	35.1	37.3	37.3	39.3	42.5	49.6	48.3	50.0
6. Surplus of government enterprises	7.1	1.9	1.9	0.6	0.5	2.8	5.3	6.6	13.4	13.2	1.3
B. Payments by individuals	53.5	61.7	84.5	91.4	88.8	91.4	99.8	84.4	96.3	92.6	196.2
1. Social security contributions	4.9	5.7	7.1	6.0	6.4	6.9	7.6	8.0	8.8	20.7	120.0
2. Personal taxes											
3. Other	48.6	56.0	77.4	85.4	82.4	84.5	92.2	76.4	87.5	71.9	76.2
C. Transfer payments from abroad				3.3	23.6	16.6	27.8	26.7	54.9	44.3	52.5
E. Total receipts	658.9	819.4	842.0	859.8	950.0	1,046.0	1,140.1	1,150.8	1,204.9	1,236.0	1,415.8
Current Expenditures											
F. Government current expenditures	342.2	399.5	440.6	470.0	483.8	530.8	568.1	638.4	745.6	831.5	873.8
1. General expenditures	96.2	118.0	121.9	144.5	150.6	166.1	179.9	209.0	245.5	260.8	270.0
a. Administration	88.6	106.9	103.5	115.3	120.4	138.6	148.7	167.8	179.3	188.9	198.7

b. Defense	7.6	11.1	18.4	29.2	30.2	27.5	31.2	41.2	66.2	71.9	71.3
c. Community services	246.0	281.5	318.7	325.5	333.2	364.7	388.2	429.4	500.1	570.7	603.8
2. Developmental expenditures	97.8	108.9	122.8	126.8	125.5	134.7	149.9	171.9	198.5	232.3	201.0
a. Education	65.2	72.6	84.7	88.9	91.7	95.3	104.0	112.4	126.4	144.6	146.4
b. Health	7.2	9.8	12.8	12.5	22.0	22.3	22.9	18.7	33.1	51.6	95.1
c. Other social ⎱											
d. Agriculture ⎰	75.8	90.2	98.4	97.3	94.0	112.4	111.4	126.4	142.1	142.2	161.3
e. Transport and communications	13.9	14.8	17.1	27.0	25.7	96.9	106.8	141.9	177.5	174.6	192.7
f. Other industry	0.8	0.3	0.1	1.7	8.9	55.5	43.4	68.8	85.1	89.3	124.9
G. Subsidies											
1. To food producers	6.8	8.5	10.9	18.1	14.6	36.4	55.1	55.4	61.4	62.4	57.9
2. To government enterprises and public corporations	6.3	6.0	6.1	7.2	2.2	5.0	8.3	17.7	31.0	22.9	9.9
3. To private firms	20.2	21.9	24.8	31.1	35.3	33.6	34.2	35.7	37.9	46.3	57.0
H. Interest on public debt	138.0	250.7	323.3	201.9	116.5	101.0	177.2	195.4	215.1	256.3	276.7
I. Transfer payments to individuals											
1. Social security benefits	31.4	35.5	40.4	43.4	50.7	52.1	63.4	70.2	80.5	91.8	94.8
2. Food "subsidy"	59.0	160.4	217.5	96.7	9.5	− 8.6	42.6	38.3	35.5	68.8	81.9
3. Other	47.6	54.8	65.4	61.8	56.3	57.5	71.2	86.9	99.1	95.7	100.0
J. Transfer payments to abroad											
K. Surplus on current account	144.6	132.5	36.2	129.8	288.7	283.7	253.8	139.4	28.8	− 72.7	15.6
L. Total current expenditures and surplus	658.9	819.4	842.0	859.8	950.0	1,046.0	1,140.1	1,150.8	1,204.9	1,236.0	1,415.8

(A brace "}" in the original joins the items "c. Other social" and "d. Agriculture," whose combined figures are shown on the single line.)

TABLE A-6

External Transactions

(Rs. Millions)

	1950	1951	1952	1953	1954	1955	1956	1957	1958	1959	1960
Receipts from Abroad											
A. Exports of goods and services	1,617.0	1,967.7	1,564.7	1,698.2	1,914.3	2,070.5	1,845.9	1,795.5	1,912.1	2,079.2	2,078.5
1. Merchandise	1,485.0	1,842.8	1,411.8	1,490.0	1,719.3	1,872.1	1,652.3	1,588.3	1,690.8	1,834.1	1,863.9
a. Food		914.2		937.7	1,249.1		1,155.5	1,117.4	1,240.4	1,156.7	1,199.1
b. Beverages and tobacco		1.8			1.6		2.2	1.1		0.7	
c. Crude materials, inedible		661.2		405.3	376.8		380.5	382.8	327.5	400.0	474.6
d. Mineral fuels		66.9		60.5	55.6		66.8	0.3	0.2	0.2	0.3
e. Oils and fats		227.1		142.0	100.2		99.2	67.9	61.9	117.3	79.8
f. Chemicals		16.0		5.1	7.4		10.0	10.6	8.1	8.8	8.2
g. Manufactured goods		13.2		9.4	9.3		7.9	7.8	6.5	7.8	8.5
h. Machinery and transport equipment		2.0		3.1	5.8		4.2	1.9	4.9	5.9	3.4
i. Miscellaneous manufactured articles		0.6		0.8	1.2		1.1	1.1	1.6	2.1	3.2
j. Miscellaneous n.e.c.		1.4		2.5	2.3		7.0	90.6	59.5	54.6	54.4
k. Statistical discrepancy		−61.6		−78.0	−90.0		−82.1	−93.2	−19.8	80.0	32.4
2. Other	132.0	124.9	152.9	208.2	195.0	198.4	193.6	207.2	221.3	245.1	214.6
B. Factor income from abroad	18.1	26.2	21.7	23.3	21.5	33.1	42.2	40.5	36.6	32.7	31.8
C. Transfer payments to individuals	11.4	12.7	13.2	7.1	4.6	7.0	6.4	8.8	7.4	7.6	7.2
D. Transfer payments to government				3.3	23.6	16.6	27.8	26.7	54.9	44.3	52.5
E. Current receipts from abroad	1,646.5	2,006.6	1,599.6	1,731.9	1,964.0	2,127.2	1,922.3	1,871.5	2,011.0	2,163.8	2,170.0
Payments to Abroad											
F. Imports of goods and services	1,344.0	1,737.3	1,856.7	1,774.8	1,540.1	1,658.8	1,857.5	2,057.5	2,001.3	2,236.7	2,276.4
1. Merchandise	1,158.0	1,516.2	1,612.0	1,529.7	1,307.3	1,391.8	1,547.0	1,710.9	1,683.2	1,915.2	1,965.0
a. Food	583.1	676.3	767.0	774.8	645.5	604.1	680.6	712.2	693.4	788.7	741.8
b. Beverages and tobacco	12.6	19.4	22.0	21.7	18.6	20.6	22.0	24.0	21.9	22.9	22.8
c. Crude materials, inedible	40.9	70.6	62.5	58.4	57.1	23.3	28.0	29.9	22.8	30.9	34.0

d. Mineral fuels	100.8	126.9	151.9	145.1	102.8	143.8	127.0	224.0	141.5	151.3	144.2
e. Oils and fats	2.0	4.2	3.5	3.1	3.3	0.6	1.3	3.0	3.8	4.6	5.0
f. Chemicals	23.6	39.3	41.4	38.4	39.8	90.8	98.7	120.8	104.4	134.9	128.4
g. Manufactured goods	259.2	373.5	382.6	322.0	298.1	312.9	372.0	383.0	374.1	408.6	434.5
h. Machinery and transport equipment	90.8	165.1	194.6	176.4	128.7	156.3	187.9	202.3	234.7	330.5	292.8
i. Miscellaneous manufactured articles	53.0	81.1	75.3	66.8	102.1	83.3	89.4	93.7	95.7	124.9	155.3
j. Miscellaneous n.e.c.	0.8	2.2	1.7	1.2	1.0	23.9	22.5	11.1	24.2	7.7	0.9
k. Statistical discrepancy	− 8.8	− 42.4	− 172.8	− 78.2	− 89.7	− 67.8	− 82.4	− 93.1	− 33.3	− 89.8	5.3
2. Other	186.0	221.1	244.7	245.1	232.8	267.0	310.5	346.6	318.1	321.5	311.4
G. Factor income paid abroad	72.0	90.4	67.2	61.1	68.1	94.4	97.6	91.6	77.2	69.4	76.0
H. Transfer payments from individuals	80.5	89.8	116.8	65.8	71.4	84.5	89.7	75.1	85.4	63.5	38.7
I. Transfer payments from governments											
J. Surplus of nation on current account	150.0	89.1	− 441.1	− 169.8	284.4	289.5	− 122.5	− 352.7	− 152.9	− 205.8	− 221.1
K. Current payments to abroad and surplus	1,646.5	2,006.6	1,599.6	1,731.9	1,964.0	2,127.2	1,922.3	1,871.5	2,011.0	2,163.8	2,170.0

TABLE A-7

GROSS DOMESTIC CAPITAL FORMATION AND SAVING

(Rs. Millions)

	1950	1951	1952	1953	1954	1955	1956	1957	1958	1959	1960
Gross Domestic Capital Formation											
A. Gross fixed capital formation	401.1	525.1	616.8	546.9	478.2	588.0	608.0	673.6	683.5	821.0	840.8
1. Government fixed capital formation	222.4	241.3	308.3	292.9	264.2	315.3	335.1	328.2	345.4	355.2	378.7
2. Residential construction	75.4	117.1	131.7	104.6	118.7	156.2	157.7	164.4	160.7	164.9	156.4
Of which subsistence	20.3	22.5	21.0	23.9	22.5	22.4	26.0	25.4	25.9	27.3	26.9
3. Enterprise fixed capital formation	112.3	166.7	176.8	149.4	95.3	116.5	115.2	181.0	177.4	300.9	305.7
B. Change in stocks	−19.6	9.5	− 4.1	89.7	− 32.6	22.2	24.1	36.2	73.3	− 9.2	− 56.1
C. Gross Domestic Capital Formation	381.5	534.6	612.7	636.6	445.6	610.2	632.1	709.8	756.8	811.8	784.7
Gross Domestic Saving											
D. Income retained by producers	251.7	278.4	256.6	267.8	293.7	215.5	269.0	276.6	296.1	373.0	373.0
1. Capital consumption allowances	139.0	143.0	138.0	148.0	167.0	169.0	183.0	210.0	235.0	305.0	305.0*
2. Retained earnings of corporations	112.7	135.4	118.6	119.8	126.7	46.5	86.0	66.6	61.1	68.0	68.0*
a. Resident companies	77.3	105.6	77.6	85.7	83.2	46.1	67.1	54.2	46.7	.....	.....
b. Non-resident companies	34.1	28.9	37.8	31.1	41.4	−4.4	13.7	4.9	5.6	.....	.....
c. Co-operative institutions	1.3	0.9	3.2	3.0	2.1	4.5	5.2	7.5	8.8		
E. Personal saving	266.0	266.0	− 20.0	79.0	226.0	302.0	255.0	126.0	256.0	284.0	284.0*
F. Government surplus on current account	144.6	132.5	36.2	129.8	288.7	283.7	253.8	139.4	28.8	− 72.7	15.6
G. *Less:* Surplus of nation on current account	150.0	89.1	−441.1	−169.8	284.4	289.5	−122.5	−352.7	−152.9	−205.8	−221.1
H. Statistical discrepancy	−130.8	− 53.2	−101.2	− 9.8	− 78.4	98.5	−268.2	−184.9	23.0	21.7	−109.0
I. Gross Domestic Saving	381.5	534.6	612.7	636.6	445.6	610.2	632.1	709.8	756.8	811.8	784.7

*Preliminary.

TABLE A-8

INDUSTRIAL ORIGIN OF GROSS DOMESTIC PRODUCT AT FACTOR COST

(Rs. Millions)

	1950	1951	1952	1953	1954	1955	1956	1957	1958	1959	1960
A. Agriculture, fishing, forestry	1,963.7	2,247.0	2,034.3	2,275.0	2,406.7	2,772.8	2,069.0	2,300.6	2,446.9	2,542.4	2,716.7
1. Tea and minor estate crops	660.6	645.9	565.9	666.0	962.5	849.0	835.0	735.9	718.9	765.1	817.3
2. Rubber	387.3	491.3	291.3	291.5	227.1	262.2	302.8	245.6	202.6	248.1	210.2
3. Coconut	398.0	495.4	337.1	395.6	354.2	332.0	327.1	284.2	301.1	402.6	331.1
4. Other	517.8	614.4	840.0	921.9	862.9	1,329.6	604.1	1,034.9	1,224.3	1,126.6	1,358.1
B. Mining and quarrying	6.2	8.1	6.2	4.1	4.7	7.2	7.4	6.6	3.8	5.2	5.8
C. Manufacturing	154.6	188.3	196.0	216.1	215.4	311.7	233.5	217.6	243.6	286.7	314.2
D. Construction	278.8	412.5	417.0	392.2	373.5	465.4	485.0	504.4	537.9	583.5	571.7
E. Electricity, gas and water	17.6	19.9	22.3	24.0	25.0	28.5	28.7	28.6	39.9	41.6	47.6
F. Transport and communications	294.1	340.3	191.0	222.6	222.2	250.5	270.9	290.3	300.7	328.3	347.3
G. Wholesale and retail trade	325.0	386.0	407.0	403.4	369.1	386.0	413.0	429.4	432.5	454.0	473.0
H. Banking, insurance, real estate	14.0	19.7	19.8	18.2	22.7	24.2	30.3	35.6	47.3	50.3	52.5
I. Ownership of dwellings	281.7	295.5	307.2	316.6	319.0	338.5	359.8	385.7	389.1	394.5	406.5
J. Public administration and defense	199.6	231.5	259.5	257.8	308.0	368.3	426.2	435.3	465.8	473.0	482.8
K. Services n.e.c.	406.9	463.9	445.4	464.8	483.7	519.3	546.1	575.7	596.2	603.3	654.6
L. Gross Domestic Product at factor cost	3,942.2	4,612.7	4,305.7	4,594.8	4,750.0	5,472.4	4,869.9	5,209.8	5,503.7	5,789.8	6,072.7

Notes on Sources and Methods

SOURCES

1. Central Bank of Ceylon, *Annual Report of the Monetary Board to the Minister of Finance.*
2. _____, *Survey of Ceylon's Consumer Finances, 1953* (1954).
3. *Accounts of the Government of Ceylon.* Sessional Paper (annual).
4. *A.R. of the Commissioner of Inland Revenue* (earlier title: *A.R. of the Commissioner of Income Tax, Estate Duty and Stamps*) (annual).
5. *A.R. of the Commissioner of Labour* (annual).
6. *A.R. of the Food Commissioner* (annual).
7. *A.R. of the Rubber Controller* (annual).
8. *A.R. of the Tea Controller* (annual).
9. Department of Census and Statistics. *Census of Ceylon, 1946* (1951–).
10. _____, *Census of Ceylon, 1953* (1957–).
11. *Report of the Registrar-General on Vital Statistics.* Sessional Paper (annual).
12. Department of Census and Statistics, *Statistical Abstract of Ceylon* (annual).
13. National Planning Council, *The Ten-Year Plan* (1959).
14. "Labour Conditions in Ceylon," *International Labour Review* (December, 1949), pp. 572–616, and (January, 1950), pp. 1–20.
15. W. Rasaputram, "Gross National Product of Ceylon at Constant (1948) Prices," *Central Bank of Ceylon Bulletin* (January, 1956), pp. 8–16.
16. _____, "Savings of the Ceylon Economy, 1950–59", *Central Bank of Ceylon Bulletin* (January, 1961), pp. 10–31.
17. United Nations, Statistical Office, *Yearbook of National Accounts Statistics* (annual) 1957–.

Table A-2. Gross National Income and Expenditure at Current Market Prices

2A. *Private consumption expenditures:* Item 1 from UN Table 1 [17], plus "rural house rents" (see 2A3 below).

2A1. *Food:* Item 1 from UN Table 5 [17].

2A2. *Clothing:* Item 4 from UN Table 5 [17].

2A3. *Rent:* Item 5 from UN Table 5 [17] (which includes urban rents only), plus "rural house rents".

Rural house rents: Rural population was estimated from the censuses ([9], [10]) and the Registrar-General's estimates [11]; average household size taken from 1946 Census [9] and 1953 CBC Survey [2], with the implied growth interpolated and extrapolated to provide estimates for other years; number of rural houses in each year estimated by dividing rural population by average size of household; monthly rent on *rented* rural houses shown by 1953 Census [10] assumed to apply to *all* rural houses, deflated by CPI (lagged one year) to obtain rent for other years; resulting average rent multiplied by number of houses to yield total rent bills.

2A4. *Durables:* ⎫ Total of items 2, 3, and 6–15 from UN Table 5 [17].
2A5. *Other:*   ⎭ Durables expenditure is not available separately.
Central government; Item 17 from CBC Table 20[1] [1] (purchase of goods and services), plus item 21 (a) (i) (defense capital formation) and "expenditure on capital maintenance" from the same table, minus item 1 (charges and sales) from CBC Table 20, minus current expenditures of the Railway and Electrical Departments [3]; all adjusted to calendar year from budget year (October–September) by the simple process of calling three-fourths of 1959/60 expenditure plus one-fourth of 1960/61 expenditure the total for 1960.[2]

Local government: Total expenditures of municipal councils, urban councils, town councils, and village committees [12], other than those identified as capital formation or transfers to the public (see items 2C1 and 4B, below).

2B1. *General expenditures:* Sum of:
Central government: Item 17(a) from CBC Table 20 [1] (purchases of goods and services: administration), plus item 21 (a) (i) (defense capital formation) from the same table, adjusted to the calendar year.

Local government: 25 percent of total expenditures (rough estimate) [12].

2B2. Developmental expenditures: A residual, 2B minus 2B1.

2C. *Gross fixed capital formation:* Item 1a–1b from the lower half of UN Table 4 [17] (fixed capital formation by private enterprises and public corporations), plus subsistence construction (see 2C2, below), plus government fixed capital formation (see 2C1, below).

2C1. *Government fixed capital formation:* Sum of:
Central government: Item 21 from CBC Table 20 [1] (capital formation), minus "expenditure on capital maintenance" from the same table, minus item 21 (a) (i) (defense capital formation), adjusted to the calendar year.

Local government: 80 percent of "public works" expenditure of municipal councils [12] (20 percent is assumed to be maintenance work), plus 20 percent of the expenditures of other local governments (a rough estimate based on the assumption that other local governments spend the same percentage of their budgets on capital formation as municipal councils do).

2C2. *Residential construction:* Sum of:
Market construction: Given in *Ten-Year Plan* [13], p. 474, as Rs. 139,000,000 for 1957; this is 44.3 percent of all building construction in that year and the same percentage is assumed to apply in all years, i.e., item 1a–1b from the top half of UN Table 4 [17] is multiplied by .443.

Subsistence construction: The change in the estimated number of rural houses from year to year (see 2C2) is multiplied by the estimated cost of building a rural house; the latter was given for 1959 in [13] and this figure was deflated by the CPI for other years; multiplying by the number of houses added during the year gives the estimate (it is a conservative one, since the assumed average cost of building a new house is conservative and no allowance is made for the replacement of existing houses).

Of which subsistence: Subsistence proportion just described.

2C3. *Enterprise fixed capital formation:* Residual: Item 1a–1b from the lower half of UN Table 4 [17] (fixed capital formation by private enterprises and public corporations), minus the marketed proportion of item 2C2, above.

2D. *Change in stocks:* Sum of:
Tea and rubber: Production, minus exports and local consumption ([8], [9]), valued at Colombo market prices.

Livestock: Change in livestock population returns [12], smoothed by a three-year moving average to even out idiosyncratic year-to-year variations

---

[1] References to table numbers in the Central Bank of Ceylon, *Annual Report of the Monetary Board to the Minister of Finance* are to the 1961 edition; similar tables appear in *Reports* of other years, but their numbers vary.

[2] All central government data have been adjusted in this way.

arising from the unreliability of the reporting system, valued at 1960 prices (unpublished CSD data), deflated by the CPI for earlier years.

Government-held food (includes rice, flour, raw sugar, and white sugar): Changes in stock data (from [6]), valued at Colombo wholesale prices.

Trade inventories of imports and domestically produced goods: these inventories were assumed to be one percent of the total of imports and domestic nonexport production (this is the U.S. ratio, which was used for want of better data) at all times; the item turned out to be very small in practice.

2E. *Exports of goods and services:* Item 5 from UN Table 1 [17].

2F. Less: *Imports of goods and services:* Item 6 from UN Table 1 [17].

2G. *Gross Domestic Product:* Sum of Items 2A–2F, above.

2H. *Net factor income from abroad:* Item 7 from UN Table 1 [17].

2I. *Gross National Product:* Sum of items 2G and 2H, above.

2J. *Payments by producers to individuals:* Sum of Items 2J1–2J3, below.

2J1. *Compensation of employees:* Item 1 from UN Table 3 [17] (called "compensation of employees" there, but actually including only wages and salaries), plus:

Social security contributions: Employees' Provident Fund Scheme came into existence in 1958 and the first contributions were made in 1959; because the act provides for minimum contributions of 6 percent by employers and 4 percent by employees the employers' share was assumed to be 60 percent of total collections [5].

Income in kind: Comprises estimates of free food provided to estate laborers (the largest payment in kind by corporate employers and the only one estimated here); an estimate for 1948 (from [14]) has been extended to later years by multiplying by indexes of rice prices and estate population.

2J2. *Entrepreneurial and property income:* ⎫ Items 2 and 3 from UN Table
2J3. *Business transfer payments:* ⎬ 3 [17], plus "rural house rents"
(see 2A3, above), plus subsistence construction (see 2C2, above), plus statistical discrepancy (since "income of unincorporated enterprises" is a residual item in the UN system, any further residual which emerged in equating Gross National Income to Gross National Product in this table was added in here); business transfer payments cannot be identified separately.

2K. *Income retained by producers:* From [16]; 1959 figures are used for 1960 as well, pending the extension of the series.

2K1. *Capital consumption allowances:* From [16].

2K2. *Retained earnings of corporations:* From [16].

2L. *Payments by producers to governments:* See 5A, below.

2M. *Less: Adjustments:* Sum of Items 2M2–2M3, below.

2M1. *Subsidies:* Sum of:

Food subsidy (producer part): Quantities of paddy and minor food crops purchased under Guaranteed Price Scheme, times the difference between prices paid producers and the f.o.b. import price.

Subsidies to government enterprises and public corporations: Deficits of Railway and Electrical Departments [3], plus item 17(d) from CBC Table 20 [1] (payments to government enterprises), minus current expenditures of Railway and Electrical Departments.

Subsidies to private firms: Item 18(a)(v) from CBC Table 20 [1] ("other transfer payments to private current accounts").

2M2. *Interest on public debt:* Item 7 from UN Table 3 [17].

2M3. *Statistical discrepancy:* Included in 2J2 above; see note for that item.

2N. *Gross National Income:* Sum of 2J–2M, above.

Table A–3. Gross National Expenditure at Constant (1953) Prices

Note: Items in this table correspond to those in Table A–2, except that they are deflated to 1953 prices by the price indexes indicated.

3A. *Private consumption expenditures:* All items CPI up to 1953; implied deflator in UN Table 1 [17] thereafter.

3A1. *Food:* Food component of CPI.

3A2. *Clothing:* Clothing component of CPI.

3A3. *Rent:* All items CPI, lagged one year (this is a better deflator than the rent component of the CPI, which severely understates price increases).

3A4. *Durables:* ⎫
3A5. *Other:* ⎭ A residual item; 3A minus 3A1, 3A2 and 3A3 above.

3B. *Government current expenditures:* Rasaputram–CBC Index [15] up to 1953; implied deflator in UN Table 1 [17] thereafter.

3C. *Gross fixed capital formation:* Same as 3B.

3D. *Change in stocks:* Deflated by an index computed using the prices of the various items in the stock estimate, currently weighted (double-weighted by an average of the value of the stock and value of change in the stock).

3E. *Exports of goods and services:* CBC export price index [1].

3F. *Less: Imports of goods and services:* CBC import price index [1].

3G. *Real Gross Domestic Product:* Sum of 3A–3F, above.

3H. *Net factor income from abroad:* Deflator implied by comparing GDP here with GDP in Table A–2 used to deflate this item.

3I. *Real Gross National Product:* Real GNP is the sum of 3G and 3H, above; *Real Gross National Income:* Real GNI is the sum of 3A, 3D, 3H, and "net foreign investment" (i.e., 2E minus 2F in Table A–2), the last item deflated by the import price index.

Table A–4. Personal Income, Outlay, and Saving

4A. *Payments by producers to individuals:* 2J.

4A1. *Compensation of employees:* 2J1.

4A1a. *Wages and salaries:* See 2J1.

4A1b. *Social security contributions:* See 2J1.

4A1c. *Income in kind:* See 2J1.

4A2. *Entrepreneurial and property income:* 2J2; includes business transfer payments.

4A2a. *Unincorporated farm income:*   A residual: 4A2, minus the sum
4A2b. *Unincorporated nonfarm income:* of 4A2c, 4A2d and 4A2e; because this item is a pure residual, division into farm and nonfarm income is impossible.

4A2c. *Rental income:* Item 9 from UN Table 2 [17] (urban rental income), plus "rural house rents" (see item 2A3, above).

Of which owner occupied: Proportions of urban and rural rental incomes, based on percentage of houses reported as owner occupied in the 1946 and 1953 censuses [10], [11], with interpolated or extrapolated proportions used for other years.

4A2d. *Interest and dividends:* Items 3b–3d from UN Table 3 [17]; also includes corporate transfer payments.

4A2e. *Less: Interest on consumer debt:* Item 8 from UN Table 3 [17].

4A3. *Business transfer payments:* Included in 4A2d, above; the value of this item is probably very small.

4B. *Transfer payments from government:* Sum of:
Central government transfer payments to individuals: Items 18(a)(iii) ("pensions to government employees") and 18(a)(iv) ("direct relief") from CBC Table 20 [1], plus the part of item 18(a)(i) ("food subsidies") remaining after the producer part of the "subsidy" (see 2M1, above) has been removed, all adjusted to the calendar year.

Local government transfer payments to individuals: Expenditures on "assistance and poor relief" by municipal councils [12], plus ten percent of the expenditures of other local governments (the percentage is based on the expenditures of municipal councils on "assistance and poor relief").

4C. *Transfer payments from abroad:* Credit item 9 from CBC Table 25A [1].

4D. *Personal Income:* Sum of 4A–4C, above.

4E. *Private consumption expenditures:* 2A.

4E1. *Food:* 2A1.

Of which subsistence: A constant proportion of certain domestic crops (proportions taken from [1], 1961 total value of net output for each crop being taken from the CSD national accounts [12]: 60 percent of rice, 40 percent of coconuts and coconut oil, 50 percent of other food crops, and 5 percent of fish.

4E2. *Clothing:* 2A2.

4E3. *Rent:* 2A3.

Of which owner occupied: See 4A2c, above.

4E4. *Durables:* ⎱
4E5. *Other:*   ⎰ 2A4–2A5.

4F. *Payments to government:* Sum of 4F1 and 4F2–4F3, below.

4F1. *Social security contributions:* Item 3 from CBC Table 20 [1] (social insurance contributions), plus total contributions to the Employees' Provident Fund [5] (1959 and 1960 only).

4F2. *Personal taxes:*

4F3. *Other:* Items 2 ("taxes on income, profits and personal expenditure"), 4 ("death duties, wealth tax and gift tax", and 7 ("other taxes and levies") from CBC Table 20 [1], minus allowances for direct taxes estimated to have been paid by corporations: a part of the income tax and surcharge on income tax based on assessments made by the commissioner of inland revenue [4] (these taxes apply to both firms and individuals and no data are published on collections from each; the division of assessments between the two, year by year, was smoothed by a three-year moving average, lagged two years to allow collections to catch up with assessments, and applied to total collections to estimate the amounts collected from persons and companies respectively), all of the profits and excess profits taxes and of contributions by government departments and enterprises in lieu of income tax, and 40 percent of the bank debits tax (representing the proportion of demand deposits held by corporations, according to CBC data) (the source for all of these was [3]); "other," item 4F3, refers to fees and fines paid by individuals to government, a small item which cannot be separately identified.

4G. *Transfer payments to abroad:* Debit item 9 from CBC Table 25 [1].

4H. *Personal saving:* Rasaputram's "average estimate" from his Table 11 [16].

4I. *Statistical discrepancy:* Arises because the estimate of personal saving used (4H), which is believed to be the best available, does not match perfectly the difference between personal receipts and outlays; "personal outlays and saving (4J) is therefore set equal to "personal income" (4D) and this statistical discrepancy serves as the balancing item.

4J. *Personal Outlay and Saving:* Sum of 4E–4I, above.

Table A–5. General Government Revenue and Current Expenditure

5A. *Payments by Producers:* Sum of 5A1–5A6, below.

5A1. *Corporate profits taxes:* The part of the income tax and surcharge on income tax judged to have been paid by companies (see 4F2–4F3, above), plus profits tax, excess profits tax, and contributions in lieu of tax by government departments and enterprises; separating current from noncurrent tax payments is impossible, so both of these are included here.

5A2. *Property taxes:* Property taxes of municipal and urban councils, plus ten percent of total revenues of other local governments (proportions based on experience with municipal and urban councils).

5A3. *Commodity and transaction taxes:* Sum of 5A3a–5A3e, below.

5A3a. *Excise:* Item 6 (other taxes on goods and services) from CBC Table 20 [1]; includes commodity taxes.

5A3b. *Sales:* Nil throughout.

5A3c. *Turnover:* Nil throughout.

5A3d. *Customs:* Item 5 from CBC Table 20 [1].

5A3d1. *Import duties:* Item 5(b) from CBC Table 20 [1].

5A3d2. *Export duties:* Item 5(a) from CBC Table 20 [1].

5A3e. *Other:* Commodity taxes (e.g., on liquor and gasoline) are included under 5A3a, above.

5A4. *Other business taxes and fees:* Item 7 ("other taxes and levies") from CBC Table 20 [1]; certain items of municipal council revenues: other taxes, markets, licenses; judicial fines, and slaughterhouses and cattle marts; "other taxes" of urban councils; and ten percent of the total revenues of other local governments [12].

5A5. *Property income paid to government:* Item 9 ("income from property") from CBC Table 20 [1]; certain items of municipal council revenues: water supply, drainage and conservancy fees, rents, electricity, and miscellaneous revenues; utility services and electric lighting revenues of urban councils; and 55 percent of total revenues of other local governments [12]; public utility enterprises run by local governments are included here on a gross basis, but this is only a small inflation of the item.

5A6. *Surplus of government enterprises:* Item 8 ("receipts from government enterprises") from CBC Table 20 [1], adjusted to alter Railway and Electrical Department revenues from a gross to a net basis [3].

5B. *Payments by individuals:* 4F.

5B1. *Social security contributions:* 4F1.

5B2. *Personal taxes:* } 4F2–4F3.
5B3. *Other:*

5C. *Transfer payments from abroad:* Credit item 10 from CBC Table 25A [1].

5E. *Total Receipts:* Sum of 5A–5C, above.

5F. *Government current expenditures:* 2B.

5F1. *General expenditures:* 2B1.

5F1a. *Administration:* Includes items mentioned under 2B1, above, minus 5F1b, below.

5F1b. *Defense:* Items 17(a)(i) ("purchases of goods and services: defense") and 21(a)(i) ("defense capital formation") from CBC Table 20 [1].

5F1c. *Community services:* This item, an extremely small one, is included under 5F2, below.

5F2. *Developmental expenditures:* 2B2.

5F2a. *Education:* Expenditures of the Education Department, less capital expenditures (given in [3] since 1959 and taken as three precent of total expenditures for previous years).

5F2b. *Health:* Expenditures of the Health Department less capital expenditures (given in [3] since 1959 and taken as six percent of total expenditures for earlier years), plus public health expenditures of municipal councils, plus ten percent of the expenditures of other local governments.

5F2c. *Other social:* Item 17(b) ("purchases of goods and services: social services") from CBC Table 20 [1], minus 4F2a and the central government part of 4F2b, above; plus ten percent of local government expenditures (a very rough estimate).

5F2d. *Agriculture:* } A residual; 4F2, minus the sum of
5F2e. *Transport and communications:* } 4F2a, 4F2b, and 4F2c; no division of current expenditures on
5F2f. *Other industry:* } economic services by sector has been made by the CBC and none was attempted here.

5G. *Subsidies:* 2M1; the nonstandard breakdown given below has been substituted for the standard one because the latter is not feasible and this provides a useful alternative; any social subsidies are included in 5G3, while among economic subsidies, 5G1 and part of 5G3 go to agriculture (5G1 to peasant producers, part of 5G3 to estates), while 5G2 and the remainder of 5G3 go to industry.

5G1. *To food producers:* Described under 2M1, above.

5G2. *To government enterprises and public corporations:* See 2M1, above.

5G3. *To private firms:* See 2M1, above.

5H. *Interest on public debt:* 2M2.

5I. *Transfer payments to individuals:* 4B.

5I1. *Social security benefits:* Item 18(a)(iii) ("pensions to government employees") from CBC Table 20 [1]; through 1960, no benefits had been paid out by the Employees' Provident Fund.

5I2. *Food "subsidy":* This describes the remaining "food subsidy" after the producer subsidy portion has been removed; since some food items are sold at a profit by the government, the subsidy can be negative, as it was in 1955; once again, a nonstandard breakdown has been applied here because the standard one is not available and this one is meaningful.

5I3. *Other:* A residual: 5I minus the sum of 5I1 and 5I2; this item includes various transfers, mostly for poor relief, made by local and central governments.

5J. *Transfer payments to abroad:* Nil throughout.

5K. *Surplus on current account:* Item 5E, above, minus the sum of Items 5F–5J.

5L. *Total current expenditures and surplus:* Sum of Items 5F–5K, above.

Table A-6. External Transactions

6A. *Exports of goods and services:* 2E.

6A1. *Merchandise:* Item 1a from UN Table 6 [17].

6A1a–6A1k. Breakdown: Exports by ISIC one-digit group; source: Customs data (this has been classified by the ISIC since 1956; figures for earlier years derive from a reclassification) [12]; 1950, 1952, and 1955 have not been reclassified.

6A2. *Other:* Item 1b from UN Table 6 [17].

6B. *Factor income from abroad:* Item 2 from UN Table 6 [17].

6C. *Transfer payments to individuals:* 4B.

6D. *Transfer payments to government:* 5C.

6E. *Current receipts from abroad:* Sum of 6A–6D, above.

6F. *Imports of goods and services:* Item 4 from UN Table 6 [17].

6F1. *Merchandise:* Item 4a from UN Table 6 [17].

6F1a.–6F1k. Breakdown: Imports by ISIC group; see 6A1a–6A1k, above.

6F2. *Other:* Item 4b from UN Table 6 [17].

6G. *Factor income paid abroad:* Item 5 from UN Table 6 [17].

6H. *Transfer payments from individuals:* Debit item 9 from CBC Table 25A [1].

6I. *Transfer payments from government:* Debit item 10 from CBC Table 25A [1].

6J. *Surplus of nation on current account:* Item 6E, above, minus the sum of Items 6F–6I.

6K. *Current payments to abroad and surplus:* Sum of items 6F–6J, above.

Table A-7. Gross Domestic Capital Formation and Saving

7A. *Gross fixed capital formation:* 2C.

7A1. *Government fixed capital formation:* 2C1.

7A2. *Residential construction:* 2C2.

Of which subsistence: See 2C2.

7A3. *Enterprise capital formation:* 2C3.

7B. *Change in stocks:* 2D.

7C. *Gross domestic capital formation:* Sum of 7A and 7B, above.

7D. *Income retained by producers:* 2K.

7D1. *Capital consumption allowances:* 2K1.

7D2. *Retained earnings of corporations:* 2K2.

7D2a. *Resident companies:*
7D2b. *Nonresident companies:* } From Rasaputram [16]; the standard breakdown is not available.
7D2c. *Co-operative institutions:*

7E. *Personal saving:* 4H.

7F. *Government surplus on current account:* 5K.

7G. *Less: Surplus of nation on current account:* 6J.

7H. *Statistical discrepancy:* Item 7C, above, minus the sum of items 7D–7G.

7I. *Gross domestic saving:* 7C.

*Table A–8. Industrial Origin of Gross Domestic Product
At Factor Cost*

8A. *Agriculture, fishing, forestry:* Item 1 from UN Table 2 [17], plus the statistical discrepancy which arises when GDP at factor cost, calculated from the expenditure side (i.e., item 2G, plus item 2M1, minus indirect taxes, which is the sum of items 5A2, 5A3, 5A3d(1), and 5A4) is compared with the sum of the items in this table (see page 265).

8A1. *Tea and minor estate crops:* Gross value of output, minus an allowance for raw material inputs, all based on CSD national accounts [12].

8A2. *Rubber:* Same as 8A1.

8A3. *Coconut:* Same as 8A1.

8A4. *Other:* A residual: Item 8A, above, minus the sum of 8A1–8A3.

8B. *Mining and quarrying:* Item 2 from UN Table 2 [17].

8C. *Manufacturing:* Item 3 from UN Table 2 [17].

8D. *Construction:* Item 4 from UN Table 2 [17], plus subsistence construction (see item 2C2, above).

8E. *Electricity, gas, water:* Item 5 from UN Table 2 [17].

8F. *Transport and communications:* Item 6 from UN Table 2 [17].

8G. *Wholesale and retail trade:* Item 7 from UN Table 2 [17].

8H. *Banking, insurance, real estate:* Item 8 from UN Table 2 [17].

8I. *Ownership of dwellings:* Item 9 from UN Table 2 [17], plus rural house rents (see item 2A3, above).

8J. *Public administration and defense:* Item 10 from UN Table 2 [17].

8K. *Services n.e.c.:* Item 11 from UN Table 2 [17].

8L. *Gross Domestic Product at factor cost:* Sum of items 8A-8K, above.

C. TRENDS IN LABOR SUPPLY AND USE, 1946–60

1. Sources of Information

The reader is asked to start with this minimal premise: if one is to study the economic development of Ceylon in the period 1946 to 1960 it is necessary to have estimates of the growth of labor supply and also of the extent to which the available labor has been utilized in the economy. Given this premise it is clear that whatever materials are available and whatever past surveys have been made must be used to develop the best possible estimates, however weak those materials—and, thus, the estimates themselves—may be.

Ceylon has no regular series of data on labor force, no good data on unemployment, and only a spotty coverage of employment by industry. There have been sporadic investigations, though, which can be used to put together a proximate picture of trends in labor supply and use:

(1) The population censuses of 1946 and 1953 included questions on the economic status of the populace—whether gainfully occupied or not and, if so, in what area and in what status (whether paid employee, employer, own account worker, etc.). The censuses also asked those who considered gainful employment their normal activity whether they were actually employed at present, but the answers received are of little value, since they obviously yield too low a total for unemployment (which, in any case, is defined so as to exclude first-time job seekers). Moreover, there is definitional variation between the two censuses: while the 1953 census provides a fairly conventional industrial classification the 1946 census uses an older and less useful system of classification, which combines industrial and functional status (e.g., it identifies "paddy cultivators" and "paddy landowners" but lumps all "land cultivators" and "landowners" of other food crops together); while the 1953 census includes unpaid family workers in the "economically active population" the 1946 census excludes them. The difficulties of using census data as inputs into these estimates are evident enough.

(2) A census of the unemployed was conducted in 1949,[23] but its results are of little value for the present purpose, being rendered utterly noncomparable with any other data by their exclusion of all job seekers who were over 60 or under 17 in age from the ranks of the unemployed, as well as all those who desired seasonal rather than year-round employment. It is not surprising that these constricted terms of definition resulted in the low implied all-island unemployment rate of 3.1 percent (based on estimates made here of the labor force at the time).

(3) An annual series of the numbers of unemployed registered at employment exchanges throughout the island has been in existence since 1939 but is of no use at all for these estimates. As is the case in nearly every country where this type of data exist, the amount of unemployment is grossly understated. Moreover, the degree of understatement is not ascertainable and it does not even seem likely that the trend in registered employment can be taken as equivalent to the trend in total unemployment, since the number of employment exchanges has changed from time to time.

(4) Employment data for selected industries, generated by the operation of the Wages Boards Ordinance, have been published

---

[23]See Department of Census and Statistics, *Statistical Abstract* 1952, pp. 155–56.

since 1948. They are of some value. For the plantation industries they can be taken as equivalent to industry employment figures. For some other industries they are good, but for yet other industries the collection of data started only in more recent years and in still others the number of establishments reporting varies too much from year to year for the figures to afford much help.

(5) The Central Bank of Ceylon, *Survey of Ceylon's Consumer Finances* of 1953 also canvassed people on their economic status: not in the labor force, unemployed, or employed (and if so in what industrial group). The survey obtained a labor force equal to 40 percent of the population sample and an unemployment rate of 16.6 percent of that labor force. Its sample, however, was extremely small for this purpose—just over 5,000, or about .06 percent of the population—and since labor supply and use were not the main concerns of the study the investigation of them was not overly intensive (e.g., no attempt was made to determine the degree of seasonality in the unemployment that was found).

(6) The most recent sample survey dealing with the problem—and one that was specifically designed to do so—was the *Employment, Unemployment and Underemployment Sample Survey* of 1959.[24] It investigated the anatomy of employment, unemployment, and the many borderline states that can lie between the two, especially in an underdeveloped country. Although there are some difficulties involved in interpreting the EUUSS (as it can be abbreviated) it has served as a basic source for the calculations made here.

In summary, there is no absolute shortage of materials bearing on the supply and use of labor in the 1946–60 period. There are instead great problems of comparability and, of course, sizable gaps in the existing knowledge as well. The task that must be undertaken is to try to provide as accurate and complete a picture of labor availability and use as possible, given the basic materials which are at hand.

2. Labor Force

The most important measure of labor availability is probably the labor force, defined as the total number of persons who are either working or seeking work at a given point in time. It is true,

---

[24]The full "Report to the Government of Ceylon on the Employment, Unemployment and Underemployment Sample Survey of Ceylon, 1959" by the International Labour Organisation team which conducted the survey is still unpublished but a summary has been released as "A Survey of Employment, Unemployment and Underemployment in Ceylon," *International Labour Review* (March, 1963), pp. 247–57.

as the EUUSS notes, that the labor force concept presents certain difficulties of interpretation in underdeveloped countries, where seasonal unemployment, perpetual underemployment, and multiple jobholding are endemic. Under these conditions, the specific identification of a severely limited time frame of reference made by the labor force concept may be misleading. The alternative is the "gainfully occupied worker" or "economically active population" concept, which classifies people on the basis of what they state their "normal" activity to be, with no mention made of any explicit time horizon over which the respondent should make his judgement about a "normal" activity. Actually, as far as labor supply goes, the conceptual difference seems to matter little in practice. The EUUSS estimated the labor force to be 32.4 percent of its sample population and the gainfully occupied 30.7.

The simplest way to estimate the size of the labor force in various years would be to take an estimate of it as a percentage of total population (e.g., for 1953 from the Central Bank survey; for 1959 from the EUUSS) and apply that percentage to the estimated population for other years. In some circumstances this simple procedure would yield an adequate measure. In the specific context involved here, however, this will not do. At least two important trends in Ceylonese society lead one to expect a changing ratio of labor force to population. For one thing, population started to grow very rapidly in 1946; the cause was a falling death rate and the main beneficiaries of the falling death rate were infants and mothers. As a result, the proportions of young people and women in the population should have risen and this would be expected to reduce the labor force-population ratio. The other notable trend is the striking spread of education, both in terms of the increasing numbers who attend school and the lengthening period of time for which they attend. This, too, should have worked for a falling ratio of labor force to population.

Allowances should be made for the effects of these two trends on the labor force. They can be made using three tools: the breakdown in the 1953 census of the gainfully occupied by age and sex groups, a projection of the 1953 participation rates by age-sex group to other years, and some calculations about the student population. A precondition of this operation is the need to work with the "economically active population" concept, since it is the one employed in the census. What is measured, then, is actually the "economically active population," but this is unlikely to differ much in practice from the labor force and for that reason the latter term, which is more convenient and familiar, will continue to be used.

Use will be made of a well-known and generally accepted fact of labor economics: over a span of just a few years the size of the labor force relative to population is almost entirely determined by the age and sex structure of the population, the other possible determinant, the "participation rates" of the various age and sex groups in the labor force, being institutionally determined and changing only very gradually over time. The basic technique of the estimates made here is to apply age-specific participation rates taken from the 1953 census to the estimated population of each age-sex group in other years, thus obtaining an estimate of labor force in each of those years. This procedure, used in conjunction with estimates of the changing age-sex structure of the population, automatically corrects for the rising ratios of young people and women in the population; a special correction will have to be made subsequently for the spread of education.

The participation rates implied in the 1953 census are as follows:

TABLE A–9

PARTICIPATION RATES FROM THE 1953 CENSUS

(Percent)

Age Group	Male	Female
0–14	2.9*	2.7*
15–19	46.5	27.7
20–24	81.4	28.7
25–54	95.1	31.9
55–59	91.2	34.1
60–	73.6	25.6
All ages	53.1	18.9

*The rates for the 0–14 age group were not based directly on the census totals but on those totals corrected for underenumeration in the 0–4 age bracket, which the Registrar-General's Department says amounted to some 135,000 children. See *Report of the Registrar-General on Vital Statistics for 1960*, p. 11.

These rates yield a labor force on the census day (March 20, 1953) of 2,993,000, or 36.4 percent of population. This ratio is a very low one relative to those found in many other countries but is not too surprising in a country whose population is growing very rapidly and is thus heavily weighted toward the age brackets with the lowest participation rates and in which the participation rates of women are very low. It is somewhat lower than the ratio found by the Central Bank for May of the same year (which was 40.0 percent) but seasonal fluctuation and statistical error in both sources could easily explain the discrepancy. In the light of the findings of the EUUSS for 1959, the fact that we are working with "economically active population" and not directly with the labor force concept may result in some slight understatement.

TABLE A–10

SCHOOL AND NONSCHOOL POPULATION, AGE 0–19*

(Thousands)

| Year | Age 0–14 | | Age 15–19 | |
	In School	Not in School	In School	Not in School
1946..........	872	1,812	73	729
1947..........	956	1,814	85	766
1948..........	1,046	1,832	100	673
1949..........	1,147	1,832	116	654
1950..........	1,176	1,913	127	623
1951..........	1,411	1,776	132	596
1952..........	1,348	1,927	136	588
1953..........	1,416	1,974	165	558
1954..........	1,437	2,064	191	539
1955..........	1,475	2,100	184	576
1956..........	1,537	2,120	184	623
1957..........	1,679	2,083	211	633
1958..........	1,785	2,076	235	647
1959..........	1,892	2,073	267	653
1960..........	1,963	2,107	293	659

*Source: *A.R.s of the Director of Education;* age-sex group projections (see text).

The labor force estimates for other years were obtained by the following means. First the age-sex structure of the population in each year was calculated. The 1953 census, with the addition of 135,000 children in the 0–4 bracket, was the starting point in this. Estimates were then made of the numbers at each year-end back to 1945. This was done by "demoting" the population of the preceding year by one year and adding in deaths by age and net emigration registered during the year following the year-end in question (previously, a modification of this procedure had been used to convert the census day figures to an end-of-1952 basis). In some cases, upward adjustments had to be made in the lowest age brackets because the number of infants projected from the census totals plus registered deaths in the intervening period was less than the number of registered births in the year in question (births tend to be underregistered, never overregistered, so such a thing is impossible). For the years after 1952 the procedure was reversed: the population at each age was "promoted" by one year, deaths by age were subtracted out, births were added, and net emigration was removed. The final results for all years accorded well with the estimates of total population made by the Registrar-General's Department, but gave in addition a reasonable estimate of the age-sex structure in the various years, something the department does not provide.

The 1953 participation rates times the estimated numbers in each age-sex category yielded the "uncorrected estimates" of Table A–11.

TABLE A–11

Mid-Year Labor Force Estimates, 1946–60

(Thousands)

Year	Uncorrected Estimates	Student Correction	Corrected Estimates	Percent of Population
1946	2,516	67	2,583	37.7
1947	2,573	57	2,630	37.4
1948	2,643	47	2,690	37.1
1949	2,721	37	2,758	37.0
1950	2,801	30	2,831	36.9
1951	2,871	15	2,886	36.6
1952	2,939	18	2,957	36.6
1953	3,012	—	3,012	36.3
1954	3,087	−10	3,077	36.1
1955	3,165	− 3	3,162	35.8
1956	3,234	1	3,235	36.2
1957	3,308	−30	3,268	35.7
1958	3,377	−23	3,354	35.7
1959	3,451	−36	3,415	35.5
1960	3,549	−47	3,502	35.4

The correction to allow for the spread of education was made by taking the 1953 census totals for the gainfully occupied in the 0–14 and 15–19 brackets and comparing these with estimates of the participation rates of nonstudents in 1953. The *A.R. of the Director of Education* gives the numbers in school by age. Using the residual, nonstudent population, as the divisor, the new (nonstudent) participation rates turned out to be 4.9 percent for the 0–14 group and 48.4 percent for 15–19. These new rates were assumed to hold among nonstudents in all years of the period. This new estimate of labor force in the 0–19 age group minus the original uncorrected estimate (i.e., total population at these ages times overall 1953 participation rates) gives the student correction, a measure of the number of potential labor force participants whose entry into labor supply has been delayed by the continuation of their education.

All that remains is to add the student correction to the uncorrected estimate and thus obtain the "corrected estimate" of Table A–11. A measure of the reliability of the labor force estimates which result from these calculations is provided by a comparison of the total obtained for 1959 by the methods just described with the findings of the EUUSS. The author's total is 3,415,000, as compared with the EUUSS figure of 3,320,000. The EUUSS estimate, which was reached using an entirely different procedure from the one described here, thus differs from the author's figure by only 2.8 percent.

3. *Employment*

The ideal way to measure the degree and pattern of labor use in the economy would be to use data that are completely independent of those used to estimate labor supply. If both independent estimates were accurate, a comparison of their totals would yield an accurate measure of unemployment. This, however, would require a very high degree of accuracy: unemployment, as a small number found as the difference between two much larger numbers, would absorb the errors of both—unless they happened to be offsetting—and have its total distorted by a much larger degree. Here the ideal of independent estimates can be only a goal; in some industries there are good independent data, but in others some reliance on census information will be necessary.

First among the industries with reliable independent data is the plantation sector, where there are good wages boards employment totals. There is some independent indication of trends and fluctuations in manufacturing employment and government employment can also be directly estimated. For the other sectors of the economy, unfortunately, the information on labor use must come from sources which, strictly speaking, deal with labor supply: the population censuses of 1946 and 1953 and the EUUSS of 1959. Still, with appropriate adjustments, these data can be used to gain at least a partially independent view of labor use.

The employment estimates for the 1946–60 period are given in Table 5–2, page 101. Their method of calculation is explained in detail in the source notes below on pages 296–297. Some general comments are necessary in addition, however.

(1) In those industries where 1946 and 1953 census data serve as a basic source, the two have been rendered comparable by an adjustment of the earlier totals to include unpaid family workers,

who were included among the "gainfully employed" in the 1953 inquiry but not in 1946. This adjustment is made on the assumption that unpaid family workers bore the same ratio to total "gainful employment" in each industry in 1946 as they later proved to bear in 1953.

(2) A particularly knotty problem concerns the interpretation of the EUUSS relative to the censuses. Since there was no census during the later years of the period studied[25] the EUUSS is essential as a source taken from near the end of the period for industries for which there were no independent estimates. But how is it to be interpreted? The EUUSS found the "gainfully employed" to be an extremely small—an unbelievably small—proportion of total population: only 30.7 percent. By contrast, the percentage calculated for the 1959 labor force here was 35.5, itself very low in a world context. This poses a dilemma: if the EUUSS finding were to be utilized in estimating 1959 employment, absolute totals substantially below 1953 levels would be the result. Yet the EUUSS did furnish figures on the distribution of the gainfully employed by groups which are essential to the present estimates. A solution to the dilemma, though not an entirely satisfactory one, is to assume that the EUUSS reflects sampling error in putting the labor force-population ratio so low but that its breakdown by industry reflects the correct proportions. These proportions are applied to the labor force total obtained here to yield the estimates shown in Table 5–2. The trouble with this is, of course, that the question of whether employment in these sectors has grown over the 1953–59 period has to some extent been begged. But, since the only alternative was to accept utterly incredible totals, the unpleasant choice has been made.

(3) Where the data used are of the "gainfully occupied" type there is the difficulty that they obviously overstate actual employment according to the concept of current—as opposed to "normal"—status. Some deflation must be made, but how much? Here the simple assumption has been made that there was five percent unemployment among the "gainfully occupied" in "other" (i.e., traditional) agriculture and ten percent in all other industries where data on the "gainfully occupied" are used. The assumption of a lower percentage in peasant agriculture is founded on the general notion that the sector is characterized more by underemployment than by outright unemployment, but obviously nothing very so-

---

[25]Information on the economic activity of the population from the 1963 census was not yet available as this book went to press.

phisticated is meant by this (unemployment in the sector probably varies between nil and a level far above five percent on a seasonal basis). These assumptions are probably not too far off the mark in the employment estimates they provide. They do go a very long way, however, toward begging the question of unemployment (see below pages 298–300).

Source notes to Table 5–2 (page 101):

"Agriculture, fishing, etc.": "agriculture" plus "fishing, hunting, forestry," below.

"Agriculture": "estates" plus "other," below.

"Estates": Wages boards data back to 1948. For earlier years, other data reported to the Labour Department (on labor strength) were used, corrected for the underreporting they seem to exhibit relative to the later data. The three components of estate employment are from the same source. Each includes only estate employment and so to a certain extent underestimates the total amount of labor involved in all (i.e., estate *and* smallholder) cultivation of each crop.

"Other": For 1946, 1953, and 1959 the census and EUUSS totals for the whole "agriculture, fishing, etc." group were reduced by the "estates" and "fishing, hunting, forestry" totals and by the five percent assumed unemployment, leaving nonestate agriculture as a residual. The figures for other years were interpolated and extrapolated.

"Fishing, hunting, forestry": Census totals for 1946 and 1953 were simply interpolated and extrapolated.

"Mining and quarrying": 1946 and 1953 census and 1959 EUUSS were deflated by the assumed ten percent unemployment, interpolated and extrapolated.

"Construction": From the 1946, 1953, and 1959 figures (minus the ten percent unemployment allowance), a trend was established. Fluctuations around this trend were allowed, based on the fluctuations of estate employment around *its* trend (this was taken as a rough indicator of how employment in the construction industry might have fluctuated).

"Manufacturing": A trend was determined from the usual three figures, minus assumed unemployment. An allowance for short-run fluctuations was made as follows. Six Wages Boards industries were chosen for which the year-to-year employment changes were identifiable. The percentage fluctuations from trend for these six industries were taken to be those for total manufacturing employment from its trend. For the pre-Wages Boards years of 1946 and 1947 employment in the six industries was assumed to be, respectively 110 percent and 105 percent of 1948, on the assumption that there was during these years a general declining phase, caused by the eclipse of war-born industry.

"Electric, gas, water": The 1946 and 1953 census totals, interpolation, and extrapolation were used. (The EUUSS total for some reason, probably sampling error, was far too large to be believed.)

"Trade, commerce, finance": Censuses, EUUSS, unemployment allowance, interpolation, and extrapolation were used to develop a trend. Fluctuations were based on an index of the total value of foreign trade.

"Transport and communications": Same procedure as with trade.

"Services n.e.c.": Census and EUUSS data, interpolation, extrapolation, and an unemployment allowance of ten percent.

"Government n.e.c.": This total excludes government services already classified elsewhere (transport, communication, utilities, health, education, etc.). For 1946 and 1953 estimates were based on census figures. The years 1947–52 were interpolated. From 1954 on the figures are based on an examination of comprehensive figures on central and local government employment published each year in the *Statistical Abstract* of the Department of Census and Statistics.

TABLE A–12

ESTIMATED EMPLOYMENT WITHIN THE PRIMARY SECTOR BY INDUSTRY, 1946–60

(Thousands)

Year	Tea*	Rubber†	Coconut‡	Other Primary Activity§	Total: Agriculture, Fishing and Forestry
1946	536	194	67	628	1,425
1947	537	190	71	655	1,453
1948	538	190	76	666	1,470
1949	539	189	81	651	1,460
1950	544	192	86	703	1,525
1951	548	207	93	682	1,530
1952	520	202	97	744	1,563
1953	523	200	91	760	1,574
1954	545	187	93	762	1,587
1955	542	194	91	791	1,618
1956	547	204	92	804	1,647
1957	557	203	93	823	1,676
1958	559	195	83	855	1,692
1959	566	186	87	870	1,709
1960	576	192	85	876	1,729

*From 1950 on, estate employment is divided by the ratio of acreage covered by estates to total acreage under the crop and the product is multiplied by .86 (this is an allowance for overstatement, obtained by comparing an estimate made by this method for 1953 with the figure from the 1953 census, assuming 95 percent actual employment among the "gainfully employed"). The 1946–49 totals are derived from total acreage on the basis of an assumed constancy of the .97 labor/land ratio which held in 1950.

†For 1950–, the same as for tea, except that the overstatement allowance for rubber works out to .84. The 1946 figure is 95 percent of the census total and the 1947–49 estimates depend on the assumed constancy of a labor/land ratio of .3 (the average of 1946 and 1950).

‡For 1950–60 the method is as above, but the hazard of estimating employment in this way is greater for coconut because total acreage is not precisely known. It was taken as constant at 1,070,000 acres throughout. The overstatement allowance for coconut is .664. The 1946 figure is 95 percent of the census total and the figures for 1947–49 are simply interpolated.

§A residual: the total minus the three preceding items.

After an exposition of methodology such as this, it hardly seems necessary to say that the employment estimates must be used with great care. Only for the estates and, since 1954, government n.e.c. is a literal interpretation of both growth trends and year-to-year fluctuations fully justified. For other industries, there are control figures which keep the growth rate of employment close to the true mark (subject to the problems of interpreting the EUUSS already mentioned), but year-to-year fluctuations have either been ignored altogether (in cases where they were not thought to be important) or assumed to be related to some outside variable (in cases where it was felt that such a rough approximation of probable fluctuations was preferable to implying no fluctuations at all). Obviously, for these industries the yearly fluctuations cannot be treated as legitimate research findings. For the economy as a whole there is slightly more justification for viewing them that way. But even there the "findings" are heavily dependent on the assumptions made for the various industries. Probably, little more can be said about employment trends than is hazarded above; see Chapter 5, pages 100–103.

For some purposes (e.g., for estimating output per worker in various industries; see above) it is desirable to have employment within the primary sector broken down on a strictly industrial basis, as opposed to the estate versus other approach used in Table 5–2 and elsewhere. Table A–12 shows the results of such a recalculation.

4. Unemployment

It is inevitable that estimates of labor force and employment in an economy must also constitute estimates of unemployment, since the latter is simply the difference between the former two concepts. The estimates of the preceding two sections of the present essay are no exception. Even though they were made with the measurement of labor force and employment as primary objectives, still they do yield unemployment estimates and these should be examined, if only briefly. The reason that they should be examined is only partly that it would be desirable to know what actual trends and levels of unemployment have been. Approached in that light, the unemployment estimates presented here must be judged most unsatisfactory. For one thing, their general level is heavily dependent on the assumed ten percent unemployment among the "gainfully occupied" in several industries. For another, as already suggested, unemployment is so small a quantity compared to employment or labor force that estimates which give a reasonably accurate view of the growth and fluctuation of these may be very bad representations of the degree—or even direction—of change in unemployment. Really, the main question that should be asked about unemployment is only whether the implied size of it is reasonably credible. If the question can be answered in the affirmative, a check on the estimates of labor force and employment will be obtained.

Not surprisingly, the level of unemployment implied by the present estimates hovers around ten percent. Through time there is perhaps some very slight tendency for the level to rise, but certainly not so much as popular discussion—to say nothing of the data on registered unemployment—would lead one to expect. The apparent cycles in percentage unemployment shown in Table A–13 do make some sense in terms of economic events of these years and also conform loosely to cycles in registered unemployment. The really interesting and important question, though, is whether the virtual failure of unemployment to rise as a percentage of the labor force is credible.

TABLE A–13

ESTIMATED LABOR FORCE, EMPLOYMENT, AND UNEMPLOYMENT, 1946–60

(Thousands)

Year	Labor Force	Employ- ment	Unemploy- ment	Unemploy- ment as a % of Labor Force	Registered Unemploy- ment*
1946...........	2,583	2,299	284	11.0	29
1947...........	2,630	2,348	282	10.7	37
1948...........	2,690	2,370	320	11.9	51
1949...........	2,758	2,415	343	12.4	68
1950...........	2,831	2,493	338	11.9	67
1951...........	2,886	2,535	351	12.2	59
1952...........	2,957	2,633	324	11.0	53
1953...........	3,012	2,676	336	11.2	52
1954...........	3,077	2,689	388	12.6	57
1955...........	3,162	2,791	371	11.7	67
1956...........	3,235	2,852	383	11.8	99
1957...........	3,268	2,911	357	10.9	99
1958...........	3,354	2,936	418	12.5	115
1959...........	3,415	3,043	372	10.9	123
1960...........	3,502	3,102	400	11.4	140

*Source: *A.R.s of the Labour Commissioner.*

On this little can be said in the light of the evidence at hand. The various surveys and censuses which have been conducted from time to time have differed too much in definitional framework to make even rough temporal comparisons possible. Only one real piece of evidence exists and it does support one unemployment figure in Table A–13—the 10.9 percent estimate for 1959. The corroborating evidence, already mentioned in the text (page 103) is from the EUUSS and puts 1959 unemployment at 10.5 percent.[26] The evidence is important because it shows the author's estimates for the later years to be reasonably close to the true percentage and implies that if percentage unemployment rose markedly during the

---

[26]"A Survey of Employment, Unemployment and Underemployment in Ceylon," *op. cit.*, p. 251.

1950's it must have started from a relatively low level (closer to five percent than ten, say), which is possible though unlikely.

The whole question of levels of unemployment and trends in them loses much of its importance, though, when underemployment is taken into account. The EUUSS found very high degrees of underemployment, particularly in rural areas (page 103) and it may well be that while open unemployment rose relatively little in percentage terms underemployment in traditional agriculture worsened rapidly. The fact that there has been increasing pressure of peasant population on the cultivated land area (see Table 2–8, page 48) suggests that this may have been the case.

D. HISTORICAL DATA

1. Introductory Notes

The body of economic statistics available for Ceylon must certainly rank as one of the most complete and accurate in the world for a country of such low per capita income. A number of circumstances have combined to produce this result: (1) the administrative efficiency of British colonial rule and the traditions it established; (2) the relatively high standard of literacy in the island; (3) the smallness of the country in area and population; (4) the cohesion created by the early development of relatively good internal transportation and communications facilities; and (5) the simplicity of the economic structure and its heavy orientation toward large-scale estate production for the world market. Except for fields where recent developments have altered either the economic structure (e.g., the emergence of an embryonic manufacturing sector in the late 1950's) or the kinds of things which one would like to know about any economy (e.g., input-output, flow of funds, or even conventional national accounts data), the collection of data has gone on long enough for suitable routines of collection and processing to be set up and the public to become accustomed to the activities of the data gatherers.

This section of the Appendix consists of two parts: (1) short introductory notes designed to assist those who wish to make use of the data included below (as well as anyone desiring a general overview of the economic data system of the country) and (2) the tables of basic economic data. Both the notes and the tables are divided into seven categories: (a) population and labor force; (b) agriculture; (c) industry; (d) international transactions; (e) money and finance; (f) government finance; and (g) prices. The notes provide general information on the various categories of data, while specific footnotes on sources and methods, as well as comments on the accuracy, inclusiveness, etc., of particular tables, are appended to each table.

Most of the tables go back in time as far as data are available, in a few cases as far back as the 1870's. Where appropriate, possible, and worth the effort involved, annual figures are given. In other cases, there are data only for selected years. In these instances, two groups of years are usually included: the census years of 1871, 1881, 1891, 1901, 1911, 1921, 1931, 1946, and 1953 and another set of years, consisting of 1900, 1913, 1929, 1939, 1949, and 1959. The latter set was chosen in the belief that it was a particularly apt one for international comparisons.

a. Population and Labor Force. The registration of births and deaths started in 1867 and the first population census was taken in 1871, so there has been ample time for a tradition of collecting population data to grow up in Ceylon. In the early days the official registration data understated births (especially female births and births of children who died soon after), deaths, and net immigration. Later experience suggests that births were less completely registered than deaths. Net immigration was understated because a count was kept only of the movements of Indian estate laborers, but since they made up by far the largest part of migratory flows, the degree of underestimation was relatively slight. On balance, then, population estimates based on all these registrations tended to be too low. Much of the understatement had been purged from the figures by the turn of the century, though. In 1893 penalties were enacted for failure to register births and deaths. This measure apparently required a few years to produce an effect, but after 1897 birth rates based on registrations ceased to rise, a sure sign that the data had become fairly reliable, since any apparent rise is much more likely to be statistical than actual. On similar grounds, death rates appear to be reliable from about 1885 on. Comprehensive migration statistics began to be collected only in 1921.

Censuses appear to have markedly underenumerated the population. Sarkar, relying mainly on comparisons of the age structure of the population shown in the censuses with hypothetical age structures which he considers to be more plausible, has made estimates of the degree of underenumeration of the various censuses.[27] He puts underenumeration at about 15 percent in 1871, approximately 10 percent in 1881 and 1891, 12 percent in 1901, 13 in 1911, and 15 percent in 1921. By 1946, he estimated, the error had fallen to 6.5

[27] N. K. Sarkar, *The Demography of Ceylon* (Colombo: Government Press, 1957), pp. 23–68.

percent. He made no estimates for 1953. The relative constancy of the degree of underenumeration as estimated by Sarkar means that his revised population growth rates for most periods differ little from those based on official census totals.

When compared with the enormous errors which have been discovered in the population statistics of some underdeveloped countries, where experience with population censuses and birth and death registration is of short duration, the defects of Ceylon's data seem relatively small. Indeed, they can usually be ignored by the investigator into economics or other subjects where population data are used as a mere adjunct to the main field of study.

The same can certainly not be said about Ceylon's data on labor supply and use. There is no unified data collecting system on labor force or employment and the registration data on unemployment are unusable. What fragmentary information there is falls into two categories: (1) data from population censuses, consisting of the answers of census respondents to questions about their economic status; and (2) unrelated bits and pieces of information on various categories of employment, which have been generated as a by-product of the enforcement of some law or by some kind of special inquiry. Thus there is a continuing series of total employment on estates using Indian labor and another of employment in industries to which the Wages Boards Ordinance had been applied. Industrial censuses and similar sporadic inquiries furnish additional information, but it is usually incomplete and difficult to relate to data from any other source. An effort to create some sort of a unified whole out of these bits and pieces is reported on elsewhere in this monograph. Though the result is imperfect, it is a necessary first step. The overall paucity of information on labor supply and use is truly deplorable, since the subject lies at the very heart of Ceylon's current economic plight.

b. Agriculture. Acreage and output data for the major crops go well back in time. However, they have undergone considerable refinement in method and improvement in accuracy in recent years. The main means used to improve the data has been to lessen the reliance put in untrained primary reporters in the villages (mostly village headmen) and unscientific rule-of-thumb estimation techniques. Figures for tea and rubber, because of the highly commercialized nature of the production of these crops, have always been best. Since the establishment of the Offices of Tea Controller and Rubber Controller in the 1930's, though, they have improved still further and are now very thorough and accurate. The other plantation crop, coconuts, is much less well served. Coconut output is estimated by working backward from exports of coconut products and estimated local consumption, using standard nut equivalents; acreage planted and yield per acre are still near mysteries, but a sample survey now being conducted by the Department of Census and Statistics promises to provide accurate and current—though not continuing—information on these. Paddy acreage is still estimated by traditional methods but a continuing semiannual sample survey has replaced the extremely inaccurate old way of calculating yields; total output continues to be estimated by multiplying acreage by yield. Minor crops are still covered by the old methods and some fairly important ones—e.g., palmyra palms—are not covered at all.

Other agricultural data, touching on ownership and tenure, production methods, size of holdings, and other matters come from agricultural censuses and other special inquiries. The information they provide has a strong tendency to be nonadditive but they are nevertheless valuable in that they are the only sources of knowledge on these important aspects of agricultural production. Data on prices of agricultural products are sparse and disorganized, except for the most recent years and for the major export products, for which long series exist (see part *d*, below).

In summary, data on the important crops—except coconuts—are good. Since agriculture in Ceylon is so heavily concentrated in four crops, the overall coverage must be judged good.

c. Industry. Industrial production is still in its infancy in Ceylon and so is the production of statistics to describe it. It is safe to predict that as industrial activity increases in volume and scope statistical coverage will rise apace. So far, putting together an index of industrial or manufacturing output has been made very difficult by the marked year-to-year changes in both the industrial structure itself and the quantity and kinds of data available. Only a few kinds of statistics which touch upon international trade (e.g., imports of various kinds of industrial or construction raw materials) go back very far in time. Data on prices of industrial products are totally lacking. Finally, a special note might be recorded here: the two forms of industrial activity with a long history in Ceylon—the processing of tea and rubber—are never included in industrial production statistics because they generally take place on the estate where the product is grown and are hard to separate out statistically from the agricultural aspects of its production.

d. International Transactions. The conduct of international trade, especially when the revenue of the government is made to depend heavily upon customs duties, virtually demands good statistics, and Ceylon, which has always relied so much on trade, has them. The Standard International Trade Classification has been used only since 1956 but the similar United Kingdom Board of Trade Classification preceded it, so functional breakdowns of Ceylon's trade back to 1921 are easy to do. Modern balance of payments accounts have been kept only since 1948. It is necessary, though, to issue a warning concerning the various indexes of import volume and price: the structure of import trade changed sharply after World War II and again around 1960, so these indexes are heavily dependent upon the base years chosen in their construction.

e. Money and Finance. The establishment of the Central Bank of Ceylon in 1950 provided the impetus for a very good set of monetary statistics, covering elements of the money supply, the operations of the banking system, interest rates, etc. The data seldom go back before 1950, though. Other financial data, of the kind needed for flow of funds or national balance sheet calculations, are largely lacking. In part, this is a reflection of the generally underdeveloped state of the island's financial system.

f. Government Finance. Central government accounts have been published on a conventional basis far back into history, but the economic and functional reclassification of these accounts is a product of the last few years, carried out by the Central Bank. As a result of this work, budget data in a nearly ideal form for analysis now exist for 1948 and subsequent years. Local government accounts are in a much less desirable state, having been only partially reclassified into economically meaningful categories. These data have been utilized for 1950 and later years as raw material for the national accounts of section B; they are repeated here so as to give the information in their original form (for central and local governments separately and by budget, rather than calendar, years for the former) and to extend the figures back in time to 1928/29. Information on related subjects—the financing of the central government deficit, public debt outstanding, and the state industrial corporations—is also given in this section.

g. Prices. A fair number of price data are collected but their combination into useful indexes has lagged a bit. At present, the most important price indexes are the Colombo Consumer Price Index, the import and export price indexes (see part *d*), and the implicit GNP deflator. The first of these has several weaknesses, which have been exposed by an official investigatory committee, and an improved index has been drawn up—but not officially adopted and published, because of its implications for the wages of government employees. As already mentioned, any import price index is heavily dependent on the base year chosen. No wholesale price index has been produced as yet; so far this has been no great pity because most wholesale goods were imported and the import price index served the purpose; but times are changing and the compilation of an index covering all wholesale goods, both imported and domestically produced, will become increasingly desirable as local production comes to account for more and more of the goods entering into trade. A reliable index of construction costs is another item which has not been produced so far, in this case because the basic statistical inputs are lacking.

TABLE A–14

TOTAL POPULATION, BIRTH RATE, DEATH RATE, AND RATE OF NATURAL
INCREASE, ANNUALLY, 1867–1960*

Year	Midyear Population (000s)	Births per 1,000	Deaths per 1,000	Deaths under 1 Year of Age per 1,000 Live Births	Rate of Natural Increase
	A. Annual Figures				
1867..............	2,329	10.0	11.7	...	−0.2
1868..............	2,355	20.1	25.3	...	−0.5
1869..............	2,363	22.4	20.3	...	0.2
1870..............	2,382	26.7	17.7	...	0.9
1871..............	2,417	28.5	19.4	...	0.9
1872..............	2,451	28.4	21.8	...	0.7
1873..............	2,462	28.3	20.0	...	0.8
1874..............	2,517	29.7	20.8	...	0.9
1875..............	2,531	28.1	22.0	...	0.6
1876..............	2,573	30.1	24.3	...	0.6
1877..............	2,670	26.8	31.8	...	−0.5
1878..............	2,741	23.1	27.6	...	−0.5
1879..............	2,772	25.1	20.8	...	0.4
1880..............	2,759	26.2	18.3	128	0.8
1881..............	2,756	27.1	27.2	170	0.0
1882..............	2,773	26.7	19.7	138	0.7
1883..............	2,782	29.6	19.3	136	1.0
1884..............	2,794	31.3	22.3	157	0.9
1885..............	2,815	28.1	29.1	189	−0.1
1886..............	2,830	27.1	23.7	153	0.3
1887..............	2,855	32.7	24.0	152	0.9
1888..............	2,901	31.8	26.4	167	0.5
1889..............	2,939	27.7	28.5	174	−0.1
1890..............	2,980	31.9	23.0	146	0.9
1891..............	3,022	31.9	28.7	170	0.3
1892..............	3,088	30.2	27.5	162	0.3
1893..............	3,121	31.3	29.6	177	0.2
1894..............	3,145	33.2	27.9	165	0.5
1895..............	3,194	31.8	27.6	169	0.4
1896..............	3,241	32.0	25.3	158	0.7
1897..............	3,352	37.7	23.7	140	1.4

(Continued on next page)

TABLE A–14 (CONTINUED)

TOTAL POPULATION, BIRTH RATE, DEATH RATE, AND RATE OF NATURAL INCREASE, ANNUALLY, 1867–1960*

Year	Midyear Population (000s)	Births per 1,000	Deaths per 1,000	Deaths under 1 Year of Age per 1,000 Live Births	Rate of Natural Increase
1898............	3,396	38.8	26.6	169	1.2
1899............	3,430	38.5	30.6	197	0.8
1900............	3,521	38.6	28.7	178	1.0
1901............	3,583	37.5	27.6	170	1.0
1902............	3,630	39.1	27.5	173	1.2
1903............	3,704	40.0	25.9	164	1.4
1904............	3,768	38.6	24.9	174	1.4
1905............	3,902	38.6	27.7	176	1.1
1906............	3,883	36.5	35.1	198	0.1
1907............	3,886	33.6	30.7	186	0.3
1908............	3,923	40.8	30.1	183	1.1
1909............	3,970	37.5	31.0	202	0.7
1910............	4,035	39.0	27.3	176	1.2
1911............	4,121	38.0	34.8	218	0.3
1912............	4,151	33.3	32.4	215	0.1
1913............	4,220	38.6	28.4	189	1.0
1914............	4,251	38.2	32.2	213	0.6
1915............	4,355	37.0	25.2	171	1.2
1916............	4,483	39.0	26.8	184	1.2
1917............	4,590	40.1	24.7	174	1.5
1918............	4,677	39.2	31.9	188	0.7
1919............	4,480	36.0	37.6	223	−0.2
1920............	4,486	36.5	29.6	182	0.7
1921............	4,522	40.7	31.1	192	1.0
1922............	4,603	39.1	27.6	188	1.2
1923............	4,684	38.7	30.3	212	0.8
1924............	4,765	37.5	25.8	186	1.2
1925............	4,847	39.9	24.3	172	1.6
1926............	4,928	42.0	25.3	174	1.7
1927............	5,009	41.0	22.6	160	1.8
1928............	5,091	41.9	26.0	177	1.6
1929............	5,172	38.3	26.2	187	1.2
1930............	5,252	39.0	25.5	175	1.4
1931............	5,326	37.4	22.1	158	1.5
1932............	5,389	37.0	20.5	162	1.7
1933............	5,419	38.6	21.2	157	1.7
1934............	5,560	37.1	22.9	173	1.4
1935............	5,608	34.4	36.5	263	−0.2
1936............	5,642	34.0	21.8	166	1.2
1937............	5,725	37.7	21.7	158	1.6
1938............	5,826	35.8	21.0	161	1.5
1939............	5,916	35.9	22.0	166	1.4
1940............	5,972	35.7	20.6	149	1.5
1941............	6,178	35.6	18.3	129	1.7
1942............	6,179	35.8	18.1	120	1.8
1943............	6,296	39.5	20.8	132	1.9
1944............	6,442	36.1	20.8	135	1.5

TABLE A–14 (Continued)

Total Population, Birth Rate, Death Rate, and Rate of Natural
Increase, Annually, 1867–1960*

Year	Midyear Population (000s)	Births per 1,000	Deaths per 1,000	Deaths under 1 Year of Age per 1,000 Live Births	Rate of Natural Increase
1945............	6,650	35.9	21.5	140	1.4
1946............	6,854	37.5	19.8	141	1.8
1947............	7,037	38.5	14.0	101	2.5
1948............	7,244	39.7	12.9	92	2.7
1949............	7,455	39.1	12.3	87	2.7
1950............	7,678	40.2	12.4	82	2.8
1951............	7,876	39.8	12.7	82	2.7
1952............	8,074	38.8	11.8	78	2.7
1953............	8,290	38.7	10.7	71	2.8
1954............	8,520	35.7	10.2	72	2.6
1955............	8,723	37.3	10.8	71	2.7
1956............	8,929	36.4	9.8	67	2.7
1957............	9,165	36.5	10.1	68	2.6
1958............	9,388	35.8	9.7	64	2.6
1959............	9,625	37.0	9.1	58	2.8
1960............	9,896	36.6	8.6	57	2.8
		B. Decade Averages			
1870–79..........	2,552	27.5	22.6	...	0.5
1880–89..........	2,820	28.8	23.9	156	0.5
1890–99..........	3,197	33.7	27.1	165	0.7
1900–09..........	3,777	38.1	28.9	180	0.9
1910–19..........	4,336	37.8	30.1	195	0.8
1920–29..........	4,811	39.6	26.9	183	1.3
1930–39..........	5,566	36.7	23.5	174	1.3
1940–49..........	6,631	37.3	17.9	123	2.0
1950–59..........	8,627	37.6	10.7	71	2.7

*These are all official data issued by the Registrar-General's Department. The department com-putes midyear population by adding births and net immigration to the previous year's population and subtracting deaths; the resulting estimate is revised from time to time in the light of census findings. The birth and death rate figures are based on registered births and deaths and estimated population. It is clear that there was a fairly high—though decreasing—degree of underregistration of both births and deaths up through the mid-1890's. Births seem to have been less completely regis-tered than deaths, though, so the rates of natural increase in the first three decades are understated. Sarkar (see pages 301–302) estimated that all censuses prior to 1953 significantly underestimated total population. His corrected totals (in thousands) are 1871–2,820; 1881–3,044; 1891–3,330; 1901–4,031; 1911–4,702; 1921–5,304; and 1946–7,122 (the 1931 census did not provide sufficient detail for him to derive a corrected figure). *Demography of Ceylon* (Colombo: Government Press 1957), pp. 57–61.

Source: *Report of the Registrar-General on Vital Statistics*, S.P., various years.

TABLE A–15

Net Immigration, 1871–1960*

(Thousands)

Year	Net Immigration	Year	Net Immigration
1871	29.9	1917	15.2
1872	6.1	1918	20.0
1873	8.4	1919	78.1
1874	35.4	1920	18.4
1875	8.8		
1876	72.8	1921	29.3
1877	78.6	1922	28.2
1878	9.9	1923	41.7
1879	3.9	1924	25.4
1880	28.1	1925	5.6
1881	9.4	1926	− 0.7
1882	6.9	1927	−11.2
1883	13.8	1928	0.3
1884	4.3	1929	18.5
1885	1.1	1930	9.9
1886	5.3	1931	−31.9
1887	17.5	1932	−29.8
1888	26.8	1933	−60.1
1889	9.1	1934	97.6
1890	38.4	1935	− 8.1
1891	43.1	1936	− 8.2
1892	48.9	1937	9.9
1893	18.5	1938	− 1.4
1894	19.0	1939	−26.4
1895	42.9	1940	−33.0
1896	35.1	1941	−27.0
1897	43.9	1942	−89.7
1898	31.2	1943	− 4.1
1899	13.2	1944	90.6
1900	95.1	1945	111.2
1901	2.3	1946	57.1
1902	23.8	1947	22.5
1903	15.7	1948	20.2
1904	21.1	1949	30.7
1905	94.6	1950	−20.4
1906	29.3	1951	−14.0
1907	7.9	1952	−16.3
1908	7.7	1953	−12.6
1909	18.6	1954	− 8.0
1910	54.0	1955	−23.0
1911	38.6	1956	−17.9
1912	39.6	1957	−12.3
1913	30.0	1958	−15.3
1914	29.6	1959	− 7.7
1915	56.5	1960	− 6.0
1916	68.1		

*Prior to 1921 the data refer to estate laborers only, the migration of other groups not being known. Since that year the data are comprehensive and generally reliable, except that in the 1950's they exclude illegal immigration (perhaps substantial) into Ceylon from India.

Source: *Report of the Registrar-General on Vital Statistics*, S.P., various years.

TABLE A–16

POPULATION BY AGE AND SEX, CENSUS YEARS 1881–1959*

(Thousands)

Age	1881			1891		
	Male	Female	Total	Male	Female	Total
0– 4........	255.3	240.8	496.1	276.5	259.2	535.7
5– 9........	227.9	198.6	426.5	247.1	217.6	464.7
10–14........	156.7	122.0	278.7	169.4	136.5	305.9
15–19........	134.3	163.6	297.9	141.2	172.0	313.2
20–24........	131.6	131.0	262.6	142.4	137.5	279.9
25–29........	145.1	125.0	270.1	155.1	143.7	298.8
30–34........	84.9	55.9	140.8	97.5	65.7	163.2
35–39........	90.3	74.5	164.8	103.8	86.2	190.0
40–44........	46.0	31.9	77.9	55.8	37.3	93.1
45–49........	53.9	57.6	111.5	55.4	62.0	117.4
50–54........	33.3	21.5	54.8	34.4	23.8	58.2
55–59........	56.9	32.8	89.7	58.7	37.8	96.5
60–64........	16.7	7.9	24.6	19.6	9.6	29.2
65–69........	16.3	11.4	27.7	18.5	12.7	31.2
70–.........	17.2	12.8	30.0	17.3	12.5	29.8
Unspecified...	3.1	2.8	5.9	0.6	0.3	0.9
Total........	1,469.6	1,290.2	2,759.8	1,593.4	1,414.4	3,007.8

Age	1901			1911		
0– 4........	328.7	310.1	638.8	311.9	296.1	608.0
5– 9........	263.9	240.1	504.0	289.0	275.5	564.5
10–14........	201.6	161.4	363.0	271.5	235.7	507.2
15–19........	179.8	206.2	386.0	178.0	168.9	346.9
20–24........	182.7	173.7	356.4	193.9	195.1	389.0
25–29........	194.7	171.2	365.9	207.2	189.7	396.9
30–34........	121.0	82.2	203.2	165.3	139.2	304.5
35–39........	126.1	101.2	227.3	151.1	103.1	254.2
40–44........	68.1	48.5	116.6	104.6	89.9	194.5
45–49........	68.5	70.0	138.5	85.5	60.9	146.4
50–54........	41.9	27.4	69.3	65.0	70.2	135.2
55–59........	61.0	39.0	100.0	51.7	31.1	82.8
60–64...... }				45.6	36.3	81.9
65–69...... }	58.0	38.5	96.5	20.3	12.6	32.9
70–......... }				34.4	27.1	61.5
Unspecified...	0.2	0.1	0.3	—	—	—
Total........	1,896.2	1,669.7	3,565.9	2,175.0	1,931.3	4,106.3

*These are official census figures, except for 1959, which has been computed by the author on the basis of a projection of the 1953 census in the light of birth and death registration in the intervening years. Minor discrepancies are attributable to rounding.

Source: Department of Census and Statistics, *Statistical Abstracts.*

TABLE A–16 (CONTINUED)

Age	———1921———			———1946———		
	Male	Female	Total	Male	Female	Total
0– 4........	328.5	315.0	643.5	437.4	424.0	861.4
5– 9........	293.3	281.6	574.9	411.8	399.5	811.3
10–14.......	295.2	257.8	553.0	414.6	391.0	805.6
15–19.......	214.5	199.3	413.8	364.5	316.1	680.6
20–24.......	221.5	220.1	441.6	327.8	313.7	641.5
25–29.......	219.1	201.5	420.6	307.3	270.3	577.6
30–34.......	174.2	150.5	324.7	246.5	203.4	449.9
35–39.......	174.1	123.1	297.2	261.1	207.2	468.3
40–44.......	117.2	99.7	216.9	182.4	139.9	322.3
45–49.......	102.8	73.8	176.6	183.4	136.1	319.5
50–54.......	71.2	73.7	144.9	104.8	91.3	196.1
55–59.......	58.9	35.9	94.8	94.7	68.5	163.2
60–64.......	49.1	39.0	88.1	71.2	59.3	130.5
65–69.......	24.3	15.9	40.2	} 124.8	104.7	229.5
70–.........	37.8	29.9	67.7			
Unspecified...	0.1	——	0.1	——	——	——
Total........	2,381.8	2,116.8	4,498.6	3,532.2	3,125.1	6,657.3

Age	———1953———			———1959———		
0– 4........	609.0	599.8	1,208.8	751	734	1,485
5– 9........	550.0	535.9	1,085.9	669	655	1,324
10–14.......	474.7	445.4	920.1	579	564	1,143
15–19.......	364.4	339.4	703.8	469	456	925
20–24.......	395.2	372.3	767.5	372	348	720
25–29.......	371.2	337.7	708.9	371	356	727
30–34.......	285.3	235.5	520.8	391	350	741
35–39.......	292.1	243.5	535.6	304	255	559
40–44.......	210.6	161.5	372.1	278	225	503
45–49.......	211.4	159.0	370.4	238	173	411
50–54.......	159.7	118.5	278.2	189	144	333
55–59.......	108.9	79.7	188.6	161	122	283
60–64.......	84.0	69.5	153.5	} 263	208	471
65–69.......} 70–.........}	152.2	131.6	283.8			
Unspecified...	——	——	——	——	——	——
Total........	4,268.7	3,829.2	8,097.9	5,035	4,590	9,625

TABLE A–17

POPULATION BY PROVINCE, SELECTED YEARS, 1871–1959*

(Thousands)

Province	1871	1881	1891	1900	1901	1911	1913	1921
Western........	575.7	671.5	762.5	909	920.7	1,106.2	1,143	1,246.8
Central.........	365.6	473.7	474.5	609	622.8	672.3	687	717.7
Southern........	398.6	433.5	489.8	560	566.7	628.8	641	671.2
Northern........	281.7	302.5	319.3	342	340.9	369.7	375	374.8
Eastern.........	112.6	127.6	148.4	173	173.6	183.7	190	192.8
North-Western...	276.1	293.3	320.1	352	353.6	434.1	451	492.2
North-Central....	63.7	66.1	75.3	77	79.1	86.3	89	96.5
Uva............	129.0	165.7	159.2	183	186.7	216.7	223	233.9
Sabaragamuwa...	197.5	225.8	258.6	317	321.8	408.5	422	471.8
Total..........	2,400.4	2,759.7	3,007.8	3,521	3,566.0	4,106.4	4,220	4,498.6†

Province	1929	1931	1939	1946	1949	1953	1954	1959
Western.........	1,421	1,445.0	1,642	1,876.9	2,080	2,232.3	2,342	2,599
Central.........	878	953.4	1,037	1,135.3	1,267	1,366.7	1,431	1,586
Southern........	760	771.2	854	961.4	1,059	1,129.3	1,193	1,362
Northern........	408	398.9	433	479.6	529	570.6	597	670
Eastern.........	217	212.4	243	279.1	321	354.4	375	444
North-Western...	548	547.0	599	667.9	768	855.2	906	1,050
North-Central....	103	97.4	119	139.5	179	229.3	245	302
Uva............	284	303.2	332	372.2	425	466.9	491	561
Sabaragamuwa...	553	578.4	658	745.4	828	893.2	939	1,051
Total..........	5,172	5,306.9	5,916	6,657.3	7,455	8,097.9	8,520	9,625

*For census years, figures are from official census returns and are given to the nearest 100,000; figures for other years, given to the nearest thousand, are estimates: those for 1954 and 1959 were made by the Registrar-General's office, while those for 1900, 1913, 1929, 1939, and 1949 are author's estimates based on the total population estimate of the Registrar-General's Department and the provincial population relative to the total in the preceding and following census years. Minor discrepancies are attributable to rounding.

†There is a discrepancy of nearly 1,000,000 in the source.

Source: Department of Census and Statistics, *Statistical Abstract* (1960).

TABLE A-18

Distribution of Population by Size of Community, Selected Years, 1871–1959*

	1871	1881	1891	1900	1901	1911	1913	1921
Total population of Ceylon	2,400.4	2,759.7	3,007.8	3,521	3,566.0	4,106.4	4,220	4,498.6
Colombo†								
Population (000s)	92.6	110.5	126.8	152	154.7	211.3	216	244.2
Percent of total	3.9	4.0	4.2	4.3	4.3	5.1	5.1	5.4
Communities of 20–100,000								
Population of (000s)	81.8	93.6	97.2	124	127.1	137.6	142	164.0
Percent of total	3.4	3.4	3.2	3.5	3.6	3.4	3.4	3.6
Other urban communities‡								
Population (000s)	2,226.0	2,555.6	97.4	124	126.5	154.6	158	172.6
Percent of total	92.7	92.6	3.2	3.5	3.5	3.8	3.7	3.8
Rural								
Population (000s)			2,686.4	3,121	3,157.7	3,602.9	3,704	3,917.8
Percent of total			89.3	88.6	88.6	87.7	87.8	87.1

	1929	1931	1939	1946	1949	1953	1954	1959
Total population of Ceylon	5,172	5,306.9	5,916	6,657.3	7,455	8,097.9	8,520	9,625.0
Colombo								
Population (000s)	277	284.2	320	362.1	400	426.1	437	490.8
Percent of total	5.4	5.4	5.4	5.4	5.4	5.3	5.1	5.1
Communities of 20–100,000								
Population (000s)	177	178.9	240	301.4	336	363.3	383	733.9§
Percent of total	3.4	3.4	4.1	4.5	4.5	4.5	4.5	7.6
Other urban communities								
Population (000s)	225	236.3	297	359.5	408	449.7	477	216.1
Percent of total	4.4	4.5	5.0	5.4	5.5	5.6	5.6	2.2
Rural								
Population (000s)	4,493	4,607.5	5,059	5,634.3	6,311	6,858.8	7,223	8,184.2
Percent of total	86.9	86.8	85.5	84.6	84.7	84.7	84.8	85.0

*Figures for 1871, 1881, 1891, 1901, 1911, 1921, 1946 and 1953 represent census findings; 1931 figures are Department of Census and Statistics estimates (the partial 1931 census did not provide estimates of population by community); the figures for 1900, 1913, 1929, 1939 and 1949 are author's estimates, based on interpolation; the 1954 estimate is an extrapolation assuming a continuation of the 1946-53 growth rate for each class of community (both the interpolated and the extrapolated estimates are adjusted to add to the Department of Census and Statistics midyear population estimate); the 1959 estimates are those of the Registrar-General's Department. Minor discrepancies are attributable to rounding.

†Colombo is the only city to exceed 100,000 in population.

‡Includes all population residing within the legal limits of urban or municipal councils of less than 20,000 total population.

§Several local government reorganizations account for the sudden upsurge in the population living in cities of 20,000 and over.

Sources: Department of Census and Statistics, *Statistical Abstract* (1960); *Report of the Registrar-General on Vital Statistics* for 1959.

TABLE A–19

TOTAL SCHOOL AND UNIVERSITY ENROLLMENT,
SELECTED YEARS, 1871–1959

Year	Total (000s)	Total as a Percent of Population Age 5–19*
1871....................	38.4	....
1881....................	93.7	9.3
1891....................	153.8	14.2
1900....................	208.3	....
1901....................	218.5	17.4
1911....................	359.7	25.4
1913....................	374.3	....
1921....................	404.8†	26.3
1929....................	562.9	....
1931....................	593.8	....
1939....................	828.8	....
1946....................	944.5	41.1
1949....................	1,262.5	....
1953....................	1,580.7	58.3
1954....................	1,628.2	....
1959....................	2,158.5	61.9

*I.e., total school and university enrollment (regardless of age) divided by total population in 5–19 age group (latter figures are from the censuses, except for 1959).

†Includes 400 students of Ceylon University College (there was no university education in Ceylon in earlier years).

Sources: *A.R. of the Director of Education*, various years; Department of Census and Statistics, *Census of Ceylon*, various years.

TABLE A–20

School and University Enrollment by Type of Institution, Selected Years, 1929–59*

(Thousands)

	1929	1931	1939	1946	1949	1953	1954	1959
English Schools								
Primary†	58.7	1.8	8.4	8.6	11.4	12.3	12.9	15.0
Junior secondary‡		26.1	24.1	11.6	62.4	87.0	89.7	2.1
Senior secondary§		31.4	36.1	76.6	120.6	171.5	175.5	160.6
Collegiate‖		3.4	6.6	11.5	14.8	26.1	30.5	291.2
Night	1.2	1.8	4.6	4.1	4.0	3.7	3.6	3.6
Other and unspecified#		3.6	6.6	22.4	27.8	14.2	13.6	0.4
Sinhalese Schools								
Infant¶								21.8
Primary†	442.6	491.5	524.6	618.7	793.4	990.8	1,021.1	90.4
Junior Secondary‡								267.5
Senior Secondary§								916.5
Estate**			0.3***	0.2***	0.3***	0.4	0.4	0.6
Other and unspecified††								0.6
Tamil Schools								
Primary†			118.6	131.7	163.2	199.0	203.9	64.7
Junior secondary‡								73.3
Senior secondary§								131.3
Estate**			43.9***	35.7***	55.9***	64.3	65.9	77.1
Other and unspecified								¶¶

(Continued on next page)

TABLE A-20 (CONTINUED)

	1929	1931	1939	1946	1949	1953	1954	1959
Training Colleges‡‡	1.7	1.8	2.1	1.5	2.0	2.8	3.1	4.4
Pirivenas§§	2.9	2.7	5.6	4.8	4.9	6.2	5.6	7.1
Other and unspecified‖‖‖	55.3	29.3	46.2	15.8	—	—	—	24.7
Total school enrollment	562.6	593.4	828.1	943.2	1,260.7	1,578.3	1,625.8	2,153.0
University##	0.3	0.4	0.7	1.3	1.8	2.4	2.4	5.5
Total school and university enrollment	562.9	593.8	828.8	944.5	1,262.5	1,580.7	1,628.2	2,158.5

*This breakdown of enrollment by type of institution is not the most informative one for understanding the level at which education is being pursued at any particular time; it is, though, the only one which can be traced through a considerable period of time. The more pertinent data relating to school enrollment by class and age are given for recent benchmark years in Tables A-21–A-23

†Schools offering classes above standard 2 but not above standard 5.
‡Schools offering classes above standard 5 but not above standard 8.
§Schools offering classes above standard 8 but not above the Senior School Certificate (S.S.C.) level.
‖Schools offering classes above the S.S.C. level (i.e., Higher School Certificate [H.S.C.] preparatory and H.S.C.).
#Students in special schools in 1946–59; students in unassisted schools in 1921–54; students in "Central" schools in 1946; students in junior schools in 1946; and students in English-language industrial schools in 1939; see footnote ‖‖‖.
¶Schools which offer no classes above standard 2.
**All estate schools are primary schools.
††Students in special schools in 1959.
‡‡Teachers and technical training institutions.
§§A kind of Buddhist religious school.
‖‖‖Students in unassisted schools in 1959; students in bilingual schools in 1929–46; figures through 1939 refer to its enrollment; it was replaced by the University of Ceylon in 1942 and in Pansala and Koran schools in 1929–39.
##Ceylon University College opened in 1921 and figures through 1939 refer to its enrollment; it was replaced by the University of Ceylon in 1942 and the 1946–54 totals represent enrollment in this university only; the 1959 figures reflect in addition the enrollment of the new Vidyodaya and Vidyalankara universities.
¶¶Unassisted schools cannot be identified as to language medium in the 1959 *Administration Report of the Director of Education*.
***Only total enrollment in estate schools is given in the original source; the separate Sinhalese and Tamil enrollments given here are estimates based on relative enrollments in other years.
Source: *A.R. of the Director of Education* (in earlier years, Director of Public Instruction), various years.

TABLE A–21

SCHOOL AND UNIVERSITY ENROLLMENT BY CLASS, 1953, 1954,
AND 1959

(Thousands)

Class	1953	1954	1959
Standard			
1(a) (lower kindergarten)...	338.7	329.9	413.0
1(b) (upper kindergarten)..	230.1	246.7	305.7
2	209.8	216.3	270.5
3	185.2	190.2	239.2
4	153.2	158.5	201.8
5	120.2	125.0	169.0
6	97.9	97.3	140.0
7	89.4	80.6	106.9
8	52.7	72.1	86.8
Pre-S.S.C.	38.1	42.3	76.9
S.S.C.	43.7	47.6	114.8
Pre-H.S.C.	3.1	3.6	9.9
H.S.C.	2.8	2.7	6.2
Other school classes	0.8	0.8	0.9
School total*	1,565.7	1,613.5	2,141.6
University			
Undergraduate	2.4	2.4	5.5
Postgraduate	——†	——†	——†
School and university total*	1,568.1	1,615.9	2,147.1

*Excludes training colleges, night schools and pirivenas; note, however, that these totals—because of discrepancies in the source—do not precisely tally with the supposedly identical totals of Table A–20.

†Less than 50.

Source: *A.R. of the Director of Education.*

TABLE A–22

School Enrollment by Age, 1953, 1954, and 1959

(Thousands)

Age	1953	1954	1959
0– 5	46.1	37.1	50.1
5– 6	192.7	165.0	211.0
6– 7	183.1	190.3	238.1
7– 8	177.1	185.7	237.4
8– 9	167.8	173.0	231.0
9–10	150.8	159.1	212.0
10–11	138.2	144.8	192.8
11–12	117.1	125.9	169.1
12–13	100.5	107.8	146.8
13–14	80.1	82.1	113.9
14–15	61.8	66.7	89.8
15–	150.4	176.1	246.1
All ages*	1,565.7	1,613.5	2,138.0
Percentage of population 5–14 (compulsory school attendance ages) enrolled in schools	71.7	73.9	75.7

*Excludes training colleges, night schools and pirivenas; the failure of this total (in some instances) to match the supposedly identical totals in Tables A–20 and A–21 is attributable to errors of enumeration. Minor discrepancies within the present table are attributable to rounding.
Source: *A.R. of the Director of Education.*

TABLE A–23

Literacy of the Population Age 5+, Census Years, 1881–1953*

Census Year	Literate (000s)			Illiterate (000s)			% of Popuation Age 5+ Literate		
	Male	Female	Total	Male	Female	Total	Male	Female	Total
1881	361.7	32.6	394.3	851.0	1,015.4	1,866.3	29.8	3.1	17.4
1891	475.8	61.6	537.4	841.0	1,093.6	1,934.6	36.1	5.6	21.7
1901	657.6	115.6	773.2	908.5	1,243.0	2,151.4	42.0	8.5	26.4
1911	878.8	204.0	1,082.8	984.4	1,431.2	2,415.5	47.2	12.5	30.9
1921	1,155.5	381.4	1,536.9	897.4	1,420.3	2,317.5	56.3	21.2	39.9
1931†	....	....	....	....	....	....	....	....	....
1946‡	2,170.7	1,182.0	3,352.8	924.1	1,519.1	2,443.2	70.1	43.8	57.8
1953‡	2,776.7	1,732.1	4,508.8	883.0	1,497.3	2,380.3	75.9	53.6	65.4

*"For Census purposes a 'literate' person is one who can both read *and* write a language." (Department of Census and Statistics, *Ceylon Year Book 1960*, p. 34). "The test of ability to read and write a language [is] whether the person is able to write a short letter and read the reply to it." (Department of Census and Statistics, *Census of Ceylon 1953*, vol. I, p. 75). However, census enumerators have never been specifically instructed to make such a test and, in any case, school enrollment has always been accepted as prima facie evidence of literacy. Thus, the data probably overstate the number of persons who can read and write effectively. Minor discrepancies in the table are attributable to rounding.
†The partial 1931 census took no account of literacy.
‡Percentage of the population age 15+ literate:

	Male	Female	Total
1946	77.9	45.2	62.9
1953	80.5	52.7	67.7

Earlier years do not give literacy totals by age, so this calculation can be made only for 1946 and 1953.

CAUSE OF DEATH: GENERAL HEADINGS AND SELECTED CATEGORIES, SELECTED YEARS, 1891–1959*

(In Number per 100,000 Deaths)

Cause	1891	1900	1901	1913	1921	1929	1931	1939	1946	1949	1953	1954	1959
I. Infective and parasitic diseases	50,653	53,961	53,755	18,109	20,020	15,887	16,287	19,756	21,093	15,882	10,604	10,414	7,667
Tuberculosis	3,015	3,443	3,991	3,559	2,406	2,611	2,993	2,815	2,951	4,501	2,708	2,277	2,093
Typhoid fever	3,922	5,390	4,961	328	475	544	678	756	953	949	452	417	173
Cholera	3,922	215	53	62	2	14	5	4	23		12	1	3
Dysentery		5,342	6,867	3,498	3,023	3,148	2,125	1,637	1,342	770	773	727	676
Diphtheria	7	2	3	5	8	13	15	33	108	139	188	240	172
Whooping cough	59	115	54	36	61	35	84	39	50	82	54	121	76
Plague					133	52	39						
Leprosy	68	87	105	51	52	70	58	99	58	69	31	62	9
Tetanus	179	364	465	308	163	237	284	216	282	367	374	364	467
Yellow fever								1					
Rabies	47	53	41	17	13	46	40	37	49	121	111	135	168
Typhus				2		1	1		4	2	1	1	
Malaria	660	2,559	2,953	1,778	1,395	1,720	1,414	7,806	9,259	2,615	811	515	93
Ankylostomiasis and other diseases due to helminths	3,439	4,119	3,527	4,331	5,137	4,804	5,315	3,850	3,706	4,324	4,723	5,263	3,272
II. Cancer and other tumors	149	231	229	442	318	345	415	538	610	1,152	2,081	2,150	2,546
III. Endocrine, metabolic and blood diseases	3,341	3,006	3,461	2,934	3,484	6,167	5,325	5,049	7,019	8,462	8,646	8,849	9,225
Vitamin deficiencies							3,701	2,666	4,487	5,536	4,808	4,787	3,790
IV. Diseases of the nervous system and sense organs	15,821	11,152	10,655	12,128	11,812	14,619	12,709	13,565	12,095	11,874	12,400	12,160	11,478
V. Diseases of the circulatory system	383	544	542	1,512	1,715	2,378	2,692	3,448	4,178	5,954	5,784	6,019	7,019

(Continued on next page)

TABLE A-24 (CONTINUED)

Cause	1891	1900	1901	1913	1921	1929	1931	1939	1946	1949	1953	1954	1959
VI. Diseases of the respiratory system	2,543	6,823	6,825	6,914	8,320	10,261	10,640	10,956	10,662	10,993	10,259	9,927	9,813
Bronchitis	376	611	705	887	890	1,011	1,263	1,288	1,112	1,211	979	1,149	997
Pneumonia	757	2,794	2,947	3,584	4,766	6,638	6,493	7,324	7,681	7,888	7,181	6,798	7,190
VII. Diseases of the digestive system	953	1,164	1,276	13,762	12,085	8,143	7,037	6,780	6,443	7,302	5,550	7,002	6,633
VIII. Diseases of the genitourinary system	127	463	427	516	1,294	1,352	1,678	1,471	1,301	1,602	1,354	1,194	1,053
IX. Diseases of pregnancy, childbirth, and the puerperium	2,565	2,322	2,093	2,753	2,744	2,980	3,527	3,008	2,933	2,074	1,751	1,599	1,372
X. Diseases of the skin and musculo-skeletal system	13,877	8,727	8,248	8,112	7,714	7,536	8,050	7,665	6,065	4,515	4,255	4,498	3,592
XI. Diseases of the new born	332†	763†	758†	5,257	5,494	7,583	7,790	8,198	8,814	11,138	13,128	12,482	12,886
XII. Senility without mention of psychosis	1,441	2,005	2,107	2,641	3,498	4,399	5,109	5,360	6,169	8,456	10,837	11,011	13,947
XIII. Violent or accidental death	1,808	1,789	1,947	1,969	1,891	2,010	2,294	2,330	2,495	3,531	3,936	4,486	4,699
Suicide	98	129	148	194	173	206	265	301	288	529	645	771	900
Homicide	52	122	137	161	154	228	285	271	299	326	349	478	900
Accidents	1,634	1,507	1,627	1,597	1,528	1,551	1,722	1,737	1,957	2,637	2,922	3,210	3,327
XIV. Ill-defined and unknown causes of death	6,008	7,050	7,676	22,951	19,612	16,339	16,446	11,876	10,122	7,063	9,418	8,130	8,069
Total deaths‡	86,663	100,873	98,813	120,008	140,749	135,274	117,452	128,611	135,937	91,889	89,003	86,794	87,971

*The data refer to officially registered deaths. The hazards of long-term comparisons of figures of this kind are well known; the two main biases which are likely to be present are improvements in the techniques of medical diagnosis and increasing inclusiveness of the registration system over time. Thus the apparent increases in such causes of death as cancer and heart ailments may be ascribed to the presence of the first kind of bias while the rise of others (e.g., deaths among the newborn) results from the second. Other trends—the general fall in the relative importance of infectious diseases, the decline in death connected with pregnancy, and the rise in deaths of simple old age—are undoubtedly genuine. Although it is difficult to make or assess such a generalization, one's impression in working with the data is that they are of a high standard of reliability back at least through 1913.

†Severely understated, mainly through underregistration of infant deaths.
‡Actual total deaths per year (not the sum of the columns, which is 100,000 in all cases, except for rounding error).
Sources: *Report of the Registrar-General on Vital Statistics,* various years.

TABLE A-25

DAILY PER CAPITA CALORIE INTAKE: TOTAL AND MAIN CONSTITUENTS,
SELECTED YEARS, 1952-59*

	1952-53	1954-56	1957	1958	1959
Cereals........................	1,163	1,228	1,229	1,150	1,304
Potatoes and other starchy roots..	96	94	61	65	57
Sugar.........................	171	169	164	186	212
Pulses and nuts.................	351	365	451	417	304
Fruits and vegetables...........	31	31	34	36	37
Meat.........................	14	13	11	11	12
Eggs.........................	6	5	4	4	4
Fish.........................	36	33	36	71	43
Milk.........................	27	34	35	32	38
Fats and oils..................	95	90	89	88	88
Total....................	1,990	2,062	2,114	2,060	2,099
Animal..................	86	88	89	121	100
Vegetable...............	1,904	1,974	2,025	1,939	1,999

*The data have been compiled from "food balance sheets." Total supply from production and imports, with allowance made for losses in distribution, is divided by population. The resulting quantity of each type of food is then evaluated as to calorie content. The F.A.O. notes that the figures should be comparable from year to year but are undoubtedly understated in all years (because of the inadequate account taken of consumption of food which never passes through the market). Also, though, slight inaccuracies in population estimates, distribution losses, etc., make the year-to-year estimates less than perfectly comparable.

Sources: Food and Agricultural Organization of the United Nations, *Production Yearbook 1959* and *1960* (Rome, 1960, 1961); Department of Census and Statistics, *Statistical Abstract* (1960).

TABLE A–26
INDUSTRY ATTACHMENT, CENSUS YEARS, 1881–1953*
(Thousands)

Industry	1881	1891	1901	1911	1921	1946	1953
Agriculture *et. al*..........	643.1	...	1,089.6	1,133.1	1,386.1	1,381.6	1,584.1
Agriculture...........	622.8	...	1,064.2	1,101.3	1,353.7	1,339.2	1,536.5
Estates...............	....	...	440.6	561.7	619.6	782.9	856.1
Tea................	....	...	312.7	369.1	323.7	467.7	550.2
Rubber............	....	...	.....	38.4	109.6	204.2	210.2
Coconut...........	....	...	73.2	104.2	119.2	69.7	95.7
Other and unspecified	....	...	54.7	49.9	67.1	41.3	#
Paddy.............	....	...	391.9	453.3	645.7	282.9	378.3
Livestock...........	....	...	6.7	5.0	6.3	5.8	7.2
Other..............	....	...	224.9	81.3	82.2	267.6	294.9
Forestry.............	0.1	...	0.7	1.4	3.7	4.2	4.4
Hunting.............	0.2	...	‖	0.1	‖	‖	0.2
Fishing..............	20.0	...	24.7	30.3	28.6	38.1	43.1
Mining and quarrying........	2.6	...	17.9	16.8	2.8	9.1	13.8
Plumbago mining........	....	...	17.9	15.4	1.6	2.8	1.8
Other.................	....	...	‖	1.4	1.2	6.3	12.0
Manufacturing.............	86.4	...	163.0	151.3	239.4	224.1	303.0
Food................ ⎰	13.1	...	11.8	15.0	33.5	15.4	25.0
Beverages............ ⎱		...	8.8	6.0	89.6	18.0	14.6
Tobacco.............	3.6	...	6.2	1.9	4.6	6.5	8.5
Textiles..............	4.6	...	4.9	40.2	68.5	33.5	73.8
Apparel..............	5.9	...	26.6	7.6	11.5	15.4	19.1
Wood†.............	35.5	...	83.8	50.1	77.1	79.5	22.9
Furniture.............	....	...	0.1	0.1	0.2	1.2	49.9
Paper...............	—	...	—	—	—	‖	0.2
Printing..............	0.5	...	1.3	1.7	2.1	4.4	8.0
Leather..............	0.3	...	0.2	0.4	0.5	0.4	0.3
Rubber..............	——	...	—	—	—	—	1.9
Chemicals............	2.3	...	0.1	0.9	1.1	1.7	9.5
Petroleum and coal......	—	...	—	—	—	—	0.3
Nonmetallic minerals....	8.3	...	10.2	7.3	11.6	11.0	19.5
Basic metals...........	—	...	—	—	—	—	1.7
Metal products.........	5.3	...	16.5	10.6	17.8	27.7	12.4
Machinery.............	—	...	—	—	—	—	1.1
Electrical.............	—	...	—	—	—	—	2.2
Transportation equipment	....	...	0.1	0.4	0.6	7.0	14.7
Miscellaneous..........	6.9	...	0.6	9.1	0.7	2.4	17.6
Construction‡..............	24.0	...	22.8	14.3	16.1	30.7	56.7
Electricity, gas, water, sanitary	....	...	0.7	1.7	2.5	8.3	5.3
Electricity and gas......	....	...	0.2	0.5	0.4	3.6	2.6
Water and sanitary......	....	...	0.5	1.2	2.1	4.7	2.7
Commerce................	71.0	...	133.5	133.9	148.9	205.1	246.2
Trade................	....	...	132.7	132.8	147.9	203.9	240.2
Finance..............	....	...	0.8	1.0	0.9	1.2	6.0
Transport, storage, communi-							
cations...................	18.9	...	25.0	50.1	78.5	94.0	104.3
Transport and storage....	....	...	.....	48.8	75.7	87.5	95.3
Communications........	....	...	....	1.4	2.9	6.5	9.0
Services§...................	97.4	...	142.5	143.6	207.6	386.0	482.1
Government............	12.9	...	21.3	12.4	14.2	66.8	116.2
Professional............	19.7	...	32.6	37.4	48.1	80.2	110.3
Religion..............	8.8	...	17.0	16.6	18.8	11.2	13.1

TABLE A–26 (CONTINUED)

INDUSTRY ATTACHMENT, CENSUS YEARS, 1881–1953*

(Thousands)

Industry	1881	1891	1901	1911	1921	1946	1953
Education	2.7	...	4.6	7.0	11.3	31.8	53.2
Medicine	3.7	...	5.1	6.7	8.2	19.9	32.2
Other	4.4	...	5.8	7.1	9.8	17.3	11.7
Personal	18.3	...	28.4	24.1	30.2	34.7	39.2
Hotels and restaurants	1.7	...	3.3	2.5	13.5	46.9	50.2
Domestic	44.8	...	56.9	66.0	101.2	154.0	111.5
Other	—	...	0.1	1.2	0.4	3.4	54.7
Insufficiently described	87.5	...	49.4	108.0	135.9	272.7	186.1
Total	1,031.0	...	1,652.7	1,752.8	2,217.9	2,611.5	2,981.7

ATTACHMENT TO SELECTED INDUSTRIES AS A PERCENT OF TOTAL, 1881–1953

Industry	1881	1891	1901	1911	1921	1946	1953
Primary	63	...	67	66	63	53	54
Agriculture	60	...	64	63	61	51	52
Estates	...	...	27	32	28	30	29
Other agriculture	...	...	38	31	33	21	23
Other primary	2	...	3	3	2	2	2
Secondary	11	...	11	9	12	10	12
Manufacturing	8	...	10	9	11	9	10
Construction	2	...	1	1	1	1	2
Tertiary	18	...	19	19	20	27	28
Professional	2	...	2	2	2	3	4
Government	1	...	1	1	1	3	4
Other tertiary	15	...	15	16	17	21	21
Insufficiently described	8	...	3	6	6	10	6
Total	100	...	100	100	100	100	100

*The source of these data is the occupational section included in each complete population census back to 1881. In the original source, in all censuses prior to 1953, the figures are broken down by some occupation scheme rather than an industry classification, e.g., "carpenters" is a typical heading, with no indication of how many are employed in construction, furniture manufacturing, etc. Moreover, the scheme used varies several times between censuses. The arrangement of the data into the industry classification of this table—which conforms, with two exceptions, to the International Standard Industrial Classification (ISIC)—involves a certain unavoidable amount of guessing and arbitrary allocation. The figures should not be taken as actual employment totals—the respondent was simply asked what he considered to be his normal economic activity—but are referred to here as "industry attachment" data instead. This concept gives a total which is closer to labor force than to total employment. Still, the census data go back for a great stretch of time and can be used to gain an idea of long-term trends in the employment structure in Ceylon. The broad picture is summarized in the second part of the table. In analyzing changes in the relative importance of the industries listed here, one should bear in mind that there is an "insufficiently described" residual which varies from census to census in size and possibly in makeup. No figures are available for 1891 because in that year the census only identified the total population by occupation (i.e., of the head of families), making no distinction between working and nonworking members of the family.

†Includes cane, coir and related manufactures, except in 1953, when some of these trades have apparently been classified as furniture manufacturing by the census takers and cannot be separated out.

‡Figures for all but the 1953 census are quite unreliable.

§Services are not broken down according to the ISIC because its subcategories—government community, business, recreation, and personal services—are not capable of being broken out of most of these data and also because the breakdown used here was thought to be of interest.

‖Less than 50 persons.

#Included under "other agriculture."

Source: Department of Census and Statistics, *Census of Ceylon*, various years.

TABLE A–27

TYPE OF EMPLOYMENT, 1946, 1953 AND 1959*

Type of Employment	In Thousands			Percent of Total		
	1946	1953	1959	1946	1953	1959
Professional, technical and related..........	76	114	99	2.9	3.8	3.5
Managerial and adminis- trative..............	5	4	8	0.2	0.1	0.3
Clerical and related.....	66†	128	105	2.5	4.3	3.7
Sales and related.......	188	221	217	7.2	7.4	7.6
Farming, forestry, hunt- ing, fishing...........	1,382	1,536	1,503	52.9	51.3	52.7
Mining and quarrying....	9	14	8	0.3	0.5	0.3
Transport operating occupations..........	87	78	106	3.3	2.6	3.7
Crafts, production process and related., ...	227†	397	373	10.6	13.3	13.1
Service occupations......	278†	439	207	10.6	14.7	7.3
Miscellaneous and unspecified...........	244	63	227	9.3	2.1	8.0
Employment............	2,612	2,993	2,853	100.0	100.0	100.0

*As in Table A–28, possible definitional variations, certain differences in the completeness with which occupations are assigned to type categories, and probable sample errors in the 1950 EUUSS severely limit the comparability of these figures.

†Obviously understated relative to 1953.

Sources: Department of Census and Statistics, *Census of Ceylon 1946, Census of Ceylon 1953; Employment, Unemployment and Underemployment Sample Survey.*

TABLE A–28

EMPLOYMENT STATUS, 1953 AND 1959*

Employment Status	In Thousands		Percent of Total	
	1953	1959	1953	1959
Employers.............	94	22	3.1	0.8
Self-employed..........	898	793	30.0	27.8
Paid employees........	1,832	1,848	61.2	64.8
Unpaid family workers..	169	160	5.6	5.6
Other and unclassified...	———	30	———	1.1
Employment............	2,993	2,853	100.0	100.0

*It seems obvious that these figures, especially as they relate to employers, are misleading. There are apparently no differences in definitions of the categories be- tween the two data sources so a sampling error in the 1959 *Employment, Unemploy- ment and Underemployment Sample Survey* is the most probable explanation for the startling apparent diminution in the number of employers.

Sources: Department of Census and Statistics, *Census of Ceylon 1953; Employ- ment, Unemployment and Underemployment Sample Survey.*

TABLE A-29

AVERAGE HOURLY EARNINGS AND AVERAGE WEEKLY HOURS OF NONSUPERVISORY WORKERS IN SELECTED INDUSTRIES: MARCH, 1948–60*

Industry	1948		1949		1950		1951		1952		1953		1954	
	A.H.E.	A.W.H.	A.H.E.	A.W.H.	A.H.E.	A.W.H.	A.H.E.	A.W.H.	A.H.E.	A.W.H.	A.H.E.	A.W.H.	A.H.E.	A.W.H.
Tea growing and manufacturing....	.18	40.1	.19	35.9	.21	40.8	.26	31.7	.27	37.6	.27	37.8	.27	38.8
Rubber growing and manufacturing.	.18	38.8	.19	36.5	.20	39.7	.28	36.2	.31	37.5	.34	31.7	.31	33.8
Coconut growing..............	..	....	.18	36.6	.18	36.8	.21	36.8	.22	32.1	.22	34.9	.26	36.2
Coconut manufacturing.........	..	....	.26†	25.9†	.26	34.2	.29	36.4	.33	33.1	.33	41.0	.35	39.7
Engineering.................	.42	44.4	.39	49.0	.40	41.6	.43	43.5	.44	42.3	.45	44.8	.46	36.6
Printing....................	.42	42.2	.49	48.4	.48	51.0	.48	48.2	.54	45.4	.54	47.4	.56	46.6

Industry	1955		1956		1957		1958		1959		1960	
	A.H.E.	A.W.H.	A.H.E.	A.W.H.	A.H.E.	A.W.H.	A.H.E.	A.W.H.	A.H.E.	A.W.H.	A.H.E.	A.W.H.
Tea growing and manufacturing....	.28	37.8	.28	35.1	.30	37.4	.29	36.7	.29	33.6	.30	39.1
Rubber growing and manufacturing.	.31	34.5	.32	36.2	.32	36.0	.32	33.9	.31	34.9	.33	39.2
Coconut growing..............	.23	37.0	.23	34.6	.25	34.5	.26	33.8	.26	33.8	.28	35.5
Coconut manufacturing.........	.38	37.1	.36	34.0	.35	34.1	.38	36.5	.50	38.7	.54	34.9
Engineering.................	.51	46.7	.49	49.0	.54	42.7	.76	40.5	.68	40.4	.81	44.0
Printing....................	.56	49.3	.56	50.1	.67	46.2	.79	46.5	.94	45.9	1.14	56.5

*Data on hours and earnings are collected by the Department of Labour in connection with the administration of the Wages Boards Ordinances. They cover only those industries to which that ordinance has been applied, a total which has grown from 7 in 1948 to 14 in 1960. Of these, six of the most significant industries are included here. The Labour Department collects information on hours and earnings twice annually, in March and September, but because of the large amount of computation work required to convert the data to the form in which they appear here, only the March figures are given.

†Includes coconut manufacturing outside of Colombo only.

Source: A.R. of the Commissioner of Labour, various years.

TABLE A–30

MINIMUM WAGE RATES FOR KEY OCCUPATIONS IN SELECTED INDUSTRIES, 1945–59*

(Rupees)

Industry	1945	1949	1953	1954	1959
			(Daily Rates)		
Tea growing and manufacturing					
Male workers, age 16	1.30	1.55	1.23	2.27	2.42
Female workers, age 15	1.04	1.20	1.74	1.79	1.92
Child workers	.92	1.08	1.42	1.47	1.60
Rubber growing and manufacturing					
Male workers, age 16	1.30	1.41	2.43	2.41	2.57
Female workers, age 15	1.04	1.11	2.04	2.03	2.17
Child workers	.92	.99	1.72	1.71	1.85
Copra manufacturing					
Kanganies (overseers)	1.48	1.53	2.23	2.21	2.27
Male workers, age 18—†	1.30	1.53	1.88	1.86	2.19
Female workers, age 18—†	.96	1.11	1.44	1.42	1.74
Child workers	.79	.94	1.27	1.26	1.56
Engineering					
Kanganies	2.45	2.66	3.04	3.03	3.97
Skilled laborers	2.65	2.86	3.24	3.23	4.17
Semiskilled laborers					
Grade I	2.29	2.50	2.88	2.87	3.82
Grade II	2.13	2.34	2.72	2.71	3.62
Unskilled laborers	1.99	2.20	2.58	2.57	3.47
Watchers	2.35	2.56	2.94	2.93	3.87
Learners and apprentices					
4th year	1.54‡	1.66	1.93	1.92	2.78
3rd year	1.18‡	1.30	1.54	1.53	2.37
2nd year	.89‡	.95	1.09	1.09	1.87
1st year	.65‡	.71	.83	.83	1.62
Match manufacturing					
Adults					
Grade I					
Men	2.83§	2.86	3.24	3.23	3.67
Women	2.37§	2.46	2.78	2.77	3.21
Grade II					
Men	2.43§	2.46	2.84	2.83	3.27
Women	2.05§	2.08	2.46	2.45	2.89
Grade III					
Men	2.17§	2.20	2.58	2.57	2.97
Women	1.81§	1.84	2.22	2.21	2.60
Grade IV					
Men (Watchers)	2.56§	2.53	2.94	2.93	3.37
Young persons					
Grade I					
Age 14–17	1.43§	1.44	1.70	1.70	2.51
Age 17	1.86§	1.87	2.20	2.19	2.51
Grade II					
Age 14–17	1.28§	1.29	1.55	1.55	2.26
Age 17	1.61§	1.62	1.95	1.94	2.26
Grade III					
Age 14–17	1.18§	1.19	1.45	1.45	1.75
Age 17	1.52§	1.51	1.85	1.84	2.16

TABLE A–30 (CONTINUED)

MINIMUM WAGE RATES FOR KEY OCCUPATIONS IN SELECTED INDUSTRIES, 1945–59*

(Rupees)

Industry	1945	1949	1953	1954	1959
			(Monthly Rates)		
Printers					
Class					
A	150.00	162.50	179.50	178.83	210.92
B	112.50‡	121.18	135.88	135.88	168.80
C, Grade I	81.25‡	89.60	101.56	101.15	136.48
C, Grade II	‖	‖	91.82	91.45	126.48
D	65.00‡	71.25	82.25	81.92	111.67
E	60.75‡	66.82	77.47	77.15	101.27
F	29.25‡	32.06	39.76	39.61	60.08
G	65.00‡	71.25	82.25	81.92	105.67
Learners and apprentices					
Class A					
1st year	45.12‡	48.75	54.85	54.65	76.47
2nd year	60.16‡	65.00	72.80	72.53	95.82
3rd year	75.20‡	81.25	90.75	90.42	116.17
4th year	97.71‡	109.09	117.43	116.99	143.45
5th year	120.32‡	130.00	144.60	144.07	173.22
Class B					
1st year	33.84‡	56.56	41.76	41.61	63.58
2nd year	56.40‡	60.94	68.44	68.19	85.86
3rd year	67.68‡	73.12	82.03	82.03	105.25
4th year	84.57‡	91.35	102.07	101.70	129.48
Class C					
1st year	32.60‡	35.62	41.13	40.96	63.55
2nd year	40.72‡	44.48	51.20	50.99	73.86
3rd year	49.80‡	53.44	61.44	61.19	86.36
4th year	61.14‡	66.82	76.47	76.15	102.35
Class D					
1st year	26.68‡	28.50	33.40	33.27	54.62
2nd year	32.60‡	35.72	41.63	41.46	63.05
3rd year	39.12‡	42.75	49.85	49.65	72.47
4th year	48.90‡	53.44	61.94	61.69	84.86
Motor transport					
Class					
A	130.20§	131.25	142.25	141.92	161.67
B	120.20§	121.25	132.25	131.92	151.67
C	112.70§	113.75	124.75	124.42	144.17
D	130.20§	131.25	142.25	141.92	161.67
E	95.20§	96.25	107.25	106.92	126.67
F	97.70§	98.75	109.75	109.42	129.17
G	87.18§	88.12	98.53	98.23	117.75
H	77.18§	78.12	88.53	88.23	107.75
I	87.18§	88.12	98.53	98.23	117.75
J	117.18§	118.12	128.53	128.23	147.75
K	63.92§	64.69	74.19	73.94	93.11
Dock, harbour, and port transport					
manual work					
Special grade	....	93.25#	97.69	97.44	99.19
Skilled	....	79.25#	83.69	83.44	85.19

(Continued on next page)

TABLE A–30 (CONTINUED)

MINIMUM WAGE RATES FOR KEY OCCUPATIONS IN SELECTED INDUSTRIES, 1945–59*

(Rupees)

Industry	1945	1949	1953	1954	1959
		(Monthly Rates)			
Semiskilled.................	.....	66.25#	70.69	70.44	72.19
Unskilled, Grade I...........	.....	58.25#	62.69	62.44	64.19
Unskilled, Grade II..........	.....	52.25#	56.69	56.44	58.19
Female kanganies...........	.....	56.25#	60.69	60.44	62.19
Female laborers.............	.....	53.19#	55.69	55.44	57.19
Nonmanual work					
Special Grade................	.....	109.92#	113.25	112.92	115.25
Grade I.....................	.....	81.19#	83.69	83.44	85.19
		(Daily Rates)			
Building					
Male laborers, age 18..........	.....	2.31#	2.58	2.57	3.47
Female laborers, age 18........	.....	2.07#	2.34	2.33	3.17
Laborers, under 18............	.....	1.87#	2.14	2.13	2.97
Semiskilled					
Grade II..................	.....	2.61#	2.88	2.87	3.82
Grade I...................	.....	2.77#	3.04	3.03	3.97
Skilled.....................	.....	2.97#	3.24	3.23	4.17

*These minimum wage rates refer to certain industries for which wages boards have been established. The first wages boards were instituted in 1945 and subsequently others were set up to apply to other industries. In most of these industries the legal minimum rates are the actual rates paid to almost all workers in the relevant category.

†Redefined in 1957 to include male workers age 16 and over and female workers age 15 and over.

‡1946.

§1947.

‖Minimum wage not established until 1952.

#1950.

Source: *A.R. of the Commissioner of Labour*, various years.

TABLE A–31
Indexes of Agricultural Production, 1946–60*
(1953 = 100)

Year	Official (1934–38 Base) Indexes† Major Crops	Minor Crops	All Crops	Unofficial (1960 Base) Indexes‡ Major Crops	Minor Crops	All Crops	Live-stock	Agricultural Output
1946....	.....	.....	.....	80.4	.....	.....	.....	.....
1947....	.....	.....	.....	81.4	.....	.....	109.0	.....
1948....	.....	.....	.....	87.0	.....	.....	84.5	.....
1949....	86.9	61.6	86.1	90.2	47.2	88.2	113.0	88.6
1950....	94.5	80.6	94.0	94.7	80.4	94.0	−9.3	92.5
1951....	97.9	94.6	97.8	98.0	82.9	97.3	91.5	97.2
1952....	99.9	100.6	99.9	103.2	94.9	102.8	101.5	102.8
1953....	100.0	100.0	100.0	100.0	100.0	100.0	100.0	100.0
1954....	106.6	102.2	106.5	110.9	104.1	110.6	115.3	110.6
1955....	113.9	110.4	113.8	119.1	122.4	119.3	140.2	119.6
1956....	109.3	87.6	108.6	110.6	108.3	110.5	84.3	110.0
1957....	114.9	72.4	113.6	114.9	109.8	114.7	62.7	113.9
1958....	115.3	75.6	113.9	121.5	97.1	120.4	76.7	119.7
1959....	114.2	68.7	112.7	121.7	94.3	120.4	120.3	120.3
1960....	118.2	72.9	116.1	131.5	109.1	130.4	111.4	130.2

*The Department of Census and Statistics publishes an index of agricultural production which goes back to 1949. The department computes separate indexes for tea, rubber, coconut, paddy, and cocoa, and a combined index for nine minor (highland) crops. As an expression of trends in agriculture since World War II this index has two serious weaknesses: (1) its base period (1934–38) is so far back in time as to reduce the relevance of the index for recent years—and, incidentally, to make its value weights depend on price and output figures which are quite unreliable in some cases—and (2) its inclusiveness leaves something to be desired—fruits, most vegetables, livestock, and livestock products are all excluded. Since much information now exists which can be used to remedy some of these defects, the author essayed a new index, which is presented here along with the official one. The first three columns of this table present the old index and the remaining five, the new one.

†These are Census and Statistics indexes, converted to a 1953 = 100 basis by simple division. The five major crop indexes (for tea, rubber, paddy, coconuts, and cocoa) have been combined by the author into a single index, each crop's weight corresponding to the department's 1934–38 weighting.

‡The unofficial index compiled by the author uses official output data for 21 crops, including 16 minor ones—several fairly important minor crops (e.g., onions, chillies) have been added which are excluded from the official index. The price data used represent the first attempt in Ceylon to ascertain the prices received by producers of a wide range of agricultural produce (from an unpublished Census and Statistics survey) and are thus probably superior to value figures which use wholesale or retail prices, even if adjusted to allow for transportation and middlemen's margins —though these price data have their weaknesses too; they are unweighted averages of provincial prices for products which are sometimes none too specifically defined (e.g., cattle, coconuts). Thus it can be hoped that the unofficial crop index is both more relevant to the period it covers and more inclusive of the whole range of agricultural activity in the island than the official index. On the latter score, an index of livestock production is provided here for the first time. This is based on livestock population and slaughter figures reported to Census and Statistics by village headmen and local sanitary and health bodies respectively and published by the department. These data have never been included in the official index because they are not considered trustworthy: the stock figures because they are based on the estimates, often made on some rough and ready method, of the village headmen and the slaughter figures because they exclude rural slaughter for the most part. The unofficial index faces up to these problems as follows: (1) it takes the stock figures as reported, assuming that errors in estimation are random and will tend to offset each other; and (2) it accepts the official slaughter data on cattle, sheep and goats—which are thought to be slaughtered almost entirely in urban areas—but rejects the published figures for buffalo and pigs, substituting the "reasonable guesses" made by the Department of Census and Statistics in another connection that 10 percent and 50 percent of buffaloes and pigs, respectively, are slaughtered each year. Livestock production was taken as slaughter plus change in stock and the aforementioned 1960 producer prices were used for weighting to produce a livestock output index.

The last column lists the author's index of total agricultural output. How good an indicator of all agricultural production is it? For one thing, well over 90 percent of agricultural output by value is included. The remaining exclusions among crop products are slight. Livestock products, especially poultry, egg, and milk production, are important remaining omissions. All three have risen rapidly in the past decade. Were at all reliable statistics on them available, they would doubtless raise the index slightly for recent years—particularly when 1960 value weights are used. Otherwise, the picture presented by the index should be reliable.

Sources: Department of Census and Statistics, *Statistical Abstract*, various years, *Mid-year Bulletin of Statistics* (June, 1961), unpublished producer price data.

TABLE A-32

VOLUME OF OUTPUT OF MAIN INDIVIDUAL CROPS, 1933-60*

Year	Tea† (000 Lbs.)	Rubber† (Metric Tons)	Paddy‡ (000 Bu.) Maha	Yala	Total	Coconut§ (000,000 Nuts)
1933......	220,740	....	......	......	......	.....
1934......	224,680	....	......	......	......	.....
1935......	220,860	....	......	......	......	.....
1936......	226,355	....	......	......	......	.....
1937......	226,105	73,664	......	......	......	1,746
1938......	246,931	50,803	......	......	......	1,854
1939......	237,272	60,963	......	......	......	1,675
1940......	265,099	91,445	......	......	......	1,399
1941......	247,870	101,097	......	......	......	1,475
1942......	291,400	103,129	......	......	......	1,488
1943......	268,798	107,089	......	......	......	1,852
1944......	296,851	100,081	13,800	6,700	20,500	1,581
1945......	276,903	98,968	12,000	4,400	16,400	1,670
1946......	282,911	95,416	11,900	5,300	17,200	1,361
1947......	298,526	90,340	11,400	5,300	16,700	1,339
1948......	298,791	96,431	12,100	6,600	18,700	1,765
1949......	298,559	90,936	13,700	9,400	23,100	1,763
1950......	306,215	115,322	14,300	7,700	22,000	1,877
1951......	326,279	106,685	12,400	9,600	22,000	2,129
1952......	316,842	98,049	18,400	10,500	28,900	2,344
1953......	343,034	100,193	13,200	8,700	21,900	2,223
1954......	366,738	95,443	19,300	11,800	31,100	2,159
1955......	380,013	95,336	21,700	14,000	35,700	2,485
1956......	375,578	96,914	19,400	8,100	27,500	2,391
1957......	397,775	99,395	20,200	11,080	31,280	1,965
1958......	413,155	101,804	21,200	15,400	36,600	1,836
1959......	413,130	93,168	21,900	14,500	36,400	2,099
1960......	437,704	98,836	26,300	16,700	43,000	1,964

*Includes all crops accounting for 10 percent of acreage sown in recent decades and all reliable output data.

†From the annual returns made by all producers to the tea and rubber controllers (rubber data were converted from long tons to metric tons by multiplying by 1.01605).

‡Estimated by the Department of Census and Statistics. Acreage figures reported by village headmen—see Table A-37, footnote‖. Average yield was originally estimated by the village headmen also, but since 1952 an annual sample survey has provided an improved yield estimate. Output is simply the product of acreage planted and average yield.

§Estimated by the Department of Census and Statistics. Local consumption calculated using the Central Bank of Ceylon, *Survey of Ceylon's Consumer Finances* for 1953 and adjusting for population change. The main items of coconut export are converted to a nut basis using standard conversion factors. Local consumption plus export is taken as production; there is no allowance for changes in inventories.

Sources: Department of Census and Statistics, *Statistical Abstract*, various years, *Mid-Year Bulletin of Statistics* (June, 1961), unpublished data; Ministry of Finance, *Economic and Social Development of Ceylon (a Survey) 1926–1954* (1955).

TABLE A–33

AVERAGE PADDY YIELD, 1951–60*

(Bushels per Acre Harvested)

Year	*Maha*	*Yala*	Average
1951.................	25.14	27.28	26.01
1952.................	30.85	30.70	30.80
1953.................	26.44	27.90	26.99
1954.................	30.47	30.13	30.34
1955.................	32.15	32.93	32.46
1956.................	30.85	28.23	30.05
1957.................	32.69	31.76	27.34
1958.................	34.06	34.87	34.38
1959.................	34.04	37.17	35.17
1960.................	36.10	36.82	36.36

*These yield data have been gathered on a sample survey basis by the Department of Census and Statistics twice annually since 1951. Earlier yield figures, based on extremely crude estimation techniques employed by the village headmen and reported through the Divisional Revenue Offices, were much lower—they averaged around 14 bushels per acre— but are now seen to have been considerably underestimated. The *Maha* season is the major one each year, being harvested during the first quarter of the year, while the *Yala* crop is generally harvested during the third quarter.

Source: Department of Census and Statistics, *Statistical Abstracts.*

TABLE A–34

ANNUAL FISH CATCH, 1950–60*

(Hundredweight)

Year	Catch	Year	Catch
1950........	833,774	1956.......	765,312
1951........	713,064	1957........	732,348
1952........	494,538	1958.......	779,484
1953........	479,515	1959.......	873,819
1954........	557,790	1960.......	959,463
1955........	592,526		

*These figures are thought to be considerably understated. There is, however, no reason to suspect that the degree of understatement has changed markedly through time, so the general pattern of output change that the data present may be taken as essentially accurate.

Source: *A.R. of the Director of Fisheries*, various years.

TABLE A-35

Estimated Distribution of Total Land Area by Use, 1954*

(Thousand Hectares)

Use	Area
Arable farm land†	570
Land under permanent (tree) crops†	953
Land under permanent meadows and pastures‡	185
Forest land§	3,546
Nonagricultural use‖	439
All other uses#	781
Total land area¶	6,474

*As can be seen in the notes below, the material for this table comes from a variety of sources and has been subjected to several kinds of rough estimates —both by the present author and, earlier in the process, by previous sources. The resulting numbers must therefore be regarded as very rough estimates only.

†The *Production Yearbook 1960* of the United Nations Food and Agricultural Organization (FAO) gives 1,523,000 acres as total cultivated land in 1954 (its source is a questionnaire filled out by the Ceylon government). The division of this area between temporary and permanent (tree) crops poses a problem. Acreage figures by crop yield a total of 4,026,000 acres (see *Economic and Social Development of Ceylon (a Survey) 1926–1954*); since this is 1,629,000 hectares it is evident that there is duplication, attributable to interplanting and double cropping. In the absence of any direct knowledge about the relative extent of duplication in tree crop or arable acreages, it was assumed by the author that the extent is the same in both cases. In other words, if one assumed that tree crops account for 62.6 percent of the net area cultivated, as they do of the gross area, the above figures result.

‡The figure is for 1952, from the Food and Agricultural Organization of the United Nations, *Production Yearbook* and, ultimately, a questionnaire filled in by the Ceylon government.

§Source: FAO *World Forest Inventory*, 1958.

‖Includes land under roads, towns, and villages, and small inland bodies of water. Source: *Economic and Social Development of Ceylon (a Survey) 1926–1954.*

#A residual; includes waste land and land available for future agricultural development but not falling into any other category.

¶Excludes major inland bodies of water.

Sources: *Production Yearbook 1960*, FAO; *Production Yearbook 1953*, FAO; Department of Census and Statistics, *Census of Agriculture 1952;* Ministry of Finance, *Economic and Social Development of Ceylon (a Survey) 1926–1954* (1955).

TABLE A-36

CROP DISTRIBUTION OF TOTAL AREA UNDER CULTIVATION, SELECTED YEARS, 1871–1959*

(Absolute Totals in Thousand Hectares)

Crops	1871 Absolute	1871 %	1881 Absolute	1881 %	1891 Absolute	1891 %	1900 Absolute	1900 %	1901 Absolute	1901 %	1911 Absolute	1911 %	1913 Absolute	1913 %	1921 Absolute	1921 %
Tea	—	—	6	1	106	14	164	20	164	19	185	18	195	20	169	15
Rubber	—	—	—	—	—	—	1	—	1	—	75	7	94	9	158	14
Coconuts	202	37	213	34	307	42	342	41	343	41	417	41	384	39	415	37
Paddy	220	40	222	36	228	31	272	32	271	32	261	26	272	27	294	26
Others	131	24	183‡	29	98	13	59	7	63	7	80	8	52	5	87	8
Total	553	100	624	100	739	100	838	100	842	100	1,018	100	997	100	1,123	100

Crops	1929 Absolute	1929 %	1931 Absolute	1931 %	1939 Absolute	1939 %	1946 Absolute	1946 %	1949 Absolute	1949 %	1953 Absolute	1953 %	1954 Absolute	1954 %	1959 Absolute	1959 %
Tea	185	15	205	16	224	17	224	16	226	16	232	16	233	16	235	15
Rubber	216	17	228	18	249	19	267	19	265	19	266	18	266	18	270	18
Coconuts	436	35	435	34	434	33	433	31	433	31	433	30†	433	29	433	28
Paddy	324	26	328	26	344	26	370	26	364	26	390	27	393	26	455	30
Others	76	6	77	6	75	6	123	9	124	9	144	10	146	10	128	8
Total	1,237	100	1,273	100	1,326	100	1,417	100	1,411	100	1,465	100	1,471	100	1,521	100

*The table lists—in thousands of hectares and as a percentage of estimated total area cultivated—the area under each of the main crops of Table A-37 (i.e., all those which account for ten percent or more of the total cultivated extent). The estimates of hectares cultivated in each main crop are those which are stated and described in Table A-37 except that for years where no figure is given in that table interpolations have been made. For 1954 the total area sown in minor crops—and thus in all crops—has been estimated by the Department of Census and Statistics to be 361,476 acres (see Department of Census and Statistics, *Census of Agriculture 1952*, Vol. 4, pp. 30–31). This figure is net—both of the interplanting of two or more crops on the same land and of the replanting of the same land twice or more

(Continued on next page)

TABLE A-36 (CONTINUED)

often during the year with seasonal crops. This is the only year for which such a figure is available; for other years only the gross area sown with each of the minor crops is known. It was thus necessary to make the assumption that the net acreage sown with all minor crops—many of which are seasonal and/or interplanted—bore the same relation to the known gross area in all years that it did in 1954—that is, that the net area was 48 percent of the gross. The "other" totals have thus been calculated in this way, except for the special cases of 1871, 1881 and 1891, which are discussed below in footnote‡. The gross area under minor crops was obtained by summing the individual crop estimates listed in *Economic and Social Development of Ceylon (a Survey) 1926–1954*, the *Statistical Abstracts*, and—for the years prior to 1929—the *Ceylon Blue Books*. Absolute totals have been converted from acres to hectares by dividing by 2.471. Small discrepancies are attributable to rounding.

†The slight decline in the relative importance of coconut cultivation in the 1950's may be more apparent than real, since no estimates of coconut acreage have been made since 1946 and it was simply assumed constant since then.

‡Coffee was near its zenith in 1881. That year it covered 115,000 hectares—23 percent of the estimated total extent cultivated. The corresponding 1871 figures are 100,000 hectares and 18 percent. By 1891 it was down to 23,000 hectares (3 percent) and by 1901 to a bare 2,500 hectares. As a major crop and a nonseasonal one, coffee acres have not been deflated to 48 percent of the official figure as was done with the other crops making up the "other" total. It was felt that here the stated acreage could be regarded as a reasonable approximation of the actual net extent.

Sources: Department of Census and Statistics, *Census of Agriculture 1952* (1956), *Census of Ceylon 1946* (1951–), *Statistical Abstracts*; Department of Statistics and Office Systems, *Ceylon Blue Books*; Ministry of Finance, *Economic and Social Development of Ceylon (a Survey) 1926–1954* (1955).

AREA UNDER CULTIVATION: MAIN CROPS, 1860–1960*
(Thousand Hectares)

Year	Tea†	Rubber‡	Coconuts§	Paddy‖	Coffee#
1860	———	....	101.2	....	81
1861	———	....	....	....	83
1862	———	....	....	....	88
1863	———	....	....	....	84
1864	———	....	....	186.6	87
1865	———	....	....	188.1	93
1866	———	....	....	200.3	97
1867	¶	....	....	182.5	100
1868	....	....	....	186.7	100
1869	....	....	....	170.6	98
1870	0.1	....	....	211.3	100
1871	....	....	....	214.7	108
1872	....	....	....	228.3	113
1873	....	....	....	215.1	117
1874	....	....	....	148.0	121
1875	0.4	....	....	211.9	127
1876	0.7	....	....	....	128
1877	1.1	....	....	....	130
1878	1.9	....	....	247.0	127
1879	2.6	....	....	235.4	116
1880	3.8	....	212.2	236.0	116
1881	5.5	....	212.5	232.3	115
1882	6.1	....	224.9	234.4	100
1883	8.0	....	225.1	245.2	78
1884	23.3	....	233.8	244.6	66
1885	48.9	....	222.7	242.0	52
1886	66.7	....	245.3	244.9	45
1887	80.8	....	254.3	227.4	42.1
1888	93.7	....	260.5	232.4	29.5
1889	83.9	....	265.8	236.9	28.8
1890	95.4	....	263.0	217.1	26.9
1891	105.7	....	307.4	228.0	22.6
1892	109.2	....	310.2	248.2	17.4
1893	123.0	....	314.4	220.9	13.4
1894	134.2	....	345.7	228.6	8.5
1895	130.6	....	349.1	238.4	9.1
1896	149.3	....	352.6	250.7	9.3
1897	163.7	....	355.7	256.0	7.9
1898	172.0	....	349.8	262.2	7.7
1899	168.9	....	362.4	261.2	4.8
1900	164.1	0.7	342.4	272.2	2.9
1901	164.4	....	342.6	271.3	2.5
1902	175.8	1.7	345.3	283.6	2.3
1903	186.4	4.7	356.3	288.1	2.0
1904	169.7	5.3	374.9	287.9	1.6
1905	185.4	14.5	373.7	282.4	1.5
1906	175.6	20.4	399.4	256.8	1.3
1907	177.3	40.8	402.2	278.8	1.0
1908	223.9	53.3	370.5	275.3	0.8
1909	216.8	62.5	419.2	274.5	0.7
1910	235.0	75.5	381.5	275.4	0.6
1911	185.1	74.7	417.0	260.9	0.6
1912	185.2	90.1	418.5	324.2	0.6
1913	195.3	94.2	383.8	271.8	0.4

(Continued on next page)

Year	Tea†	Rubber‡	Coconuts§	Paddy‖	Coffee#
1914	196.9	68.1	394.8	277.3	0.4
1915	193.0	80.4	395.7	317.7	0.4
1916	201.6	89.7	392.0	272.0	0.3
1917	205.9	92.8	366.1	284.2	0.3
1918	204.7	105.0	374.7	274.7	....
1919	202.1	124.9	409.4	287.7	....
1920	.....	.....	.....	.....	....
1921	169.2	157.9	.....	.....	....
1922	.....	.....	.....	.....	....
1923	.....	.....	.....	301.4	....
1924	.....	.....	.....	.....	....
1925	178.1	177.6	.....	336.0	....
1926	178.9	192.3	.....	337.6	....
1927	182.1	198.3	.....	337.7	....
1928	185.1	216.0	.....	339.0	....
1929	184.9	216.1	435.5	323.8	....
1930	.....	.....	.....	.....	....
1931	.....	.....	.....	.....	....
1932	.....	.....	.....	.....	....
1933	225.5	.....	.....	.....	....
1934	226.1	245.2	.....	.....	....
1935	225.7	254.4	.....	.....	....
1936	226.3	244.9	.....	.....	....
1937	225.3	244.5	.....	.....	....
1938	225.2	244.5	.....	344.0	....
1939	224.1	248.9	.....	.....	....
1940	223.4	258.3	.....	.....	....
1941	223.2	258.0	.....	.....	....
1942	222.5	258.0	.....	.....	....
1943	222.4	226.2	.....	.....	....
1944	222.4	266.1	.....	.....	....
1945	222.5	267.0	.....	346.4	....
1946	223.7	266.9	433.4	369.6	....
1947	224.2	266.7	.....	369.6	....
1948	224.6	266.4	.....	364.1	....
1949	225.2	265.1	.....	364.2	....
1950	227.0	265.2	.....	364.8	....
1951	229.6	265.3	.....	367.2	....
1952	231.5	265.8	.....	390.3	....
1953	232.4	266.1	.....	390.3	....
1954	232.9	266.8	.....	393.2	....
1955	229.2	267.5	.....	417.5	....
1956	230.9	266.8	.....	.....	....
1957	230.9	267.4	.....	.....	....
1958	231.8	269.1	.....	.....	....
1959	234.6	270.4	.....	.....	....
1960	235.5	270.4	.....	464.8	....

*"Main crops" are defined as those which account for ten percent or more of the total cultivated area. For several decades now tea, rubber, coconuts, and paddy have each represented more than a tenth of total cultivation and have been the only crops to do so. The only other crop ever in modern times to exceed the ten percent level is coffee, which had a meteoric rise and fall in the nineteenth century. Some statistics of coffee acreage are thus included here for historical interest. (All figures are converted from acres to hectares by dividing by 2.471.)

†The most recent data—back through 1933—are from the tea controller's official registration figures and should be quite accurate. The 1921 and 1925–29 estimates are based on the *Censuses of Production* of 1921, 1924 and 1929 and estimates based on these censuses made by the authors of *Economic and Social Development of Ceylon (a Survey) 1926–1954*. In the 1883–1919 period the estimates have been taken from the *Ceylon Blue Books* and derive from the returns of the village

headmen and the divisional revenue officers (D.R.O.'s). These last figures should be taken as rough estimates only.

‡Back to 1934 the data are from the rubber controller's registration and can be regarded as accurate. The 1921 and 1925–29 estimates are based on the 1921–24, and 1929 Censuses of Production. Earlier figures, back to 1902, are from the *Ceylon Blue Books*. The 1900 estimate is from *Ferguson's Ceylon Handbook and Directory*. Rubber was cultivated in Ceylon all through the late nineteenth century but only in minute quantities.

§The 1946 estimate, based on the 1946 *Census of Ceylon*, is the most recent one made of coconut acreage—it enumerated 920,942 acres but excluded town and village gardens, which were thought to add another 150,000 acres. The 1929 estimate is from that year's *Census of Production*. The 1921 *Census of Production* provided a figure of 820,000 acres (about 331,800 hectares) but this is so obviously a gross underenumeration that it is not included in the tables. All earlier data are from the *Ceylon Blue Books*. In view of the formidable difficulties encountered by efforts to gage coconut acreage in recent years, these precise year-by-year early figures cannot be taken seriously.

‖The data refer to total "asweddumized" area (that is, the amount of land ridged and made ready for paddy cultivation) in existence each year, whether actually seeded or not. Figures on the area seeded are available—by growing season—only since 1951 (see below). The asweddumized area totals have long been reported by the village headmen, the information being channeled through the divisional revenue officers. Since 1954 sown acreage totals have been compiled by a complete enumeration process under the supervision of the Department of Census and Statistics. These totals (listed below) should thus be quite accurate. However, the collecting of this information has interfered with the old reporting system (i.e., of asweddumized area) and no data are available on that basis for the last years in the table. An estimate of asweddumized acreage in 1962 was obtained directly from the Department of Census and Statistics by the author, though. This figure (1,195,146 acres, or some 483,700 hectares) was used, along with the 1955 total, as the basis for an interpolated 1960 estimate and this is the origin of the most recent figure in the column. The 1946 and 1945 totals come respectively from the 1946 *Census of Ceylon* and from *Economic and Social Development of Ceylon (a Survey) 1926–1954*. The 1938 figure is the result of the paddy survey of that year and the 1923 and 1925–29 totals are based on the *Censuses of Production* of 1921, 1924 and 1929. For 1919 and earlier years the source is the annual D.R.O. returns, as listed in the *Ceylon Blue Books*. As with coconuts, these oldest estimates should be regarded as rough approximations only.

The aforementioned sown acreage figures are on a seasonal basis. There are two main growing seasons in Ceylon. The *Maha* ("great") season involves sowing sometime between August and November and harvest in January to March; the *Yala* ("lesser") season covers the other months of the year. Some notion of the extent of replanting twice a year is given by the recent data on separate *Maha* and *Yala* acreages (in each case the *Maha* acreage is listed under the year in which the crop is harvested; i.e., *Maha* 1959–60 is listed under 1960):

PADDY CULTIVATION: AREA SOWN
(Thousand Hectares)

Year	Maha	Yala
1951	257.4	177.1
1952	298.7	171.5
1953	264.9	159.3
1954	311.8	195.6
1955	333.7	211.4
1956	339.5	147.6
1957	315.5	173.3
1958	340.2	219.2
1959	343.2**	195.1**
1960	372.6**	221.6**

**Data from 1959 on are not strictly comparable with earlier years, since they include acreage under the Gal Oya scheme which had previously been excluded. Gal Oya acreage amounted to 5,800 hectares in *Maha* 1958–59 and 2,700 in *Yala* 1959.

#Source: Figures from Ferguson for 1860–86, supplemented by indirect estimates of nonestate acreage: output of estates and peasants was known, as was estate acreage and hence yield per acre; it was assumed that in all years per acre yield on peasant cultivations was 56 percent of the estate yield, as a survey taken in 1856 showed it to be; peasant acres were taken as exports divided by the yield figure thus derived; a three-year moving average was used to smooth out random variations in this measure. From 1887 on, *Ceylon Blue Book* data are used. These figures refer to coffee in its heyday, but the crop continues to be cultivated in very small quantities up to the present time. In 1951 a minimum estimate of area planted is 622 acres (252 hectares). The 1952 agricultural census reported 271,125 coffee trees on 922 estates. If one accepts as a rough estimate 10 feet as the average distance between trees then 435.6 trees can be cultivated on an acre and 622 acres of cultivation are implied. (See V. D. Wickizer, *The World Coffee Economy* [Stanford, California: Food Research Institute, Stanford University, 1943,] p. 38, who says that any distance from 6 to 14 feet can be used.)

¶1867 was the first year of commercial tea cultivation in Ceylon.

Sources: *Ferguson's Ceylon Handbook and Directory*.

Department of Census and Statistics, *Census of Agriculture 1952* (1956), *Census of Ceylon 1946* (1951—), *Statistical Abstracts*; Ministry of Finance, *Economic and Social Development of Ceylon (a Survey) 1926–1954* (1955).

TABLE A-38

Ownership and Tenure of Agricultural Holdings, Selected Years, 1946-59*

A. Tea†

	1951		1953		1954		1959	
	Acres	%	Acres	%	Acres	%	Acres	%
Rupee companies‡........	.....		62,585	10.9	75,153	13.1	123,360	21.3
Ceylonese individuals								
Estates........	.....		220,012	38.3	217,568	37.8	133,010	22.9
Small holdings........							77,640	13.4
Sterling companies§........	.....		291,653	50.8	282,783	49.1	211,337	36.5
Non-Ceylonese individuals....							34,305	5.9
Total........	.....		574,250	100.0	575,504	100.0	579,652	100.0

1946		1949‖		1951		1953		1954		1959		
Acres	%	Acres	%	Acres	%	Acres	%	Acres	%	Number	Acres	%

B. Rubber

	Acres	%	Acres	%	Acres	%	Acres	%	Number	Acres	%
Rupee companies	365,055	58.0	410,258	62.6	416,981	63.4	421,326	63.9	239	88,590	13.3
Ceylonese individuals									142,721	474,974	71.1
Sterling companies	264,350	42.0	245,243	37.4	240,446	36.6	237,883	36.1	133	88,458	13.2
Non-Ceylonese individuals									165	16,156	2.4
Total	629,405	100.0	655,501	100.0	657,427	100.0	659,209	100.0	143,258	668,178	100.0

C. Coconuts—1951#

	Acres	%
Rupee companies	17,680	7.4
Ceylonese individuals	202,365	84.9
Sterling companies	6,614	2.8
Non-Ceylonese individuals	11,765	4.9
Total	238,424	100.0

D. Paddy

	Holdings—1946¶				—Parcels 1955§§—
	Number of Holdings	%	Acres	%	Percent of All Parcels
Owner cultivated	469,701	60.8	495,525	55.1	55.0
Share cropped**	199,934	25.9	212,151	23.6	28.7
Leased	28,069	3.6	81,918	9.1	13.7
Thatumaru††	52,190	6.8	58,572	6.5	2.6
Others‡‡	22,014	2.9	51,805	5.8	
Total	771,908	100.0	899,971	100.0	100.0

TABLE A–38 (CONTINUED)

	Acres	%
E. Smallholdings—1951‖‖‖		
Owner cultivated		
Fully owned.................................	131,483	58.2
Jointly owned..............................	40,491	17.9
Leased......................................	20,213	9.0
Share cropped.............................	12,391	5.5
Other.......................................	21,198	9.4
Total.................................	225,776	100.0

*Five types of agricultural holdings are usually distinguished in Ceylon: (1) Estate: a holding of 20 acres or more, worked with hired labor; (2) Asweddumized paddy land: mud land prepared for the cultivation of paddy; (3) Chena: land covered with secondary forest which is slashed and burned for the temporary cultivation of food grains; (4) Town and village garden: a holding of one acre or less—usually forming the compound of a dwelling place—with cultivation of any kind; (5) Smallholding: any other holding between 1 and 20 acres on which there exists any kind of cultivation. This table assembles the available fragments of information on land ownership and tenure on each type of land. No information on the tenure of chena cultivation or town and village gardens is available.

†Figures for tea and rubber refer to the end of the year except for tea data prior to 1959, which are for March 31 of the following year. Source: *Administration Reports of tea and rubber controllers.*

‡I.e., companies incorporated in Ceylon.

§I.e., companies incorporated in the United Kingdom.

‖For 1949 only the percentages of foreign and Ceylonese ownership are stated in the *Administration Report;* the absolute totals have been inferred.

#Source: Department of Census and Statistics, *Census of Agriculture 1952*, Part 3. It is estimated that 103,060 acres of estate cultivation, 579,458 acres in smallholdings, and some 150,000 in town and village gardens failed to be enumerated in the census. Nothing is known about the ownership of the omitted estate acreage but the smallholdings and town and village garden cultivation is almost entirely—perhaps completely—owned by Ceylonese individuals. The foreign owned share of total acreage may thus have been only 2 percent or so, rather than 7.7 percent suggested by the census.

¶Source: Department of Census and Statistics, *Census of Ceylon 1946*, Vol. 1, Part 2 (1951–). The data refer to paddy holdings, i.e., to total acreage under a single ownership, whether contiguous or not. Excludes paddy growing on estates.

**Locally known as "ande" tenure.

††A system by which co-owners of a plot of land rotate the cultivation of it and the enjoyment of its fruits.

‡‡Includes usufructuary mortgages (i.e., creditors who have obtained possession of land in lieu of debt repayment), hired cultivators, those who have been allotted Crown land under the Land Development Ordinance, etc.

§§The data are from a sample survey taken by the Department of Census and Statistics and are published in *A Report on Paddy Statistics* (1956). They refer to the *Maha* 1954–55 and *Yala* 1955 seasons and, by contrast to the 1946 holdings statistics, to paddy *parcels*, individual contiguous plots of land under individual or co-operative cultivation.

‖‖‖Source: Department of Census and Statistics, *Census of Agriculture 1952*, Vol. 4 (1956). The data refer to the 90,524 smallholdings—comprising 225,776 acres—for which census returns were filed. Judging from 1946 census totals, no more than a fourth of all smallholdings are represented and of course the sample is not a random one. The data should thus be regarded as suggestive only.

Sources: A.R. *of the Tea Controller; A.R. of the Rubber Controller;* Department of Census and Statistics, *Census of Ceylon, 1946*, Vol. 1, Part 2 (1951–), *Census of Agriculture 1952*, Vol. 4 (1956), *A Report of Paddy Statistics*, Monograph No. 9 (1956).

TABLE A-39

Size Distribution of Agricultural Holdings, Selected Years, 1935–59*

A. Tea†

	1935			1939			1946			1949		
	Number	Acres	%	Number	Acres	%	Number	Acres	%	Number	Acres	%
Smallholdings (−10 acres)	68,982	65,938	11.8	76,826	61,322	11.1	77,668	63,158	11.4	78,339	63,796	11.5
Estates: 10–100 acres‡												
Estates: 100–500 acres	2,369	491,801	88.2	2,348	492,523	88.9	2,367	489,695	88.6	2,402	491,780	88.5
Estates: 500– acres												
Total	71,351	557,739	100.0	79,174	553,845	100.0	80,035	552,853	100.0	80,471	555,576	100.0

A. Tea†

	1951			1953			1954			1959		
	Number	Acres	%	Number	Acres	%	Number	Acres	%	Number	Acres	%
Smallholdings (−10 acres)	84,363	67,414	11.9	87,715	69,781	12.2	87,628	70,628	12.2	92,083	77,640	13.4
Estates: 10–100 acres‡	1,540	43,128	7.6	1,599	44,178	7.7	1,700	46,062	8.0	1,959	52,277	9.0
Estates: 100–500 acres	593	168,127	29.6	594	169,814	29.6	578	165,208	28.7	620	160,347	27.7
Estates: 500– acres	346	288,619	50.9	347	290,477	50.6	346	293,863	51.1	342	289,388	49.9
Total	86,842	567,288	100.0	90,255	574,250	100.0	90,252	575,504	100.0	95,004	579,652	100.0

B. Rubber

	1936			1939			1946			1949		
	Number	Acres	%	Number	Acres	%	Number	Acres	%	Number	Acres	%
Smallholdings (−10 acres)	……	128,984	21.3	99,095	131,566	21.8	112,670	146,767	23.1	112,951	149,800	23.8
Estates: 10–100 acres‡				4,930	123,531	20.4	5,369	133,732	21.1	5,181	131,942	21.0
Estates: 100–500 acres	……	476,168	78.7	876	349,100	57.8	882	354,752	55.8	658	150,641	23.9
Estates: 500– acres										215	197,022	31.3
Total	……	605,152	100.0	104,901	604,197	100.0	118,921	635,251	100.0	119,005	629,405	100.0

(Continued on next page)

TABLE A-39 (CONTINUED)

B. Rubber

	1951			1953			1954			1959		
	Number	Acres	%	Number	Acres	%	Number	Acres	%	Number	Acres	%
Smallholdings (−10 acres)	124,487	171,542	26.2	127,045	175,843	26.7	128,740	178,609	27.1	136,421	191,068	28.6
Estates: 10–100 acres‡	5,554	140,715	21.5	5,619	142,708	21.7	5,679	144,159	21.9	5,983	157,094	23.5
Estates: 100–500 acres	651	148,052	22.6	636	145,910	22.2	657	157,849	23.9	667	148,451	22.2
Estates: 500– acres	216	195,192	29.8	216	192,966	29.4	195	178,592	27.1	187	171,565	25.7
Total	130,908	655,501	100.0	133,516	657,427	100.0	135,271	659,209	100.0	143,258	668,178	100.0

C. Coconut—1951§

	Number	Acres	%
Town and village gardens	......	150,000	14.0
Smallholdings	......	579,458	54.1
Estates: −10 acres‖	413	1,991	0.2
Estates: 10–100 acres	1,993	53,773	5.0
Estates: 100–500 acres	1,241	150,576	14.1
Estates: 500– acres	43	32,084	3.0
Size unknown	......	103,060	9.6
Total	......	1,070,942	100.0

TABLE A-39 (CONTINUED)

D. Paddy

Size (Acres)	Number	Holdings, 1946# %	Acres	%	Size (Acres)	Parcels, Maha 1953–54¶ Number	%	Acres
0 – ½	242,690	31.4	58,005	6.4	0 – ½	339,914	36.2	....
½–1	253,823	32.9	147,376	16.4	½–1½	421,504	44.9	....
1–2	162,120	21.0	193,794	21.5	1½–2½	87,431	9.3	....
2–5	85,310	11.1	231,726	25.7	2½–3½	36,268	3.9	....
5–10	19,705	2.6	122,073	13.6	3½–5	24,160	2.6	....
10–	8,260	1.1	146,996	16.3	5–10	22,601	2.4	....
					10–	7,538	0.8	....
Total	771,908	100.0	899,970	100.0	Total	939,416	100.0	981,997

E. Smallholdings—1951**

Size (acres)	Number	%	Acres	%
0 – ½	18,330	20.2	3,890	1.7
½–1	16,790	18.5	9,855	4.4
1–2½	29,370	32.4	43,691	19.4
2½–5	15,072	16.6	50,485	22.4
5–10	7,574	8.4	49,682	22.0
10–20	2,646	2.9	34,797	15.4
20–	742	0.8	33,376	14.8
Total	90,524	100.0	225,776	100.0

(Continued on next page)

TABLE A-39 (CONTINUED)

*The *Census of Ceylon 1946* estimated the total cultivated and cultivable land on all agricultural holdings to be divided among the five commonly distinguished types of holdings—see Table A-33, footnote *, for their definitions—as follows:

AGRICULTURAL HOLDINGS BY TYPE, 1946

Type of Holding	Number	Acres Cultivated	Acres Suitable but not Cultivated	Total Acres excluding Wasteland	Acreage Size of Holding (Acres)
Estates..............................	10,812	1,343,697	290,372	1,634,069	151.1
Paddy land..........................	771,908	607,510	292,461	899,971	1.2
Chena...............................	91,996	46,322	175,073	221,395	2.4
Town and village gardens...........	858,892	309,381	91,832	401,213	0.5
Smallholdings.......................	394,782	903,191	207,559	1,110,750	2.8
Total...........................	2,128,390	3,210,101	1,057,297	4,267,398	2.0

These data give some idea of the breakdown of all agricultural land into the five types of holding and also of the average size of each type. The further step of providing size distributions of holdings for each type can be taken only on a selective basis and this is done in the body of the table. No such information is available for chena or town and village gardens.

†Figures are for December 21, except for tea data before 1959 which refer to March 31 of the following year. Source: *Administration Reports of the tea and rubber controllers*. Earliest data given are for first year with reliable statistics.

‡In every case a span of acres includes holdings equal to its lower and excludes its upper limit (i.e., 10–100 acres means from 10 to under 100).

§For the estates for which size is given in the table the source is Department of Census and Statistics, *Census of Agriculture 1952* (1956). If total estate acreage is assumed to have remained constant since the 1946 census, the authors of Vol. 4 of the 1952 census observe (p. 6), then the later census elicited only a 69.82 percent response in terms of estate acreage. The assumption is a fairly reasonable one since coconut acreage seems to have been nearly constant for some decades (see Table A-37)—though no one knows what happened to it in the 1950's; hence the acreage figure for "estates: size unknown." If one assumes further that all coconut acreage was the same in 1951 as in 1946 then figures can be filled in for cultivation on smallholdings and in town and village gardens. Thus the figure used here for smallholders is acreage enumerated in 1946; for gardens the estimate made at that time is used.

‖Refers to coconut plots of less than 10 acres on estates of 20 acres or more.

#Source: Department of Census and Statistics, *Census of Ceylon 1946*, Vol. 1, Part 2 (1951–). See footnote ¶, Table A–38.

¶The data are from the total enumeration made by the Department of Census and Statistics—see Table A–37, footnote ‖—and are published in *A Report on Paddy Statistics*. See footnote §§, Table A–38.

**The data—from the *Census of Agriculture 1952*—are incomplete. See footnote ‖‖, Table A–38.

††The data.—from the *Census of Agriculture 1952*—are incomplete. See footnote ‖‖, Table A–38.

‖‖The data.—from the *Census of Agriculture 1952*—are incomplete. See footnote ‖‖, Table A–38.

§§The data—from the *Census of Agriculture 1952*—are incomplete. See footnote ‖‖, Table A–38.

Sources: *A.R. of the Tea Controller*; *A.R. of the Rubber Controller*; Department of Census and Statistics, *Census of Agriculture 1952*, Vol. 4 (1956); *Census of Ceylon 1946*, Vol. 1, Part 2 (1951–), *A Report on Paddy Statistics* (1956).

TABLE A–40

(Thousands)

Year	Buffaloes	Neat Cattle	Goats	Sheep	Swine	Horses
1871........	.....	996.7	88.9	67.7	.....	6.7
1881........	280.9	1,056.0	79.6	60.6	.....	4.3
1891........	392.5	1,064.8	134.2	87.4	40.9	4.7
1900........	493.2	1,397.8	158.0	89.9	91.5	4.8
1901........	520.6	1,476.7	151.1	91.3	88.0	4.0
1911........	461.7	1,465.4	195.2	90.4	86.5	4.8
1913........	458.7	1,484.3	203.4	90.0	85.6	5.0
1921........	418.6	1,386.0	150.0	57.2	46.1	2.0
1929........	550.0	1,100.0	184.0	57.0	45.0	2.0
1931........	528.0	1,052.0	194.0	65.0	41.0	1.1
1939........	545.6	1,119.7	246.7	55.9	35.7	1.3
1946........	522.0	1,079.5	306.4	63.8	74.1	1.3
1949........	656.1	1,248.7	400.7	57.3	103.8	...
1953........	655.6	1,228.7	499.0	103.9	74.4	2.5
1954........	706.6	1,277.3	563.9	95.0	83.3	...
1959........	780.8	1,486.1	487.4	49.3	76.7	...

*The figures are all based on annual returns of the district revenue officers with the sole exception that the 1921 data are from the *Census of Production* of that year. Exactly how the district revenue officers calculate the livestock population of their districts is not specified in the sources, but a fairly high degree of inaccuracy must be assumed. Data from the 1946 census of agriculture do not jibe well with the D.R.O.'s estimates for the year (they are 410,000 buffaloes, 1,166,900 cattle, 63,300 sheep, and 296,200 goats); there is no way of telling which comes nearer to the truth. The *Census of Agriculture 1952* contains only a partial livestock enumeration and is thus no help in making an islandwide assessment.

Sources: Department of Census and Statistics, *Statistical Abstract*, various years; Department of Statistics and Office Systems, *Ceylon Blue Book*, various years.

TABLE A–41

Indexes of Industrial Production, 1952–61*

	1954	1955	1956	1957	1958	1959
A. 1952 Gross Value—Weighted†						
(1952 = 100)						
Mining and quarrying.. ⎫ Manufacturing........ ⎭	93.6	105.4	102.2	99.5	93.4	119.3
Food..............	102.3	110.3	115.3	112.5	115.3	112.7
Beverages..........	89.5	89.7	83.7	82.1	90.5	80.2
Tobacco............	104.0	99.6	106.1	116.4	114.9	139.4
Wood, cork, etc.....	92.3	83.6	80.8	86.4	85.4	224.4
Leather............	107.6	101.4	87.4	157.8	137.3	145.0
Paper..............	.....	.....	.....	100.0	83.2	303.5
Chemicals..........	81.8	105.6	93.8	75.0	68.6	79.9
Mineral products....	161.9	161.2	159.3	124.7	170.8	187.9
Metal products.....	73.1	213.9	1,292.8	1,372.8	1,054.4	1,166.6
Textiles............	137.5	183.8	229.2	347.1	404.7	449.8
Apparel (incl. foot-wear)............	362.2	844.8	1,053.7	1,405.7	2,367.3	2,635.0
Rubber products....	125.8	156.4	223.6	307.1	381.2	486.3
Miscellaneous manu-facturing........	136.3	136.3	138.6	191.4	153.8	157.4
Electricity and gas....	124.1	137.9	147.4	160.5	175.4	193.3
Industrial output (ex-cluding construction).	96.6	108.6	106.7	105.5	101.5	126.6
Construction‡........	89.6	111.6	116.3	121.0	129.0	139.9
Industrial output......	92.4	110.3	112.9	115.8	119.4	135.1

(Continued on next page)

TABLE A–41 (CONTINUED)

	1957	1958	1959	1960	1961
B. 1952–56 Value Added—Weighted§ (1952–56 = 100)					
Mining and quarrying......	116.0	53.3	73.0	101.1	87.1
Manufacturing.............	107.4	113.8	124.5	133.0	139.0
Food................. Beverages.............	107.4	115.2	115.0	123.6	127.9
Tobacco.................	115.7	126.9	231.7	200.5	204.2
Textiles.................	146.2	173.8	214.1	192.2	198.3
Apparel (incl. footwear)...	251.0	421.9	602.4	602.2	648.1
Wood, cork, etc..........	124.4	98.2	113.2	491.9	113.8
Furniture...............	110.2	113.5	116.9	120.4	124.1
Paper..................	266.0	236.0	476.2	493.8	495.7
Printing................	112.1	117.7	121.3	124.9	128.7
Leather................	150.7	126.6	167.8	180.2	211.0
Rubber................	104.4	96.1	99.6	107.1	109.2
Chemicals..............	89.4	84.0	105.3	98.8	140.0
Mineral products........	104.4	146.6	163.1	156.8	155.6
Metal products.........	308.1	255.5	367.1	1,267.0	2,014.1
Miscellaneous...........	123.2	122.5	131.0	205.6	131.2
Electricity and gas........	128.0	140.7	157.5	174.4	185.0
Industrial output (excluding construction)............	108.7	114.2	125.1	135.0	141.1
Construction‡.............	118.2	126.1	136.8	134.0	.....
Industrial output..........	115.0	122.0	132.5	134.4	.....

*Because of the extreme newness of many kinds of industrial activity in Ceylon and the paucity of data available, the construction of indexes of physical output poses a number of theoretical and practical problems. The two series presented here are, except where otherwise specified, the product of work done by the Statistics Section, Development Division, Department of Industries. Given the considerable shortcomings of the basic data with which they had to work, the Statistics Section produced series which give a reasonably accurate picture of the rate of industrial progress—within the particular definitional framework specified in each of the two cases. It should be pointed out, though, that there is probably some upward bias present in both indexes, for several reasons: (1) both indexes are based on current weights, thus giving heavier weighting to expanding industries; (2) in some cases as new data were uncovered by the Statistics Section they were added in at the current year, even though no corresponding entries had been made for earlier years; and (3) construction (see footnote ‡, below) has been added in on a value rather than a volume basis, so any price increases are reflected here and thus inflate the index.

†Each unit within an industry and each industry within a wider industrial group is here weighted by the gross value of its output. Insofar as there are interfirm and interindustry buyer-seller relationships this procedure exaggerates the growth of the broader indexes (e.g., all manufacturing). Such relationships are rare in the Ceylon economy, however.

‡In the absence of any even reasonably credible measure of physical volume of construction, the necessity to provide some sort of estimate here led the author to convert the value of income originating in the sector (see Table A–8) into an index and use it in this connection. The result is, of course, to some extent inaccurate, generally overstated; since the upward trend of prices has been very slow in Ceylon over the period concerned, the degree of bias is really quite limited.

§To avoid the bias mentioned in footnote †, above, the Statistics Section shifted in 1960 from a gross value to a value-added weighting system. The base period was also altered, from 1952 to 1952–56.

Sources: Department of Census and Statistics, *Statistical Abstract*, 1960 and 1961; Statistics Section, Development Division, Department of Industries (unpublished data).

TABLE A–42

COAL AND OIL CONSUMPTION, SELECTED YEARS, 1871–1959*

Year	Coal (000 Metric Tons)†	———Oil Products (000 Imperial Gallons)———				
		Motor Fuel	Crude Petroleum	Kerosene	Lubricating Oil	Total
1871.......	86‡	———	......	.....§	....§	......
1881.......	105‡	———	......	.....§	....§	......
1891.......	338‡	———	......	.....§	....§	......
1900.......	599	———	897	2,422	92	3,411
1901.......	638	———	2,186	2,792	76	5,054
1911.......	675	206	3,527	4,427	165	8,325
1913.......	757	383	5,188	4,693	249	10,513
1921.......	652	1,382	17,489	4,307	414	23,592
1929.......	826	10,502	53,365	8,628	913	73,408
1931.......	502	8,845	52,006	7,920	716	69,487
1939.......	479	12,909	91,991	8,397	809	114,106
1946.......	349	17,080	96,650	9,850	1,090	124,670
1949.......	316	25,927	159,571	15,808	1,964	203,270
1953.......	389	40,631	151,833	16,682	1,241	210,387
1954.......	289	38,652	130,033	22,150	1,587	192,422
1959.......	176	48,908	156,799	37,135	3,264	246,106

*Total apparent consumption, i.e., total domestic supply—in this case entirely imports—each year with no allowance made for changes in inventories. In evaluating these figures in terms of energy use in the economy of Ceylon, it should be recalled that Colombo has long been an important fueling port for ocean traffic and much of the coal and crude petroleum imported over the years has gone for this purpose.

†Figures converted from long tons by multiplying by 1.01605.

‡Includes coke.

§Some information on imports is given in the customs returns but it is expressed in nonstandard units (e.g., so many "cases" of kerosene).

Sources: *Ceylon Customs Returns* (December), various years; Department of Commerce, *Thirty Years Trade Statistics of Ceylon (1925–1954)*, Pt. 1; Department of Statistics and Office Systems, *Ceylon Blue Books*, various years.

TABLE A-43

ELECTRIC POWER CONSUMPTION, SELECTED YEARS, 1939–59*

(Million Kilowatt-Hours)

Year	Government Generation	Private Generation	Total
1939............	31	107	138
1946............	53	130	183
1949............	70	141	211
1950............	81	158	239
1953............	144	169	313
1954............	162	174	336
1959............	270	194	464

*Figures for government generation consist of the total generation reported by the Department of Electrical Undertakings. To these official figures has been added an estimate of the substantial amounts of power generated by private enterprises, consisting mainly of tea and rubber estates, but also of coconut and rice mills, a few private industrial operations, and, since 1960, public corporations. The estimate for 1950 was made by the World Bank team and appears in their report; it was extended by analogy to other years by the author by deflating the estimates for each sector (e.g., tea factories) by an output index for the sector.

Sources: Department of Census and Statistics, *Statistical Abstract* 1960; International Bank for Reconstruction and Development, *The Economic Development of Ceylon* (Baltimore, Maryland, Johns Hopkins Press, 1953), pp. 460–62; Ceylon Cement Corporation (formerly Kankesanturai Cement Corporation), *Annual Reports;* Eastern Paper Mills Corporation, *Annual Reports;* Kantalai Sugar Corporation, *Annual Reports.*

TABLE A–44

IRON AND STEEL CONSUMPTION, SELECTED YEARS, 1871–1959*

(Thousand Metric Tons)

Year	Pig Iron	Imports Other†	Total	Domestic Production‡	Total Consumption
1871	§	2	2	—	2
1881	§	1	1	—	1
1891	§	4	4	—	4
1900	§	7	7	—	7
1901	§	7	7	—	7
1911	§	21	21	—	21
1913	1	31	32	—	32
1921	§	7	7	—	7
1929	1	83	84	—	84
1931	§	36	36	—	36
1939	1	45	46	—	46
1946	1	28	29	1	30
1949	1	49	50	1	51
1953	§	63	63	—	63
1954	1	59	60	—	60
1959	1	72	73	—	73

*Total apparent consumption—i.e., total domestic supply with no allowance made for changes in inventories—of pig iron, crude steel, and basic iron and steel forms, such as angles, beams, plates, tubes, wire, etc. No attempt has been made to convert consumption figures for the various forms to crude iron or steel equivalents or to gage the iron and steel content of imported ferrous metalware.

†Includes minute quantities of crude steel.

‡The war-inspired government rolling mill, which used scrap as its raw material, functioned from 1943 through 1950.

§Less than 5,000 metric tons.

Sources: *Ceylon Customs Returns* (December), various years; Department of Commerce, *Thirty Years Trade Statistics of Ceylon (1925–1954)*, Pt. I.; Department of Statistics and Office Systems, *Ceylon Blue Book*, various years.

TABLE A-45

CONSUMPTION OF THE MAIN BUILDING MATERIALS, SELECTED YEARS, 1871–1959*

Year	Cement (Hydraulic) (000 Metric Tons)			Tiles‡ (000,000)			Lumber (Sawn)‖ Thousand Cubic Metres		
	Production	Imports	Consumption	Production	Imports	Consumption	Production	Imports	Consumption
1871.........	—	†	†	....	0.4§	....	..	..	..
1881.........	—	1	1	....	0.6§	....	..	..	..
1891.........	—	3	3	....	0.5§	....	..	..	..
1900.........	—	6	6	....	2.7§	....	..	..	..
1901.........	—	5	5	....	2.5§	....	..	..	..
1911.........	—	18	18	....	4.2§	....	..	..	..
1913.........	—	22	22	....	5.6§	....	..	..	..
1921.........	—	10	10	....	1.8	....	..	11	..
1929.........	—	82	82	....	10.9	....	..	32	..
1931.........	—	48	48	....	4.6	....	..	1	..
1939.........	—	70	70	....	5.8	....	1	4	5
1946.........	—	73	73	....	7.0	....	1	10	11
1949.........	—	139	139	6.0	16.2	22.2	18	2	20
1953.........	66	131	197	10.9	24.7	35.6	15	1	16
1954.........	84	114	198	23.9	17.2	41.1	11	1	12
1959.........	89	199	288	29.2	21.8	51.0	13	3	16

*Apparent consumption defined as production plus imports minus exports (exports in all cases being nil). Cement and tiles (mainly roofing tiles) are probably the best indications of building activity—of the more substantial sort. Village homes (for all but the most substantial rural citizens) are entirely of local materials and are not reflected in this table.

†Less than half the unit.

‡Production figures are understated because of the incompleteness of returns from the many small producers.

§Includes bricks.

‖Production figures are collected by the Forest Department—in cubic feet—and should be relatively accurate. Imports are sometimes stated in square feet and sometimes in tons and arbitrary assumptions were used to convert these units to cubic feet. It was assumed that imported lumber was on the average one inch thick and that one ton of wood equals 1,057 square feet (as was the case with part of the 1959 imports, which are stated in both units). Prior to 1921 imports of sawn lumber were not distinguished in the customs returns from other types of "worked timber." Cubic feet have been converted to cubic metres by multiplying by 0.028317. Included under "lumber (sawn)" is lumber intended primarily for building purposes; railroad ties, barrel staves, etc., are excluded, as is unworked timber.

Sources: *Ceylon Customs Returns* (December), various years; Department of Census and Statistics, *Statistical Abstract*, various years; Department of Statistics and Office Systems, *Ceylon Blue Books*, various years.

TABLE A-46
FREIGHT TRAFFIC: RAIL AND OCEAN, SELECTED YEARS, 1871–1959*

Year	Rail† Metric Tons Carried	Rail† Thousand Metric Ton Kilometer	Ocean Imports Colombo Coal and Petroleum§	Ocean Imports Colombo Total	Ocean Imports Other Ports	Ocean Imports Total	Ocean Exports Colombo	Ocean Exports Other Ports	Ocean Exports Total	Thousand Metric Tons Entered and Cleared, All Ports Entered	Thousand Metric Tons Entered and Cleared, All Ports Cleared
1871	151,427	13,276	....	....	....	....	....	....	....	841	838
1881	322,590	31,663	....	....	....	....	....	....	....	1,576	1,543
1891	286,020	29,923	....	....	....	....	....	....	....	2,904	2,576
1900	396,283	44,471	....	....	....	....	....	....	....	4,319	4,306
1901	373,098	42,187	....	....	....	....	....	....	....	4,631	4,543
1911	708,753	86,140	....	....	....	....	....	....	....	9,716	9,697
1913	845,817	102,995	777	1,851	....	....	517	....	....	10,266	10,194
1921	893,679	116,181	808	1,538	....	....	556	....	....	9,280	9,333
1929	1,404,770	192,143	1,009	2,280	....	....	616	....	....	14,377	14,234
1931	1,036,898	143,577	704	1,708	....	....	726	....	....	13,471	13,035
1939	916,366	133,096	955	2,113	....	....	625	....	....	13,998	13,914
1946	1,391,206	210,304	862	2,278	....	....	592	....	....	5,900	5,920
1949	1,288,305	198,024	1,167	2,700	230	2,930	694	73	767	12,554	12,820
1953	1,622,159	254,797	1,104	2,956	80	3,036	879	150	1,029	14,717	13,643
1954	1,672,850	261,008	1,070	2,878	226	3,104	961	121	1,082	17,046	14,956
1959	1,599,302	300,752	1,235	3,353	....	....	632	....	....	12,030	12,148

*These data outline adequately the long-term growth of two types of freight traffic. No data exist on traffic carried by road or by inland or coastal waterways.

†Tons carried information for the Ceylon Government Railways is available for all years. Ton-miles data were published only for the last three years and for 1891. These showed the average haul rising from 65 miles in 1891 to about 100 miles in the 1950's; for other years ton-miles were estimated by interpolating an average average haul (i.e., by assuming that the average haul increased at a constant rate over the period). For 1871 to 1881, average haul figures were extrapolated. Long length of haul (i.e., by assuming that the average haul increased at a constant rate over the period). For 1871 to 1881, average haul figures were extrapolated. Long tons were converted to metric tons by multiplying by 1.01605 and ton-miles to metric ton-kilometers by multiplying by 1.46.

‡This, of course, measures goods actually loaded and unloaded in Ceylon, as opposed to the "entered and cleared" figures, which include transit traffic.

§By and large, this measures imports for the purpose of servicing shipping. However, "petroleum" includes kerosene and gasoline intended primarily for internal use.

Sources: Ceylon Government Railway, *Administration Report*, various years; *Administration Report on the Customs and Shipping; Administration Report of the Principal Collector of Customs* (title varies), various years.

TABLE A–47

SIZE OF INDUSTRIAL ESTABLISHMENT, 1952*

	Average Number Employed	
Industry	Operatives	All Employees
Estate agriculture†	. . .	112
Mining and quarrying		
Plumbago	187	218
Salt	31	36
Manufacturing		
Milk products	6	9
Grain milling	11	14
Confectionery and tanning	37	42
Distilling and brewing	41	52
Bottled soft drinks	19	22
Tobacco	580	640
Textiles and thread	364	381
Coir fibre and coir goods	41	44
Footwear (except rubber)	58	63
Plywood and timber sawing	25	28
Printing and publishing	37	47
Leather and leather goods (excluding footwear)	35	39
Rubber goods	85	100
Fertilizers	40	55
Coconut oil milling	93	103
Soap, glycerine, and perfumes	35	43
Matches	172	180
Brick and tiles	50	53
Ceramics, glass and cement	309	338
Engineering	265	294
Jewelry and plastics	31	35
Electricity, gas, water and sanitary		
Electricity	32	38
Gas	92	95

*These data, all from the *Census of Industry 1952* (with one exception; see below), are presented here even though they are almost impossible to evaluate. Of one thing one can be sure: the census limited itself to establishments which met three conditions: (1) they had not less than five paid employees; (2) they had invested capital of not less than Rs. 3,000; and (3) they used mechanical power in at least part of their production process. Thus the actual average size of all establishments in industries where small-scale production is common—like tobacco (native tobacco products), textiles, coconut milling, brick and tile, etc.— is obviously much smaller than the table indicates. A source of error which cannot be adjusted for, though, is the failure of the census to enumerate all units within its chosen field of purview. No one can even guess at the size of establishments which failed to file census returns and this means that the figures above contain errors which are unassessable either as to direction or amount.

†From the *Census of Agriculture 1952*. An estate here is defined as a holding of 20 acres or more, other than paddy and chena land.

Source: Department of Census and Statistics, *Census of Industry 1952*, (1954).

TABLE A–48

IMPORT VOLUME INDEXES, 1938–61*

(1953 = 100)

Year	Food and Drink	Textiles	Others	Total	Inter- mediate Goods	Invest- ment Goods	All Imports
			—Consumer Goods—				
		A. Central Bank Import Volume Indexes					
1938......	69	55	34	60	71	57	61
1948......	84	64	60	77	73	63	74
1949......	85	82	67	81	88	72	81
1950......	94	90	66	88	90	82	88
1951......	95	86	107	96	107	101	99
1952......	95	99	100	96	102	104	99
1953......	100	100	100	100	100	100	100
1954......	95	94	75	91	105	85	93
1955......	95	103	109	99	110	124	104
1956......	108	119	125	112	106	154	116
1957......	109	97	134	111	152	151	124
1958......	116	128	149	123	116	149	125
1959......	129	114	193	138	141	196	145
1960......	121	110	221	137	141	175	141
1961......	112	96	73	102	137	152	114

Year	All Imports	Year	All Imports	Year	All Imports
		B. Census and Statistics Volume Index			
1938......	64	1946......	55	1954......	99
1939......	66	1947......	68	1955......	97
1940......	65	1948......	69	1956......	106
1941......	60	1949......	76	1957......	112
1942......	40	1950......	84	1958......	113
1943......	44	1951......	94	1959......	125
1944......	46	1952......	96	1960......	118
1945......	51	1953......	100	1961......	110

*The two official import volume indexes are presented here for all the years for which they have been calculated by the bodies responsible for them, the Central Bank Research Department and the Department of Census and Statistics respectively. In both cases the indexes are of the Laspeyres type, the Central Bank Index having 1954–58 value weights and the Census and Statistics Index 1948 value weights. In choosing between the two indexes, the former is probably preferable for most analytical purposes because of its more recent base, its greater inclusiveness (some 75–80 percent of imports by value in the base period) and its breakdown. Much of the difference which can be noted between the figures generated by the two indexes for given years is no reflection on the Census and Statistics Index, though; it simply reflects the great influence of the choice of a base period on this kind of index. No single index can give an entirely adequate expression of changes in the volume of imports when the structure of import trade has undergone considerable changes over the period of study. Both indexes have been converted to a 1953 = 100 base by simple division.

Source: Central Bank of Ceylon, *Annual Report of the Monetary Board to the Minister of Finance* (1961).

TABLE A–49

EXPORT VOLUME INDEXES, 1938–61*

(1953 = 100)

Year	Tea	Rubber	3 Main Coconut Products	18 Minor Products	All Exports
A. Central Bank Export Volume Indexes					
1938.............	72	52	91	109	72
1948.............	89	95	72	80	86
1949.............	90	90	71	93	86
1950.............	90	122	81	102	95
1951.............	91	106	98	108	96
1952.............	94	97	113	93	98
1953.............	100	100	100	100	100
1954.............	109	97	93	110	103
1955.............	109	103	119	110	109
1956.............	105	90	112	104	102
1957.............	111	96	78	100	100
1958.............	123	95	73	94	106
1959.............	115	94	93	98	104
1960.............	123	108	80	105	110
1961.............	128	90	112	102	114

Year	All Exports	Year	All Exports	Year	All Exports
B. Census and Statistics Export Volume Index					
1938......	73	1946......	78	1954......	103
1939......	72	1947......	74	1955......	109
1940......	73	1948......	84	1956......	104
1941......	71	1949......	84	1957......	99
1942......	80	1950......	92	1958......	107
1943......	81	1951......	93	1959......	105
1944......	78	1952......	98	1960......	110
1945......	70	1953......	100	1961......	115

*As in Table A–48, these are the two official indexes for all the years for which they have been calculated. Again, they are Laspeyres indexes with 1954–58 and 1948 value weights respectively. The comparable figures differ much less between the two indexes than was the case with the import indexes because the coverage of the two export indexes is much more similar—both come within two or three percentage points of total coverage by base-period value—and because the structure of export trade was changed much less than the structure of import trade, making the choice of a base period much less crucial. Both indexes have been converted to a 1953 = 100 basis by simple division.

Source: Central Bank of Ceylon, *Annual Report to the Monetary Board to the Minister of Finance* (1961).

TABLE A–50

IMPORT PRICE INDEXES, 1938–61*

(1953 = 100)

Year	Food and Drink	—Consumer Goods— Textiles	Other	Total	Intermediate Goods	Investment Goods	All Imports
			A. Central Bank Import Price Indexes				
1938......	19	26	28	22	35	31	25
1948......	75	130	70	57	84	63	61
1949......	74	103	63	77	74	63	75
1950......	76	110	69	80	81	70	79
1951......	85	127	91	103	98	86	101
1952......	98	103	95	99	107	93	100
1953......	100	100	100	100	100	100	100
1954......	89	92	99	92	94	95	93
1955......	81	88	106	87	98	95	89
1956......	82	89	106	87	97	94	89
1957......	85	97	102	91	108	101	95
1958......	76	87	106	83	99	98	88
1959......	78	90	104	84	94	109	89
1960......	77	94	104	84	93	118	89
1961......	76	97	102	83	88	110	89

Year	All Imports	Year	All Imports	Year	All Imports
		B. Census and Statistics Import Price Index			
1938......	23	1946......	73	1954......	88
1939......	22	1947......	82	1955......	89
1940......	26	1948......	88	1956......	99
1941......	31	1949......	84	1957......	96
1942......	46	1950......	86	1958......	83
1943......	64	1951......	102	1959......	91
1944......	76	1952......	110	1960......	91
1945......	71	1953......	100	1961......	89

*These indexes correspond with the volume indexes of Table A–48. All comments made in the note there apply here as well, with one exception pertaining to the Census and Statistics Import Price Index: it is Paasche index through 1958, after which it becomes a 1948-weighted Laspeyres index.

Source: Central Bank of Ceylon, *Annual Report of the Monetary Board to the Minister of Finance* (1961).

TABLE A–51
EXPORT PRICE INDEXES, 1938–61*
(1953 = 100)

Year	Tea	Rubber	3 Major Coconut Products	18 Minor Products	All Exports
A. Central Bank Export Price Indexes					
1938.............	30	25	12	20	24
1948.............	80	45	90	80	73
1949.............	89	41	96	84	78
1950.............	102	99	119	108	105
1951.............	107	164	131	144	127
1952.............	93	115	81	113	98
1953.............	100	100	100	100	100
1954.............	126	88	93	113	111
1955.............	133	102	75	114	116
1956.............	121	98	77	123	108
1957.............	112	93	82	132	104
1958.............	111	81	93	127	102
1959.............	110	94	108	118	106
1960.............	108	105	95	130	106
1961.............	106	85	74	118	97

Year	Tea	Rubber	Coconut Products	All Products
B. Census and Statistics Export Price Indexes				
1938.............	30	26	12	26
1939.............	33	32	14	29
1940.............	34	37	14	32
1941.............	39	38	16	35
1942.............	40	45	28	40
1943.............	41	50	28	42
1944.............	46	64	31	49
1945.............	48	66	37	52
1946.............	52	64	49	56
1947.............	80	49	77	72
1948.............	81	45	79	72
1949.............	89	41	92	77
1950.............	102	100	114	104
1951.............	106	165	134	126
1952.............	94	114	83	98
1953.............	100	100	100	100
1954.............	126	88	94	112
1955.............	134	101	79	117
1956.............	122	98	79	109
1957.............	113	93	85	104
1958.............	111	81	98	102
1959.............	110	93	112	106
1960.............	108	104	101	106
1961.............	106	85	82	99

*These price indexes correspond with the volume indexes of Table A–49 and all comments made in the footnote to that table apply here also.
Source: Central Bank of Ceylon, *Annual Report of the Monetary Board to the Minister of Finance* (1961).

VALUE, VOLUME, AND PRICE OF MAIN EXPORTS, 1870–1960

Year	Tea Quantity (000,000 Lbs.)	Tea Unit Value	Tea Value (Rs. 000)	Rubber Quantity (000,000 Lbs.)	Rubber Unit Value	Rubber Value (Rs. 000)	Coconut Oil Quantity (000 Cwt.)	Coconut Oil Unit Value	Coconut Oil Value (Rs. 000)	Copra Quantity (000 Cwt.)	Copra Unit Value	Copra Value (Rs. 000)
1870	...	...	...	...	...	...	136	12.50	1,700	41	8.00	329
1871	...	...	...	...	...	...	207	12.50	2,588	51	8.00	408
1872	...	...	...	...	...	...	278	11.90	3,307	41	6.76	277
1873	...	...	...	...	...	...	114	12.44	1,418	34	5.62	191
1874	...	...	...	...	...	...	145	12.46	1,807	29	6.48	188
1875	...	...	...	...	...	...	124	12.44	1,542	8	6.25	50
1876	...	...	...	...	...	...	213	12.46	2,653	28	6.21	174
1877	...	...	...	...	...	...	133	12.42	1,652	20	7.95	159
1878	...	...	...	...	...	...	175	12.47	2,183	46	8.67	399
1879	...	...	...	...	...	...	218	12.47	2,718	65	8.15	530
1880	...	...	...	...	...	...	352	12.46	4,386	93	9.81	912
1881	...	...	...	...	...	...	202	12.42	2,508	54	6.76	365
1882	1	.85	592	...	...	...	211	12.44	2,625	96	7.47	717
1883	2	.46	916	...	...	...	348	12.46	4,335	171	8.75	1,496
1884	2	.72	1,436	...	...	...	384	12.44	4,778	202	8.14	1,644
1885	4	.71	2,482	...	...	...	265	12.45	3,300	162	7.88	1,277
1886	8	.64	5,102	...	...	...	277	12.46	3,451	157	8.77	1,377
1887	14	.59	8,300	...	...	...	323	12.46	4,025	136	7.88	1,071
1888	24	.53	12,625	...	...	...	364	12.45	4,531	147	8.54	1,255
1889	34	.52	17,859	...	...	...	380	12.44	4,728	55	7.81	429
1890	46	.50	22,900	...	...	...	369	12.44	4,589	156	9.48	1,480
1891	68	.45	30,473	...	...	...	427	12.44	5,310	69	13.37	921
1892	72	.45	32,526	...	...	...	565	12.44	7,026	169	9.61	1,625
1893	82	.50	40,723	...	...	...	389	15.56	6,045	87	14.36	1,251
1894	85	.54	46,103	...	...	...	450	15.56	6,993	46	12.66	579
1895	99	.50	49,291	...	...	...	419	15.56	6,522	41	11.13	451
1896	110	.38	41,836	...	...	...	391	15.56	6,080	58	9.81	565

(Continued on next page)

TABLE A-52 (Continued)

Year	Tea Quan-tity (000,000 Lbs.)	Tea Unit Value	Tea Value (Rs. 000)	Rubber Quan-tity (000,000 Lbs.)	Rubber Unit Value	Rubber Value (Rs. 000)	Coconut Oil Quan-tity (000 Cwt.)	Coconut Oil Unit Value	Coconut Oil Value (Rs. 000)	Copra Quan-tity (000 Cwt.)	Copra Unit Value	Copra Value (Rs. 000)
1897	114	.41	46,931	……	……	……	488	13.07	6,383	140	9.46	1,328
1898	122	.38	47,734	……	……	……	467	13.07	6,109	517	9.71	5,024
1899	149	.36	53,735	……	……	……	468	14.25	6,673	403	9.76	3,931
1900	149	.36	53,735	……	……	……	468	14.25	6,673	403	9.76	3,931
1901	144	.33	47,611	……	……	……	474	16.03	7,601	458	9.92	4,541
1902	151	.36	54,299	……	……	……	551	18.15	10,008	378	10.85	4,099
1903	149	.38	58,199	……	……	……	688	16.03	11,023	732	10.29	7,532
1904	158	.36	56,855	……	……	……	511	18.00	9,197	723	11.03	7,974
1905	142	.42	59,564	……	……	……	587	16.71	9,816	391	12.53	4,904
1906	171	.36	61,390	……	……	……	539	17.71	9,546	449	12.62	5,661
1907	180	.42	74,635	……	……	……	479	24.72	11,830	384	13.85	5,322
1908	179	.41	73,553	……	……	……	644	18.60	11,985	749	11.16	8,356
1909	193	.42	81,012	……	……	……	600	21.91	13,142	785	12.76	10,008
1910	184	.46	84,137	……	……	……	528	26.05	13,741	624	16.80	10,479
1911	187	.46	84,900	……	……	……	505	26.03	13,146	822	16.03	13,173
1912	192	.44	83,817	……	……	……	402	26.35	10,587	614	16.42	10,083
1913	192	.46	87,788	25	2.42	61,269	547	30.60	16,738	1,117	18.76	20,959
1914	194	.46	89,726	34	1.67	57,220	486	27.54	13,392	1,412	16.47	23,248
1915	216	.57	122,458	49	1.62	78,997	502	25.84	12,959	1,209	14.61	17,657
1916	203	.52	105,266	55	1.90	103,812	323	27.66	8,935	1,310	13.58	21,868
1917	195	.49	95,663	72	1.81	130,968	435	23.19	10,081	1,079	12.25	13,216
1918	181	.46	83,176	46	1.34	62,252	527	29.57	15,693	1,272	10.03	12,758
1919	209	.56	116,502	101	1.31	132,071	676	37.97	25,674	1,760	18.39	32,357
1920	185	.44	80,782	88	1.02	89,961	508	39.14	19,865	1,358	20.92	28,405
1921	162	.70	112,708	88	.59	51,602	485	31.00	15,025	1,367	17.78	24,304
1922	172	.84	146,036	105	.54	56,970	555	26.91	14,925	1,687	17.07	28,804
1923	182	1.02	185,686	84	.88	73,594	481	29.00	13,935	1,015	17.86	18,123
1924	205	1.05	214,965	83	.77	63,750	553	28.64	15,827	1,769	17.53	31,008

Year												
1925....	209	.93	199,697	102	1.66	169,992	617	27.24	16,813	2,274	16.83	38,268
1926....	217	.98	213,164	130	1.29	170,078	570	27.17	15,489	2,419	16.47	39,848
1927....	227	.94	213,775	125	.95	119,174	673	24.62	16,568	1,982	16.07	31,845
1928....	237	.85	201,311	128	.58	73,986	779	24.73	19,266	1,977	16.09	31,802
1929....	252	.82	205,194	181	.48	86,631	879	20.51	18,024	2,042	12.89	26,316
1930....	243	.75	182,038	171	.28	47,158	764	17.26	13,190	1,813	9.94	18,029
1931....	244	.57	138,699	138	.14	19,842	963	12.60	12,130	1,877	6.77	12,715
1932....	253	.43	107,693	111	.12	13,233	1,025	14.12	14,475	914	9.06	8,284
1933....	216	.55	117,910	142	.16	22,995	1,061	10.18	10,800	1,287	5.31	6,828
1934....	219	.66	145,063	179	.32	56,615	1,397	7.49	10,461	2,109	4.38	9,244
1935....	212	.69	145,764	120	.32	38,394	1,109	12.31	13,647	975	8.02	7,818
1936....	218	.70	153,392	112	.42	46,840	689	14.44	9,949	1,035	9.74	10,077
1937....	213	.80	170,587	156	.49	77,010	1,337	15.00	20,061	1,417	8.83	12,511
1938....	236	.73	172,421	115	.39	45,275	1,508	9.32	14,057	1,504	5.84	8,783
1939....	228	.82	188,029	135	.50	67,564	1,258	10.56	13,286	1,061	6.69	7,102
1940....	246	.84	207,910	197	.57	113,101	597	11.33	6,763	1,566	6.32	9,892
1941....	238	.95	224,736	202	.58	118,287	563	13.58	7,643	2,138	6.92	14,799
1942....	266	.96	253,762	251	.69	171,824	497	23.15	11,504	2,297	12.14	27,887
1943....	264	1.02	269,374	220	.77	169,006	961	21.90	21,049	2,953	12.67	37,403
1944....	276	1.13	311,271	224	.99	222,791	827	23.59	19,509	2,020	14.17	28,625
1945....	232	1.20	278,476	215	1.02	218,404	774	27.60	21,359	2,274	17.06	38,803
1946....	292	1.30	380,545	228	.99	226,665	861	34.56	29,758	776	21.14	16,407
1947....	287	1.97	566,523	181	.75	135,502	846	57.31	48,488	595	35.94	21,387
1948....	296	1.99	590,271	206	.69	141,619	1,515	55.49	84,061	1,089	38.74	42,191
1949....	298	2.18	649,845	195	.63	122,862	1,784	68.01	121,327	431	50.04	21,567
1950....	298	2.52	751,651	262	1.53	401,120	1,514	84.13	127,374	422	60.27	25,436
1951....	305	2.62	800,036	226	2.53	572,439	2,195	103.44	227,061	387	69.92	27,059
1952....	315	2.30	723,048	206	1.76	363,060	2,134	62.36	133,084	815	40.73	33,194
1953....	336	2.46	825,090	213	1.54	328,893	1,871	75.98	142,153	428	53.40	22,825
1954....	361	3.11	1,122,798	203	1.36	275,967	1,378	72.71	100,191	920	49.40	45,445
1955....	362	3.30	1,194,227	222	1.58	350,348	1,945	58.25	113,291	1,531	37.41	57,281
1956....	348	3.00	1,043,847	190	1.54	292,553	1,699	58.40	99,221	1,160	42.23	48,989
1957....	366	2.77	1,015,896	209	1.44	300,298	1,081	62.83	67,920	700	47.63	33,343
1958....	411	2.75	1,130,969	207	1.25	258,109	887	69.78	61,897	560	52.40	29,346
1959....	384	2.72	1,045,013	206	1.45	297,820	1,390	84.36	117,264	860	59.97	51,572
1960....	410	2.67	1,095,679	235	1.61	378,374	1,110	71.85	79,753	580	55.48	32,181

TABLE A-52 (CONTINUED)

VALUE, VOLUME, AND PRICE OF MAIN EXPORTS, 1870–1960

Desiccated Coconut

Year	Quantity (000 Cwt.)	Unit Value	Value (Rs. 000)	Year	Quantity (000 Cwt.)	Unit Value	Value (Rs. 000)
1870				1916	306	28.44	8,705
1871				1917	272	34.41	9,361
1872				1918	203	25.47	5,180
1873				1919	675	36.93	24,928
1874				1920	519	35.34	18,330
1875				1921	871	30.56	26,602
1876				1922	768	26.24	20,159
1877				1923	819	27.74	22,716
1878				1924	871	25.21	21,964
1879				1925	794	23.65	18,778
1880				1926	754	22.91	17,276
1881				1927	873	23.46	20,482
1882				1928	787	25.21	19,840
1883				1929	690	17.21	11,876
1884				1930	705	14.24	10,036
1885				1931	669	10.21	6,832
1886				1932	599	11.94	7,150
1887				1933	790	8.54	6,747
1888				1934	647	6.39	4,135
1889				1935	664	11.01	7,308
1890				1936	602	11.70	7,042
1891				1937	589	11.51	6,780
1892	16	23.10	370	1938	594	7.41	4,399

Year			
1893	27	21.91	597
1894	43	23.45	1,001
1895	73	22.66	1,658
1896	94	21.81	2,051
1897	103	20.69	2,152
1898	121	19.20	2,332
1899	130	17.67	2,295
1900	126	17.74	2,238
1901	126	18.38	2,315
1902	239	11.99	2,871
1903	164	18.91	3,105
1904	169	18.31	3,094
1905	184	17.94	3,301
1906	182	18.72	3,404
1907	205	21.78	4,471
1908	246	17.44	4,299
1909	231	19.09	4,407
1910	264	23.76	6,276
1911	292	24.03	7,023
1912	279	23.99	6,689
1913	304	25.89	7,867
1914	312	25.13	7,839
1915	349	24.78	8,647

Year			
1939	673	10.60	7,132
1940	285	9.61	2,738
1941	106	10.37	1,099
1942	112	19.28	2,159
1943	66	25.76	1,700
1944	58	26.00	1,516
1945	107	30.37	3,250
1946	194	52.71	10,226
1947	231	100.01	23,103
1948	236	106.97	25,245
1949	312	81.73	25,500
1950	898	106.06	95,238
1951	795	82.63	65,687
1952	1,112	58.71	65,280
1953	1,146	68.79	78,838
1954	1,104	60.01	66,250
1955	1,157	47.37	54,807
1956	1,275	50.85	64,836
1957	978	56.08	54,846
1958	1,135	63.71	72,310
1959	1,050	71.43	75,003
1960	604	65.60	39,625

Source: Department of Statistics and Office Systems, *Ceylon Blue Book*, various years; Department of Commerce, *Thirty Years Trade Statistics of Ceylon (1925–1954)*, Vol. I; Department of Census and Statistics, *Statistical Abstract*, various years.

TABLE A–53

COMMODITY DISTRIBUTION OF MERCHANDISE IMPORTS, DOMESTIC EXPORTS, AND REEXPORTS, SELECTED YEARS, 1871–1959*

(Thousand Rupees)

Year	Food, Drink and Tobacco	% of Total	Raw Materials Mainly Manufac- tured	% of Total	Articles Wholly or Mainly Manufac- tured	% of Total	Animals not for Food	% of Total	Total
			A. Imports (Total)						
1871....	....	....	....	....	....	....	...	...	39,128
1881....	....	....	....	....	....	....	.....	...	43,139
1891....	....	....	....	....	....	....	.....	...	59,037
1900....	....	....	....	....	....	....	...	...	114,544
1901....	....	....	....	....	....	....	...	...	104,050
1911....	....	....	....	....	....	....	...	...	156,986
1913....	....	....	....	....	....	....	...	...	186,073
1921....	....	....	....	....	....	....	...	...	261,543
1929....	181,058	44.9	62,305	15.5	159,508	39.6	134	—	403,001
1931....	102,202	46.8	34,264	15.7	81,787	37.5	90	—	218,129
1939....	114,104	47.3	37,048	15.4	89,626	37.2	206	0.1	242,422
1946....	384,971	56.7	70,684	10.4	222,741	32.8	342	0.1	695,541
1949....	518,273	50.4	110,011	10.7	399,869	38.9	690	0.1	1,028,843
1953....	796,445	49.5	163,497	10.2	646,677	40.2	1,219	0.1	1,607,838
1954....	664,067	47.5	137,932	9.9	594,274	42.5	982	0.1	1,397,256
1959....	811,654	40.6	186,755	9.3	998,849	50.0	210	—	2,004,924
			B. Domestic Exports						
1871....	....	....	....	....	.....	...	...	..	31,434
1881....	....	....	....	....	.....	...	...	..	33,645
1891....	....	....	....	....	.....	...	...	..	56,150
1900....	....	....	....	....	.....	...	...	..	90,869
1901....	....	....	....	....	.....	...	...	..	85,977
1911....	....	....	....	....	.....	...	...	..	170,111
1913....	....	....	....	....	....	...	...	..	224,236
1921....	....	....	....	....	.....	...	...	..	248,121
1929....	243,754	61.8	141,152	37.2	3,653	1.0	4	—	379,564
1931....	155,989	74.7	51,033	24.5	1,623	0.8	1	—	208,645
1939....	203,784	67.0	98,901	32.5	1,473	0.5	3	—	304,167
1946....	415,508	58.0	297,978	41.6	2,599	0.4	112	—	716,197
1949....	703,943	70.1	296,004	29.5	4,873	0.5	10	—	1,004,830
1953....	934,397	62.9	545,717	36.7	5,394	0.4	27	—	1,485,536
1954....	1,232,430	71.9	477,431	27.8	4,753	0.3	62	—	1,714,676
1959....	1,152,264	68.5	514,593	30.6	15,814	0.9	11	—	1,685,349

COMMODITY DISTRIBUTION OF MERCHANDISE IMPORTS, DOMESTIC EXPORTS, AND REEXPORTS, SELECTED YEARS, 1871–1959*

(Thousand Rupees)

Year	Food, Drink and Tobacco	% of Total	Raw Materials Mainly Manufactured	% of Total	Articles Wholly or Mainly Manufactured	% of Total	Animals not for Food	% of Total	Total
			C. Reexports						
1871....	.....	....	......	....	......	....	...	...	4,095
1881....	.....	....	......	....	......	....	...	...	2,543
1891....	.....	....	......	....	......	....	...	...	2,650
1900....	.....	....	......	....	......	....	...	...	4,094
1901....	.....	....	......	....	......	....	...	...	3,932
1911....	.....	....	......	....	......	....	...	...	10,416
1913....	.....	....	......	....	......	....	...	...	8,751
1921....	.....	....	......	....	......	....	...	...	8,480
1929....	2,726	7.0	32,089	82.2	4,117	10.5	100	0.3	39,032
1931....	974	4.2	19,104	82.4	2,944	12.7	166	0.7	23,188
1939....	657	2.9	20,070	88.3	1,905	8.4	94	0.4	22,726
1946....	12,264	22.8	29,459	66.7	2,237	5.1	187	0.4	44,147
1949....	4,128	7.5	45,801	82.7	5,331	9.7	19	—	54,778
1953....	4,949	6.3	63,628	81.5	9,387	12.0	100	0.1	78,064
1954....	18,272	20.3	58,349	64.8	13,402	14.9	26	—	90,049
1959....	5,056	30.4	2,910	17.5	8,692	52.2	...		61,736
			D. Exports (Total)						
1871....	....	....	....	....	......	...	...	...	35,529
1881....	....	....	....	....	......	...	...	...	36,189
1891....	....	....	....	....	......	...	...	...	58,800
1900....	....	....	....	....	......	...	...	...	94,962
1901....	....	....	....	....	......	...	...	...	89,909
1911....	....	....	....	....	......	...	...	...	180,527
1913....	....	....	....	....	......	...	...	...	232,987
1921....	....	....	....	....	......	...	...	...	256,600
1929....	237,480	56.7	173,242	41.4	7,771	1.9	104	—	422,581
1931....	156,963	67.7	70,137	30.2	4,567	2.0	167	0.1	233,129
1939....	204,442	62.6	118,971	36.4	3,378	1.0	97	—	328,111
1946....	427,712	56.3	327,438	43.1	4,836	0.6	298	—	764,686
1949....	708,071	66.8	341,305	32.2	10,204	1.0	28	—	1,063,240
1953....	939,346	59.9	609,346	38.9	14,781	0.9	127	—	1,568,036
1954....	1,250,794	69.3	535,780	29.7	18,155	1.0	88	—	1,809,297
1959....	1,157,320	68.1	517,503	30.5	24,506	1.4	11	—	1,753,876

*The percentage figures refer to the percentage of all imports or exports which are classified by type in the customs returns. For imports, this includes all imports but postal packets during October-December, 1939, 1946, and 1959; returned goods and special transactions are also excluded in 1959. For exports, postal packages are excluded in all years and special transactions and returned goods are excluded in 1959 only. In all cases, values which cannot be assigned to a category are included in total imports or exports and this, along with rounding error and a few slight discrepancies in the original data, account for the failure of the parts to add to the whole in some years.

The classificatory system used between midyear 1921 and 1955 is that recommended by the United Kingdom Board of Trade. In 1956 a shift was made to the Standard International Trade Classification of the United Nations and the 1959 figures thus represent this system. They are, therefore, not strictly comparable to the earlier figures but the differences between the two systems are relatively slight and no very misleading impression should be created by the shift. Prior to July, 1921 various systems were used at various times and no attempt has been made to reconcile these with the Board of Trade Classification.

Sources: Department of Commerce, *Thirty Years Trade Statistics of Ceylon* (1925–1954), Vol. I; Department of Census and Statistics, *Statistical Abstract*, 1960.

TABLE A–54

REGIONAL AND COUNTRY DISTRIBUTION OF IMPORTS, SELECTED YEARS, 1871–1959

Region or Country	1871	1881	1891	1900	1901	1911	1913	1921
	A. Value (Million Rupees)*							
North America.........	—	—	0.2	0.7	0.4	1.7	2.4	7.8
Canada†	—	—	—	0.1	—	—	—	0.7
United States......	—	—	0.2	0.6	0.4	1.7	2.4	7.1
Central and South America............								
	—	—	—	—	—	0.1	0.1	—
Europe...............:	14.7	13.2	20.2	43.1	37.5	54.2	69.4	75.0
France...........	0.1	0.1	0.2	1.1	0.8	1.1	1.5	1.9
Germany‡.........	—	—	0.4	2.6	1.9	4.8	6.0	1.5
Holland..........	—	—	—	0.9	0.4	1.2	1.3	2.8
Italy.............	—	0.1	—	0.3	0.2	0.5	1.0	1.2
United Kingdom...	14.6	12.8	19.3	33.7	30.9	42.7	54.3	65.4
Other Western... ⎱ Eastern Europe§. ⎰	—	0.2	0.2	4.5	3.3	3.9	5.2	2.2
Africa................	1.3	—	0.1	0.3	0.1	0.3	2.3	11.9
Egypt.............	1.3	—	—	0.2	—	0.1	0.1	0.1
Union of South Africa‖.........	—	—	—	—	—	0.1	1.5	8.9
Others...........	—	—	—	—	—	0.1	0.7	2.9
Asia and Oceania......	32.0	33.9	46.2	78.2	74.6	100.5	111.9	163.8
Australia.........	1.8**	0.6**	0.7**	1.1	3.9	2.2	2.9	3.6
Burma...........	—	—	—	4.7	4.4	5.9	7.1	60.0
China#...........	—	—	0.1	1.6	1.4	0.1	0.7	0.8
India¶...........	29.6	32.6	44.1	64.6	60.5	72.5	76.6	64.0
Iran.............	—	—	—	—	—	—	—	4.0
Japan............	—	—	0.1	1.1	1.0	1.9	4.1	4.1
New Zealand......	††	††	††	—	—	—	0.1	0.1
Others...........	0.6	0.6	1.3	5.1	3.4	17.8	20.5	27.0
Total........	48.0	47.1	66.6	122.3	112.6	156.7	186.1	260.9

Region or Country	1929	1931	1939	1946	1949	1953	1954	1959
	A. Value (Million Rupees)*							
North America.........	15.2	9.4	7.0	61.0	83.7	68.6	49.0	157.6
Canada†..........	1.8	0.4	1.1	18.8	10.7	16.7	12.4	20.0
United States......	13.5	9.1	6.0	42.3	73.0	51.9	36.7	137.6
Central and South America............	1.0	0.3	0.8	45.8	17.3	27.6	24.3	—
Europe...............	125.0	55.8	62.1	127.8	265.5	532.4	472.9	708.1
France...........	4.8	2.3	1.8	1.2	3.7	24.3	20.0	30.5
Germany‡.........	10.5	4.3	4.6	—	7.0	23.8	22.4	74.3
Holland..........	4.9	1.9	1.9	1.0	5.5	34.3	29.0	34.3
Italy.............	3.3	0.9	0.6	1.5	21.3	41.4	38.1	20.5
United Kingdom...	89.5	40.5	45.4	115.4	185.3	361.4	292.9	495.2
Other Western...⎱ Eastern Europe§..⎰	11.9	6.0	7.7	8.8 ⎰	34.2	35.2	59.0	29.5
					8.4	11.9	11.4	23.8

TABLE A–54 (Continued)

Region or County	1929	1931	1939	1946	1949	1953	1954	1959
Africa..................	8.3	4.5	3.0	124.2	79.4	59.0	40.0	17.1
Egypt.............	1.5	0.7	0.7	81.7	35.3	7.6	15.2	11.9
Union of South Africa‖..........	6.6	3.3	1.6	12.8	1.4	6.2	4.8	5.2
Others............	0.3	0.4	0.7	29.7	42.6	45.2	20.0	——
Asia and Oceania.......	253.6	148.0	168.3	339.7	581.4	920.0	811.0	903.3
Australia..........	10.7	5.1	6.1	96.8	102.1	174.3	105.7	96.7
Burma............	78.3	40.8	37.4	4.4	153.0	129.0	125.2	132.4
China#.............	1.8	1.6	1.1	0.6	2.1	209.0	158.6	150.0
India¶.............	84.9	50.1	52.6	177.9	152.6	200.0	191.4	246.7
Iran...............	10.7	8.6	5.7	33.9	28.3	1.9	11.4	69.5
Japan.............	10.8	10.7	14.2	0.4	18.1	69.5	76.2	147.6
New Zealand......	0.1	0.1	——	0.3	0.3	0.5	1.0	——
Others............	56.3	30.9	51.3	25.5	122.0	135.7	141.4	60.5
Total.........	403.0	218.1	240.5	695.5	1,028.8	1,607.8	1,397.3	2,004.9

Region or Country	1871	1881	1891	1900	1901	1911	1913	1921
			B. Percentage of All Imports‡‡					
North America........	——	——	0.3	0.6	0.4	1.1	1.3	3.0
Canada†...........	——	——				——	——	0.3
United States......	——	——	0.3	0.6	0.4	1.1	1.3	2.7
Central and South America.............			——	——	——	0.1	0.1	——
Europe...............	30.6	28.0	30.3	35.2	33.3	34.6	37.3	29.0
France............	0.2	0.2	0.3	0.9	0.7	0.7	0.8	0.7
Germany‡.........	——	——	0.6	2.1	1.7	3.1	3.2	0.6
Holland...........	——	——	——	0.7	0.4	0.8	0.7	1.1
Italy.............	——	0.2	——	0.2	0.2	0.3	0.5	0.5
United Kingdom...	30.4	27.2	28.9	27.6	27.4	27.2	29.2	25.3
Other Western...⎱ Eastern Europe§..⎰	——	0.4	0.3	3.7	2.9	2.5	2.8	0.9
Africa.................	2.7	——	0.1	0.2	0.1	0.2	1.2	4.6
Egypt.............	2.7	——	——	0.2	——	0.1	0.1	——
Union of South Africa‖..........	——	——	——	——	——	0.1	0.8	3.4
Others............	——	——	——	——	——	0.1	0.4	1.1
Asia and Oceania.......	66.7	72.0	69.3	63.9	66.3	64.1	60.1	63.4
Australia..........	3.8‖	1.3‖	1.0‖	0.9	3.5	1.4	1.6	1.4
Burma............	——	——	——	3.8	3.9	3.8	3.8	23.2
China#.............	——	——	0.1	1.3	1.2	0.1	0.4	0.3
India¶.............	61.7	69.6	66.1	52.8	53.7	46.2	41.2	24.8
Iran..............	——	——	——	——	——	——	——	1.5
Japan.............	——	——	0.1	0.9	0.9	1.2	2.2	1.6
New Zealand......	††	††	††	——	——	——	0.1	——
Others............	1.3	1.3	1.9	4.2	3.0	11.4	11.0	10.4
Total.........	100.0	100.0	100.0	100.0	100.0	100.0	100.0	100.0

(Continued on next page)

TABLE A-54 (CONTINUED)

REGIONAL AND COUNTRY DISTRIBUTION OF IMPORTS, SELECTED YEARS, 1871–1959

Region or Country	1929	1931	1939	1946	1949	1953	1954	1959
	B. Percentage of All Imports‡‡							
North America.........	3.8	4.3	2.9	8.7	8.1	4.3	3.5	8.8
Canada†..........	0.4	0.1	0.5	2.7	1.0	1.0	0.9	1.1
United States......	3.3	4.2	2.5	6.1	7.1	3.2	2.6	7.7
Central and South America............	0.2	0.1	0.3	6.6	1.7	1.7	1.7	——
Europe...............	31.0	25.6	25.7	18.3	25.8	33.1	33.9	39.6
France...........	1.2	1.1	0.7	0.2	0.4	1.5	1.4	1.7
Germany‡.........	2.6	1.9	0.9	——	0.7	1.5	1.6	4.2
Holland..........	1.2	0.9	0.8	0.1	0.5	2.1	2.1	1.9
Italy.............	0.8	0.4	0.2	0.2	2.1	2.6	2.7	1.1
United Kingdom...	22.2	18.5	18.8	16.5	18.0	22.5	21.0	27.7
Other Western...⎫ Eastern Europe§..⎭	3.0	2.8	3.2	1.3 {	3.3 / 0.8	2.2 / 0.7	4.2 / 0.8	1.7 / 1.3
Africa.................	2.1	2.1	1.2	17.8	7.7	3.7	2.9	1.0
Egypt............	0.4	0.3	0.3	11.7	3.4	0.5	1.1	0.7
Union of South Africa‖.........	1.7	1.5	0.7	1.8	0.1	0.4	0.3	0.3
Others...........	0.1	0.2	0.3	4.3	4.1	2.8	1.4	——
Asia and Oceania.......	62.9	67.9	69.8	48.6	56.6	57.2	58.1	50.6
Australia.........	2.7	2.3	2.5	13.9	9.9	10.8	7.6	5.4
Burma...........	19.4	18.7	15.5	0.6	14.9	8.0	9.0	7.4
China#...........	0.5	0.7	0.5	0.1	0.2	13.0	11.4	8.4
India¶...........	21.1	23.0	21.8	25.5	14.9	12.4	13.7	13.8
Iran.............	2.7	4.0	2.4	4.9	2.8	0.1	0.8	3.9
Japan............	2.7	4.9	5.9	0.1	1.8	4.3	5.5	8.3
New Zealand......	——	——	——	——	——	——	0.1	
Others...........	14.0	14.2	21.3	3.7	11.9	8.4	10.1	3.4
Total........	100.0	100.0	100.0	100.0	100.0	100.0	100.0	100.0

*Components may not add to total because of rounding, inability to attribute some imports to a country of origin, and discrepancies in the original data.

†Includes Newfoundland, both before and after its confederation with Canada.

‡From 1946 on refers to West Germany (East Germany included under "Eastern Europe").

§Refers to the Soviet bloc nations, including Yugoslavia, and is thus identified separately only from 1949 on.

‖Refers to Cape and Natal colonies prior to the formation of the Union of South Africa.

#From 1949 on, refers to Mainland China (Taiwan is included in "Other Asia and Oceania").

¶Includes all India through 1946; after 1946, it refers only to independent India (Pakistan and foreign enclaves in India are thereafter included under "Other Asia and Oceania").

**Includes New Zealand.

††Included under Australia.

‡‡Refers to the percentage of total imports whose country of origin is known.

Sources: Department of Commerce, *Thirty Years Trade Statistics of Ceylon (1925–1954)*, Vol. I; *Ceylon Customs Returns* (December), various years; Department of Statistics and Office Systems, *Ceylon Blue Book*, various years; United Nations, Statistical Office, *Direction of International Trade*, various years.

TABLE A–55

REGIONAL AND COUNTRY DISTRIBUTION OF EXPORTS (TOTAL), SELECTED YEARS, 1871–1959

A. Value (Million Rupees)*

Region or Country	1871	1881	1891	1900	1901	1911	1913	1921
North America	0.7	2.5	3.9	7.7	6.7	28.6	42.6	60.9
Canada†	—	—	—	1.0	1.2	3.5	3.9	4.6
United States	0.7	2.5	3.9	6.6	5.5	25.1	38.7	56.3
Central and South America	—	—	—	—	—	0.3	0.4	0.6
Europe	27.2	26.2	44.8	69.8	64.5	118.0	159.3	155.1
France	0.3	1.2	0.3	0.8	1.2	1.1	0.9	1.5
Germany‡	0.4	0.1	1.5	4.4	5.3	15.0	22.8	10.1
Holland	—	—	—	0.1	0.1	0.6	0.6	7.5
Italy	—	0.9	0.2	0.6	0.4	0.3	0.4	4.7
United Kingdom	26.3	21.5	41.5	56.3	50.2	80.1	105.6	118.6
Other Western... Eastern Europe§..	0.2	2.5	1.2	7.6	7.4	21.0	29.0	12.6
Africa	0.3	0.1	0.1	1.7	0.3	1.7	2.1	7.7
Egypt	0.3	—	—	0.2	0.2	0.4	0.6	3.4
Union of South Africa‖	—	—	—	0.1	0.1	1.0	1.1	3.5
Others	0.1	0.1	0.1	1.4	0.1	0.3	0.4	0.8
Asia and Oceania	8.0	7.4	10.0	15.8	18.4	23.6	30.8	27.3
Australia	0.5**	1.0**	2.3**	5.7	6.2	9.4	13.6	7.0
Burma	—	—	—	—	0.4	0.1	0.1	0.2
China#	—	0.1	0.1	0.2	0.8	3.3	3.8	0.1
India¶	7.1	5.9	6.7	7.8	9.0	6.7	7.3	11.2
Iran	—	—	—	—	—			
Japan	—	—	—	—	—	0.3	0.9	1.2
New Zealand	††	††	††	1.2	1.1	2.2	2.5	3.6
Others	0.4	0.4	1.0	0.9	0.8	1.6	2.5	3.9
Total	36.3	36.2	58.8	95.0	89.9	172.2	233.0	251.6

A. Value (Million Rupees)*

Region or Country	1929	1931	1939	1946	1949	1953	1954	1959
North America	85.8	31.1	74.9	100.7	160.5	201.4	189.5	250.0
Canada†	7.2	5.4	12.6	12.8	45.9	80.0	70.5	86.2
United States	78.6	25.7	62.3	87.9	114.6	121.0	119.0	163.8
Central and South America	4.9	3.6	3.3	5.1	11.2	9.5	13.8	8.6
Europe	221.9	132.2	174.1	420.3	474.8	582.4	665.2	724.8
France	3.9	2.2	6.4	0.5	11.8	13.3	13.8	19.0
Germany‡	18.0	6.4	2.3	—	41.9	43.3	35.2	92.9
Holland	4.0	3.2	1.7	1.5	34.9	64.3	41.7	43.3
Italy	11.6	5.8	3.1	0.1	20.3	33.8	33.8	43.8
United Kingdom	161.7	102.7	151.3	400.6	335.7	389.0	501.9	479.5
Other Western...	22.7	12.0	9.3	17.5 {	29.5	35.2	36.2	14.8
Eastern Europe§..					0.7	3.3	2.4	31.4

(Continued on next page)

TABLE A–55 (CONTINUED)

Region or County	1929	1931	1939	1946	1949	1953	1954	1959
Africa..............	20.6	15.1	17.8	56.4	113.7	141.0	196.2	116.7
Egypt............	8.5	5.3	4.7	18.3	57.5	60.5	87.6	27.6
Union of South								
Africa‖.........	7.8	6.6	10.3	23.6	41.8	66.7	85.7	80.0
Others...........	4.4	3.2	2.8	14.5	14.3	13.8	22.9	9.0
Asia and Oceania......	54.4	29.7	38.0	144.5	237.3	565.2	686.7	332.4
Australia.........	22.7	7.4	9.8	73.5	83.6	131.9	172.9	106.2
Burma...........	0.2	0.2	0.3	1.0	0.2	0.5	7.6	1.4
China#...........	0.3	0.2	0.2	0.3	1.7	241.9	221.4	77.6
India¶...........	14.2	10.4	12.0	38.8	22.3	41.9	74.3	53.3
Iran.............	0.3	0.3	0.3	—	12.7	0.5	8.6	
Japan............	2.1	1.3	2.7	—	4.2	10.0	14.3	41.9
New Zealand......	8.6	6.4	7.9	17.6	33.2	33.3	41.0	38.6
Others...........	6.2	3.5	4.8	13.4	79.3	105.2	146.7	13.3
Total........	390.7	212.2	326.9	764.7	1,059.6	1,563.6	1,804.7	1,702.6

Region or Country	1871	1881	1891	1900	1901	1911	1913	1921
	B. Percentage of All Exports‡‡							
North America........	1.9	6.9	6.6	8.1	7.5	16.6	18.1	24.2
Canada†..........	—	—	—	1.1	1.3	2.0	1.7	1.9
United States......	1.9	6.9	6.6	6.9	6.1	14.6	16.5	22.4
Central and South								
America............	—	—	—	—	0.2	0.2	0.2	0.2
Europe..............	75.1	72.4	76.2	73.5	71.7	68.5	67.7	61.6
France............	0.8	3.3	0.5	0.8	1.3	0.6	0.4	0.6
Germany‡.........	1.1	0.3	2.6	4.6	5.9	8.7	9.7	4.0
Holland...........	—	—	—	0.1	0.1	0.3	0.3	3.0
Italy..............	—	2.5	0.3	0.6	0.4	0.2	0.2	1.9
United Kingdom...	72.7	59.4	70.6	59.3	55.8	46.5	44.9	47.1
Other Western... ⎫								
Eastern Europe§.. ⎭	0.6	6.9	2.0	8.0	8.2	12.2	12.3	5.0
Africa.................	0.8	0.3	0.2	1.8	0.3	1.0	0.9	3.1
Egypt............	0.8			0.2	0.2	0.2	0.3	1.4
Union of South								
Africa‖..........	—	—	—	0.1	0.1	0.6	0.5	1.4
Others...........	0.3	0.3	0.2	1.5	0.1	0.2	0.2	0.3
Asia and Oceania......	22.1	20.4	17.0	16.6	20.5	13.7	13.1	10.9
Australia.........	13.8**	2.8**	3.9**	6.0	6.9	5.5	5.8	2.8
Burma...........	—	—	—	—	0.4	0.1	—	0.1
China#...........	—	0.3	0.2	0.2	0.9	1.9	1.6	—
India¶...........	19.6	16.3	11.4	8.2	10.0	3.9	3.1	4.5
Iran.............					⋅			
Japan............	—	—	—	—	—	0.2	0.4	0.5
New Zealand......	††	††	††	1.3	1.2	1.3	1.1	1.4
Others...........	1.1	1.1	1.7	0.9	0.9	0.9	1.1	1.6
Total........	100.0	100.0	100.0	100.0	100.0	100.0	100.0	100.0

TABLE A-55 (Continued)

Region or Country	1929	1931	1939	1946	1949	1953	1954	1959
B. Percentage of All Exports‡‡								
North America.........	22.1	14.7	24.3	13.9	16.1	13.4	10.8	17.5
Canada†..........	1.9	2.6	4.1	1.8	4.6	5.3	4.0	6.0
United States......	20.3	12.1	20.2	12.1	11.5	8.1	6.8	11.4
Central and South America............	1.3	1.7	1.1	0.7	1.1	0.6	0.8	0.6
Europe...............	57.2	62.4	56.5	57.8	47.6	38.8	38.0	50.6
France...........	1.0	1.0	2.1	0.1	1.2	0.9	0.8	1.3
Germany‡.........	4.6	3.0	0.7	—	4.2	2.9	2.0	6.5
Holland..........	1.0	1.5	0.6	0.2	3.5	4.3	2.4	3.0
Italy.............	3.0	2.7	1.0	—	2.0	2.3	1.9	3.1
United Kingdom...	41.7	48.5	49.1	55.1	33.7	25.9	28.7	33.5
Other Western...⎫ Eastern Europe§..⎭	5.9	5.7	3.0	2.4⎰	2.9 0.1	2.3 0.2	2.1 0.1	1.0 2.2
Africa...............	5.3	7.1	5.8	7.8	11.4	9.4	11.2	8.1
Egypt............	2.2	2.5	1.5	2.5	5.8	4.0	5.0	1.9
Union of South Africa‖.........	2.0	3.1	3.3	3.2	4.2	4.4	4.9	5.6
Others...........	1.1	1.5	0.9	2.0	1.4	0.9	1.3	0.6
Asia and Oceania.......	14.0	14.0	12.3	19.9	23.8	37.7	39.2	23.2
Australia.........	5.9	3.5	3.2	10.1	8.4	8.8	9.9	7.4
Burma...........	0.1	0.1	0.1	0.1	—	—	0.4	0.1
China#...........	0.1	0.1	0.1	—	0.2	16.1	12.6	5.4
India¶...........	3.7	4.9	3.9	5.3	2.2	2.8	4.2	3.7
Iran.............	0.1	0.1	0.1	—	1.3	—	0.5	—
Japan...........	0.5	0.6	0.9	—	0.4	0.7	0.8	2.9
New Zealand.....	2.2	3.0	2.6	2.4	3.3	2.2	2.3	2.7
Others...........	1.6	1.7	1.6	1.8	7.9	7.0	8.4	0.9
Total........	100.0	100.0	100.0	100.0	100.0	100.0	100.0	100.0

*Components may not add to totals because of rounding, inability to attribute some exports to a country of destination, and discrepancies in the original data.
†Includes Newfoundland, both before and after its confederation with Canada.
‡From 1946 on, refers to West Germany (East Germany included under "Eastern Europe").
§Refers to the Soviet bloc nations, including Yugoslavia, and is thus identified separately only from 1949 on.
‖Refers to Cape and Natal colonies prior to the formation of the Union of South Africa.
#From 1949 on, refers to Mainland China (Taiwan is included in "Other Asia and Oceania").
¶Includes all India through 1946; after 1946, it refers only to independent India (Pakistan and foreign enclaves in India are thereafter included under "Other Asia and Oceania").
**Includes New Zealand.
††Included under Australia.
‡‡Refers to the percentage of total exports whose country of destination is known.
Sources: Department of Commerce, *Thirty Years Trade Statistics of Ceylon (1925–1954)*, Vol. I; *Ceylon Customs Returns* (December), various years; Department of Commerce, *Ceylon Blue Book*, various years; United Nations, Statistical Office, *Direction of International Trade*, various years.

TABLE A–56

Imports, Exports, and the Balance of Trade, 1871–1947*

(Million Rupees)

Year	—Merchandise—		Balance Excluding Bullion and Specie	Bullion and Specie		Balance Including Bullion and Specie
	Imports	Exports		Imports	Exports	
1871.........	39.1	35.5	− 3.6	8.9	0.8	− 11.6
1881.........	43.1	35.7	− 7.5	4.0	0.5	− 10.9
1891.........	59.0	58.3	− 0.7	7.6	0.5	− 7.8
1900.........	114.5	92.0	− 22.5	7.8	2.9	− 27.4
1901.........	104.1	87.3	− 16.8	8.6	2.7	− 22.7
1902.........	97.9	98.2	0.4	11.6	1.2	− 10.1
1903.........	100.9	102.2	1.3	15.4	6.5	− 7.5
1904.........	105.3	101.1	− 4.2	11.2	3.2	− 12.2
1905.........	108.3	102.2	− 6.1	6.9	0.3	− 12.7
1906.........	112.8	109.7	− 3.1	10.7	2.8	− 11.0
1907.........	120.1	129.4	9.3	9.3	0.3	0.3
1908.........	122.4	129.0	6.5	7.9	1.2	− 0.1
1909.........	125.4	146.9	21.5	8.3	0.1	13.2
1910.........	151.5	173.6	22.1	13.3	0.1	8.9
1911.........	157.0	180.5	23.5	7.4	1.5	17.6
1912.........	175.3	199.0	23.6	6.7	—	17.0
1913.........	186.1	233.0	46.9	13.6	1.9	35.2
1914.........	172.3	218.4	46.0	4.6	1.0	42.4
1915.........	163.6	273.4	109.7	4.8	—	104.9
1916.........	211.5	297.5	86.0	8.5	—	77.5
1917.........	184.1	304.2	120.0	1.0	2.8	121.8
1918.........	177.7	212.1	34.4	—	1.8	36.2
1919.........	239.3	367.1	127.7	3.4	—	124.3
1920.........	221.3	268.5	47.2	39.7	7.8	15.4
1921.........	261.5	256.6	− 4.9	0.5	—	− 5.5
1922.........	280.3	297.8	17.5	1.5	—	16.0
1923.........	287.8	376.9	89.1	4.4	0.2	84.9
1924.........	302.4	414.0	111.6	10.0	—	101.7
1925.........	350.9	522.2	171.3	9.5	0.1	162.0
1926.........	394.7	532.3	137.5	13.1	0.4	124.8
1927.........	406.2	479.4	73.3	15.0	1.5	59.8
1928.........	400.1	417.6	17.5	12.0	4.0	9.5
1929.........	403.0	422.6	19.6	26.3	16.7	9.9
1930.........	302.0	323.0	20.9	22.2	10.3	9.0
1931.........	218.1	233.1	15.0	9.9	14.5	19.6
1932.........	196.1	188.8	− 7.2	0.3	0.2	− 7.3
1933.........	177.1	200.2	23.0	0.2	0.1	22.9
1934.........	217.0	263.8	46.8	0.1	0.1	46.8
1935.........	227.5	253.1	25.6	—	—	25.6
1936.........	214.3	268.5	54.1	0.1	0.1	54.2
1937.........	242.6	332.1	89.5	0.5	—	89.0
1938.........	235.5	284.8	49.3	0.7	0.1	48.6
1939.........	242.4	328.1	85.7	0.2	—	85.6
1940.........	282.6	386.8	104.2	0.2	1.7	105.7

TABLE A–56 (Continued)

Year	—Merchandise— Imports	Exports	Balance (Excluding Bullion and Specie)	Bullion and Specie Imports	Exports	Balance Including Bullion and Specie
1941.........	287.1	423.8	136.6	——	15.3	151.9
1942.........	295.8	530.7	234.9	0.3	——	234.6
1943.........	446.8	569.9	123.1	0.2	0.3	123.2
1944.........	517.7	679.9	162.3	——	——	162.3
1945.........	621.3	666.0	44.7	0.1	——	44.6
1946.........	695.5	764.7	69.1	0.1	——	69.1
1947.........	963.2	889.2	— 74.0	7.5	——	81.6

*The table summarizes the little knowledge there is about international finance in the years before a full balance of payments was drawn up. All totals are as they appear in the customs records and no adjustments have been made for probable under- or overvaluation, to obtain a consistent f.o.b. and c.i.f. listing, etc.

Sources: Department of Commerce, *Thirty Years Trade Statistics of Ceylon (1925–1954)*, Vol. I; Department of Statistics and Office Systems *Ceylon Blue Book*, various years.

TABLE A-57

BALANCE OF PAYMENTS, 1948-61*

(Million Rupees)

	1948	1949	1950	1951	1952	1953	1954	1955	1956	1957	1958	1959	1960	1961
I. *Current account*														
A. Merchandise														
1. Exports f.o.b.†	985	1,064	1,412	1,783	1,410	1,495	1,724	1,893	1,772	1,669	1,624	1,773	1,796	1,720
2. Imports c.i.f.†	−891	−1,027	−1,173	−1,545	−1,707	−1,633	−1,384	−1,478	−1,576	−1,764	−1,713	−1,956	−1,999	−1,782
3. *Trade balance*	94	37	239	238	−297	−138	340	415	196	−95	−89	−183	−203	−62
B. Other current transactions (net)														
1. Nonmonetary gold movements	+	−1	−2	−2	−3	−2	—	−2	−4	−2	—	−2	−2	−2
2. Foreign travel	+	−29	−32	−44	−48	−38	−28	−27	−28	−27	−30	−31	−24	−18
3. Transportation and insurance	+	−7	21	30	39	94	78	56	41	44	76	73	76	69
4. Investment income	−49	−29	−55	−64	−46	−38	−47	−61	−50	−53	−41	−37	−44	−40
a. Direct investment		−33	−27	−44	−41	−42	−57	−79	−79	−79	−63	−53	−56	−46
b. Other interest and dividends		4	−28	−20	−5	4	10	18	29	26	22	16	12	6
5. Government expenditure	+	37	6	17	21	24	26	30	17	12	−4	11	−21	−15
6. Miscellaneous services	−21	23	29	−9	−8	−15	−20	−27	−35	−35	−42	−27	−24	−27
7. Private remittances and migrants' transfers	+	−59	−69	−77	−104	−59	−67	−78	−83	−66	−78	−56	−31	−29
8. Official donations§	+					14	24	17	28	27	55	44	53	50
C. *Current Account balance*	24	−28	137	89	−446	−158	306	323	82	−195	−153	−208	−220	−75

II. Capital account (net)

A. Private capital movements.	-22	-22	-41	25	-38	-49	-57	-20	-38	-4	2	-5	-6
1. Direct investment.	....	-2	-49	-5	-7	-13	-25	-25	-38	-12	-9	3	-8
2. Other long-term investment.		-24	-16	-12	-14	-7	-25	-24	-3	-3	1	-1	-1
3. Other short-term investment.	-42‖	4	24	42	-17	-29	-7	29	3	11	10	-7	3
B. Official and banking institution capital movements.	55	-167	-94	366	211	-235	-279	-46	233	173	205	196	94
1. Long-term capital.		-4	-84	-75	265	53	-1	-38	-10	40	-43	105	-5
2. Short-term capital.		-163	-10	441	-54	-288	-278	-8	-243	133	248	91	99
C. *Capital account balance.*	33	-189	-135	391	173	-284	-336	-66	195	169	207	191	88
III. Monetary gold account.	18	—	—	—	—	—	—	—	—	—	—	—	—
IV. *Errors and omissions (net).*	-5	52	46	55	-15	-22	13	-16	-16	-16	1	29	-13

(Note: the −42‖ figure is bracketed jointly against "Other long-term investment" and "Other short-term investment.")

*The data from 1950 on are highly sophisticated and fully comparable from year to year. By contrast, the 1948 and 1949 figures are rough estimates, initial attempts at making this type of statistical presentation. The other notes point to particular instances in which care must be exercised in using them. The basic source for all data is the Department of Exchange Control.

†The estimates differ slightly from Customs totals, because in 1948 and 1949 adjustments were made to allow for a probable overvaluation of imports and undervaluation of exports and because in later years exports were valued on a consistent f.o.b. basis and imports on a consistent c.i.f. basis (Customs had not been entirely consistent on this).

‡Included under "miscellaneous services."

§Includes gifts in cash and amounts released from counterpart funds under U.S. Public Law 480, only.

‖Represents the increase in Ceylon's external assets, only.

Sources: *A.R. of the Controller of Exchange,* 1948 and 1949; *Central Bank of Ceylon, Annual Report of the Monetary Board to the Minister of Finance,* 1961.

TABLE A–58

OFFICIAL EXCHANGE RATE BETWEEN U.S. DOLLAR AND CEYLON
RUPEE, 1939–60*

(Rupees per Dollar, End of Year)
(Selling Rate)

Year	Rate	Year	Rate
1939	3.033	1950	4.775
1940	3.327	1951	4.785
1941	3.325	1952	4.762
1942	3.322	1953	4.762
1943	3.322	1954	4.795
1944	3.322	1955	4.772
1945	3.322	1956	4.800
1946	3.315	1957	4.765
1947	3.315	1958	4.760
1948	3.315	1959	4.762
1949	4.775	1960	4.762

*The rupee has been officially fixed at 13.33 rupees per pound sterling
since 1941; dollar-rupee rates thus fluctuate only as the dollar-sterling
rate in London varies.

Source: International Monetary Fund, *International Financial Statistics*,
various years.

TABLE A-59

Selected Foreign Assets in Ceylon, Selected Years, 1939-59*

A. Bank Deposits and Borrowings

Year	Demand Deposits Rs. 000,000	Demand Deposits % of All Deposits	Commercial Bank Time Deposits Rs. 000,000	Time Deposits % of All Time Deposits	Total Deposits Rs. 000,000	Total Deposits % of All Deposits	Borrowings Rs. 000,000	Borrowings % of All Borrowings	Total Liabilities Rs. 000,000	Total Liabilities % of All Liabilities	Central Bank: Deposits of International Organizations Rs. 000,000	Deposits of International Organizations % of All Deposits	All Banks: Total Liability to Foreigners Rs. 000,000†	Total Liability to Foreigners % of All Liabilities
1949†	15.0	2.0	5.5	8.2	20.5	2.5	13.1	100.0	33.6	4.1	—	—	33.6	4.1
1953	21.0	3.8	1.2	1.2	22.2	3.4	7.0	39.3	29.2	4.4	0.9	1.3	30.1	2.6
1954	14.2	2.2	2.3	1.6	16.5	2.1	4.4	41.5	20.9	2.5	0.8	0.6	21.7	1.6
1959	11.7	1.7	6.3	2.0	18.0	1.8	9.0	19.7	27.0	2.4	74.5	41.0	101.5	5.0

B. Government Debt

Year	Sterling Loans (Rs. 000,000)	I.B.R.D. Loans (Rs. 000,000)	Other Loans§ (Rs. 000,000)	Total Foreign Debt (Rs. 000,000)	Total Public Debt (Rs. 000,000)	Percentage of Debt in Foreign Hands
1939	163.4	—	—	163.4	203.7	80.2
1946	125.4	—	—	125.4	447.6	28.0
1949	125.4	—	—	125.4	565.3	22.2
1953	125.4	—	—	125.4	1,169.0	10.7
1954	192.1	—	—	125.4	1,145.0	11.0
1959	178.6	60.9	38.0	277.5	1,837.0	15.1

(Continued on next page)

TABLE A–59 (CONTINUED)

C. Estate Land‖

Year	Tea Acres (000)	Tea % of Total	Rubber Acres (000)	Rubber % of Total	Coconut Acres (000)	Coconut % of Total
1939	.....	.....	.....	.....	.....	.....
1946	.....	.....	.....	.....	.....	.....
1949	.....	.....	264.4	42.0	.....	.....
1951	.....	.....	245.2	37.4	18.4	1.7#
1953	291.7	50.8	240.4	36.6	.....	.....
1954	282.8	49.1	237.9	36.1	.....	.....
1959	245.6	42.4	104.6	15.7	.....	.....

*Subject to the limitations mentioned in the other footnotes, the table gives an idea of the foreigner's share in some leading types of assets. Foreign holdings of other assets—e.g., nonestate businesses, currency—are not known.

†Includes deposits of foreign banks and nonbank constituents.

‡Includes only *known* foreign assets; e.g., currency holdings by foreigners, a liability of the Central Bank, are not included.

§From the U.S, U.S.S.R., Canada, and China.

‖In all cases, the foreign holding is taken to be the sum of the holdings of sterling companies and non-Ceylonese individuals. There is, however, some further foreign ownership, which is indirectly exercised through ownership of stock in rupee companies.

#The percentage is approximate, since the total acreage is not precisely known.

Sources: Central Bank of Ceylon, *Annual Report of the Monetary Board to the Minister of Finance, 1961*; *A.R. of the Tea Controller*, various years; *A.R. of the Rubber Controller*, various years; Department of Census and Statistics, *Census of Ceylon 1946*, Vol. 1.

TABLE A–60

EXTERNAL ASSETS OF CEYLON, 1939–60*

(Million Rupees)

Year	Govern- ment†	Government Agencies and Institutions‡	Central Bank§	Commer- cial Banks‖	Total	Changes between Periods
1939#......	23.5	106.3	60.8	84.5	275.1	.....
1940.......	29.3	67.2	80.2	147.7	324.4	+ 49.3
1941.......	99.9	95.6	105.9	133.3	434.7	+110.3
1942.......	51.6	66.4	192.0	211.4	521.4	+ 86.7
1943.......	135.8	81.5	229.7	224.6	671.6	+150.2
1944.......	259.8	103.7	313.9	282.6	960.0	+288.4
1945.......	420.6	142.3	460.5	236.5	1,259.9	+299.9
1946.......	393.5	184.4	415.2	217.2	1,210.3	− 49.6
1947.......	178.9	206.9	440.5	121.0	947.3	−263.0
1948.......	157.4	222.3	459.9	158.3	997.9	+ 50.6
1949.......	86.8	235.8	514.9	126.2	963.7	− 34.2
1950.......	76.8	265.7	565.1	225.3	1,132.9	+169.2
1951.......	76.1	291.3	668.4	181.0	1,216.8	+ 83.9
1952.......	65.9	310.6	401.1	96.2	873.8	−343.0
1953.......	70.2	228.4	245.1	96.7	640.4	−233.4
1954.......	61.5	225.8	524.5	132.5	944.3	+303.9
1955.......	111.7	237.2	655.2	224.7	1,228.8	+284.5
1956.......	134.6	243.1	737.0	161.0	1,275.7	+ 46.9
1957.......	112.3	249.4	590.8	109.4	1,061.9	−213.8
1958.......	24.5	255.5	538.7	114.5	933.2	−128.7
1959.......	16.0	229.7	386.7	101.6	734.0	−199.2
1960.......	20.0	219.4	190.2	111.7	541.3	−192.7

*The figures refer to the liquid asset holdings of the institutions listed and, within this definition, provide quite comprehensive information. Types of assets which are excluded are foreign bank deposits and other intangible assets held by individuals and all foreign tangible assets held by Ceylon residents.

†Includes amounts receivable under bilateral trade and payments agreements with China.

‡Valued at face value.

§Prior to the establishment of the Central Bank in 1950, the figures refer to the external assets of the Currency Board. The reserve is valued at cost or face value, whichever is less. It includes balances due to Ceylon from bilateral clearings with all countries except China.

‖Amounts to the sum of foreign currency on hand in local banks, balances due to local banks from abroad, and export bills purchased and discounted by them.

#All figures are year-end.

Source: Central Bank of Ceylon, *Annual Report of the Monetary Board to the Minister of Finance*, 1961.

TABLE A–61

The Money Supply and Its Components, 1938–60*

(Million Rupees)

Year	Currency Held by Public†	Demand Deposits Held by Public			"Money Supply"§	Time and Savings Deposits				Savings Certificates
		Resident‖	Nonresident	Total‡		Commercial Banks		Other Institutions#	Total¶	
						Resident‖	Nonresident‖			
1938‡	33.9	.....	.....	.....	.....	.....	.....	38.4	.....	1.2
1939	41.5	.....	.....	.....	.....	.....	.....	39.2	.....	1.6
1940	50.4	.....	.....	.....	.....	.....	.....	38.0	.....	3.1
1941	82.2	.....	.....	.....	.....	.....	.....	37.5	.....	3.4
1942	163.5	.....	.....	267.2	430.7	.....	.....	33.4	.....	2.5
1943	193.2	.....	.....	245.1	438.3	41.4	.....	48.0	89.4	10.7
1944	281.9	.....	.....	334.2	616.1	51.3	.....	71.9	123.2	18.2
1945	330.4	.....	.....	399.0	729.4	63.6	.....	116.5	180.1	25.8
1946	274.7	.....	.....	392.1	666.8	61.0	.....	164.4	225.4	27.8
1947	238.1	.....	.....	324.4	562.5	63.6	.....	177.5	241.1	27.0
1948	241.1	.....	.....	365.7	606.8	67.5	.....	184.9	252.4	33.2

1949......	243.9	396.1	9.4	404.9	648.8	46.5	5.2	191.5	243.5	32.1
1950......	325.4	572.1	13.2	575.1	900.5	67.5	5.4	222.1	295.0	27.0
1951......	377.4	609.6	15.1	618.4	995.8	83.9	2.9	270.1	356.9	26.8
1952......	356.6	524.8	12.7	531.1	887.7	100.0	1.1	289.0	390.1	27.5
1953......	335.3	481.7	9.3	477.6	812.9	98.7	1.2	287.5	387.4	26.6
1954......	341.8	591.2	9.9	603.9	945.7	133.6	2.3	284.1	420.0	25.5
1955......	384.5	664.3	11.2	670.3	1,054.8	150.2	1.8	299.4	451.4	24.8
1956......	401.1	709.7	8.9	703.5	1,104.6	185.7	1.7	324.7	512.1	26.6
1957......	434.9	593.1	8.3	585.6	1,020.5	213.9	1.7	343.9	559.5	29.2
1958......	529.8	536.3	9.9	511.3	1,041.1	253.3	7.7	363.9	624.9	29.7
1959......	565.0	599.8	8.9	589.2	1,154.2	293.5	6.3	394.1	693.9	31.2
1960......	595.3	595.6	11.8	588.9	1,184.2	357.0	6.6	418.9	782.5	32.2

*Since there is no single definition of the "money supply" which is completely acceptable for all analytic purposes, various possible components of different concepts of "money supply" are presented here.

†Includes subsidiary notes and coins. Consists of the total currency issue of the Central Bank (before 1950, of the Currency Board) minus cash balances known to be held by the central government and the commercial banks.

‡From 1949 on, excludes central government and interbank deposits, as well as float. Prior to 1949, no data on float exist, so it is included in total deposits. From 1950 on the total includes a small amount of deposits held in the Central Bank by others than the central government and commercial banks. The "total demand deposits" figure differs from the sum of the "resident" and "nonresident" columns by this figure plus the float.

§"Money supply" here refers to the sum of public currency holdings and public demand deposits, as defined in footnotes † and ‡.

‖Time and savings deposits are not identifiable by type prior to 1949; resident and nonresident accounts are thus lumped together and central government accounts —which are excluded from 1949 on—are included in this total. For reference, the government accounts amounted to Rs. 14,700,000 in 1949.

#Refers to the Post Office Savings Bank and the Ceylon Savings Bank.

¶After 1948, excludes government time and savings deposits (all in commercial banks). These deposits are included through 1948—see footnote ‖.

Source: Central Bank of Ceylon, *Annual Report of the Monetary Board to the Minister of Finance*, various years.

TABLE A-62

Ownership of Commercial Bank Deposits, 1956–61*

Year	Financial Institutions Rs. 000,000	%	Plantations Rs. 000,000	%	Trading Business Rs. 000,000	%	Other Business Rs. 000,000	%	Local Government Rs. 000,000	%	Nonbusiness Institutions Rs. 000,000	%	Individual Rs. 000,000	%	Total Rs. 000,000	%
A. Demand Deposits																
1956	53.7	8.4	179.0	28.0	99.8	15.6			43.1	6.8	29.2	4.6	233.3	36.6	638.1	100.0
1957	50.3	8.4	154.7	26.0	100.9	17.0			19.5	3.3	25.9	4.4	243.5	40.9	594.8	100.0
1958	44.4	8.0	133.3	24.2	117.3	21.3			17.7	3.2	27.4	5.0	211.8	38.4	551.9	100.0
1959	42.3	7.6	135.6	24.2	(60.5)	10.8	65.1	11.6	12.2	2.2	25.5	4.6	218.9	39.1	560.1	100.0
1960	48.7	8.3	129.3	22.0	73.3	12.5	50.7	8.6	16.9	2.9	26.8	4.6	241.7	41.1	587.4	100.0
1961	46.5	7.8	101.4	17.1	91.2	15.4	68.9	11.8	21.0	3.5	33.8	5.7	230.0	38.8	592.8	100.0
B. Time and Savings Deposits																
1956	26.9	15.1	35.5	19.9	8.5	4.8			8.3	4.7	8.2	4.6	91.0	51.0	178.3	100.0
1957	29.3	13.3	25.4	11.5	24.9	11.3			21.7	9.9	5.4	2.5	113.4	51.5	220.0	100.0
1958	49.2	21.1	17.5	7.5	21.3	9.1			16.8	7.2	3.8	1.6	125.1	53.6	233.6	100.0
1959	46.6	16.6	36.5	13.0	(9.4)	3.3	27.4	9.8	10.2	3.6	8.0	2.8	142.7	50.8	280.9	100.0
1960	56.6	16.8	53.8	15.9	12.7	3.8	39.9	11.8	6.3	1.9	10.7	3.2	157.5	46.7	337.4	100.0
1961	58.7	17.6	44.5	13.3	14.4	4.3	19.3	5.8	19.2	5.7	9.6	2.9	168.7	50.5	334.3	100.0

C. All Deposits

Year	Amt	%	Amt	%	Amt	%	Amt	%	Amt	%	Amt	%	Amt	%	Total	%
1956	80.6	9.9	214.5	26.3	108.2	13.3			51.4	6.3	37.4	4.6	324.3	39.7	816.4	100.0
1957	79.6	9.8	180.1	22.1	125.8	15.4			41.2	5.1	31.3	3.8	336.9	43.8	814.8	100.0
1958	93.6	11.9	150.8	19.2	138.6	17.6			34.5	4.4	31.2	4.0	336.9	42.9	785.5	100.0
1959	88.9	10.6	172.1	20.5	(69.9)	8.3	92.5	(11.0)	22.4	2.7	33.5	4.0	361.6	43.0	841.0	100.0
1960	105.3	11.4	183.1	19.8	86.0	9.3	90.6	9.8	23.2	2.5	37.5	4.1	399.2	43.2	924.8	100.0
1961	105.2	11.3	145.9	15.7	105.6	11.4	88.2	9.5	40.2	4.3	43.4	4.7	398.7	43.0	927.1	100.0

*This table provides a detailed breakdown by type of ownership of total commercial bank demand, time, and savings deposits held by the resident public (i.e., excluding holdings by the central government and foreigners and interbank deposits). The data refer to September 30 of each year. They originate in special semiannual surveys conducted by the Central Bank Research Department and are available only for the indicated years.

Source: *Central Bank of Ceylon Bulletin*, various issues; *Annual Report of the Monetary Board to the Minister of Finance*, various years.

TABLE A-63
SELECTED INTEREST RATES, 1946-60*
(Percent per Annum)

Year	Treasury Bills†	Central Bank Advances‡	Commercial Banks§ Fixed Deposits||	Commercial Banks§ Savings Deposits	Post Office Savings Bank	Ceylon Savings Bank	Savings Certificates
1946	...	...	...	...	2.0	...	3.3–3.5
1947	...	...	...	...	2.0	...	3.3–3.5
1948	...	...	...	...	2.0	...	3.3–3.5
1949	...	...	...	...	2.0	2.5	3.3–3.5
1950	0.52	...	...	...	2.0	2.5	3.3–3.5
1951	0.40	2.5	0.5–2.5	1.0–2.5	2.0	2.5	3.3–3.5
1952	0.92	2.5	0.75	1.0–2.0	2.0	2.5	3.3–3.5
1953	2.48	3.0	1.50	1.0–2.0	2.0	2.5	3.3–3.5
1954	0.87	2.5	0.75	1.0–2.0	2.0	2.5	3.3–3.5
1955	0.76	2.5	0.50	2.0	2.0	2.5	3.3–3.5
1956	0.64	2.5	0.50	2.0	2.0	2.5	5.0
1957	1.22	2.5	1.25–2.0	2.0	2.0	2.5	5.0
1958	1.76	2.5	1.25–2.0	2.0	2.0	2.5	5.0
1959	2.02	2.5	1.25–2.0	2.0	2.0	2.5	5.0
1960	2.60	4.0	2.5	2.0	2.0	2.5	5.0

Year	Commercial Banks# Discounts¶	Loans I**	Loans II††	Loans III‡‡	IV§§	Long-Term Loans||||	Long-Term Government Bonds##
1946	...	...	...	...	...	...	...
1947	...	...	...	...	...	...	...

Year							
1948	.....	.....	.....	.....	.....	.....	.....
1949	.....	.....	.....	.....	.....	.....	.....
1950	.....	.....	.....	.....	.....	3.5–6.5	.....
1951	2.5–7.5	2.25–5.0	3.0–8.0	3.0–12.0	3.0–15.0	3.5–6.5	2.57
1952	2.5–6.0	2.25–5.0	3.0–8.0	4.0–7.0	3.0–8.0	3.5–6.5	2.53
1953	3.0–6.5	3.5–5.0	4.0–8.0	4.5–7.5	3.5–8.0	3.5–6.5	3.36
1954	3.0–6.5	3.0–4.5	4.0–8.0	4.5–7.5	3.5–8.0	3.0–6.5	2.93
1955	3.0–6.5	3.0–4.5	4.0–8.0	4.5–7.5	4.0–8.0	3.0–6.5	3.06
1956	3.0–6.5	3.0–4.5	4.5–8.0	4.5–7.5	4.0–8.0	3.0–6.5	3.00
1957	3.0–6.5	3.0–5.0	4.5–8.0	4.5–7.5	4.5–8.0	3.0–6.5	2.98
1958	3.0–6.5	3.0–5.0	4.5–8.0	4.5–7.5	4.5–8.0	3.0–5.5	2.90
1959	3.0–6.5	3.0–5.0	4.5–8.0	4.5–7.5	4.5–8.0	3.0–5.5	2.82
1960	4.0–8.0	4.5–7.5	4.5–8.0	5.5–8.0	4.5–8.0	3.0–5.5	3.24

*This table lists only certain selected rates, yet should give a good general picture of the levels and trends of short and long-term interest rates on various kinds of transactions in recent years. The information is valid though only in regard to the institutions specifically mentioned here; it takes no account of the activities of noninstitutional lenders like pawnbrokers and rural moneylenders, whose rates at any given time are certain to be much higher than those listed here. Where a range of rates were charged by different institutions for a specific transaction and no simple means of taking a weighted average presented itself, the range of rates itself was entered in the table. Most of these data have been compiled by the Central Bank and this explains the paucity of data prior to the bank's founding in 1950. All rates are those prevailing on December 31, unless otherwise noted.

†A weighted average rate on all bills issued during December of the year in question.

‡Rate on advances secured by the pledge of government securities.

§Rates prevailing on the last Friday in December. The data refer only to the larger commercial banks. In general, no interest is paid on demand deposits. "Fixed deposits" cannot be withdrawn for a given period of time—3, 6, or 12 months—and pay interest only for that fixed period. The rates given here are those paid on six-month deposits.

#All rates are those prevailing on the last Friday in December.

¶Rates on trade bills purchased and discounted.

**Loans secured by government securities.

††Loans secured by stock in trade.

‡‡Loans secured by immovable property.

§§Unsecured loans.

‖Mortgages and other long-term loans made by the Agricultural and Industrial Credit Corporation, the Ceylon Savings Bank, the State Mortgage Bank, and the Loan Board.

##Represents the redemption yield if held until the latest redemption date of the long-term bond issue with a latest redemption date nearest to ten years after the year in question.

Source: Central Bank of Ceylon, *Annual Report of the Monetary Board to the Minister of Finance*, various years, Department of Economic Research (unpublished data).

TABLE A–64

LOCAL COMPANIES REGISTERED AND LIQUIDATED, 1944–60

Years	Number Regis- tered*	Nominal Share Capital† (Rs. 000)	Number Liqui- dated	Net Change
1944............	47	13,585	10	+ 37
1945............	138	89,910	12	126
1946............	212	160,961	13	199
1947............	176	117,940	19	157
1948............	114	85,375	16	98
1949............	108	117,955	26	82
1950............	115	91,536	16	99
1951............	179	177,625	26	153
1952............	161	184,815	17	144
1953............	145	179,245	31	114
1954............	131	144,474	35	96
1955............	125	174,273	35	90
1956............	127	232,267	15	102
1957............	112	117,850	25	87
1958............	82	216,297	33	49
1959............	89	218,905	16	73
1960............	63	117,859	20	43

*Excludes companies with no share capital.
†Initial capital only; excludes any increase after registration.
Source: *A.R. of the Registrar of Companies*, various years.

TABLE A-65

CENTRAL GOVERNMENT REVENUE, SELECTED YEARS, 1928/29—1960/61*

(Rs. Million)

	1928/29	1930/31	1938/39	1945/46	1946/47	1947/48	1948/49	1949/50	1950/51	1951/52
Customs duties................	52.8	43.4	55.3	146.6	250.0	314.0	329.3	355.9	527.7	487.2
Export duties.................	11.9	9.9	3.4	13.9	83.3	137.0	149.1	167.6	282.7	227.3
Import duties.................	40.9	33.5	51.9	132.6	166.7	177.0	180.2	188.3	245.0	259.9
Direct taxes..................	3.0	2.7	20.4	108.7	92.0	100.5	117.7	128.0	144.3	218.1
Income tax...................	—	—	17.4	61.8	55.2	62.0	76.6	78.5	96.4	146.9
On individuals†............	—	—	7.3	32.1	25.9	32.1	41.2	41.6	45.0	70.0
On companies†.............	—	—	10.1	29.7	29.3	29.9	35.4	36.9	51.4	76.9
Other: individuals...........	3.0	2.7	3.0	5.4	6.2	8.0	7.2	11.0	9.3	13.3
Social security contributions..	1.2	1.5	1.9	2.7	3.7	4.2	4.6	4.8	5.1	7.4
Other‡....................	1.8	1.2	1.1	2.7	2.5	3.8	2.6	6.2	4.2	5.9
Other: companies§..........	—	—	—	41.5	30.7	30.6	33.8	38.5	38.6	57.9
Commodity taxes‖............	17.4	14.2	14.7	67.8	63.0	64.0	62.8	65.0	84.6	78.3
Nontax revenue...............	34.6	41.5	26.5	60.2	56.2	62.1	66.2	74.4	75.7	86.2
Charges and sales#...........	20.4	18.3	16.7	31.0	31.5	39.4	45.6	52.5	57.7	66.2
Receipts from government enterprises¶...	—	—	0.3	0.1	4.4	9.9	7.0	8.8	1.8	2.3
Income from property**........	12.0	6.8	4.1	15.3	11.0	10.7	11.4	11.0	13.6	13.7
Annuity payments and repayments of advances made from revenue††......	2.2	16.4	5.4	13.8	9.3	2.1	2.2	2.1	2.6	4.0
Total revenue................	107.8	101.7	116.9	383.3	461.2	540.6	576.0	623.3	832.3	869.8
Surplus.....................	−18.1	1.1	−33.0	34.4	23.7	−52.3	−115.1	−172.4	−58.3	−287.7

(Continued on next page)

TABLE A-65 (Continued)

	1952/53	1953/54	1954/55	1955/56	1956/57	1957/58	1958/59	1959/60	1960/61
Customs duties..........	443.8	503.3	628.9	608.4	627.5	617.0	695.9	733.7	738.9
Export duties...........	193.2	259.1	370.7	322.1	323.9	325.0	328.9	327.2	303.6
Import duties...........	250.6	244.1	258.2	286.3	303.6	292.0	367.0	406.5	435.3
Direct taxes...........	243.5	231.3	219.7	313.6	282.6	278.7	218.2	215.2	313.9
Income tax............	163.2	155.0	153.2	213.0	202.2	192.4	194.8	189.5	258.8
On individuals†	81.1	76.2	73.4	85.1	84.6	85.3	68.2	58.7	......
On companies†	82.2	78.8	79.9	127.9	117.6	107.1	126.6	130.8	......
Other: individuals.....	11.1	13.5	13.3	13.9	11.1	13.9	17.0	21.0	50.9
Social security contributions.....	5.9	6.2	6.6	7.5	7.9	8.5	9.5	10.9	12.2
Other...........	5.2	7.3	6.7	6.4	3.2	5.4	7.5	10.1	38.7
Other: companies§	69.2	62.8	53.2	86.7	69.4	72.5	6.4	4.7	4.2
Commodity taxes‖	92.8	100.6	95.4	112.1	131.9	147.9	160.9	190.9	190.6
Nontax revenue.........	87.8	99.6	119.8	122.8	112.6	137.1	142.5	143.6	147.1
Charges and sales#.....	65.6	73.8	79.4	84.8	85.0	90.1	99.1	107.0	110.5
Receipts from government enterprises¶...	0.8	—	1.8	5.9	3.3	16.6	3.9	1.2	1.5
Income from property**.........	14.6	15.6	19.4	18.2	18.6	24.5	21.5	21.3	20.5

Annuity payments and repayments of advances made from revenue††	6.8	10.2	19.2	13.9	5.7	5.9	18.0	14.1	14.6
Total revenue	867.8	934.8	1,063.8	1,156.9	1,154.6	1,180.7	1,217.5	1,283.4	1,390.5
Surplus	−247.0	5.0	90.5	−65.5	−245.5	−273.3	−442.8	−458.6	−490.9

*This table and the one that follows are based on a reclassification of the official accounts (which are embodied in *The Accounts of the Government of Ceylon*) made by the Department of Economic Research of the Central Bank of Ceylon. By and large the bank's reclassification conforms with UN usage, but in one important instance—the treatment of government enterprises—it does not. It includes the railway and electrical departments on a gross basis (though public corporations are treated on a net basis). Insofar as possible the present table converts these two major commercial departments to a net basis in the accounts—that is, they are included only so far as they remit profits or losses to the government (they keep no balances, so their total deficit or surplus can be treated as a subsidy or tax). Also, their capital expenditure has been removed from that of the government. Other departments than these two which provide services to the public—post and tele-communications, medical, port, etc.—have been included here on a gross basis. The Central Bank data go back to 1947/48; for earlier years, data from the auditor-general's report were used. Revenues were reclassified by the author in accordance with the scheme used for later years, but the much more difficult reclassification of expenditures was not undertaken. All data refer to the budget year, October 1 to September 30.

†Estimates based on tax assessments by the relevant department.
‡Includes estate duty, wealth, gift, and personal expenditure taxes (last three from 1959/60 only).
§Includes profits and excess profits taxes.
‖Includes excise taxes, licenses, etc.
#Includes both the sale of property—stores and Crown land—and returns from the provision of services to the public by the post office, port, etc.
¶Transfers from the Railway and Electrical Department and the autonomously organized government enterprises.
**Interest and rent.
††Loan repayments by autonomous government enterprises.
Source: Central Bank of Ceylon, *Annual Report of the Monetary Board to the Minister of Finance*, 1962, *Accounts of the Government of Ceylon*, S.P. (annual; 1948–); *Auditor-General's Report*, S.P. (annual; before 1948).

TABLE A-66

CENTRAL GOVERNMENT EXPENDITURE, 1928/29–1960/61*

(Rs. Million)

	1928/29	1930/31	1938/39	1945/46	1946/47	1947/48	1948/49	1949/50	1950/51	1951/52
Current expenditure on goods and services.....	.....	.....	.....	.....	.....	260.6	293.6	321.7	383.6	420.7
Administration.....	.....	.....	.....	.....	.....	60.4	67.6	69.8	99.7	86.0
Defense†.....	.....	.....	.....	.....	.....	2.9	4.5	6.9	9.7	15.0
Social services.....	.....	.....	.....	.....	.....	128.6	139.2	156.6	172.1	207.5
Economic services.....	.....	.....	.....	.....	.....	68.7	82.3	88.4	102.1	112.2
Transfer payments.....	.....	.....	.....	.....	.....	172.7	158.6	141.5	246.4	382.7
To private sector.....	.....	.....	.....	.....	.....	142.7	135.7	114.5	219.2	353.6
Food subsidies.....	.....	.....	.....	.....	.....	77.8	55.1	35.8	131.6	247.8
Interest on national debt.	.....	.....	.....	.....	.....	17.8	18.5	19.7	21.4	23.2
Other†.....	.....	.....	.....	.....	.....	47.1	62.1	59.0	66.2	82.6
To government enterprises.	.....	.....	.....	.....	.....	4.9	6.7	6.1	8.7	7.5
To local government.....	.....	.....	.....	.....	.....	25.1	16.2	20.9	18.5	21.6
Capital expenditure.....	.....	.....	.....	.....	.....	152.5	209.2	241.6	228.7	320.7
Administration.....	.....	.....	.....	.....	.....	6.3	10.5	28.3	7.6	8.0
Social services.....	.....	.....	.....	.....	.....	18.6	34.9	52.2	48.5	62.6
Economic services.....	.....	.....	.....	.....	.....	127.6	163.8	161.1	172.6	250.1
Loans and net advances.....	.....	.....	.....	.....	.....	7.1	29.7	90.9	31.9	33.4
Total expenditure.....	126.1	100.6	134.7	348.9	437.5	592.9	691.1	795.7	890.6	1,157.5
Surplus.....	−18.1	1.1	−33.0	34.4	23.7	−52.3	−115.1	−172.4	−58.3	−287.7

	1952/53	1953/54	1954/55	1955/56	1956/57	1957/58	1958/59	1959/60	1960/61
Current expenditures on goods and services.............	457.3	470.1	526.2	547.1	595.3	684.6	790.1	847.5	871.7
Administration..........	100.7	100.4	126.7	126.7	145.8	157.0	167.2	172.4	189.9
Defense†...............	28.4	31.4	26.5	30.4	33.6	64.1	72.4	70.4	74.0
Social services........	212.8	225.0	233.9	256.9	277.9	314.4	377.4	420.2	418.5
Economic services.....	115.4	113.3	142.1	133.1	138.0	149.1	173.1	184.5	189.3
Transfer payments........	278.6	147.9	191.0	288.4	341.4	406.5	451.5	480.4	549.3
To private sector.....	234.5	115.7	137.7	208.4	261.5	313.2	353.1	385.9	458.2
Food subsidies........	127.0	12.5	36.0	79.5	105.5	112.0	146.5	193.0	248.0
Interest on national debt.	29.5	35.9	33.5	34.0	34.8	38.5	44.0	53.1	68.6
Other†................	78.0	67.3	68.2	94.9	121.2	162.7	162.6	139.8	141.6
To government enterprises.	21.0	9.4	30.0	55.6	53.6	60.7	63.6	58.8	55.1
To local government.....	23.1	22.8	23.3	24.4	26.3	32.5	34.8	35.7	36.0
Capital expenditure........	316.5	253.8	295.1	307.8	298.8	350.4	363.0	357.2	399.0
Administration..........	12.5	10.1	9.0	16.4	13.6	18.2	14.3	11.0	12.4
Social services........	76.6	60.6	80.4	100.5	86.9	79.8	76.5	70.0	78.9
Economic services.....	227.4	183.1	205.7	190.9	198.3	252.4	272.2	276.2	307.7
Loans and net advances....	62.4	57.8	−39.0	79.1	164.5	12.9	55.6	56.9	61.4
Total expenditure.........	1,114.8	929.8	973.3	1,222.4	1,400.1	1,454.2	1,660.3	1,742.0	1,881.4
Surplus...................	−247.0	5.0	90.5	−65.5	−245.5	−273.3	−442.8	−458.6	−490.9

*See footnote * Table A–65.
†By contrast with the Central Bank tables, but in accordance with UN recommended practice, all defense expenditure is considered current.
‡Includes pensions, direct relief, and subsidies and grants to private enterprises.
Sources: Central Bank of Ceylon, *Annual Reports of the Monetary Board to the Minister of Finance, Accounts of the Government of Ceylon*, S.P. (annual; 1948–); *Auditor-General's Report*, S.P. (annual; before 1948).

TABLE A-67

CENTRAL GOVERNMENT DEFICIT BY MEANS OF FINANCING, 1949/50–1960/61*

(Rs. Million)

Year	Foreign				Domestic						Total Deficit
	Grants	Loans†	Decline in External Assets‡	Total Foreign	Central Bank	Commercial Banks	Nonbank Borrowing	Administrative Borrowing§	Decline in Cash Balances and Reserves‖	Total Domestic	
1949/50#	——	——	8.2	8.2	18.8	52.1	7.5	16.8	69.0	164.2	172.4
1950/51	——	——	−46.3	−46.3	− 1.7	− 7.7	89.6	42.1	−17.7	104.6	58.3
1951/52	6.5	——	−19.6	−13.1	143.5	46.1	28.7	−22.0	104.5	300.8	287.7
1952/53	3.3	——	83.6	86.9	62.8	−11.5	153.3	18.5	−63.0	160.1	247.0
1953/54	19.1	63.3	28.2	110.6	−196.4	8.2	94.2	− 9.0	−12.6	−115.6	− 5.0
1954/55	26.0	12.1	−47.0	− 8.9	− 8.7	− 5.6	−65.9	27.2	−28.6	− 81.6	− 90.5
1955/56	23.2	5.2	− 9.0	19.4	− 7.7	41.2	10.0	−14.6	17.2	46.1	65.5
1956/57	10.5	18.6	23.0	52.1	74.8	− 1.1	92.6	5.5	21.6	193.4	245.5
1957/58	13.1	23.7	4.7	41.5	175.6	−33.3	−63.8	86.8	66.5	231.8	273.3
1958/59	18.2	33.0	36.1	87.3	144.0	3.1	144.1	20.6	43.7	355.5	442.8
1959/60	9.3	26.6	20.8	56.7	273.0	1.7	52.9	68.9	5.4	401.9	458.6
1960/61	13.3	13.3	4.8	31.4	205.1	43.1	158.3	35.5	17.4	459.4	490.8

*By budget year (October 1–September 30).
†Actual drawings during the year, net of repayments.
‡Includes assets held by government and by government agencies and institutions.
§Refers to paper borrowing from various deposits and miscellaneous trust funds.
‖Excludes, of course, decline in foreign asset holdings.
#The figure for commercial banks refers only to the last nine months of the financial year; this causes a degree of inaccuracy in the totals for nonbank borrowing and decline in cash balances and reserves, but the other figures are unaffected.
Source: Central Bank of Ceylon, *Annual Reports of the Monetary Board to the Minister of Finance.*

TABLE A-68

LOCAL GOVERNMENT REVENUE AND EXPENDITURE, 1948–60*

(Rs. Million)

	1948	1949	1950	1951	1952	1953	1954	1955	1956	1957	1959	1959†	1960†
A. Totals													
Revenue													
Municipalities	18.7	24.1	29.1	27.6	31.2	34.7	34.0	26.3	35.5	37.8	42.2	45.3	45.5
Urban councils	11.6	10.1	11.1	13.0	14.1	16.1	16.3	18.9	18.9	21.5	23.2	23.9	26.5
Town councils	...	...	...	...	1.9	2.1	2.2	1.6	2.6	2.6	3.4	3.8	...
Village committees	...	...	...	...	10.0	8.8	8.2	8.3	8.2	9.2	12.5	12.4	14.4
Total	...	...	...	...	57.2	61.8	60.8	55.0	65.2	71.1	81.2	85.5	...
Expenditure													
Municipalities	16.1	21.7	24.2	23.7	30.2	32.7	30.9	26.8	38.2	40.4	40.1	41.8	42.8
Urban councils	12.0	10.6	10.7	12.4	14.0	15.4	16.2	19.5	19.5	21.2	22.7	24.5	27.2
Town councils	...	...	...	...	2.0	2.0	2.2	2.7	2.7	2.7	3.2	3.3	...
Village committees	...	...	...	...	8.8	8.5	7.7	8.4	8.5	12.4	12.6	11.7	14.2
Total	...	...	...	...	55.0	58.6	57.0	57.4	68.9	76.7	78.6	81.4	...
B. Breakdown: Municipalities													
Revenue													
Taxes	11.3	12.7	14.1	13.8	14.4	16.7	16.7	13.5	18.2	18.5	20.3	21.6	21.7
Property	9.2	10.1	10.6	10.6	11.0	12.9	13.3	10.7	14.6	15.0	16.7	17.5	17.6
Other‡	2.1	2.6	3.6	3.3	3.4	3.8	3.4	2.8	3.6	3.5	3.6	4.1	4.1
Central government grants and refunds	4.2	5.7	8.5	6.8	8.9	9.3	8.1	7.2	9.1	10.5	13.0	13.2	13.3
Other: fees, etc.	3.2	5.7	6.5	7.0	7.9	8.7	9.2	5.8	8.2	8.8	8.9	10.5	10.5
Total	18.7	24.1	29.1	27.6	31.2	34.7	34.0	26.3	35.5	37.8	42.2	45.3	45.5
Expenditure													
Public health	2.2	3.0	3.1	3.3	3.5	3.8	3.9	3.8	4.6	4.7	5.0	9.2	9.4
Water	1.4	1.5	1.6	1.6	2.1	2.1	1.7	1.9	2.4	2.8	2.8	2.9	3.0
Public works	6.2	7.6	8.4	7.0	10.1	11.3	9.9	8.2	11.7	12.4	11.5	8.8	8.8

(Continued on next page)

TABLE A-68 (CONTINUED)

	1948	1949	1950	1951	1952	1953	1954	1955	1956	1957	1959	1959†	1960†
Assistance and poor relief...	1.0	1.7	2.3	2.0	3.2	3.4	3.8	3.0	4.0	3.8	4.0	3.2	3.2
Electricity...	—	1.6	1.9	2.3	2.7	2.9	2.0	1.4	3.4	3.3	3.4	3.7	5.1
Other...	5.3	6.3	6.9	7.5	8.6	9.2	9.6	8.5	12.1	13.4	13.4	14.0	13.3
Total...	16.1	21.7	24.2	23.7	30.2	32.7	30.9	26.8	38.2	40.4	40.1	41.8	42.8

C. Breakdown: Urban Councils

	1948	1949	1950	1951	1952	1953	1954	1955	1956	1957	1959	1959†	1960†
Revenue													
Taxes...	3.5	3.2	3.3	3.3	2.8	3.4	3.3	3.7	6.6	7.1	7.3	7.8	7.3
Property...	1.8	1.7	1.7	1.8	1.9	2.1	2.2	2.7	2.7	2.9	3.0	3.2	3.8
Other...	1.7	1.5	1.6	1.5	0.9	1.4	1.1	1.0	3.9	4.2	4.4	4.5	3.5
Central government grants and refunds§...	7.5	3.9	4.5	5.4	5.9	6.5	5.9	7.3	7.3	4.1	5.3	5.5	8.4
Other: fees, etc.‖...	0.6	3.0	3.3	4.3	5.4	6.2	7.1	7.9	5.0	10.3	10.6	10.6	10.8
Total...	11.6	10.1	11.1	13.0	14.1	16.1	16.3	18.9	18.9	21.5	23.2	23.9	26.5
Expenditure#													
Water...	0.3	0.2	0.2	0.2	0.2	0.3	0.3	0.5	0.5	0.5	0.5	0.6	0.7
Electricity...	3.4	3.2	3.5	4.0	4.5	5.3	5.8	6.9	6.9	7.2	7.8	8.8	10.2
Other‖...	8.3	7.2	7.0	8.2	9.3	9.8	10.1	12.1	12.1	14.5	14.4	15.1	16.3
Total...	12.0	10.6	10.7	12.4	14.0	15.4	16.2	19.5	19.5	22.2	22.7	24.5	27.2

*These data are of a much lower degree of reliability and consistency of classification than the corresponding central government statistics in Tables A-65 and A-66. The totals for the municipalities derive from the official records of the various municipalities themselves, while those for the other legal entities are from the Department of Local Government. They generally include local government enterprises (electricity, water, etc.) on a gross basis.
†Provisional.
‡Includes licenses.
§Includes assigned revenue from central government taxes, fees, etc.
‖In the records of the Department of Local Government, the various categories of revenue and expenditure often fail to correspond to the published totals; the reason for this, according to the Department of Census and Statistics, is improper filling in of reporting forms by some urban council officials. The procedure followed here is to accept the overall total and the figures given for the categories identified separately; "Other," however, is a residual, consisting of stated total revenue or expenditure minus the separately identified categories.
#No other important categories of expenditure can be identified.
Source: Department of Census and Statistics, Statistical Abstract, 1960 and 1961.

TABLE 11 66

Public Debt Outstanding, 1938–61*

(Rs. Million)

Year End	Rupee Debt	Sterling Debt	Other Foreign Debt†	Total Funded Debt	Floating Debt‡	Gross Debt	Sinking Funds§	Net Debt	Change in Net Debt	I.M.F. & I.B.R.D. Notes‖
1938	30.9	163.2	—	194.1	—	194.1	66.3	127.8	......	—
1939	40.3	163.4	—	203.7	—	203.7	63.2	140.5	+ 12.7	—
1940	45.3	125.4	—	170.7	—	170.7	26.3	144.4	+ 3.9	—
1941	55.3	125.4	—	180.7	—	180.7	31.4	149.3	+ 4.9	—
1942	67.1	125.4	—	192.5	10.0	202.5	36.0	166.5	+ 17.2	—
1943	103.3	125.4	—	228.7	9.5	238.2	39.8	198.4	+ 31.9	—
1944	169.2	125.4	—	294.6	12.0	306.6	43.7	262.9	+ 64.5	—
1945	266.9	125.4	—	392.3	9.0	401.3	50.1	351.2	+ 88.3	—
1946	312.2	125.4	—	437.6	10.0	447.6	60.2	387.4	+ 36.2	—
1947	343.5	125.4	—	468.9	—	468.9	73.1	395.8	+ 8.4	—
1948	367.5	125.4	—	492.9	24.0	516.9	90.4	426.5	+ 30.7	—
1949	423.7	125.4	—	549.1	16.2	565.3	105.2	460.1	+ 33.6	—
1950	436.0	125.4	—	561.4	78.6	640.0	119.7	520.3	+ 60.2	—
1951	582.0	125.4	—	707.4	30.0	737.4	162.5	575.0	+ 54.7	—
1952	684.3	125.4	—	809.7	167.2	976.9	176.3	800.6	+225.6	—
1953	730.5	125.4	—	855.9	313.1	1,169.0	177.3	991.7	+191.1	79.8
1954	782.1	192.1	—	974.2	170.8	1,145.0	193.1	951.9	− 39.8	79.8
1955	829.3	192.1	12.9	1,034.3	60.0	1,094.3	200.2	894.1	− 57.8	79.8
1956	881.9	192.1	19.3	1,093.3	68.0	1,161.3	218.7	942.7	+ 48.6	79.8
1957	961.8	192.1	39.6	1,193.5	170.4	1,363.9	240.6	1,123.3	+180.6	65.5
1958	1,006.8	192.1	65.7	1,264.6	230.8	1,495.4	283.3	1,212.1	+ 88.8	62.8
1959	1,101.8	178.6	98.9	1,379.3	457.7	1,837.0	312.4	1,524.7	+312.6	62.8
1960	1,216.8	167.9	125.8	1,510.5	719.9	2,230.4	317.5	1,912.8	+388.1	166.0
1961	1,396.6	167.9	139.1	1,703.6	947.4	2,651.0	318.3	2,332.7	+419.9	166.0

*Excludes proceeds of the War Loan raised internally and relent to the United Kingdom (fully repaid by 1959). Promissory notes given to the International Monetary Fund and World Bank are not included in the totals, but do appear separately in the last column on the right; see footnote ‖, below. All figures are end of year.

†Represents amounts withdrawn and outstanding on development loans from the United States, the U.S.S.R., Canada, and China, plus I.B.R.D. loans.

‡Consists entirely of treasury bills up to 1952; thereafter, other forms of borrowing, especially advances from the Central Bank of Ceylon, assume some importance.

§Refers to market value of securities held on behalf of sinking funds.

‖Promissory rupee notes written to the I.M.F. and I.B.R.D. are held by the Central Bank do not represent debt in any economically meaningful sense. These notes merely excuse Ceylon from paying its rupee subscription obligations to these organizations; no actual borrowing by the government has occurred. Since it is thought that the payment of these notes will never be demanded, they are not deemed to be part of the public debt.

Source: Central Bank of Ceylon, *Annual Report of the Monetary Board to the Minister of Finance*, various years.

TABLE A–70

Basic Data on the Public Industrial Corporations, 1956–61*

Year	Net Worth (Rs. 000)	Sales (Rs. 000)	Profit† (Rs. 000)	Employ-ment	Production (Tons of Paper)
1. Eastern Paper Mills (1955; Paper and Paper Bags; Rs. 22,000,000)					
1956............	20,074	349	− 846‡	...	736
1957............	17,748	1,654	−2,411	...	1,379
1958............	15,078§	1,676‖	−3,713‖	404	1,235
1959............	13,266#	4,149¶	−1,884¶	472	4,187
1960............	**	††	††	522	4,563
1961............	‡‡	§§	§§	567	.....

Year	Net Worth (Rs. 000)	Sales (Rs. 000)	Profit (Rs. 000)	Employ-ment	Production (Tons of Coconut Oil)	(Tons of Feeds)
2. Ceylon Oils and Fats (1955; Coconut Oil, Feeds; Rs. 19,800,000)						
1956.......					1,234	111
1957.......	16,019	4,835	−2,096	...	3,426	1,800
1958.......	13,647§	14,673‖	−2,372‖	...	6,678	4,700
1959.......	......	......	.....	...	7,477	3,422
1960.......	......	......	.....	...	8,112	11,723
1961.......	......	......	.....	...	10,459	23,607

Year	Net Worth (Rs. 000)	Sales (Rs. 000)	Profit (Rs. 000)	Employ-ment	Production (Tons)
3. Ceylon Ceramics (1955‖‖; Ceramic Ware; Rs. 3,000,000)					
1956............	2,602	268	−284	...	201
1957............	2,306	453	−296	147	338
1958............	2,020§	920‖	−304‖	139	368
1959............	2,217#	1,028¶	29¶	132	425
1960............	6,408**	1,443††	146††	186	466
1961............	.....	.....	...	190	417

Year	Net Worth (Rs. 000)	Sales (Rs. 000)	Profit (Rs. 000)	Employ-ment	Production (000,000 Sq. Ft.)
4. Ceylon Plywoods (1956; 3-Ply Plywood; Rs. 2.8 Million)					
1956............	2,826	2,614¶¶	386¶¶	351	5.6¶¶
1957............	3,028	3,083	368	354	7.6
1958............	3,411	2,609	−48	356	6.9
1959............	3,812#	3,778¶	844¶	389	8.3
1960............	.....	.....	....	...	9.3
1961............	.....	.....	....	...	9.8
1962............	.....	.....	....	594	...

TABLE A–70 (CONTINUED)

Year	Net Worth (Rs. 000)	Sales (Rs. 000)	Profit (Rs. 000)	Employment	Production (Value at Cost; Rs. 000)
5. D. I. Leather Products (1956; Shoes, Leather Goods; Rs. 1,700,000)					
1956........	1,702	803¶¶	− 6¶¶	221	638¶¶
1957........	1,705	1,272	44	251	1,012
1958........	1,794	1,500	215	288	1,278
1959........	1,940#	2,238¶	226¶	295	1,726¶
1960........	1,831**	1,734††	14††	298	1,523**
1961........	....	....	......	300	....

Year	Employment	Production (Tons of Caustic Soda)	(Tons of Chlorine)
6. Paranthan Chemicals (1956; Caustic Soda, etc.; Rs. 15,700,000)***			
1960.................................	223	64	70
1961.................................	222	666	183

Year	Net Worth (Rs. 000)	Sales (Rs. 000)	Profit (Rs. 000)	Employment	Production (Tons of Cement)
7. Ceylon Cement (1956†††; Cement, Concrete Products; Rs. 26,800,000)					
1956.....	20,431	1,608‡‡‡§§§	628‡‡‡	...	83,371
1957.....	24,152	9,755§§§	1,329	...	48,195
1958.....	24,508	14,407§§§	1,652	...	79,079
1959.....	32,283#	19,286‖‖‖	5,137‖‖‖	...	93,463
1960.....	48,523	15,456	4,503	972	83,623
1961.....	....	....	....	987	80,471

Year	Employment	Production (Tons of Ilmenite)
8. Ceylon Mineral Sands (1957; Ilmenite; Rs. 8,000,000)###		
1960...	100	6,264
1961...	100	3,832

Year	Employment	Production (Tons of Sugar)	(Tons of Molasses)
9. Kantalai Sugar (1957; Sugar, Molasses, Alcohol; Rs. 28,000,000)			
1960.................................	...	215	319
1961.................................	360	306	155

(Continued on next page)

TABLE A–70 (Continued)

Year	Production (Tons of Salt)
10. National Salt (1957; Salt; Rs. 14,000,000)	
1959...	4,164
1960...	11,233
1961...	

Year	Production (000 Lbs. of Yarn)
11. National Textiles (1958; Cotton Yarn; Rs. 41,100,00)	
1961...	423

12. National Small Industries (1959; Various; Rs. 5,600,000)
    Brick and tile factories under construction
13. Hardboard (1959; Hardboard; Rs. 3,000,000)
    Factory under construction
14. Industrial Estates (1960; Various; Rs. 2,500,000)
    Under construction
15. Iron and Steel (1961; Iron and Steel; Rs. 80,000,000¶¶¶)
    Construction not yet begun
16. Tire and Tube (1961; Tires and Tubes; Rs. 51,700,000¶¶¶)
    Construction not yet begun

*The table presents, in summary form, a record of the government's ventures into the field of publicly owned industrial development. The figures have been culled from the annual reports of the corporations and from the 1961 and the 1962 Central Bank of Ceylon, *Annual Reports of the Monetary Board to the Minister of Finance.* Data are presented only for those years from 1956 in which commercial production took place (i.e., preproduction costs have been included only as they have been amortized over each producing year) and are as comparable as possible. For the newest five corporations, which had not started construction by the end of 1961, status at that time is noted. All figures refer to calendar years, except where noted—with the exception of net worth totals, which refer to the last day of the year, except when otherwise noted.

†Profit before taxes but after all other costs have been charged in a conventional business accounting way.

‡This is with no allowance made for depreciation, which, based on changes for later years, should have been Rs. 400,000–500,000.

§On March 31, 1959.

‖For the 15 months ending March 31, 1959.

#On March 31, 1960.

¶For the 12 months ending March 31, 1960.

**On March 31, 1961.

††For the 12 months ending March 31, 1961.

‡‡On March 31, 1962.

§§For the 12 months ending March 31, 1962.

‖‖Took over earlier government ceramics plant.

##Took over government plywood plant which had existed since 1941; formerly called Gintota Plywoods.

¶¶For the nine months ending December 31, 1956.

***Plant was under construction and testing from 1956 on, but because of technical difficulties did not go into commercial production until 1960.

†††Took over from government cement factory opened in 1950; formerly called Kankesanturai Cement.

‡‡‡For the last two months of 1956.

§§§Includes sale of electricity to Department of Electrical Undertakings (this ceased after 1958).

‖‖‖For the 15 months ending March 31, 1960.

###Technical difficulties delayed the start of commercial production until 1960.

¶¶¶Refers to the initial investment only.

TABLE A–71

COLOMBO CONSUMER PRICE INDEX, 1939–61*

(1953 = 100)

Year	All Items	Food	Clothing	Fuel and Light	Rent	Miscel- laneous
1939	38	32	32	45	81	39
1940	39	34	36	46	81	41
1941	43	39	43	48	80	43
1942	57	55	55	76	78	54
1943	69	64	88	90	83	72
1944	70	64	98	90	84	77
1945	77	69	104	90	89	96
1946	80	71	113	107	98	95
1947	88	79	134	116	108	95
1948	91	86	119	97	111	96
1949	90	90	98	93	102	90
1950	95	96	98	98	97	94
1951	99	96	125	108	97	98
1952	98.4	94.3	120.8	100.2	98.7	102.9
1953	100.0	100.0	100.0	100.0	100.0	100.0
1954	99.5	100.1	96.0	103.5	100.2	97.1
1955	98.9	99.2	97.2	102.5	100.2	97.3
1956	98.6	97.5	98.8	101.5	100.2	101.4
1957	101.2	99.0	101.9	97.5	100.2	110.0
1958	103.3	99.8	105.7	101.2	100.2	116.4
1959	103.5	98.8	111.2	102.6	100.2	118.6
1960	101.9	95.1	114.9	102.9	100.2	120.9
1961	103.1	94.2	125.5	104.6	100.2	126.3

*Two separate indexes, linked together in 1952, are shown in this table. Prior to 1952, the reference of the index was to a "working-class" budget in Colombo, with weights based on a 1938–39 budget study. In 1952 this index was replaced by a "Colombo Consumer Price Index," weighted according to the budgets of Colombo working-class families, as revealed in a 1949-50 budget study. Here, both indexes are recalculated on a 1953 = 100 basis.

That the indexes understate to some degree the recent price increases for many Ceylonese consumers cannot seriously be doubted. A 1958 committee (see *Report of the Committee to Revise the Cost-of-Living Index*, Sessional Paper II of 1959) recommended a number of improvements in the index, designed to account for recent price changes—mostly increases—more accurately, but so far no action has been taken on their recommendations. The committee's main points were that (1) price movements based on a "middle income" budget have been quite different from those reflected in the index and (2) the pattern of consumption had shifted noticeably since 1949–50 (as revealed by the committee's 1958 budget study). Simple calculations based on a reweighting of the five major categories of the index suggest understatement attributable to these shortcomings of at least one to three percentage points. The main factors producing downward bias in the present index—especially where "middle income" consumers are concerned—are (1) the heavy weighting and constant price of subsidized rice and (2) the method used to price housing (the rent index is based on the assessed value of a sample of "working-class" houses in Colombo—this has not changed since 1953—rather than on rents actually paid).

All these criticisms of the Colombo Consumer Price Index, it should be mentioned, do not shake the basic point of this table: that consumer price increases in Ceylon have been very small when compared with those in most other countries over the same period.

Sources: Central Bank of Ceylon, *Annual Report of the Monetary Board to the Minister of Finance*, various years; Department of Census and Statistics, *Statistical Abstract*, various years.

TABLE A–72

IMPLIED G.N.P. AND G.N.I. DEFLATORS, 1950–60*

(1953 = 100)

Year	G.N.P. Deflators	G.N.I. Deflators
1950	104.2	92.5
1951	109.6	99.4
1952	98.9	99.5
1953	100.0	100.0
1954	102.4	95.9
1955	107.8	97.8
1956	106.1	99.7
1957	103.9	100.8
1958	104.2	98.9
1959	104.4	98.1
1960	102.6	96.7

*These implied indexes grow out of the integrated tables (see pages 269–271). The G.N.P. deflator is an index of prices paid for the Gross National Product of Ceylon. The G.N.I. deflator is an index of the prices paid by Ceylonese nationals in converting their Gross National Income into goods and services. They differ only because the terms of trade vary (if the terms of trade improve, the G.N.I. deflator falls relative to the G.N.P. deflator; if they deteriorate, the opposite movement takes place). The indexes are only as reliable as the indexes which were used to deflate various elements of G.N.P. and this is not always too reliable.

TABLE A-73
COLOMBO MARKET PRICE OF MAIN EXPORT COMMODITIES, 1937-61*
(Rupees)

Year	Tea (per Lb.)	Rubber (per Lb.)	Copra† (per Candy)	Coconut Oil (per Ton)	Desiccated Coconut (per Lb.)	Cocoa (per Cwt.)
1937.........	0.76	0.50	47.23	302.72	0.10	33.65
1938.........	0.70	0.37	27.74	184.22	0.06	19.33
1939.........	0.76	0.47	34.58	218.90	0.09	20.02
1940.........	0.81	0.55	32.79	225.00	0.08	22.77
1941.........	1.09	0.56	32.38	262.30	0.09	30.15
1942.........	0.80‡	0.67	54.16	468.70	0.19	29.18
1943.........	0.96‡	0.71	59.00	438.33	0.23	29.40
1944.........	1.07‡	0.98	65.00	477.33	0.23	37.44
1945.........	1.16‡	0.96	80.44	569.72	0.27	56.48
1946.........	1.23‡	0.93	100.00	696.75	0.45	106.37
1947.........	1.60	0.64	122.00	995.59	0.80	91.00
1948.........	1.55	0.63	134.90	1,022.38	0.66	149.43
1949.........	1.96	0.57	150.00	1,021.75	0.51	110.66
1950.........	2.11	1.55	208.84	1,412.01	0.83	169.24
1951.........	1.94	2.15	244.74	1,623.58	0.61	177.47
1952.........	1.75	1.38	155.52	980.95	0.44	165.13
1953.........	1.92	1.35	202.98	1,275.03	0.53	157.95
1954.........	2.61	1.11	180.78	1,118.06	0.44	251.72
1955.........	2.20	1.28	146.04	945.14	0.35	170.95
1956.........	2.19	1.45	159.90	982.75	0.41	125.63
1957.........	1.86	1.16	183.07	1,031.54	0.44	169.41
1958.........	1.73	0.93	209.84	1,222.56	0.51	208.97
1959.........	1.85	1.25	238.94	1,487.82	0.56	176.50
1960.........	1.88	1.24	191.06	1,158.31	0.47	152.64
1961.........	1.83	1.01	141.54	893.76	0.35	118.49

*These are annual arithmetic averages of weekly prices in the Colombo market for these commodities. In all cases but tea and desiccated coconut (where the price is an average for all grades) it is the highest grade to which the prices refer: R.S.S. No. 1 for rubber; Estate No. 1 for copra; white, naked, warf delivered for coconut oil; and Estate No. 1 for cocoa. The ultimate sources of the data are the trading associations dealing with the various commodities and the Ceylon Chamber of Commerce.

†A candy equals five hundredweights.

‡These are not free market prices, but are contract prices for bulk delivery (most Ceylon tea was sold in this way during World War II).

Sources: Central Bank of Ceylon, *Annual Report of the Monetary Board to the Minister of Finance,* 1961; Department of Census and Statistics, *Statistical Abstract,* 1949.

TABLE A-74

INDEXES OF SHARE PRICES, 1939-61*

(1953 = 100)

Year	Tea	Rubber	Commer- cial and Industrial	Year	Tea	Rubber	Commer- cial and Industrial
			A. Rupee Companies				
1939......	50	53	32	1951.......	116	156	98
1940......	55	59	35	1952.......	99	133	107
1941......	55	68	39	1953......	100	100	100
1942......	60	88	46	1954......	118	87	96
1943......	72	142	59	1955......	128	112	93
1944......	79	153	62	1956......	115	109	87
1945......	82	128	55	1957.......	101	108	73
1946......	88	117	55	1958.......	67	74	62
1947......	100	91	124	1959......	62	83	57
1948......	85	56	89	1960......	69	108	62
1949......	83	48	78	1961.......	59	84	55
1950......	110	96	81				

Year		Tea	Rubber	Year		Tea	Rubber
			B. Sterling Companies				
1939..............		66	110	1951..............		146	242
1940..............		59	103	1952..............		101	146
1941..............		62	115	1953..............		100	100
1942..............		66	125	1954..............		146	109
1943..............		106	219	1955..............		152	132
1944..............		108	223	1956..............		126	190
1945..............		126	222	1957..............		123	268
1946..............		129	205	1958..............		94	173
1947..............		135	225	1959..............		96	195
1948..............		125	148	1960..............		99	258
1949..............		103	78	1961..............		74	177
1950..............		128	135				

*These indexes, which were prepared by the Department of Census and Statistics and the Central Bank of Ceylon, originally were based on January-June 1939 = 100 and were recalculated on a 1953 = 100 basis.

Source: Central Bank of Ceylon, *Annual Report of the Monetary Board to the Minister of Finance*, various years.

Selected Bibliography

I. OFFICIAL PUBLICATIONS

Accounts of the Government of Ceylon, Sessional Paper. (annual).
Administration Report of the Commissioner of Agrarian Services. (annual).
Administration Report of the Commissioner of Inland Revenue. (annual).
Administration Report of the Commissioner of Labour. (annual).
Administration Report of the Director of Agriculture. (annual).
Administration Report of the Director of Census and Statistics. (annual).
Administration Report of the Director of Commerce. (annual).
Administration Report of the Director of Education. (annual).
Administration Report of the Director of Fisheries. (annual).
Administration Report of the Director of Health Services. (annual).
Administration Report of the Director of Industries. (annual).
Administration Report of the Director of Irrigation. (annual).
Administration Report of the Director of Rural Development. (annual).
Administration Report of the Director of Social Services. (annual).
Administration Report of the Food Commissioner (Supply). 1952.
Administration Report of the Principal Collector of Customs. (annual).
Administration Report of the Registrar of Companies. (annual).
Administration Report of the Rubber Controller. (annual).
Administration Report of the Tea Controller. (annual).
Administration Report on the Customs and Shipping. (annual).
Auditor-General's Report. Sessional Paper. (annual; before 1948).
Ceylon Customs Returns. (monthly).
Economic Survey of Rural Ceylon 1950–1951. Final Report. Sessional Paper XI of 1954.
Estimates of Revenue and Expenditure of the Government of Ceylon. (annual).
The New Consumer Price Index. Sessional Paper VI of 1953.
New State-Owned Factories. Sessional Paper XXIII of 1947.
Postwar Development Proposals. 1946.
Public Accounts in Ceylon. 1956.
Report of the Coconut Commission. Sessional Paper XII of 1949.
The Report of the Colonial Auditor for 1928/29.
Report of the Commission on Government Commercial Undertakings. Sessional Paper XIX of 1953.
Report of the Commission on Social Services. Sessional Paper VII of 1947.
Report of the Committee on Coconut Duties. Sessional Paper XVIII of 1955.
Report of the Committee to Revise the Cost-of-Living Index. Sessional Paper II of 1959.
Report of the Development Division, 1961–62.

Report of the Joint United Kingdom and Australian Mission on Rice Production in Ceylon—1954. Sessional Paper II of 1955.

Report of the Kandyan Peasant Commission. Sessional Paper XVIII of 1951.

Report of the Land Commission. Sessional Paper X of 1958.

Report of the National Wage Policy Commission. Sessional Paper VIII of 1961.

Report of the Registrar-General on Vital Statistics. Sessional Paper (annual).

Report of the Taxation Commission. Sessional Paper XVII of 1955.

Report on Industrial Development and Policy. Sessional Paper XV of 1946.

Report on Soil and Paddy Problems in Ceylon. Sessional Paper XIX of 1956.

Report on the Rubber Industry. Sessional Paper XVIII of 1947.

Report on the Survey of Landlessness. Sessional Paper XIII of 1952.

CENTRAL BANK OF CEYLON. *Annual Report of the Monetary Board to the Minister of Finance.* (annual).

———— *Bulletin* (monthly), 1950–.

———— *Ceylon Consumer Survey 1963. Preliminary Report.* 1963.

———— *Survey of Ceylon's Consumer Finances.* 1954.

CEYLON GOVERNMENT RAILWAY. *Administration Report.* (annual).

DEPARTMENT OF CENSUS AND STATISTICS. *Census of Agriculture 1952.* 4 vols., 1956.

———— *Census of Ceylon 1946.* 1951–.

———— *Census of Ceylon 1953.* 1957–.

———— *Census of Industry 1952.* 1954.

———— *Ceylon Year Book.* (annual), 1948–.

———— *Mid-Year Bulletin of Statistics.* June, 1961.

———— *Preliminary Report on the Economic Survey of Rural Ceylon 1950.* Sessional Paper XI of 1951.

———— *Quarterly Bulletin of Statistics.* 1951–60.

———— *Report of the Committee on National Income Estimates.* 1957.

———— *A Report on Paddy Statistics.* 1956.

———— *Report on the Census of Government and Local Government Employees 1951.* 1952.

———— *Report on the Survey of Landlessness.* Sessional Paper VIII of 1952.

———— *Statistical Abstract.* (annual), 1951–.

———— *Survey of Private Investment 1954.* 1956.

DEPARTMENT OF COMMERCE. *Thirty Years Trade Statistics of Ceylon (1925–1954).* 5 vols., 1955–57.

DEPARTMENT OF INDUSTRIES. *Directory of Industrial Establishments.* 3rd ed., 1962.

———— *Span of Industrial Production in Ceylon 1962.* 1962.

DEPARTMENT OF INFORMATION. *Budget Speeches.* 1947/48–1962/63.

———— *A Six-Year Plan for Ceylon.* 1950.

DEPARTMENT OF INLAND REVENUE. *The New Tax System.* 2 vols., 1959.

DEPARTMENT OF NATIONAL PLANNING. *Draft Short-Term Implementation Programme.* 1962.

DEPARTMENT OF STATISTICS AND OFFICE SYSTEMS. *The Ceylon Blue Book.* (annual) to 1948.

KALDOR, NICHOLAS. *Suggestions for a Comprehensive Reform of Direct Taxation*. Sessional Paper IV of 1960.

MINISTRY OF AGRICULTURE. *The Agricultural Plan*. 1958.

MINISTRY OF FINANCE. *The Budget and Economic Growth*. 1961.

———— *Economic and Social Development of Ceylon (a Survey) 1926–1954*. 1955.

———— *Economic and Social Progress 1956–62*. 1963.

———— *Foreign Economic Aid*. 1962.

———— *Governmental Policy in Respect of Private Foreign Investment in Ceylon*. 1955.

———— *Revision of the Existing Law Relating to Direct Taxation*. 1961.

MINISTRY OF INDUSTRIES. *Investors' Guide*. Bulletin One, Series I, 1961.

———— *Investor's Guide to Industrial Possibilities*. 1961.

———— *State Industrial Projects*. Bulletin One, Series II, 1961.

MINISTRY OF INDUSTRIES, HOME AND CULTURAL AFFAIRS. *Industrial Programme Public Sector 1962–66*. 1962.

NATIONAL PLANNING COUNCIL. *First Interim Report*. 1957.

———— *Papers by Visiting Economists*. 1959.

———— *Reports of Committees and Technical Working Groups*. 1959.

———— *Six-Year Programme of Investment 1954/55 to 1959/60*. 1955.

———— *The Ten-Year Plan*. 1959.

NEWMAN, PETER. *Studies in the Import Structure of Ceylon*. Planning Secretariat, 1958.

RAY, P. K. *Report to the Government of Ceylon on a Pilot Crop (Paddy) Insurance Scheme*. Sessional Paper I of 1959.

———— *Report to the Government of Ceylon on Crop (Paddy) Insurance*. Sessional Paper XIV of 1957.

SARKAR, N. K. *The Demography of Ceylon*. Colombo: Government Press, 1957.

WILLIAMS, K. *The National Income of Ceylon*. Colombo, 1952.

II. BOOKS

BAUER, P. T. *The Rubber Industry*. Cambridge, Massachusetts: Harvard University Press, 1948.

BOEKE, J. H. *Economics and Economic Policy of Dual Societies as Exemplified by Indonesia*. New York: Institute of Pacific Relations, 1953.

DE SILVA, COLVIN R. *Ceylon Under the British Occupation, 1795–1833*, vol. 2. Colombo, 1962.

Far Eastern Economic Review 1965 Yearbook. Hong Kong, 1964.

FARMER, B. H. *Ceylon: A Divided Nation*. London: Oxford University Press, 1963.

———— *Pioneer Peasant Colonization in Ceylon*. London: Oxford University Press, 1957.

FEI, JOHN C. H. AND GUSTAV RANIS. *Development of the Labor Surplus Economy*. Homewood, Illinois: Richard D. Irwin, Inc., 1964.

FERGUSON, A. M. AND J. *The Ceylon Directory for 1874*. Colombo, 1874.

Ferguson's Ceylon Directory 1963. Colombo, 1963.

GUNASEKERA, H. A. DE S. *From Dependent Currency to Central Banking in Ceylon*. London: G. Bell and Sons, Ltd., 1962.

HICKS, J. R. *Essays in World Economics*. London: Oxford University Press, 1959.

HICKS, URSULA K. *Development from Below.* London: Oxford University Press, 1961.
HIGGINS, BENJAMIN H. *Economic Development.* New York: W. W. Norton & Co., Inc., 1959.
Industries of Ceylon. Colombo, 1963.
INTERNATIONAL BANK FOR RECONSTRUCTION AND DEVELOPMENT. *The Economic Development of Ceylon.* Baltimore, Maryland: Johns Hopkins Press, 1953.
JEFFRIES, SIR CHARLES, *Ceylon—The Path to Independence.* London: Pall Mall Press, Ltd., 1962.
JENNINGS, SIR WILLIAM IVOR. *The Economy of Ceylon,* 2nd ed. London: Oxford University Press, 1951.
KÖVARY, R. *Investment Policy and Investment Legislation in Underdeveloped Countries.* New York: Taplinger Publishing Co., 1960.
LEACH, E. R. *Pul Eliya. A Village in Ceylon.* London: Cambridge University Press, 1961.
LEVIN, JONATHAN V. *The Export Economies.* Cambridge, Massachusetts: Harvard University Press, 1960.
LUDOWYK, E. F. C. *The Story of Ceylon.* London: Faber & Faber, Ltd., 1962.
MILLS, LENNOX A. *Ceylon under British Rule, 1795–1932.* London: Oxford University Press, 1933.
NEWMAN, PETER. *Malaria Eradication and Population Growth.* Ann Arbor, Michigan: University of Michigan (to be published).
OLIVER, HENRY M. *Economic Opinion and Policy in Ceylon.* Durham, North Carolina: Duke University Press, 1957.
PAKEMAN, S. A. *Ceylon.* New York: Frederick A. Praeger, Inc., 1964.
RAMACHANDRAN, N. *Foreign Plantation Investment in Ceylon, 1889–1958.* Colombo, 1963.
RYAN, BRYCE AND OTHERS. *Sinhalese Village.* Coral Gables, Florida: University of Miami Press, 1958.
SURIYAKUMARAN, C. *The Economics of Full Employment in Agricultural Countries.* Colombo: K. V. G de Silva & Sons, 1957.
TILAKARATNA, W. M. *Agricultural Credit in a Developing Economy— Ceylon.* Colombo, 1963.
UNITED NATIONS. ECONOMIC AND SOCIAL COUNCIL. ECONOMIC COMMISSION FOR ASIA AND THE FAR EAST. *Mobilization of Domestic Capital in Certain Countries of Asia and the Far East.* Bangkok, 1951.
UNITED NATIONS. STATISTICAL OFFICE. *Methods of National Income Estimation,* Series F. No. 8. New York, 1955.
———— *A System of National Accounts and Supporting Tables,* Studies in Methods, Series F, No. 2, Rev. 1. New York, 1960.
UNIVERSITY OF CEYLON. *The Disintegrating Village.* Colombo, 1957.
VITTACHI, TARZIE. *Brown Sahib.* London: Andre Deutsch, Ltd., 1962.
WALLICH, HENRY CHRISTOPHER. *Monetary Problems of an Export Economy.* Cambridge, Massachusetts: Harvard University Press, 1950.
WEERAWARDANA, I. D. S. *Ceylon General Election, 1956.* Colombo: M. D. Gunasena & Co., Ltd., 1960.
WICKIZER, V. D. *Coffee, Tea and Cocoa: An Economic and Political Analysis.* Stanford, California: Stanford University Press, 1951.
WRIGGINS, W. HOWARD. *Ceylon: Dilemmas of a New Nation.* Princeton, New Jersey: Princeton University Press, 1960.

III. ARTICLES

ABEYRATNE, E. L. J. "Dry Land Farming in Ceylon," *Tropical Agriculturalist* (July/September, 1956), pp. 191–229.

"Acceleration of Population Growth in ECAFE Countries since the Second World War," *Economic Bulletin for Asia and the Far East* (May, 1955), pp. 1–12.

"Analysis of National Income in Selected Asian Countries," *Economic Bulletin for Asia and the Far East* (January-June, 1952), pp. 13–26.

ARULPRAGASAM, L. C. "A Consideration of the Problems Arising from the Size and Sub-Division of Paddy Holdings in Ceylon and the Principles and Provisions of the Paddy Lands Act Pertaining to Them," *Ceylon Journal of Historical and Social Studies* (January/June, 1961), pp. 59–70.

"Aspects of Urbanization in ECAFE Countries," *Economic Bulletin for Asia and the Far East* (May, 1953), pp. 1–15.

BEHRMAN, J. N. "State Trading by Underdeveloped Countries: Ceylon," *Law and Contemporary Problems* (Summer, 1959), pp. 460–467.

"Ceylon and the South-East Asian Common Market," *Industry* (January, 1962), pp. 13–15, 27.

"Ceylon Sugar in the Market," *Ceylon Commerce* (July/August, 1960), pp. 8–9.

"Ceylon's Central Banking Experiment," *The Banker* (July, 1950), pp. 33–38.

"Ceylon's State-Operated Industries," *Far Eastern Economic Review* (June 12, 1952), pp. 756–758.

CHENERY, HOLLIS B. "Comparative Advantage and Development Policy," *American Economic Review* (March, 1961).

COREA, G. "Overall Budgetary Policy in an Export Economy," *Ceylon Economist* (November, 1950), pp. 177–190.

———— "The Scope for Industrial Development," *Ceylon Economist* (November, 1957), pp. 28–36.

———— "Some Problems of Economic Development in Ceylon," *Ceylon Economist* (August, 1950), pp. 39–54.

DAS GUPTA, B. B. "The Theory and Reality of Economic Development," *Central Bank of Ceylon Bulletin* (November, 1955), pp. 10–14.

"Deficit Financing for Economic Development," *Economic Bulletin for Asia and the Far East* (November, 1954), pp. 1–18.

DE SILVA, G. V. S. "The Budget: An Iniquitous Transference of Wealth," *Ceylon Economist* (August, 1950), pp. 10–21.

———— "The World Bank Mission's Report," *Ceylon Economist*, Vol. 2, No. 3 (1952), pp. 115–125.

DE SILVA, K. M. "Indian Immigration to Ceylon—The First Phase c. 1840–1855," *Ceylon Journal of Historical and Social Studies* (July-December, 1961), pp. 106–137.

"Devaluation, Price Movements and Changes in External Trade in ECAFE Countries," *Economic Bulletin for Asia and the Far East* (2nd quarter, 1950), pp. 21–46.

"Development Planning in Ceylon," *International Labour Review* (February, 1956), pp. 194–209.

"Development Policies and Means of Implementing Development Programs, with Special Reference to ECAFE Countries," *Economic Bulletin for Asia and the Far East* (November, 1956), pp. 21–69.

DIAS, W. P. H. "The Rubber Replanting Subsidy Scheme," *Ceylon Today* (June, 1960), pp. 22–26.

DON MICHAEL, W. "The Paddy Lands Bill—A Comment," *Ceylon Economist* (January, 1958), pp. 125–130.

————— "Some Aspects of Land Settlement and Land Reform in Ceylon," *Ceylon Economist* (January, 1958), pp. 25–71.

ECKAUS, R. S. "The Factor Proportions Problem in Underdeveloped Areas," *American Economic Review* (September, 1955).

"Economic Indicators of Inflation in ECAFE Countries," *Economic Bulletin for Asia and the Far East* (May, 1955), pp. 13–22.

ELLSWORTH, P. T. "Factors in the Economic Development of Ceylon," *American Economic Review* (May, 1953), pp. 115–125.

FARMER, B. H. "The Ceylon Ten-Year Plan, 1959–68," *Pacific Viewpoint* (September, 1961), pp. 123–136.

————— "Peasant Colonization in Ceylon," *Pacific Affairs* (December, 1952), pp. 387–398.

FERNANDO, C. W. "The Progress of Industry in Ceylon," *Industry* (January, 1960), pp. 15–18.

FERNANDO, MRS. E. C. "The Coir Industry," *Coconut Journal* (July/September, 1958), pp. 77–84.

————— "Some Aspects of the Production and Sale of Tea—Particularly Low Grown Tea," *Central Bank of Ceylon Bulletin* (February, 1958), pp. 16–27.

FERNANDO, M. "The Present Financial Crisis," *Ceylon Economist* (January, 1961).

FERNANDO, W. S. M. "The Soap Industry in Ceylon," *Ceylon Economist* (March, 1956), pp. 91–99.

FRANK, ANDREW GUNDER. "Policy Decisions and the Economic Development of Ceylon," *Economa Internazionale* (November, 1955), pp. 797–809.

GOODE, R. "The New System of Direct Taxation in Ceylon," *National Tax Journal* (December, 1960).

"Government Policy towards Foreign Private Investment in Ceylon," *Ceylon Commerce* (May/August, 1958), pp. 19–21.

GREEN, R. H. "Theory, Plan and Practice: Aspects of Economic Change in Ceylon," Harvard University, Graduate School of Public Administration, *Public Policy* (eds. CARL FRIEDRICH AND SEYMOUR E. HARRIS). Cambridge, Massachusetts: The School, 1959–60, pp. 273–308.

GREENBERG, MICHAEL. "Central Banking in Ceylon," Gethyn Davies, *Central Banking in South and East Asia*. Hong Kong: Hong Kong University Press, 1960, pp. 9–26.

GUNASEKERA, H. A. DE S. "Banking Arrangements in Ceylon," *Banking in the British Commonwealth* (ed. R. S. SAYERS). London: Oxford University Press, 1952, pp. 401–420.

————— "The Money Supply and the Balance of Payments in Ceylon," *Banca Nazionale del Lavoro Quarterly Review* (September, 1954), pp. 146–157.

————— "A Review of Central Banking in Ceylon," *Ceylon Journal of Historical and Social Studies* (July, 1959), pp. 125–147.

———— "Thoughts on Full Employment," *Ceylon Economist* (November, 1950), pp. 191–198.

GUNAWARDENA, ELAINE. "The Development of External Trade in the Nineteenth Century and the First Half of the Twentieth Century," *Ceylon Economist* (March, 1960), pp. 55–66.

———— "The Structure and Movement of Earnings and Income of Workers in Plantation Industries in Ceylon," *Central Bank of Ceylon Bulletin* (November, 1960), pp. 11–28.

GUNAWARDENE, PHILIP. "Nationalization of Foreign Owned Tea Plantations," *Ceylon Economist* (June, 1958), pp. 131–148.

HEWAVITHARNANA, B. "Insurance in Ceylon and Nationalisation," *Ceylon Economist* (December, 1958), pp. 321–340.

HICKS, J. R. "Reflections on the Economic Problems of Ceylon," in *Papers by Visiting Economists*, pp. 7–22.

HICKS, URSULA K. "Local Government and Finance in Ceylon," in *Papers by Visiting Economists*, pp. 105–114.

HIGGINS, BENJAMIN, "The Dualistic Theory of Underdeveloped Areas," *Economic Development and Cultural Change* (January, 1956).

"History of Industrial Development in Ceylon," *Ceylon Commerce* (May/August, 1958), pp. 57–59.

HSIEH, CHIANG. "Underemployment in Asia: I. Nature and Extent," *International Labour Review* (June, 1952), pp. 703–725.

———— "Underemployment in Asia: II. Its Relation to Investment Policy," *International Labour Review* (July, 1952), pp. 30–39.

INDRARATNE, A. D. V. DE S. "An Analysis of Agricultural Credit in Underdeveloped Countries with Special Reference to Ceylon," *Ceylon Journal of Historical and Social Studies* (July, 1959), pp. 182–202.

"Industrial Organization in the Public Sector in ECAFE Region," *Economic Bulletin for Asia and the Far East* (July/September, 1951, pp. 35–44.

IVERSON, C. "The Role of the Central Bank in the Ceylon Economy," *Central Bank of Ceylon Bulletin* (February, 1956), pp. 8–11.

JAYASURIYA, F. R. "The Future of the Tea Industry in Ceylon," *Ceylon Economist* (March, 1956), pp. 134–165.

JAYASURIYA, F. R., AND SARKAR, N. K. "The Place of Small Scale Industry in National Planning," *Ceylon Economist* (March, 1956), pp. 114–121.

JAYATILAKA, E. L. P. "Social Accounts for Ceylon," *Yorkshire Bulletin of Economic and Social Research* (February, 1953), pp. 17–52.

JAYAWARDENA, N. V. "The Problem of Liquidity in an Under-Developed Country," *Ceylon Economist,* (2nd quarter, 1952), pp. 93–101.

KAHAWITA, R. "Gal Oya Scheme: Facts and Fallacies," *Ceylon Economist* (September, 1951), pp. 57–68.

KALDOR, N. "An Economic Survey of Ceylon," *Ceylon Commerce* (May/August, 1958), pp. 7–13.

———— "Observations on the Problem of Economic Development in Ceylon," in *Papers by Visiting Economists*, pp. 25–33.

KANDIAH, P. "An Analysis of Peasant Economy in Ceylon," *Ceylon Economist* (February, 1951), pp. 242–258.

———— "Land and Agriculture in Ceylon" Pt. I, *Ceylon Economist* (November, 1950), pp. 169–176.

_____ "Unemployment in Ceylon," *Ceylon Economist* (August, 1950), pp. 32–38.

KANESALINGAM, V. "Problems of Financial Administration in a New State with Particular Reference to Ceylon," *Public Finance*, No. 1 (1962), pp. 66–81.

KANESATHASAN, S. "Export Instability and Contracyclical Policy in Under-developed Export Economies, A Case Study of Ceylon since 1948," *International Monetary Fund Staff Papers* (April, 1959), pp. 46–74.

_____ "Foreign Capital in the Economic Development of Ceylon," *Ceylon Journal of Historical and Social Studies* (January/June, 1963), pp. 84–98.

KANNANGARA, D. M. "Formative Influences in Ceylon's Banking Development," *Ceylon Journal of Historical and Social Studies* (January/July, 1960), pp. 82–95.

_____ "The Role of Exports in Ceylon's Short-Run Income Fluctuations," *Ceylon Journal of Historical and Social Studies* (January/June, 1963), pp. 41–58.

KARUNATILLEKE, N. S. "Development of Banking in Ceylon," *Asian Studies*, Bombay, (February, 1963), pp. 57–69.

_____ "Our Banking Systems," *Ceylon Today* (June, 1962) pp. 25–27; (July, 1962), pp. 27–29; (August, 1962), pp. 22–25.

KELEGAMA, J. B. "The Ceylon Economy in the War and Post-War Years," *Ceylon Economist* (May, 1957), pp. 318–370.

_____ "The Economic Significance of the Paddy Lands Bill," *Ceylon Economist* (January, 1958), pp. 81–124.

_____ "Economics of Food Subsidies," *Ceylon Economist* (June, 1951), pp. 350–357.

_____ "The Economy of Rural Ceylon and the Problem of the Peasantry," *Ceylon Economist* (September, 1959), pp. 341-370.

_____ "The Kandyan Peasantry Problem," *Ceylon Economist* (3rd quarter, 1952), pp. 181–193; Vol. II (July, 1953), pp. 264–276.

KULARATNAM, K. "Minerals and the Economic Development of Ceylon," *Ceylon Economist* (September, 1954), pp. 11–26.

KUZNETS, S. "Economic Growth of Small Nations," International Economics Association, *Economic Consequences of the Size of Nations* (ed. E. A. G. ROBINSON), New York: St. Martins Press, 1960.

"Labour Conditions in Ceylon," *International Labour Review* (December, 1949), pp. 572–616, (January, 1950), pp. 1–20.

LEEMBRUGGEN, J. A.: "Exchange Control in Ceylon," *Ceylon Economist* (June, 1951), pp. 375–386.

LEWIS, W. ARTHUR. "Economic Development with Unlimited Supplies of Labour," *The Manchester School* (May, 1954).

LOGANATHAN, C. "Some Problems of the Ceylon Economy," *Ceylon Economist*, No. 2 (1952), pp. 102–110.

_____ "The Tax on Bank Debits," *Ceylon Commerce* (July, 1957), pp. 20–26.

MORGAN, THEODORE. "Distribution of Income in Ceylon, Puerto Rico, the United States and the United Kingdom," *Economic Journal* (December, 1953), pp. 821–34.

_____ "The Economic Development of Ceylon," *The Annals of the American Academy of Political and Social Science* (May, 1956), pp. 92–100.

"The Movement of Indian Estate Labour to and from Ceylon, 1950–59," *Industry and Labour* (September 15, 1960), pp. 230–231.

MUKERJI, K. P. "The Ceylon Wage Boards," *Ceylon Economist* (November, 1950), pp. 115–123; erratum (February, 1951), p. 222.

NAVARATNE, V. T. "Crop Insurance and Its Application to Ceylon," *Ceylon Economist* (June, 1958).

OLIVER, HENRY M., JR. "The Economy of Ceylon," *Economic Systems of the Commonwealth* (ed. CALVIN B. HOOVER), Duke University Commonwealth Studies Center, Publication No. 16. Durham, North Carolina: Duke University Press, 1962, pp. 202–237.

———— "The Industrialization of Ceylon: Opinions—Policies, 1916–1951," *Ceylon Economist* (November, 1956), pp. 175–225.

PANABOKKE, C. R. "The Problems of Dry Zone Agriculture," *Ceylon Economist* (January, 1958), pp. 72–80.

PAUL, E. C. S. "An Anatomy of the Public Corporation in Ceylon," *Ceylon Commerce* (May/August, 1958), pp. 65–70.

PERERA, DUNCAN. "Interest Rates in Ceylon," *Ceylon Economist* (September, 1959), pp. 371–400.

PERERA, M. P. "The Industrial Products Act and the Protection of Local Industry," *Central Bank of Ceylon Bulletin* (February, 1957), pp. 8–14.

PERERA, M. S. "Cottage and Small Scale Industries," *Industrial Ceylon* (December, 1961), pp. 93–96.

———— "The Role of Small Industries in National Development," *Ceylon Today* (May, 1960), pp. 11–19.

PERERA, N. M. "Financial Procedure in the House of Representatives," *Ceylon Economist* (September, 1951), pp. 9–13.

PERERA, S. N. "Industrial Products Act," *Ceylon Economist* (July, 1961).

"Population and Food Supplies in Asia and the Far East," *Economic Bulletin for Asia and the Far East* (May, 1956), pp. 1–10.

"Population Trends and Related Problems of Economic Development in the ECAFE Region," *Economic Bulletin for Asia and the Far East* (June, 1959), pp. 1–45.

PREBISCH, RAOUL. "The Role of Commercial Policies in Underdeveloped Countries," *American Economic Review Papers and Proceedings* (May, 1959).

"Problems of Cottage and Small Industries," *Ceylon Today* (February, 1961).

"Problems of National Income Estimation in ECAFE Countries," *Economic Bulletin for Asia and the Far East* (January/March, 1951), pp. 20–32.

"Problems of Nationalisation of Insurance in Ceylon," *Ceylon Commerce* (June, 1957), pp. 7–11.

RAJARATNAM, S. "The Ceylon Tea Industry, 1886–1931," *Ceylon Journal of Historical and Social Studies* (July/December, 1961), pp. 169–202.

———— "The Growth of Plantation Agriculture in Ceylon, 1886–1931," *Ceylon Journal of Historical and Social Studies* (January/June, 1961), pp. 1–20.

RAMACHANDRAN, M. "Finances of Manufacturing Companies in the Post-War Period," *Central Bank of Ceylon Bulletin* (December, 1963).

RANGNEKAR, D. K. "The Nationalist Revolution in Ceylon," *Pacific Affairs* (December, 1960), pp. 361–374.

RASAPUTRAM, W. "Economic Expansion and the Balance of Trade in Ceylon," *Ceylon Economist* (March, 1960), pp. 67–84, (July, 1961), pp. 208–220.

―――― "The Government Component in the Gross National Product of Ceylon," *Central Bank of Ceylon Bulletin* (June, 1960), pp. 10–16.

―――― "Gross National Product of Ceylon at Constant (1948) Prices," *Central Bank of Ceylon Bulletin* (January, 1956), pp. 8–16.

―――― "Inflation in Ceylon," *Ceylon Economist* (June, 1951), pp. 322–330.

―――― "Savings of the Ceylon Economy, 1950–59," *Central Bank of Ceylon Bulletin* (January, 1961), pp. 10–31.

REID, MARGARET G. "Survey of Ceylon's Consumer Finances," *American Economic Review* (December, 1956), pp. 956–964.

RIPPY, J. FRED. "Trinidad and Ceylon, Two Profitable British Crown Colonies," *Underdeveloped Areas* (ed. L. W. SHANNON). New York: Harper and Brothers, 1957, pp. 247–252.

ROBINSON, JOAN. "Economic Possibilities of Ceylon," *Papers by Visiting Economists*, pp. 35–71.

RUPESINGHE, W. "The Paddy Lands Bill," *Ceylon Economist* (July, 1953), pp. 277–285.

SALGADO, M. R. P. "Planned Industrial Development and the Problem of Markets," *Ceylon Economist* (January, 1958), pp. 4–24.

―――― "Reflections on an Economic Policy for Development," *Ceylon Journal of Historical and Social Studies* (January/June, 1963), pp. 1–24.

SARKAR, N. K. "A Method of Estimating Surplus Labour in Peasant Agriculture in Over-Populated Under-developed Countries," *Journal of the Royal Statistical Society*, Series A, Part 2 (1957), pp. 209–214.

―――― "Population Trends and Population Policy in Ceylon. A Summary of Findings," *Population Studies* (March, 1956), pp. 195–216.

SELVARATNAM, S. "Some Implications of Population Growth in Ceylon," *Ceylon Journal of Historical and Social Studies* (January/June, 1961).

SENEWIRATNE, S. T. "A Study of the Gal Oya Project," *Ceylon Economist* (September, 1951), pp. 69–76.

SINGER, HANS. "The Distribution of Gains between Investing and Borrowing Countries," *American Economic Review Papers and Proceedings* (May, 1950).

SIRIWARDENE, D. R. "The External Value of the Ceylon Rupee," *Ceylon Economist* (September, 1951), pp. 40–50.

"Some Commercial and Economic Aspects of Public Enterprises in Certain Asian Countries," *Economic Bulletin for Asia and the Far East* (May, 1954), pp. 29–35.

STEIN, B. "Development Problems in Ceylon," Robert I. Crane, *Aspects of Economic Development in South Asia* (supplement BURTON STEIN). New York: Institute of Pacific Relations, 1954.

STRAUS, MURRAY L. "Cultural Factors in the Functioning of Agricultural Extension in Ceylon," *Rural Sociology* (September, 1953), pp. 249–256.

"A Survey of Employment, Unemployment and Underemployment in Ceylon," *International Labour Review* (March, 1963), pp. 247–257.

TAEUBER, IRENE B. "Ceylon as a Demographic Laboratory: Preface to Analysis," *Population Index* (October, 1949), pp. 293–304.

"Taxation and Economic Development in Asian Countries," *Economic Bulletin for Asia and the Far East* (November, 1953), pp. 1–15.

STALEY, C. E. "Export Taxes in Ceylon, 1948–52," *Public Finance*, No. 314 (1959), pp. 249–268.

TILAKARATNA, W. M. "Changes in the Distribution of Income in Ceylon, 1939 and 1948," *Ceylon Economist*, No. 2 (1952), pp. 127–135.

———— "Rural Indebtedness in Ceylon," *Ceylon Economist* (June, 1958), pp. 149 ff.

USWATTE-ARATCHI, G. "The Guaranteed Price Scheme for Paddy—The Subsidy to the Producer," *Ceylon Economist* (January, 1961), pp. 142–151.

WADINAMBIARATCHI, G. H. "Postscript to Devaluation," *Ceylon Economist* (3rd quarter, 1952), pp. 200–206.

WAI, U. TUN. "Report of the Ceylon Taxation Commission," *Public Finance*, No. 2 (1957), pp. 122–144.

WEERAWARDANA, I. D. S. "Parliamentary Control of Finance," *Ceylon Economist* (September, 1951), pp. 28–39.

WICKREMASINGHE, S. A. "The Gal Oya Project and the Crisis of Agriculture," *Ceylon Economist* (June, 1951), pp. 358–374.

WIGNARAJA, P. "Some Relationships between Population Growth, Capital Formation and Employment Opportunities," *Central Bank of Ceylon Bulletin* (November, 1956), pp. 8–11.

WILSON, A. J. "Ceylonese Cabinet Ministers 1947–1960, Their Political, Economic and Social Backgrounds," *Ceylon Economist* (March, 1960), pp. 1–54.

WRIGGINS, W. HOWARD. "Impediments to Unity in New Nations: The Case of Ceylon," *American Political Science Review* (June, 1961), pp. 313–320.

IV. OTHER MATERIALS

COMMONWEALTH CONSULTATIVE COMMITTEE ON SOUTH AND SOUTH-EAST ASIA. *The Colombo Plan for Co-operative Economic Development in South and South-East Asia.* London, 1953.

———— *Report on the Colombo Plan for Co-operative Economic Development in South and South-East Asia.* London (annual), 1950–

ECONOMIC GROWTH CENTER AT YALE UNIVERSITY. *A System of National Economic Accounts and Historical Data.* New Haven, Connecticut: Economic Growth Center, Yale University 1963.

Food and Agricultural Organization of the United Nations. *Production Yearbook 1953.* 1960.

GREEN, REGINALD HERBOLD. "The International Impact on Southeast Asian Economies: Analytical and Theoretical Explorations in the Economic Development of Burma, Malaya, and Ceylon." (unpublished dissertation). Cambridge, Massachusetts: Harvard University, 1960.

INTERNATIONAL LABOUR ORGANIZATION. *Rapid Survey of Handicrafts and Small-Scale Industries.* Report to the Government of Ceylon (mimeographed), 1951.

———— *Report to the Government of Ceylon on the Development of a Textile Industry on a Decentralized Basis.* (mimeographed), 1958/59.

———— "Report to the Government of Ceylon on the Employment, Unemployment and Underemployment Sample Survey of Ceylon, 1959." (unpublished draft report), 1960.

INTERNATIONAL MONETARY FUND. *International Financial Statistics.* (monthly).

RASAPUTRAM, WARNASENA. "The Influence of Foreign Trade on the Level and Growth of National Income of Ceylon, 1926–57." (unpublished Ph.D. dissertation), University of Wisconsin, 1959.

Three-Monthly Review of Ceylon. London, Economist Intelligence Unit. (quarterly), November, 1955–. (formerly called *Quarterly Economic Review of Ceylon*).

UNITED NATIONS. ECONOMIC AND SOCIAL COUNCIL. ECONOMIC COMMISSION FOR ASIA AND THE FAR EAST. *Economic Survey of Asia and the Far East.* (annual), New York: Columbia University Press, 1949–1950.

UNITED NATIONS. Statistical Office. *Direction of International Trade* (various years).

———— *Yearbook of International Trade Statistics.* New York, 1950–.

———— *Yearbook of National Accounts Statistics.* (annual), 1957–.

VAN DEN DRIESEN, I. H. *The Economic History of Ceylon in the Nineteenth Century.* Vol. 1. *Plantations, Land and Capital.* (unpublished English manuscript of Sinhalese book), 1961.

———— "The Need for Immigrant Labour." (unpublished manuscript), 1963.

Index

413